The Choctaw Route:
History Through the Miles

Barton Jennings

The Choctaw Route: History Through the Miles
Copyright © 2021 by Barton Jennings

Publisher's Cataloging-in-Publication Data
Jennings, Barton

The Choctaw Route: History Through the Miles
767p.; 23cm.
ISBN: 978-1-7327888-6-2

Library of Congress Control Number: 2021949022

Front cover photo by Barton Jennings. The ghost of The Choctaw Route at Perry, AR.
Back cover photo by Sarah Jennings
All interior photos by Barton Jennings unless otherwise noted.

Please send comments or corrections to sarah@techscribes.com

TechScribes, Inc.
PO Box 2199
Alma, AR 72921
www.techscribes.com

Printed in the United States of America

Contents

Other books by Barton Jennings

History Through the Miles

Arkansas & Missouri Railroad: History Through the Miles
Alaska Railroad: History Through the Miles
Iowa Interstate Railroad: History Through the Miles
Everett Railroad: History Through the Miles
Tennessee Central Railway: History Through the Miles
Whitewater Valley Railroad: History Through the Miles
Oregon's Joseph Branch: History Through the Miles
Missouri & North Arkansas Railroad:
History Through the Miles
Hennepin Canal Parkway: History Through the Miles
Delta Heritage Trail (Missouri Pacific's Wynne
Subdivision): History Through the Miles

Textbook

The Basics of Transportation: Policies, Practices and
Pricing – An Applied Perspective

Acknowledgements

The Rock Island Choctaw Route was torn apart about forty years ago, so you can't just go out and see how things were done. The author has been fortunate enough to know some of the employees who worked for the railroad over the last few years of the Rock Island. Additionally, he has had the pleasure to get to know a number of the people who have researched the railroad, or who operate parts of it today under new names. These all deserve a thanks for their help.

A number of documents were also used in writing this book. It is amazing what can be found on the internet these days. Copies of the *Official Guide*, the annual reports of various state railroad and corporation commissions, Interstate Commerce Commission reports, and other such documents were great resources.

The Rock Island itself produced numerous documents that are still available. These include timetables, track charts, lists of stations, contracts, and even its own magazine, which changed its name several times over the years. Issues of *The Choctaw*, the promotional newspaper published during the construction of the Choctaw, Oklahoma & Gulf, also make great reading. An interesting source about the route's history can be found in the railroad's centennial issue of the *Rock Island Lines News Digest*, dated October 1952. This issue had a major article entitled "1852 – 100 Years of Progress – 1952."

Related sources such as the *Arkansas Marketing and Industrial Guide*, *The Coal Dealers Blue Book*, local histories published by the Goodspeed Publishing Company, Sanborn Insurance Maps, and others were a great aid. Newspapers also reported heavily on the construction and operations of the Choctaw Route. David Hoge is a master of newspaper research; his collection of more than 3000 pages of railroad-related newspaper articles from Arkansas is an incredible source of information, and he deserves a thanks for sharing this resource. The *Arkansas Railroad History* website is also a jewel with some of the best researchers around sharing information. Finally, the author has a house with several rooms full of books, timetables and other documents about this and other railroads – important research items from a time long before today's internet.

6

What Is The Choctaw Route?

The Choctaw Route was the almost 900-mile Rock Island Railroad route between Memphis, Tennessee, and Tucumcari, New Mexico. The line was built by a number of companies, but spent most of its life as a mainline of the Chicago, Rock Island & Pacific. The oldest use of the term *Choctaw Route* dates to the Choctaw Coal & Railway Company, and later the Choctaw, Oklahoma & Gulf which acquired it. During the late 1800s, the railroad had special Congressional permission to build across the Choctaw lands of the Indian Territory, now part of Oklahoma. The Choctaw once lived in the south of the United States, east of the Mississippi River. They were one of the "Five Civilized Tribes" who obtained that title because they adopted numerous practices of white settlers. Eventually, much of the tribe was moved to eastern Oklahoma, generally along the coal fields and route of this railroad.

Over the years, the railroad route also carried several other names. The name of *The 35th Parallel Route* dates back to when the railroad was being planned as one of a number of proposed transcontinental railroads. The 35th Parallel is actually the 35th Parallel North, a circle of latitude that is 35 degrees north of the Earth's equator. The line defines the southern border of Tennessee, the border between North Carolina and Georgia, and the southernmost point of Nevada.

Before the Civil War, a number of railroads were proposed at just about every Parallel. The 35th Parallel Route favored the southern states and was promoted by William E. Woodruff, founder of the *Arkansas Gazette*. While some construction took place before the war, it lost out to the 41st Parallel Route used by Union Pacific, chosen by the United States during the Civil War.

The Sunbelt Line was a name used to show a connection to the Sunbelt Route of the Southern Pacific, an important link to the Rock Island's Golden State Route at Tucumcari, New Mexico. The term was heavily used after the 1975 bankruptcy of the Chicago, Rock Island & Pacific to show a new beginning for the company. Many of the preservation plans for the Memphis to Tucumcari line used the Sunbelt Line name, even those created by governments and other railroad companies.

No matter the nickname used, the line was not saved as one piece after the labor strike and bankruptcy of the late 1970s. Much of the Rock Island Railroad was sold to other companies, such as the original mainline between Chicago and Council Bluffs becoming the Iowa Interstate Railroad. The Golden State Route (Kansas City to Tucumcari) was acquired by the St. Louis Southwestern Railway Company, and some of the Mid-Continent Route from Kansas City to Fort Worth became part of the Oklahoma, Kansas & Texas Railroad Company.

Both of these latter two lines directly connected to the Choctaw Route and eventually became part of Union Pacific Railroad.

During the early 1980s, there were a number of similar proposals to save most of the Choctaw Route. Generally, this was for the track between Memphis and El Reno, Oklahoma, where most of the local and through freight traffic existed. The first major proposal submitted to the Interstate Commerce Commission was a joint plan by the Arkansas Transportation Commission and the Oklahoma Department of Transportation. Submitted in 1980, this would have created a regional railroad "(1) between El Reno, OK and Memphis, TN (513 miles); (2) between Little Rock, AR and Alexandria, LA (227.6 miles); and (3) between Mesa and Stuttgart, AR (20.8 miles)." This plan never came to fruition due to a lack of confirmed funding and the inability to obtain a commitment from an operating railroad to lease the trackage.

Other proposals were made, including an effort by the Atchison, Topeka & Santa Fe to acquire the line across Arkansas and Oklahoma in 1981, and there were several reports through 1985 that the Choctaw Nation would buy part of the line west of Perry, Arkansas. However, the Choctaw Route was not saved as a whole and was eventually split up into a number of smaller operating segments.

As of the writing of this book, the following is the status of the line.

* Memphis (TN) to Brinkley (AR) – Owned and operated by Union Pacific Railroad.
* Brinkley (AR) to Galloway (AR) – Abandoned.
* Galloway (AR) to North Little Rock (AR) – Owned and operated by Arkansas Midland Railroad.
* North Little Rock (AR) to Little Rock (AR) – Abandoned.
* Little Rock (AR) to Pulaski (AR) – Owned and operated by Union Pacific Railroad, some short sections abandoned.
* Pulaski (AR) to Perry (AR) – Owned and operated by Little Rock & Western Railway.
* Perry (OK) to Danville (AR) – Owned by Continental Grain Company, operated by Little Rock & Western Railway, out of service.
* Danville (AR) to Howe (OK) – Abandoned.
* Howe (OK) to McAlester (OK) – Owned and operated by Arkansas-Oklahoma Railroad, with track in the McAlester area owned by Union Pacific Railroad.
* McAlester (OK) to Shawnee (OK) – Owned by Union Pacific Railroad, out of service.
* Shawnee (OK) to Oklahoma City (OK) area – Owned by Union Pacific Railroad, operated by Arkansas-Oklahoma Railroad.
* Oklahoma City (OK) area to El Reno (OK) – Owned by Union Pacific Railroad, operated by Union Pacific Railroad and AT&L Railroad.
* El Reno (OK) to Geary (OK) – Owned and operated by AT&L Railroad.

- Geary (OK) to Bridgeport (OK) – Owned by the State of Oklahoma, operated by AT&L Railroad.
- Bridgeport (OK) to Weatherford (OK) – Owned by the State of Oklahoma, out of service.
- Weatherford (OK) to Erick (OK) – Owned by the State of Oklahoma, operated by the Farmrail Corporation.
- Erick (OK) to Amarillo (TX) area – Abandoned.
- Amarillo (TX) area – Owned and operated by BNSF Railway.
- Amarillo (TX) area to Tucumcari (NM) – Abandoned.

This book will cover the Choctaw Route, broken down by the status of the line. Please note that this status can change quickly, as there are efforts to re-open parts of the line, and the loss of a single shipper can result in the closure of another.

Creating a Rock Island Railroad Choctaw Route Guide

This book is designed to provide a guide to *The Choctaw Route*, also once known as the *The 35th Parallel Route* and later as *The Sunbelt Line*. Much of the route is abandoned, while other parts are operated by modern railroads, both shortline and Class I companies. Even with these changes, much of the line's history can still be found along its route. There are several museums along the line, a number of stations and bridges, and lots of trains that can still be photographed.

The Chicago, Rock Island & Pacific Railroad shut down in 1980, and parts were sold off over the next few years, followed by scrappers removing much of the rest of the line by the late 1980s. This means that a large part of the railroad has been gone for almost forty years. During this time, portions of the route have become roadways, parks, trails, lots for houses and businesses, farm fields, or just left to erode away. However, an amazing amount of the railroad can still be found and followed, and a number of bridges and structures still exist.

There is always the question about how much detail to provide in a book like this. One reader told the author that in a previous book, if someone once tied a mule to a she-shed along the line, it was reported. While that is not quite the goal, there is an effort to explain the history of each community along the line, what shippers were located there, and what facilities the railroad had. Obviously, all of these changed over the one hundred years of the railroad's history, so the challenge is how much information to report. In writing this book, the author attempted to include information about the first few years of the railroad's existence, the peak of a community's activity, and what remains today. Not everything is reported, but enough history is provided to give the reader an idea of what happened at each location.

The railroad historically used east-west as the line's description, although in some areas it curves greatly from these directions. The route description will use the east-west railroad directions, but will often use the real directions when describing certain features along the route. Additionally, the tracks were often described by their car-lengths. These car-lengths varied over the years, but were generally around 45 feet per car. Therefore, a track listed as being 20 cars in length could hold about 900 feet of train.

Another help in following the railroad and knowing what was at many of the locations are the many maps available on the internet. County road maps, topographic (topo) maps, and many other maps from the era can be found. Comparing these older maps with newer maps can often make finding the railroad easier. One map site that was very helpful while following the railroad is TopoZone (www.topozone.com), whose maps generally showed the railroad grade. The U.S. Geological Survey has also been very active making their Historical Topographic Map Collection available through TopoView. Both are recommended.

A final issue deals with all of the names that were used to represent the railroad over its one-hundred-plus years. To simplify the issue, the term Rock Island or Rock Island Railroad will generally be used, even when another railroad originally built the line. Additionally, an ampersand (&) will be used in railroad company names to make them easier to identify. Especially with companies like the Memphis & Little Rock, mixing the railroad name and the cities that it served can get very confusing. Therefore, even if the firm did not use or always use an ampersand, one will be used in this book. Please forgive these simplifications.

The Rock Island Divisions and Districts

Over the years, the railroad changed its management assignments many times, leading to the use of different division and district names. New names would be created, divisions would be merged, and many other changes took place in the more than one hundred years that part or all of the Choctaw Route existed. The eastern end of the route lasted more than 120 years before the end of the Chicago, Rock Island & Pacific, while the very western end lasted about seventy years. Because of this, the status of different parts of the line can seem confusing.

For example, in 1907, the Chicago, Rock Island & Pacific redrew divisions across the entire railroad. The Choctaw Route was broken down into four different divisions. The Arkansas Division covered the track from Memphis to the east yard limit board at Booneville, with its offices at Little Rock. From Booneville to the west yard limit board at Shawnee was the Indian Territory Division, based in Haileyville, Oklahoma. The Oklahoma Division included the track west from Shawnee to the east yard limit board at Geary, and its offices were at Chickasha, Oklahoma. Finally, the Panhandle Division was based at Geary, Oklahoma, and was responsible for the track westward to Texola, with the track on to Tucumcari not yet built. Later, the Missouri-Kansas Division was assigned the track west of Amarillo, with this area becoming the Amarillo Division a few years later.

In May 1921, another reorganization of the divisions on the Rock Island was announced in the *Rock Island Magazine*. The changes impacted the Choctaw Route in several ways. First, the Louisiana Division was made a part of the Arkansas Division, creating the Arkansas-Louisiana Division. Next, the Indian Territory Division and the Panhandle Division were consolidated into the new Panhandle-Indian Territory Division. Finally, the Amarillo Division was merged with the El Paso-Mexico Division, creating the El Paso-Amarillo Division.

A challenge for the railroad was that the Choctaw Route, while a through line between Memphis and Tucumcari, varied greatly in different places along the line. A perfect example was the different freight tonnages and commodities that moved over different parts of the line. In 1932, one of the slowest years during the Great Depression, the volumes varied significantly from place to place, as reported by the Office of Chief Engineer of the Rock Island Lines. On the very east end of the line where agriculture and timber still dominated, 550 net tons of freight moved westward between Memphis and Little Rock daily, while 1250 tons moved eastward daily. Between Little Rock and Haileyville, there were 700 net tons moving westward each day, and 1150 tons eastward.

The line between Haileyville and El Reno saw the greatest volume of freight on the Choctaw Route due to the oil and coal businesses, plus the traffic from the Oklahoma City area. Between Haileyville and Shawnee there were 1560 daily tons westward and 1380 tons eastward, while between Shawnee and El Reno, there were 2630 tons of freight westward and 1360 tons moving eastward. West of El Reno to Sayre, where wheat farming dominated, there was only an average of 650 westbound daily tons of freight, with 1000 daily tons moving to the east. Sayre to Amarillo, the volumes dropped further to about 220 tons westward and 750 tons eastward. The traffic west of Amarillo was very light, with 180 tons moving west and 200 tons moving east each day.

Shipments of wheat on the western end of the line were an important part of the finances of the railroad. In many years, the volume of wheat determined whether the Rock Island made a profit or not. These volumes across the railroad could vary from a few thousand shipments (a bad year) to several hundred thousand shipments (a great year).

By 1947, the track west of Amarillo was part of the larger Panhandle Division. The track from Shawnee to Tucumcari was part of the Southern Division by the early 1960s. At the same time, the eastern end of the Choctaw Route was the Arkansas Division, which also included the line south into Louisiana. At the time, rice, soybeans, cotton, and other agricultural products accounted for 8.9% of the originating traffic on the Arkansas Division. Manufactured and miscellaneous products produced in Little Rock and other towns along the line accounted for 21.9% of the originating traffic. However, paper, lumber, bauxite, and other similar products accounted for more than 50%, and much of this was funneled onto the Choctaw Route at Biddle Yard in Little Rock.

During the early 1960s, the Rock Island reported that the line east of El Reno averaged six million gross tons a year (freight cars and freight combined), while to the west the average was only two million gross tons. Because of the volume of these movements, the track from Memphis west to Perry, Arkansas, and from Oklahoma City to El Reno, were protected by Automatic Block Signals (ABS).

Because of the challenge of describing a railroad built over more than fifty years, the names of the divisions will generally be quoted along with a date. It should be noted that this was also a challenge for the railroad, and by *Southern Division Time Table No. 7*, dated July 30, 1967, the entire route from Memphis to Tucumcari was finally controlled by one division. To show the status of the railroad under the Southern Division, the station codes used in *Time Table No. 7* will be noted after the station name throughout this route guide.

History of The Choctaw Route

Like many railroads, it took a number of companies to create the Rock Island Railroad between Memphis, Tennessee, and Tucumcari, New Mexico. There have also been many more who have operated parts of the railroad after its failure. An attempt is made to report on all of these in this book.

The rail line also had very different personalities depending upon where it was. Across Arkansas, timber and lumber initially dominated, with several dozen large lumber companies shipping on the railroad. Most of these lumber companies had their own logging railroads, many of which were investigated as part of the Interstate Commerce Commission Tap Lines hearings. Coal was also a major early commodity moved from Western Arkansas and Eastern Oklahoma stations. At Little Rock, the Rock Island's rail line towards New Orleans added more timber, oil and other shipments to the Choctaw Route. Later, cotton, hay, rice and other crops became the primary sources of business for the railroad in Arkansas.

Across Oklahoma, first coal, and then oil dominated, with cotton in the east and wheat in the west providing more business. Wheat was grown across the panhandle of Texas, where oil and carbon black plants were also along the railroad. West of Amarillo, the number of on-line shippers dwindled, with a few wheat and hay shippers keeping the line busy during harvest season.

The terrain also varied from the many wetlands found in Eastern Arkansas to the mountains of Western Arkansas. Heading across Western Oklahoma, the rail line climbed as it headed west to the high and dry panhandle of Texas. Most of the railroad passed through rural country, but it still had to wind its way through the urban areas of Memphis, Little Rock, Oklahoma City, and Amarillo.

Creating *The Choctaw Route*, also known as *The 35th Parallel Route* or *The Sunbelt Line*, involved many companies, some that actually operated parts of the line and others that were subsidiaries and existed only on paper. The railroad runs east-west, and like most such railroads, the line was built primarily from east (Memphis) to west (Tucumcari). However, parts of the route were built west to east, with miles of track completed in Oklahoma years before the last of the track was built in Arkansas. Much of this was possible because the Choctaw Route was actually a younger railroad route, with parts built years after other railroads had already begun serving the region.

This history of companies involved with building the Chicago, Rock Island & Pacific from Memphis, Tennessee, west to Tucumcari, New Mexico, follows the companies as they were created. A brief history of each of the railroad companies is provided here. An issue with this company history, and the history of the route, is that some of these companies existed at the same time. Another issue deals with all of the names that were used to represent the railroad over its more than 160 years of existence. To simplify the issue, the name Rock Island or CRI&P (Chicago, Rock Island & Pacific) will generally be used through the route guide materials, even when another railroad originally built the line. The names of the communities along the route often changed, and every effort was made to be consistent with their current use. Again, please forgive these simplifications.

Memphis & Little Rock Railroad Company (1853-1873)

The Memphis and Little Rock Railroad had a very hectic history. Because of periodic high waters between the Mississippi and the St Francis Rivers, with no levee control whatever, the building of a railroad taxed engineering skill. Its progress was slow, it ran into financial difficulties, and it changed hands four times between its inception and 1887. The 55-pound rails would not hold the ties to the fill in high water, and the engineers had to anchor the track to the trees with cable and chains to keep from losing it altogether.

"1852 - 100 Years of Progress - 1952"
Rock Island Lines News Digest (October 1952)

The Memphis & Little Rock Plank or Railroad Company was the start of the Rock Island line westward from Memphis, Tennessee. The company was organized by Special Act of the Arkansas General Assembly, approved January 11, 1853. When created, there was a plan for a railroad between the two cities in the company's name, but the Act did say that if $400,000 in capital stock for the railroad was not subscribed, then the owners could build a plank road instead along the same route. The territory between Memphis and Little Rock was probably the hardest part of the entire railroad to build as it covered almost 100 miles of rivers, swamps, sloughs, and hardwood river bottoms. There was little access except by riverboat, and the soils were generally not good for building a stable railroad grade.

While the railroad was incorporated in Arkansas, it was strongly backed by Memphis businessmen, and the city itself issued $350,000 of bonds to assist the new enterprise. At the time, a number of Mississippi River towns were battling to see who would control the western trade. For years, Memphis had benefitted from the trade that riverboats brought it, but now rail was becoming the key. By the 1850s, Memphis had railroad service from several Atlantic coast cities, but realized that it needed rail service into the growing west to keep and control the market. To further assist with the construction of the railroad westward, the United States Congress authorized a land grant of 438,647 acres of mostly Arkansas swampland on February 3, 1853.

The influence of Memphis on the railroad was clear for decades. Even as the Choctaw, Oklahoma & Gulf consolidated the system and built westward, Memphis was an obvious backer and point of pride. The December 1899 issue of *The Choctaw* magazine was dedicated to Memphis, Tennessee, and included the following.

>*Memphis is a phenomenal city. It is essentially a city of exchange, of barter between the producers of raw products, and the manufacturers on one side and consumers on the other. It creates very little; it adds very little to the raw wealth or its raw products; its additions to the wealth it handles, in the shape of new forms and accretions, are a minimum.*
>
>*And yet, commercially, as a city of exchange solely or nearly so, it ranks in business actually done with any city in the United States of equal, or even double, its population. For nearly a half century, despite now and then accumulating but, happily, temporary disasters, its record shows the smallest percentage of failures, whether considering capital or population as the basis, of any city in America.*

James M. Williamson was the first president of the Memphis & Little Rock Railroad and also served as a director. Based in Memphis, Williamson signed a contract in June 1854 with John H. Bradley & Company to build the railroad. Reports from the time state that Bradley & Company was an "experienced and energetic Railroad building firm of Indiana." The contract provided two years to build 40 miles of track from Hopefield (across the Mississippi River from Memphis) to the St. Francis River, and four years to complete the remainder of the railroad. The original gauge was to be 5 feet, 6 inches.

Surveys for the Memphis & Little Rock Railroad were made quickly, and the town of Hopefield became the eastern end of the railroad, cited as the location of the company offices in the company's charter. Hopefield was located on the Arkansas shore of the Mississippi River and provided a landing for boats and ferries to reach Memphis. The first rails of the company were installed in early June of 1857, and the first train ran west in August, obviously not meeting the two year requirement for service to the St. Francis River. About the same time, John Robertson replaced Williamson as president of the company. Despite financial difficulties, the track reached the St. Francis River at Madison, Arkansas, by November 1858, and trains started running daily in January 1859.

The second part of the Memphis & Little Rock to be built was the west end from the north bank of the Arkansas River near Little Rock, eastward to the White River at DeValls Bluff. This part of the railroad was easier to build as much of it crossed the Grand Prairie of Arkansas. Newspapers reported that by late 1860, hundreds of men were working east across this prairie, and that construction of the grade to the White River had nearly been completed. About the same time, a contract had been let for construction of the St. Francis River bridge and 1000 tons of "high quality English rails" were being delivered monthly at New Orleans for completion of the line. On January 26, 1862, William Woodruff (founder of the *Arkansas Gazette*) and General Albert Pike (a writer and legal scholar who often represented Native American tribes in their claims against the federal government) participated in driving the last spike of the track between Little Rock and DeValls Bluff. Reports were that the spike was driven about ten miles east of what was later named Argenta, and today's North Little Rock, at a point short of Bayou Meto.

As the east end of the railroad was being built, passenger and freight services soon started up. The first public service operated late in 1859, and the receipts from hauling of passengers, mail, express and freight amounted to $6,859.06 in just three months. 1860 saw $32,528.40 in revenues, and the first eight months of 1861 produced revenues of $41,826.27. Reports from the time show that more than half of the revenue came from passenger service.

With the two parts of the railroad built, the railroad started offering regular service between the two cities in its name. The service included train Memphis to Madison, stagecoach to Clarendon, riverboat to DeValls Bluff, and then railroad on to near Little Rock. About this time, a rumor began that would last for several decades that the Memphis & Little Rock Railroad would merge with the Little Rock & Fort Smith Railroad to create a line across Arkansas. In fact, the June 1893 *Travelers' Official Guide* still clearly listed Little Rock-Fort Smith connecting trains. While logical, the merger never did take place, although numerous newspaper reports about the action were published.

Impact of the Civil War

The timing could hardly have been worse for the railroad as the Civil War began with the capture of Fort Sumter in April 1861, followed by Arkansas' secession on May 6, 1861. This action made the railroad a target for both Union and Confederate military forces, depending upon who controlled the railroad at the time. The railroad operated for about a year as if the Civil War did not exist, but as Union forces captured the cities of Memphis and Little Rock the railroad became a vital resource for the Union Army, which operated the line for the last several years of the war. This led to some issues as a loan from the State of Arkansas was due in January 1864, but the amount and terms were not known as the paperwork was in the hands of the Confederacy. By April 1864, the Memphis & Little Rock was the only railroad in Arkansas still operating, and that was only between the north bank of the Arkansas River at Little Rock, and DeValls Bluff. In May 1864, the Arkansas General Assembly ordered the railroad to provide a report on the fiscal condition of the company, but it was hard to do as the Quartermaster Corps and the U.S. Military Railroad were running the line.

This historical marker at DeValls Bluff tells the basic story of the Memphis & Little Rock Railroad. Several other markers and signs in town provide more detail.

After the Civil War, the railroad was returned to the Memphis & Little Rock Railroad, which found that it had a wrecked railroad. Soon, Robert Campbell Brinkley was made president of the railroad company, adding some stability to the organization. R. C. Brinkley was well known as a key player in the development of railroads across the south, having been president of the Memphis & Charleston Railroad. He immediately initiated a program to rehabilitate and complete the whole railroad, while at the same time he developed a number of businesses in Memphis.

To assist with the repairs and pay the company for its use during the Civil War, the United States Congress issued another land grant of 365,539 acres on July 28, 1866. By 1868, the railroad had a reported one thousand men rebuilding the old lines and building the new line between the St. Francis and White Rivers. A number of contractors were cited in reports from the time, and men and companies seemed to change quickly as the company's finances also changed. By March 31, 1868, the Memphis & Little Rock Railroad was back to where it had been in early 1862.

1869 was an important year for the railroad as the line had crossed the St. Francis River and the first bale of cotton was shipped east from Forrest City, arriving at Memphis on July 15, 1869. By September, the railroad had reached the L'Anguille River and work was underway on the White River Bridge at DeValls Bluff.

The 1869 Board War

A dispute came about in 1869 as the old Board of Directors of the company failed to hold a stockholders' meeting, and a number of stockholders called their own meeting and elected new company leadership. Both boards then obtained court orders to stop the actions of the other board, and things went as far as having the company's rolling stock seized on Friday, November 19, 1869, to protect the assets of the railroad. With one board based in Memphis and the other one in Little Rock, a sheriff was eventually put in charge until a solution could be found. Things became even more uncertain when company president John C. Fremont claimed that the railroad was actually owned by the Memphis, El Paso & Pacific Railroad Company, a proposed transcontinental railroad that built some track in Texas. At the time, Fremont was also president of the Memphis, El Paso & Pacific. Little came of this announcement, and the Memphis & Little Rock Railroad remained an independent company.

The two groups of directors soon went to court, but the case was settled out of court during January 1870. The old board was given temporary authority and a special meeting of stockholders was scheduled for February 15th at Hopefield. A representative of the Pulaski County, Arkansas, bonds failed to show up and the Memphis delegation won all of the board seats but one. This unity allowed construction to begin again and ended much of the internal bickering.

Completion of the Railroad

Construction continued through the late 1860s and early 1870s. Much of the railroad was built on wooden trestles, but the last spike was finally driven the afternoon of April 11, 1871. The spike was driven at DeValls Bluff, celebrating the opening of the White River bridge. The focus of the work turned to improving the railroad, including raising the tracks above flood levels and filling in the numerous trestles. In 1871, it was reported that eight hundred men were at work on these tasks.

On January 12, 1872, the Memphis & Little Rock changed its track gauge to five feet to match the gauge of its primary connections at Memphis, the Memphis & Charleston Railroad and the Memphis, Clarksville & Louisville Railroad. By late 1872, a new and improved inclined plane was built at Hopefield so that railcars could be moved across the Mississippi River by ferry to these other railroads. While this work made the railroad more reliable, the lack of sufficient business and the heavy expenses caused it to fail, and on December 12, 1873, it was sold to the Memphis & Little Rock Railway Company.

U.S. Military Railroad (1862-1865)

During the Civil War, Congress had authorized President Abraham Lincoln to seize control of all railroads and telegraphs as part of the war effort. However, only southern railroads were actually seized during the war, made possible due to the creation of the U.S. Military Railroad (USMRR), a part of the United States War Department.

The Union Army seized Little Rock in 1863, and their Quartermaster Corps operated the Memphis & Little Rock Railroad until May 1, 1865, after which the U.S. Military Railroad took over. There is some evidence that the U.S. Military Railroad played a role in the operations and later destruction of the line near Memphis, especially after Hopefield was burned by Union troops on February 19, 1863. Operations were based across the Arkansas River from Little Rock, at a location known as Huntersville by Union forces. The Quartermaster Corps made a number of improvements at Huntersville (Argenta, later North Little Rock) during the war, including improvements at the railroad's roundhouse and the construction of several warehouses as a part of the United States Army depot. At the other end of the railroad at Hopefield, the United States Army destroyed the shops and much of the railroad to prevent Confederate troops from using the railroad to attack Memphis.

One of the challenges for the U.S. Military was the 5-foot 6-inch gauge of the railroad. At least two steam locomotives of that gauge were brought up the Mississippi and Arkansas rivers from the New Orleans, Opelousas & Great Western Railroad. Other equipment such as freight cars were also built specifically for the operation.

By April 1864, the Memphis & Little Rock Railroad's line to DeValls Bluff was the last rail line actually operating in Arkansas, and Confederate soldiers continued to attack trains operating over the line, and to tear up the railroad. At the end of the Civil War, the U.S. Military Railroad was in charge. On June 30, 1865, the military had ten steam locomotives and ninety-eight cars operating on the Little Rock to DeValls Bluff railroad, with the east end out of service. On November 1, 1865, the USMRR packed up and left, returning the mostly-destroyed property to the Memphis & Little Rock Railroad.

Memphis & Little Rock Railway Company (1873-1877)

The cost to rebuild and complete the railroad was too much for the Memphis & Little Rock Railroad to actually cover, and soon the bond payments were not being made. An auction of the railroad was announced for March 17, 1873, to settle the claims of the holders of the second mortgage bonds of the railroad, who's coupons had not been paid according to agreement. Henry F. Vail, a bank

21

and railroad official who was trustee of the second mortgage bondholders, handled the sale where the railroad was sold for $3,181,000 to Stillman Witt, a railroad and steel industry executive. Witt then turned the railroad over to the Memphis & Little Rock Railway Company on December 12, 1873.

In reality, there were few changes in the owners of the railroad as the bond holders were the ones who acquired the company, using the money owed to them as the acquisition payment. Something else that didn't change was the inability of the railroad to pay its bills. By 1875, the Trustees of the first mortgage bondholders were in control of the company. The railroad also seemed to be in chaos as company president W. G. Greenlaw (an early business partner with R. C. Brinkley) stated that he was working to prevent a foreclosure of the mortgage to guarantee the employees their wages, and that the company directors had failed to meet to take any actions on the railroad's problems.

In August 1875, Robert K. Dow, a major stockholder, was appointed receiver of the Memphis & Little Rock Railway. On December 1, 1876, the United States circuit court ordered the sale of the railroad, setting the sale date of February 27, 1877. However, the sale actually didn't take place until April 27, 1877. The sale was not a simple auction of the company. Instead, there were plans to sell the railroad property in multiple parts, covering the federal land grants that hadn't yet been sold; Arkansas land grants that hadn't yet been sold; the railroad itself; all property guaranteed and held by bonds and mortgages issued on May 1, 1860; and all the property guaranteed and held by bonds and mortgages issued on December 1, 1873. For the reader's information, the *Poor's Manual* of 1877-78 stated that there were 133,948 acres of land grant property still available. On December 31, 1879, the Memphis & Little Rock Railroad Company reported that the railroad had received 142,802.63 land grant acres from the federal government, of which only 54,104.38 acres had been sold at an average price of $2.89 an acre. At the time, the railroad was also entitled to an additional 661,383 acres, but no patents had been issued.

On April 27, 1877, the entire property was apparently sold on the steps of the United States courthouse in Little Rock to the trustees for the bondholders for $500,000. The property was then reorganized on April 30th under the original charter of the Memphis & Little Rock Railroad Company.

Memphis & Little Rock Railroad Company (1877-1887)

The railroad was back to using the name Memphis & Little Rock Railroad Company, starting on April 30, 1877. The change in the corporate organization created an opportunity for the St. Louis, Iron Mountain & Southern Railway to purchase the Memphis & Little Rock Railroad. Numerous reports in 1880 covered the purchase, which apparently was a stock exchange, but a full purchase was apparently stopped by a large block of security holders. For the next several years, Jay Gould of the St. Louis, Iron Mountain & Southern was shown as president of the Memphis & Little Rock Railroad, and a number of his business associates were on the Board of Directors.

Newspapers reported that Jay Gould was spending money to improve the conditions of the Memphis & Little Rock. However, financial issues again quickly came up, and on June 24, 1882, E. K. Sibley was appointed receiver of the railroad. The reason for the receiver was a lawsuit filed by Russell Sage for the non-payment of a $125,921.13 debt, as reported in *The Daily Arkansas Gazette* of June 25, 1882.

Data collected for the 1880 U.S. Census (*Report of the Agencies of Transportation in the United States*) showed that cotton (19,219 tons), merchandise and miscellaneous (14.031 tons), manufactures (manufactured products - 12,910 tons), and lumber and other forest products (8749 tons) were the major products moved on the railroad. Other products like provisions (foods and household supplies – 5663 tons), livestock (3728 tons), flour (3133 tons), and stone, brick, lime, cement, sand and clay (1004 tons) added to the 70,347 tons moved in the reported year (July 1, 1879 - June 30, 1880). At the time, the railroad also had 14 steam locomotives (coal and wood-fired); 8 passenger cars; 4 mail, baggage and express cars; 270 freight cars; and 8 other cars. The railroad had an agreement with the Southern Express Company to provide space in their baggage and express cars, with revenues of $5224.37 in 1879. The Memphis & Little Rock Railroad Company also paid $2049.30 in car hire to a sleeping-car company.

The railroad was well-staffed. There were 6 general officers and 8 office clerks, plus 60 station men. To operate the trains, there were 15 engineers, 6 conductors, and 33 other trainmen. Maintaining the equipment were 9 machinists, 25 carpenters, and 24 other shop men. There were also 213 employees maintaining the track, plus 76 other employees, with a total annual payroll of $144,487.30.

The Memphis & Little Rock Railroad Company was shown to have 145.32 miles of track (135.0 route miles), all using 58-pound-per-yard iron rail. The railroad had installed 33,000 ties the year before, most being white oak which were bought at 32 cents per tie. The company reported that a white oak tie had an average life span of six years.

The revenues were more than enough to cover the operating costs, but the funded debt ($2.85 million) was another story. The receivership ended on December 1, 1883. However, more unpaid bills forced the company back into receivership on March 24, 1884, with Rudolph Fink as the receiver. Fink would be involved with efforts to save the railroad for years, and was also involved with building other railroads across the country.

A sale of the railroad was ordered and then delayed as the property was turned over to the trustees of the mortgage holders on August 7, 1884. Fink then became the general manager for the trustees. Over the next few years, owners of the mortgage bonds changed several times and the sale was delayed. Jay Gould also delayed the sale, trying to protect the $750,000 that he had invested in company stock. While the operations remained under the control of trustees and the courts, the gauge of the railroad was changed again to standard gauge on May 30, 1886.

A sale of the Memphis & Little Rock, known as the "Old Reliable" in some reporting, took place on April 13, 1887. However, this sale was contested and a new one was held on September 1, 1887, where the railroad was sold for $2 million to Robert K. Dow, one of those who were owed money by the railroad. Almost immediately, the new owners held a stockholders meetings and elected Rudolph Fink as president of the new company, the Little Rock & Memphis Railroad.

The Chicago, Rock Island & Pacific Railway Company (1880-1948)

The history of The Chicago, Rock Island & Pacific Railway Company dates back to the beginning of the Rock Island family, which started with the Illinois incorporation of the Rock Island & LaSalle Railroad Company on February 27, 1847. Little was done until the company amended its charter on February 7, 1851, to make the company the Chicago & Rock Island Railroad Company. Construction started on October 1, 1851, and the first train reached Joliet, Illinois, on October 10, 1852. On February 22, 1854, the railroad was the first to reach the Mississippi River when it was built to Rock Island, Illinois. On August 20, 1866, as the firm continued to grow, it became the Chicago, Rock Island & Pacific Railroad Company.

On June 2, 1880, the Chicago, Rock Island & Pacific Railroad Company consolidated with five other railroads to create The Chicago, Rock Island & Pacific Railway Company. These other railroads showed the direction of growth, and included The Iowa Southern & Missouri Northern Railroad Company; The Newton & Monroe Railroad Company; Atlantic & Audubon Railroad Company; Atlantic Southern Railroad Company; and The Avoca, Macedonia & South Western Railroad Company.

This is the Rock Island Railroad that purchased a controlling interest in the Choctaw, Oklahoma & Gulf Railroad in 1902. On March 3,1905, Congress passed *An Act Granting to the Choctaw, Oklahoma and Gulf Railroad Company the power to sell and convey to the Chicago, Rock Island and Pacific Railway Company all the railway property, rights, franchises, and privileges of the Choctaw, Oklahoma and Gulf Railroad Company, and for other purposes.* This act was required because the Choctaw, Oklahoma & Gulf had been built on the lands of Indian Territory, which was under the protection and control of the Secretary of the Interior.

About the same time, the Reid-Moore Syndicate (Judge William H. Moore, his brother J. H. Moore, Daniel G. Reid and William B. Leeds) gained control of the Rock Island Railroad, and eventually the St. Louis & San Francisco Railway and the Chicago & Eastern Illinois Railroad. The Reid-Moore Syndicate developed plans to grow the railroads and to control most of the Midwest and Southern rail operations. Numerous subsidiaries and controlling companies, including the Rock Island Company and the Chicago, Rock Island & Pacific Railroad, were used to sell debt to pay for the expansion.

In 1904-1905, the Choctaw, Oklahoma & Gulf was consolidated with the Chicago, Rock Island & Pacific. Concerns about competing railroads coordinating their actions led the State of Oklahoma to pass legislation (1908) requiring that the Chicago, Rock Island & Pacific; the St. Louis & San Francisco; and the Choctaw, Oklahoma & Gulf be split up by their owners, the Rock Island Company of New Jersey. Economic issues also began to impact the Reid-Moore Syndicate, and in 1909, the St. Louis & San Francisco was purchased by a group headed by Benjamin F. Yoakum and P. L. Winchell. Yoakum was the former chairman of the executive committee for the Chicago, Rock Island & Pacific, and the former chairman of the St. Louis & San Francisco. Winchell was the former president of the Chicago, Rock Island & Pacific, and became the president of the St. Louis & San Francisco with the split.

The Rock Island was able to fight off financial troubles for a few years due to the agricultural products and coal that it hauled, but when the debt began to hit, the railroad entered bankruptcy in 1915 and Moore and Reid were mostly gone. The CRI&P was reorganized in 1917, thanks to its receiver, Jacob McGavock Dickinson. Dickinson was the receiver April 20, 1915 - June 21, 1917, and had a distinguished career in the railroad industry and in politics. He worked as an attorney for railroads like the Illinois Central Railroad and the Louisville & Nashville Railroad. He taught law at the Vanderbilt University Law School, served on the Tennessee Supreme Court, helped to organize the American Society of International Law, and was president of the American Bar Association. Dickinson served as the United States Secretary of War under President William Howard Taft from 1909 to 1911, and after serving as the Rock Island's receiver, was the president of the Izaak Walton League a decade later. After two years of Jacob Dickinson's care, the railroad was reorganized without a foreclosure sale, keeping the same company name.

Despite the successful reorganization in 1917, the Rock Island was again in receivership in 1933. The company was still tied down with debt created by the Reid-Moore Syndicate (about $400 million in funded debt with almost $14 million in interest payments every year for the company), and revenues were hurt by the Great Depression. After almost fifteen years, the Chicago, Rock Island & Pacific Railroad Company was chartered in Delaware on December 16, 1947, and became the official operator of the railroad on January 1, 1948.

Little Rock & Memphis Railroad Company (1887-1898)

Despite the name change, the pattern of the Memphis to Little Rock railroad was again the same. The bond holders took over the railroad, the company couldn't pay its debt, and a receiver was appointed. Another common factor was that there were plenty of rumors about other companies taking over the Little Rock & Memphis Railroad (LR&M). Companies like Illinois Central; Atchison, Topeka & Santa Fe; Southern Railway; St. Louis Southwestern; and the Kansas City, Pittsburg & Gulf are a few of the companies that reporters just knew were interested in buying the rail line.

There were also plenty of rumors about the railroad building west. Routes to Texas and Oklahoma were reportedly surveyed by the Little Rock & Memphis, or by companies who were going to buy the railroad and then extend it. Reports about building a line to Hot Springs were common, especially after the railroad built a ticket office there. In reality, the Little Rock & Memphis was interested in the Hot Springs traffic, with passengers using the Hot Springs Railroad and the St. Louis, Iron Mountain & Southern for travel between Hot Springs and Little Rock, and then the Little Rock & Memphis on east to Memphis. However, as part of the battle with the Iron Mountain, LR&M tickets were not being sold by the Iron Mountain at Hot Springs, so the Little Rock & Memphis opened their own ticket office there.

In September 1887, the Little Rock & Memphis sold $3,186,000 in bonds secured by a mortgage on the railroad. The money was used to pay off old debts and to make improvements at various locations along the line. The improvements included raising the roadbed even more and filling in additional trestles.

In 1889, the Interstate Commerce Commission surveyed railroads about "relations existing between railway corporations and their employes." The results were reported in the *Third Annual Report of the Interstate Commerce Commission* (1889). Company president Rudulph Fink of the Little Rock & Memphis Railroad Company submitted the following.

> *This company has not provided any insurance fund or guaranty fund of any sort, for its employees.*

> *The company has provided sleeping cars for its employees at Hopefield, Ark., where on account of the encroachments of the Mississippi River upon the Arkansas shore, no permanent quarters could be maintained. A reading-room has been provided at Memphis, Tenn.*

> *No provision is made for technical education in our shops.*

> *There is a recognition system of promotion in the service, based upon length of service and peculiar fitness.*

There is no special rule in force as regards competency of lo-
comotive engineers. Most of the engineers on the line have been
trained upon it, beginning as firemen.

The *Eleventh Census of the United States* (1890) included a great deal of additional detail about the Little Rock & Memphis Railroad Company. The report
included information about expenses and revenues, employment, equipment,
and various operations. It stated that the number of mainline miles operated
by the railroad had been reduced from 135.00 miles to 131.25 miles, due to
"track straightened in 1888." This left the railroad operating 130.60 miles in
Arkansas, and 0.65 miles in Tennessee, with 85.00 miles of track consisting of
steel rails, and 46.25 miles of iron rails. The railroad operated 13 "ordinary"
passenger cars and 7 baggage, postal and express cars. No sleeper or parlor cars
were listed. For the freight service, there were 123 boxcars, 84 flat cars, 17 stock
cars, 40 coal cars, 2 refrigerator cars, 114 company service cars, and 7 "other"
cars. To pull the trains, there were 8 freight, 5 passenger, and 3 switching steam
locomotives. An ICC report dated April 1, 1896, showed that the passenger
equipment of the railroad totaled 20 cars, all with Westinghouse train brakes.
Six of the cars were equipped with Miller automatic couplers. The railroad also
had 269 freight cars, none with automatic couplers or train brakes.

The 1890 Census stated that the railroad had 15 general administration
employees, 167 in maintenance of way and structures, 50 in maintenance of
equipment, and 168 "conducting transportation." Passenger operations for
the previous year produced $270,912.43 in revenue ($233,134.21 passenger,
$20,772.99 express, $15,205.23 mail, $1800.00 other) while the movement of
131,854 tons of freight produced $311,062.10.

By December 1890, Pullman Buffet Sleepers were running between Little
Rock and Louisville, Kentucky. Another passenger train improvement was the
decision in 1892 to start using the Frisco Bridge to reach Memphis, saving almost an hour over the ferry at Hopefield. However, freight moves continued to
use Hopefield.

This was all good news, but it changed with the default on bond interest in
early 1893. In explaining the lack of payments, Rudolph Fink stated that the
St. Louis, Iron Mountain & Southern had blocked the railroad from many of
the sources of business in Little Rock, and that earnings had plummeted from
when the net earnings had averaged $150,000 per year. It was pointed out that
the "Gould interests" were working to harm the property, possibly as revenge
for the earlier losses that Jay Gould had experienced when owning the company.

On May 31, 1893, the Central Trust Company of New York filed claims on
the property and Rudolph Fink was appointed as receiver. Almost immediately, the east end of the railroad was under water from flooding, halting traffic
for a few days. With bills and interest unpaid, the United States Court at Little
Rock ordered the railroad sold. A series of sales were announced and then

postponed. The cause cited was the heavy debt ($3,000,000) that any buyer would assume. Approximately a half-dozen sales were postponed before the property was sold to the Choctaw & Memphis on October 25, 1898. It was December 31, 1898, before the new company actually took over the railroad, and the receivership didn't end until December 23, 1899. The last official action of the Little Rock & Memphis was to turn over $19,409.23 in earnings that were acquired from November 19, 1898 to December 31, 1898.

Choctaw Coal & Railway Company (1888-1894)

There are not many railroads that can trace their history back to a turkey hunt, but the Choctaw Coal & Railway Company can. During the 1880s, Edward D. Chadrick, a financier and newspaper man from Minneapolis, started hearing about coal being found and mined in Oklahoma. Recognizing the demand for coal across the Midwest, Chadrick started looking for solutions on how to mine the coal and transport it to the market.

In 1885, Chadrick was introduced to mining and railroad experts from the coal region of Pennsylvania, and worked to introduce them to the potential of Oklahoma, then part of Indian Territory. Later that year, a team of experts went to Indian Territory to explore potential mine locations and routes for a railroad. The trip was disguised as a turkey hunt, but executives of the Lehigh Valley Railroad came away convinced that there was money in the project. Plans were made over the next two years, and on February 1, 1888, the Choctaw Coal & Railway Company was incorporated in Minnesota.

On February 18, 1888, Congress passed an act that authorized the Choctaw Coal & Railway Company to construct and operate a railway through the Indian Territory, as well as telegraph and telephone lines. The Congressional Act provided a number of clear conditions associated with permission to build the railroad. Some of these are included here.

> *That said corporation is authorized to take and use for all purposes of railway, and for no other purpose, a right of way one hundred feet in width through said Indian Territory for said mainline and branch of the Choctaw Coal and Railway Company; and to take and use a strip of land two hundred feet in width, with a length of three thousand feet, in addition to right of way, for stations, for every ten miles of road, with the right to use such additional ground where there are heavy cuts or fills as may be necessary for the construction and maintenance of the road-bed, not exceeding one hundred feet in width on each side of said right of way, or as much thereof as may be included in said cut or fill.*

That said company shall cause maps showing the route of its located lines through said Territory to be filed in the office of the Secretary of the Interior, and also to be filed in the office of the principal chief of each of the nations or tribes through whose lands said railway may be located.

That said railway company shall build at least one hundred miles of its railway in said Territory within three years after the passage of this act, and complete the main line of the same within said Territory within one year thereafter.

Additionally, the company was to pay $15 per mile, per year, to the Secretary of the Interior. The payment was to benefit the Indian tribes in the general area through which the railroad was constructed. Although the initial route was designated by Congress, there was a great deal of speculation about where the Choctaw Coal & Railway Company would actually build. Newspaper reports went as far as stating that the company would build in Texas, Arkansas and the Indian Territory, reaching places like Little Rock, El Paso, and Texas at the Red River.

By early 1890, the Garvey Brothers were building track in Indian Territory, heading east and west from South McAlester and were expected to reach the Frisco at Wister by May 1, 1890. Coal mines were already being opened along the line, with plans to have coal ready to ship when the railroad was completed. Later that year, sixty-seven miles of track were in service between Wister and South McAlester. While the line at McAlester was being built, the company was also building track further west. The October 1952 issue of the *Rock Island Lines News Digest* reported on the construction of the line, and included the following information.

In 1888 this Company surveyed a line, beginning at Fort Reno (near El Reno) and extending eastward via Yukon to and through the site of the present Oklahoma City, where the U.S. Government had already surveyed and reserved a townsite area for the future city. The formal opening was scheduled for April 22, 1889. Controversy developed over the right-of-way and the line between El Reno and Oklahoma City was not completed and placed in operation until February, 1892, although portions of the line between Fort Reno, El Reno and Yukon seem to have been built in 1889.

The year 1890 was not a good one for the Choctaw Coal & Railway Company. The Choctaw Council of the Choctaw Nation filed complaints about the company, stating that it attempted to obtain more land than allowed, was planning routes not in its charter, had built fences along the right-of-way without permission of the council, had created coal and rail syndicates, and was locating and creating new town sites. Additionally, a receiver was appointed in December 1890 because the company defaulted on interest on the bonds and also failed to make payments on loans taken out to build the railroad.

The *Eleventh Census of the United States* (1890) included some basic details about the Choctaw Coal & Railway Company. It stated that there were 39.80 miles of track in Indian Territory, which commenced operations in 1890. The railroad owned three steam locomotives used for freight service, and no passenger equipment. The freight was moved on 210 coal cars, 25 flat cars, and 10 boxcars. There were also two cars used in company service. For the year ending on June 30, 1890, the railroad handled 16,404 tons of bituminous coal, all originating on-line. No other freight was reported.

Plans for more construction were announced in 1891, but a report in the June 1893 *Traveler's Official Guide* stated that the railroad still consisted of two parts. The first was 64.7 miles of track between South McAlester and Wister Junction in Indian Territory, while the second was 31.2 miles of track from Fort Reno to Oklahoma City in Oklahoma Territory. More talk of connecting South McAlester with Oklahoma City took place in 1894, but on August 24, 1894, the United States Congress granted the railroad the right to sell the company, including its rights to build in the Indian Territory. On August 8, 1894, the Choctaw Coal & Railway Company was sold to George H. Earl for $3,500,000, and then was transferred to the Choctaw, Oklahoma & Gulf Railroad Company on October 3, 1894.

Choctaw, Oklahoma & Gulf Railroad Company (1894-1948)

As stated by the Interstate Commerce Commission (ICC), the "Choctaw, Oklahoma and Gulf was incorporated under an act of Congress, approved August 24, 1894, for the purpose of acquiring the property, rights, and franchises of the Choctaw Coal and Railway Company." The Choctaw Coal & Railway Company was sold to a reorganization committee on September 8, 1894, and then transferred to the Choctaw, Oklahoma & Gulf on October 3, 1894.

The new Choctaw, Oklahoma & Gulf (CO&G) was controlled by businessmen from Philadelphia, Pennsylvania, and for the first time, seemed to have ample capital to complete the railroad as had been discussed for decades. An expansion program began almost immediately, and track was built between South McAlester and Oklahoma City by October 1895. To continue track construction, and the acquisition of existing railroads, several new subsidiaries were created. These included the Choctaw & Memphis Railroad; the Western Oklahoma Railroad; and the Choctaw, Oklahoma & Texas Railroad.

With the new construction and acquisitions, the railroad basically operated from near Memphis, Tennessee, to east of Amarillo, Texas. The ICC described the company as "a single-track, standard-gauge, steam railroad, of which the main line extends from Hopefield, Ark., a point on the Mississippi River opposite Memphis, Tenn., westwardly through the States of Arkansas and Oklahoma, to the Texas-Oklahoma boundary at Texola, Okla. Branch lines extend from Benton to Hot Springs and Malvern, Ark.; Branch Junction to Ardmore, Okla.; Tecumseh Junction to Asher, Okla.; and Geary, Okla., to Anthony, Kans."

One issue with the creation of the Choctaw, Oklahoma & Gulf was that many of the founders were investors and were willing to sell their stocks and bonds for a profit. Additionally, a number of the early investors were connected to The Chicago, Rock Island & Pacific Railway Company, and by 1902, control of the CO&G stock was in the hands of the Rock Island.

To further control the Choctaw Route, the CRI&P leased the railroad on March 24, 1904, for a period of 999 years. At the time, *Poor's Railroad Manual* reported that the Rock Island owned the entire capital stock of the CO&G, and the lease terms were to simply pay the funded debt and any lease payments for which the Choctaw, Oklahoma & Gulf was responsible.

However, even with this ownership and lease, The Chicago, Rock Island & Pacific Railway Company could not officially acquire the Choctaw, Oklahoma & Gulf Railroad Company. This was because the original charter of the CO&G was issued by the United States Congress due to its location in Indian Territory. On March 3, 1905, Congress passed *An Act Granting to the Choctaw, Oklahoma and Gulf Railroad Company the power to sell and convey to the Chicago, Rock Island and Pacific Railway Company all the railway property, rights, franchises, and privileges of the Choctaw, Oklahoma and Gulf Railroad Company, and for other purposes.*

Despite approval from Congress to acquire the Choctaw, Oklahoma & Gulf, the lease continued and the CO&G remained as an invisible but separate company, but completely controlled by The Chicago, Rock Island & Pacific Railway. The lease ended when the CO&G was formally merged into the Rock Island on January 1, 1948.

This builder's photo of Choctaw, Oklahoma & Gulf #107, which became an 1800-series Rock Island locomotive, seems like an odd design for Oklahoma and Arkansas. #107 was built by Baldwin in 1902 to a design known as a Camelback. This design allowed the firebox to be large by placing the cab over the boiler and the driving wheels. This larger firebox allowed the steam locomotive to burn fines and lower quality coal from the railroad's own mines. While the engineer rode in the cab, the fireman rode the back by the firebox, often preventing reliable communications between these members of the crew. About 3000 Camelback locomotives were built for service in the United States. Photo from the author's collection.

Choctaw & Memphis Railroad Company (1898-1900)

The purchase of the Little Rock & Memphis Railroad by the Choctaw & Memphis Railroad Company was only a part of a larger plan to connect Memphis with cities further west. The original charter showed that the Choctaw & Memphis Railroad had been created to "acquire the property of the Little Rock & Memphis Railroad Company, and also to construct a railroad between the City of Little Rock and the Arkansas-Indian Territory State line." This goal to go west was actually a plan of the Choctaw, Oklahoma & Gulf, the owner and creator of the Choctaw & Memphis.

Fredric P. Alcott, a trustee, actually bought the Little Rock & Memphis on October 25, 1898. He then turned the property over to the Choctaw & Memphis Railroad Company, which had been incorporated in Arkansas on September 15, 1898. The Choctaw & Memphis Railroad was well funded thanks to its ownership by the Choctaw, Oklahoma & Gulf, and construction started all along the extended route. Alcott remained trustee through the existence of the Choctaw & Memphis, protecting the interests of the bondholders.

The Choctaw & Memphis Railroad basically handled the construction of the railroad from Argenta (North Little Rock), Arkansas, to Howe, Oklahoma. Almost as soon as the construction ended, the railroad was bought by the Choctaw, Oklahoma & Gulf Railroad for $1,621,500 on June 30, 1900. At the time, the railroad had a reported 282 miles of track, which included the new Arkansas River Bridge.

Little Rock Bridge Company (1899)

To build the Arkansas River Bridge at Little Rock, the Little Rock Bridge Company was created by the Choctaw & Memphis Railroad. The name Little Rock Bridge Company can be confusing, because this was the third company that used that name at Little Rock. The first was created in 1872 and was to build a railroad bridge that could be used by all railroads, but was believed to be controlled by the Cairo & Fulton Railroad from the beginning. The second incorporation came in October 1892 with the purpose of building a toll bridge over the Arkansas River at Little Rock, since it was "too burdensome" for taxpayers to build a free bridge.

The third Little Rock Bridge Company was organized in May 1899 by the Choctaw & Memphis Railroad as part of a plan by the Choctaw, Oklahoma & Gulf Railroad to extend the railroad westward. In January 1899, Congress had passed legislation authorizing the construction of the Arkansas River bridge, and the Little Rock Bridge Company was formed to create the plans. According to the 1907 *Moody's Manual of Railroads and Corporation Securities*, the Little Rock Bridge Company issued $375,000 in 20-year bonds on June 19, 1899. *Moody's* stated that the bonds were "Secured by first lien on bridge and appurtenances across the Arkansas River at Little Rock, Ark." By late 1899, the Little Rock Bridge Company was rolled into the Choctaw & Memphis Railroad for $1 since the deed allowed the bridge company to sell or lease the bridge to the Choctaw & Memphis as long as the railroad took over paying the principal and interests on the bonds.

Despite the bridge originally being a part of the Little Rock Bridge Company, that name has never been used to describe the bridge. Instead, Choctaw Bridge or Rock Island Bridge have been the commonly used names.

Western Oklahoma Railroad Company (1900-1902)

The Western Oklahoma Railroad Company was incorporated in the Territory of Oklahoma on December 11, 1900. The company was organized by the Choctaw, Oklahoma & Gulf Railroad to build several lines in Oklahoma. On the Choctaw Route, the company built forty miles of track from Elk (Elk City) to the Oklahoma-Texas State Line.

The *Annual Report of the Governor of Oklahoma to the Secretary of the Interior for the Fiscal Year Ended June 30, 1902*, stated that the "following is a statement of miles of track laid and depots built by the construction department on the Choctaw, Oklahoma and Gulf Railroad system in Oklahoma Territory for the year ending June 30, 1902." The report showed 39.400 miles of main line and 6.105 miles of sidings, for a total of 45.505 miles of track.

In addition to the Choctaw Route, the company built almost 120 miles of track south from Haileyville, on the Choctaw Route, to Ardmore, Oklahoma. Both lines were nearly complete when the Choctaw, Oklahoma & Gulf Railroad officially purchased the Western Oklahoma Railroad Company on May 1, 1902. The Western Oklahoma Railroad Company was never an operating company, but instead was used to obtain right-of-way and to build track.

Chicago, Rock Island & El Paso Railway Company (1900-1910)

The Chicago, Rock Island & El Paso Railway Company was incorporated in the Territory of New Mexico on December 18, 1900. The railroad was initially created to build what became the Golden State line from the Texas-New Mexico state line, to the southwest through Tucumcari and on to Santa Rosa, New Mexico, a total of 112 miles. There, the line connected with the El Paso & Rock Island, later Southern Pacific. Eventually, an agreement was reached to allow Southern Pacific to operate and control the line to Tucumcari.

On July 31, 1903, the property rights and franchises, as well as the grading performed on the Choctaw Route by the Chicago, Rock Island & Choctaw Railway, was conveyed by deed to the Chicago, Rock Island & El Paso Railway Company. This route eastward from Tucumcari toward Amarillo was held up by financial issues across the country. On January 9, 1909, the Tucumcari & Memphis Railway Company was incorporated to complete the work started by the Chicago, Rock Island & Choctaw. According to *The Railway and Engineering Review* (December 31, 1910), the railroad from Tucumcari eastward to the Texas-New Mexico state line at Glenrio included 41.46 miles of mainline, as well as 1.07 miles of sidings. Construction was completed by May 9, 1910. When completed, the route was conveyed back to the Chicago, Rock Island & El Paso Railway Company, which turned all of the track over to The Chicago, Rock Island & Pacific Railway on December 31, 1910, since the CRI&P owned one-hundred percent of the capital stock and funded debt of the company.

The Chicago, Rock Island & El Paso Railway Company was a part of a May 2, 1907, agreement with the El Paso & Rock Island Railway, and the Dawson Railway Company. This agreement dealt with the operations, maintenance and management of the terminal at Tucumcari. The agreement had Southern Pacific (El Paso & Rock Island) furnish all employees, tracks, engine house, turntable and other facilities at Tucumcari. The railroads would have equal and joint use of these facilities, thus eliminating the need for duplicate facilities and investments.

The Chicago, Rock Island & El Paso Railway Company remained one of the major parts of the company, in addition to The Chicago, Rock Island & Pacific Railway Company and The Chicago, Rock Island & Gulf Railway Company. These three railroads formed what was called the Rock Island Lines. When the property of the Chicago, Rock Island & El Paso Railway was conveyed to the CRI&P, its funded obligations were also conveyed with the property.

Choctaw, Oklahoma & Texas Railroad Company (1901-1903)

For many years, the Texas Constitution required that railroads operating in the state be based there. To do this, most railroads created a Texas subsidiary. The Choctaw, Oklahoma & Texas Railroad Company is one of these organizations, incorporated in Texas on June 22, 1901. The company, with a capital value of $1,680,000, was to build the railroad west from the Oklahoma-Texas state line to Amarillo. From the beginning, the Choctaw, Oklahoma & Texas Railroad was a subsidiary of the Choctaw, Oklahoma & Gulf. The track reached Yarnall, Texas, a distance of almost 100 miles, by July 6, 1902. There, it used trackage rights on another railroad to reach Amarillo, before the Choctaw Route built its own route.

The charter was amended on November 24, 1902, to allow construction further west to the Texas-New Mexico border. About this time, the Choctaw, Oklahoma & Texas Railroad was falling under the control of the Chicago, Rock Island & Pacific, and it was merged into the Chicago, Rock Island & Gulf Railway Company, a Rock Island subsidiary, on September 25, 1903. Actual control of the railroad took place on December 1, 1903.

Chicago, Rock Island & Gulf Railway Company (1902-1948)

The Chicago, Rock Island & Pacific Railway chartered the Chicago, Rock Island & Gulf Railway Company on May 13, 1902. The purpose of the company was to comply with Texas law while building a rail route from Fort Worth to the Gulf Coast at Galveston, Texas. In 1903, a few more than thirty miles of track was built between Fort Worth and Dallas, but the purchase of half-interest in the Trinity & Brazos Valley to Houston and Galveston ended the need for new construction.

With the Chicago, Rock Island & Gulf Railway (CRI&G) established in Texas, three other Rock Island subsidiaries in the state were merged into the CRI&G. These included the Chicago, Rock Island & Mexico Railway; Choctaw, Oklahoma & Texas Railroad, and the Chicago, Rock Island & Texas Railway. The company then completed the route from Amarillo west to the Texas-New Mexico border at Glenrio in 1910, connecting to the Tucumcari & Memphis

Railway. This final construction connected Memphis with Tucumcari and then on to the West Coast. A line from Liberal, Kansas, to Amarillo was built in the late 1920s. By the 1930s, the railroad was large enough to be considered a Class 1 railroad, even though it was a subsidiary of the Rock Island.

Owned by The Chicago, Rock Island & Pacific Railway, the CRI&G jointly entered receivership in 1933. On September 1, 1939, the Rock Island officially leased the CRI&G. When the new Chicago, Rock Island & Pacific Railroad Company was created on January 1, 1948, the Chicago, Rock Island & Gulf Railway was included.

Chicago, Rock Island & Choctaw Railway Company (1903)

The Chicago, Rock Island & Choctaw Railway was another railroad company created to build track for the Memphis to Tucumcari route. According to the Rock Island Railroad:

> *The Chicago, Rock Island and Choctaw Railway was incorporated under the laws of New Mexico on January 26, 1903, for the purposes of building the line from Tucumcari to the New Mexico-Texas State Line, and there connect with the extension from Amarillo. March 31, 1903, this Company let a contract for completion of the entire line and most of the grading and some other work was done under this contract up to July 16, 1903, when construction work was ordered discontinued. On July 31, 1903, property rights and franchises of this Company were conveyed by deed to Chicago, Rock Island and El Paso Railway Company.*

The work on the Chicago, Rock Island & Choctaw Railway was halted in 1903 after funding became difficult to obtain, not just for the railroad but also the contractors involved. A series of financial crises occurred in the early 1900s, including 1901, 1903 and 1907. All of them were based upon sudden price drops of important stocks, or individuals and firms suddenly needing cash, leading to more interest in selling stocks than in buying them. This impacted banks as many became short of cash, making loans impossible to issue and many trying to collect owed debt.

Moving the property rights and franchise of the Chicago, Rock Island & Choctaw to the Chicago, Rock Island & El Paso Railway was done simply to protect the right to build the railroad and the work that had already been done. The Chicago, Rock Island & El Paso performed no more work on the railroad. The grades of the Chicago, Rock Island & Choctaw were not completed, and when the railroad was opened less than a decade later by the Tucumcari & Memphis Railway, much of the original work had to be done again.

Tucumcari & Memphis Railway (1909-1910)

The Tucumcari & Memphis Railway Company was incorporated January 9, 1909, under the laws of the Territory of New Mexico, to complete the work started by the Chicago, Rock Island & Choctaw Railway Company. The Tucumcari & Memphis Railway actually "purchased from the Chicago, Rock Island & El Paso Railway Company, the property, rights and franchises of the Chicago, Rock Island and Choctaw Railway Company which the El Paso had purchased July 31, 1903." New contracts were issued and the railroad from Tucumcari eastward to Glenrio at the Texas-New Mexico state line was completed by May 9, 1910.

The Tucumcari & Memphis Railway Company was always a construction company, and as soon as the railroad was completed, it was deeded back to the Chicago, Rock Island & El Paso Railway Company. A few months later on December 31, 1910, the El Paso Line was conveyed by deed to The Chicago, Rock Island & Pacific Railway Company.

Arkansas & Memphis Railway Bridge & Terminal Company (1912-Present)

Plans for this bridge began during the early 1900s when several railroads started looking at alternatives to using the Frisco Bridge over the Mississippi River at Memphis. By 1910, location engineers of the Chicago, Rock Island & Pacific were reported to be looking for sites for a new railroad bridge to be built over the Mississippi River between Hopefield, Arkansas, and Memphis, Tennessee.

The Arkansas & Memphis Railway Bridge & Terminal Company was incorporated in Tennessee and Arkansas on January 3, 1912, under the general laws of the State of Tennessee. Three railroads were involved, The Chicago, Rock Island & Pacific Railway; St. Louis Southwestern Railway; and the St. Louis, Iron Mountain & Southern Railway, each owning an equal share of the stock. All were impacted by the lack of capacity on the Great Bridge, also known as the Frisco Bridge. The companies also complained about the high rates being charged to use the bridge.

Acts of Congress on July 20, 1912, and August 23, 1912, approved the construction of the bridge, and design work began the following year. On May 13, 1913, the plans were submitted to the War Department for approval, which was received on August 15, 1913. To ensure the revenue needed to build and maintain the bridge, the three owning railroads agreed on March 2, 1914, to use the bridge and terminal facilities of the Arkansas & Memphis Railway Bridge & Terminal Company for 50 years, and all three extended the agreement to September 1, 1975, right after World War II. Using a number of noted bridge companies and contractors, construction proceeded quickly and the bridge opened to rail traffic on July 14, 1916. At first, the bridge was known as The Rock Island Bridge, but later became officially known as the Harahan Bridge, to honor James Theodore Harahan, former president of the Illinois Central Railroad.

The Arkansas & Memphis Railway Bridge & Terminal Company was more than just the bridge, it also included two mainlines and some terminal tracks in Memphis. A report from 1918 stated that the railroad had 1.998 miles of double track bridge over the Mississippi River, 1.427 miles of second main track, and 0.409 miles of yard track and sidings. However, the firm owned no equipment.

The company's *Special Instruction No. 4*, dated June 16, 1950, stated that there were "Two main tracks, extending from Kentucky Street (Memphis, Tenn.), to connections with Missouri Pacific Railroad Company and The Chicago, Rock Island & Pacific Railroad Company, distances of 2.85 and 2.88 miles, respectively, at Briark, Ark." The document also listed a West Siding at Briark, located south of South Track and measuring approximately 0.61 miles, as well as a 0.45 mile long East Siding, located north of North Track and west of Kansas Street. The company also had their Government Spur, located near Briark and breaking off of West Siding.

During the 1970s, the Rock Island stated in their employee timetable that the "Arkansas & Memphis Railway Bridge & Terminal Co. operates two main tracks designated as 'North Track' and 'South Track' extending for 2.89 miles between Kentucky St., Memphis, Tenn., and Briark, Ark., via Harahan Bridge across Mississippi River."

Union Pacific eventually absorbed the stock of all three owners of the bridge, and now shows the Arkansas & Memphis Railway Bridge and Terminal as a subsidiary. There is an interesting note about this as the original company spelling is with two ampersands, while Union Pacific spells the name with only one ampersand. The bridge is part of the Memphis Subdivision of the North Little Rock Area, and trains of the Brinkley Subdivision also use the bridge, with approximately twenty trains a day crossing the structure.

Rock Island Memphis Terminal Railway Company (1913-1948)

Another little-known company that played a role in creating the Choctaw Route was the Rock Island Memphis Terminal Railway Company, incorporated in Tennessee on August 19, 1913. This company raised the funds and built the Rock Island's terminal in Memphis, according to *Poor's Manual of Railroads* (1922). The report stated that the "CRIP acquired all stock and bonds in return for advances made for construction of a freight terminal in Memphis, together with about three miles of track. Construction of a freight station and terminal and switching tracks have been completed." The Interstate Commerce Commission stated that the company owned a "freight station and

2.721 miles of yard tracks and sidings," and leased "certain terminal property of the Arkansas & Memphis Railway Bridge & Terminal Company."

The Rock Island Memphis Terminal Railway was another paper railroad created and owned by the Rock Island, which advanced the funds for the railway's construction in return for all bonds issued by the company. To make things even more complex, the terminal facilities of the Rock Island Memphis Terminal were conveyed to the Arkansas & Memphis Railway Bridge & Terminal Company on April 1, 1915. They were then leased back by the Rock Island Memphis Terminal and used by the CRI&P. The firm was merged into the Rock Island with its reorganization in 1948.

Chicago, Rock Island & Pacific Railroad Company (1948-1980)

The last version of the Chicago, Rock Island & Pacific was chartered in Delaware on December 16, 1947, and with the reorganization, exited receivership on January 1, 1948. The reorganization eliminated a number of subsidiaries and streamlined the organization, and included the Chicago, Rock Island & Gulf Railway. This is the Rock Island that most people remember, and is the last company to operate the entire Choctaw Route between Memphis and Tucumcari.

At first, the railroad invested in track and equipment improvements across the system. However, the move toward more highway traffic, both for passengers and freight, quickly impacted the company. Its main northern route was closely followed by Interstate 80, and the Choctaw Route was followed by Interstate 40. Other highways, and the consolidation of competing railroads, also impacted the railroad company. Several attempted mergers, including the famous failure of a merger with Union Pacific, led to uncertain management practices and financial concerns. However, during this same time, the railroad converted to diesel locomotives and modernized many of its track maintenance practices. Nevertheless, the investments in track and equipment soon fell behind what was required.

In 1964, Union Pacific proposed an acquisition (some sources used the term merger) of the Rock Island, with the lines to the south and west of Kansas City, including the Choctaw Route, being sold to Southern Pacific. This started one of the longest series of hearings in the history of the Interstate Commerce Commission (ICC). After producing more than 150,000 pages of documents, the ICC approved the merger in 1974 after taking three years to fully release their findings. One of the many requirements imposed was that the Amarillo-Memphis line would be sold to the Atchison, Topeka & Santa Fe.

Meanwhile, in 1965, the Chicago, Rock Island & Pacific earned its final profit and the company survived off of previous profits, borrowed money, and sold assets. The railroad abandoned a number of branch lines, but the slow actions of the Interstate Commerce Commission meant it could take years for steps to be taken. With all of the conditions that would be enforced by the ICC, Union Pacific announced that it no longer was interested in acquiring the CRI&P. The result was that the Rock Island Railroad entered bankruptcy in 1975.

Attempted savings led salaries to be lower than many of the more prosperous railroads, and in August 1979, its clerks went on strike. With no one to do the paperwork, and the operating unions refusing to cross the picket lines, the Rock Island was basically shut down. Despite President Carter's order to return to work, strikers remained on the picket lines. Management soon was operating trains, serving as much as half of the previous volumes and actually turning a profit. However, with a concern about the cash available and the long-term future of the property, Bankruptcy Judge Frank J. McGarr ordered the CRI&P liquidated in January 1980, the largest liquidation of any American company to that point. Trains stopped running in early 1980, except for a few runs to move equipment to interchange, sale or scrapping locations. Soon, the Interstate Commerce Commission (ICC) had the Kansas City Terminal and its owners operate the core of the railroad, a plan lasting until March 23, 1980. After that, railroads began to lease or buy sections of track for operations from the Rock Island estate. Additionally, a few railroads were issued service orders by the ICC. However, the Rock Island Railroad of old was gone.

One of the goals of Bankruptcy Judge Frank J. McGarr was to pay off the debts of the railroad and have some funds left over for the stock and bond holders. Rock Island president John W. Ingram resigned and William M. Gibbons, who had been appointed trustee during the bankruptcy of March 17, 1975, became president. Gibbons began a program to sell what he could sell, and scrap the rest. Track was quickly put up for sale at a price of about $50,000 a mile for mainlines, and $35,000 a mile for branch lines. Locomotives, rail cars and other equipment were evaluated and sold or scrapped, with some being repaired to increase their value.

Some parts of the railroad were quickly sold, while others were clearly destined for scrap. During March 1982, the firm L. B. Foster was contracted to remove about 3000 miles of track across the system. The one hundred miles of track from Bushland (Texas) to Tucumcari was some of the first removed. Most of the track across the panhandle of Texas was also abandoned after no offers were made to buy it.

After the Rock Island Railroad was shut down, locomotives were gathered up to be returned to their owners, sold off, or simply scrapped. In December 1984, GP40 #4713 was stored in North Little Rock, Arkansas, looking the worse for wear.

The Arkansas track from Hazen to Carlisle was abandoned in 1982 after the last of several trustee moves, but it held on until late 1984 when the 33.5 miles of track from Brinkley to Hazen was scrapped by Determan-Merrill, Inc., a subcontractor for L. B. Foster. In January 1985, a contract was issued to L. B. Foster to scrap the track between Perry and McAlester, but much of the line was saved. However, the track between Danville and Howe was removed.

Real estate was also sold off, and the company raised more than $500 million, paying off all debts in full. On June 1, 1984, Gibbons ended his presidency of the estate of the Chicago, Rock Island & Pacific Railroad. On that date, the company became the Chicago Pacific Corporation and used the profits from the railroad property sales to buy several companies, including the Hoover appliance company. In late 1988, the Maytag Corporation acquired the company for about $1 billion.

Passenger Trains of The Choctaw Route

Since this book provides a route guide from the perspective of someone riding the Choctaw Route, it only makes sense that some of the route's passenger train history be included. The Choctaw Route was never the busiest passenger train route on the Rock Island, and certainly didn't match many of the nearby and connecting lines of railroads like Missouri Pacific, Southern Pacific, and Illinois Central. However, the Choctaw Route did see a number of named trains that connected Memphis to Little Rock, Hot Springs, Oklahoma City, Amarillo, and even the west coast.

The earliest passenger trains covered the Memphis to Little Rock route, initially with the assistance of riverboats and stagecoaches. The first copy of the *Travelers' Official Railway Guide of the United States and Canada* (June 1868) had only a short listing about the Memphis & Little Rock Railway.

> *A train leaves Memphis for Madison at 7:00 a.m. Returning, leaves Madison at 2:00 p.m. Distance, 40 miles. Fare, $2.00.*

> *At Madison connects with stages to and from Little Rock, and Overland Mail Route to San Francisco.*

The first major expansion of service occurred when the railroad was completed to Little Rock, but the construction west to Oklahoma, and south to Hot Springs, added greatly to the number of trains and services provided. Hot Springs in particular increased the interest in and quality of the passenger service over the route. Hot Springs, with its spas, resorts, illegal gambling and other activities, drew large and important crowds, especially from the Chicago connections of the Illinois Central.

In the June 1893 *Travelers' Official Guide* the Little Rock & Memphis Railroad listing (dated October 9, 1892) advertised "Double Daily Trains Between Memphis and Little Rock" and "schedule one hour faster than competitors." Along with this, the listing stated "shortest and quickest route to the celebrated Hot Springs" and "elegant Woodruff and Pullman Buffet Sleepers between Little Rock and Memphis." At the time, trains left Memphis daily at 8:30am and 8:30pm, arriving at Little Rock at 2:25pm and 1:55am, respectively. Heading east, a train departed daily at 2:15am, arriving at Memphis at 8:05am, with an afternoon daily train leaving at 1:50pm and arriving at Memphis at 7:55pm. Connecting rail service was shown to Texas through both Brinkley (St. Louis South-western Ry.) and Little Rock (St. Louis, Iron Mountain & Southern Ry.), and on to Fort Smith via the Little Rock & Fort Smith Railway.

Choctaw Route Passenger Trains in 1910

By 1910, the Choctaw Route was open all the way to Amarillo and the passenger service had begun to stabilize, with odd-numbered trains heading west and even-numbered trains heading east. At the time, only train Nos. **45-41** and **42-46** covered the entire route. Known as the *Western Express*, these trains had a complex consist that involved dropping off and picking up cars along the line. These included drawing-room sleeping cars that operated Chicago-Memphis on the Illinois Central. For the important Hot Springs service (train Nos. **45** and **46**), the trains carried a parlor car, coach and partitioned smoker. A dining car and first-class coaches operated Memphis-Little Rock, and a drawing-room sleeping car handled Little Rock-Oklahoma City traffic and a parlor car handled Oklahoma City-Amarillo. A coach was added for the Shawnee-Sayre business. Covering the entire Memphis-Amarillo route were chair cars and a partitioned smoker.

Train Nos. **43** and **44**, known as the *Memphis Mail*, operated daily between Memphis and El Reno. The trains made limited stops east of Booneville, Arkansas, and then stops at all stations to the west. The trains had drawing-room sleepers Memphis-Oklahoma City and Memphis-Hot Springs, and chair cars and a partitioned smoker Memphis-El Reno. There was an additional Shawnee-El Reno chair car.

A number of other passenger trains worked the line as locals. Train No. **41** worked as a local between Memphis and Little Rock, where through westbound passengers could connect to train No. 45-41. Likewise, train No. **42** handled local stops in the other direction for train No. 42-46. Other trains like Nos. **649** and **650** (Wister-McAlester), Nos. **769** and **770** (Oklahoma City-Geary), and Nos. **47** and **48** (McAlester-Sayre) also handled local passenger traffic.

A very unusual set of trains (Nos. **601** and **602**) on the schedule operated Memphis-Mansfield, with a Frisco connecting train handling some cars on to Monett, Missouri. This daily operation featured coaches and a combination smoker Memphis-Monett. A sleeping car, coach and combination smoker came up from Hot Springs to Little Rock, and then went on to Mansfield, Fort Smith, and Monett.

Choctaw Route Passenger Trains in 1926

During the next decade or more, the Choctaw Route was extended westward to Tucumcari, New Mexico, where connections were made with what became the Golden State Route – CRI&P and Southern Pacific service between Chicago and California via Kansas City. Changes were made in the services provided, and some train consolidations took place, until what was about the peak of service in 1926. In that year, train Nos. **111** and **112** (*Memphis-Californian*) were the only trains to cover the entire Memphis to Tucumcari line. These trains connected at Tucumcari with Southern Pacific train Nos. 11 and

12, providing service on to El Paso and Los Angeles. Nos. 111 and 112 handled a number of sleepers (Memphis-Los Angeles, Memphis-Little Rock, and Memphis-Amarillo), plus chair cars (Memphis-Tucumcari) and a dining car that was shown to serve all meals en route.

Train Nos. **41** and **42** had become the *Choctaw Limited* and operated between Memphis and Amarillo. While coaches operated the entire length of the run, sleeping cars only operated Memphis-Oklahoma City and McAlester-Oklahoma City. No. 42 also had an Amarillo-Oklahoma City-Memphis sleeper that it picked up off train No. 112. Meals were provided by a dining car between Little Rock and Booneville.

As earlier, much of the Choctaw Route was covered by local passenger trains that served city pairs. Train Nos. **47** and **48** (*Hot Springs – Panama Limited*) handled sleepers and coach cars Memphis-Little Rock-Hot Springs, plus sleepers that started and ended in Chicago on the Illinois Central. A dining car served all meals. The Hot Springs business was so important that train Nos. **45** and **46** (*Hot Springs Limited*) also handled sleepers, coaches and dining cars between Memphis and Hot Springs. Some of these sleepers also came off of the Illinois Central at Memphis. Train Nos. **601** and **602** also handled local service between Memphis and Little Rock.

Similar to 1910, a number of locals handled service along certain sections of the Choctaw Route. However, the general rule about the line was that passenger service reduced in quality and volume as you headed west. Train No. **45-605** operated Memphis to Little Rock as No. 45, then on west to Booneville as No. 605. Meanwhile, No. **606** operated Booneville to Little Rock. Heading west from Booneville, train Nos. **43** and **44** provided daytime local service as far west as El Reno. At least three trains daily operated each way Oklahoma City-El Reno. West of El Reno, train Nos. **41** and **42** provided local service as far west as Amarillo. West of Amarillo, only the *Memphis-Californian* operated, providing all passenger services.

Choctaw Route Passenger Trains in 1934

The Great Depression negatively impacted the passenger service on the Choctaw Route, much like on most rail lines across the country. Trains that were operated for tourists were eliminated, and sleeper trains began to handle more local service. Train Nos. **111** and **112** (*Memphis-Californian*) were still the only trains to cover the entire Memphis to Tucumcari line. A 12-section drawing-room sleeper operated Memphis-Tucumcari-El Paso, while a similar sleeper operated Little Rock-Oklahoma City. Chair cars operated Memphis-Tucumcari-Los Angeles. To provide meal service, a cafe-lounge car operated Little Rock-Amarillo.

Train Nos. **45** and **50** (*Hot Springs Limited*) still handled a 10-section, 1 drawing room, 2 compartment sleeper to and from Chicago via the Illinois Central at Memphis. Coaches, an observation parlor car, and a dining car op-

45

erated Memphis-Hot Springs. Train No. **42** operated each morning from Little Rock to Memphis, and then returned as No. **41** during the afternoon, handling all local traffic. Further west, train No. **606** consisted of a "motor" and operated in the morning from Booneville to Little Rock, and then returned as No. **605** during the late afternoon.

Train No. **44** provided eastbound Oklahoma City to McAlester "motor" service in the morning, while train No. **43** went back west to El Reno in the afternoon. No. 43 had the task of hauling a 12-section, drawing room sleeper from Oklahoma City to El Reno for a connection to Kansas City on train No. 32. Meanwhile, train Nos. **703** and **704** provided "motor" service between Oklahoma City and Bridgeport. Train Nos. **51** and **52** (*Choctaw Limited*) provided overnight service between Oklahoma City and Amarillo. These trains were shown to carry a 12-section, drawing room sleeper, plus coaches. Additionally, they carried several El Reno-Oklahoma City sleepers connecting with Dallas and Kansas City.

Choctaw Route Passenger Trains During and After World War II

As the Great Depression started to end with the beginning of World War II, railroads were investing in modern passenger trains, attempting to attract riders and lower costs. For the Choctaw Route, this meant the debut of the *Choctaw Rocket* on November 17, 1940. This train consisted of Pullman-Standard equipment (chair, sleepers, and observation-parlor-dining cars) pulled by an EMD E-6 diesel-electric locomotive. This new train reduced the existing 44-hour travel time between Memphis and Amarillo by more than ten hours.

The war years produced a great deal of passenger and freight business, but equipment was limited. In June 1941, the railroad operated a very limited number of trains across the Choctaw Route. The *Memphis-Californian* (Nos. **111** and **112**) provided Memphis-Tucumcari service that connected with Southern Pacific for service on to Los Angeles. The train included Memphis-Los Angeles 12-section, 1-drawing room sleepers and a chair car. Coaches operated Memphis-Tucumcari, and a cafe-lounge car operated Little Rock-Tucumcari.

The *Choctaw Rocket* (Nos. **51** and **52**) provided limited stops Memphis-Amarillo. These trains had chair cars, 8-section and 5-double bedroom sleepers, and an observation-parlor-dining car. The Hot Springs Limited (Nos. **45** and **50**) operated Memphis-Hot Springs and had through sleepers from Chicago, in addition to the coaches, chair cars, parlor car, and dining car Memphis-Hot Springs. Further west, several trains (Nos. **511**, **512**, **513**, and **514**) provided Oklahoma City-El Reno service to connect to trains on the Dallas-Kansas City mainline.

Troop trains were common during the war with a number of military installations along the line. Some of the biggest moves involved troops of the

German Afrika Korps being taken to Fort Reno as prisoners of war. As with most lines, the existing trains had to handle the traffic growth, and few major changes were made in the service. Even after the war ended, it took a few years for major changes to take place, and in December 1945, there were few differences from 1941.

The next moves by the Rock Island involved reducing the number of trains. By early 1947, there were only three trains operating between Memphis and Little Rock: Nos. **45** and **50** (Memphis-Little Rock-Hot Springs *Hot Springs Limited*), Nos. **51** and **52** (Memphis-Amarillo *Choctaw Rocket*), and Nos. **111** and **112** (Memphis-Tucumcari *Memphis-Californian*). Several additional trains still provided Oklahoma City-El Reno service to connect to trains on the Dallas-Kansas City mainline, but the other Oklahoma local trains were gone.

The Final Two Decades of Choctaw Route Passenger Trains

Ridership began to drop sharply after World War II, and it didn't take long for the Rock Island to start reducing services. Two major changes took place during the late 1940s. The first involved the elimination of the *Hot Springs Limited*, with the *Choctaw Rocket* (Nos. **51** and **52**) hauling Hot Springs cars to Little Rock, which then operated as train Nos. **151** and **152** to and from the spa city. The *Choctaw Rocket* was officially a Memphis-Oklahoma City train starting in 1950, with the train continuing Oklahoma City-Amarillo as a nameless local. The second change was Nos. **111** and **112** becoming the *Cherokee* in March 1949.

In February 1952, the *Choctaw Rocket* was replaced by local trains Memphis-Oklahoma City. The next year, the railroad brought in two RDC-3 cars to handle the Little Rock-Oklahoma City business, primarily the mail and package/express business. The RDC-3s were modified for the business, with the baggage section replaced by an expanded RPO section. This equipment started running in August 1953, and in September began covering Memphis-Oklahoma City as the *Choctaw Rockette* (Nos. **51** and **52**). The operation was so successful that it was extended all the way to Amarillo in July 1955.

About this time, Nos. **111** and **112** (*Cherokee*) were down to their last sleeper, a Memphis-Los Angeles 10-section, 1-drawing room, 2-compartment car that was generally owned by Southern Pacific and operated by Pullman. In the November 1956 public timetable, the train was renumbered as **14** and **15**. With the number change, coaches operated Memphis-Tucumcari and Memphis-Los Angeles, but an 8-section, 5-double bedroom sleeper only operated Memphis-Oklahoma City. This sleeper was gone by the Spring-Summer 1958 timetable. During this time, Rock Island timetables began to call this line the "Route of the Cherokee."

The *Cherokee* name was gone by the Spring-Summer 1959 public timetable, and it was simply shown as a Memphis-Tucumcari daily train. Nos. **51** and **52** were simply shown as *Choctaw*, although it was still informally known as the

47

Choctaw Rockette. Everything was renumbered in 1959 with the *Choctaw* now Nos. **23** and **24**, and the Tucumcari trains becoming Nos. **21** and **22**.

Both pairs of trains remained until the mid-1960s. Nos. **23** and **24** last operated on August 8, 1964. Train Nos. **21** and **22** survived for the mail and express shipments. Consists generally included a single locomotive pulling a half-dozen baggage cars full of pouched mail and railway express shipments, a Railway Post Office (RPO), and a single coach. Much of this mail business was soon lost, with the last Memphis & McAlester RPO operating on September 29, 1967. Train Nos. **21** and **22** made their last trips on November 10, 1967.

Additional details about the various passenger trains can be found throughout the descriptions of each route.

Maps and Timetables

PREVENT INJURY

SAFETY FIRST

From the *Chicago, Rock Island & Pacific Railroad Southern Division Timetable No. 9.* Dec. 28, 1969. Back Cover. Employee timetable from the author's collection.

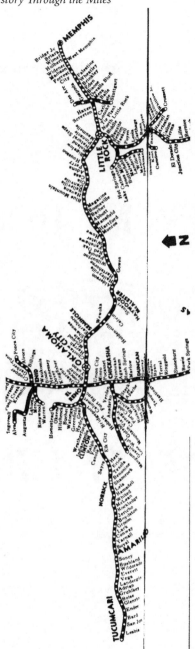

Map of the Southern Division, *Rock Island Employee Timetable No. 1*, page 82-83, March 18, 1979. From the author's collection.

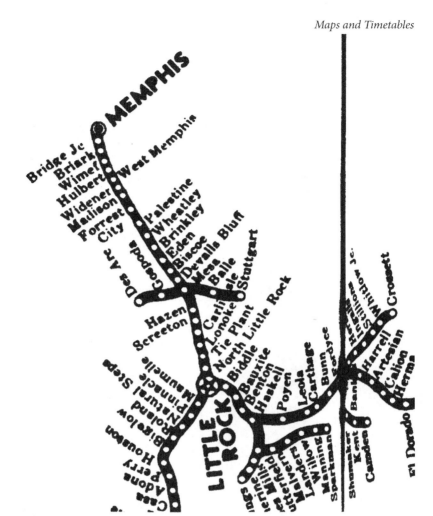

Map of the Southern Division, *Rock Island Employee Timetable No. 1*, page 82-83, March 18, 1979. Enlarged to show Memphis to Little Rock. From the author's collection.

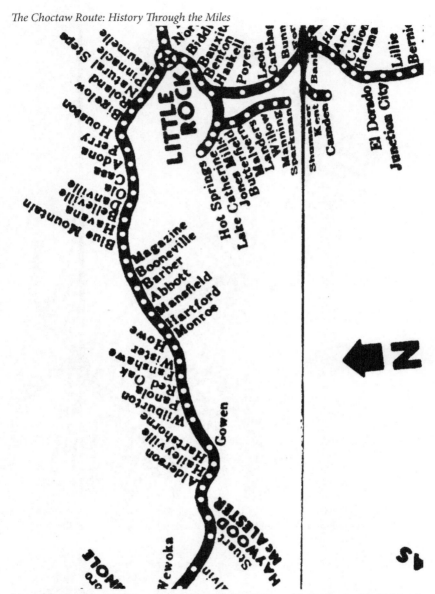

Map of the Southern Division, *Rock Island Employee Timetable No. 1*, page 82-83, March 18, 1979. Enlarged to show Little Rock to Haywood. From the author's collection.

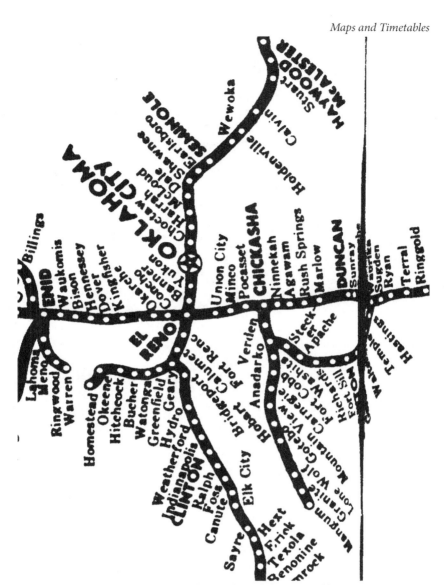

Map of the Southern Division, *Rock Island Employee Timetable No. 1*, page 82-83, March 18, 1979. Enlarged to show Haywood to Sayre. From the author's collection.

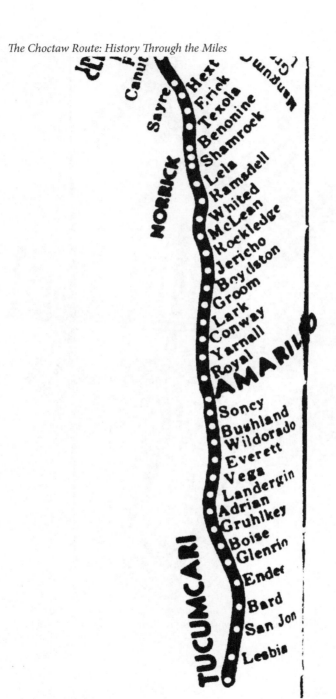

Map of the Southern Division, *Rock Island Employee Timetable No. 1*, page 82-83, March 18, 1979. Enlarged to show Sayre to Tucumcari. From the author's collection.

Chicago, Rock Island & Pacific Railroad

SOUTHERN DIVISION

TIME TABLE

No. 9

EFFECTIVE AT 12:01 A.M.
CENTRAL STANDARD TIME

SUNDAY, DEC. 28, 1969

W. C. HOENIG
Superintendent

G. H. VOSS
Asst. General Manager

C. R. HURT
Asst. General Manager

W. F. THOMPSON
General Manager

This Time Table for the exclusive use
and guidance of Employees

Chicago, Rock Island & Pacific Railroad Southern Division Timetable No. 9. Dec. 28, 1969. Front Cover. Employee timetable from the author's collection.

Main Line

Footage Capacity of Sidings	Car Capacity of Other Tracks	Station Numbers		SUBDIVISION 29 STATIONS TIME TABLE NO. 9 December 28, 1969	M.P. from Memphis	Signs
....	Yard	30000	FO-GO-US	..MEMPHIS, TENN............*TO	....	RFWY BC
				— 1.2		
....	......	....	K....	KENTUCKY ST., TENN...TO	1.2	R
				— 2.2		
....	......	....		SL-SF Crossing..................	3.4	....
....	......	30004	......	BRIDGE JCT., ARK..........	3.4	....
				— 0.7		
....	......	30005	......	BRIARK..................	4.1	....
				— 5.3		
4130	250	30009	YD..	WEST MEMPHIS........ TO (N)	9.4	WYd
				— 4.3		
5319	......	30013	......	MOUNDS.....................P	13.7	....
				— 6.0		
4631	2	30020	......	PROCTOR...................P	19.7	....
				— 7.2		
8391	......	30027	......	HETH.......................P	26.9	....
				—11.6		
4017	20	30038	......	WIDENER..................P	38.5	....
				— 2.2		
....	115	30041	......	MADISON ....P	40.7	....
				— 4.1		
3713	206	30045	FC..	FORREST CITY .... *TO	44.8	W
				MoPac Crossing..............		
				— 5.1		
....	70E	30050	......	LONGINO...................P	49.9	....
				— 1.9		
8391	30	30052	......	PALESTINE.................P	51.8	....
				— 7.2		
....	8W	30059	......	GOODWIN.................P	59.0	....
				— 5.5		
4392	44	30064	WY..	WHEATLEY.................TO	64.5	....
				— 4.0		
....	......	....	......	COTTON BELT JCT. .... P	68.5	Yd
				— 0.6		
....	......	....	......	BR JUNCTION	69.1	Yd
				— 0.1		
W4585 E4322	98	30069	B...	StLSW Crossing................ BRINKLEY............*TO (N)	69.2	RWY YdBC
				—11.3		
....	11W	30080	......	BRASFIELD ....P	80.5	....
				— 7.8		
4434	47	30088	......	MESA ....P	88.3	Y
				— 5.0		
4091	59	30093	HA..	HAZEN.....................TO	93.3	W
				— 5.0		
4612	18	30098	......	SCREETON ....P	98.3	....
				— 4.4		
4112	101	30103	NE..	CARLISLE ....TO (N)	102.8	W
				— 6.1		
....	18W	30110	......	SISEMORE...................P	108.9	....
				— 2.6		
4586	117	30111	KO..	LONOKE......................TO	111.5	W
				—13.1		
4594	E4	30124	......	GALLOWAY..................P	124.6	....
				— 6.0		
....	......	....	......	StLSW Crossing ....P	130.5	....
				— 1.4		
2862	550	31132	......	NORTH LITTLE ROCK.....P	131.9	Yd
				— 0.9		
....	......	....	......	MoPac Crossing..................	132.8	....
				— 0.1		
....	258	31133	......	LITTLE ROCK..................	132.9	Yd
				— 2.3		
....	Yard	31136	RK..	BIDDLE.................*TO (N)	135.2	RFWT YdBC
				135.2		

Chicago, Rock Island & Pacific Railroad Southern Division Timetable No. 9. Dec. 28, 1969. Memphis to Biddle. Employee timetable from the author's collection.

Main Line

Footage Capacity of Sidings	Car Capacity Of Other Tracks	Station Numbers			SUBDIVISION 30 **STATIONS** TIME TABLE NO. 9 December 28, 1969	M.P. from Memphis	Signs
......	Yard	31136	RK...	Rules 400 to 406	BIDDLE..............*TO (N) — 1.2	135.2	RFWT YdBC
......	......	....	....		HOT SPRINGS JCT.......P — 3.5	136.4	Y
......	......	....	....		MoPac Crossing.............. — 1.8	139.9	....
4609	14	31142	....	AUTOMATIC BLOCK SYSTEM Biddle to MP 185-34	PULASKI....................P — 8.7	141.7	....
......	W10	32150	....		MAUMELLE.................. — 2.5	150.4	....
4753	14	32153	....		PINNACLE.................P — 6.4	152.9	....
4581	20	32159	....		ROLAND....................P — 7.4	159.5	....
......	5E	32167	....		LEDWIDGE.................P — 5.4	166.9	....
3408	16	32172	....		BIGELOW....................P — 4.3	172.3	....
......	W10	32177	....		HOUSTON...................P — 7.2	176.6	....
4301	62	32184	RY...		PERRY.....................TO — 10.5	183.8	....
3586	......	32194	....		HOMEWOOD................P — 4.1	194.3	....
......	15	32198	....		CASA.........................P — 10.2	198.4	....
4583	41	32209	AO...........		OLA.........................TO — 10.9	208.6	W
1782	66	32219	DA...........		DANVILLE................TO — 4.3	219.5	W
4619	24	32224	UN...........		BELLEVILLE............TO — 4.8	223.8	....
......	8E	32229	....		HAVANA...................... — 5.9	228.6	....
4585	......	32234	....		WAVELAND................P — 4.9	234.5	....
......	5E	32239	....		BLUE MOUNTAIN.........P — 5.7	239.4	....
......	W5	32245	....		MAGAZINE.................. — 6.6	245.1	....
4424	80	32252	BO...........		BOONEVILLE.......... *TO 116.5	251.7	YdRYW BC

Chicago, Rock Island & Pacific Railroad Southern Division Timetable No. 9. Dec. 28, 1969. Biddle to Booneville. Employee timetable from the author's collection.

Main Line

Footage Capacity of Sidings	Car Capacity Of Other Tracks	Station Numbers	SUBDIVISION 31 STATIONS TIME TABLE NO. 9 December 28, 1969	M.P. from Memphis	Signs
4424	80	32252	BO.........BOONEVILLE............ *TO	251.7	WBC YdRY
......	25	32272	——— 19.8 ——— MF.........MANSFIELD ....TO	271.5	....
3683	37	32280	——— 8.5 ——— ....HARTFORD, ARK...........P	280.0	....
3705	56	32295	——— 15.4 ——— ....KCS Crossing.................. BX.........HOWE, OKLA................TO	295.4	....
3125	31	32302	——— 6.4 ——— ....SL-SF Crossing............UX ....WISTER.........................P	301.8	W
	24	32322	——— 20.5 ——— RO.........RED OAK.....................TO	322.3	....
	10	32330	——— 7.7 ——— ....PANOLA.......................P	330.0	....
3273	73	32335	——— 5.6 ——— WN.........WILBURTON................TO	335.6	W
7558	......	32340	——— 4.4 ——— ....LIMESTONE ....P	340.0	....
......	18	32352	——— 11.5 ——— HN.........HARTSHORNE .... *TO 99.8	351.5	RWBC

Chicago, Rock Island & Pacific Railroad Southern Division Timetable No. 9. Dec. 28, 1969. Booneville to Hartshorne. Employee timetable from the author's collection.

Main Line

Footage Capacity of Sidings	Car Capacity Of Other Tracks	Station Numbers	SUBDIVISION 32 **STATIONS** TIME TABLE NO. 9 December 28, 1969	M.P. from Memphis	Signs
......	14	32352	HN..........HARTSHORNE............*TO	351.5	R W B C
			8.9		
3604	......	32361	...............ALDERSON...................P	360.9	....
			5.5		
6538	282	32366	MA.........McALESTER................TO	366.4	W Y d C
			0.0		
......	......	....	..............MKT Crossing..................	366.4	....
			11.0		
3845	74	32377	..............HAYWOOD....................P	377.4	Y d
			9.1		
4080	11	32387	..............STUART.....................P	386.5	....
			4.6		
2239	......	32391	..............HILLTOP....................P	391.1	....
			5.2		
......	......	....	..............KO&G Crossing................	396.3	....
			0.9		
4486	64	32397	CA.........CALVIN......................TO	397.2	....
			13.5		
7215	140	32411	HD.........HOLDENVILLE...........TO	410.7	W
			..............SL-SF Crossing................		
			7.9		
5605	61	32419	WA.........WEWOKA....................TO	418.7	W
			6.3		
5189	......	32426	..............LIMA.....................P	425.0	....
			6.2		
3292	259	32431	DM.........SEMINOLE...................TO	431.2	W
			4.6		
4448	......	32436	..............TRACY......................P	435.8	
			10.1		
......	......	....	..............OCA JCT.......................	445.9	
			2.3		
......	Yard	32448	JE ....SHAWNEE .... *TO 96.7	448.2	R Y d W F B C

Chicago, Rock Island & Pacific Railroad Southern Division Timetable No. 9. Dec. 28, 1969. Hartshorne to Shawnee. Employee timetable from the author's collection.

Main Line

Footage Capacity of Sidings	Car Capacity of Other Tracks	Station Numbers	SUBDIVISION 33 **STATIONS** TIME TABLE NO. 9 December 28, 1969	M.P. from Memphis	Signs
......	Yard	32448	JE ....SHAWNEE ....*TO (N)	448.9	RYdB FWYC
			— 7.7 —		
4588	......	32456	..............DALE.....................P	457.0	....
			— 4.0 —		
......	17E	32461	..............McCLOUD.....................P	461.0	....
			— 5.1 —		
4613	32	32466	RH........HARRAH.................,.......TO	466.1	....
			— 6.5 —		
......	15	32473	..............CHOCTAW....................P	472.6	....
			— 9.9 —		
......	......	......	..............SL-SF Crossing.................	482.5	....
			— 1.5 —		
......	......	......	..............MKT Crossing...........P UX	484.1	....
			— 1.6 —		
......	......	......	..............MKT Crossing..............UX	485.6	....
			— 0.0 —		
5532	Yard	32485	KX........HARTER................... *TO	485.6	FWYd YBC
			— 0.3 —		
......	......	......	..............MKT Crossing..............UX	485.9	....
			— 0.6 —		
......	......	......	...... SL-SF Crossing..............UX	486.5	....
			— 0.3 —		
......	......	......	...... SL-SF Crossing..............UX	486.8	....
			— 0.9 —		
......	......	......	...... SL-SF Crossing..............UX	487.7	....
			— 6.8 —		
......	6E	32495	...... COUNCIL.....................P	494.5	....
			— 6.4 —		
7668	198	32501	KU.. YUKON.....................TO	500.9	....
			— 5.8 —		
......	20	32507	...... BANNER.....................P	506.7	....
			— 5.6 —		
......	......	......	...... BELT JCT....................P	512.3	....
			— 1.0 —		
......	Yard	21232	FO.. EL RENO YARD.....*TO (N)	513.3	RYdB FWTC
			64.4		

(Vertical annotation: AUTOMATIC BLOCK SYSTEM MP 488.9 to MP 510.8)

Chicago, Rock Island & Pacific Railroad Southern Division Timetable No. 9. Dec. 28, 1969. Shawnee to El Reno. Employee timetable from the author's collection.

Main Line

Footage Capacity of Sidings	Car Capacity of Other Tracks	Station Numbers		SUBDIVISION 34 **STATIONS** TIME TABLE NO. 9 December 28, 1969		M.P. from Memphis	Signs
......	Yard	21232	FO..	EL RENO YARD......*TO (N)		513.3	R Y d B F W T C
				— 2.5 —			
......	......	....	......	ROCK ISLAND JCT.	..P	514.2	Yd
				— 0.1 —			
......	......	....	......	CRI&P Crossing.....	..P	514.3	....
				— 0.2 —			
......	......	....	......	PANHANDLE JCT..	....	514.4	Yd
				— 8.6 —			
5162	36	33523	......	CALUMET....................P		523.2	....
				— 11.6 —			
4354	161	33535	GY..	GEARY....................TO		534.8	RCWY
				— 8.6 —			
......	W18	33540	......	BRIDGEPORT..................		543.4	....
				— 11.2 —			
3847	45	33554	CO..	HYDRO....................TO		554.6	....
				— 8.0 —			
2491	152	33563	WF..	WEATHERFORD..........TO		562.6	W
				— 10.4 —			
5160	13	33573	......	INDIANAPOLIS.............P		573.0	....
				— 7.5 —			
......	......	....	......	SL-SF Crossing...........UX		580.5	....
				— 0.2 —			
5085	20	33582	......	CLINTON.........................		580.7	Y
				— 2.6 —			
......	......	....	......	P&SF Crossing............UX		583.2	....
				— 11.0 —			
5160	......	33594	......	.............FOSS...................P		594.3	....
				— 7.4 —			
......	29E	33602	......	.............CANUTE.........................P		601.7	....
				— 7.6 —			
3816	190	33609	KC	.......ELK CITY...................TO		609.3	W
				— 17.0 —			
......	Yard	33627	SA	..........SAYRE.................*TO (N)		626.3	YdRF WYBC
				113.0			

The left labels "AUTOMATIC BLOCK SYSTEM MP513.4 to MP514.4" and "Rules 400-406" appear vertically between the station number and stations columns.

Chicago, Rock Island & Pacific Railroad Southern Division Timetable No. 9. Dec. 28, 1969. El Reno to Sayre. Employee timetable from the author's collection.

Main Line

Footage Capacity of Sidings	Car Capacity of Other Tracks	Station Numbers	SUBDIVISION 35 **STATIONS** TIME TABLE NO. 9 December 28, 1969	M.P. from Memphis	Signs
4158	Yard	33627	SA ....SAYRE ....*TO (N)	626.4	RYYd FWBC
			——— 14.6 ———		
2920	80	33641	.............ERICK.............................	640.9	....
			——— 7.6 ———		
......	10E	33649	.............TEXOLA, OKLA.............P	648.5	....
			——— 5.4 ———		
3700	......	33654	.............FULLER, TEXAS ....P	653.9	....
			——— 10.6 ———		
2740	125	33665	SK ....SHAMROCK ....TO	664.5	....
			——— 0.5 ———		
......	......	....	.............FW&D Crossing.................	665.0	....
			——— 22.3 ———		
2680	105	33687	.............McLEAN ....P	687.2	W
			——— 15.2 ———		
2700	......	33702	.............ROCKLEDGE.................P	702.4	....
			——— 11.4 ———		
......	36	33714	.............BOYDSTON ....P	713.8	....
			——— 5.5 ———		
4150	76	33719	GR.........GROOM.......................TO	719.3	Y
			——— 7.4 ———		
......	36	33727	.............LARK............................P	726.7	....
			——— 8.5 ———		
......	40	33735	.............CONWAY.................P	735.2	....
			——— 8.5 ———		
2290	......	33744	.............YARNALL.................P	743.7	....
			——— 12.1 ———		
......	......	....	.............FW&D Crossing............UX	755.6	....
			——— 3.5 ———		
......	......	....	.............P&SF Crossing	759.3	....
			——— 1.3 ———		
......	Yard	34762	VN.........AMARILLO............*TO (N)	760.6	RFWY YdBC
			134.2		

Chicago, Rock Island & Pacific Railroad Southern Division Timetable No. 9. Dec. 28, 1969. Sayre to Amarillo. Employee timetable from the author's collection.

Main Line

Footage Capacity of Sidings	Car Capacity of Other Tracks	Station Numbers	SUBDIVISION 36 STATIONS TIME TABLE NO. 9 December 28, 1969	M.P. from Memphis	Signs
......	Yard	34762	VN..........AMARILLO.............*TO (N)	760.6	RFWY YdBC
			6.5		
......	33	34768	..............SONCY	767.1	....
			6.9		
......	33	34775	..............BUSHLAND	774.0	....
			8.0		
1580	57	34783	..............WILDORADO.....................	782.0	....
			7.5		
......	32	34789	..............EVERETT.....................	789.5	....
			5.5		
2940	69	34796	GA..........VEGA........................TO	795.0	Y
			7.7		
......	19	34804	..............LANDERGIN.....................	802.7	....
			6.1		
2680	53	34810	..............ADRIAN.....................	808.8	....
			4.2		
......	W19	34813	..............GRUHLKEY.....................	813.0	....
			8.5		
2450	......	34821	..............BOISE	821.5	....
			10.8		
......	13	34833	..............GLENRIO, TEX................	832.2	....
			17.9		
......	22	34851	..............SAN JON, N. MEX..............	850.3	....
			15.0		
......	20	34866	..............LESBIA	865.3	....
			8.7		
......	Yard	16137	XN..........TUCUMCARI..........*TO (N)	874.0	RYdFW TYBC
			113.4		

Chicago, Rock Island & Pacific Railroad Southern Division Timetable No. 9. Dec. 28, 1969. Amarillo to Tucumcari. Employee timetable from the author's collection.

ROCK ISLAND LINES
1941   16702
PASS Mr. V. J. Tannlund***

Traffic Agent - C.G.W. RR

BETWEEN ALL STATIONS UNTIL JANUARY 31, 1942
UNLESS OTHERWISE LIMITED ABOVE

COUNTERSIGNATURE   CHIEF EXECUTIVE OFFICER

Rock Island Lines rail pass, circa 1942. From the author's collection.

Memphis (TN) to Brinkley (AR)
Union Pacific Railroad

This part of the railroad still exists and serves as the Brinkley Subdivision of Union Pacific Railroad. This is due to an action that began on April 1, 1912, when St. Louis Southwestern Railway (Cotton Belt or SSW) passenger trains moved from the Fair Oaks to Memphis route over Missouri Pacific, to the Brinkley to Memphis route over the Rock Island. The original decision to operate to Memphis over the St. Louis, Iron Mountain & Southern was due to Gould's ownership of the two railroads, and began in 1892.

A contract for the use of the Rock Island's track by the Cotton Belt stated that 64.67 miles of track would be used. During the mid-1910s, the cost for the Cotton Belt was $0.55 per train mile for all movements of passenger trains and light engines. The Cotton Belt was also charged 2.5% of the costs of any betterments or facility additions.

After several years, the Missouri Pacific decided that the Cotton Belt's freight service should also move, and on March 1, 1920, a one-year notice was issued to the Cotton Belt that their Fair Oaks-Memphis freight rights were ending. On February 28, 1921, the Cotton Belt signed a trackage rights agreement with the Rock Island, allowing Cotton Belt trains and crews to operate over the Brinkley to Memphis line of the Arkansas-Louisiana Division. At the same time, the SSW moved from the Missouri Pacific freight terminal to that operated by the Illinois Central at Memphis.

While freight traffic over the route grew, passenger service never became a major factor. For example, in 1950, Rock Island timetables showed that each railroad operated two passenger trains in each direction. The same number of scheduled freight trains were operated by each railroad, plus many extras. The Cotton Belt operated their *Lone Star Limited* train between Memphis and Dallas, Texas. The second passenger train was a connection to the St. Louis-Dallas *Morning Star* train. Passenger service ended on November 1, 1952, also ending the Cotton Belt's Railroad Post Office (RPO) service to and from Memphis.

By the 1961 Rock Island timetable, the St. Louis Southwestern operated more freight trains over the Memphis-Brinkley line than did the owner. At the time, the track from Memphis, Tennessee, to Biddle Yard in Little Rock, Arkansas, was Subdivision 52 of the Arkansas Division. By 1979, this was Subdivision 29 of the Southern Division, and handled about 14 million gross tons a year, the most on the entire Choctaw Route. The track between Memphis and Brinkley also had the highest speeds on the Memphis-Tucumcari line at 50mph. The subdivision was the eastern end of the Choctaw Route, an almost direct line between Memphis and Amarillo, Texas, and on to Tucumcari, New Mexico.

Later in 1979, when a number of unions went on strike and the Rock Island Railroad shut down, a decision had to be made to continue the Cotton Belt Memphis service. On September 26, 1979, the Interstate Commerce Commission ruled that the bankrupt Chicago, Rock Island & Pacific Railroad would be operated by other railroads to preserve the freight service. On the evening of March 23, 1980, Extra 4436 west departed from Memphis, making it the last common carrier service by the Chicago, Rock Island & Pacific on the east end of the Choctaw Route. Late that night, the Cotton Belt took over the Brinkley-Memphis line, closing all of the offices along the route except for those at the ends.

However, a few Rock Island trains operated by the railroad's trustees moved equipment along the line as late as June 26, 1981. Cotton Belt train register reports for the track between Brinkley and Briark (near West Memphis) indicate that railroad trustee trains operated at least five times to and from Memphis, with the last one on June 26th. All of the train movements featured a caboose-hop eastward, but a train of about forty cars westward back to Biddle Yard in Little Rock. Each train was pulled by Rock Island #829, an SW8 switcher assigned to Biddle Yard and used to collect cars from along the railroad and to switch the assets of the railroad at Biddle. These trips were intended to remove cars stored in the Fourth Street Yard at Memphis and get them to Mesa, Arkansas, where they were scrapped, or to Biddle Yard in Little Rock, where cars were being sold or returned to their owners.

The Cotton Belt was owned by Southern Pacific, which was acquired by Union Pacific in 1996. As a part of the purchase agreement, BNSF was granted trackage rights over the line between Briark and Brinkley. Since that time, the line has been improved with heavier rail, new bridges and signals, and lots of changes in sidings and spur tracks. This part of the route description will include details from all eras and ownerships.

0.0   MEMPHIS (FO-GO-US) – Don't get confused by the three station calls, different offices at Memphis used different station or telegraph calls. The 1979 Rock Island timetable showed that Memphis had almost everything, including general order boards and books, a standard clock, fuel station, train register station, water station, wye, and wayside radio. Because the Cotton Belt also needed access to the general orders, they were also kept at the Illinois Central Gulf Iowa Yard and roundhouse, as well as at Central Station. However, Memphis wasn't the original eastern terminal of the Choctaw Route, it was Hopefield, Arkansas.

Hopefield

The Memphis & Little Rock Railroad, and the railroad companies that followed, used a ferry at Hopefield, Arkansas, to cross the Mississippi River and reach the railroads in Memphis, Tennessee. Shown as Milepost 2.0 by the Choctaw & Memphis Railroad, Hopefield was located across the river from what was called North Memphis, just north of the west end of the current Interstate 40 bridge. Hopefield had an interesting Dutch-Spanish beginning in 1795. The Spanish wanted to discourage Americans from crossing the Mississippi River and settling in what at the time was Spanish territory. To do so, they hired Dutch immigrant Benjamin Fooy (or Foy) to create a base to regulate river traffic and American settlement. He also collected river tolls and served as agent to the local Native American tribes. The community went through several names – Foy's Point, Campo de la Esperanza, and then finally Hopefield in 1803 with the Louisiana Purchase. Fooy quickly went to work performing many of the same jobs for the United States. However, Hopefield also later became known as a safe place for gambling and dueling.

The charter for the Memphis & Little Rock Railroad listed Hopefield as the location of the company offices, and it was the eastern base for construction of the railroad. Materials like rail and spikes were delivered here, often up the Mississippi River from New Orleans, where shipments were received from Europe. The June 6, 1857, issue of the *Arkansas State Gazette and Democrat* reported that the first rails of the Memphis & Little Rock had just been installed at Hopefield. The railroad's first locomotive also arrived at Hopefield. This was the *Little Rock*, which arrived in August 1857 and operated westward shortly afterwards. Hopefield soon became an important station of the railroad as it was the east end of the tracks and the connection with Mississippi River traffic. It was also the dock location for service to the railroads at Memphis, initially provided by the ferryboat *Nevada*. This became historically important as on November 7, 1857, the Memphis & Little Rock hauled six bales of cotton to Hopefield and on to Memphis, making this the first freight revenue on a railroad in Arkansas.

Initially, Hopefield housed the railroad shops, which were turned into an armory for the Confederacy. During the Civil War, the tracks were destroyed. A major attack by Union troops on February 19, 1863, resulted in the burning of Hopefield, and it took a number of years to get the railroad back in service. Because of this, the heirs of the Winchesters, who had provided land for the railroad as long as it was in service, wanted their land back. However, the Arkansas Supreme Court ruled that the railroad had never abandoned the tracks, but had only been delayed in repairing them and starting service again.

Hopefield was a well-known railroad location, and it was considered to be an important destination for a number of planned railroads. After the Memphis & Little Rock, the next railroad to include Hopefield in their plans was The Mississippi Valley, Upper Division Railroad, incorporated on November 30, 1868, to build 50 miles from Hopefield to Helena, Arkansas. Next was the Memphis & Kansas City, which completed a survey from Hopefield to Batesville, Arkansas, in 1871-1872. On March 2, 1881, a second Memphis & Kansas City was organized at Hopefield. During 1879, the Memphis & Great Southwestern Railway Company was incorporated to build a railroad from Hopefield through Pine Bluff and on to Jefferson, Texas, with branches to Shreveport and Texarkana. It was incorporated in Arkansas a number of times, including November 18, 1880, December 21, 1880, and February 9, 1881, however it wasn't built. In 1910, the Memphis, Dallas & Gulf amended its charter to include an extension to Hopefield.

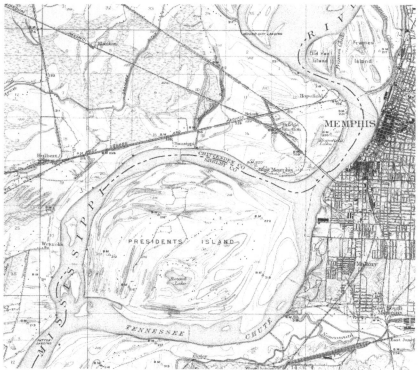

This map from 1916 shows the Hopefield area, as well as the junction at Briark and Bridge Junction. Note that it shows a loop track at Hopefield that was used to turn trains. U.S. Geological Survey Historical File, Topographic Division. https://ngmdb. usgs.gov/ht-bin/tv_browse.pl?id=845237e91c5cd0de252818486d530197.

Even though a number of railroads planned to build to Hopefield, the Memphis & Little Rock and its later versions were the only ones to actually operate to here. As the bridges were built across the Mississippi River, and flood levees were built, Hopefield lost its importance and began to regularly flood. However, as late as July 1907, the Chicago, Rock Island & Pacific was still making investments in track and the Mississippi River incline at Hopefield, and then plans were announced in 1908 for more track improvements and a new coal chute there. In 1909, Hulbert Yard at today's West Memphis opened to replace the yard at Hopefield, but the boat transfer incline was still being used. Trains soon moved to the Frisco Bridge, and eventually the Harahan Bridge of the Arkansas & Memphis Railway Bridge & Terminal Company. This ended the need for the Hopefield tracks and they were removed. This area is now farmland.

The Rock Island at Memphis

After the construction of the Frisco Bridge, the Rock Island kept changing their operations, sometimes using the bridge and sometimes the ferry. The railroad also used different passenger stations over the years. However, the opening of the Harahan Bridge changed this and led to further improvements in the Memphis area. The improvements included a new freight station on Calhoun Street at East Fourth, replacing the older freight house located just south of the Poplar Street depot of the Illinois Central.

According to the *Rock Island Employee's Magazine*, the red brick freight house was 46 feet wide and 484 feet long, and replaced an earlier facility on Front Street at the foot of Adams Avenue. Offices were located in a 155-foot two-story section. The building was part of the Fourth Street Rock Island Yard, located at the east end of the series of freight houses and stations in Memphis. Because it was one of the last terminals built, city streets were an issue and the tracks bridged Georgia Avenue between Fourth and Wellington.

The freight house was opened on July 7, 1914, and it stayed busy for many decades. Nearby was the coach yard and roundhouse at Pennsylvania Avenue, today's Riverside Drive. The coach yard was located west of Pennsylvania Avenue and between Virginia and Carolina Streets. The tracks in this area have been moved some to allow the construction of the nearby Interstate 55 interchange, and BNSF and Television Channel 3 have offices in the general area. A report on the railroad's operations stated that arriving and departing freight engines were moved between Fourth Street Yard and the roundhouse by switch engine, while passenger crews moved their own trains to and from Central Station.

However, the end of passenger and less-than-carload service reduced the need for the complex. In late 1966, the railroad offices were moved to a smaller concrete building at Fourth and Broadway. The tracks were removed and the freight house was leased for storage by 1975. Today, the elevated grade to the freight house still stands immediately east of Fifth Street, and the freight house and rail yard area is now parking and a large church.

The Fourth Street Yard, which once contained 24 tracks and handled 7000 interchange cars a month, would be at Union Pacific Milepost 379.3. Union Pacific's Memphis Subdivision continues to the east with the stations of K.C. Junction (Milepost 380.6) and Memphis (Milepost 380.7).

Rock Island Railroad Passenger Service to Memphis

Memphis was always an important connection for passenger trains operating over the Choctaw Route of the Rock Island Railroad. It provided connections to the east via Southern Railway; the Louisville & Nashville; the Nashville, Chattanooga & St. Louis; and the St. Louis-San Francisco. It also provided connections to Chicago and New Orleans via the Illinois Central. The connection with the Illinois Central was especially important as a large number of Chicago passengers transferred to trains heading to Hot Springs, Arkansas, a noted resort town with plenty of connections to the Chicago mob.

There is little detail about what stations the Memphis & Little Rock used initially in Memphis, but first-class coaches were shown to operate between Atlanta and Little Rock, using both the Louisville & Nashville and the Memphis & Charleston (Southern) routes. However, sleeping car passengers had to change equipment since Pullman provided the cars to the east while Woodruff Buffet Sleepers provided cars on the Memphis & Little Rock. By the late 1800s, timetables of the Little Rock & Memphis Railroad stated that trains served the Louisville & Nashville station in Memphis.

During the late 1800s and early 1900s, passenger trains swapped back and forth from using the transfer ferry at Hopefield and using the new Frisco Bridge. These changes may have helped determine which Memphis station was used, as during December 1899, an announcement was made that the Choctaw & Memphis would begin using the Illinois Central's Calhoun Street station on December 10th. Newspapers added that the "station is one of the most complete and elegant depot buildings in any city in the South where there is not a union station. There is not a depot building in the city that compares with it in any respect." The Rock Island remained at this station, although some other railroads continued to bounce back and forth between stations in Memphis.

In 1914, the new Grand Central Station opened on the site of the former Calhoun Street Station. Owned by Illinois Central Railroad, the station also housed "offices of the Illinois Central and Yazoo & Mississippi Valley roads, including those of the passenger and freight traffic departments, the general, division and terminal superintendents, the superintendent of motive power and the claims department," according to the February 1915 issue of the *Illinois Central Magazine*. Besides the Illinois Central and the Yazoo & Mississippi Valley, the station handled the passenger business of the Rock Island and the Frisco.

Known as Central Station by the end of World War II, the station was the scene of the display of one of Rock Island's original *Rocket* trains on September 20, 1937. The streamlined *Choctaw Rocket* began service westward on November 17, 1940, claimed by some to be the first diesel passenger train to regularly serve Memphis. Service and demand soon peaked, and the last Memphis Pullman sleeper service on the Choctaw Route operated on January 6, 1958. The last Railway Post Office (RPO) operated Memphis-McAlester on Trains No. 21 and No. 22 on September 29, 1967. The last Rock Island passenger trains left and arrived at Memphis on November 9, 1967.

City of Memphis

Memphis has long been an important Mississippi River town, and today has a population of more than 650,000, making it the second largest city in Tennessee. The entire metropolitan area includes approximately 1,350,000 people. The bluffs that Memphis sit on were noted by a number of explorers, but it wasn't until May 22, 1819, that the city was founded. Its founders included Andrew Jackson (military leader and future president), James Winchester (military leader in the American Revolutionary War and War of 1812), and John Overton (Tennessee Superior Court judge and political leader). The development gave the state a market city on the Mississippi River. The city was named after a similar ancient city, the Egyptian capital that was located on the Nile River.

Because of its markets, railroads were quickly attracted to Memphis. In 1857, the Memphis & Charleston Railroad arrived, providing a route between the cities in the railroad's name. It was the only railroad completed between the Atlantic coast and the Mississippi River before the beginning of the Civil War. After the war, Memphis grew quickly and more railroads were built to Memphis to reach the cotton markets, and the produce from further west. The Memphis & Charleston and the other railroads encouraged rail construction across Arkansas to create further freight and passenger demand for their lines. The Memphis & Little Rock was just the first of these railroads.

0.9   **TOWER 17** – Located at Union Pacific Milepost 378.4 and known as Control Point Y381, this was not an official station in timetables of the Chicago, Rock Island & Pacific. Tower 17, a two-story buff brick tower, guarded the wye to Memphis Union Station. Union Station was located on Calhoun Street between South Second Street and South Third Street, just west of Central Station. Union Station was used by the St. Louis Southwestern Railway Company and the St. Louis, Iron Mountain, & Southern Railway Company; as well as eastern roads Southern Railway; Louisville & Nashville Railroad; and Nashville, Chattanooga & St. Louis Railway.

Tower 17 also handles the switches east of the crossing with Canadian National, the former Illinois Central line. The line to the north sees little use, but the line to the south curves across the Canadian National line and then connects to it from the west due to a lack of available space.

1.0   **CN CROSSING** – This location is at Union Pacific Milepost 378.3. The diamonds are protected by Tower 17 to the east, and Texas Street to the west. The north-south track is the passenger mainline for what was the Illinois Central's Chicago to New Orleans route. Five blocks north of here is Memphis Central Station, once used by Illinois Central, Yazoo & Mississippi Valley, Rock Island, and Frisco. Memphis Central Station, referred to as Grand Central Station prior to 1944, is the second station built on the site. The first was known as Calhoun Street Station, and it was also owned by the Illinois Central or its predecessors, and Calhoun was sometimes used by Rock Island trains as early as the late 1800s. On November 9, 1967, the last Rock Island passenger trains arrived and departed Memphis from Central Station.

The Memphis Area Transit Authority Trolley

Central Station opened on October 4, 1914, and featured five through tracks and five stub tracks. The building had a five-story office building on top of the station complex. For years it was rated as the worst Amtrak station in the country, serving the *City of New Orleans*. During the late 1990s, the Memphis Area Transit Authority acquired and restored the building, adding meeting and museum space, and converting the former offices into condominiums. The building reopened during November 1999 as part of a redevelopment effort.

Just north of Central Station is a line of the Memphis Area Transit Authority trolley systems. This system consists of three different routes

– Main Street Rail Line (2.1 miles), Madison Line (2.2 miles), and the Riverfront Line which passes north of Central Station (4.1 miles). All three lines mostly use restored vintage streetcars from Portugal and Australia.

Plans for the streetcar system started in January 1990, and the Main Street Line opened to the public on April 29, 1993, delayed by the restoration of enough cars to operate the line. On October 1, 1997, the Riverfront Line opened, followed by the Madison Avenue Line on March 15, 2004. Several equipment fires shut the trolley system down during June 2014, and it reopened on April 30, 2018.

At one time, Memphis may have had the most intense streetcar system in the country, and few locations were more than a block or two from a trolley stop. As happened in many places, the system started as a number of smaller streetcar companies. These included the Citizens Street Railroad, East End Street Railway, Memphis & Raleigh Springs Railroad, and the City & Suburban Railway. These systems merged into the Memphis Street Railway Company during March 1895. About 160 miles of routes were operated, but were slowly replaced by buses and electric trolleybuses until the last streetcars operated on June 15, 1947.

Central Station still stands on the south side of downtown Memphis. The building houses the local Amtrak office as well as condominiums on the upper floors.

1.1   **TEXAS STREET** – Today located at Union Pacific Milepost 378.2 and designated as Control Point Y380, this tower once protected the west side of the Illinois Central Crossing. Today, there is a crossover between several east-west tracks and a connecting track to the south.

1.2   **KENTUCKY STREET (K)** – Kentucky Street, named for the nearby north-south city street, has long been a very important tower at Memphis, and a popular railfan location. The tower was a train register and train order station, which also included a wayside radio. While the building was just a small one-story wooden structure, it also held the CTC board for the Arkansas & Memphis Railway Bridge & Terminal Company, making it responsible for the track from Texas Street to Briark in Arkansas. A second panel handled the switches at the west end of the many tracks through town, a route known as Broadway. For many years, the Frisco also had an operator and train order signal at the tower, but they moved to Tennessee Yard during the early 1980s.

Southern Pacific #6814 pulls the PBME Sprint eastward past Kentucky Street in September 1991. About the only thing that remains from this photo are the tracks.

Rock Island documents stated that Kentucky Street was the initial station for westbound St. Louis Southwestern (SSW) trains, while the initial station for Rock Island trains was Memphis. Kentucky Street was busy with many of the area railroads, and at one time westbound trains of Rock Island, Missouri Pacific and Cotton Belt all had to stop for train orders. Trains coming off of the Illinois Central also had switches lined by the Kentucky Street operator. Kentucky Street still exists, but is handled from elsewhere. Union Pacific defines it as Control Point Y379 and states that it is at Milepost 378.1.

Heading west toward the Mississippi River, the many tracks make an S-curve with several crossovers so trains can be routed over either the Harahan or Frisco Bridge. This S-curve is very different from what was here in the early 1900s. The elimination of local warehouses and yards, as well as the construction of nearby Interstate 55, all have impacted the current track design.

2.0   **HARAHAN BRIDGE** – The Harahan Bridge crosses the Mississippi River, connecting the states of Tennessee and Arkansas. It was the second railroad bridge built here, and stands just north of the first railroad bridge, which featured a single track and is used today primarily by BNSF. Known initially as the "**Memphis Bridge**" for the Memphis Route slogan of the railroad, the BNSF bridge later was known as the "**Great Bridge**" or the "**Frisco Bridge.**" The large structure was built for the **Kansas City & Memphis Railway & Bridge Company**, controlled by the Kansas City, Fort Scott & Memphis Railroad. Construction began in 1888 and the bridge opened to great fanfare on May 12, 1892. Costing nearly three million dollars, at the time the single-track structure was the southernmost bridge over the Mississippi River. There were claims that it featured the longest truss span in the United States, and was the third longest bridge in the world. In 1928, the "Great Bridge" officially became part of St. Louis-San Francisco Railway (Frisco), giving it its third name. The railroad is now owned by BNSF, which has been upgrading the structure for years and has replaced the long timber approach trestle on the west end. The bridge is listed as a Historic Civil Engineering Landmark.

By the early 1900s, the "Great Bridge" could no longer handle the traffic of the many railroads using it. Memphis Mayor E. H. Crump, a powerful Tennessee politician who effectively controlled the city for almost fifty years, pushed for a new second railroad bridge which would also feature a roadway. Soon, the Chicago, Rock Island & Pacific Railroad; St. Louis Southwestern Railway; and the St. Louis, Iron Mountain & Southern Railway incorporated the **Arkansas & Memphis Railway Bridge & Terminal Company** on January 3, 1912, under the general laws of the State of Tennessee.

Construction of the Harahan Bridge involved a number of noted politicians, railroaders, and design engineers. The leadership of the Arkansas & Memphis Railway Bridge & Terminal Company was a unique one, as identified by a plaque on the Harahan Bridge. President was A. C. Ridgway, who had previously served as general superintendent of the Florence & Cripple Creek, general manager of Rio Grande Southern, and vice president and general manager of the Denver, Northwestern &

Pacific. He became assistant second vice-president of the Rock Island during January 1910, and then later second vice-president. He replaced F. O. Meicher, who was killed at Kinmundy, Illinois, on January 22, 1912. F. H. Britton of the Cotton Belt was vice-president. Britton had worked for several railroads, but became the general superintendent of the St. Louis Southwestern Railroad in 1899, and later was president of the company and a number of its subsidiaries, such as the Paragould Southeastern Railway. G. H. Crosby, Secretary and Treasurer, held a similar position with the Rock Island. Finally, the General Counsel was J. W. Canada, who worked for various Iron Mountain railroads.

The names of the officials of the Harahan Bridge in 1916 are listed on this large plate on the east end of the bridge.

The new bridge was initially controversial as the owners of the existing railroad bridge didn't want the competition, and politicians from as far away as Alabama spoke out against it. Congressman Kenneth Mc-Kellar, from Memphis, threatened to block approval for the bridge as a "wagonway" wasn't included, although the railroads were not exactly supportive of building a free highway bridge. However, the Memphis business community heavily supported the idea, and $400,000 was appropriated for the wagonways. With the public push for a road, and a political fight between Eastern Arkansas and Memphis, and even a call for the bridge to be a "toll-free" bridge that would also accommodate trolley lines, the Rock Island suggested a $4 million bridge that would include two railroad tracks, and wagonways that would be turned over to Crittenden County (Arkansas) and the City of Memphis so they could be operated without tolls.

Several congressional hearings and debates followed throughout the year, but permission to construct a double-track bridge over the Mississippi River at Memphis was provided by Act of Congress on July 20, 1912, as amended by another Act approved on August 23, 1912, thanks to the work of Kenneth Douglas McKellar. This was only the start for McKellar, who served as a United States Representative from 1911 until 1917 and as a United States Senator from 1917 until 1953 for Tennessee. He served in Congress (House and Senate combined) longer than anyone else in Tennessee history. He rose to be the ranking member of the Appropriations Committee, where McKellar led the fight to get landowners fair market prices for their land taken by the Tennessee Valley Authority. This popular fight kept him in office until he was defeated in 1952 by Albert Gore, Sr.

On April 10, 1913, Ralph Modjeski was hired to prepare plans for the bridge. Modjeski was a logical choice, as the Polish-American civil engineer was known as the pre-eminent bridge designer in the United States, having already designed several major bridges across the Mississippi River. The Rock Island Railroad already knew him, as he was the chief engineer on the improved Mississippi River bridge at Rock Island, Illinois. Modjeski was also known for taking over the Quebec Bridge after it failed during construction due to its poor design. He was also responsible for the San Francisco-Oakland Bay Bridge and about forty other major bridges.

Design work took place quickly and an initial plan was submitted to the War Department for approval on May 13, 1913. Approval for construction was given by the War Department on August 15, 1913. The bridge was 4972 feet long, with 1194 feet in Tennessee and 3778 feet in Arkansas. Another 2.5 miles of approach spans and fills were required on the Arkansas end to reach the flood levees. The bridge is more than 100 feet above the normal level of the Mississippi River, required to reach the high ground at Memphis.

Reports state that the main structure is 2549 feet long, with 2202 feet of through truss (truss work above the bridge deck) and 347 feet of deck truss (truss work under the deck). From east to west, the spans measured 186 feet, 791 feet, 621 feet, 604 feet, and 347 feet. There are then 2424 feet of deck plate girder spans set on steel towers over the Arkansas floodplain. The War Department required that the bridge piers and spans over the Mississippi River match the lengths of the bridge spans on the older Frisco Bridge located just downstream to create no new challenges for river traffic.

A number of important bridge companies were involved in the project, including the Pennsylvania Steel Company (main bridge superstructure), Union Bridge & Construction Company of Kansas City, Missouri (substructure), and the Virginia Bridge & Iron Company (west approach superstructure). Major challenges during construction included water levels, the river current, soft soils, and a fear of possible damage to the Frisco Bridge, which was only 200 feet away. Major construction took place from February 28, 1914, to July 15, 1916, using large mats to provide stable footing for the workers and to prevent the river bed from shifting, and 21 barges for work over the river. Large pressurized caissons were used for the river piers, which helped to blow the river bottom out of the way, creating fountains in the river which were a tourist draw. The piers were built on top of the caissons, using masonry blocks of granite backed with concrete. The two longest spans were the first installed, although flooding did cause some movement of several spans and the failure of another. A series of reports and photos on Memphis and the construction of the Harahan Bridge and the new terminal were published in the March 1915 issue of the *Rock Island Employes' Magazine*.

This plate on the east end of the Harahan Bridge lists the primary contractors involved in the structure's construction.

The bridge opened to rail traffic on July 14, 1916, but without celebration due to World War I in Europe. It wasn't until September 17, 1917, that the wagonways opened due to delays in building a wooden viaduct in Arkansas. The roadways consisted of 14-foot lanes using wooden planks over a steel frame, hanging off the outside of the main structure. The roadways were used until 1949, when the U.S. Highway 70 bridge opened just south of the Frisco Bridge.

During planning of the project, the bridge was generally called The Rock Island Bridge. However, the name was changed to the Harahan Bridge to honor James Theodore Harahan, president of the Illinois Central (1906-1911). On January 22, 1912, Harahan and three other railroad executives were heading south through Kinmundy, Illinois, in a private car to negotiate the construction of the bridge. Their private car was reportedly being pulled by the locomotive that Casey Jones wrecked during his fatal collision at Vaughn, Mississippi, on April 30, 1900. Hanahan and the other executives were asleep when their train was rear ended by IC Train No. 3, *The Seminole Limited*. Harahan was killed, and the other railroads decided to honor him with the naming.

The *Railway Employees' Magazine* of February 1912 had an news article about the accident, which involved Rock Island business car #1902, which was attached to the rear of Illinois Central train No. 25, the *New Orleans Express*.

> *It was that most deplorable and unexplainable of railway disasters – a tail end collision. The victims were asleep in Vice President Melcher's private car attached to the rear of No. 25, the IC's New Orleans express. About 1 am, 25 stopped at Kinmundy for water. Flagman Broecker has testified that he ran back a block and a half and signaled No 3, the Panama Limited, and got two blasts of the whistle, but the all steel train rushed on with speed unchecked. With a crash that was heard for miles the engine of No. 3 struck the private car and tore it to bits. The standing train, for all its locked brakes, was shoved ahead 200 feet.*

Besides James Theodore Harahan, three others were killed in the car. These included Frank Otis Melchor, Second Vice President of the Rock Island System; Judge E. P. Pierce, general solicitor of the Rock Island; and Eldridge E. Wright, a Memphis lawyer and son of former Secretary of War Luke E. Wright. Four other occupants, including two porters, escaped from the car with little injury. The deaths in the wooden business car accelerated the push to require steel-frame and all-steel passenger cars on all mainline trains.

During the 1970s, the Rock Island stated in their employee timetable that the "Arkansas & Memphis Railway Bridge & Terminal Co. operates two main tracks designated as 'North Track' and 'South Track' extending for 2.89 miles between Kentucky St., Memphis, Tenn, and Briark, Ark., via Harahan Bridge across Mississippi River." The bridge deck was shown to have an elevation of 295.49 feet, with a 1.01% average grade westbound onto the bridge, and a 1.13% average grade eastbound.

In 1991, Southern Pacific #6814 East pulls off the east end of Harahan Bridge and into Memphis.

Union Pacific eventually absorbed all three owners of the bridge, and now operates approximately twenty trains a day across it. The bridge is part of the Memphis Subdivision of the North Little Rock Area. Trains moving over the Brinkley Subdivision also use the bridge.

This photo of Union Pacific #3150 West on the Harahan Bridge is taken from a train on the Frisco Bridge in 1994.

Mississippi River and the State Line

The Mississippi River is the second longest river in North America, measuring 2320 miles long. It starts in Lake Itasca in northern Minnesota, and flows south to the Gulf of Mexico south of New Orleans. At Memphis, the river changes channels often and is part of a major transportation network of barges moving grains south and fertilizers, salts, and other products back north. Its older channel serves as the border between Arkansas and Tennessee.

Tennessee became the 16th state on June 1, 1796. It is 36th largest and the 16th most populous of the fifty United States. Nashville is the state capital. Tennessee is known as *The Volunteer State*, a nickname based upon the number of volunteer soldiers from the state who reported for the War of 1812. This was not the only example, as Tennessee furnished more soldiers for the Confederate Army than any other state besides Virginia, and more soldiers for the Union Army than the rest of the Confederacy combined.

The east end of the bridge is in **Shelby County**, Tennessee's largest county in both area and population. The county had 927,644 residents during the 2010 census, mainly due to its county seat of Memphis, which is the second most populous city in the state. The county was named for the first and fifth governor of Kentucky, Isaac Shelby. He also served in the state legislatures of Virginia and North Carolina. Shelby was also a veteran of many wars, including Lord Dunmore's War, the American Revolutionary War, and the War of 1812. Shelby was awarded a ceremonial sword and a pair of pistols by the North Carolina legislature for his leadership at the Revolutionary War Battle of Kings Mountain, giving him the nickname of "Old Kings Mountain." As governor, he also led the state militia at the Battle of the Thames, also known as the Battle of Moraviantown, on October 5, 1813. This War of 1812 battle ended Tecumseh's Indian Confederacy and regained the United States' control over the Fort Detroit area. Shelby was awarded the Congressional Gold Medal for his actions. His fame led nine states to have counties named after him.

The Territory of **Arkansas** was admitted to the Union as the 25th state on June 15, 1836. It is the 29th largest state, and the 32nd most populated. Little Rock is the capitol, and the most populated city. Arkansas can be flat or mountainous depending upon where you travel. The southeast half is lowlands and river delta, while the northwest includes the highlands of the Ouachita and Ozark Mountains – the only major mountainous region between the Rocky Mountains and the Appalachian Mountains. Arkansas is also the only state where diamonds are mined, and you can go mine them yourself at the Crater of Diamonds State Park.

The west end of the bridge is in **Crittenden County**, a Mississippi River delta county that is rich in farmland, but one that often has to fight flooding. The county was created on October 22, 1825, as the twelfth county in Arkansas. While West Memphis is the largest city in the county, Marion is the county seat and the county has only 50,902 residents as of the 2010 census. Southland Greyhound dog-racing park is a major attraction in the area, and it has been turned into a casino with talk of ending the dog races. The county was named for Robert Crittenden, an attorney who served as the Secretary of the Arkansas Territory. He also served as acting Governor of the Arkansas Territory, and as a Commissioner during the negotiations of the 1824 Treaty with the Quapaw Indians. Crittenden survived a duel with a former close friend, and is credited by some as being a co-founder of the Rose Law Firm in Little Rock. The legal firm is reportedly the third oldest law firm in the United States and the oldest west of the Mississippi River, as well as the oldest company of any kind in Arkansas.

Big River Crossing

For decades, one of the challenges for locals was to climb the Harahan Bridge and walk the remains of the wagonways (roadways). This thrill attracted the interest of trail organizers, and proposals were made to reinstall the north bridge deck and turn it into a walking and biking trail. In February 2011, Union Pacific Railroad officials agreed to the idea, and in June 2012, Memphis was awarded a $14.9 million federal grant to build the walkway. Construction quickly began, and about $11 million was used for the Harahan Bridge portion, completed in 2016.

Signs like his one at the west end of the Harahan Bridge mark the route of the Big River Trail.

The mile-long walkway is the longest public pedestrian bridge across the Mississippi, and is designed to be a part of the ten-mile Main Street to Main Street project, connecting Memphis with West Memphis. The walkway is also illuminated with LED lights, which produce a programmed light show from sundown until 10pm.

2.8   **HARAHAN** – This is a set of crossovers located just west of the end of the Harahan Bridge. Union Pacific has designated this location as Control Point (CP) Y377 and it is located at Milepost 376.5 of the Memphis Subdivision. The crossover allows the two tracks west of here to be used to meet trains, and the location is obviously named for the nearby Harahan Bridge.

UP #9052W pulls the MENLNS off the west end of Harahan Bridge in 1991.

3.4   **BRIDGE JUNCTION** – Today, this diamond with BNSF is CP Y376, located at Milepost 375.9 on Union Pacific. However, historically it was the manual interlocking where the Arkansas & Memphis Railway Bridge & Terminal Company crossed the Frisco, known as SL-SF Crossing by the Rock Island. A large two-story tower once stood to the north to control the crossing.

There is also a connecting track to the south that allows westbound trains on the Frisco Bridge to head west on the Rock Island, giving the location the name of Bridge Junction. In 1979, the Rock Island Railroad cited this ability in its timetable by stating that "StLSW trains will enter or leave CR&IP main track at Briark, BR Junction or Cotton Belt Junction."

Bridge Junction is not far north of Interstate 55 at Exit 1 – Bridgeport Road. Not far to the west is an industrial lead that heads south under I-55 to BASF Corporation, the second largest producer and marketer of chemicals and related products in North America. Getting off at Exit 1 provides access to parking for the Big River Crossing of the Harahan Bridge.

3.44 = 4.25 PROPERTY LINE – Rock Island Railroad, and later Cotton Belt documents, showed that the Arkansas & Memphis Railway Bridge & Terminal Company ended here at Milepost 3.44, and the mileposts heading west started at 4.25. As stated in these documents, 3.44 A&M B&T = 4.25 CRI&P. This mileage conversion eliminated 0.8 miles from the route's distance, thanks to the replacement of the Hopefield ferry with the Harahan Bridge.

This track is located on a high fill to keep trains above flood waters. The grade was originally built using wooden trestles (almost all of the forty miles of track between Memphis and Madison were once located on trestles), but major parts of the line have been filled in. However, a large number of long trestles still exist to allow flood waters to pass through the grade. CRI&P records show some of the longer ones to be at Milepost 3.9 (82 span ballast deck pile trestle), Milepost 4.4 (37 span pile trestle), Milepost 4.5 (35 span pile trestle), Milepost 4.6 (68 span ballast deck pile trestle), Milepost 5.0 (76 span ballast deck pile trestle) and Milepost 5.3 (22 span ballast deck pile trestle). Union Pacific has strengthened or modified many parts of these trestles during recent years.

4.1   BRIARK (BR) – There is some confusion about this milepost due to the nearby property line. Union Pacific mileposts only add to the confusion.

Briark is the west end of two tracks and is where Union Pacific's Brinkley and Memphis Subdivisions split. This area was known as Bridge Siding in the Choctaw & Memphis Railroad's 1899 list of stations. Today, it is Control Point Y375 and is located at Milepost 375.3 on the Memphis Subdivision. The track that continues straight is the former St. Louis, Iron Mountain & Southern track, then Missouri Pacific. This route was the 98-mile Memphis Branch, opened in May 1888 by the St. Louis, Iron Mountain & Southern Railway, between Memphis and Bald Knob, Arkansas.

Eastbound Rock Island trains would turn from heading northeast to heading southeast at Briark. The reason for this turn is that the original mainline once headed straight to reach Hopefield. Much of this old grade can still be seen on aerial photos, and County Road 803 uses the grade for a short distance east of Dacus Lake Road. If you follow the old grade, it eventually passes under Interstate 40. North of I-40 is a large field that can be planted when not flooded. The north edge of the field is Hopefield Point, located along Hopefield Chute which was once the main channel of the Mississippi River, and still used as the dividing line between Arkansas and Tennessee.

This is another location noted by the 1979 CRI&P timetable where "StLSW trains will enter or leave CR&IP main track." Today, BNSF trains also can enter the line as they have trackage rights over the route to Brinkley.

5.0   INTERSTATE 55 – The railroad passes under I-55 at this location. I-55 stretches 965 miles from downtown Chicago, Illinois, to LaPlace, Louisiana. It basically connects Lake Michigan with the Gulf of Mexico. In this area, the highway runs north-south along the west side of the Mississippi River through Arkansas, turns east-west for a short distance to reach Memphis, and then turns north-south again to travel through Mississippi. I-55 crosses the Mississippi River using the original U.S. Highway 70 bridge, located just south of the Frisco Bridge.

5.4   MISSISSIPPI RIVER LEVEE – At this location for westbound trains, the railroad passes over a short trestle and then runs along the top of the flood levee that protects West Memphis.

This February 1937 photo from a train on the Rock Island mainline east of Forrest City shows the flood waters in that year. The Resettlement Administration photo doesn't provide an exact location, but it is likely near West Memphis. Evans, Walker, photographer. *View taken from train between Memphis, Tennessee, and Forrest City, Arkansas.* Feb 1937. Photograph. Retrieved from the Library of Congress, https://www.loc.gov/item/2017762338/.

6.8   CONSOLIDATED GRAIN AND BARGE TERMINAL – Immediately to the south of the railroad is the Mississippi River and a CGB barge terminal. This facility specializes in the movement of grains, but other bulk products can sometimes be seen here. There are no tracks to this facility today, and CRI&P records show no tracks in the past. Just west of the CGB access road, the railroad leaves the levee and uses its own embankment.

This February 1937 photo from a train on the Rock Island mainline east of Forrest City shows the flood waters in that year. The Resettlement Administration photo doesn't provide an exact location, but it is likely near West Memphis. United States Resettlement Administration, Locke, Edwin, photographer. *View taken from train en route to Forrest City, Arkansas from Memphis, Tennessee during the flood.* Feb 1937. Photograph. Retrieved from the Library of Congress, https://www.loc.gov/item/2017728297/.

7.5 **LAKE'S** – This station was listed in the 1899 list of stations published by the Choctaw & Memphis Railroad. The station was once located near the grade crossing with South Loop Drive.

8.2 **TENARK INDUSTRIAL LEAD** – This lead turns south, using the former St. Louis, Iron Mountain & Southern Railway Marianna Branch route. This line between West Memphis and Marianna, 42.9 miles long, opened for service on February 1, 1913. The line was also known as the Memphis-Marianna Cut-off. While the line once provided a shorter route to Louisiana, it also opened up large sections of timber for a number of lumber companies.

This location was known as Wimef, and the Interstate Commerce Commission stated that Wimef was a junction point for tracks of the Missouri Pacific and the Rock Island, and that it was located 1350 feet east of Hulbert. From Wimef, Missouri Pacific trains operated in accordance with Rock Island operating rules over the Rock Island tracks eastward to Memphis.

To reach this line, the St. Louis, Iron Mountain & Southern (StLIM&S) had an agreement to use 3.92 miles of Rock Island track between what was shown as Hopefield to Hulbert. In reality, it was from today's Briark to here. In a 1915 agreement, the Iron Mountain paid $0.55 to $0.65 per train mile, depending upon the number of trains per day, to use the line. The Iron Mountain would also pay 1-2/3% of all betterments made on the line. Additionally, the StLIM&S also was charged with part

87

of the cost of the signal system, prorated based on the number of trains operated by the two railroads.

During February 1973, Missouri Pacific petitioned the Interstate Commerce Commission for permission to abandon the line between Tenark and Hughes, leaving the less than four miles that still exist today. There are approximately a half-dozen shippers on the line.

8.4   **WEST MEMPHIS** – The switch at West Memphis is known as Control Point Y901 by Union Pacific. The track is controlled by CTC signaling between CP Y901 and Briark, originally installed by the Rock Island between Briark and Hulbert in 1939-1940. Centralized Traffic Control (CTC) is a form of railway signaling whereby a centralized train dispatcher's office controls the switches and signals along a route, directing the train traffic over the line.

The installation of the CTC signaling involved a hearing by the Interstate Commerce Commission (ICC) in late 1939, because the system was fought by the Order of Railroad Telegraphers, "on the ground that safety of operation would be decreased." This hearing provided a wonderful description of train operations at the time.

> *Under the existing manual-block system, operators are stationed at Hulbert and Briark. Communication between them, with respect to the movement of trains in the zone involved, is effected by telephone. Train-order and manual-block signals are provided at Hulbert and Briark. Under the present practice an absolute block for passenger trains is maintained. Freight trains are permitted to follow each other through the block at 10-minute intervals. An east-bound Missouri Pacific train is not permitted to use the Rock Island tracks until a member of the crew has telephoned the operator at Hulbert from Wimef and obtained the block clearance. When this is received a hand-operated switch at the junction is thrown, and the train proceeds into the block. There are some switching movements through the zone involved, and during the month of August 1939 an average daily total of approximately 27 train or switching movements through the territory was made. A maximum speed of 70 miles per hour for passenger trains through the zone involved is permitted under the operating rules. Freight and switching movements are made under yard-limit rules.*

To the north is the Union Pacific Hulbert Subdivision, which goes 3.5 miles north to a connection with UP's Memphis Subdivision at Presley Junction. The line actually crosses on north and connects with the

BNSF at Marion. According to both UP and BNSF documents, the track between UP's Memphis and Brinkley lines is Track Warrant Control territory and is under the jurisdiction of the UPRR dispatcher. Maps from 1930 show that the line was Frisco trackage. However, Union Pacific has a 30-year lease on the line, allowing access to the large Union Pacific container yard just west of Marion. Trains heading toward Texas from the intermodal terminal often use the route, however timetables state that "no six axle locomotives are allowed to operate from MP 476.0 to MP 479.4 on the Hulbert Branch."

This area is shown as Wimef on many maps. The United States Geological Survey (USGS) states that the name can be traced back to at least 1936, where it was found on county highway maps published by the State Department of Transportation.

City of West Memphis

West Memphis has a population of about 26,500, a level that it has maintained since about 1970. While the traditional farming income has dropped, trucking has gained an important role due to Interstates 40 and 55. Before the area was settled, it was visited by people like Hernando de Soto (Spain) and Father Jacques Marquette and Louis Jolliet (France). However, the higher land on the eastern shore of the Mississippi was more attractive to most early settlers.

In 1875, a few houses and businesses were built near the Mississippi River, often on stilts to fight flooding. The town moved some, and was located about three miles south of today's downtown. In 1883, General George Nettleton, an official of the Kansas City, Fort Scott & Memphis Railroad (later Frisco), named the town West Memphis as they built through the area. By the early 1900s, the town was moving to higher ground along the railroads, and a post office opened here in 1920. West Memphis was incorporated in 1927 with Zach T. Bragg, a local logger and sawmill operator, as mayor.

West Memphis soon developed a reputation for entertainment, and was where B. B. King and others began their public entertaining. A chain of bars, clubs and restaurants on 8th Street acquired the name "Beale Street West" due to the music scene. Another famous location was The Coffee Cup, which was located at 204 East Broadway. This is where Elvis Presley ate his first breakfast after being inducted into the U.S. Army on March 24, 1958. A true trivia detail is that the movie *Hallelujah* was filmed near West Memphis in 1929.

9.4 **WEST MEMPHIS (YD)** – This is the milepost that the Rock Island used for West Memphis in 1979. The timetable showed that there was locomotive water, a dispatcher telephone, and a yard here. Located at the Avalon Street grade crossing, this was the west end of a three-track yard to the north. In 1979 there was also 4130-foot siding. Union Pacific has instructions about the Avalon Street grade crossing. "Eastward trains over 3,500 feet in length must stop short of South Avalon Street and not proceed until authority to enter CTC has been obtained either by signal indication or verbal authority from the control operator."

By 1908, the Rock Island called this area Hulbert (Hulburt about 1900), and before that it was known as Berkley's Landing. The Hulbert post office was established during February 1909. The name Hulbert is believed to come from William R. Hulbert, a local landowner during the 1800s. One of the first businesses here was founded by Henry and Ed Dabbs, several decades before West Memphis moved north to its current location. The Dabbs store building still stands at 1320 South Avalon and is listed on the National Register of Historic Places. The Hulbert post office served the area until West Memphis got its own post office in 1920. On August 19, 1955, the community of Hulbert was annexed by West Memphis.

The railroad had several customers at Hulbert. One of these was the Choctaw Shingle Company, which located there in 1907. The mill cost $100,000 and produced 300,000 shingles a day. The company had its own railroad using Davenport locomotives, Russell logging cars, and a Russell Skidder. The company built lodging for 100 workers and their families, a hotel and a commissary. There was also a cotton gin and seed house west of Mudge Street, today's Avalon Street. H. U. Mudge was president of the Chicago, Rock Island & Pacific when the Hulbert Yard was built. On September 4, 1912, the Arkansas Railroad Commission ordered the railroad to build a depot at Hulbert, and it was located nearby.

Hulbert Yard

During the early 1900s, the Rock Island Railroad replaced the facilities at Hopefield with a new yard and shops complex at Hulbert. The first announcement came during 1907, and then the work was delayed for a year. The November 12, 1908, issue of *The Iron Age* reported that "[w]ork has begun on the construction of terminal tracks, roundhouse and shops of the Rock Island Railroad at Hulbert, Arkansas, under contract awarded to the Dalhoff Construction Company, Little Rock."

The use of the Dalhoff Construction Company had some negative impacts on the project. The construction company entered receivership in 1908 and it took the permission of a Little Rock bankruptcy court for them to complete the contract for the construction of the Hulbert Yard. As the Hulbert Yard was being built in 1909, the Hopefield yard and shops were flooded and closed starting March 1st. This pushed the effort to complete the project, but the Dalhoff Construction Company still had its problems. By late 1909, a sale of the company's assets was ordered, and the receiver reported that 17 boxcars, 2 flatcars, 1 gondola, a camp and kitchen outfit, a blacksmith outfit, 9 head of stock, and lot of track tools were located at Hulbert.

On November 15, 1909, the new Hulbert yard and terminal opened. A cost of $175,000 was cited for the yard and a press release was made that the "Chicago, Rock Island & Pacific announces that along with the St. Louis & San Francisco, the two companies will construct a connection between the two railroads from the St. Louis & San Francisco at Marion, Arkansas, to the Chicago, Rock Island & Pacific at Hulbert, Arkansas. Completion was expected by early 1910." Information from several newspaper articles also stated that the Hulbert Yard was going to handle eastbound traffic heading to Memphis and beyond. One of the facilities was a re-icing station, used to ice refrigerator cars loaded with fruits and vegetables.

The *Arkansas Gazette* reported on April 4, 1910, that the Hulbert Shops were almost finished. An article in the February 15, 1912, issue of the *St. Louis Lumberman* reported that $300,000 would be spent to build shops at the new yard in Hulbert. Just a week earlier, the Chicago, Rock Island & Pacific experienced an unusual train robbery at Hulbert. On February 7, 1912, train No. 43 was robbed by five men who used dynamite to blow the safe, taking about $60,000. A report stated that so much dynamite was used that the combination baggage and express car was blown to splinters.

The yard, turntable and roundhouse were located east of Mudge Street, now South Avalon Street. Just west of this area is now the Morning Star Cemetery, sitting on land donated by the railroad to the local black community. The Hulbert Yard didn't last long as operations were concentrated in Memphis. A National Railroad Adjustment Board report covered the closing of Hulbert Yard. On June 20, 1932, the yard at Hulbert, Arkansas, was abandoned and the freight terminal moved to Fourth Street Yard at Memphis, Tennessee, and freight engines arriving and departing were moved between Fourth Street Yard and roundhouse by switch engine. Today, there is still a three-track yard at Hulbert, with much of the land on the north side of the yard where the roundhouse stood now covered by cotton warehouses.

Hulbert Branch

At the east end of the remains of Hulbert Yard, heading north, is the Hulbert Branch, also known as Union Pacific's Hulbert Subdivision. As a part of the development of Hulbert Yard, there were plans to connect the Rock Island and Frisco Railroads near West Memphis. At the time, the Frisco and the Rock Island were part of what was known as the Rock Island-Frisco Lines. This came about when the St. Louis & San Francisco Railroad Company was reorganized on June 20, 1896, and eventually B. F. Yoakum became the President and Chairman of the Board. In 1903, the Reid-Moore Syndicate acquired the Frisco, and also the Rock Island and the Chicago & Eastern Illinois. This allowed what was called "Yoakum's Dream" to happen – the consolidation of the facilities of the Rock Island and the Frisco. During that period of time, a number of new rail lines and facilities were built, often jointly owned and operated. Hulbert Yard and the Hulbert Branch were examples of this effort. However, the coordination plans were too expensive, and at the same time the Reid-Moore Syndicate pulled enormous sums of money out of the companies. On May 27, 1913, the Frisco went into the hands of receivers and the Rock Island-Frisco Lines was dissolved. On August 24, 1916, the new St. Louis-San Francisco Railway Company was created.

The connecting line that would allow the St. Louis & San Francisco to reach the new Hulbert Yard was known in some reports as the Marion Connection. The line, which was announced in late 1909, was jointly built by the two railroads between Hulbert (CRI&P) and Marion (Frisco), Arkansas. The announcement stated that completion of the project was expected by early 1910. Reports over the next forty years sometimes conflicted, but they agreed that there were 7.05 miles of main track, plus as many as 1.90 miles of sidings.

In 1915, a joint facility contract existed between the Frisco and the Rock Island for this line. The contract stated that the 7.05 miles of joint track was owned by the Frisco and that the Rock Island Railroad was to pay a rental fee of $3855.45 (2.5% of the line's $154,218 valuation). Additionally, the Rock Island was to pay half of the line's taxes, and would pay a percentage of the line's maintenance and operating expenses, prorated on the basis of the total number of cars handled by each railroad.

Because of the access to two railroads, business developed quickly along the route. Some of these companies included the Federal Compress and Warehouse Company, West Memphis Cotton Oil Company, Dacus Lumber Company, Thompson's Cotton Gin, and the West Memphis Lumber and Supply Company. Today, the south 3.5 miles of the route is Union Pacific's Hulbert Subdivision. The north end of the line is at Presley Junction on the former Missouri Pacific Bald Knob to Memphis line, now UP's Memphis Subdivision. The line heads on north to Marion, called the Hulbert Branch and owned by BNSF.

Cotton gins and sawmills dominated the scene along the Rock Island Railroad for more than a century. This photo of the West Memphis Gin Co. shows a typical cotton gin during the 1930s. Mydans, Carl, photographer. *Cotton gin company. West Memphis, Arkansas.* West Memphis, Arkansas, Crittenden County, June 1936. Photograph. Retrieved from the Library of Congress, https://www.loc.gov/item/2017761543/.

10.2 CANNERS – To the south is the former Canners of East Arkansas facility, which once canned soft drinks, including its Scramble Cola brand. The U-shaped facility was once served by two tracks. The firm was founded on April 3, 1970, and was the subject of a short piece in *The Rocket* (September/October 1970), a magazine "published bimonthly in Chicago by the Public Relations department of the Rock Island Lines for and about its active and retired employees."

> *West Memphis – Canners of Eastern Arkansas, Inc., will build a 60,000-square-foot soft drink canning plant in Ranier Industrial Park. The plant will be located on a 20 acre site and will involve an investment of $2 million.*
>
> *This latest industrial activity brings to a total of 143 industries that have either located along the Rock Island, or expanded their present facilities, since the beginning of 1970.*

11.4 RICEVILLE - Just east of this location, the railroad crosses Tenmile Bayou on Bridge 111, which consists of a 40-foot I-beam span with three timber spans on each end. Tenmile Bayou once wandered throughout the area until this diversion ditch was built to channelize it.

Maps from as early as 1889 show Riceville, and post office records show that there was a post office here 1879-1911. A 1903 Department of Agriculture report indicated that there was some rail service here in the early 1900s, as there were 68 rail shipments of cotton from Riceville in 1902-1903.

Riceville was not listed as a Rock Island station in 1979, but a track exists here today. To the north is the new Americold Logistics freezer warehouse and distribution center. While the facility handles contract work for a number of companies, recent users have included Simplot and Schwan's Consumer Brands. Temperature-controlled railcars are often spotted at the facility.

13.7   MOUNDS – During the early 1900s, Mounds was a busy lumbering station for the Rock Island Railroad. There has been a 115-car siding here on the north side of the mainline for many years. It measured 5319 feet in 1979, and Union Pacific lists it as being 6880 feet today. The Rock Island had an active dispatcher telephone here for many years as there was no agency or train order office.

Mounds came about due to logging. The August 15, 1909, issue of *The St. Louis Lumberman* reported that the Mark H. Brown Lumber Company had been incorporated with a capital stock of $10,000 and had purchased the milling plant of the Clements-Stevens Lumber Company of Mounds, Arkansas. A great amount of detail is known about the organization through its incorporation documents. One interesting detail is that the treasurer was J. H. Allen, who also operated his own J. H. Allen and Company timber operation. Allen later managed several mills in southwest Arkansas. About the same time, *The Lumber Manufacturer and Dealer* reported that while the general offices of the Mark H. Brown Lumber Company were at Mounds, offices in Memphis had been opened "to facilitate the sale of the output of its big mill at Mounds." The company was also at the time listed as being an oak lumber manufacturer and already had a retail lumber yard in South Memphis.

To support the mill, the Mark H. Brown Lumber Company operated a logging railroad in the area. The standard gauge operation reportedly used a Shay locomotive, the most widely used slow speed geared steam locomotive in the country. Logger Ephraim Shay designed the locomotive in the late 1870s and then Lima Locomotive Works of Lima, Ohio, built the locomotives. Almost 2770 Shay locomotives were built by Lima between 1878 and 1945, weighing as little as 6 tons and as much as 160 tons.

Records indicate that the Mark H. Brown Lumber Company owned and operated a Shay they numbered 101. This locomotive (Shop Number 1508) was built April 10, 1905, as Kinchin, Beacham & Co. #101, operating at Helena, Georgia. The small two-cylinder Shay was sold to J. D. Strother of Proctor, Arkansas, in 1909, and was soon used by the Pemiscot Lumber Company at Proctor. It came to Mark H. Brown Lumber sometime after 1910.

During October 1915, the lumber company was sold to Brown & Hackney, Inc., with R. J. Hackney president. Shay #101 was included with the sale. The sawmill apparently closed about 1920, as the Mounds post office was open 1909-1921, and in 1919 the Shay was for sale through the Southern Iron & Equipment Company in Atlanta, Georgia, where it was scrapped.

It has been mentioned that Brown's logging railroad possibly used several Shay locomotives. Records show that W. H. Scott & Son of Falcon, Mississippi, acquired a small 2-truck, coal burning standard gauge Shay (Shop Number 2245 with a build date of December 4, 1909) they numbered 18. Shay #18 soon was at Farrell Locomotive Works at Brinkley, Arkansas, a major dealer in used locomotives. Records show that it was later Brown & Hackney #1 at Pulaski, Arkansas (August 1920), Mark H. Brown Lumber #18 at Transylvania, Louisiana (March 1921), and Mark H. Brown Lumber #1 at Lake Providence, Louisiana. It was reported as scrapped on November 1, 1927.

Shay Locomotives

Some readers may question the reports about Shay and other logging locomotives. However, the Shay locomotive was the most used logging design, with 2767 Shays constructed over 67 years (1878-1945). Having a Shay locomotive generally showed that a logger was serious about operating their logging railroad. Because of their rugged construction, they often lasted decades and were sold from timber company to timber company.

The Shay was known for its low speed (10-20mph), high pulling power, and the ability to climb steep grades and operate on bad track. A Shay had two or three cylinders located on the engineer's side of the locomotive which drove a drive shaft that connected to every axle. To balance the weight, the boiler was moved slightly to the fireman's side of the frame. While almost 120 Shay locomotives still exist, few of them ever operated in Arkansas.

A typical Shay locomotive.

The Mounds Wreck of 1917

On January 27, 1917, there was a rear-end collision between two sections of a CRI&P passenger train at Mounds, which resulted in the death of three passengers, and the injury of 84 passengers and one employee. In reality, the first train was a Rock Island eastbound passenger train that was running as 1st No. 604, and the second train was an eastbound St. Louis Southwestern locomotive and caboose running as 2nd No. 604. The passenger train was operating from Little Rock to Memphis, hauling a combination mail and baggage car, a baggage car, two coaches and one chair car. What helped make the accident so severe was that all of the passenger cars were of wooden construction, except for the chair car which had steel platforms and vestibules. This mix of wood and steel cars was very common on the railroad at the time. During the mid-1910s, the Rock Island had about 1200 passenger cars, and only about one-third were of steel construction.

The Interstate Commerce Commission (ICC) investigated the accident, which happened as the passenger train finished its work at Mounds and was rear-ended by the Cotton Belt train. The finding was that both trains were behind schedule, and that the passenger train (1st No. 604) was losing time due to track slow orders and the business at several stops. The Cotton Belt train was to stay ten minutes or more behind the Rock Island passenger train, but without open stations, the crew could only guess how far back they were on this foggy night. The situation was made worse as the Rock Island passenger train crew failed to drop fusees along the track to warn the following Cotton Belt train.

For those who don't understand the use of fusees, train crews used to carry a large number of these devices. They could be used to warn other crews of their presence, and to stop highway traffic when a grade crossing was blocked. Since they burned for about ten minutes, a fusee could be dropped between the rails from a caboose, letting a following train know how close they were. By looking at how much of the fusee had burned, the following crew had an idea of the time that had passed since the fusee had been lit and dropped on the track. Since none were being dropped by the Rock Island crew, the Cotton Belt crew didn't realize how close they were.

The ICC report concluded by stating that "(t)raffic of such density as exists on this line would seem to warrant the use of a block system for the protection of trains." The report also commented that more open stations with agents would help increase the line's safety. "There is no reason why a manual block signal system could not be introduced on this division, the maintenance of a few more night offices, is all that would be required to secure the additional factor of safety afforded by such a block system." It would be a few years before the signals were installed.

15.1   **TRI-STATE AGGREGATE** – To the south was once a short 450-foot spur track, used to load rail cars. The long conveyor belt still exists, and the facility is now operated by Big River Industries.

16.1   **EDMONDSON** – The Memphis & Little Rock began train service from Hopefield to Edmondson's on Wednesday, June 17, 1868, and it was shown as a telegraph station for decades. At the time, train service was provided Monday, Wednesday and Friday. Edmondson's, shown as Edmunson and Edmondson in some railroad documents, was another farm products center during the late 1800s and early 1900s. For example, a 1903 Department of Agriculture report indicated that there were 978 rail shipments of cotton from Edmondson in 1902-1903. Two railroad-owned stock pens were here in 1921. In 1950, there was a 17-car capacity spur track at Edmondson, but it was gone by 1973.

The settlement of Edmondson (or Edmondson's) began when Andrew Edmondson moved here in the 1840s from Virginia. A post office using his name opened in 1859, and it is still open in the community to the south, which had a population of 427 in 2010. Some reports state that a depot was built here in 1868, and that by 1874, Edmondson had three cotton gins and two churches. About the same time, the area was described as a "terrible canebrake full of bear, panther, wolves, possum, and squirrel."

Another effort to develop the community occurred in 1902 when the Edmondson Home and Improvement Company was created by black residents. The company acquired land and then platted lots, selling and renting both lots and completed houses to African Americans. The town was incorporated in 1911, opened a new school in 1917, and soon had a livery stable, a mule sales barn, a theater, an ice house, two sawmills, a shingle mill, four doctors, a dentist, and a drugstore. At the time, Edmondson was centered along Main Street, which ran alongside the Rock Island Railroad.

Edmondson then faced a number of disasters, including floods in 1912 and 1913, a 1916 tornado, a 1927 fire that burned most of the town, and a flood in 1937. Maybe more damaging was that the Home and Improvement Company was closed in 1939 after it was discovered that it hadn't paid property taxes for more than twenty years. Much of the town was sold after Crittenden County seized it and Harold Weaver paid the back taxes on 588 lots. A new brick school opened in 1953, but by the late 1960s, students went to Crittenden County schools in West Memphis as part of a regional desegregation plan. A new city hall opened in 1974 and the post office quickly moved in after the building it was in burned. A new post office and elementary school have been built here over the past few years.

West of Edmondson at about Milepost 18, the railroad crosses Fifteenmile Bayou, which has been moved into Ditch No. 12 and around the community.

19.7   **PROCTOR** – Today, Proctor is simply some woods and a few houses to the south, however, it was once a Rock Island siding (a 4631-foot siding to the north in 1979) with a dispatcher telephone and a spur track. A post office opened here in 1890 as farming and logging grew in the area. The Proctor Cooperage Company was operating here in 1905.

During 1909-1910, there was a small battle between the Town of Proctor and the Chicago, Rock Island & Pacific. In December 1909 and again during January 1910, the Town of Proctor petitioned the Arkansas Railroad Commission to force the railroad to build a proper station. At the time, the railroad was reportedly using half of a boxcar as a depot, and the town said that the structure was not adequate for the 500 passengers a year that boarded a train at Proctor. On February 2, 1910, the petition was dismissed because the CRI&P had built a new depot.

A number of logging railroads once operated in the area. Both J. H. Findlay and the G. W. Simms Company reportedly had logging railroads during the start of the Twentieth Century. J. D. Strother also had a sawmill and logging railroad that was better documented. He was logging in the area with a standard gauge railroad by 1905, using a Shay with Shop Number 1508 that later went to the Mark H. Brown Lumber Company at Mounds, Arkansas. In 1910, he sold his operation to the Pemiscot Lumber Company and moved to Blaine, Mississippi. Strother may have known something as the Pemiscot Lumber Company had involuntary bankruptcy proceedings started against it during January, 1914.

The December 31, 1914, issue of the *Arkansas Gazette* reported on the sale of the Pemiscot Lumber Company to the Columbia Hardwood Lumber Company. The article stated that the sale would include 2500 acres of timber, three sawmills, a "dummy railroad" which connected with the St. Louis, Iron Mountain & Southern, and a tramroad which operated to the river. The newspaper also called the Columbia Hardwood Lumber Company one of the "wealthiest corporations in eastern Arkansas".

The Tradesman, an industry magazine, had several articles about the change of ownership in January 1915. An article in the January 10, 1915, issue stated that "Columbia Hardwood Co., of Chicago, will open a general office in Memphis as a result of the purchase of the Pemiscot Lumber Co., of Crittenden County, Ark., at a price said to be $62,500. In the sale goes a tram railroad several miles long, saw mill and several hundred acres of timber land, mainly red gum." A second article in the January 25, 1915, issue, confirmed the sale and stated that the "property involved includes a 2,500 acre tract of timber land, three saw mills and a logging railroad."

The Southern Lumberman of October 12, 1918, had an interesting article on the challenges of logging in a damp environment that studied the George C. Brown & Company timbering operations. The article described how the sawmill was located at Brown, Arkansas, about one mile south of Proctor on a rail spur. Newspapers later stated that Brown closed his band saw mill at Proctor in 1922 and moved to uncut timber in Mississippi. However, Brown had a 3000-acre plantation and home at Hughes where he remained.

20.6 **TWENTYMILE BAYOU** – This is another short bridge that crosses a channelized stream. Some older maps show that "Browns" was located just west of the bridge, not to the south as described in the *The Southern Lumberman*.

21.5 **COUNTY LINE** – Look for the grade crossing with U.S. Highway 79. To the east is **Crittenden County**, while **St. Francis County** is to the west. **St. Francis County** was formed on October 13, 1827, by the Arkansas territorial legislature, and named for the St. Francis River. The St.

Francis River drains much of southeastern Missouri and northeastern Arkansas along its 425-mile route. The new county included land that was once part of Phillips County, the seventh county created in what would become the State of Arkansas. The St. Francis county seat moved about a number of times, first meeting in the home of William Strong, and then moving to Franklin. In 1840, the county seat moved to Madison, and then to Mount Vernon in 1855. The new county courthouse burned in 1856 and the county seat moved back to Madison. In 1874, the county seat moved to Forrest City, created by Nathan Bedford Forrest as a construction camp and commissary while he completed the construction of the Memphis & Little Rock Railroad, later the Chicago, Rock Island & Pacific. The county includes a great deal of farming, hunting and fishing lands, and the population is approximately 30,000.

Both Crittenden and St. Francis counties are generally rural with large farming economies. Crittenden County is first in Arkansas in the production of sorghum (6000 acres), second in soybeans (210,000 acres), and fourth in wheat (16,000 acres). Corn, rice, cotton and peanuts are also significant crops grown in the county. St. Francis is the second largest grower of sweet potatoes in Arkansas (900 acres), and also has significant acreage of soybeans, rice, cotton, wheat, corn and sorghum.

Tarsus

Early maps show a small community named Tarsus just west of the county line. A railroad line once went north from here to just west of Shearerville. The name Tarsus traces back to Eastern Turkey where a city by that name was the capital over the Roman province of Cilicia. The city, today buried beneath the modern city of Cumhuriyet Alani, was once a center of cultural and intellectual studies. It received special privileges from the Romans, such as an exemption from imperial taxes and Jewish citizens of Tarsus were granted Roman citizenship. It was also once the home of the apostle Paul, who studied there. For Tarsas, Arkansas, nothing remains and the area is now simply fields of soybeans, cotton and other grains.

23.1   **RAGGIO** – This station was found in the 1899 timetable of the Choctaw & Memphis. The name Raggio comes from a merchant who came to Arkansas from Italy and settled to the south alongside the St. Francis River. Raggio was actually a logging town that was closer to the Missouri Pacific Railroad and its bridge across the St. Francis River, located in Lee County. The town was used to bundle logs together to float them to market, and a post office opened in 1875. The town was incorporated in 1907, but it burned in 1916 and was not rebuilt.

24.4 **QUIGLEY** – In the December 8, 1907, passenger timetable of the Rock Island, Quigley was shown as a passenger stop for westbound No. 41 and eastbound No. 42. Train No. 41 was the daily *Western Express*, a Memphis to Amarillo train that was an important link to Hot Springs. It featured "Parlor and Drawing-room Sleeping Cars, Coach and partition Smoker Memphis to Hot Springs. Dining Car Memphis to Little Rock. Drawing-room Sleeping Car Little Rock to Oklahoma City. Chair Car and Smoker Memphis to Amarillo. First class Coaches Memphis to Little Rock."

Eastbound train No. 42 was the *Memphis Express*. It was also a daily train that carried cars off of many routes. The timetable stated that there was a "Drawing-room Sleeping Car Oklahoma City to Little Rock. Parlor Car, electric-lighted Coach and partition Smoker Hot Springs to Memphis. Dining Car Little Rock to Memphis. Chair Car and partition Smoker Amarillo to Memphis. Drawing-room Sleeping Car Hot Springs to Memphis (to Chicago via Illinois Central R.R.)."

The *Hardwood Record* of October 25, 1914, had an advertisement for J. H. Bonner & Sons, with mills and offices at Quigley. The ad boasted that the firm's specialty was St. Francis Basin Red Gum, and that they manufactured southern hardwoods such as gum, oak and ash. The company also had their own logging railroad that served the mill and nearby woods. The *Arkansas Marketing and Industrial Guide* of 1921 showed that the firm was at Jonquil, Arkansas. Comparing maps from the two years shows that the locations were the same.

26.9 **HETH** – There has long been a siding to the north at Heth (once Heth's), measuring 8391 feet long. In 1967, Heth was the planned meet location between westbound passenger train No. 21, and eastbound Rock Island freight No. 26, scheduled for 10:00pm. The Rock Island had a dispatcher telephone here, and a new water station was installed at Heth in 1910. Heth was a station soon after the railroad passed through the area (some maps show it as 26 Mile Siding), and the small unincorporated community has had an area post office since 1896. It is today the home of S & S Heth Farms, Inc. Heth was the mailing address of J. H. Bonner & Sons, and the Ross-Atley Lumber Company was also here. The Ross Atley Lumber Company was based in Chicago, and had a three-foot gauge logging railroad here about 1907-1911.

Heth was the subject of a report in the U.S. Department of Agriculture, Weather Bureau's *The Floods of 1913 in the Rivers of Ohio and Lower Mississippi Valleys*. It stated that in April 1913, during a period of heavy flooding, the tracks at Heth were 2 feet under water and the station platform floated away.

There were once a large number of timber panel bridges east and west of Heth. Some have been filled while others have been replaced.

Not far west of Heth is Ditch No. 6 (Blackfish Bayou), which has had its timber spans replaced by more modern materials.

This photo shows the Flood of 1937 in East Arkansas. By this time, the railroad had raised its grade so that it was one of the few things above the flood waters. This photo was taken by Edwin Locke as a part of his documentation of the flood and the relief efforts underway in February 1937. United States Resettlement Administration, Locke, Edwin, photographer. *View taken from train en route to Forrest City, Arkansas from Memphis, Tennessee during the flood.* Tennessee, Memphis, Feb 1937. Photograph. Retrieved from the Library of Congress, https://www.loc.gov/item/2017728309/.

Crittenden Railroad

Heth was also a junction with the Crittenden Railroad. This was another Tap Line, a logging railroad that also served as a common carrier railroad for its owner. The Interstate Commerce Commission reported that the railroad was incorporated July 19, 1905, for a period of 50 years under the general laws of Arkansas. The original track was built by the Crittenden Lumber Company about 1899, reportedly 13 miles from Earle to Heth. This track was sold to the newly created Crittenden Railroad when it was fully organized on August 10, 1905. The corporation papers stated that the railroad "was to construct, maintain, and operate a railroad from Earle to a point in St. Francis County, all in Arkansas, a distance of about 15 miles."

The Crittenden Railroad was somewhat unique in that it had interchange connections with two railroads: the St. Louis, Iron Mountain &

Southern Railway at Earle and the Rock Island at Heth. The railroad was based at the mill facility at Earle, and owned 22.014 miles of road and 9.493 miles of yard and side tracks, with a number of spur tracks into the woods. This included 9 miles of track from Heth that was built in 1915 by the lumber company and sold to the railroad. During this time, the lands of the lumber company were being drained as part of a project by the Tri-County Drainage Canal. Reportedly, about 55,000 acres of land in the area was drained, and the value of the land rapidly increased. This allowed the land to be sold for farming as the timber was logged.

While the railroad was examined as part of the Tap Line cases, it was important enough to be under Federal control from January 1, 1918, to February 29, 1920, as a part of the nationalization of the United States railroad industry. The Interstate Commerce Commission (ICC) reported that in 1918, the Crittenden Railroad abandoned three sections of line totaling 15.44 miles. These sections included all of the track south of Heth, four miles of mainline north from Heth, and a 3.5-mile branch line. This left the railroad as being less than thirteen miles long with only an outside connection at Earle, Arkansas, with the Missouri Pacific. The railroad closed in 1921, with the U.S. Railroad Retirement Board showing an end date of January 1, 1922. A later hearing involved a lawsuit by the railroad to receive more payments from the federal government for losses incurred while the government ran the railroad. However, the ICC stated that the loss came about because the less-than-carload freight simply disappeared and less logging was taking place.

29.0   **CICALLA** – This was listed as a station in the 1899 timetable of the Choctaw & Memphis Railroad Company. Cicalla was simply a rural passenger station stop and never had any substantial facilities. The name 29 Mile Siding was also once used for the station.

30.0   **LUCERN** – A 1936 county road map shows that Lucern (Lucerne on some maps) was just east of Whitmore, and was located where County Road 503 comes in from the north and County Road 508 crosses the tracks. County Road 503 follows the grade of the Helena, Parkin & Northern Railway to Interstate 40, and then the grade is used by Arkansas Highway 75 all the way to Parkin. Some records show that Lucern was originally named Woodville, but there was already a Woodville east of Pine Bluff, Arkansas. While there is nothing but a barn here today, there were once a number of houses and a church at Lucern.

Helena, Parkin & Northern Railway

Lucern was a connection with the Helena, Parkin & Northern Railway (HP&N), which operated north to Parkin on the St. Louis, Iron Mountain & Southern (Missouri Pacific). The HP&N was investigated as part of the Interstate Commerce Commission (ICC) Tap Line Case, a series of hearings by the ICC which evaluated a number of railroads owned by logging companies called "Tap Lines." These lines were essentially industrial railroads serving only its owner, but were established as common carriers to obtain a share of the shipment rate revenue. Many of the lines were found to not be common carriers, and they lost their ability to charge a part of the rate for their services. Initially, this was true for the HP&N, however, a challenge all the way to the U.S. Supreme Court required the ICC to review their decisions. ICC *Investigation and Suspension Docket No. 11 - The Tap Line Case*, decided on July 29, 1914, that some timber-owned railroads were more than simple logging lines. For the HP&N, the ruling reverted to the divisions and allowances as of May 1, 1912.

The Helena, Parkin & Northern Railway dates back to 1890 when the Fee brothers from Pennsylvania built a small lumber mill at Parkin, Arkansas. The next year, the Lansing Wheelbarrow Company was founded in Lansing, Michigan, and soon bought the Fee sawmill to provide the company lumber to build wheelbarrows and carts. Other lumber operations, such as the Northern Ohio Lumber Company and the Parkin Cooperage Company created a great deal of traffic for the St. Louis, Iron Mountain & Southern at Parkin. Parkin became essentially a jointly owned company town as the lumber companies built schools and other joint facilities. The Northern Ohio School, built for the children of black employees from these companies, is now located at the Parkin Archeological Park and was placed on the National Register of Historic Places in 2014.

According to the Interstate Commerce Commission, the Lansing Wheelbarrow Company owned the Helena, Parkin & Northern Railway and used it to haul logs from the woods and swamps to the south. Some records show that the Helena, Parkin & Northern Railway began operating in 1904 while others show 1908, and the *Twenty-Third Annual Report on the Statistics of Railways in the United States for the Year Ending June 30, 1910*, stated that the HP&N measured 9.89 miles long. They continued to build south, and many maps showed that it eventually reached the Choctaw Route at Lucern, earlier Woodville. However, the December 1911 issue of *The Official Railway Equipment Register* didn't show an interchange with the CRI&P here. The U.S. Railroad Retirement Board showed that the HP&N was covered October 1, 1914, until December 31, 1921. The Lansing Wheelbarrow Company later became the Lansing-Company, which ceased operations in December 2009.

The Helena, Parkin & Northern Railway used a real mix of steam locomotive types. These varied from geared logging locomotives to former Manhattan Railway Company 0-4-4 "Forney" Locomotives. Some records show that Shay Construction Number 417, built November 26, 1892, worked on the line moving logs. This Shay was built as Mitchell & McClure Logging Railroad #4, of Duluth, Minnesota. It went to the Tony & Northeastern Railway in Wisconsin, and then to the HP&N. On August 17, 1918, the locomotive went to the Little Rock Lumber & Manufacturing Company at Natural Steps, Arkansas. In 1926, it became the property of the Bemberg & Son Iron Works in Little Rock, and then the Farrell Machine Works at Brinkley.

Another locomotive that worked on the Helena, Parkin & Northern Railway was former Manistique & Northwestern Railway #1. This Baldwin-built 2-6-0 (construction number 8120, September 1886) went through the hands of the Manistique, Marquette & Northern Railroad; Manistique & Northern Railroad; and Birmingham Rail & Locomotive before being sold to HP&N on February 2, 1914.

31.1 WHITMORE – The Whitmore Gin Company was here when the State of Arkansas published its *Arkansas Marketing and Industrial Guide* in 1921, as was the Shue Crill Company, manufacturers of wagon and dimensional stock. A 1903 Department of Agriculture report indicated that there were 148 rail shipments of cotton from Whitmore in 1902-1903. In 1950, the Rock Island had a six-car capacity spur track.

Whitmore was always a farming community, and in 1960, there were about a dozen houses and two churches to the south. What is left of the community is located just east of North Blackfish Bayou, crossed using an 80-foot deck plate girder with 10 panels of ballasted deck on one end, and six on the other.

32.3 BLACKFISH – Blackfish, also once known as Black Fish and Black Fish Siding, was listed as having an 85-car-long siding in 1950, although no other tracks besides the mainline exist here today. The railroad is situated on a high fill to stay above the flood waters of Blackfish Bayou, from which the community took its name. No buildings remain here today and the site is marked simply by the junction of several farm roads to the south, and the railroad overpass over County Road 503.

The Corps of Engineers stated that "Blackfish Bayou is one of the principal drainage channels for the lower portion of the St Francis Basin. Its headwaters are in the west central portion of Crittenden County, from where it flows in a southwesterly direction through the eastern portion of St Francis County to near the south line of that county, where it empties into St Francis River 44 miles above the mouth of that stream." During the early 1900s, the Corps of Engineers annually appropriated small sums to remove snags and work on various channelization projects in the area.

34.0   ROUND POND – The small community of Round Pond still exists on the north side of the tracks. A number of small businesses once operated here according to the 1921 *Arkansas Marketing and Industrial Guide*. These included D. M. Albin (cotton gin), B. M. Perkins (timber), J. E. Wheat (lumber mill), Round Pond Gin Company (cotton), and a Rock Island one-pen stock yard. Early records also show a Round Pond Terminal Company, and it was listed as a freight connection in the August 1912 *The Official Railway Equipment Register*. This was a small railroad that stretched north to Short Bend.

The Rock Island once had a number of track workers based at Round Pond, and new section houses were constructed at Round Pond in early 1910. In 1950, the railroad still had a 20-car capacity spur track at Round Pond. The remains of a cotton gin still stand on the west side of the community.

36.4   ROUND POND CUT-OFF BRIDGE – Rock Island documents from 1973 show that this bridge consisted of 18 panels of ballast deck timber piling. A number of concrete piers are also included in the bridge today.

This waterway is shown to be the St. Francis River on some maps, but it is actually a straightened and channelized old river channel, improved to reduce flooding at Madison. Today, this is the primary route of the river, thanks to the W. G. Huxtable Pumping Station. The Corps of Engineers explains that "The Memphis District's W. G. Huxtable Pumping Station, located near Marianna, Ark., is one of the largest stormwater pumping plants in the world. Completed in 1977, the station performs a two-fold mission. First, it prevents backwater from the Mississippi River from entering the lower St. Francis Basin when the Mississippi River is at bank full stage. This is accomplished by four 27' x 28' gravity flow gates, thereby becoming a dam. Second, its 10 enormous pumps remove excess surface water impounded by the Mississippi River and St. Francis Basin levees in the most efficient manner possible. The watershed served by the plant is more than 2,000 square miles, equal to the size of the state of Delaware." This complex prevents any boats from traveling up the St. Francis River, ending for good the days of commercial river traffic.

38.5 **WIDENER** – In 1979, the Rock Island had a 4017-foot siding to the north, along with a track that served the cotton gin. The siding is gone, except for the very west end that is used as a short spur track. This change has led Union Pacific to use Milepost 39.1 for Widener. For those who look, the remains of these tracks can be found where they once crossed Arkansas Highway 50 just north of the mainline.

Among the changes made by Union Pacific are new train signals next to the Arkansas Highway 50 grade crossing.

Widener (Widener's in the 1899 Choctaw & Memphis timetable) is located at an elevation of 194 feet and was not an original railroad station along the Choctaw Route due to the swamps in the area, and common flooding. For example, in 1882, it was reported that 28 miles of the Memphis & Little Rock Railroad was under water due to Mississippi River flooding. A post office named Mead, named for postmaster Robert T. Mead, was opened along the track in 1888. A railroad depot opened the same year using the same name.

About 1895, the name of the post office became Wideners, named for businessman, farmer and logger John M. Widener, a leading citizen of St. Francis County. The importance of area farming is made clear by a 1903 Department of Agriculture report that stated that there were 1537 rail shipments of cotton from "Wideners" in 1902-1903. On July 17, 1909, Widener was incorporated, the post office became Widener in 1917, and the population grew to 449 residents by 1920. About this time, reports showed that Widener was the home of a number of regional businesses. This included the Widener Gin Company, C. H. Huffman, Linder Brothers, Tom Pelkey, Phoenix Cotton Oil Company, and a one-pen railroad-owned stockyard.

Like many small towns in eastern Arkansas, the Depression was hard on the community and the population only began to recover when crop prices began to increase. The population dropped to 187 by 1930, and then slowly grew to 381 in 1990. Businesses have come and gone, and a gas station and small grocery, as well as a small cotton gin, support the community. The population reported by the 2010 census was 273 residents.

One of the few claims-to-fame of Widener is that it is the birthplace of blues legend Luther Allison. Allison was born here on August 17, 1939, and his family moved to Chicago a few years later. Luther Allison taught himself to play the guitar and got involved with the music scene in Chicago, becoming part of a house band at a club on Chicago's West Side. He began touring, both in the United States and in Europe, and recorded for both Delmark and Motown Records. In 2000, the *Chicago Sun-Times* called Allison "the Bruce Springsteen of the blues."

40.6   ST. FRANCIS RIVER BRIDGE – The St. Francis River, a tributary of the Mississippi River, is another meandering East Arkansas river, flowing through what used to be a series of bayous and hardwood bottoms. The 425-mile river starts in Iron County, Missouri, at first flowing like a typical mountain stream. It turns south and forms the western side of the Missouri Bootheel – the border between Arkansas and Missouri in the area. The St. Francis River eventually flows into the Mississippi River seven miles north of Helena, Arkansas. Looking at the meandering and muddy river here, it is hard to imagine that the river is used each year for the Missouri Whitewater Championships.

Just north of Marked Tree, Arkansas, the Little River flows into the St. Francis River, and the river south is considered to be navigable. This explains why the Rock Island had a turn span here. However, the U.S. Code of Federal Regulations has long had a section created by the Coast Guard (33CFR – Navigation and Navigable Waterways). Part 117.137 was entitled St. Francis River and stated "The draws of the Chicago, Rock Island and Pacific railroad bridge, mile 59.7 at Madison, and all drawbridges above that point need not be opened for the passage of vessels."

The name St. Francis River has an uncertain origin. There are a number of conflicting theories, made even more complicated by having the name changed from "François" to "Francis" during the early 1900s. In Missouri, the older name still exists with St. Francois County and the St. Francois Mountains. In Arkansas, it is generally St. Francis. Some speculate that the name dates back to Jacques Marquette and his exploration of the Mississippi River, possibly named for St. Francis of Assisi or St. Francois Xavier. What is known is that Native Americans settled along the river between 1000 and 1250 A.D. A mound and village were documented by Hernando de Soto in 1541, and the remains are included in the Parkin Historic Site at the Parkin Archeological State Park in Cross County, Arkansas. Cherokees moved into the area by 1780, and then generally moved further west to avoid white settlement. No matter the name source, the United States Board on Geographic Names declared the river's name to be St. Francis in 1899.

The railroad reached here in 1861, and a bridge over the St. Francis River opened on September 30, 1861. It was described as being 600 feet long, with three spans being supported by six brick piers. The 200-foot-long center span was a drawbridge that revolved on a large circular brick pier to allow steamboats to move on the river. For a number of years, the tracks ended just west of the bridge at the Madison depot, even though the iron rails had been purchased by the end of September 1861. Additionally, some grading to the west had been completed, and Crowley's Ridge to the west had been cut through.

In April 1869, a contractor completed a new St. Francis bridge for the Memphis & Little Rock. This was the second bridge as the first one was burned during the Civil War. After several weeks of inspections and testing, the railroad accepted the bridge and began using it. The bridge was replaced again about 1899 as train sizes got larger and heavier. In 1973, Rock Island documents show that the bridge, east to west, included a 12-panel ballast deck timber pile trestle, 197 feet of through truss, a 196-foot through truss draw span, 157 feet of through truss, and a five-panel ballast deck trestle. Today, most of the bridge has been replaced by twelve 50-foot modern spans, leaving only a through truss span and the timber trestle on the east end. The pier for the turn span is used by the new bridge, a reminder of what was once here.

This through truss span on the east approach to the St. Francis River Bridge is one of the few parts not replaced recently by Union Pacific Railroad.

40.7 MADISON (MN) – Madison, a former river town on the west bank of the St. Francis River, reached its peak population of 1263 in 1990, but had a population of only 769 during the 2010 census. The town is situated between the low grounds along the river, and the higher Crowley's Ridge to the west. The town has been destroyed multiple times by fire, flood and the Civil War, so much of its early history is unclear. In 1841, Madison, which had been named for President James Madison, became the county seat of St. Francis County. Madison lost the county seat in 1855, but regained it in 1856 after the Mount Vernon courthouse and records burned.

Just before the Civil War, Madison was a regionally important port. It was known for its dances and parties on docked paddlewheelers, and it became even more important when the Memphis & Little Rock Railroad reached the east bank of the St. Francis River, just across from Madison. Madison survived the Civil War, but was impacted by a major flood and fire in 1867. The town began to regrow and benefitted when the bridge across the St. Francis River opened on April 17, 1869.

In 1874, Madison again lost the county seat, this time to Forrest City, just on the other side of Crowley's Ridge. It was some time before the county records were moved; in fact, it took a midnight raid by Forrest City residents to move them. Despite this, Madison still attracted timber and agricultural interests, and a 1903 Department of Agriculture report indicated that there were 15 rail shipments of cotton from Madison in 1902-1903. Madison was incorporated on July 1, 1914. An interesting fact about Madison is that it was the home of the first African-American millionaire in Arkansas, Scott Bond. Bond, born into slavery, had slowly bought land and businesses in Madison. Among his interests were five cotton mills and a sawmill, and he was buried in Madison with great respect in 1933. His family plot was listed on the National Register of Historic Places on June 6, 2002.

A 1921 Sanborn Map Company document showed that a Morgan & West Manufacturing Company crate factory was once south of the Rock Island mainline, served by a long spur track. The factory, shown as the Morgan & West Box Company in other sources, included a saw and planing mill, a boiler and powerhouse, the main factory, and a number of lumber sheds. The firm apparently entered bankruptcy in 1922.

The Rock Island Railroad also had a long industry track that curved north and followed the river into downtown Madison where it served several companies. These included the Prichard & Wheeler Company sawmill, the E. D. Berry Gin, the Scott Bond Gin Company, and the Prichard & Wheeler Company lumber yard.

Madison has continued to suffer through multiple floods, and only a few businesses still exist, mostly to serve area farms. The Arkansas Delta Project started in Madison in 1979 as an attempt to improve the economy of the area, but the town has continued to shrink.

Railroads at Madison

Rail service to the St. Francis River started in 1858, with reports that most of the line between Hopewell Point and Madison was laid on pile trestle bridges since the soil was not good for a stable grade, and the railroad would have had to haul in rock and earth to build any fills. Once the bridge was opened, trains heading west from Madison faced a two-mile grade of 0.81% as they climbed over Crowley's Ridge. Once the railroad crossed the peak of the ridge at 304 feet, it dropped for another two miles at a 0.77% grade. Located at an elevation of 210 feet, the Rock Island had a 5335-foot siding at Madison, as well as a house track and several industry spurs. A station once stood at Madison, and it was shown as a telegraph station and a connection "with steamers plying on St. Francis River north and south" in the railroad's October 9, 1892, timetable. In early 1917, the Rock Island petitioned the Arkansas Railroad Commission to allow the railroad to remove the depot at Madison, but it was still active in 1967.

During the late 1800s, J. G. Stern had a logging operation at Madison that used a five-foot gauge pole railroad. A pole railroad uses logs instead of rails, and the wheels are designed to ride on tops of the logs, with flanges on both the inside and the outside of the wheels. These railroads were generally hauled by mules or oxen, although some did use steam locomotives to pull log cars.

41.6 **CROW CREEK BRIDGE** – This bridge consists of three 75-foot deck plate girder spans. It once had ballast deck timber spans off of each end, but now has modern concrete spans. Crow Creek flows south and then turns east to enter the St. Francis River. The bend in the old channel of the St. Francis River that the railroad crosses is known as Crow Bend.

During the early 1900s, the Rock Island obtained ballast from Crow Creek and used it on a number of projects east towards Memphis.

41.9 **LITTLE CROW CREEK BRIDGE** – This bridge includes a 40-foot deck plate girder span with short timber trestles off each end. Little Crow Creek flows south and then east before entering Crow Creek. Heading west, the railroad follows Little Crow Creek through the pass in Crowley's Ridge.

43.8 **SUMMIT** – This station, located at the top of Crowley's Ridge, was listed in the 1899 timetable of the Choctaw & Memphis Railroad. During 1899, the Choctaw & Memphis was working on plans to lower the summit, reduce the grades, and straighten the curves involved with the climb over Crowley's Ridge.

Crowley's Ridge

Coming from the east, many people think that they have reached the mountains of Arkansas when they first see Crowley's Ridge. However, this narrow rolling hill only varies from half-a-mile to 12 miles wide, and stands only 250 to 550 feet above the surrounding delta and farmland. Crowley's Ridge stretches for about 150 miles from southeastern Missouri to near Helena, Arkansas. The ridge was named for Benjamin Crowley, credited as being the first American settler in the area, who arrived about 1820. Benjamin Crowley helped to create Greene County, was the first postmaster in the region, and founded the first church in the area. During the 1930s, the Civilian Conservation Corps built a number of buildings on his old farm, leading to the creation of Crowley's Ridge State Park.

There are two theories about how Crowley's Ridge was created. The long-held theory is that it started as an island between the Mississippi River and Ohio River. It was left isolated when the Mississippi River changed its course, and windblown sediment known as loess piled up and created the ridge. The second theory is that Crowley's Ridge was created by uplift along a fault line that captured the blowing loess. Measurements indicate that Crowley's Ridge is still growing and that it might be related to the nearby New Madrid Seismic Zone.

44.8   FORREST CITY (FC) – Just west of the top of the Crowley's Ridge grade is Forrest City, the county seat and largest city in St. Francis County. The area's higher elevation has long attracted settlers and a small community developed here by the Civil War. The war stopped area work on the Memphis & Little Rock Railroad, but in 1866, former Confederate general Nathan Bedford Forrest received a contract to build the railroad across Crowley's Ridge. Forrest chose this location to be the base of his work, and approximately 1000 Irish laborers were supported from his commissary here. A town quickly grew up around the commissary, and in early 1869, U. B. Izard had a town surveyed. Surveyor John C. Hill marked off a 36-block town on March 1, 1869. While there were plans to name the town Izardville, the Forrest City post office opened later that year, about the same time the first freight train arrived. The first store opened in 1870, operated by the Izard Brothers. The *Forrest City Free Press* started publishing the same year, and Forrest City was incorporated on May 11, 1870.

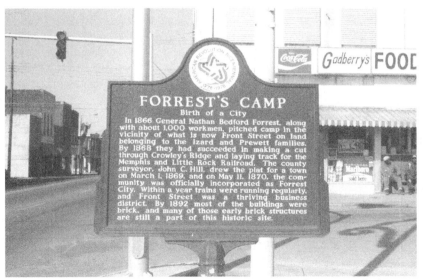

This historical marker in downtown Forrest City, photographed in 1982, tells the story of the beginning of the community.

In 1874, Forrest City became the county seat of St. Francis County, and soon thereafter a fire burned much of downtown, taking many of the county records with it. By 1880, the population had reached more than 900, and schools and churches had opened, however a yellow fever outbreak took place in late 1879. This led to several city improvements, and Forrest City had electric lights, a water and sewer system, and even paved streets by 1900. Agriculture played a major role in the city's fortune, as shown in a 1903 Department of Agriculture report that listed 5142 rail shipments of cotton from the various gins and warehouses in 1902-1903.

By 1920, Forrest City was the center of commerce for a large part of Eastern Arkansas. The *Arkansas Marketing and Industrial Guide* of 1921 showed a long list of major businesses, including the Forrest City Box Company, Forrest City Compress Company, Forrest City Gin Company, Planters Gin Company, Houston & Dillon Gin Company, Yocoma Gin Company, Forrest City Spoke & Handle Company, Forrest City Ice & Coal Company, Vacarro-Grobmyer Company (lumber), and Vanhouten Lumber Company.

The Flood of 1927 isolated Forrest City, but it was the home of one of the county's three Red Cross relief camps. It became the largest in Arkansas, housing more than 15,000 refugees. The Great Depression and another flood in 1937 hurt the community, but Forrest City was again a center for relief and refugees. World War II had little direct impact on the city, but several manufacturing plants developed afterwards. The schools were desegregated in 1964, and a number of city facilities were built in the 1960s. While the population of the county has decreased over the past several decades, the population of Forrest City was 15,371 in the 2010 census, the highest ever.

Forrest City was the birthplace (April 13, 1946) of Rock and Roll Hall of Fame member Al Green, listed as Number 65 in the *Rolling Stone* list of the 100 Greatest Artists of All Time, and Number 14 on its list of the 100 Greatest Singers. Don Kessinger, the last player-manager in American League baseball history, was also born in Forrest City (July 17, 1942). A six-time All-Star, Kessinger played shortstop for the Chicago Cubs, St. Louis Cardinals and the Chicago White Sox.

This photo shows part of the 1937 flood refugee encampment that was located at Forrest City, Arkansas. The community's location on the west slope of Crowley's Ridge kept it above the flood waters of the local rivers and bayous. Evans, Walker, and Edwin Locke, photographers. *Untitled photo, possibly related to: Flood refugee encampment at Forrest City, Arkansas.* Forrest City, Arkansas, ca. 1937. Photograph. Retrieved from the Library of Congress, https://www.loc.gov/item/2017758416/.

The Railroads of Forrest City

Forrest City features a diamond between Union Pacific's Brinkley and Helena Subdivisions, what was known by the CRI&P as MOPAC Crossing. The north-south line was for many years the Wynne Subdivision that stretched all the way to McGehee, Arkansas. However, the track south of the junction to Helena, Arkansas, has been abandoned and is slowly being turned into a rail-trail.

These signal control boxes at Forrest City show that Union Pacific's two subdivisions still cross here.

The St. Louis, Iron Mountain & Southern Railway Company's Knobel Branch, built from Knobel, Arkansas, on the Poplar Bluff to Little Rock mainline, to Forrest City, opened in December 1882. The line went from Knobel south to Paragould (now abandoned); south to Jonesboro Junction, following the Cotton Belt line (now abandoned), and then south to Forrest City (in service), a total of 97 miles. By 1883, what was known as the Crowley Ridge Branch was extended from Forrest City south to Helena, 43 miles, by the purchase of the Iron Mountain & Helena Railroad.

The Iron Mountain & Helena Railroad was actually an older line than the Knobel Branch. The Iron Mountain & Helena Railroad Company was originally created in Arkansas on December 31, 1860. However, construction didn't start until the 1870s, after the railroad made a contract in 1873 with the Southern Construction Company for the building of its road. The first work was 18 miles of track between Barton and Marianna, using a track gauge of 3½'. The unique gauge was chosen as the railroad connected with the Arkansas Midland's line into Helena, which used the same gauge. The original plan for the Iron Mountain & Helena was a 140-mile line from Helena to the St. Louis, Iron Mountain & Southern at Peach Orchard, in northeast Arkansas, and it built to Forrest City. In 1881, the line was converted to standard gauge, and then sold to the Kansas City & Southern Railway Company on February 21, 1882. On October 26, 1882, the line was sold to the St. Louis, Iron Mountain & Southern Railway, becoming part of the new Helena Branch.

The St. Louis, Iron Mountain & Southern entered receivership on August 19, 1915, and was merged with the Missouri Pacific on May 12, 1917. In 1982, the railroad became owned by Union Pacific, which first spent large sums to rebuild it for chemical trains, but then halted service in late 1986. The route south of Helena Junction to north of McGehee was abandoned in 1992 by Union Pacific, becoming the Delta Heritage Trail. The route northward was kept to connect to industry in Helena, which has been switched by the Arkansas Midland Railway Company since 1992.

Forrest City was once the home of a track gang, and in 1982 these tool sheds still stood at the east end of town.

During the early 1900s, Forrest City was full of railroad tracks, few of which remain. In 1919, the CRI&P had two tracks through the interlocking. The siding (north track) ended about West Street, and there were two spur tracks to the south that served the Forrest City Water & Light Company, along with a railroad tool house. The joint railroad station was immediately to the southeast of the diamond, a block further east and across Washington were several tracks to the south that served a cotton platform. The St. Francis County Courthouse was a block further to the east, located just east of Izard Street. To determine the charges for the area freight, a 40-foot, 100,000-pound capacity track scale was installed.

Missouri Pacific (MP or MoPac) handled most of the local business like the Forrest City Ice & Coal Co., Forrest City Gin Company, and the Planters Gin and Manufacturing Company. The MP freight house was to the north of the Rock Island, on the east side of the Missouri Pacific tracks, north of Hill Street and east of West Street. Both railroads served the large Forrest City Compress Company cotton compress on the west side of town and the CRI&P served the Forrest City Cotton Oil Mill that was southwest of Davis and West Streets, a complex that still mostly stands along the interchange connecting track. Besides the industry tracks, there were once two connecting tracks to the west in the southwest quadrant of the diamond. One still exists, which connects at Division Street where both tracks bridge over the street.

The Derailment of St. Louis Southwestern Passenger Train No. 626

While all of the industry tracks at Forrest City provided business for the railroad, one of them also caused the May 12, 1921, derailment of St. Louis Southwestern passenger train No. 626. Heading eastward about 3½ hours late, this train consisted of one baggage car, one mail and express car, one coach, one chair car and two Pullman sleeping cars (the first three cars were of steel underframe construction while the last 3 cars were of wooden construction), pulled by locomotive #657 (4-6-0). The derailment occurred at the mainline switch to the compress track at 9:25am, located about 0.8 mile west of Forrest City, and resulted in the death of one employee (engineer), and the injury of four passengers and two railroad employees.

The investigation that followed determined that a section gang was working on a spur track off the compress track, and they had lined the switch so their section motor car and push car could reach the location. The sectionman in charge apparently failed to line the switch back, leaving it lined and locked for a movement to the compress track. A westbound Rock Island passenger train ran through the switch about 9am, leaving the points gapped on each side and the connecting rod bent. When Cotton Belt Locomotive #657 hit the switch, it tried to go down the compress track, but instead rolled off the embankment to the right.

The Interstate Commerce Commission stated that the "accident was caused by the failure of Engineman Boone, of train No. 626, properly to observe and obey the stop indication of the switch target of the compress track switch." It also added that "the indication of the switch target at this point was entirely overlooked and disregarded by two engine crews; in one case the switch was run through and damaged, and in the other case the switch was split and the train derailed." Blame was also placed upon the section foreman who loaned his switch key to a sectionman, despite a Rock Island rule that stated that the section foreman must not permit his switch key to be out of his possession and must personally open and close all main track switches.

The report also described the track at the location. "Approaching the point of accident from the west the track is tangent for several miles, while the grade is 0.8 per cent ascending for a distance of about 2,100 feet. The track is laid with 90-pound rails, with 20 treated pine ties to the rail-length, single-spiked, and ballasted with about 12 inches of gravel. In the vicinity of the switch the track is on an embankment about 17 or 18 feet in height. The compress track leads from the main track toward the south, the switch being a facing-point switch for eastbound trains. The switch stand is a High Star stand, located on the engineman's side of an eastbound train."

Forrest City Union Station

As previously mentioned, immediately to the southeast of the Missouri Pacific-Rock Island diamond was Forrest City Union Station, which included a baggage room and large platform on the CRI&P. This union station was unique in that the Hotel Avery was on the second and third floors. Construction on the three-story station and hotel began in 1885, and a basement added a fourth floor since the property was on a grade. The Hotel Avery featured forty rooms and a restaurant, and opened officially with a large ball on April 28, 1886.

While a major presence in Forrest City, the hotel had a history of borderline finances. By 1898, the hotel had become the Belser Hotel, and then the Marion Hotel by 1901. The station part of the building, including the express company and located in the northwest corner of the hotel, was upgraded in 1908. By 1916, records indicate that the entire building was owned by the Rock Island, which leased the upper floors to the hotel, as well as the lobby and restaurant on the east end of the first floor. In 1917, management of the Marion Hotel was contracted to the John J. Grier Hotel Company. For a decade, the Grier Hotel Company had managed hotels, dining rooms and lunch rooms along the Rock Island, including those at Little Rock and Booneville, Arkansas. With the management change, Rock Island passenger timetables began to promote the hotel. Promotions of the dining room ended about 1920.

In 1919, the United States Railroad Administration (USRA), which managed the nationalized railroads across the United States during World War I, moved the Missouri Pacific station into the Rock Island building and away from their own station, described as being 400 yards to the north. With this change, Forrest City Union Station began to be used as the building's name. Even after Missouri Pacific passenger trains stopped running in 1938, their bus system still used the Rock Island station.

The Forrest City station was not originally built with covered platforms, but citizens at many stations across the state petitioned the Arkansas Railroad Commission during the 1920s for such improvements. In response, umbrella sheds were built along the Rock Island tracks and the front porch of the station was enclosed. In 1923, the Van Noy Interstate Railroad News Company took over management of the facility, and then the Rock Island Dining Car Department in 1929. The last timetable advertisement for the Marion Hotel is believed to be in the August 1936 Rock Island timetable. The hotel was leased again, this time to W. N. Landers and A. B. Wolfe on April 1, 1937.

The hotel closed sometime in the late 1940s. Across the tracks to the north was the CRI&P Freight Depot, which was remodeled during the mid-1950s to include a train order office/ticket office, and a small waiting room for passengers. The railroad moved all of their offices out of Union Station and into the freight house, and the large building was torn down in 1958. When passenger service ended in November 1967, the waiting room was closed, but the train order office stayed open until the railroad shut down in March 1980. The Cotton Belt took over rail operation on March 23, 1980, and the station was soon closed. The freight house was later torn down, leaving several empty blocks around the CRI&P-MP diamond, which is now Union Pacific-Union Pacific.

This view of the Rock Island station in Forrest City dates from 1982, shortly before the Cotton Belt tore the building down.

This simple station sign now marks the location where Forrest City Union Station once stood.

47.8   REDFERN – Heading west from Forrest City, U.S. Highway 70 closely follows the old Rock Island Choctaw Route to North Little Rock, Arkansas. The remains of a number of small communities and industries once served by the railroad can be seen and even explored along this part of the line.

Redfern was once a station on the railroad, and in 1950 there was a 100-car siding here. Redfern was reportedly named for the Redfern family, who farmed in the area.

48.9   BECKS – Becks was also known as Beck's, Becks Spur, or Beckspur. Today, a grade crossing with Beckspur Road marks the location, which includes several churches and houses, but no station or side tracks. A 1934 survey report indicated that the elevation of the "top of rail opposite the Chicago, Rock Island & Pacific Railway station" at Becks was 218.6 feet. The station was no longer listed by 1950.

Becks was never a large community, and it initially relied upon logging and farming for its existence. *The Daily Postal Bulletin* (July 1, 1899), "issued from the office of the General Superintendent Railway Mail Service," stated that a post office opened at Becks, Arkansas, on June 14, 1899. However, the post office closed in 1908.

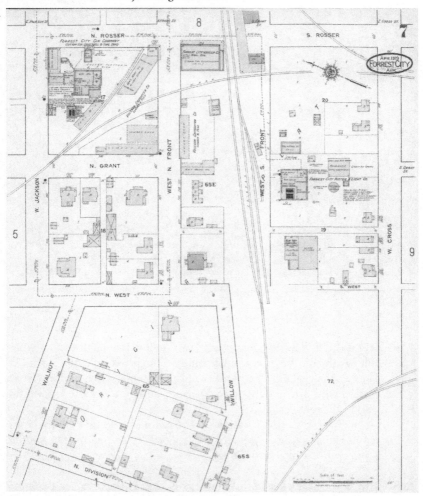

This map shows the area just west of the former Rock Island-Missouri Pacific diamond at Forrest City, Arkansas. *Sanborn Fire Insurance Map from Forrest City, Saint Francis County, Arkansas.* Sanborn Map Company, Apr, 1919. Map. Retrieved from the Library of Congress, https://www.loc.gov/item/sanborn00246_006/.

This map shows the downtown area of Forrest City, located just east of the former Rock Island-Missouri Pacific diamond. *Sanborn Fire Insurance Map from Forrest City, Saint Francis County, Arkansas.* Sanborn Map Company, Apr, 1919. Map. Retrieved from the Library of Congress, https://www.loc.gov/item/sanborn00246_006/.

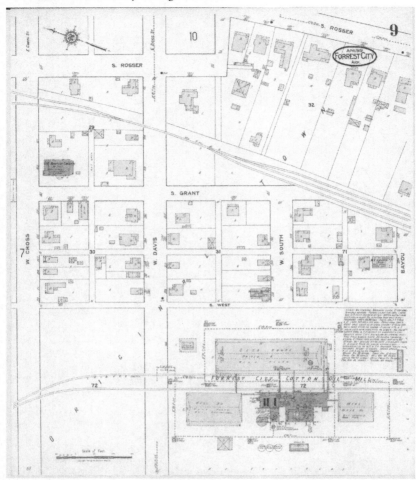

This map shows the area around the Forrest City Cotton Oil Mill, located south-west of the former Rock Island-Missouri Pacific diamond. *Sanborn Fire Insurance Map from Forrest City, Saint Francis County, Arkansas.* Sanborn Map Company, Apr, 1919. Map. Retrieved from the Library of Congress, https://www.loc.gov/item/sanborn00246_006/.

49.9 **LONGINO** – To the south is the retired Arkansas Power & Light (AP&L) Hamilton Moses Power Plant, which burned natural gas for electrical power production. Construction began in 1949, and in 1950 the Rock Island showed that the industry tracks had the capacity to hold 70 freight cars. In 1973, there were still four spur tracks at the plant. The power plant opened in 1951 to great celebration, with many area towns declaring it a holiday.

AP&L had been created by Harvey C. Couch, who also gained control of the Louisiana & Arkansas Railway and the Louisiana Navigation & Railway Company, and merged them with the Kansas City Southern, of which Couch was president. When Couch died in 1951, C. Hamilton Moses became president and CEO of AP&L, and the plant was named after him.

The name Longino honors an early business associate of Couch. In 1903, Couch borrowed money to buy wire and began stringing it to provide rural telephone service. One of the parties that he borrowed money from was Dr. H. A. Longino of Magnolia, who invested $1500 in Couch's business, and then loaned him the same amount. Eight years later, Couch sold his growing firm to Southwestern Bell Telephone for $1.5 million. Couch then purchased several electrical plants in south Arkansas and created the Arkansas Power Company in 1913, becoming the Arkansas Power & Light Company by the end of 1914. Longino's house in Magnolia, Arkansas, was added to the National Register of Historic Places in 1982.

50.7 **L'ANGUILLE RIVER BRIDGE** – The L'Anguille River is another slow-moving main channel that once flowed through the miles of swamp and bayous of eastern Arkansas. The river's name is old, appearing in French explorer reports from at least 1723, and means "eel" in French. The river forms from several creeks and drainage canals south of Jonesboro, Arkansas, and flows south, eventually joining the St. Francis River near Marianna. The only natural break in Crowley's Ridge is where the L'Anguille River passes through it.

Friedrich Gerstäcker, a German nineteenth-century author who wrote about his travels in Arkansas (1838-1842), stated that the L'Anguille River basin included "swamps and thorns, creepers, wild vines, fallen trees, half or entirely rotted, deep and muddy water-courses, bushes so thick that you could hardly stick a knife into them, and, to complete the enjoyment, clouds of mosquitoes and gnats, not to mention snakes lying about on the edges of the water-courses." Gerstäcker's reports don't seem to be exaggerated, as the L'Anguille and Cache Rivers were major obstacles for the construction of the Memphis & Little Rock Railroad. The route between the two rivers wasn't completed until 1871. Even after the railroad was completed, the line often closed due to area flooding. In particular, the floods of 1927 and 1937 greatly impacted the railroad and area farmland. However, the characteristics of the river makes it an attraction for fishing and waterfowl hunting.

The Memphis & Little Rock initially announced that the railroad's track would be laid to the L'Anguille River by July 1, 1869. However, a report in the September 19, 1869, *Daily Arkansas Gazette* stated that the bridge over the L'Anguille River was under construction, along with about 5000 feet of trestle work throughout the area. By November, the L'Anguille River bridge was completed and trains were running in the area to support track construction to the west. This has traditionally been a 51-panel ballast deck wooden trestle, crossing both the main channel and the overflow of the river. Several other trestles in the area also cross flood channels of the L'Anguille.

51.8   **PALESTINE** – Palestine is the first significant community west of Forrest City, and had a population of 681 during the 2010 census, down from 741 in 2000, and its peak population of 976 in 1980. The town is a typical East Arkansas farming community with a post office (opened in 1870), gas station and convenience store, schools, bank, farm supply store, and other businesses. Interstate 40 is located just north of Palestine and features a truck stop and more businesses.

By the opening of the post office in 1870, Palestine was a cluster of homes and farms in Prairie Township of St. Francis County. While several names had been used for the community, generally based upon the name of the most important resident, Palestine was chosen when the post office was opened to serve the township. There is no clear reason for the name, but various stories do exist. One story states that the name honors a local resident who had recently been killed in an accident at the local sawmill. A second story states that the first postmaster chose the name from his Bible.

The town's founding, and its later incorporation on April 23, 1889, makes it one of the oldest towns in St. Francis County. Located at an elevation of 207 feet, it is also the site of the first county school, opened in 1870. A number of businesses soon opened along Main Street, which paralleled the railroad. This downtown area was rebuilt during the 1890s after a large fire. Palestine was an early station on the railroad, and it was shown to be a telegraph station in 1892. A cotton gin opened by the late 1800s, and a 1903 Department of Agriculture report indicated that there were 1377 rail shipments of cotton from Palestine in 1902-1903. A report from 1905 stated that the town had five dry-goods and general supply stores, two grocery stores, and one drugstore. Telephone service also started that year.

Palestine is noted as the home of the first consolidated school district in Arkansas, with the Palestine Special School District created in

1913. To handle the larger student numbers, both the existing Palestine two-room schoolhouse and a local Baptist church were used until a new school was opened in 1914. Today, Palestine hosts the combined Palestine-Wheatley School District.

The *Arkansas Marketing and Industrial Guide* of 1921 listed the C. M. Wilkinson cooperage and lumber company, as well as The Banks Company cotton gin, as the major industries at Palestine. There are a few reports that a logging railroad operated north out of Palestine to Slonikers Mill and on north to the Missouri Pacific at Hamlin, Arkansas. As the timber was cut, Palestine relied more upon local farming, and cotton, rice and soybeans are the major crops today.

In 1950, the Rock Island had a 90-car siding, plus other tracks with a capacity of 30 railcars, at Palestine. There was also a dispatcher telephone. Today, Union Pacific has an 8391-foot siding to the north, with the east switch of the siding located just west of the Main Street grade crossing.

55.5 **MCGOFFINS** – This is another 1899 Choctaw & Memphis railroad station that no longer exists. It was located near today's grade crossing with County Road 117. The 1899 *ABC Pathfinder Shipping and Mailing Guide* listed McGoffins as a station on the Little Rock & Memphis (Choctaw & Memphis R. R.).

56.7 **WOOD SPUR** – This location was shown to be an 8-car capacity spur track in 1950. Today, there are still woods to the north, and a few houses and a small church to the south.

59.0 **GOODWIN** – Goodwin grew up as a community about the same time the railroad was built through the area, and a Goodwin post office opened here in 1873. Soon after the railroad was built, Goodwin was apparently a stop for both passenger and freight trains, as in 1878, a new 50,000-gallon, wind driven water tank was built here.

The area was first known as Goodwin Prairie, and the Goodwin Township was created to serve local farmers. The community of Goodwin soon followed. The town was never large and it is still an unincorporated community. However, it was a source of some freight and passenger traffic for the railroad. For example, 48 rail shipments of cotton moved from here in 1902-1903.

The need for a depot and agent came up at about the same time, and received the attention of the State of Arkansas. On March 23, 1905, the General Assembly of the State of Arkansas approved Act 107 that required the construction of a depot at Goodwin. The Act stated "That it is hereby made the duty of the corporation or person engaged in operating the railway on the line of which the station of Goodwin, in St Fran-

127

cis County, is located, to erect and maintain at said station a building and depot facilities suitable and sufficient to accommodate the passengers taking and leaving trains at said station, and to properly receive and care for all freight received at or offered for shipment from said station. The station and depot facilities hereby provided for shall be completed within six months from the passage of this Act." A later survey reported that the elevation of the "top of rail opposite the Chicago, Rock Island & Pacific Railway station" was 207.1 feet. An agent worked this station for a number of years, providing orders to train crews both day and night. In 1950, the Rock Island had a 101-car siding, as well as a 19-car spur track, at Goodwin.

Goodwin is the site of what some consider to be the first modern commercial aircraft disaster in the United States. On January 14, 1936, American Airlines Flight 1 was on its regular Memphis to Little Rock route when it crashed into swamps near Goodwin. Seventeen people were killed when the DC-2 crashed, making it the worst civil plane crash in the United States up to that point, and it is still the worst in Arkansas' history.

60.4   **BLOSSOM** – Look for County Road 919, also known as Blossom Road. A railroad station was once here, and in 1950 there was a 19-car capacity spur track. An Interstate Commerce Commission report from 1926 stated that the track from the east was tangent and practically level all the way from Forrest City.

64.5   **WHEATLEY (WY)** – The town of Wheatley has gone through a number of name changes since it was first settled in the mid-1800s. The town was originally known as Dennis Station, named for Wheatley Dennis. The first post office in the area opened in 1870 as Britton, named for a nearby railroad station. It was changed to Wheatley in 1872. Some early spellings also used Wheetley. The town was originally in Monroe County, but a redrawing of the county line moved it to St. Francis County.

In 1900, a second railroad announced plans to build through Wheatley. On March 10, 1900, the Maberry, Cotton Plant & Wheatley Railroad was incorporated. According to the *Arkansas Gazette* (March 9, 1900), "[t]he proposed road begins at a point on the east bank of [the] Cache river near Maberry, in Woodruff county, and runs east by way of Cotton Plant and Jent to Wheatley, its length to be thirteen miles." However, the railroad was never built.

Cotton was an early area crop and a 1903 Department of Agriculture report indicated that there had been 720 rail shipments of cotton from Wheatley during the previous shipping year. The arrival of the Missouri & North Arkansas Railroad led to the incorporation of Wheatley in

1907. In 1909, the Wheatley Rice Milling Company was built at Wheatley, with a rice dryer and storage facility near the railroad crossing.

During the 1920s, the Lee Highway, later U.S. Highway 70, was built alongside the Rock Island Railroad through Wheatley. The Arkansas Rice Growers Co-Operative rice dryer burned and then was enlarged in 1929, and became a part of Riceland Food in 1945. Besides the rice mill, the Wheatley Spoke Company and the Ark-Mo Lumber Company also operated facilities here in the early 1900s. The town's population peaked at more than 500 during the 1980s, but has declined to approximately 350 for the past decade. However, a large rice elevator still marks the location of Wheatley.

This Riceland Foods rice elevator stands over the former junction of the Rock Island Railroad and the Missouri & North Arkansas Railroad.

Wheatley was an important location on the railroad, with a 4800-foot siding on the south side of the mainline. The west switch was about 200 feet east of the station. The siding was heavily used to pass trains. An agent was generally assigned here to handle train orders and deal with interchange traffic from the Missouri & North Arkansas.

On January 5, 1926, an accident took place at the east switch of Wheatley that showed the dangers of operating trains at the time. At 1:25am in a dense fog, Cotton Belt westbound freight No. 695 ran into the rear of Rock Island freight train No. 997, killing a railroad special agent in the caboose of train No. 997. The Rock Island freight was running about an hour late, while the Cotton Belt freight was more than three hours late. Both trains had received a train order at Goodwin to meet an extra Cotton Belt eastbound freight at Wheatley. The Rock Island train had stopped to line the east switch so they could enter the 4800-foot Wheatley siding, and the Cotton Belt freight didn't see it until it was too late. Adding to the problem was that the Cotton Belt train had been instructed to not leave Goodwin until 1:22am so that it was at least ten minutes behind, but it left four minutes early. This reduced the time that the Rock Island freight crew had to stop, line the switch, and pull into the siding.

Making things more complicated was that an extra eastbound freight was in the siding at Goodwin, and that westbound passenger train No. 111 was scheduled through the area within a few minutes. The train crews were running out of tracks, and without radio or signals, were having to make decisions on the fly. The Interstate Commerce Commission pointed out that the crew of No. 977 failed to use fusees to warn any following train of their presence, and that if "an adequate block-signal system been in use on this line, this accident probably would not have occurred."

In 1979, the Rock Island showed that Wheatley was still a train register and train order station. There was also a 97-car siding to the south. Today, there is only a short spur track into the rice elevator. However, Wheatley can still be a busy railroad location. Union Pacific's employee timetable states that "[t]rains enroute to Pine Bluff must not pass MP 64.0 until authorized to occupy the Jonesboro Sub. by Dispatcher 18, channel 096-096, to prevent blocking road crossings."

Missouri & North Arkansas Diamond

The Missouri & North Arkansas Railroad (M&NA) crossed the Rock Island Railroad at Division Street and closely followed today's Union Street. The crossing was shown to be an automatic interlocking. For many years it was an important connection as many shippers had their cargo sent through Helena to avoid the high terminal fees at Memphis, Tennessee. This importance could be seen by the M&NA yard that was located just south of the CRI&P line. The yard was used for interchange business and featured a 28-car siding to the east and a 40-car track to the west. The west track connected directly to a Rock Island interchange track to the west. There was also an interchange track in the northeast quadrant of the diamond, as well as stock pens that were retired in 1927.

For many years, both railroads used a joint depot near the diamond, with the Rock Island using the telegraph code of "WY" for the station. In 1915, the station was owned by the Rock Island and the M&NA paid an annual rent of $625 to use the station, based upon a charge of 2.5% of the station's $25,000 valuation. Each railroad paid half of the agent's salary as well as any maintenance expenses related to the depot. Any other expenses were prorated on the basis of tonnage handled by each railroad.

Off and on, the Missouri & North Arkansas would have their own station as an attempt to reduce costs. The M&NA station was originally a boxcar body that was replaced in 1929 after it burned as part of the fire at the Arkansas Rice Growers Co-Operative. The nearby Chicago, Rock Island & Pacific depot was also damaged at the same time. As a result, a larger frame building was built as a joint station. Passing through Wheatley, the Missouri & North Arkansas grade is now the mill access road on the west side of the complex.

In 1950, the crossing was shown as the H&NW Crossing after the Missouri & North Arkansas went through several ownerships and names, and much of the system was eventually abandoned in the late 1940s. The line between Helena and Cotton Plant was sold to the Helena & Northwestern Railway (H&NW), primarily because of the Helena timber industry and the suppliers along the line. The area also had a history of shipping agricultural products such as cotton and rice. The H&NW was officially incorporated on October 8, 1948, and soon the 55-mile line was purchased for $300,000. Service began on September 15, 1949, but it ended on December 1, 1951. The line was quickly abandoned, but parts of the yard to the south and the track into the rice elevator were saved and used by the Rock Island to provide service to the rice mill. Some of these tracks still exist.

64.7   **COUNTY LINE** – Just west of Wheatley is the county line between **St. Francis County**, to the east, and **Monroe County**, to the west. **Monroe County** was created on November 2, 1829, by the Arkansas territorial legislature, and was named for James Monroe, the fifth President of the United States. The county seat is Clarendon, originally known as Mouth of the Cache. The county is generally a mix of rural farmland and bottomland hardwood forest. The county's population peaked at 21,601 in 1920, stayed level until the early 1940s, and has now dropped to about 7000.

This part of Arkansas has seen a steady decline in population since World War II. Much of this has been caused by the loss of farm workers. The issue of mechanical farming cannot be overstated when looking at the population of this part of the country, and its impact on employment. When land was plowed using a mule, about an acre could be done in a day. The first tractors could plow almost ten acres in the same time. Today, the most modern tractors can plow as many as 150 acres in a day. Thus, one tractor and driver are doing the work of as many as 150 laborers and mules from a century ago. Harvesting the crops has changed in much the same way, where a single cotton picker can do the work of as many as 1000 men, women and children. As farms acquired tractors, harvesters, and other such equipment, most of the farm laborer jobs went away and many of those workers headed to the larger cities where factory and service jobs could provide employment.

Monroe County farmers grow significant amounts of soybeans (105,000 acres), rice (50,000 acres), and corn (35,000 acres). Sorghum and wheat are also grown. The county is also known for its hunting and fishing, which attracts visitors from around the country.

68.5 **COTTON BELT JUNCTION** – Located just west of the Plaza Street grade crossing, Cotton Belt Junction is the east end of the Brinkley railroad complex. Brinkley was once a complicated rail community, with tracks operated by companies related to the Chicago, Rock Island & Pacific; St. Louis Southwestern; and Missouri Pacific. There were also once a number of industry tracks and private railroads. The north-south Cotton Belt line, and the Rock Island line east to Memphis still exist, as well as a few connecting tracks and yard tracks.

Cotton Belt Junction was where a Rock Island line curved to the northwest, where there is a wye to connect to the Cotton Belt mainline today, once the Rock Island Newport Branch. Cotton Belt Junction is still listed as a location on Union Pacific's Brinkley Subdivision, but few trains use the line to head north (Union Pacific east) on the former Cotton Belt mainline. This track, known as the East Leg of Wye, is now excepted track and is generally used for loading cars from an agricultural warehouse. To the south was once a several-track yard that was used to move local freight cars off and on mainline trains.

69.1 **BR JUNCTION** – This is where the junction with the St. Louis Southwestern was, and where Cotton Belt trains curved south to reach their mainline and head toward Texas and the west coast. With the diamond now gone at Brinkley, and the Rock Island track abandoned to the west, the mainline of the Union Pacific Brinkley Subdivision now curves to the south and joins the Jonesboro Subdivision, once the Cotton Belt's mainline.

69.2 **BRINKLEY (B)** – Brinkley is the west end of the former Rock Island mainline that was sold to the St. Louis Southwestern and then became the property of Union Pacific. West of here, the railroad has been abandoned.

Brinkley (AR) to Galloway (AR)
Abandoned

After the Rock Island shut down in early 1980, this part of the line was initially assigned to the St. Louis Southwestern (SSW). In fact, they had rights to operate as far west as Perry, Arkansas, to preserve service to the large paper mill there. However, the Cotton Belt did not need the line between Brinkley and North Little Rock, as they had their own line from North Little Rock to Altheimer, where it connected with their mainline between St. Louis and Pine Bluff. This line was in better shape than the Rock Island line, so the SSW used their own lines between Brinkley and North Little Rock, removing the diamond at Brinkley.

This photo shows the former Brinkley Union Station platform that was used by the Rock Island Railroad, and the now abandoned railroad grade.

Missouri Pacific acquired the line west of Hazen, and the line from Hazen to Brinkley was abandoned soon after. Service between Carlisle and Hazen ended in 1982, and the track was removed in early 1985 by Determan-Merrill, Inc., a subcontractor for L. B. Foster.

Additional track was abandoned from Carlisle to Galloway in 1994. This was done after Union Pacific sold several rail lines to the Arkansas Midland

Railroad Company in 1992. *Federal Register* Volume 59, Issue 167 (August 30, 1994), stated that the Interstate Commerce Commission permitted the Arkansas Midland Railroad "to abandon a portion of its Carlisle Branch between MP 123.80, near Galloway, AR, and MP 102.28, at Carlisle, AR, a distance of approximately 21.52 miles."

The old railroad right-of-way has generally been left to nature, but in a few places it is used as farm and timber access roads, city parks, and even paved walking trails.

69.2 **BRINKLEY (B)** – Brinkley dates back to the construction of the Rock Island Railroad, and was named for Robert Campbell Brinkley, president of the Memphis & Little Rock Railroad after the Civil War. Brinkley was responsible for rebuilding and completing the railroad from Memphis to Little Rock, using money that he raised in Great Britain. One of those who provided money to R. C. Brinkley was George Peabody, a London financier. To honor the funding and their friendship, Brinkley named the Peabody Hotel in Memphis after him. To honor Robert C. Brinkley long after his death, a tree was planted at Brinkley. For decades, the Chicago, Rock Island & Pacific planted trees to honor employees killed or injured while working, or to honor important employees upon or after their death.

The City of Brinkley is located on a natural route out of the swamps of Eastern Arkansas, and the Butterfield Overland Mail Route, one of the routes of the Trail of Tears, roads used by several Union armies, and even today's Interstate 40 pass through the area. Many are today marked by the Arkansas Heritage Trails System. A land grant to build the railroad was provided in 1852, and plans were made to establish towns along the line. The area where Brinkley was created was a logical location since it was halfway between Memphis and Little Rock.

Settlers had already arrived in the area, and railroad contractors based some of their operations here. The name Lick Skillet was used by the railroad's construction workers, believed to have come about because "when the day's work was completed, the railroad crew cooked dinner over a campfire and retired for the evening only when the last skillet was licked." Brinkley was platted in the winter of 1869-1870, and a post office opened in 1870. On August 6, 1872, Brinkley requested incorporation, which was filed with the Arkansas Secretary of State on August 21, 1872. There were 327 residents in the 1880 census, and the 1882 arrival of the Cotton Belt (Texas & St. Louis Railway) led the town to grow more, with 1510 residents in 1890. A major fire soon forced the town to rebuild, using more permanent and fire-proof materials.

The book *Biographical and Historical Memoirs of Eastern Arkansas*, released by the Goodspeed Publishing Company in 1890, had a good description of Brinkley at the time.

> *It now consists of the Monroe County Bank, seven gener-*
> *al, six grocery, three drug and two jewelry and notion stores,*
> *a boot and shoe shop, a furniture and undertaker's store, a*
> *millinery store, bakery, feed store, billiard hall, four hotels,*
> *a meat market, a meat market and restaurant, two black-*
> *smith and two barber shops, a pool hall and temperance*
> *saloon, the machine and car shops of the Batesville & Brin-*
> *kley Railroad, two livery stables, two brick-yards, a grist-*
> *mill, cotton-gin, Niffen's foundry, the Union Wood Turning*
> *Works, Brinkley Oil Mill (employing from fifty to seven-*
> *ty-five men), the Brinkley Car and Manufacturing Works*
> *(employing about 200 men), three churches (Methodist,*
> *Baptist, and Cumberland Presbyterian), also three Baptist*
> *churches and one Methodist for the colored people, a public*
> *school house for the whites (the school for colored children*
> *being taught in one of the church edifices). In addition to the*
> *foregoing, there is a lodge, each, of Masons, Knights of Pyth-*
> *ias, Knights of Honor, Knights and Ladies of Honor, and two*
> *Building & Loan Associations. The town is incorporated,*
> *and in August 1889, the school board took an actual census*
> *of the inhabitants within the corporate limits, and found a*
> *population of 1,498, and there is said to be several hundred*
> *outside of these limits. Brinkley is a railroad center, a good*
> *cotton market, and its shipments are extensive.*

Timber and lumber production was an early source of business activity, but farming soon took its place. Brinkley's population was 1648
in 1900, and a 1903 Department of Agriculture report indicated that
there were 13,833 rail shipments of cotton from Brinkley in 1902-1903.
By 1920, the city was growing and had 2714 residents and a number
of manufacturing jobs. The 1921 *Arkansas Marketing and Industrial
Guide* listed a number of Brinkley companies, including Brinkley Lumber Company, Wright Lumber Company, American Handle Company,
Ark-Mo Lumber Company, Arkansas Stave Company, Brinkley Heading Company, St. Louis Cooperage Company, and Farrell's Locomotive
Works. The report also showed that the Chicago, Rock Island & Pacific
had shops here, as well as two stock pens and a 40-foot, 100,000-pound
capacity scale. Not listed, but standing since late 1906, was a railroad
coal chute to fuel railroad locomotives.

Brinkley wasn't impacted much by World War II, but saw new jobs
from Phillips Van Heusen and Wagner Electric Corporation soon after.
However, many of the timber-based companies were gone by that time,

and agriculture was becoming mechanized, requiring fewer workers. Brinkley's population peaked at 5275 in 1970. The loss of further manufacturing and local businesses continued over the next several decades, and the 2010 census showed a population of 3188.

While Brinkley is the most populous city in Monroe County, with the change in the economy, Brinkley has attempted to add tourism to its economic base. Antique and gift shops, hotels and restaurants, and the creation of the downtown Lick Skillet Railroad Work Station Historic District (listed on the National Register of Historic Places in 1992) all work to this purpose. The creation of the Central Delta Depot Museum and Visitors Center in the former Union Station also works to attract tourists. Probably the most important tourism attraction is outdoor recreation, especially duck hunting during the winter. Another attraction is the bridal dress boutique in the Great Southern Hotel. With over 2500 wedding dresses, it is a regional destination.

Brinkley Car Works & Manufacturing Company

Located just north of the SSW-CRI&P diamond and to the east of the Cotton Belt was the Brinkley Car Works & Manufacturing Company. This firm was known by a number of names over the years and has a rather complicated history. However, it is important in the development of Brinkley and many of the railroads in the area.

The firm started as Gunn & Black, which operated a sawmill near Brinkley by 1879. To obtain lumber and to market their service to other firms, the company built a three foot, six inch gauge rail line from its mill at Brinkley, 11 miles northwest to the town of Cotton Plant, opening on July 1, 1879. The railroad was known as the Cotton Plant Railroad, although it had no incorporation as a railroad. It was finally incorporated using the name on April 16, 1881, and then the gauge was converted to three feet to connect to the new Texas & St. Louis Railroad (Cotton Belt).

The lumber and manufacturing company changed during the early 1880s as the Gunn and Black partnership broke up, and the Brinkley Car Works & Manufacturing Company was organized in 1882. A new partner with a history of railroad construction, William Black, was somehow involved with the new firm. Black had previously been involved with the carpentry and grocery businesses, and then got into the timber and railroad construction businesses, In 1884, Black established the Brinkley Lumber Company in Memphis. An 1891 history of the area stated the following about the firm.

"... they have a pay role of some 260 persons, 120 of whom are employed at the saw-mill in the woods, and cut down 68,000 feet of timber per day, the rest being employed in constructing railroads and in the general car repair shop. Every facility incident to this particular industry is embraced within the works, the tools and machinery being of the most modern and improved kind, and only skillful and experienced workmen are employed. This company ships about 220 carloads of lumber, consisting of flooring, shingles, moldings, lath, pickets, doors and window sashes, per month, to Memphis, Tenn., where they have one of the leading lumber establishments in the city, it having been established through the efforts of the late Maj. Black. Prior to Mr. Black's decease, which occurred in September, 1889, he was president and director of the company, with O. M. Norman, manager, and H. H. Myers, secretary and treasurer, but after his death Mr. Norman was made president, director and manager, and Mr. Myers became secretary, treasurer and director. This company also owns the Brinkley, Helena & Indian Bay Railroad, and about 36,000 acres of land in Monroe County."

A listing in the 1894 *Directory to the Iron and Steel Works of the United States* stated that the firm built railroad box and flat cars. Other listings included things like clap boards, blinds, and other wood parts. In 1893, the firm was sued by John Gunn for his part of the company. The court report stated that Gunn lived in Shelby County, Tennessee, and was described as "an illiterate man, that he can scarcely read, and is able to write his name only by great effort." Gunn claimed that he was "book-keepered" out of his share of the company. Little is known about the results, but the firm is long gone after leasing the railroad to the Choctaw, Oklahoma & Gulf in 1900. By the 1921 *Arkansas Marketing and Industrial Guide*, the firm was no longer listed.

Farrell's Locomotive Works

Located south of the Brinkley Union Station, south of Ash Street and on the west side of the former Cotton Belt mainline, are the remains of Farrell's Locomotive Works. This company was one of the few railroad locomotive rebuilders in the south, and certainly in Arkansas. The firm started as the J. J. Farrell Machinery Company, and then became the Farrell Machine and Boiler Works in 1898, founded by J. J. Farrell, Sr. The firm was destroyed by a tornado in 1909, but soon reopened, apparently as several divisions working on different products. For example, the firm rebuilt steam locomotives, cotton gins, sawmill equipment, well pumps, and other similar equipment. One of the most visible parts, and the one the Ash Street building was painted for, was the Farrell's Locomotive Works.

James J. Farrell was a native of Illinois who moved to Arkansas to make his fortune. He was involved with building and operating railroads, water works and light plants, and in manufacturing the machinery required. His son Paul M. Farrell, born in Brinkley, took over managing the firm when his father died in 1939. Paul added new operations, including farming, cotton gins, coal stripping projects, construction and finance, highway building, and the repair and selling of heavy construction equipment. Much of the equipment has been used internationally, including a waterworks project in Venezuela, railroad projects in Brazil, canals in Mexico, and strip mines in India. Major domestic projects have included the Shumaker Navy Ordnance Plant (Camden, Arkansas), a duPont Plant (Indiana), several shipyard projects, and the Manhattan Project (Oak Ridge, Tennessee).

Farrell's Locomotive Works specialized in buying old and worn out railroad steam locomotives, rebuilding them, and then selling them back into the industry. Many of their customers were logging and shortline railroads, but even the U.S. federal government was a major customer. During World War II, the firm rebuilt a number of steam locomotives for the U.S. Army and Navy, and for a number of foreign countries. Because of this, the company was one of the first Arkansas industries to receive an AA-1 priority during World War II. The firm was known for searching along abandoned railroads, junk yards and other places for unused locomotives and cranes that could be rebuilt and sold. After the war, the locomotive business slowed, but didn't end until the late 1950s. A bell from the firm is on display at the Central Delta Depot & Museum at Brinkley.

As stated, the firm actually was engaged in many product lines through many different subsidiary firms. In July 1957, the firm was still advertising as Farrell Industries, listing five different divisions. These were Farrell's Locomotive Works, Farrell – Cooper Lumber Company, Farrell Gin Company, Clark Farrell Construction Company, and Decatur Cotton Oil Company. A newspaper advertisement in November 1957, listed Farrell's Locomotive Works, Farrell – Cooper Lumber Company, Farrell Gin Company, and The Murfreesboro & Nashville Railroad Company. Today, most of the construction buildings are gone, but the brick office of Farrell's Locomotive Works still stands.

Brinkley and Its Railroads

Brinkley was an important station on the Rock Island, and *Rock Island Timetable No. 1,* dated March 18, 1979, stated that there were general order boards and books, a standard clock, wayside radio, and a wye here. The station was staffed and Brinkley was a train register station, but that there were no train order signals. The interlocking between the Rock Island and the Cotton Belt was shown to be a manual interlocking. In the early 1900s, this crossing was made more complicated by the Rock Island Newport Branch, which went north on the east of the Cotton Belt before crossing over and heading to Cotton Plant. South of the diamond, the Arkansas Midland Railroad came in from the south along the east side of the SSW.

The area around the **StLSW Crossing**, as listed in Rock Island timetables, was a very busy area. According to Sanborn maps in 1906, just north of the SSW-CRI&P diamond and to the east of the Cotton Belt was the Brinkley Car Works & Manufacturing Company. North of Brinkley Car Works was the H. Alfrey Heading Factory, located to the east of the CRI&P Newport Branch. To the east of the Brinkley Car Works was The Arkansas Cotton Oil Company, located on the north side of the Rock Island mainline. At one time, the Rock Island also had a north-south line next to the Cotton Belt line, and a **CRI&P Crossing** was shown to be just east of the StLSW Crossing.

The Memphis & Little Rock (Rock Island) was the first railroad here, but the Cotton Plant Railroad (Batesville & Brinkley) was built in 1879. The Texas & St. Louis Railway (Cotton Belt) was completed on August 12, 1883, as a three-foot gauge railroad. The railroad became the St. Louis, Arkansas & Texas on April 29, 1886, after the various parts of the line were consolidated. Plans were made to standard gauge the railroad, with work beginning on October 18, 1886. The railroad grew by absorbing a number of connecting railroads, but the company soon entered receivership. The St. Louis Southwestern Railway Company (Cotton Belt, or SSW) was created and acquired all of the properties by June 1, 1891. By 1930, the Cotton Belt was controlled by Southern Pacific, which became a part of Union Pacific in 1996.

The Brinkley Car Works & Manufacturing Company built a line to the south that was acquired when the Brinkley, Helena & Indian Bay Railroad was organized in Arkansas on July 19, 1889. The line eventually became the Arkansas Midland, and then later Missouri Pacific. All of these railroads created a complex network of tracks and buildings. According to Sanborn, in 1906, the Rock Island had their station just southwest of the SSW-CRI&P diamond. To the south was the Cotton Belt passenger station, later the location of their freight station. Across the Cotton Belt tracks was the Arkansas Midland Railroad passenger and freight depot. It faced east and was squeezed between the Cotton Belt and Arkansas Midland tracks. The Rock Island freight house was located just east of Main Street, on the north side of the tracks about where the current Brinkley Police Department building stands today.

To interchange freight and serve all of the rail customers, there were a number of tracks. Just east of the Rock Island freight house were several interchange tracks that curved north to connect to the Cotton Belt. Further west was the J. J. Farrell cotton gin, located on the north side of the mainline and west of New York Avenue. Next to the west was the sawmill of the National Cooperage & Wooden-Ware Company.

To the south of the SSW-CRI&P interlocking were several customers served by both the Cotton Belt and Arkansas Midland. These included the Keaton Brothers & Company stave mill, and the Brinkley Spoke Company. In this area, the Arkansas Midland had a one-track train shed, located west of the Arkansas Midland mainline between White Oak and Elm Streets. A short piece of the Arkansas Midland, later Missouri Pacific, remains south of Maple Street as it curves to the southeast. The track is used as a lead to switch the south end of the large grain elevator here.

Besides the major railroads, there were also once several logging railroads at Brinkley. Gunn & Black had their Cotton Plant Railroad, and the Brinkley Car Works & Manufacturing Company built their Brinkley & Helena Railroad to the south about 1886. Another logging railroad was operated by the Robe-Lake Lumber Company. *The Hardwood Record* of August 10, 1911, stated that the company had 12,000 acres of timber lands and that two mills were in production. The report also stated that the company was making improvements in its railroad facilities "in order to make the development of its timber holdings the more rapid." Ownership of the firm changed in early 1913. The *St. Louis Lumberman* of February 15, 1913, reported that "The Robe-Lake Lumber Company has filed a certificate with the Secretary of State, showing that the name of the company has been changed to the Brown Bros. Land and Lumber." Brown Brothers was a large regional lumber company that was based in Jonesboro, Arkansas. The firm operated various logging railroads in eastern Arkansas until 1936.

Brinkley Union Station

In 1906, each of the three railroads in Brinkley – Rock Island, Cotton Belt, and Arkansas Midland (St. Louis, Iron Mountain & Southern, then Missouri Pacific) – had their own train stations. At the time, the CRI&P passenger depot was located on the southwest side of the SSW-CRI&P diamond. South of the Rock Island station was the Cotton Belt passenger depot. Across the Cotton Belt tracks to the east was the Arkansas

Midland passenger and freight depot, with the tracks of the Arkansas Midland further to the east.

Things changed on March 8, 1909, when a tornado hit Brinkley and destroyed the CRI&P freight depot, section house and all the passenger depot except for the telegraph office. The storm led to a series of studies about a new union station, even though the Cotton Belt and Rock Island had already discussed tearing down their old stations and building a new Union Depot. Later reports indicated that some initial cost estimates had already been worked up, and at least one local official commented that much of the removal work had already been done by the tornado. By the end of the month, all three railroads had agreed to build a Union Depot at Brinkley, Arkansas. Construction began almost immediately, and the CRI&P quickly built a larger freight depot.

By 1911, all three railroads were using the repaired Rock Island station at the diamond. According to the Central Delta Depot & Museum, in that year Brinkley had 10 Rock Island passenger trains, 4 Cotton Belt passenger trains and 2 Arkansas Midland passenger trains daily, plus several mixed freights. More than 500 passengers a day passed through the station's doors. With business growing, a decision was made to build a single union station for the three railroads. Additionally, on July 7, 1911, the Arkansas Railroad Commission ordered that the small wooden Rock Island station be replaced by a larger union station. The new station, built of brick for a cost of $26,000, faced the diamond and featured wings alongside the Rock Island and Cotton Belt. The building wings included office space and freight rooms for each railroad, and the building officially opened on September 16, 1912.

The new Brinkley Union Station was owned by the Rock Island Railroad, and the Rock Island and St. Louis Southwestern each paid half of the operating and maintenance expenses. The St. Louis, Iron Mountain & Southern (earlier the Arkansas Midland, later Missouri Pacific) paid the Rock Island $30 per month for each train using the station, with a minimum of $60 a month.

Passenger volumes stayed steady until after World War II, but then they soon dropped. Nevertheless, the Chicago, Rock Island & Pacific installed 63 miles of automatic block signals between Brinkley and North Little Rock by the end of 1949. Meanwhile, the Missouri Pacific passenger service was down to mixed trains (both freight and passenger) operating daily except Sunday from Barton Junction. By 1950, the service was down to a mixed train operating between Brinkley and B&B Junction (Pine City) three days a week, connecting with the Barton Junction-Clarendon mixed train. By 1952, all Missouri Pacific passenger service to Brinkley had ended.

The Cotton Belt passenger service also declined sharply during the 1950s. The last Cotton Belt passenger trains from Memphis were No. 1

141

and No. 2, the *Lone Star*, which operated Memphis to Texarkana. They last operated on October 31, 1952. This left only the St. Louis to Texas trains, and the last operated as No. 8 between Pine Bluff and East St. Louis on November 30, 1959. The Rock Island held on longer to its passenger service, using self-propelled Rail Diesel Cars. The last trains (No. 21 and No. 22) ran on November 10, 1967, between Memphis and Tucumcari, New Mexico.

The building became a train order station that handled the interlocking. After the Rock Island closed, the Cotton Belt became the building's owner. Not needing the structure, the Cotton Belt announced plans on December 21, 1986, to tear down the Union Station and Cotton Belt freight house to the south. The building was fortunately saved, and was listed on the National Register of Historic Places in 1992 as a part of the Lick Skillet Railroad Work Station Historic District. This District includes a number of buildings in downtown Brinkley, including the Rusher Hotel, now the Great Southern Hotel.

By 1984, the Union Station at Brinkley was abandoned and looking sad. Today, it has been restored and is used as the Central Delta Depot & Museum.

By 2020, the Brinkley Union Station was restored and the home of the Central Delta Depot & Museum.

On August 11, 1996, Union Pacific acquired Southern Pacific, and the Brinkley Union Station was included. In 1999, a letter writing campaign began to obtain the station, and during February 2001, Union Pacific deeded the property to the City of Brinkley. The building was leased to the Central Delta Historical Society to restore the structure and turn it into a museum. Restoration began on May 4, 2001, and was completed by May 2003. It now serves as the Central Delta Depot & Museum and a visitor center for the nearby Louisiana Purchase State Park.

Besides the former Union Station, the Central Delta Depot & Museum includes a number of other structures, including the former Missouri Pacific depot from Monroe (on the Arkansas Midland Railroad to the south), a furnished tenant farm house, and Southern Pacific Caboose #4746 (Class C-50-9 caboose, built in 1981).

This former Arkansas Midland Railroad/Missouri Pacific Railroad depot from Monroe, Arkansas, is located just north of the Central Delta Depot & Museum at Brinkley.

Cotton Plant Railroad

As previously stated, the Cotton Plant Railroad dates back to the 1870s when the partnership of Gunn & Black built a sawmill at Brinkley to support their door, sash and blind factory in Memphis, Tennessee. They built a private 3'-6" gauge railroad north from Brinkley to Cotton Plant by July 1, 1879. In 1881, the Texas & St. Louis Railroad, later the Cotton Belt, built a 3-foot gauge railroad through Brinkley. In response, Gunn & Black changed their railroad to the same gauge and incorporated it as the Cotton Plant Railroad.

On June 22, 1882, the Batesville & Brinkley Railroad was created with the intentions of buying the Cotton Plant Railroad and extending it north to Newton, on what became the Missouri Pacific main line, and then up the White River to Batesville, Arkansas. The railroad was extended 19 miles to Patterson, and then the Augusta & Southeastern Railway Company was purchased to further extend the line. During late 1886, the St. Louis, Arkansas & Texas Railway (Cotton Belt) rebuilt its line to standard gauge, and the Batesville & Brinkley Railroad did the same by 1888.

On January 10, 1890, the White & Black River Valley Railroad Company (W&BRV) was incorporated to consolidate the various lines. The route was expanded further to the two White River ports of Newport and Jacksonport. On July 1, 1900, the railroad was leased for 80 years by the Choctaw, Oklahoma & Gulf Railroad Company, which connected to the line at Brinkley. *The Commercial and Financial Chronicle* (January 25, 1902) provided a list of the railroad equipment acquired with the W&BRV. It listed 4 locomotives, 8 passenger cars of various types, 47 box cars, 32 flat cars, 1 stock car, 1 caboose, and 3 miscellaneous cars.

The Chicago, Rock Island & Pacific leased the Choctaw, Oklahoma & Gulf on March 24, 1904. Not long after, the Interstate Commerce Commission provided a description of the White & Black River Valley Railway, stating that it "is a single-track, standard-gauge, steam railroad, located entirely in Arkansas. The main line extends from Brinkley to Jacksonport, 56.472 miles, and a branch line extends from Wiville to Gregory, 5.963 miles, a total of 62.435 miles of main tracks owned. Other tracks wholly owned aggregate 7.182 miles, making a total of 69.617 miles of all tracks wholly owned. The White & Black River Valley Railway also owns jointly with the St. Louis, Iron Mountain & Southern Railway Company 0.112 mile of yard tracks and sidings at Brinkley."

As river traffic was replaced by railroads, towns like Jacksonport lost their importance, and the four miles of railroad from there to Newport was abandoned by June 1928. The rest of the railroad was abandoned on March 9, 1941, with a track or two in Newport being sold to the Missouri Pacific, and a few tracks in Cotton Plant going to the Missouri & Arkansas. The track that heads northwest at Cotton Belt Junction once connected to the Newport Branch.

Arkansas Midland Railroad

The Arkansas Midland Railroad Company actually had a fairly complex history. It started as the Arkansas Midland Railroad, created on November 7, 1853, and chartered on January 20, 1855. The route was planned as a 115-mile line from Helena to Little Rock, and some discussion had it as a narrow gauge line. While some grading was done, the company never built any track due to a lack of funding and the Civil War. On August 31, 1870, the Arkansas Central Railway Company was organized and acquired the work of the Arkansas Midland. The firm completed track with a gauge of 3½' from Helena to Duncan and on to Clarendon, a total of approximately fifty miles. Train service began in 1872.

In 1872, a railroad map was published by G. W. & C. B. Colton & Company that showed the Arkansas Central as a part of a much larger network of railroads. The map was labeled as showing "the Arkansas Central, the Helena & Corinth, and the Pine Bluff & Southwestern Railways, together forming the Texas & Northeastern Railway." The map showed an existing route from Corinth (Mississippi) to Helena to Pine Bluff, and on to Shreveport (Louisiana), with projected lines and connections to places like Nashville (Tennessee), Chicago (Illinois), Houston and San Antonio (Texas), and even Los Angeles (California).

However, the railroad almost immediately failed financially and was sold to the Arkansas Midland Railroad Company (chartered May 15, 1878) on January 3. 1880. On the same date, the Arkansas Midland acquired the Little Rock & Helena Railroad Company. The new owner of the railroad was Sidney Hornor, a member of the Hornor family that would later develop West Helena and the interurban railroad between Helena and West Helena.

When the Cotton Belt built through the area in 1883, the Arkansas Midland converted its track to 3-foot gauge. The railroad then converted to standard gauge in 1887. The line expanded further on August 1, 1891, when it bought the Brinkley, Helena & Indian Bay Railroad, organized in Arkansas on July 19, 1889.

The railroad ran from Pine City to Brinkley, and was built to 3-foot gauge. The northern-most eight miles of track had previously been built by the Brinkley Car Works & Manufacturing Company, and had been acquired as part of the plan to build a larger railroad. When purchased, the Arkansas Midland changed the gauge of the Brinkley, Helena & Indian Bay Railroad to standard gauge.

In 1901, Jay Gould gained control of the railroads, resulting in some joint operations. For example, on June 20, 1907, the Railroad Commission of Arkansas ordered that by July 1, 1907, the St. Louis, Iron Mountain & Southern Railway, Arkansas Midland Railroad, and the Brinkley, Helena & Indian Bay Railroad had to establish joint freight and passenger rates. The railroads were fully merged into the St. Louis, Iron Mountain & Southern on September 1, 1909, which then merged with the Missouri Pacific on May 12, 1917. The line to Clarendon was abandoned about 1917. Because Missouri Pacific had two routes west from Helena, the Arkansas Midland route was abandoned east of Barton, Arkansas, in 1932, and the line west of Barton was abandoned during the 1950s.

Brinkley and the Interstate Commerce Commission

During the 1920s, the Interstate Commerce Commission sponsored a number of studies to consolidate the nation's railroads into a smaller but more healthy system. This work came about thanks to the Transportation Act of 1920, which instructed the Interstate Commerce Commission to create such plans. William Z. Ripley, a professor of political economy at Harvard University, created a number of consolidation plans during 1920-1923, creating what became known as the Ripley Plan. The planning took so long that a number of railroads consolidated on their own, leading to today's large railroads.

One of these consolidated systems included the Rock Island, the Frisco, the Louisiana & Arkansas, and parts of other regional railroads. One proposal split the St. Louis Southwestern, with the track north of Brinkley going to the Rock Island Railroad. Brinkley, with its connections in all directions, was also included in several other proposals, generally with the goal of connecting Midwest industrial and population centers with ports on the Gulf of Mexico.

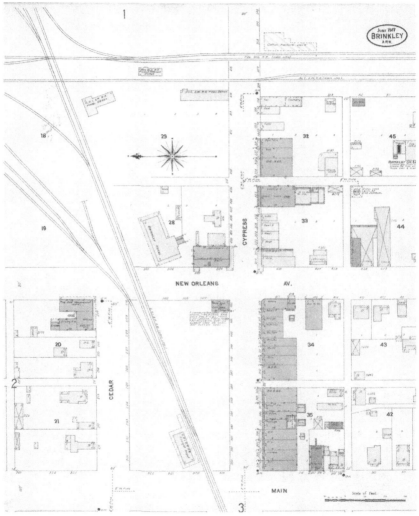

The station area at Brinkley in 1907. *Sanborn Fire Insurance Map from Brinkley, Monroe County, Arkansas.* Sanborn Map Company, June, 1907. Map. Retrieved from the Library of Congress, https://www.loc.gov/item/sanborn00209_003/.

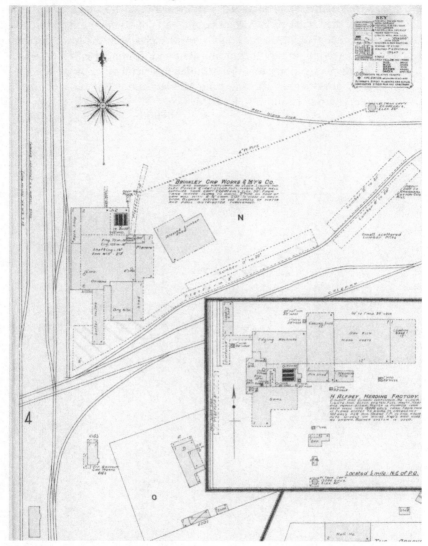

This map shows the area around the Brinkley Car Works & Manufacturing Company in 1907. *Sanborn Fire Insurance Map from Brinkley, Monroe County, Arkansas.* Sanborn Map Company, June, 1907. Map. Retrieved from the Library of Congress, https://www.loc.gov/item/sanborn00209_003/.

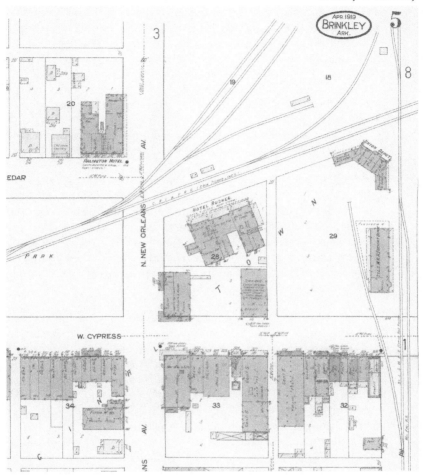

This map shows the area around the Brinkley Union Depot in 1919. *Sanborn Fire Insurance Map from Brinkley, Monroe County, Arkansas.* Sanborn Map Company, Apr, 1919. Map. Retrieved from the Library of Congress, https://www.loc.gov/item/sanborn00209_005/.

74.3   EDEN – Heading west, U.S. Highway 70 turns south and then west, not getting back to the CRI&P grade until the Cache River. This highway route misses Eden, Arkansas, which was located just east of Bayou DeView at an elevation of 179 feet. Eden was one of many stations used for loading logs onto Rock Island trains, and some of the roads and foundations can still be seen here. In 1950, Eden was shown to be a 99-car siding with a 9-car spur track. By the 1970s, there were no side tracks here.

Eden was earlier known as Jones's Island, surrounded by channels of "Bayou De Vue." The location's name was changed in early 1902.

75.0   BAYOU DE VIEW BRIDGE – This 29-panel ballast deck timber trestle still stands and is used for vehicle access to the area. The name Devue, De Vue or De View, is used for a number of features in the area. This stream is Bayou de View, a part of the Cache and White River basins. The stream is less than 100 miles long and drains parts of Woodruff, Monroe and Prairie Counties. There are efforts to expand the Cache River National Wildlife Refuge to include more than 30 miles of Bayou de View.

75.9   DAGMAR – The location of Dagmar can be found at the Wildlife Management Area work base on Dagmar Road, north of U.S. Highway 70. Old maps show that a large mill building once stood here, located next to Big Robe Creek. The *ABC Pathfinder Shipping and Mailing Guide* of January 1915 stated that the Rock Island had a depot here that was served by RPO route 237-103, as well as the American Express Company for express freight service. In 1917, Dagmar was a flag stop for a morning and afternoon local passenger train in each direction.

Dagmar was considered to be the east end of a "mudhole" and flood area that often closed the nearby highway, and sometimes the railroad. The area is now the Sheffield Nelson Dagmar Wildlife Management Area (WMA), founded in 1952 as the Dagmar Wildlife Management Area and consisting of a bottomland hardwood overflow area with many lakes, ponds, sloughs and bayous. The WMA began with the purchase of 5265 acres from the Dacus Lumber Company, a lumber company based in West Memphis. In 1955, another 1209 acres was obtained from the Townsend Lumber Company. Land was also obtained from the Deview Water Company, 1262 acres in 1971, and from other smaller owners. Today, the WMA is approximately 8000 acres in size. The Dagmar name came from a small farming community located along the railroad prior to the Flood of 1927. The Wildlife Management Area was renamed after former commissioner Sheffield Nelson on March 20, 2008.

In this area, the former Rock Island Railroad grade can be driven east to the Bayou de View bridge. Heading west, the grade is used as part of the Conway George Foot Trail, an access route used by hunters. Immediately to the north of the railroad grade was once a road that was used to reach a number of farms and logging camps. The area to the west was notorious for flooding, and a report from April 26, 1928, stated that flood waters were 28 inches over the main highway along a five-mile segment between Dagmar and Brasfield.

80.4 CACHE RIVER BRIDGE – The Cache River, slightly longer than 200 miles, drains much of northeast Arkansas before flowing south to join the White River at Clarendon, Arkansas. The river was originally a slow and muddy river. Parts of the river's watershed include sloughs, swamps, and oxbow lakes. Little of the river could ever be called straight or swift flowing. However, the river was used as part of a drainage system to make farmland from area swamps. Because of this, parts of its upper channel have been channelized and straightened. During the 1970s, there were plans for the U.S. Army Corps of Engineers to dredge and straighten more of the river, but duck hunters and other groups fought the plan. In 1986, much of the lower part of the river, more than 90 miles of channel, was saved by the creation of the Cache River National Wildlife Refuge. This refuge includes the largest tract of contiguous bottomland hardwood forest remaining in the United States.

While the Cache River was a mix of flooded swamp land and meandering channels, it was an important food source for early natives, and a number of Indian mounds were built along its course. As white settlers arrived, the heavy swamps discouraged development. But, as some land was cleared and drained, cotton and other cash crops became common in the area. This led to steamboat service during the early 1800s and the creation of several river towns along its route. However, more reliable water conditions on the nearby White River prevented any major development.

There is no clear source of the name Cache, but some sources state that in the Picardie language, the word for hunt is similar to Cache. Picardie is a part of northern France where residents historically spoke a unique form of French. Several early French explorers who visited Arkansas were from Picardie.

The Cache River at this location serves as the county line between **Monroe County**, to the east, and **Prairie County** to the west. **Prairie County** was created on November 25, 1846, after having been part of the reservation for the Western band of Cherokee from 1812 to 1836. The county's population in 2010 was 8715, down from a peak of 17,447 in 1920. The county received its name from the Grand Prairie, a large, flat grassland area west of the swamps and bayous. The area was used initially for the production of hay and cotton, but the production of soybeans (100,000 acres), rice (55,000 acres), corn, sorghum and wheat is common today. The county has a northern and southern district, each with a county seat. DeValls Bluff is the southern county seat, while Des Arc is the northern district county seat.

The Railroad Bridge

During the late 1860s as the railroad was being rebuilt after the Civil War, a number of contractors changed while projects were underway. Some reports show that this happened with the original Cache River bridge. A report in the *American Railroad Journal* in 1868 seems to indicate that this bridge was impacted by this change in contractors. The report did state that the contractor was building a 360-foot bridge and 1200 feet of trestle at the Cache River. This area was always a challenge for the railroad, and much of the trestle simply crossed stagnate sloughs and backwaters. Letters from the time apparently show that the original bridge was temporary, and a more permanent bridge was started after April 1871.

The bridge built in 1871 was also replaced and a steel bridge was eventually installed. However, even this Cache River bridge has been removed, although the piers of the bridge can still be seen in the river to the north of U.S. Highway 70. From east to west, Rock Island records state that the bridge consisted of five ballast deck wooden pile trestle spans, one 70-foot deck plate girder span, a 150-foot deck plate girder turn span to allow river navigation, and two 70-foot deck plate girder spans.

This pier once supported the turnspan of the Cache River Bridge. While the spans are gone, the piers remain.

80.5 **BRASFIELD** – Brasfield was founded based upon railroading and grew based upon logging. The railroad arrived in 1871, and the west bank of the Cache River was used as a stop for firewood, where local settlers could sell wood to the railroad for its steam locomotives. The location also provided a connection to the river traffic on the Cache River. The name used for the stop by the railroad was Cache River and Cache Flagstop. Many sources state that the stop became Brasfield in 1907.

The town was a logging and sawmill center by that time, and the Antioch Baptist Church once had a cornerstone with the date of 1891. The first large sawmill was operated by the Penrod-Abbott Lumber Company. It became the Penrod-Jurden-McCowen Lumber Company, according to the February 1, 1913, issue of *The St. Louis Lumberman*. The article stated that the "company owns several large tracts of hardwood stumpage, principally gum and oak on Cache river, in fact, sufficient to run the mill for ten years. The plant is a 9-foot band with re-saw and is cutting about 45,000 feet log scale per day." The company's general offices were in Kansas City. Reports also state that the lumber company operated a standard-gauge logging railroad. Records show that Farrell Locomotive Works of Brinkley sold a small Class B-24-2 Shay (Shop Number 365, built August 1891) to Penrod, Jurden & McCowen about 1912. Up until that time, the locomotive had only worked in Wisconsin.

Brasfield became even more of a lumber company town in late 1916 when the mill was acquired by the W. P. Brown & Sons Lumber Company of Louisville, Kentucky. The purchase was announced by an advertisement on the cover of the January 25, 1917, *Lumber World Review*. The ad stated that the firm had purchased 14,000 acres of timber in "the famous St. Francis Basin" in 1910. It also stated that the company had "eight mills located in various parts of the Southern lumber field." The Great Depression ended the construction boom, and the sawmill operated off and on until it closed for good in 1936. During its final years, the company was known as Brown Brothers Land & Lumber Company. A post office was located at Brasfield from 1907 until 1958. Today, Brasfield is a community of about 100 people and an attraction for activities on the Cache River.

For the railroad, Brasfield was never a major facility, but it was a steady source of lumber shipments until the Great Depression. In 1917, Brasfield was a flag stop for a morning and afternoon local passenger train in each direction. In 1950, there was an 11-car spur track. Not long after, the track was removed.

82.3 **BISCOE (BS)** – Biscoe, located to the north of the Rock Island grade, is another small eastern Arkansas farm town. The first name used for the area was Fredonia, a name borrowed from the Republic of Fredonia, a temporary result of the Fredonian Rebellion during late 1826 and early

1827. The Fredonian Rebellion was the first Anglo attempt to secede parts of Texas from Mexico. A number of settlers led by Empresario Haden Edwards, and initially supported by area Cherokee tribes, created the Republic of Fredonia near Nacogdoches, Texas. A small Mexican army arrived on January 31, 1827, and ended the rebellion, with Haden and his brother Benjamin fleeing back into the United States.

This area was noted in many journals for its slightly higher elevation, an important advantage when the lands to the east flooded. The area became known as Surrounded Hill, and it was surveyed by the federal government in 1849. The first land in the area was settled officially in 1853. Little became of the settlement until the railroad arrived in 1871. A depot was quickly built and the Fredonia post office opened in 1872. Confusion over the name, and the new major property owner Eldridge Atkins, led the post office to be renamed Surrounded Hill in 1875. The post office went back to Fredonia in 1881 after Abraham Boyd acquired much of the land and laid out a town using the name Fredonia. The name would not stick, and by the end of the year, the post office was back to being Surrounded Hill.

By 1890, the community had two general stores, two grocery stores, two saloons, a post office, a hotel, a blacksmith shop, a steam-powered cotton gin and a gristmill. Records show the post office was again renamed, this time Biscoe by 1902. On July 26, 1909, the town of Fredonia was officially incorporated, but using the name Biscoe to honor landowner John Biscoe. However, most locals still used the name Fredonia.

In 1909, the Rock Island had a depot at Biscoe, but with only a day agent. To allow the depot's use by nighttime trains, the depot was left open at night. This detail comes from an *Arkansas Gazette* article on August 31, 1909, which reported on a robbery of three express packages on August 28, 1909. The article reported that the thieves entered the unlocked depot and then smashed the ticket window to gain access to the office where the packages were stored.

The high ground around Biscoe made it a refugee camp during the Great Flood of 1927. By 1940, Biscoe featured a community hall, two schools, eight general stores, a drugstore, a barber shop, two bus stations, two blacksmith shops, two cotton gins, three filling stations, a train depot, and a post office. There were also five churches, all African-American.

Timber was an early industry at Biscoe, and then it became cotton. The *Arkansas Marketing and Industrial Guide* of 1921 stated that at the time the Biscoe Gin Company was here. The Rock Island also had a one-pen stockyard. Today, rice, soybeans, cotton and wheat are the major crops grown in the area. Biscoe's population was 363 residents in the 2010 census.

In 1950, the Chicago, Rock Island & Pacific Railroad had a 90-car-length siding, plus spur tracks that could handle 43 freight cars. During July 1959, the railroad petitioned the Arkansas Commerce Commission for permission to close the freight agency at Biscoe. The railroad cited poor economics in the area as a reason for closing the agency. During the early 1970s, the siding was still on the north side of the mainline. Today, only a faint grade still passes through town. Heading west, the railroad turns to the southwest before turning sharply to the west to cross the White River. Some stories from Rock Island newsletters state that the curve was made so that the railroad would cross the White River on property owned by developers of the railroad.

85.3   **WHITE RIVER BRIDGE** – The White River starts as several branches in the Ozark/Boston Mountains in northwest Arkansas. It flows north into Missouri, and then east and southeast back into Arkansas. It eventually flows into the Mississippi River south of Helena, across from Rosedale, Mississippi. The river is navigable from the Mississippi River as far upstream as Batesville, Arkansas. At one time, Locks #1, #2, and #3 in the Batesville area allowed barge movements even further upstream, but in May 1952, Lock and Dam #1 was leased to the City of Batesville for recreation and hydroelectric purposes. On June 20, 1952, the lock gates at dams #2 and #3 were made inoperative by securing them closed. During April 1957, Lock #1 was heavily damaged by flooding and the lower gate was destroyed, ending any ability to navigate further upstream. However, the waters that this bridge crosses are navigable, requiring the lift span.

The swift waters and frequent flooding made bridging the White River difficult, and the Memphis & Little Rock Railroad bridge didn't open until April 1871. The bridge consisted of a number of Pratt through truss spans, and because of boats using the river, it featured a center pier with a swing span. It was the largest bridge between North Little Rock and West Memphis, and was often cited as being a problem for the railroad.

In 1920, pier 4 started leaning excessively, twisting the bridge spans and leading to cracking on pier 5. New piles were driven to share the load on pier 4, but it continued to lean even further. Floods in 1921 and 1922 caused more damage, and pier 4 was replaced. However, almost immediately, pier 3 was damaged when it was struck by a steamboat on February 26, 1923. With the capacity limitations of the bridge, and the multiple damages to repair, it was decided to build a new bridge.

Throughout 1923, a new bridge was designed and the American Bridge Company and the Kansas City Bridge Company were hired to manufacture and assemble the bridge. The American Bridge Company was formed as a J. P. Morgan & Company engineered merger of 28 steel companies in April 1900. The firm has dominated the industry since. The Kansas City Bridge Company erected bridges across the Midwest, especially during the first half of the Twentieth Century. The firm was found in 1893, and includes the Huey P. Long Bridge in Louisiana as one of its major projects. The firm closed during the early 1960s.

The White River Bridge took more than three years to design and build, and it opened on January 15, 1927, at a cost exceeding $800,000. Reports state that the bridge was 2671 feet long, including timber trestles on each end. Over the White River from east to west, there was a single through truss span, a 187-foot center lift span, and then two more through truss spans. The lift span could raise 55 feet and was of a unique design also used on the Rock Island Railroad bridge over the Des Plaines River at Joliet, Illinois. Both bridges were built by the American Bridge Company, with the Joliet Lift Bridge installed in 1932. An interesting design feature of this bridge is that the lift machinery is incorporated into the two towers instead of being placed directly on the lift span.

The bridge had a 25-mph speed restriction in 1950. For years, the Code of Federal Regulations covered the operations of the bridge.

> *White River, Ark.; Chicago, Rock Island and Pacific Railway Company bridge near DeValls Bluff. At least 12 hours' advance notice required for openings to be given to the Chief Dispatcher, Chicago, Rock Island and Pacific Railway Company, Little Rock, Arkansas. Whenever any vessel passing through the bridge intends to return through it within 12 hours and informs the draw tender of the probable time of its return, the draw shall be opened promptly on signal for the passage of the vessel on its return trip without further notice.*

Later, the Code of Federal Regulations stated that the bridge remained in the waterway and is open to navigation. However, the rail line, including the bridge, is no longer in use. It was shown to be at Mile 122 of the White River and located in the Eighth Coast Guard District.

The last regular Rock Island train, freight No. 39, reportedly crossed the bridge early on March 24, 1980. After the railroad closed, a few Rock Island trustee trains operated to remove freight cars. The Cotton Belt was assigned operating rights over the line, but never ran a train. Eventually, the bridge was abandoned after the tracks were removed, with the lift span raised and locked in the open position. The former Rock Island bridge has been deemed a navigation hazard, but it still stands.

Originally, the historic U.S. Highway 70 bridge was located about 1500 feet downstream of the Rock Island bridge. It also featured a lift bridge to clear river traffic. It was listed on the National Register of Historic Places on April 9, 1990. However, a new bridge opened in early 2004, and the original highway bridge was blown up on July 20, 2004. The old highway grade can still be followed to new boat ramps, while the new Highway 70 bridge is immediately south of the Rock Island lift bridge, providing a great close-up view of the rail structure.

The lift span of the White River bridge still stands just north of the new U.S. Highway 70 bridge.

86.3   DE VALLS BLUFF – This is a town that has gone through a number of versions of the same name. As reflected by the post office, the name has been Duvall's Bluff (1851-1856), Devall's Bluff (1856-1894), Devalls (1894-1896), Devall Bluff (1896-1919), and De Valls Bluff (1919-Today). What hasn't changed is that the community is alongside the White River, at the west end of the Rock Island bridge.

De Valls Bluff is somewhat unique in that it existed before the Memphis & Little Rock was built. A store, warehouse and a few houses were here before the Civil War, connecting boats on the White River with Little Rock by stagecoach. A number of steamboats stopped here to resupply and to pick up and drop off loads. Much of the business was conducted by C. S. Duvall, who had moved here from Georgia. The

157

construction of the Memphis & Little Rock Railroad, and its direct connection to the Little Rock area, made the river port even more important. During the Civil War, De Valls Bluff became a military supply base for the Union Army. It was also a base for military units, although it had a reputation of being a poor assignment due to frequent bouts of malaria, called "Clarendon shakes" by the troops.

After the Civil War, De Valls Bluff remained busy with the railroad to the west. In 1871, the railroad completed their route and opened the bridge across the White River, ending most of the freight and passenger business on the river. The population dropped from almost 2000 to only 186 by the 1880 census, and there were only three stores, one druggist, and one sawmill. Even though railroads were drawing passenger and freight business away from the rivers, the June 1893 *Travelers' Official Guide* showed that trains still connected "with steamers plying on White River north and south." DeVall's Bluff was also shown to be a telegraph station at the time.

Timber in the area attracted new businesses and residents, and F. P. and A. J. Wells opened a factory that made a number of wooden products, including boat oars and wooden blanks (large blocks of wood used by other factories to manufacture specific products) for factories around the world. An *Arkansas Gazette* article stated that the firm supplied eight train car loads of wooden blanks for a Liverpool customer, and eventual use in English cotton mills.

Other factories also showed up to use natural resources from the area. Maxwell & Company located a handle factory here, and F. Gates & Company built a sawmill, producing "three to five million feet of ash, gum and cypress lumber, and is principally for local demand." A pearl button factory, using mussel shells from the White River, opened at De Valls Bluff, but went through multiple owners (Erie Pearl Button Company and Rockport Pearl Button Company, for example) before closing during World War I. With all of the local industry, De Valls Bluff reached its peak population of 924 in the 1910 census.

De Valls Bluff also served the local farming community, which grew as loggers cleared local forests. The U.S. Department of Agriculture reported that 738 rail shipments of cotton were made from De Valls Bluff in the 1902-1903 shipping season. The *Arkansas Marketing and Industrial Guide* of 1921 listed a number of businesses at De Valls Bluff, including Ayer-Lord Tie Company, Cleveland Stave Company, De Valls Bluff Gin & Mill Company, De Valls Bluff Pearl Button Company, Hammers Land & Lumber Company, Kesl Brothers Company (furniture stock), and Oak Grove Handle Company.

The 1910s and 1920s were the peak of De Valls Bluff development, and many of the brick buildings along the two-block business district have dates from that era. These include Hill 1924, Hipolite 1924, Murphy 1916, Alcoon 1917, and Robinson 1913. One of the few two-story brick buildings was the Castleberry Hotel, built in 1925. This was the main lodging until the 1960s, and while closed today, was placed on the National Register of Historic Places in 2007. The population during the 1920s was almost 900, but it soon dropped as logging ended and the Great Depression started. Another early industry that still exists today is duck hunting and fishing. A number of private clubs have been in the area since the 1800s.

Today, De Valls Bluff has a population of about 600 and features a post office, convenience store and gas station, several restaurants, and a few businesses related to the fishing and hunting industry.

The Rock Island Shuttle Train

The area to the east of the White River, and the river itself, has long experienced frequent flooding. Because of this, the railroad and roads across the area were often closed by heavy rains. The Rock Island spent years and lots of money elevating their grade, and often could run while local roads were closed. This led to the idea of running a shuttle train to get cars and trucks across the flooded areas.

In 1928, the first use of the idea took place. Eighteen railroad flat cars were modified to allow cars and trucks to drive from end to end. Beginning on July 3, 1928, the shuttle operated between Brinkley and De Valls Bluff, allowing highway traffic to reopen. Reports from the time state that drivers could stay in their car or ride in one of several passenger cars on the train, but that passengers in the cars had to use the coaches. Prices for the shuttle were listed as being $3.50 a vehicle, plus $0.63 per adult passenger and $0.32 for children 5-12. The train basically operated back and forth between the high ground at Brinkley and De Valls Bluff, leaving Brinkley at 7:00 a.m., 11:00 a.m., and 3:00 p.m., and leaving De Valls Bluff at 9:00 a.m., 1:00 p.m., and 5:00 p.m.

Several hundred cars used the service daily in 1928, and local communities supported the service by publishing schedules and having snacks available at the boarding locations. The service ended by July 24, 1928, as the waters receded. The railroad heavily promoted their service, gaining goodwill across the region, although the highway industry was somewhat embarrassed. A great deal of highway work took place over the next several years to prevent it from ever happening again, but the Rock Island Shuttle Train was back in January 1930. In this case, sections of other roads were improved and a detour route was created via Cotton Plant and Des Arc, ending the need for the train.

The Railroad at De Valls Bluff

The Rock Island Railroad made a long S-curve between the White River bridge and the west side of De Valls Bluff. Some of this grade is now used by the new U.S. Highway 70 route. Heading west, the railroad faced a curving one-mile grade of 0.65%, climbing back to an elevation of 219 feet from 185 feet at the White River Bridge.

A 1950 Sanborn map shows that the CRI&P railroad station once sat between the mainline and a siding. With the mainline to the north, it was located near the parking lot on Railroad Street, just west of Main Street/Highway 70. This parking lot provides access to the De Valls Bluff Rail Trail, a paved ¼-mile trail heading west along the former Rock Island grade. The De Valls Bluff Lumber Company once stood where the convenience store stands today, and the Rock Island had a spur track swinging east, located just south of the lumber company. This spur track crossed Main Street to serve several businesses along the White River. During the 1920s, branches off of this track reached many of the industries in town. In 1950, there was no siding listed in the employee timetable. However, it did state that the spur tracks had a capacity of 86 railcars.

The Rock Island Railroad is paved for about ¼ mile as it heads west from De Valls Bluff, forming the De Valls Bluff Rail Trail. A number of signs at the parking lot provide information about the railroad and its role in the town's development.

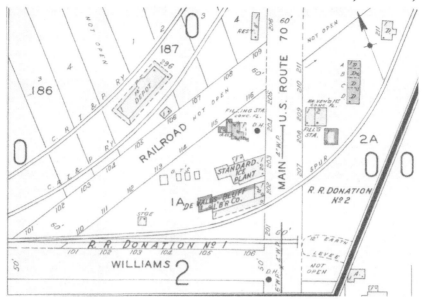

The station area at De Valls Bluff. *Sanborn Fire Insurance Map from De Valls Bluff, Prairie County, Arkansas.* Sanborn Map Company, Apr, 1950. Map. Retrieved from the Library of Congress, https://www.loc.gov/item/sanborn00230_004/.

88.3   MESA – Heading west, the railroad curved through the west side of De Valls Bluff, and a short distance of the grade is used by Argo Road. Just west of Argo Road was the east end of the Mesa rail yard, where the Searcy Branch once curved north off the east end of the siding. For years, Mesa, known earlier as 88 Mile Post, was an important station on the railroad, with branch lines to the north and south. There was a small depot with semaphores since it served as a train register station, and the railroad had two stock pens here during the 1920s. The 98-car siding and other tracks were protected by yard limits. The siding was on the north side of the mainline, and the Stuttgart Branch wye was once to the south at about the middle of the siding.

   After the railroad shut down, Missouri Pacific acquired the line from North Little Rock to Hazen, but made a number of trips further east to Mesa. The reason for these trips were the large number of stored freight cars here. The A. Tennenbaum Company purchased many of the stored cars at Mesa and cut them up for scrap. Missouri Pacific hauled a number of gondola loads of scrap back west to their yard at North Little Rock.

Searcy Branch

To the north was once the Searcy Branch, a 37.6-mile line that has a complex history involving four smaller railroads that each built a part of the line. The oldest part of the Rock Island Searcy Branch is the Searcy & West Point Railroad Company, incorporated on July 3, 1882, to "commence at the town of Searcy and run from thence via Kensett, on the St. Louis, Iron Mountain & Southern Railway, on the most direct and practicable route, to West Point, on the Little Red River; the termini and the line thereof being about nine miles." An 1896 Sanborn map showed the Searcy facilities of the Searcy & West Point Railroad. The railroad started at the corner of West Pleasure Avenue and Spring Street. On the northeast corner, across the street from today's White County Public Library, was the express and freight depot. From here, the railroad ran eastward down the middle of Pleasure Avenue. There was a cotton platform on the north side of Pleasure just east of Oak Street, with a 2-stall shop complex further to the east, just west of Charles Street. While the line to Kensett and West Point was abandoned, the downtown property was later used by the CRI&P.

On August 26, 1897, the Des Arc & Northern Railway Company was incorporated to build and operate a railroad and telegraph line between Searcy and Des Arc, as well as an extension on to Bee Rock on the Little Red River. The company built the 24 miles between Des Arc and Searcy. On June 29, 1899, the Searcy & Des Arc Railroad Company was incorporated to consolidate the two railroads "to form a continuous line of railroad from Searcy, in White County, to Des Arc, in Prairie County, in the State of Arkansas – 25 miles." At the same time, the route of the Searcy & West Point Railroad was abandoned, leaving just the line south of Searcy.

On November 28, 1902, the next part of the railroad was incorporated when the Hazen & Northern Railroad Company was created to build a railroad and telegraph line from a connection with the Searcy & Des Arc Railroad southward to the Choctaw, Oklahoma & Gulf Railroad (CO&G) near Hazen, Arkansas. The railroad was built further east than planned and connected to the CO&G at Mesa, five miles to the east. The plan for the railroad also included a line from Searcy to Heber Springs. This second line was never built and the route later became part of the Missouri & North Arkansas. The CO&G supported the completion of the Hazen & Northern Railroad, which was shown to be 14 miles long.

The *Third Annual Report of the Railroad Commission of the State of Arkansas* (1903) included a statement that the Searcy & Des Arc Railroad Company was a part of the Rock Island System, and that the Choctaw, Oklahoma & Gulf "took possession of the road on May 1,

1902, and upon taking charge found that there were neither books nor records to show what had been done prior to that date." On March 24, 1904, all of these lines were sold to the Chicago, Rock Island & Pacific Railway Company. Initially the railroad handled a great deal of timber, but then slowly saw a reduction in freight traffic to just handling the spring and fall agricultural moves. Mixed passenger and freight service was still being provided in the early 1950s. However, in late 1959, the line between Searcy and Des Arc was abandoned. By the late 1960s, the railroad embargoed the track that remained, using the first few miles of the branch to store old freight cars. The line between Mesa and Des Arc was abandoned in 1980 when the Rock Island shut down.

There is one additional story related to this line that involves the Missouri & North Arkansas (M&NA). This railroad also had a route across the White and Cache River bottoms. There were proposals that the M&NA use the Rock Island from Searcy to Mesa and then east to Wheatley, where it would get back on its line to Helena. This would have allowed the two railroads to share the costs of some of the most expensive track to maintain. While the Rock Island favored the agreement, the M&NA never felt that it could afford the change.

Stuttgart Branch

Heading south from Mesa was the Stuttgart Branch, originally built as the Stuttgart & Rice Belt Railroad in 1911. The line was projected to provide an alternative rail route for the booming rice industry at Stuttgart. However, the revenue didn't come close to covering the construction costs, and the line was sold to the Rock Island, Stuttgart & Southern Railway Company at a foreclosure sale on January 22, 1913. The Rock Island, Stuttgart & Southern Railway was itself incorporated on January 20, 1913, and then leased to the Chicago, Rock Island & Pacific on February 1, 1914, for 999 years. This was somewhat of a formality as the CRI&P already owned the entire capital stock of the smaller railroad. The lease payments were reported by the 1915 *Poor's Manual of Railroads* to be "paying all amounts necessary to keep up corporate existence of lessor, taxes assessments, interest on outstanding obligations, etc."

Also according to the 1915 *Poor's*, the Rock Island, Stuttgart & Southern Railway consisted of 21.01 miles of track, with 1.87 miles of sidings and other tracks. The rail weighed 65 and 67 pounds per yard. The company had one locomotive, two passenger cars and two freight cars. The CRI&P acquired the line to get access to the rice business at Stuttgart. The line was never a major route, having passenger and freight service provided by a mixed train until the 1950s. However, the Stuttgart station, designed similar to the one at Hazen, gave the appearance that there were once greater plans for the route.

In late 1980, the Arkansas Transportation Commission and Oklahoma Department of Transportation jointly submitted a plan to acquire the Choctaw Route between El Reno, Oklahoma, and Memphis, Tennessee. The two states specifically included the 20.8 miles of track between Mesa and Stuttgart in their plans. However, the purchase was never made as the two states could not get an operating commitment from a major railroad. The line was removed in 1982 after the CRI&P went bankrupt.

91.2   BOGARD – There was once a short 405-foot spur track here, known as Green by the late 1960s. In 1980, while the Cotton Belt was originally assigned the line from Memphis to Perry, Arkansas, the SSW decided to use their own lines between Brinkley and North Little Rock. To provide service to grain elevators and other customers, Missouri Pacific was assigned the route between Bogard and North Little Rock. Missouri Pacific also made a few trips east to Mesa to handle the scrap business. However, the railroad later cut their service to Carlisle-west.

Heading west from Mesa, the abandoned railroad grade is often part of the Railroad Prairie Natural Area. As stated by the Arkansas Natural Heritage Commission, the "Railroad Prairie Natural Area occupies portions of the abandoned right-of-way of the former Chicago, Rock Island, and Pacific railroad along U.S. Highway 70 between Carlisle and De Valls Bluff. Its long, linear shape encompasses a variety of habitats and communities including prairie, herbaceous wetland, oak woodland, and forest. A large portion of Railroad Prairie consists of tallgrass prairie, a habitat that was once much more common across the Grand Prairie of eastern Arkansas....The natural area also provides critical habitat for several species now considered rare throughout the state."

The right-of-way for the Railroad Prairie Natural Area was originally acquired by the Arkansas Nature Conservancy, which purchased 13 miles of grade from DeValls Bluff to near Carlisle during December 1986. There were statements that the right-of-way contained some of the last remaining untouched and untilled portion of the Arkansas prairie. The land was then sold to the Arkansas Natural Heritage Commission on January 12, 1987.

Bogard is also at the east end of a thirty-one mile stretch of straight track that goes from Milepost 90.5 to Milepost 121.5, located at the Pulaski County line.

Much of the railroad grade in this area is now preserved as the Railroad Prairie Natural Area, returning the right-of-way to its original look before farming plowed the native grasses.

93.3 HAZEN (HA) – Hazen, like many agricultural-based towns in the area, has a large grain elevator towering over the community. On the west side of town is the Riceland Foods elevator, which handles rice and soybeans. The elevator has the capacity of more than four million bushels. During the early 1920s, Hazen was the home of the Hazen Milling Company and Ark-Mo Lumber Company. Cotton was also an early business, as the U.S. Department of Agriculture reported 1946 rail shipments of cotton from here in 1902-1903. Livestock was also shipped, using two railroad-owned stock pens. The railroad had a number of section houses at Hazen, which were replaced with newer buildings in 1904.

    Once the Memphis & Little Rock Railroad arrived at Hazen, the town became a target for other railroads. On October 6, 1882, the Meadow Valley Railroad was incorporated to build a railroad from Hazen to Arkansas City, Arkansas. Meetings of stockholders and directors of the company continued for about a year, but no construction took place.

This large Riceland Foods rice elevator is located on the west side of Hazen. It clearly marks the approach to Hazen when traveling from the west.

From the 1910s until the 1930s, Hazen was a railroad junction town between the Rock Island and the Cotton Belt (Central Arkansas & Eastern Railroad). The Rock Island station was used by both railroads, with the Cotton Belt paying $540 annual rent in 1915. It also equally covered any maintenance and improvement costs, and annually paid 2.5% of the station's $3142 valuation ($78.55)

The 1950 employee timetable of the Rock Island Railroad stated that there was a 90-car long siding, plus a 59-car-long industry track. In 1973, the Rock Island had sidings to the north and to the south of the mainline. The north siding was just east of the depot, while the south siding stretched to the west. The railroad's 1979 timetable stated that the siding was 4091 feet long.

On Monday, June 1, 1980, the Missouri Pacific (MP) began operating the Chicago, Rock Island & Pacific line between Little Rock and Hazen. At the same time, Missouri Pacific began using Biddle Yard. MP soon cut their service back to Carlisle. With the abandonment of the Rock Island, the grade through town is now the Hazen Rail-Trail, a paved walking trail. Also known as the T. A. Cowan Parkway, the trail through the former Rock Island right-of-way also connects a series of city parks. Outside of town, parts of the grade are also the Railroad Prairie State Natural Area.

Hazen was named for Dr. William Cogswell Hazen, who was born in Charlottesville, Virginia, in 1808. Hazen moved west to Tennessee, married well and bought a plantation, and then moved to the Grand Prairie of Arkansas in 1854. During the Civil War, he moved to Texas to avoid the fighting, and then returned after the war to start a business in Des Arc. He died poor in 1872, but in the first house built on the site of today's Hazen. By this time, a cotton gin was working here, located next to the newly rebuilt railroad. In 1873, the town of Hazen was surveyed and platted for Dr. Hazen's widow, who began selling lots. A post office opened the same year.

On July 8, 1884, the City of Hazen was officially incorporated. The first weekly newspaper opened in 1889, and the population was 458 in 1890. By this time, cream and milk was being shipped to Little Rock and Memphis, and Hazen was becoming a regional farming center. The construction of U.S. Highway 70 and Interstate 40 has drawn some of the local businesses away. Although small, Hazen has been the home of three Miss Arkansas winners: Pam Jackson (1963), Micki Petrus (1981), and Eudora Mosby (2005). The population in the 2010 census was 1468, down from the peak of 1668 in 1990.

Central Arkansas & Eastern Railroad

The Central Arkansas & Eastern Railroad once operated south out of Hazen. The company was incorporated on May 18, 1901, for the purpose of constructing a railroad from England, Arkansas, to Ryan, Arkansas. Ryan is less than ten miles east of England in a farming region, providing shipments of rice, lumber and hay. The charter was soon amended to include an 18-mile extension from Ryan to Stuttgart, as well as a 17-mile line from Rice Junction (just north of Stuttgart) to Hazen.

On July 1, 1910, the St. Louis Southwestern leased the railroad for thirty years and completed the two new lines by October 22, 1911. The railroad described the routes as passing "through a virgin forest of fine timber and a good agricultural country producing cotton and rice in abundance." While the lines were originally profitable, by the 1930s service was down to three days a week, and the Southwestern Transportation Company bus and truck company was providing local service for the railroad. The railroad line was abandoned in 1937.

The Hazen Depot

A distinctive building in downtown Hazen is the Rock Island Depot, placed on the National Register of Historic Places in 1987. Located on the southeast corner of Livermore and North Front Streets, the single-story stuccoed brick building faces south toward the grade of the abandoned Rock Island Railroad. The building features the typical bay window in the agent's office and has a tile roof. The freight storage area that was at the east end of the building is missing, having been torn down due to its deteriorated condition.

This depot replaced the original Memphis & Little Rock station, which was used by both the Rock Island and the St. Louis Southwestern. A larger station was needed due to the freight and passenger volumes at the time, and the Rock Island agreed to build a modern structure that the community could be proud of. When built in 1915, the building contained two waiting rooms, four restrooms, the combination ticket/telegrapher's office, and the conductor's room. The building was built with the design of the era – a white waiting room at the west end of the building, and a black waiting room to the east. There were separate restrooms for the two waiting rooms.

In 1984, the Hazen depot was near collapse, especially the freight room on the east end.

This restored depot still stands on its original foundation, clearing marking the route of the railroad through Hazen.

With the abandonment of the railroad, the Arkansas Nature Conservancy purchased 13 miles of right-of-way between Carlisle and De Valls Bluff. The property was then transferred to the Arkansas Natural Heritage Commission for the Railroad Prairie Natural Area. On February 14, 1987, 2.5 miles of the right-way, along with the depot, was transferred to the City of Hazen. About 400 feet of track was left so that visitors can get a better idea of what the area looked like in the past. Union Pacific caboose #25501 is also here, donated to Hazen during September 1989. Caboose #25501 is a Class CA-8 caboose, built in June 1964. It was retired on May 25, 1989. White Water Regional Irrigation currently occupies the station building.

96.5   CUNEO – Cuneo was shown on several maps during the late 1800s, but records today call it a historical community, or a ghost town. A government survey report from the 1920s stated that there was a switch and sign board here with this name. Cuneo is a family name found in the area.

98.3   SCREETON – During the 1970s, Screeton was a 4612-foot siding on the south side of the mainline. There was also a short house track off of the siding near its west end. Today, there are a few houses to the north and a farm complex to the south, all alongside U.S. Highway 70. A station stood here during the early 1900s.

The Screeton family lived in the area, with Dr. G. T. Screeton serving as the railroad agent at Carlisle starting on January 2, 1870. The July 1899 issue of *The Choctaw* reported on Edward Screeton by stating the following.

> *Right here it will not be out of place to mention the fact that Mr. E. R. Screeton, the county sheriff, has within the last year erected at Hazen a fine, up-to-date flour mill, and is through it offering substantial encouragement to the growing of grain in the county. The mill has a capacity of 100 barrels a day, and the neighboring farmers have in some heavy crops of wheat which are in promising condition.*

Edward Screeton was the County Judge by 1910, and several members of his family operated a grocery store.

99.4   **COUNTY LINE** – This is the county line between **Prairie County** to the east, and **Lonoke County** to the west. **Lonoke County** is one of the fastest growing counties in Central Arkansas, generally caused by families moving out of Pulaski County for the past several decades. In 1970, the county's population was 26,249, with 34,518 in 1980, 39,268 in 1990, 52,828 in 2000, and 68,356 in 2010. Lonoke County was formed on April 16, 1873, from parts of Pulaski and Prairie Counties. The county seat is also named Lonoke, a name that came from a lone oak used as a survey landmark by the Memphis & Little Rock Railroad.

Lonoke County is a mix of Grand Prairie along the Rock Island Railroad, with rolling hills to the north and some delta lands to the south. The Grand Prairie has been a driving force for the county, with dairy and hay production, then cotton production followed by rice, which with 90,000 acres, is the fifth most of any Arkansas county. Farmers also grow corn (fifth most with 40,000 acres), pecans (third most of any county with 500 acres), soybeans (110,000 acres), sorghum and wheat. Today, cities like Lonoke and Cabot have become bedroom communities for the Little Rock area.

99.7   **PRAIRIE CENTER** – Prairie Center, also spelled Prairie Centre, had a post office during the 1870s and 1880s when it was a dairy and hay production area. Area survey records state that the elevation of the top of rail opposite the Prairie Center railroad station was 239.5 feet during the 1910s and 1920s.

102.3 END OF TRACK IN 1994 – Union Pacific records show that they acquired the line to here on November 17, 1983. For almost a decade, it was operated as the Carlisle Branch, a part of the Little Rock Terminal. When the Arkansas Midland Railroad acquired the Carlisle Branch in 1992, this was the end of Union Pacific's line. The track was kept to here so the railroad could serve the agricultural businesses at Carlisle. Unfortunately, many of the elevators in the area relied upon Mississippi River ports or company facilities in southeast Arkansas. With the abandonment of the railroad to the east, the rail route became indirect, and trucking began to handle much of the business.

The August 30, 1994, *Federal Register* reported that the Interstate Commerce Commission had approved the abandonment of the Arkansas Midland Railroad line from near Carlisle (MP 102.28) to near Galloway (123.80).

102.8 CARLISLE (NE) – During the 1980s, there were two sidings at Carlisle to the south. The long one was west of the depot, and the short one went from the depot to the east. These tracks had been here for a long time, and the Rock Island showed one as a 90-car siding in 1950, with the other part of a series of tracks with a capacity of 92 railcars. Several tracks also served the grain facility at the west end of town, now the Riviana Foods facility. As late as 1979, the Rock Island showed a depot, locomotive water, and a dispatcher telephone at Carlisle. Earlier, there had been a two-pen stockyard here, owned by the railroad.

Many of these facilities were important to the railroad, and they were updated and modernized on a regular basis. For example, in 1910, the *Arkansas Gazette* reported that improvements to the 30' x 74' foot depot at Carlisle were almost finished (other reports stated that it was a new depot). The article also reported that the CRI&P was planning to replace an old wooden water tank with a new 65,000-gallon steel water tank. Additionally, standpipes would be installed at each end of the depot so that trains could take on water without making two stops.

Farm products were always the major source of rail freight at Carlisle. Cotton was grown initially, and in 1902-1903, 252 rail shipments of cotton were made from Carlisle. However, rice soon became the dominant crop in the area, with the Arkansas State Rice Milling Company having a facility here. Arkansas State Rice started as the Carlisle Rice Mill, chartered in January 1909. The mill was sold to Arkansas State Rice in 1917, which operated it until 1965, when it was sold to Riviana Foods. One of the famous products made here is the crisped rice for the Nestle Crunch candy bar. Kraft Foods also had a plant here from the late 1920s until the late 1940s.

This large rice elevator can be found on the abandoned Rock Island grade on the east side of Carlisle.

Located on the southeast corner of Court and Main Streets is the Rock Island Depot, built about 1920. Like at Hazen, a new station was required and built as the region experienced a population boom, and rice production increased the rail freight volumes. The depot, which was listed on the National Register of Historic Places in 1990, is described as being a one-and-one-half story masonry and frame structure, finished in brick with half-timbered stucco. The look is typically known as the Tudor Revival style. The building floor layout was typical for the area, with a central ticketing and agent office with a telegrapher's bay window. For passengers, there were waiting rooms on either side of the ticket office, one for whites on the west end, and one for blacks on the east end. There is also a covered porch on the west end with its original waiting benches. Today, the depot is used as office space.

With the railroad abandoned, much of the former right-of-way has been turned into a series of parks. Other parts of the grade are now covered with new buildings.

Designed very much like the Hazen depot, the CRI&P depot at Carlisle was preserved after the railroad shut down and turned into office space for a local insurance company. This photo was taken in 1984.

The City of Carlisle

Carlisle, although located in Lonoke County, is the easternmost municipality within the Little Rock – North Little Rock – Conway Metropolitan Statistical Area. Carlisle is located in Arkansas' Grand Prairie, a tall grass area that attracted farmers from the early 1800s. However, it wasn't until the arrival of the railroad after the Civil War that towns began to develop and farm products could be shipped to national markets. The Memphis & Little Rock Railroad was built through here in 1858, but it was soon destroyed, rebuilt, and destroyed again during the Civil War. By the early 1870s, the line was again open and was completed between the end points in its name.

About this time, Samuel McCormick and his wife, L. J. McCormick, settled in the area and platted a town here on August 1, 1872. A post office opened the following year. Using the name Carlisle, the town grew and was incorporated on August 28, 1878. Originally the town was in Prairie County, but moved to Lonoke County when the county line was resurveyed. The reason for the name Carlisle is unclear, but there are several stories that try to explain it. One is that the McCormicks once lived in Carlisle, Pennsylvania, and used the name of their former home. The second story is that Carlisle was a senator in another state who was a friend of the McCormicks.

By 1880, the population of Carlisle was 159. The first major business in the area was cutting the natural grasses for hay. Soon, the hay was used locally by several dairies, who shipped milk and cream to regional markets. Farming began with cotton, but about 1900, W. H. Fuller began growing rice in the area. After several failures due to unreliable water sources, he produced 5225 bushels of rice from just 70 acres, and the rice boom was on. Today, Arkansas reportedly produces about half of the nation's rice.

The boom in rice production caused Carlisle to quickly double in size (212 residents in 1900 and 516 in 1910). Since then, Carlisle has slowly grown, with the population peaking in 1980 at 2567 residents. During the 2010 census, the population was 2214. Carlisle hosts the typical schools, stores, restaurants and other businesses found in towns of its size that support area farming. Most of the town is north of the old railroad grade, which passes through town several blocks north of U.S. Highway 70.

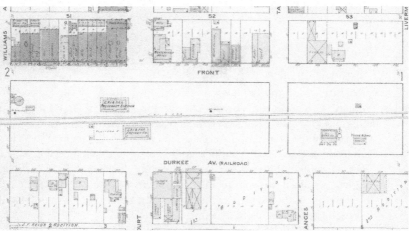

The railroad station area at Carlisle. *Sanborn Fire Insurance Map from Carlisle, Lonoke County, Arkansas.* Sanborn Map Company, Feb, 1918. Map. Retrieved from the Library of Congress, https://www.loc.gov/item/sanborn00215_002/.

Heading west, another major agricultural crop is often seen. This area is one of the leading producers of baitfish. These include Golden Shiners, black and pink fathead minnows, goldfish, black salty, and other fish sold across the country in bait shops. These farms often include hatcheries and hundreds of large ponds.

Battle of Ashley's Station

During the latter part of the Civil War, Union forces built a number of facilities to protect the Memphis & Little Rock Railroad, and the supplies that moved through the area. A number of these were small bases built of logs, dirt and hay that protected the cutting of hay and the grazing of cattle and horses. Throughout early August, 1864, Confederate forces began to attack isolated forts and capture Union troops and supplies. Many of the captured troops had been busy cutting hay for the calvary forces based at DeValls Bluff. On August 24, 1864, Confederate Brigadier General Joseph Shelby attacked a series of these forts between Carlisle and Hazen, capturing a number of Union troops and their arms and supplies. Ashley's Station was one of these forts.

The battle was the last major action by General Shelby during his efforts in northeastern Arkansas throughout the summer of 1864. Shelby and his 2500 troops had been ordered to the region with orders to tame lawless deserters and bushwhackers and to hinder Union operations. At the top of his list was to attack the Memphis & Little Rock Railroad and shipping on the White River. Shelby lost 173 men, killed and wounded, and produced the following report about the action.

> *The immediate and tangible fruits of my expedition are 577 prisoners, including 1 field officer and 11 line officers; over 200 Federals killed and wounded; ten miles of railroad track destroyed completely – the ties torn up and burned, the iron heated and bent, telegraph destroyed, bridges and trestle-works ruined; 3,000 bales of hay destroyed by fire; 20 hay machines chopped to pieces; 5 forts razed to the ground; 500 stand of small arms distributed to my unarmed men; many fine horses captured; 12 barrels of salt brought off the field and given to a command suffering for it, besides supplying many needy soldiers with blankets, shoes, boots, hats, and clothing. All this was done within six miles of Devall's Bluff, and my detail was tearing up the track while the enemy's bullets, fired at the covering regiments, were throwing the splinters from the ties into their very faces.*

Today, 10.8 miles of the railroad right-of-way from west of Carlisle to near Hazen is listed on the Arkansas Register of Historic Places as the Ashley's and Jones' Station Battlefield.

104.7 BAYOU TWO PRAIRIE BRIDGE – The railroad actually crossed this stream using several timber pile ballast deck trestles. Bayou Two Prairie, also known as Two Prairie Bayou, flows to the southeast and joins with a number of other streams along the route. The Bayou is lined with minnow farms that use the Bayou's water in their operations.

There was once a community along the stream using the same name, Bayou Two Prairies, that had a post office for a short time in 1849.

105.8 MCCREANOR – McCreanor, McCreanors, or McCreanor's, was another small community built along the railroad. Area histories state that the railroad sold land in the area, often to new immigrants. By the 1890s, most of the landowners were African-Americans, located away from the larger communities. There was a McCreanor post office 1900-1908, at the town's population peak. However, as farms consolidated, many landowners sold their small farms and moved away, and the town was mostly gone by 1950.

McCreanor was once a railroad junction town with the Pine Bluff & Northern Railway heading south. There was a siding, sign board and depot here during the early 1900s. According to survey reports, the top of the rail opposite the train station was at 228.9 feet of elevation. The town was once located near where the Lonoke County Co-op is today, and the Pine Bluff & Northern Railway headed south along today's Arkansas Highway 381.

Pine Bluff & Northern Railway Company

The Pine Bluff & Northern Railway Company (PB&N) once operated southward from McCreanor, creating a junction here with the Rock Island Railroad. The railroad started as the Meto Valley Railway Company, which was incorporated under the general laws of Arkansas on October 29, 1908. The company planned to build a 16-mile line southward. According to Interstate Commerce Commission records, the railroad leased the rail from the Chicago, Rock Island & Pacific. Never financially successful, the railroad entered receivership on April 12, 1910.

The Meto & Arkansas Valley Railway Company was incorporated on October 1, 1910, with the goal of constructing "not more than 25 miles of railroad, extending southerly from McCreanor to the town of Tomberlin. While the records are not clear, apparently the Meto & Arkansas Valley Railway Company acquired the Meto Valley Railway Company and consisted of many of the same owners and managers.

On May 26, 1910, the Pine Bluff & Northern Railway Company was incorporated to build an 80-mile railroad between Pine Bluff and Searcy, Arkansas. Records show that the Meto & Arkansas Valley sold its property on October 21, 1911, and that the deeds were dated March

26, 1912. There are reports that the railroad again was controlled by a receiver and was sold to an individual on February 26, 1916, for $5000, with the receiver controlling the company until the purchase price was paid in full.

The Interstate Commerce Commission described the railroad as a single-track standard-gauge steam railroad, extending "southerly from McCreanor, Ark., to Cullor, Ark., a distance of 6.779 miles. The carrier also owns yard and side tracks totaling 0.305 mile. Its road thus embraces 7.084 miles of all tracks owned." The PB&N shut down and was abandoned in 1927. Arkansas Highway 381 uses parts of the grade as it heads directly south.

108.9 SISEMORE – Until the end of the Rock Island's operations, Sisemore was a short spur track to the south. In 1950 and 1969, it was listed as being 18 cars long. There was also a dispatcher telephone here in 1979.

Hick's Station

Hick's Station was an original station on the Memphis & Little Rock Railroad, located several miles east of what later became Lonoke. During the Civil War, the station was a Confederate base that guarded the eastern approaches to Little Rock. After the Battle of Brownsville and the Battle at Reeds Bridge, the area became a Union army field hospital. After the railroad was rebuilt by Federal forces, Union troops established a permanent presence to guard the railroad. However, on July 6, 1864, Confederate skirmishers destroyed the tracks nearby, derailing a train. A historical marker noting this military action at Hick's Station can be found east of Lonoke at Sunset Memorial Gardens Cemetery.

When the railroad was rebuilt after the Civil War, the line was straightened, avoiding Brownsville. As a part of the change, the depot at Hick's Station was moved to the new community of Lonoke.

111.5 LONOKE (KO) – Lonoke owes its existence to the railroad, as it came about when the railroad was rebuilt after the Civil War. The first freight moved was basic products for the community, as well as hay and livestock. In 1879, the Memphis & Little Rock Railroad built hay and cotton sheds at Lonoke. About 1883, a new depot, described as "the neatest by far" of any on the railroad, was built at Lonoke on the north side of the tracks between Richmond (Park) and Center avenues.

These improvements quickly paid off. By 1900, cotton was being grown across the region and the railroad moved 7746 rail shipments in 1902-1903. By 1920, the farming market was diversified and rice had become a major commodity being moved from Lonoke. At the time, the railroad served the Lonoke Flour Mill, Lonoke Rice Milling Company, Lonoke Rice Products Company, and a railroad-owned stockyard that included three pens. Today, rice and soybeans are the major crops grown in the area, plus the many minnow and fish farms. At the west edge of Lonoke is the large white Riceland Foods elevator.

In 1950, Lonoke was a maze of tracks. A 98-car siding was here, and the other tracks had a capacity of 137 cars. A 1973 track chart shows three sidings, with the eastern-most to the north of the mainline. Then there were lapped sidings to the south and then another to the north when heading west. The Lonoke railway station was on the south side of the tracks, just east of the middle siding. The depot was a train orders station, and also had locomotive water. Later, the siding was shown to be 4586 feet long.

Lonoke Depot

Lonoke is the fourth Arkansas town since West Memphis that still has its Rock Island Railroad depot. Like the others, it is listed on the National Register of Historic Places (October 4, 1984). It was restored thanks to a $144,000 grant, and then dedicated on May 10, 1987, with Senator Dale Bumpers delivering the keynote address. Today, it is used by the Lonoke Area Chamber of Commerce. The station is easy to find as it is located on Front Street – U.S. Highway 70.

In 1984, the CRI&P Lonoke depot still looked as if a passenger train was about to arrive. It has since been restored and is used by the Lonoke Area Chamber of Commerce.

The former railroad right-of-way is now a series of parks and parking lots, with a short stretch of track to the east that is used to display a boxcar and a caboose. The caboose is former Missouri Pacific #13664, the last of a series of sixty cabooses manufactured in 1973-1974 by the International Car Corporation. These cabooses featured an extended vision, off-center cupola. Assigned Union Pacific caboose Class CA-31, the car last worked at Sedalia, Missouri, was removed from service on July 25, 1986, and donated to the City of Lonoke in 1988. Alongside the caboose is the beginning of a paved trail that heads east along the railroad right-of-way. It is about a mile long and ends at the Lonoke Municipal Ball Park on the east side of town.

This station opened during November 1912 at a reported cost of $26,000. It replaced an earlier frame depot that had been built in 1899. It is a one-story red brick structure, measuring 28 x 100 feet. In the center is the agent's office, which features a bay window on what was the track side, still with its train order semaphore signals. To the west was the 28 x 20 foot freight room, used for LCL (less-than-carload) shipments. To the east was a large passenger waiting area. The building has gabled ends which are above the roof level, using the Jacobethan style. Each end also features a cast stone plaque with "Lonoke" engraved in it.

Besides the Lonoke name, the depot also featured painted Rock Island emblems on the red brick end walls of the station, as shown here in 1984.

179

On October 10, 1922, in honor of the railroad's 70th anniversary, a tree was planted at Lonoke in recognition of Rudolph Fink. Rudolph Fink had worked for a number of railroads in Mexico and the United States, and then became receiver and then president of the Memphis & Little Rock Railroad. His brother, Albert Fink, led much of the construction of the Louisville & Nashville, creating a system of cost accounting that was soon adopted by many other railroads. The third brother, Henry Fink, was known as the "Railroad Doctor" because of his success in turning around failing railroads, eventually becoming the chairman of the Norfolk & Western Railroad.

The Battle of the Lonoke Depot

For some reason, while the Rock Island Railroad and the City of Lonoke had an important business relationship, there also seemed to be a number of legal battles between the two. For example, on December 4, 1907, the Railroad Commission of Arkansas ordered the railroad to build "a stock pen for the use of shippers in loading live stock for shipment and a spur track contiguous to same. Said stock pen and spur track shall be commensurate with the needs of the shippers of live stock of said territory and the business done by said railroad company at said point." This was not the last legal action between Lonoke and the CRI&P.

The station that stands today at Lonoke almost wasn't built thanks to a tremendous amount of local conflict. By early 1908, the Chicago, Rock Island & Pacific had plans to build a new passenger depot at Lonoke, located about two blocks west of the existing passenger depot. A major reason for the new location was to ease traffic congestion on the adjacent highway grade crossing. However, by summer, a number of battles were underway. In August, the Lonoke town council condemned the freight depot, two seed houses and the cotton platform as part of a series of demands for more modern rail facilities in town. The railroad had already moved its stock yard and pens, and the town was threatening to tear all the buildings down as a way to force the railroad to build the new buildings.

On September 1, 1908, some sort of truce was reached and an agreement had been made to build a new freight depot and a new passenger depot two blocks west of their original location. The cotton platform was also to be moved 150 yards west of the freight and passenger depots. However, as work began, a group of citizens sued the railroad to keep the station where it was. With the injunction in place, work stopped, so the City of Lonoke began tearing down seed houses and other railroad buildings. Soon, citizens, the town, and the railroad were all suing each other for a solution. A court injunction allowed the railroad to build new seed houses and a cotton platform. Eventually a new depot was built, but only after a few more lawsuits and a court case that went all the way to the Arkansas Supreme Court.

White River, Lonoke & Western Railway

For a few years, Lonoke was a junction town. *The Railway Age* (February 11, 1898) reported that the White River, Lonoke & Western had been incorporated to build a railroad from the Wooley Mine No. 2, north of Jacksonville, Arkansas, to Lonoke, "thence in an easterly direction through the counties of Lonoke and Arkansas to some point on or near White river, a distance of 50 miles." Most of the subscribers were from Jacksonville, but a few were from places like St. Louis, Kansas City, Lonoke and Little Rock. Later reports showed J. N. Wooley as owner of the White River, Lonoke & Western. *Poor's Manual of Railroads* (1899) reported that the railroad was chartered on February 3, 1898, and that 16 miles of track from Wooley to Lonoke was completed on July 1, 1899. The railroad was built with 35-pound rail and had three locomotives and eight freight cars.

Soon, there was talk about building the route on to the southeast to Seaton, Arkansas, with mention of the extension in *Poor's Manual of Railroads* (1899) and *The Railway Age* (July 5, 1901). However, the railroad was soon in trouble. *The Railway Age* of October 4, 1901, reported that the Arkansas Railroad Commission had cited the White River, Lonoke & Western for failure to file their annual reports with the commission before September 15, as required by law.

Additionally, a lawsuit had started against the railroad for failure to pay rent on the track materials used to build the railroad. The court records stated that the "lease provided in substance that the McLeod Lumber Company agreed to lease to the White River, Lonoke & Western Railway Company certain steel rails, straps, nuts, bolts and spikes for the term of two years, beginning August 20, 1898, on the conditions that the lessee should pay $550 in quarterly payments of $137.50 each." The report stated that no payment had been made for more than a year on the 220 tons of track material, and the court ordered the payments made, the materials returned, or the property sold.

The end of the "Wooley Line" railroad came quickly. The *Third Annual Report of the Railroad Commission of the State of Arkansas* (1903) explained the actions taken, stating "[o]n September 17, 1901, the White River, Lonoke & Western Railway was purchased by the Choctaw, Oklahoma & Gulf Railway Company, and the rails and all material were removed and the road abandoned from Wooleys to Lonoke, Arkansas, a distance of 16 miles."

The story is actually a bit more complicated. In June 1901, Pulaski County chancery Judge Martin ordered the railroad sold in response to a foreclosure suit by Memphis and St. Louis creditors. After several attempts, Allen N. Johnson purchased the railroad for $16,500 on August 15, 1901. A month later on September 17th, the railroad was sold to the Choctaw, Oklahoma & Gulf (CO&G), which immediately scrapped the railroad. Some reports stated that the rails were actually already owned by the CO&G and the company simply reclaimed their own materials. Today, only a few fence lines and some highway grades mark the route of this railroad.

The City of Lonoke

Today, U.S. Highway 70 and the Rock Island Railroad grade go through the center of Lonoke. Lonoke was not the first town in this area. The first was Brownsville, located about three miles to the north. In 1858, the Memphis & Little Rock Railroad curved its route so that it would pass through what at the time was the county seat of Prairie County. During the Civil War, Brownsville and the railroad was destroyed during the Union assault on Little Rock. When the railroad was rebuilt, a new straighter route was chosen, and the remains of Brownsville were no longer on the railroad.

A new station, using the name of Hick's Station, was built about 1868 to serve the area. A year later, a decision was made to move the station west about two miles. Memphis & Little Rock civil engineer Major G. P. C. Rumbough was assigned the job of finding the new location, and he is generally credited with coming up with the name. Rombaugh named the new town after a lone red oak that had been used as a landmark for the railroad's construction. While he pronounced the town's name "Lo-no-kah" to make it sound Native American, it quickly became "Lone-oak." The first spelling of the name was Loneoak, but Rumbough soon changed it to Lonoke.

In 1869, Isaac C. Hicks and Hamilton Reynolds surveyed and platted the new townsite on the estate of Major L. W. Monroe. A general store soon opened. Lonoke was incorporated as a town on January 22, 1872. The post office, which had started at Brownsville (1851-1868) and then moved to Hicks Station (1867-1872), relocated to Lonoke that same year. Lonoke County was created from parts of Prairie and Pulaski counties in 1873, and Lonoke was incorporated and became the new county's seat. The first courthouse was the former Prairie County Courthouse that was still standing in Brownsville, moved to Lonoke soon after. A three-story brick county courthouse was built in 1928.

The population boomed from 1900 (951) to 1910 (1547). This was when the focus changed from cattle and lumber, to cotton, corn and hay.

Rice became another crop during the early 1900s, and then soybeans in the 1940s. World War I also stimulated the economy with the construction of the Eberts Training Field, used by the United States Army for pilot training during World War I and World War II. After Interstate 40 was built, Lonoke has essentially become a part of the Little Rock area. Its population has grown to about 4000, with 4245 in the 2010 census, making it the second most populous city in Lonoke County.

Eberts Training Field

Eberts Training Field, named for Melchior McEwan Eberts, an early Arkansas aviator and West Point graduate, was built in 1917 as an aviation training center. The facility came about as a plan to have communities bid on these facilities, and Lonoke was able to underbid nearby Pulaski County by providing 960 acres and a rail spur at no cost. Construction of the airfield began during December 1917 and the first cadets and soldiers arrived in the spring of 1918. Soon the facility was one of the largest in the United States.

With cadets arriving so quickly, the local school gymnasium was used as housing. Officers were housed in the Frank Barton home at 220 Park Street, a house that still stands. A popular story from the era involved the Lonoke Cemetery. The Airfield was built on the northwest side of town and across the street from the Cemetery. Reportedly, instructors introduced the cemetery to all new cadets as a reminder of how dangerous flying could be. The first training planes used were the famous "Flying Jenny" (Curtis JN-4D), which also had the nickname of the "flying coffin."

The speed of World War I caught many by surprise, and when it ended on November 11, 1918, the first class had yet to graduate. The airfield was closed at the end of November 1919, but wasn't abandoned as it served as the Lonoke Municipal Airport. The airfield was used at the start of World War II for contract glider training, and was closed in 1943. No signs of the airfield remain today.

114.0 DANIEL – Look for the Tulls Road grade crossing – basically a farm field access road from the north. This spur track, active during the first several decades of the 1900s, was named for the nearby W. M. Daniel's plantation. Daniel once owned the Lonoke Flouring Mill, built 1917. W. M. Daniel was also involved as an engineer with the installation of the Lonoke water system in 1897.

114.7 BAYOU METO BRIDGE – This bridge was shown to be a 222-foot ballast deck, timber pile trestle, by Union Pacific. Older Rock Island Railroad records showed that it was a 17-panel timber trestle.

Bayou Meto is a well-known name in central Arkansas because it is a slow-moving stream that forms in northwestern Pulaski County, and then flows around the east side of North Little Rock. There is a lot of confusion about the name as some early French documents have it named "Bayou Metre." This could mean that the water is about a meter deep, or that it is a bad spelling of mi-terre which could mean minor or unimportant land, or for halfway between major rivers. Even the English spelling has changed, with Bayou Metoe being used some until the early twentieth century.

The stream, it is known as a river in some sources, winds greatly as it flows east and south, entering the Arkansas River a few miles southwest of Gillett, Arkansas. The distance is about 100 miles by road, but 150 miles by the stream. Bayou Meto serves as part of the county line between Lonoke and Prairie counties, and Arkansas and Jefferson counties. It is also considered to be an important habitat for a wide variety of fish, waterfowl, mammals and reptiles. Parts of the stream are protected as wildlife management areas. The stream's channel can vary by the water level, and it was large enough to be part of Little Rock's defensive line during the Civil War.

While Bayou Meto was used by some for transportation, it was generally unsettled until the land became available through the Swamplands Act of 1850. This Act allowed some states to claim federal lands if they drained the swamps. Lumbering and then farming used much of the land as it was drained.

Additional projects continued over the years, with a floodgate installed near the Arkansas River during the 1920s by the U.S. Army Corps of Engineers. However, after World War II, wildlife preservation became important and large sections of the Bayou were protected through the creation of Wildlife Management Areas. Now, some areas are flooded on purpose to attract ducks for hunting.

116.5 BAYOU METO BRIDGE – As stated, Bayou Meto is a winding stream, and the railroad was forced to bridge it several times in this area. Union Pacific showed that this bridge was a timber pile trestle with a ballast deck, measuring 263 feet long. CRI&P records stated that it was a 20-panel timber trestle.

117.0 METO – Meto, named for Bayou Meto, was located just west of the Arkansas Highway 15 grade crossing (Milepost 116.8), which leads north to Interstate 40. This station was originally Perkins, listed as being five miles west of Lonoke by the Railroad Commission of Arkansas in 1904. The station of Meto was in the 1950 Arkansas Division timetable, with a 94-car siding. By 1979, the siding was gone, but the location was known as Remington Arms, with 2025 feet of track capacity heading north to the manufacturer's plant. The old grade can be made out as it winds through trees just west of the Remington Arms Gun Club, located just north of the former tracks and west of Highway 15.

The former railroad mainline grade here is now Blackmon Road, built as the entrance to the large auction yard. Blackmon Auctions was started in 1938, founded by Eddie Blackmon, Sr. Blackmon Auctions handles large and small auction across the country, and has handled a number of locomotive and other equipment auctions for Union Pacific Railroad.

This sign is located at the entrance to Blackmon Auctions. While the railroad is gone, a number of railroad equipment auctions are based out of this facility.

To the north is the large Remington Arms Company facility. The firm was founded in 1816 by Eliphalet Remington, and the company is still considered to be America's oldest gun maker, and largest U.S. producer of shotguns and rifles. In 1986, Remington moved its ammunition manufacturing from Bridgeport, Connecticut, to this plant to have it nearer the sporting market. Remington has undergone several ownership changes as it was acquired by the DuPont Corporation during the Great Depression and then sold to an investment firm in 1993. It has also acquired a number of other firms in the industry, often to expand their market. The firm went through a quick bankruptcy in 2018 to straighten out some of its finances, but is still operating under its name. This plant, known as the Lonoke Plant, is where all Remington ammunition is made, and is also the home to Remington's Industrial Products Division and Ammunition Product Services.

185

North of the former station of Meto is the Remington Arms Lonoke Plant.

There were several early settlements along the stream that used the name Bayou Meto or Meto, and this location was no different, especially after the railroad was rebuilt following the Civil War. There was a post office at Meto 1912-1922, and the A. C. Martineau cotton gin was located here during the 1910s and 1920s. A U.S. Coast and Geodetic Survey made during the fall of 1916, under the command of Captain Edwin H. Pagenhart, indicated that the elevation of the top of rail at the Meto station was 237.4 feet. Captain Pagenhart was an early surveyor and engineer for the Coast and Geodetic Survey. During the 1930s, he was Director of the Survey in the Philippines for the United States.

117.5 BAYOU METO BRIDGE – This is another crossing of the wandering stream. Rock Island Railroad records showed it to be a 20-panel timber trestle, while Union Pacific records showed it to be a 248-foot timber pile trestle with a ballast deck.

120.8 KERR – Coming into Kerr from the east, the railroad again passes a series of minnow ponds. Kerr was located at the Kerr Road grade crossing, just south of Exit 165 on Interstate 40. A post office opened and closed in 1876 at Kerr, and then reopened two years later and lasted until 1935.

Initially the railroad simply had a basic passenger station at Kerr. Starting on September 1, 1909, the railroad opened a freight and telegraph station at Kerr, designed to handle the growing cotton business. In 1916, a survey report stated that the elevation of the top of rail opposite the Kerr depot was 245.1 feet. The station was out of the railroad's timetable by 1950.

121.6 COUNTY LINE – This is the west end of the thirty-one miles of tangent track that started near Bogard. This is also the county line between **Lonoke County** to the east, and **Pulaski County** to the west. **Pulaski County** is the crossroads of Arkansas, where the major north-south and east-west highways meet, and once where the major railroads also met. It is the most populous county in Arkansas with about 400,000 residents. Little Rock is the county seat, and is also the state capital and largest city in the state. Pulaski County was created on December 15, 1818, as the fifth in Arkansas, and has been broken up several times to form other counties.

Seven states (Arkansas, Georgia, Illinois, Indiana, Kentucky, Missouri and Virginia) have a county named after Casimir Pulaski, a Polish nobleman and military commander. Pulaski supported the idea of political freedom and came to North America to fight with the Continental Army in the American Revolutionary War. Having experience with calvary forces, he led a calvary charge at the Battle of Brandywine that was credited with saving the life of George Washington. He was soon promoted to Brigadier General, with the title of "Commander of the Horse." He then taught calvary concepts to parts of the Continental Army and created his own Pulaski Cavalry Legion, which he led until his death in a calvary charge at the Battle of Savannah on October 11, 1779. He has since been one of the few people to be awarded honorary United States citizenship, and is one of several who have been called "the father of the American cavalry."

For many years, Pulaski County was a large farming area, but with the expansion of the Little Rock urban area, less land is now used for that purpose. However, Pulaski County still ranks as fifth in the production of sweet potatoes for Arkansas, and significant acreage of corn and soybeans can also be found.

123.8 END OF ARKANSAS MIDLAND RAILROAD – The track east of here is gone, but west of this location it is still in service, operated by the Arkansas Midland Railroad. The track to the east to near Carlisle was abandoned by the Arkansas Midland in 1994 after it was acquired from Union Pacific.

GOOD OVER LINES OF
The Chicago, Rock Island & Pacific Ry. Co.
Frank O. Lowden, James E. Gorman,
Joseph B. Fleming, Trustees
Unless Territory Otherwise Limited
E. M. DURHAM, Jr., Chief Executive Officer

RESTRICTIONS
NOT GOOD ON ROCKET TRAINS

Not Good in Suburban Territory Between
Chicago and New Lenox

This pass is a license, non-transferable and revocable without notice, which is issued gratuitously without any consideration whatever, to the person or persons named hereon, and is restricted as herein set out. Its acceptance or use is with the understanding that neither company named herein nor their Trustees, nor their successors in ownership, or operation of their lines of railroad, shall be liable in damages for injury to or death of the user, or for loss of or damage to the property of the user, no matter whether such death or injury, or loss or damage, is due to negligence or otherwise, and the user hereby releases all claims and causes of action against said companies, their Trustees or the r said successors, for any such damages. This pass must not be used in violation of law, and the users must not be prohibited by law from receiving free transportation.

I accept the above conditions

This pass will not be honored unless signed in ink.

Rock Island Lines rail pass, back side, circa 1942. From the author's collection.

Galloway (AR) to North Little Rock (AR)
Arkansas Midland Railroad

As previously stated, after the Rock Island Railroad shut down in early 1980, the eastern end of the Choctaw Route was initially assigned to the St. Louis Southwestern (SSW), including as far west as Perry, Arkansas, to preserve service to the large papermill there. However, the Rock Island track between Brinkley and North Little Rock wasn't used as the SSW had their own route.

Missouri Pacific acquired the rights to operate the line from Mesa to Little Rock, and then purchased much of the line on November 17, 1983, operating between Hazen and Biddle Yard in Little Rock. Service between Carlisle and Hazen ended in 1982, and the track was removed in early 1985 by Determan-Merrill, Inc., a subcontractor for L. B. Foster. This left the line as the Carlisle Branch, in service as far west as Biddle Yard.

In 1992, Union Pacific sold several rail lines to the Arkansas Midland Railroad Company (AKMD), including much of the Carlisle Branch. When created, the AKMD was a subsidiary of Pinsly Railroad Company, a holding company of short line railroads. The firm, based in Westfield, Massachusetts, was started in 1938 by Samuel M. Pinsly and was one of the oldest such companies in the United States. The Arkansas Midland abandoned the track from Carlisle to Galloway in 1994. On December 5, 2014, Genesee & Wyoming (G&W) filed a Notice of Exemption with the Surface Transportation Board to acquire the Arkansas Midland from Pinsly. The G&W is the largest short line holding company in the country and operates a number of rail operations in Arkansas.

The Arkansas Midland now operates several different lines across Arkansas. This part is known as the North Little Rock Branch. It includes 7.8 miles of former Rock Island track from North Little Rock to Galloway, and 6.8 miles of former Cotton Belt trackage, once used by the SSW to avoid the Brinkley to North Little Rock trackage of the Rock Island.

123.8 END OF ARKANSAS MIDLAND RAILROAD – This is the location of the end of active track, located just west of Arkansas Highway 391 (Exit 161 on I-40). This area is a growing exit full of truck stops, warehouses, and the home of Maverick Transportation, a large trucking company. The end of track is just long enough to allow lumber to be delivered to the nearby Quality Wholesale Building lumberyard.

The track west of here is operated by the Arkansas Midland Railroad as far as Milepost 131.7 at North Cornish Street in North Little Rock, Arkansas.

124.6 GALLOWAY – Galloway, or Galloway Station, was named for Walter A. Galloway, a resident and merchant who once operated a general merchandise store here. Walter Galloway was born in Pulaski County on November 22, 1844, to parents who arrived in the area in 1830 from Virginia. Walter fought in Company F of the First Arkansas Mounted Riflemen in numerous area battles during the Civil War, and then returned to farming. In 1871, Galloway opened a store on the Memphis & Little Rock Railroad and the town there took his name. In 1874, he moved to Kerrs where he operated a store and a nearby farm. In 1879, he moved to Jacksonville, Arkansas, northeast of Little Rock, where he started another business. He also owned several large farms in Pulaski and Lonoke counties. He became the postmaster at Jacksonville in 1882.

During the early 1900s, there was a railroad station here, built in late 1905. There was also a siding at Galloway. This area was a challenge for the railroad to maintain, and crews regularly worked on the grade and track. Because of this, new 90-pound steel rails, 33 feet long, were installed here in March 1913, along with new creosoted pine ties. During August 1914, several crews were working in the area lining and raising the track. In some places the track required a raise of as much as ten inches due to the sagging fill. The high heat of summer was also an issue, causing sun kinks. Records show that the railroad routinely placed slow orders in this area because of the track work and heat.

On August 21, 1914, Rock Island westbound passenger train No. 45 derailed at 1:47pm about a mile west of the east passing track switch at Galloway due to these conditions. The train was operating from Memphis to Hot Springs with a combination baggage and mail car, one combination baggage and coach car, one coach, one dining car, one parlor car, and three sleeping cars, The investigation reported that the "cars were of steel construction except one sleeping car and the parlor car, which were of wooden construction, and the dining car, which had a steel under frame."

An investigation by the railroad and the Interstate Commerce Commission determined that the track moved under the train, causing the derailment. The conductor reported that the front trucks of the fifth "car jerk around, followed by a similar movement of the rear trucks", which led him to believe that the track kinked under the fifth car. Wheel marks showed that the "rear truck of the sixth car and the forward truck of the seventh car dropped inside and rode the rail." After about 500 feet, the rear cars "broke loose from the train and turned over on their sides to the north, the head end of the train continuing on for a distance of about 500 feet." Two "bridgemen working on the cattle guard near the station board...were crushed under the seventh car of that train when it turned over on its side." Additionally, 26 passengers, three employees, and one Pullman porter were injured. Sun kinks and grade settlement remained a problem for the railroad until the end of the company.

In 1950, there was a 100-car siding here to the south. Union Pacific later reported that it was 4594 feet long. Today, this is an industrial area with warehouses, truckstops, and large stores. It is very different from what it was like during the late 1800s and early 1900s when it was a small rural community that supported area farming. There was a post office here from 1871 until 1903, until it was moved to the larger cities to the west.

126.5 INTERSTATE 440 – The railroad passes under the East Belt Freeway that connects Interstate 40, just north of here, with Interstate 30 and Interstate 530/U.S. Highway 65 south of Little Rock. At I-40, it connects with the North Belt Freeway, Arkansas Highway 440, to head on north to U.S. Highways 67/167 near Jacksonville. The East Belt is about 14 miles long and was completed in 2003.

At one time, the railroad had a station near here named Shingle Switch. The industry located here can easily be determined from the station's name.

127.9 NIEMEYER – Neimeyer was an early station on the railroad and was listed by the Choctaw & Memphis in their 1899 timetable. Niemeyer was an early farm community and had a post office for only a few years (1883-1885). It was located just west of the old horseshoe lake east of North Little Rock, near the Eureka Garden Road grade crossing.

129.6 TIE PLANT – The March 3, 1907, issue of the *Arkansas Gazette* had a headline reading "Begin Work Soon on Big Creosoting Plant," with a subheading stating "Ayer & Lord Tie Co. Has Purchased Tract of Land Near Argenta and Will Erect Plant." The article stated that Ayer & Lord had purchased 150 acres along the Rock Island Railroad to build a "four-cylinder creosoting plant" for about $150,000. This plant was designed to manufacture 8-12,000 ties a day, operating day and night, using the four pressure cylinders. The *Arkansas Gazette* also stated that the ties were to be used primarily by the Rock Island.

As a part of the tie plant's construction, Ayer & Lord built a hotel, homes, and a boarding house for workers, most of whom were African-American. Reports from the time stated that as many as 300 workers were employed at the plant, which was located at Tie Plant Station on the Rock Island. A post office using the name Tie Plant opened here during January 1909. In November, the railroad opened a station and agency at Tie Plant, what the railroad had called the Ayer Lord Tie Plant. Koppers Company acquired the plant in 1944 and has operated it since. For many years, Koppers and the Rock Island Railroad had a very close relationship. In 1960, the CRI&P reported that Koppers at Tie Plant treated almost all of the pilings, bridge timbers, poles and ties for the entire railroad.

A recent environmental report on the facility states that the 157-acre plant currently employs 90 workers and treats over 1.5 million crossties a year. Other products treated include lumber and utility poles, switch ties, road crossings and framed bridge timbers. The materials treated come from Arkansas, southern Missouri, western Tennessee, and northern Mississippi. Union Pacific Railroad is the primary customer.

To move ties around the property, the tie plant used a two-foot gauge railroad. For many years, these in-plant trains were moved using small fireless locomotives that obtained their steam from the plant's main steam plant. One of the last of these was a Heisler fireless locomotive, which was scrapped in 1971.

In 1950, the railroad had a 58-car-long siding to the north of the main track, the same side as the tie plant. Several lead tracks into the tie plant broke off of this siding. At the west end of the siding was a connecting track to the St. Louis Southwestern. Union Pacific documents from the late 1980s show no changes in the track design. Today, many of these tracks are gone or unused, as Union Pacific built their own lead into the tie plant from their mainline to the north. A short piece of the siding is still in existence to handle deliveries and storage of chemical tank cars.

130.5 STLSW CROSSING – In 1904, the Railroad Commission of Arkansas called this Dixie Mills and described it as a crossing of a spur of the St. Louis Southwestern Railway (SSW). This Cotton Belt line operated under a number of different names, including the Little Rock Branch, the England Branch, and earlier as the Altheimer Branch. The rail line was built through the original charter of the Little Rock & Eastern Railway, incorporated on February 17, 1887. The purpose of the company was to build a railroad from Altheimer, on the mainline of the St. Louis, Arkansas & Texas Railway, to Argenta, (now North Little Rock), a bit more than forty miles away. On August 15, 1887, the rights and franchises of the Little Rock & Eastern (LR&E) were conveyed to the Arkansas & Southern Railway Company, which had created the LR&E to obtain permission to build the line.

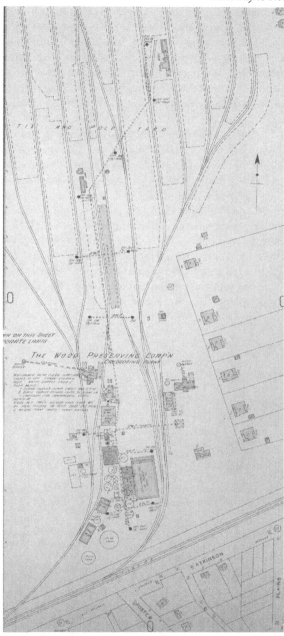

Tie plant in 1939. *Sanborn Fire Insurance Map from Little Rock, Pulaski County, Arkansas.* Sanborn Map Company, Vol. 2, 1939. Map. Retrieved from the Library of Congress, https://www.loc.gov/item/sanborn00285_008/.

On August 18, 1887, the Arkansas & Southern became an official part of the St. Louis, Arkansas & Texas Railway, and construction began, with the line being completed in 1888. While the line was built to connect the railroad with the Little Rock area, it mainly served as an agricultural line serving small farming towns. However, it did provide some competition to the Missouri Pacific (St. Louis, Iron Mountain & Southern) and Rock Island for some shippers in the North Little Rock area.

In 1985, the Cotton Belt obtained trackage rights from Baldwin, near Pine Bluff, to North Little Rock over the former Missouri Pacific Pine Bluff Subdivision. These trackage rights were part of a series of trackage rights created by the consolidation of railroad routes in the Pine Bluff area. The daily Little Rock Local began to operate on the new route, and the Little Rock Branch was served by only an occasional local. This local service ended during April 1989 and 35.8 miles of the line were abandoned on July 1, 1991. Only a few miles of the line still remain in the Sherry, Rose City, and Broadway areas of North Little Rock. The Arkansas Midland Railroad operates what is left, 6.8 miles of track as far southeast as the Tarco Roofing Plant near Interstate 440, according to several Union Pacific sources.

Arkansas Midland Railroad #2502 operates on the former Cotton Belt route just north of the Rock Island diamond at North Little Rock, Arkansas.

The Crossing Area

This area has historically been an industrial zone with a number of both large and small manufacturing and support facilities. In 1939, Fones Brothers Hardware had a warehouse north of the Rock Island and west of the Cotton Belt, served by the SSW. Across the SSW tracks to the east was the furniture manufacturing plant for Fones Brothers. The Dixie Gin Company cotton gin was across the Rock Island to the south and served by the Rock Island.

During the early 1970s, there were two interchange tracks between the Rock Island and the Cotton Belt. The first was in the northeast quadrant of the junction, allowing westbound Rock Island trains to head northwest to the Missouri Pacific North Little Rock Yard. The second interchange track was in the southwest quadrant, allowing westbound trains on the Cotton Belt to head west on the Rock Island. This was a long track that was also used to serve several shippers.

Until 1979, this was an automatic interlocking, supported by a dispatcher telephone. Cotton Belt track charts from 1982 showed that there was an industrial area along the SSW that included leads into industries listed as joint tracks between the SSW and CRI&P. The northeast quadrant track still exists, but the southwest quadrant track has been removed. A new industrial lead has been built in the southeast quadrant to serve the All American Poly facility. The 1982 SSW track charts show the Cotton Belt line to the Missouri Pacific Yard as the "Old Main."

Almost all of the buildings in the area are now gone. However, still towering over the diamond area is the abandoned W. R. Grace facility. This plant was involved with vermiculite exfoliation from at least 1953. The Environmental Protection Agency reported that W. R. Grace acquired the plant in 1964 and "approximately 85,050 tons of vermiculite were shipped from the Libby, Montana, mine to the North Little Rock facility from January 1966 to September 1989."

What is vermiculite exfoliation? Vermiculite expands greatly like popcorn when heated in furnaces with temperatures of approximately 1000-1500°F. The expanded vermiculite has a very low density and thermal conductivity. It is used as a soil amendment, lightweight construction aggregate, and thermal insulation filler. Its active surface area makes it useful as an absorbent in some chemical processes. It can also be ground into a fine powder and used as a filler in inks, paints, and plastics.

Standing north of the Rock Island-Cotton Belt diamond is the former W. R. Grace facility, once a processor of vermiculite.

131.3 BUCKEYE – Between North Palm Street (131.0) and North Buckeye Street (131.3) was once the massive Buckeye Cotton Oil Company. The Buckeye Cotton Oil Company was formed in 1901 as a subsidiary of The Procter & Gamble Company (P&G). At the time, P&G was facing shortages of cottonseed oil, used in making soap and other P&G products. To solve the problem, P&G leased a cotton seed crushing mill at West Point, Mississippi, and built a series of new mills over the next several years. Among these was the Little Rock Mill (actually located in North Little Rock), where construction began in 1902.

Over the years, P&G needed other products that could be produced at the Buckeye mills. These included cellulose and crushed soybeans at this plant. This led some records to show the plant as the Buckeye Cellulose Cotton Seed and Oil Mill. In 1992, P&G broke up Buckeye and sold it as several different divisions. Today, the Buckeye facility is mostly gone with just a few of the buildings still standing.

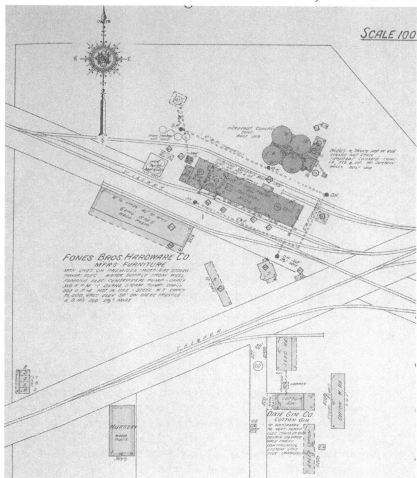

This map shows the area around the former Rock Island-Cotton Belt diamond near North Little Rock, Arkansas. *Sanborn Fire Insurance Map from Little Rock, Pulaski County, Arkansas.* Sanborn Map Company, Vol. 2, 1939. Map. Retrieved from the Library of Congress, https://www.loc.gov/item/sanborn00285_008/.

While little of the former Buckeye Cotton Oil Company remains, this towering warehouse still marks the location.

Buckeye was not the only large industry that once was here. To the south of the Rock Island was the Southern Cotton Oil Company, which manufactured cottonseed oil and meal for animal feed. The cottonseed oil was used in products like Wesson cooking oil. To the north of Buckeye was the Arkansas Fertilizer Company. A 1907 hearing by the Arkansas Railroad Commission focused on "switching cotton seed and cotton seed products from the plant of the Buckeye Cotton Oil Co., Argenta, Ark., to this plant of the complainant, the Arkansas Fertilizer Company, within the limits of the same station, a distance of about one eighth of a mile away." Apparently, the Arkansas Fertilizer Company was a customer of Buckeye and the Rock Island regularly moved freight cars between the two facilities, although sometimes at a rate and level of service that didn't please everyone. In 1939, Buckeye and Arkansas Fertilizer were both still served by the Rock Island Railroad, as well as the Cotton Belt, which reached them from the north via an industrial lead off of their Old Main track. A block to the west of Buckeye and to the north of the Rock Island was McLean Arkansas Lumber Company, built in 1916. None of these are here today.

Arkansas Midland Railroad

The Arkansas Midland Railroad has developed a number of facilities in this area. At 5th and Buckeye are the offices of the railroad, with a sign calling the small locomotive storage area the John P. Gill Yard. Gill was an area historian who worked with The Little Rock Convention & Visitors Bureau to produce several tours of the area's history. Just to the south and east of Buckeye Street is the North Little Rock Logistics Center, a transload and warehousing facility being developed by the railroad on parts of the old Buckeye Cotton Oil Company property.

This sign marks the property of the Arkansas Midland Railroad in North Little Rock, Arkansas.

131.7 END OF ARKANSAS MIDLAND RAILROAD – At North Cornish Street, the remains of the Rock Island curve north to serve the now-closed Onesource Home Building Centers lumber yard. The mainline west of here was removed by the early 1990s.

Rock Island Lines rail pass, circa 1925. From the author's collection.

GOOD OVER LINES OF
The Chicago, Rock Island & Gulf Ry.
Unless Territory Otherwise Limited
J. E. GORMAN, PRESIDENT.

RESTRICTIONS
Not Good Locally Between Chicago and Points
East of Joliet
NOT GOOD ON TRAINS 3 AND 4
Not Good on Trains 7 and 8 For Trips East of
Wilton, Ia.

This pass is a license, non-transferable and revocable without notice, which is issued gratuitously,
without any consideration whatever, to the person
or persons named hereon, and is restricted as herein
set out. Its acceptance or use is with the understanding that neither the Chicago, Rock Island &
Pacific Railway Company nor any other company
named herein shall be liable in damages for injury
to or death of the user, or for loss of or damage to
the property of the user, no matter whether such
death or injury, or loss or damage, is due to negligence or otherwise, and the user hereby releases all
claims and causes of action against said company
or companies for any such damages. This pass
must not be used in violation of law, and the user
must not be prohibited by law from receiving free
transportation.
I consent to the above restrictions.

This pass will not be honored unless signed in ink

North Little Rock (AR) to Little Rock (AR)
Abandoned

This short stretch of track was abandoned as Union Pacific did not need it. Their North Little Rock yard was the destination of trains off of the remains of the Carlisle Branch, and the costly Arkansas River Bridge and track was not justified. Only the Argenta Depot, the Arkansas River Bridge and the Choctaw Station in Little Rock still remain along this short stretch of track, although a number of grade crossings still include the rails of the former railroad.

131.7 END OF ARKANSAS MIDLAND RAILROAD – West of North Cornish Street in North Little Rock, the railroad has been removed. The tracks once continued west, running just north of East 4th Street. The abandoned track was part of Union Pacific's Carlisle Branch after it acquired the line from the Rock Island estate. The Carlisle Branch started at Biddle Yard in Little Rock, headed north across the Arkansas River and then east to Carlisle. With access to the line from their North Little Rock yard, and the west end from Biddle Yard, the costly center part across the Arkansas River was unneeded and abandoned by the early 1990s.

In this location, a series of tracks to the north of the mainline also headed west, ending at the old CRI&P freight house. The freight house was located on the northeast corner of East 4th Street and North Main in North Little Rock (Argenta), to the east of the two-story building that stands there today. Heading west from the mainline, the railroad once served the George W. Pitman wood handle factory before passing under Interstate 30. This underpass is still there and is used as a basketball court. Immediately to the west, the Rock Island had a series of diamonds across the Missouri Pacific's line to Pine Bluff and on south. The Rock Island then served the Cameron Feed Mills, located on the west side of the Missouri Pacific line and south of East 5th Street, before the line ended at Main Street. All of these tracks and industries are gone today, many being replaced by modern apartments and condominiums. However, a few of the rails can still be seen in today's streets and parking lots.

CRI&P During the Argenta Era

Before the Arkansas River bridge was built and the mainline turned south to cross it, the mainline continued west. This route connected to the St. Louis, Iron Mountain & Southern to get across the Arkansas River. The route also featured the Little Rock & Memphis Railroad shops and a number of rail customers. During late 1873, the Memphis & Little Rock Railroad was encouraged by the Cairo & Fulton to extend their track to near the Fort Smith Crossing and use the Baring Cross Bridge across the Arkansas River. An *Arkansas Gazette* advertisement announced the move.

> *Notice to Passengers – Arrangements having been made to cross the trains of this road over the Cairo and Fulton bridge, from and after this date, January 5, 1874, passengers will be received and delivered at the depot of the Cairo and Fulton, in Little Rock. A similar arrangement will be made for freight on completion of the freight depot in Little Rock, which will be within twenty or 30 days.*
> *A. S. Livermore, General Superintendent*

Almost immediately, the St. Louis, Iron Mountain & Southern attempted to prevent the M&LR from using the Baring Cross Bridge. However, in late 1877, the courts ruled against the Iron Mountain and forbade them from removing the connection between the two railroads.

In 1892, the Little Rock & Memphis Railroad had two routes through North Little Rock, then known as Argenta. Both routes connected to the St. Louis, Iron Mountain & Southern to cross the Arkansas River to reach Little Rock. One route went through town between 4th (Bulah, later Madison) and 5th (Allen) to reach the Iron Mountain, and a depot was built at Newton Street, today's Main Street. The other route turned north up Newton and then curved west through the Little Rock Oil & Compress to connect to the Iron Mountain. At the time, Little Rock Oil & Compress had both a cotton seed oil mill and stock yards. The cotton seed oil facility was where the Rock Region Metro offices and bus barns are today. By 1914, the tracks no longer went west following 4th Street.

Until about 1910, the Argenta railroad shops were not far west on this line. These shops were located east of Olive, south of Monroe, west of Locust, and north of Madison (today's 4th Street), and were originally built and owned by the Memphis & Little Rock. Today, Locust is the frontage road to the east of Interstate 30 and Olive is a block west of the Interstate, thus the freeway uses much of the site of the former Rock Island shop complex. According to an 1897 Sanborn insurance map, a lead to the turntable came in from the east, passing through a series of coal bins. Clockwise and to the south were seven tracks, and then a lead to the yard to the southwest. There was then a lead to the "Car Shop" and lumber sheds, plus a west spur into the "Machine Shop." A lead went to the northwest and passed by the "Blacksmith Shop." There were then three spur tracks to the north, and then a two-stall "Car Repair and Painting" roundhouse. The yard also featured several other buildings such as a supply warehouse, offices, and changing rooms. Starting not long after the Rock Island built its new line around Little Rock, parts of the shop were moved to the new Biddle Yard complex. By 1910, most of the shops were closed, and the location was completely cleared by 1917.

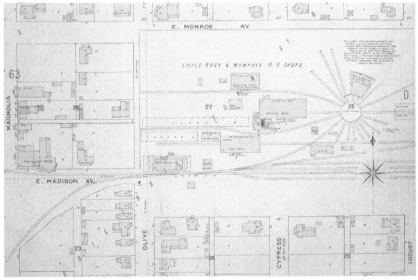

Sanborn Map of Little Rock & Memphis Railroad Shops (NLR/Argenta) – 1897. *Sanborn Fire Insurance Map from Little Rock, Pulaski County, Arkansas.* Sanborn Map Company, 1897. Map. Retrieved from the Library of Congress, https://www.loc.gov/item/sanborn00285_004/.

Besides the shops, and the nearby passenger depot, the Rock Island also once had stockyards in North Little Rock that consisted of ten pens and a quarantine area. The railroad also installed a 40-foot, 100,000-pound capacity track scale in 1921 to weigh shipments originating in the area.

131.9 NORTH LITTLE ROCK – For years, the Rock Island station was the only intercity railroad passenger station in North Little Rock. Known as the Argenta Depot, the building was built in 1912 as part of a consolation prize for losing the railroad's shops. The building was relatively small, but it featured a Mediterranean style design common in larger buildings. Located on the south side of the mainline along 4th Street, the single-story brick depot used a roughly cruciform plan, with the telegrapher's bay and corresponding cargo room on the street side forming the transept (the arms of the cross shape). Arkansas stations at Mansfield and Lonoke also featured similar designs.

The station was placed on the National Register of Historic Places in 1989, and the application includes a full description of the building. It states that there were two waiting rooms – one for whites and one for African-Americans – in the east end of the station. The waiting rooms were located to either side of the ticket window, which opened onto a hall which connected the two rooms. To the west was the separate cargo room, with cargo doors to the south and the north.

The Argenta Depot featured a gabled red tile roof with parapeted gable ends. At one time, the trackside featured a full-length porch to shelter passengers. In 1914, tracks of the local trolley system, the Intercity Terminal Company, were extended to the Rock Island depot. Rock Island passenger service continued until the station was closed in the 1960s, and all passenger services moved to the Little Rock station.

In 1977, the North Little Rock History Commission announced plans to acquire or lease the Argenta Depot, the first public attempt to preserve it. On January 23, 1985, the City of North Little Rock made a similar announcement, but still no action took place. Several more announcements were made, and by 1988, details were being finalized to turn the depot over to the City. Today, the building still features the Argenta lettering and painted Rock Island signs. It is used as a community center for the area. Note how 4th Street loops around the south side of the Argenta Station, demonstrating that the station was actually built in the middle of the street.

The basic design used for the Argenta Depot is similar to others used along the Choctaw Route. Like many others, this station sits beside an abandoned grade instead of an active railroad.

The depot at North Little Rock still displays the Argenta lettering, typical of many of the stations built along the line.

Argenta

The area known as North Little Rock has gone through a number of names and organizations. At first, it was just a collection of homes, sheds and docks along the Arkansas River, across from the state capital of Little Rock. By 1838, several investors created the Town of D'Cantillon on the north side of the Arkansas River, "immediately opposite the State-house." However, much of the town soon washed away. With the Memphis & Little Rock reaching here, the area became very important during the Civil War. The Confederate States of American first developed the site as a supply depot, and when captured by Union forces in 1863, the facilities were further expanded. These facilities included a large railroad terminal and roundhouse, ferry and ship docks, and a number of warehouses. During this time, the community became known as Huntersville, believed by some to be a kind of insult about how less sophisticated the residents were compared to the capital city. However, at least one newspaper report from early 1865 referred to a Mr. Hunter, "of railroad and stage office notoriety." Apparently, the Union military superintendent of the railroad was William Hunter, and some believe that his name was used for the community which grew up around the Union facilities.

By the early 1870s, Huntersville was the terminus of three railroads, causing the community to grow. A plat for the City of Argenta was created in March 1866, and a post office opened on April 18, 1871, using the name Argenta. The term argenta comes from the Latin word for silver, Argentum. The idea for the name Argenta came from Colonel Robert C. Newton, the son of Thomas Newton, a farmer and president of the Arkansas Mining Company. There were reports that the mining company had found some silver in their Kellogg Mine, located just north of Argenta. By Spring 1872, the Memphis & Little Rock Railroad was using the name Argenta for the community.

In 1890, an effort was made to incorporate the City of Argenta, but Little Rock annexed the area before the incorporation could take place. The case went to the Arkansas Supreme Court, but the annexation was found to be legal. In March 1903, the Hoxie-Walnut Ridge Bill was passed that allowed the annexation or consolidation of cities within one mile of each other as long as the residents of both cities approved. Land just north of Argenta was incorporated as North Little Rock, and efforts immediately began to annex the Argenta part of Little Rock. A July 1903 election resulted in the merger, and Little Rock was again located just south of the Arkansas River. The city became North Little Rock in 1904, back to Argenta in 1906, and then finally back to North Little Rock during October 1917.

Today, North Little Rock is the home of Union Pacific's Jenks Shops and the North Little Rock Hump Yard. It is also the home of about 70,000 residents, making it the seventh-most populous city in Arkansas. While mainly a residential city with plenty of shopping, it is an important transportation junction for rail and highway, with Interstates 30 and 40 meeting here, as well as U.S. Highway 67. It is also the home of what is believed to be the last structure used in the movie *Gone with the Wind* – the Old Mill – now the site of more than 200 weddings and the destination of more than 100,000 visitors each year. There are few sources better for the entire history of North Little Rock than the book *North Little Rock: The Unique City* by Walter Adams.

The Argenta Railroad Shops and Mainline

The Memphis & Little Rock Railroad had some sort of railroad shop at Argenta (North Little Rock) since the railroad was built. Until the late 1860s, the Memphis & Little Rock was still actually two lines, consisting of the eastern tracks based at Hopefield, and the western lines based at Argenta, which didn't even have that name yet. Few reports about the details of these early shops have been found, except that a number of improvements were made by the U.S. Military Railroad during the Civil War.

Several newspaper statements put the initial Memphis & Little Rock shops on the north side of the Arkansas River, "almost opposite the little rock." These shops reportedly included a turntable connecting an engine house and a small machine shop. Reports also placed the "little ramshackle railroad station" about 2000 feet to the east.

The Union Army took charge of the railroad at North Little Rock on September 10, 1863. Because of the volume of use and the effort by the Confederates to destroy the railroad shops, the Union Army added a new six-stall roundhouse and a machine shop to the railroad's facilities. Near the depot, warehouses and corrals were built. Reports indicate that until May 1, 1865, the railroad was operated by the Quartermaster Corps of the Union Army, with the U.S. Military Railroad taking over after that. By December, the military had many of their facilities for sale. These included a 160' x 54' warehouse, four mess houses, and a 360' x 80' covered freight platform with five railroad offices.

A March 1866 plat map for Argenta showed the "Depot Grounds of the Memphis and Little Rock R.R." south of Arkansas Street (today called Brother Paul Drive). The grounds were located between Goodson (today's Olive Street) and Woodruff (today's Locust Street) streets. This area is under the north end of the Interstate 30 Arkansas River bridge.

Historical marker along the River Trail just west of Main Street Bridge in North Little Rock. Photo by David Vogt.

One of the first detailed reports on the Argenta Shops can be found in the *Daily Arkansas Gazette* (February 16, 1873). This article is basically a report on a tour that one or more employees of the newspaper took of the shops. This report is included here.

> At Argenta, on the other side of the river, are situated the repair shops of the Memphis and Little Rock Railroad company, and they are no small item of interest to this city. The shops embrace a machine shop, carpenter shop, blacksmith's shop, engine room, and steel and iron store room, all of which are under the control and management of Thomas Reynolds, master mechanic. Our reporter first visited the carpenter shop, over which Mr. Preston Twitchell presides, and found there at work about eighteen carpenters in the different branches of car building and repairing. There are now building in the shop three freight cars and a caboose, with the new style of zinc roofs. The company do not pretend to manufacture their own cars, being able to buy them much cheaper than they can be made here. The shop is 200 feet in length by 60 in width, and contains the latest machinery used in the business, among which are planers of the Dainels

[sic] and cylinder make. Adjoining the carpenter shop is the steel and iron store room, a building 20x30 feet, in which are stored all the surplus iron and steel owned by the company. The blacksmith shop, although a dirty smoky place, is not uninteresting. The "bone and sinew" of the land is there displayed. At present the force is employed in making locomotive springs.

The engine room, in which is the power of the whole establishment, is of especial interest. The engine is from the Metropolitan works, Richmond, Va.; 50-horse power, with a 24-inch cylinder, and is nearly new. In this room is a powerful force pump, by the aid of which water is brought from the river and placed in the water tank in the yard. And now, last but not least comes the machine shop, in which ten skillful machinists display their ingenuity. Among the machinery we noticed lathes, planers, bolt cutters and a wheel press. The locomotives Nos. 6, 7, 8 and 9, which have all been badly wrecked by running into the ditch, have come out of this shop almost as good as new. In front of the round house a fine cast iron turn-table was observed. The Huntsville, a little engine purchased from the Memphis and Charleston company, does the necessary switching. In these shops there are about sixty hard-working mechanics, just such citizens as Little Rock is in need of, and we hope it will not be long before there will be more of these establishments in our city. We learn from the master mechanic that the rolling stock of the road, at present, consists of fourteen locomotives, ten passenger cars, and two hundred freight cars, all of which are in almost daily use. Mr. Twitchell, the boss carpenter in these shops, claims for himself the credit of building the first two passengers cars in this state. They are at present running on the road. We would recommend such of our citizens as take an interest in the industries of the city to take a look through these very extensive shops.

It didn't take long for changes to occur at the Argenta shops. A fire in late January 1875 started in the stationery engine room and burned down the engine room, blacksmith shop, machine shop, the 10-stall roundhouse, and the 200' x 45' carpenter building. Additionally, locomotive No. 6, locomotive No. 8's tender, and baggage car No. 2 were also burned, although employees were able to save several other locomotives by running them out of the shops. The shops soon reopened using temporary buildings.

It took a few years, but in 1878, the Memphis & Little Rock announced plans for new shops at Argenta. The first step was the purchase of 30 acres, with today's Olive Street to the west and Locust Street to the east, and between Fourth and Fifth Streets. This property was to the north of the original shop area which was near the Arkansas River. Today, Interstate 30 uses much of this new shop property, with the warehouse of Halbert Pipe & Steel using much of the rest.

The new shops were to include a 15-stall roundhouse and turntable, machine shop (120' x 52'), blacksmith shop (50' x 80'), car shop (100' x 50'), stationary engine house (24' x 30'), and an elevated water tank. Plans were also announced to straighten the mainline along the river to direct it toward the new shops. By October of 1878, the new shops were open and the old shops near the river had been torn down. However, the original ticket and telegraph office were kept where they were.

These new shops apparently were productive for the railroad as the company even built several wooden passenger cars about 1880. The cars were 52 feet long and used six axles. The Memphis & Little Rock boasted that the cars were built of Arkansas wood such as pine, oak, poplar, walnut and ash. The shop also built wooden freight cars and rebuilt a number of locomotives, changing them from burning wood to burning coal.

The new Argenta Shops became the west end of the Memphis & Little Rock Railroad. However, the railroad wanted to directly serve Little Rock. Trains of the Cairo, Arkansas & Texas Railroad (later Missouri Pacific) reached the Arkansas River at today's North Little Rock on January 11, 1873. The Baring Cross Bridge was built across the Arkansas River by December 20th of the same year. This provided an opportunity for the M&LR to reach Little Rock.

The railroad built west through what is today downtown North Little Rock, passing just south of the Federal Building (Old Post Office) on Main Street. At today's Willow Street, the Memphis & Little Rock entered property owned by the Cairo, Arkansas & Texas Railroad (CA&T), and then curved south to join the CA&T about where the Fourth Street underpass exists today. The route can still be found where tracks curve east off of the mainline just north of Union Pacific's Fourth Street offices. The CA&T became part of the St. Louis, Iron Mountain & Southern, which forced the Little Rock & Memphis out of its Little Rock Station in 1893. Within a few years, the Iron Mountain also forced the abandonment of the tracks west of Willow Street. The tracks were removed all the way east to the feed mill, located a block east of Main Street.

This action eventually led to plans to extend the Little Rock & Memphis through Little Rock and on west using its own route. This was accelerated when the Choctaw & Memphis Railroad acquired the Little Rock & Memphis Railroad on October 25, 1898. As a bridge over the

Arkansas River was being built, rumors began that the Argenta Shops would be closed and moved to Little Rock. Several meetings of Argenta citizens were held in 1899, with the purpose of "securing the retention of the Choctaw and Memphis railway shops." Choctaw & Memphis general manager Henry Wood promised that the shops would stay in Argenta if the community matched a $50,000 and land offer from another nearby place (probably Little Rock). Argenta citizens raised $10,000 and the railroad promised that the shops would stay where they were.

Notice to the Traveling Public.
Change of Passenger Depots, Little Rock

Having abandoned the Newton Avenue station, Argenta, effective December 10, all Choctaw Route trains will arrive and depart from the passenger station, Third and McLean streets. As soon as possible a passenger depot for the use of residents of the North Side will be erected between Cedar and Walnut streets.
J. F. Holden, Traffic Manager
John H. Harris, General Superintendent

This December 10, 1899, notice was the start of moving the base of operations from Argenta (North Little Rock) to Little Rock. A new passenger station was opened about four blocks south of the Choctaw bridge in 1899. Things remained quiet for several more years, but an article in the May 7, 1904, issue of the *Arkansas Gazette* again stated that there was no basis for the rumors that the shops would be moved. However, by August, the Argenta Shops were closed temporarily due to an economic slowdown. Concern about the future of the shops wasn't helped when the old master mechanic office building was moved from the shops to Fourth and Magnolia Streets in Argenta to be used as a freight depot. Next, some of the equipment from the machine shops was shipped to the shops at Haileyville, Indian Territory. Over the next several years, the rumors were reported on more and more frequently with repeated denials by the railroad.

By 1907, construction on the new Biddle Yard in Little Rock was underway. A report late in 1908 stated that Biddle Yard would become the primary yard in the area and that the yard at Argenta would be designated an industrial yard and the Argenta roundhouse would be shut down. However, business picked up and the shops at Argenta remained, even receiving a new 70-foot turntable at the roundhouse. Other improvements were made at Argenta in 1909, including new flooring in the roundhouse and a new employee washroom with lockers. But comments were being made that the Argenta Shops were in the wrong location to handle the "New Orleans" and "Louisiana" traffic hitting the mainline at Hot Springs Junction.

In 1912, the Chicago, Rock Island & Pacific announced plans to build a new brick passenger depot in North Little Rock (Argenta), but on November 1, 1912, the railroad began moving trainmen and their families to Little Rock. The new Argenta station opened by the end of the year and most of the Argenta Shop forces were transferred to Little Rock in June 1913. A few employees remained at Argenta to handle car repairs in a series of new car sheds. These employees were moved to Biddle by 1918, and in June, the city council of North Little Rock ordered the railroad to remove the abandoned shop buildings and tracks, ending the history of the Argenta Railroad Shops.

The New Line

The new 1899 mainline passed today's Argenta Depot and then curved to the south to cross the Arkansas River. The curve measured seven degrees, one of the sharpest on the line. The line climbed about ten feet to reach the Arkansas River Bridge, first using a long timber trestle. Later, the grade was filled, leaving just a few bridges over various streets.

Three streets were crossed by the new fill, initially using the timber trestles. However, steel bridges were quickly installed. East Broadway (Milepost 132.2), originally East 3rd Street, was an 82-foot-long steel and concrete viaduct. East 2nd Street (Milepost 132.3) was crossed using a 68-foot-long concrete viaduct. Finally, East Washington Street (Milepost 132.4) was a 60-foot steel viaduct, installed in November 1906. The river bridge then began, crossing over East Arkansas Street, now named Brother Paul Drive. This street was interesting as the Cotton Belt ran down the middle of the street to reach its passenger station in Argenta. The Cotton Belt built a new passenger station and freight station that opened on August 1, 1910, ending service to the Little Rock Union Station via the Iron Mountain's Baring Cross Bridge. The new station was located at Washington and Orange streets, next to the Main Street bridge. Passenger service didn't last long, ending on December 9, 1928, when buses replaced the train service. By the 1960s, the station was being used as a warehouse. The passenger station burned on July 2, 1967, and was removed. The freight house came down in late 1971 as part of an urban renewal project.

The Automatic Block System (ABS) signals on the Rock Island that started at Briark ended at Milepost 132.3 as the railroad approached the Arkansas River Bridge.

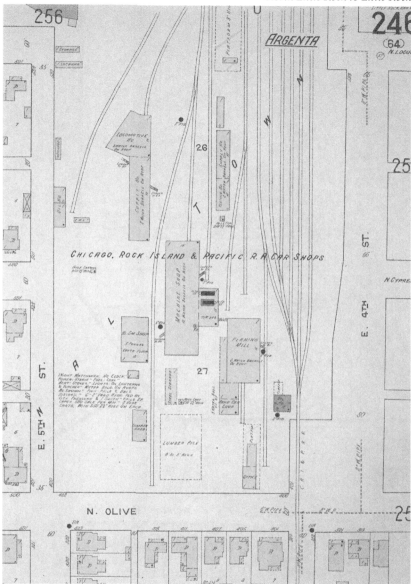

Sanborn Map of CRI&P Car Shops (NLR/Argenta) – 1913. *Sanborn Fire Insurance Map from Little Rock, Pulaski County, Arkansas.* Sanborn Map Company, Vol.1, 1913. Map. Retrieved from the Library of Congress, https://www.loc.gov/item/sanborn00285_005/.

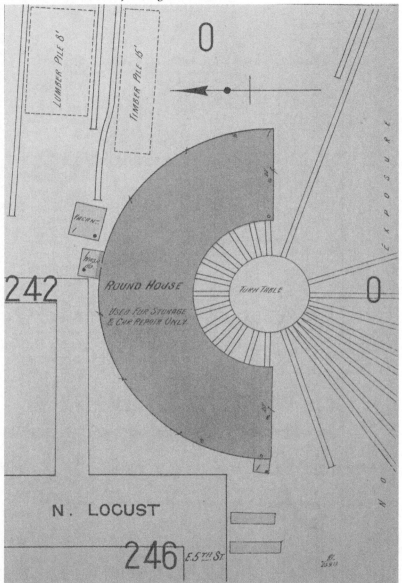

Sanborn Map of CRI&P Roundhouse (NLR/Argenta) – 1913. *Sanborn Fire Insurance Map from Little Rock, Pulaski County, Arkansas.* Sanborn Map Company, Vol.1, 1913. Map. Retrieved from the Library of Congress, https://www.loc.gov/item/sanborn00285_005/.

132.5 CHOCTAW ARKANSAS RIVER BRIDGE – This bridge was an essential component of the new Choctaw Route through Little Rock, Arkansas. The railroad quickly applied to Congress for approval to build the bridge, and on December 20, 1898, the Committee on Interstate and Foreign Commerce authorized the Choctaw & Memphis Railroad Company to construct the bridge across the Arkansas River. On January 10, 1899, Congress made their final approval, and the Secretary of War approved the plans on March 1, 1899.

To build the bridge, the Little Rock Bridge Company was created. According to the 1907 *Moody's Manual of Railroads and Corporation Securities*, the Little Rock Bridge Company issued $375,000 in 20-year bonds on June 19, 1899. *Moody's* stated that the bonds were "Secured by first lien on bridge and appurtenances across the Arkansas River at Little Rock, Ark." By late 1899, the Little Rock Bridge Company was rolled into the Choctaw & Memphis Railroad.

Articles in *The Railway and Engineering Review* (April 8, 1899) and *The Railroad Gazette* (April 14, 1899) provided more detail. Both articles stated that McGee, Kahmann & Co., had the contract to build the bridge. The company was based in Kansas City and was involved in building a number of railroads across the region. *The Railroad Gazette* article provided more detail, including that McGee, Kahmann & Co., was responsible for the substructure. It also stated that the Pencoyd Iron Works has the contract for the superstructure, which included "four spans of 400 ft. each."

The Pencoyd Iron Works came about from the success of the A. & P. Roberts Company, a specialty iron foundry. They had the contract to manufacture the structural elements of the Main Exhibition Building and Machinery Hall at the 1876 Centennial Exposition. At the time, it was the largest building in the world. The firm was also building bridge components, and soon became the Pencoyd Iron Works. The company was bought by J. P. Morgan in 1900 as a part of his creation of the American Bridge Company. This new firm was assembled from 28 existing bridge companies and was soon part of United States Steel. The Pencoyd Iron Works facility was closed during the 1940s and torn down in the 1950s.

When built, the Arkansas River Bridge was described as having four 14-panel Pennsylvania through truss spans, measuring 1614 feet long. The first train crossed the bridge on December 10, 1899, and it became the main route for all trains on the Choctaw Route and also provided a connection to the Rock Island lines in southern Arkansas and northern Louisiana.

The bridge included a turn span to allow tall ships to pass through the structure. However, reports indicate that the bridge was seldom opened. A 1955 article in the *Arkansas Gazette* stated that the bridge had only been opened twice since 1938, and that during January 1953, the bridge became stuck when being opened for a pile driver going up river. It apparently took three days to actually open the turn span. As a result, the Army Corps of Engineers required a 48-hour notice from any boat needing the bridge to be opened.

In 1972, the third span from the north end (railroad-east) was replaced with a 12-panel, polygonal Warren through truss vertical lift span. The lift span was part of the work to make the Arkansas River navigable. The bridge remained in service until the early 1980s when the Rock Island was liquidated in bankruptcy and the bridge was acquired by the Union Pacific.

The Arkansas River Bridge was rebuilt in 1972 with a lift span. This view from downstream shows the difference in the design of the lift span versus the traditional Pennsylvania through truss spans. Note that the lift span is now permanently raised and the bridge deck has been rebuilt to allow the Arkansas River Trail to use it to cross the river.

During Fall 1989, all of the trestles off the north end of the bridge were removed, but work on the main bridge was stopped due to the need for Corps of Engineers permitting. With the trestles removed, the railroad sold the property from the river to a block north of Broadway in January 1990. In February 1990, Union Pacific announced plans to dismantle the old Chicago, Rock Island & Pacific bridge over the Arkansas River, but the work was not undertaken.

As the Clinton Presidential Center was being planned, it was decided that the former Rock Island and Missouri Pacific tracks on the south side of the Arkansas River were in the way. By this time, they were all owned by Union Pacific, which sold the tracks and property along the Little Rock riverfront and in the area of the Clinton Presidential Center for $3 million during late December 2001. As a part of the deal, the railroad included the Missouri Pacific Junction Bridge and the Rock Island Bridge for free. Little Rock became the bridge's owner on December 27, 2001. It was rebuilt at a cost of $10.5 million for pedestrian use as a part of the Clinton Presidential Center, and tied into the Arkansas River Trail. It reopened on October 1, 2011, but as a trail instead of a railroad bridge.

The Arkansas River Bridge has been rebuilt to allow the Arkansas River Trail to use it to cross the river. This ramp takes users up to the deck of the raised span.

The Arkansas River

The Arkansas River is a 1469-mile tributary of the Mississippi River, flowing from Lake County, Colorado, near Leadville, southeast across Kansas, Oklahoma and Arkansas until entering the Mississippi River at Napoleon, Arkansas. The river is the second-longest tributary of the Mississippi-Missouri River system, the sixth-longest river in the country, and the 45th longest river in the world. The Arkansas River was

217

once the border between the United States and Mexico, as created by the Adams-Onís Treaty of 1821. This ended with the Texas Annexation, also known as the Treaty of Guadalupe Hidalgo.

The Arkansas River is now used by the McClellan-Kerr Arkansas River Navigation System. The commercial river was named for Senators John L. McClellan of Arkansas, and Robert S. Kerr of Oklahoma. The work by the U.S. Corps of Engineers has made the river navigable from the Mississippi River as far west as the Tulsa Port of Catoosa. The McClellan-Kerr System officially opened on June 5, 1971, with President Richard M. Nixon attending the opening ceremony.

Arkansas River Trail

This series of trails connects parts of Little Rock and North Little Rock using a core trail alongside the Arkansas River. Much of the route generally parallels the former Rock Island Railroad westward to Pinnacle Mountain State Park. The original trail contained 16 miles of walkways from the Rock Island Bridge (Clinton Bridge) westward to the Two Rivers Park Bridge alongside the Rock Island line at Interstate 430. The trail has since been extended to Pinnacle Mountain State Park with many branches and plans for additional routes. In 2011, the American Automobile Association *Southern Traveler* magazine declared the Arkansas River Trail to be the "Best Bike Trail in the South."

132.8 MOPAC CROSSING – Immediately south of the Arkansas River Bridge, the Rock Island crossed a Missouri Pacific line. The crossing had an automatic interlocking in 1979, but a switch tower in the northeast quadrant in 1913, using the station code of UX in 1950. This line was originally the Little Rock, Mississippi River & Texas Railway, built in several parts over a decade.

This rail line's history began with the Mississippi, Ouachita & Red River Railroad Company (MO&RR). The MO&RR was the first Arkansas railroad under construction. It was officially chartered in Arkansas on January 22, 1855, although some sources state it was chartered in 1852. The railroad completed about seven miles of track westward from the Mississippi River at Ferguson's Point before the Civil War. Following the war, land grants were issued, but by 1871, only twenty-nine miles of track were in operation between Chicot and Collins, Arkansas, and another forty miles were graded, bridged, and tied. However, money soon ran out and bills could not be paid.

On November 24, 1868, the Little Rock, Pine Bluff & New Orleans Railroad Company (LRPB&NO) was chartered. In 1870, the company was planning a line between New Orleans and Pine Bluff, and 55 miles of track was graded, bridged and tied, with 16 miles of track in place. The company promised that the line would be completed in March, 1871. This didn't come true, and by 1872, the company was in financial trouble with about 65 miles of track completed between Chicot and Pine Bluff.

On November 11, 1873, the MO&RR and the LRPB&NO were merged to create the Texas, Mississippi & Northwestern Railroad Company (TM&NW). This plan didn't work, and the TM&NW was sold at foreclosure to the bondholders on December 16, 1875, and then to the Little Rock, Mississippi River & Texas Railway (LRMR&T) on December 18, 1875. New construction didn't take place for a while, but the railroad was extended to Little Rock by 1881, when passenger service to Little Rock Union Depot began via a riverfront line. On January 28, 1887, the LRMR&T was acquired by the St. Louis, Iron Mountain & Southern Railway, and eventually Missouri Pacific and then Union Pacific. During the 1980s, this was Union Pacific's Rock Street Industrial Lead.

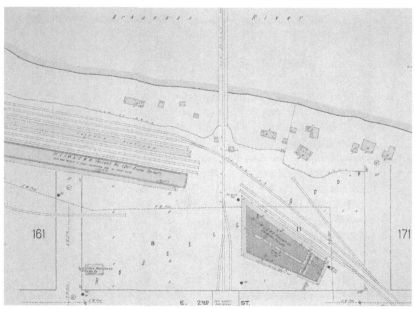

Sanborn Map of MOPAC Crossing at Little Rock – 1913. *Sanborn Fire Insurance Map from Little Rock, Pulaski County, Arkansas.* Sanborn Map Company, Vol.1, 1913. Map. Retrieved from the Library of Congress, https://www.loc.gov/item/sanborn00285_005/.

This area was a busy one for both railroads with freight houses and passenger stations within feet of the diamond. The St. Louis, Iron Mountain & Southern had two freight houses here. To the east was the inbound freight house, a relatively small and compact building served by two spur tracks. To the west was the larger outbound freight terminal which had four spur tracks and a long covered shed and building. This complex was located north of East Second Street and east of Collins Street. It would be on the south side of today's President Clinton Avenue.

East Second Street Bridge

For years, East Second Street bridged across the railroad using a concrete arch bridge, built in 1915 and paid for by the Rock Island Railroad. The Historic American Engineering Record conducted a study on the bridge after the railroad shut down, and produced the following statement about its significance.

> *Almost certainly designed by the bridge engineers of the Chicago, Rock Island and Pacific Railroad Company, the bridge over their lines at Second Street is one of the most important small bridges in the state. Its pony arch construction is unique in Arkansas, and its early date, 1915, precedes the period when such through arch concrete structures became comparatively popular.*

The bridge was built by the Fox Construction Company of El Reno, Oklahoma. The company built a number of structures along the Choctaw Route, including parts of the new terminal built in Memphis. Fox Construction Company advertised as a general railroad contractor providing crushed stone, ballast, grading and concrete work in the *Rock Island Employes' Magazine*. Like many of the other historic structures in the area, the East Second Street Bridge was removed during the early 2000s for the construction of the William J. Clinton Presidential Center and Park.

The Historic American Engineering Record report included a number of photos of the East Second Street Bridge. This view is from the northeast and includes the Rock Island's Little Rock Station in the background. Historic American Engineering Record, C., Chicago, R. I. &. P. R. C. & Fox Construction Company. (1968) *Second Street Bridge, Spanning Union Pacific Railroad lines, Little Rock, Pulaski County, AR.* Pulaski County Arkansas Little Rock, 1968. Documentation Compiled After. Photograph. Retrieved from the Library of Congress, https://www.loc.gov/item/ar0099/.

132.9 LITTLE ROCK (RK) – This area today cannot be recognized except for the former Choctaw Station (station code DS in 1950), as the entire area from the Arkansas River south to 5th Avenue has been razed for the William J. Clinton Presidential Center and Park. Clinton was the 42nd President of the United States, serving from 1993 until 2001. Ground breaking for the complex took place on December 5, 2001, and it was dedicated on November 18, 2004, during a major event that featured musical and dance acts, celebrities, and four former presidents. The facility contains 2 million photographs, 80 million pages of documents, 21 million e-mail messages, and 79,000 artifacts from the Clinton presidency. Additional facilities are also here, including the Heifer Village and Urban Farm located on East Third Street, which used to dead end at the railroad, but was extended eastward for the project.

This photo from the Historic American Engineering Record looks down upon the Rock Island station from the East Second Street Bridge. Historic American Engineering Record, C., Chicago, R. I. &. P. R. C. & Fox Construction Company. (1968) *Second Street Bridge, Spanning Union Pacific Railroad lines, Little Rock, Pulaski County, AR.* Pulaski County Arkansas Little Rock, 1968. Documentation Compiled After. Photograph. Retrieved from the Library of Congress, https://www.loc.gov/item/ar0099/.

A controversy came about during the planning for the Presidential Center as a number of historic buildings were in the area and were to be torn down to make way for the complex. Of these, only the Choctaw Station was saved, converted into the Clinton School of Public Service.

Choctaw Station

Located just south of East 2nd Street, which bridged over the tracks, was the Choctaw Station. In September 1899, the Choctaw & Memphis purchased the old Little Rock Infirmary property on Second Street, installing the railroad's general offices in the former Alexander George house. More property was acquired for freight and passenger stations, rail yards, and other facilities. In 1899, the Choctaw, Oklahoma & Gulf Railroad opened the station to serve Little Rock. The building featured a central two-story concourse. This was the most decorated part of the station, with terra cotta frieze surrounding the second story. Off each end of the station were smaller one-story wings. When opened, the building was described as being one of the architecturally finest stations in Arkansas.

The main two-story structure measures 125 feet by 56 feet. The central part served as the ticket office and waiting rooms. The restaurant and dining hall filled the area to the north (railroad-east) while the baggage room was to the south (railroad-west). The second floor was used as general offices, as were the one-story wings. There was also a one-story porch that covered the passenger platforms along the east side (track-side) of the building.

Passenger service used the station until the Rock Island ended it in November 1967. The building was soon abandoned and sold for other uses. The station was listed on the National Register of Historic Places in 1975, owned by the Arkansas Building Company according to various reports. It was also once owned by the *Arkansas Gazette* newspaper.

The former Rock Island station in Little Rock still proudly displays its "The Choctaw Route" lettering.

The Choctaw Station now serves as the Clinton School of Public Service.

On October 14, 1990, the Choctaw Railway Station opened as the Spaghetti Warehouse, part of a national restaurant chain. The company spent $2 million to restore and alter the building. One feature of the restaurant was the 1924 Pullman car *Mount Sheridan*, which was used as a private dining room. The *Mount Sheridan* had once operated on the St. Louis Southwestern train *Lone Star* between Memphis and Shreveport. This means that the car had operated over the eastern end of the Rock Island for decades. The car was retired in 1952 and was used as an SSW instruction car. It then was sold to an individual in Oklahoma before coming to Little Rock's Spaghetti Warehouse. The restaurant closed on February, 4, 1996, after sales had dropped by more than a third. The building later was the home of The Edge nightclub. Now it houses the classrooms of the Clinton School of Public Service.

1940 - The Chicago, Rock Island & Pacific Railroad (CRI&P) unveiled the first diesel-powered streamlined train, which was called the Choctaw Rocket. The Choctaw Rocket Pullford-Standard was the first streamliner to operate out of Memphis and the first to operate in Arkansas.

As a part of the creation of the Clinton Presidential Center and Park, a number of signs about the area's railroad history were erected. However, they don't always have the details correct. For example, this sign uses the name "Pullford-Standard" instead of "Pullman-Standard."

Choctaw Freight Terminal

The Choctaw Freight Terminal was a sad part of the construction of the William J. Clinton Presidential Center and Park, and deserves having the full story told. Over the years, the Rock Island and its predecessors had three freight houses in Little Rock. The first one was actually located north of Union Depot (today's Amtrak station) at North and Victory streets, on the west side of downtown. This structure was built when the Little Rock & Memphis was using the Baring Cross Bridge to reach Little Rock. The railroad moved out of the building in 1896. It was being used by the Little Rock Wheelbarrow Manufacturing Company when it burned down on December 4, 1899.

When the Choctaw Passenger Station opened, the freight station in Argenta (North Little Rock) was still being used. However, a new Little Rock freight terminal was needed to transfer freight between railroad boxcars and wagons or trucks, and a contract was issued to C. W. Clark of Malvern to build the new facility just east of the passenger station, a structure designed by future Arkansas governor George Washington Donaghey, who designed a number of structures along the Choctaw, Oklahoma & Gulf Railroad. The building, which measured 40 feet by 215 feet, was noted for its distinctive brick work, including Gothic arches and Florentine patterns over the doorways and windows. The fancy brickwork was credited to free former slaves who hand cut each brick to create the designs. With great ceremony, the freight house opened on April 9, 1900.

225

When the freight house and passenger station were completed, the area was a very busy rail terminal. There were twelve tracks here, with two mainline tracks to the west. To their east were four tracks in a small yard used to switch both passenger and freight trains. Further to the east were six tracks used by the freight house, or to hold cars for other local customers.

Business grew quickly, and by 1910, a new freight station was needed, which opened in 1911. This new freight terminal was located west of the passenger station between 3rd and 4th Streets, where the *Arkansas Democrat* buildings were built and stand today. The new Rock Island freight station was twice as big as the original Little Rock complex, being 46 feet wide and 500 feet long. The westernmost part of the structure featured a 46 foot by 100 foot two-story area that included office space for Rock Island freight clerks. The railroad tracks were along the north side of the building, and several covered platforms allowed access to more tracks and rail cars. More platforms were built in 1926 to allow the loading and unloading of automobiles in boxcars. By the 1960s, the complex was unused, and it was acquired by the *Arkansas Gazette* in 1968.

When the new freight house opened, the old freight house building from 1900 was leased to a variety of businesses and used as a warehouse or for equipment storage. For many years, the building and its six stub tracks, which came from the south, were leased by the Reaves Transfer Company.

During the late 1930s, Fisher Cement & Roofing Company leased the building. Fisher used the second floor for their offices and stored building materials in the former freight area. The office space on the first floor was used by the Rock Island to store equipment. May Supply Company leased the building in 1944, acquired a long term lease on March 1, 1947, and soon built an addition to the building for office space. In 1961, the 1900-era freight house was acquired by May Supply. In 1962, May Supply built a larger building around part of the freight house, both hiding it from public view and preserving it. In 2001, the Choctaw Freight House again became public as the May Supply Company complex was being torn down for the Clinton Presidential Center. With the historic nature of the building, a number of preservationists, including the National Trust for Historic Preservation, tried to save the structure, but to no avail as it was torn down on November 21, 2001, the day after Thanksgiving. Reportedly, the destruction of the freight terminal was hastened by a court hearing at the request of the Friends of the Choctaw Terminal, where a restraining order to block the demolition of the building was being discussed. At the time of its demolition, the Choctaw Freight House was the last surviving example of a traditional two-story brick freight station in Arkansas. The nearby Alexander George house, once the Choctaw, Oklahoma & Gulf's general office building, was another historic building connected to the railroad that was torn down quickly for the project.

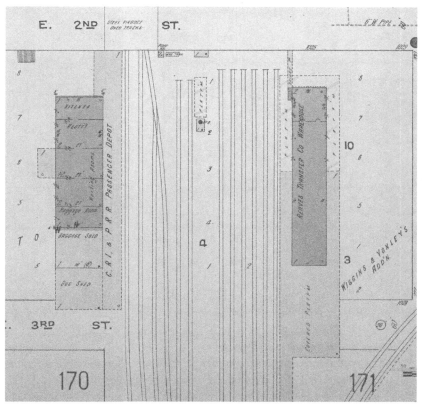

Sanborn Map of CRIP Station at Little Rock – 1913. *Sanborn Fire Insurance Map from Little Rock, Pulaski County, Arkansas.* Sanborn Map Company, Vol.1, 1913. Map. Retrieved from the Library of Congress, https://www.loc.gov/item/sanborn00285_005/.

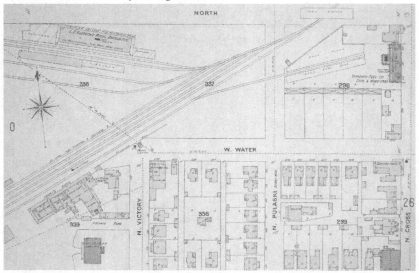

Sanborn Map of Original 1897 CRIP Freighthouse at Little Rock – 1897. *Sanborn Fire Insurance Map from Little Rock, Pulaski County, Arkansas.* Sanborn Map Company, 1897. Map. Retrieved from the Library of Congress, https://www.loc.gov/item/sanborn00285_004/.

City of Little Rock

Little Rock is located on the south bank of the Arkansas River near the center of the State of Arkansas. It serves as the county seat of Pulaski County and the capital of Arkansas. With a population of about 200,000, it is the most populous city in the state. Spanish explorer Hernando de Soto crossed parts of Arkansas in 1541, but did not reach the Little Rock area. However, French explorer Bernard de la Harpe did in 1722 while surveying the Arkansas River. He found a bluff here that he named La Petite Roch, or "The Little Rock." A rock located here is still recognized as the official La Petite Roch, and is a significant tourist attraction.

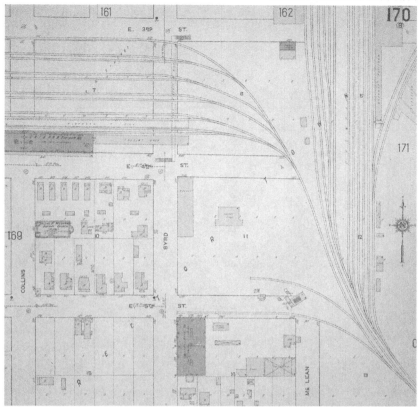

Sanborn Map of New 1911 CRIP Freighthouse at Little Rock – 1913. *Sanborn Fire Insurance Map from Little Rock, Pulaski County, Arkansas.* Sanborn Map Company, Vol.1, 1913. Map. https://www.loc.gov/item/sanborn00285_005/.

The bluff noted by La Harpe was the first significant rock outcropping on the Arkansas River and was near a Quapaw Indian settlement and a popular river crossing, so he established a trading post here. The trading post attracted settlers, and when Arkansas became a territory in 1819, it was one of the largest communities in the territory. However, the capital was located at the older community of Arkansas Post until 1821 when it moved to Little Rock. On June 1, 1821, the community was officially founded, but there were some fights about its name. While Little Rock was popular, the name Arkopolis was also popular and appeared on several maps published by the U.S. Geological Survey. Little Rock was incorporated as a town on November 7, 1831, and a city on November 2, 1835. It became the capital of the State of Arkansas on June 15, 1836.

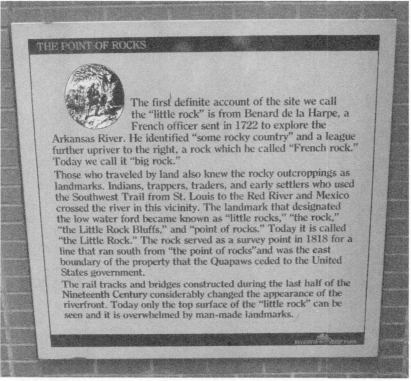

THE POINT OF ROCKS

The first definite account of the site we call the "little rock" is from Benard de la Harpe, a French officer sent in 1722 to explore the Arkansas River. He identified "some rocky country" and a league further upriver to the right, a rock which he called "French rock." Today we call it "big rock."

Those who traveled by land also knew the rocky outcroppings as landmarks. Indians, trappers, traders, and early settlers who used the Southwest Trail from St. Louis to the Red River and Mexico crossed the river in this vicinity. The landmark that designated the low water ford became known as "little rocks," "the rock," "the Little Rock Bluffs," and "point of rocks." Today it is called "the Little Rock." The rock served as a survey point in 1818 for a line that ran south from "the point of rocks" and was the east boundary of the property that the Quapaws ceded to the United States government.

The rail tracks and bridges constructed during the last half of the Nineteenth Century considerably changed the appearance of the riverfront. Today only the top surface of the "little rock" can be seen and it is overwhelmed by man-made landmarks.

A number of signs along the riverfront explain the history of Little Rock, including this one about The Little Rock.

133.1 NORTH END CARLISLE BRANCH – The railroad still has some industrial customers south of here, so the railroad was preserved to this point, located about East 4th Street. For many years, even this stub of track was still shown to be the Carlisle Branch.

In this area is the World & 3rd Street stop of the Metro Streetcar system. This is the end of the line that serves the Clinton Presidential Center and Park. The River Rail Streetcar originally opened on November 1, 2004, and then was expanded to the William J. Clinton Presidential Center and Heifer International headquarters on February 16, 2007. The system, now known as Metro Streetcar, operates five replica streetcars over 3.4 miles of track in Little Rock and North Little Rock.

The original Little Rock trolley service began in 1876 when the first horsecar line opened, lasting until 1895. Steam-powered streetcars operated in 1888 and 1889. On December 23, 1891, electric traction began to be used as the system was consolidated. The electric streetcars operated until September 1, 1947.

Trolley car #411 waits for passengers with the Choctaw Station standing just to the north.

Building the Railroad Westward

When the Choctaw, Oklahoma & Gulf acquired the Little Rock & Memphis through its Choctaw & Memphis, plans were created to connect the properties of the two railroads. This required the construction of approximately 170 miles of track through the Ouachita Mountains between Little Rock and Howe in the Indian Territory. This work was well documented by *The Choctaw*, a newspaper "[i]ssued monthly by authority of the Choctaw, Oklahoma and Gulf, and the Choctaw and Memphis Railroads." In the October 1899 issue, the construction of the railroad was described in great detail.

> *It will be remembered that the old Little Rock and Memphis property was sold to the Choctaw, Oklahoma and Gulf Railroad, October 25, 1898. Grade work was commenced at Ferguson's Mill [later Belleville, located in Yell County south of Russellville, Arkansas], November 1, and on December 1, 1898, it began with a full force and with great earnestness at both ends of the line. Track laying began at Howe April 20, 1899, but owing to the heavier work at this end of the line and especially at Ross Hollow, where there is a cut of 135*

> *feet, the track laying here was delayed until two months ago. The gap between Little Rock and Howe was 166 miles. The Roberts track-laying machine was used on the west end of the line under the supervision of McCabe & Steen. By the use of this machine it was possible to make 2 miles a day. The best day's work was 11,460 feet. All the work has been pushed with the greatest speed consistent with the best results. The first 100 miles east from Howe was under contract to the Choctaw Construction Company, sub-let to McCabe & Steen, and the contract for 66 miles west from Little Rock was held by McCarthy & Reichardt, of Little Rock, who sub-let 43 miles to McCabe & Steen. Track laying at Ferguson's Mill began August 11. The results accomplished since then have been highly satisfactory.*

The railroad looped around the south and west sides of Little Rock and then westward, following a series of streams into the mountains where timber immediately became a source of revenue. The line was built eastward from Howe and westward from Little Rock, plus in both directions from the Belleville area. This allowed the 170-mile railroad connection to be built in one year. *The Choctaw* reported that the railroad was "finished at 9:44am on October 13, 1899, 22 miles west of Little Rock."

Little Rock (AR) to
Little Rock Junction (AR)
Union Pacific

Union Pacific acquired this track using Missouri Pacific, and then rebuilt part of it as a new mainline. The rest was defined as the Carlisle Branch and is used to serve a number of customers in southeast Little Rock. In reality, the track north of the Pine Bluff mainline is a patchwork of former Rock Island and Missouri Pacific lines, many of them once simply industrial leads. Some parts of the line were easily mixed with the former Missouri Pacific Rock Street Branch, the original mainline between Little Rock and Pine Bluff, Arkansas.

133.1 NORTH END CARLISLE BRANCH – The railroad still has some industrial customers south of here, so the railroad was preserved to this point, located about East 4th Street. For many years, even this stub of track was still shown by Union Pacific to be the Carlisle Branch.

The track comes this far and curves to the west on the south side of East 3rd Street, ending at the *Arkansas Democrat* warehouse just east of Rector Street. This is the area where the third Rock Island Little Rock Freight Terminal once was. At one time, the Rock Island had a spur track to the east at East 4th Street that served the St. Louis Cotton Compress Company's Compress No. 1 facility. On the east side of the compress was a large Missouri Pacific rail yard, located on what was once the Little Rock, Mississippi River & Texas Railway. There were a number of industries in this area, but the Missouri Pacific served them long before the CRI&P showed up. The Little Rock, Mississippi River & Texas Railway line was also partly abandoned to make space for the Clinton Presidential Center. The tracks still exist to serve shippers south of East 6th Street and several blocks to the east.

The spur to the *Arkansas Democrat* warehouse passes by the brick streets of the former Rock Island freight house that was built in 1911.

133.3 EAST 6TH STREET – The railroad bridges over this street, where there is a short runaround track that allows trains to switch in the area. There is also an S-curve connecting track to the east to reach the former Missouri Pacific track, shortening the distance to switch area customers.

133.5 EAST 9TH STREET – On the west side of the tracks and just north of East 9th Street is a switch into the scrap metals complex of the Sol Alman Company. The Sol Alman Company started in 1905 when Charles Alman, a Russian immigrant, founded the Charles Alman Waste Materials Company in Little Rock, Arkansas. His son, Sol, acquired the business in August 1942 and the company became the Sol Alman Company. It is now run by the third generation of Almans and recycles non-ferrous metals including copper, aluminum, brass, stainless steel, zinc, aluminum cans, and lead as well as ferrous metals including iron and steel. They also cut up and process structures as large as bridges.

Where the Sol Alman Company now operates was once the Purified Petroleum Products Company oil purifying station. On the east side of the mainline was the Gay Oil Company. Both companies were here and being served by the Rock Island by the 1910s.

133.9 EAST 15TH STREET – In this area there are currently several tracks to the east (railroad-south) that serve AFCO Steel. AFCO Steel dates back to 1909, and is involved with producing steel components for various construction projects.

To the west are a series of cemeteries. The one to the north is the Oakland & Fraternal Historic Cemetery Park, established in 1862. The cemetery was created when Little Rock purchased a 160-acre estate to have a place to bury the Civil War dead. Several articles from the time in the *Arkansas Gazette* provide more information. One stated that the city cemetery was needed as there were "many soldiers dying almost daily in the emergency hospitals of Little Rock." The paper also explained the name by reporting that the land was "christened Oakland, probably because the site which was chosen for it was natural forest, wooded principally with oaks."

The southern part of the cemetery complex is the Little Rock National Cemetery. In 1863, Union forces captured Little Rock and troops set up an encampment in the cemetery, where they began burying their dead. The federal government acquired 9.1 acres in September 1866, and then 3.2 more acres in April 1868, and created the Little Rock National Cemetery on April 9, 1868. In 1884, an 11-acre Confederate cemetery was created adjacent to the national cemetery, and the remains of 640 Confederate soldiers were removed from Mt. Holly Cemetery and reburied there. In 1913, the Confederate Cemetery became a federal cemetery, set aside for Confederate veterans only. In 1938, the Confederate Cemetery became the Confederate Section of Little Rock National Cemetery. More land has been added to the Little Rock National Cemetery over the years, making it more than 31 acres. The cemetery was listed on the National Register of Historic Places in 1996.

Since the original purchase, the 160-acre estate has been broken up into seven different cemeteries. These include the National Cemetery, two Confederate cemeteries, the main Oakland Cemetery, a Fraternal cemetery, a Jewish cemetery, and Agudath Achim, a Jewish Orthodox cemetery. About 108 of the acres are used for the more than 62,000 burials located on the site.

Heading railroad-west, the Union Pacific tracks curve east, cross Commercial Street (MP 134.6) at-grade, curve back to the south and cross Bolton Avenue (MP 135.0). This area includes a number of warehouses, but none are currently served by the railroad. Originally, the Rock Island mainline continued directly south alongside the National Cemetery, crossed Roosevelt Road at the south end of the cemetery, and then curved west to Biddle. This short track realignment reduces the conflict at the east end of Biddle Yard and loops the Carlisle Branch through an industrial area once served by Missouri Pacific.

135.1 EAST ROOSEVELT ROAD – Roosevelt Road is a major east-west street across the southern part of Little Rock. Its western end is also designated as U.S. Highway 70B. Just south of the crossing is a track into the large CertainTeed construction materials manufacturing facility. This location is part of the Roofing Products Group. During the 1930s, this area was the home of the Arkansas District Headquarters of the Civilian Conservation Corps. It was part of the Seventh Corps Area, based in Omaha, Nebraska.

South of here, the former Rock Island Railroad curved to the west to arrive at Biddle Yard. Today, it has a junction with Union Pacific's White Bluff Subdivision, the name now used for the line to Pine Bluff. This is an important part of the story of Missouri Pacific/Union Pacific acquiring parts of the Rock Island in the Little Rock area. Until 1984, MP/UP trains heading from North Little Rock to Pine Bluff and on to New Orleans (the Valley Route) faced a tough route out of town. Trains would curve south out of the North Little Rock yard, running just west of Interstate 30. They would then cross the Arkansas River on the Junction Bridge. The bridge and part of the route was built by the Little Rock Junction Railway Company, incorporated on December 8, 1883, to connect the Little Rock, Mississippi River & Texas Railway with the Little Rock & Fort Smith Railway that served North Little Rock. The bridge and 0.42 miles of track opened on December 9, 1884. In 1984, the route was replaced and on December 27, 2001, Union Pacific donated the bridge to the City of Little Rock. Like the Rock Island bridge, it was turned into a pedestrian bridge as a part of the Arkansas River Trail, opening on May 17, 2008.

Heading south off of the Little Rock Junction Bridge at Rock Street Junction, trains would curve east using a twenty degree curve, too sharp for some modern railroad equipment. Trains would then cross the Rock Island Railroad and curve around the east side of Little Rock, several blocks to the east of the Rock Island route. Near the Little Rock airport, the line headed south toward Pine Bluff.

This torturous route was replaced in early 1984 with a route using part of the Rock Island. Union Pacific made it a significant event by having their steam locomotive #8444 (4-8-4) inaugurate the new Valley Route. This route used the Baring Cross Bridge and the Missouri Pacific mainline to a set of new crossovers and a switch to the former Rock Island mainline at 16th Street, named Little Rock Junction. From here, Union Pacific used the Rock Island to Biddle Yard. East of Biddle Yard, Union Pacific used the former Rock Island route to the Port of Little Rock to reach 25th Street, located near the airport runway. There, the tracks were realigned to connect to the southward Valley Route main.

135.2 BIDDLE (JC) – Biddle (station code became RK in 1968 after passenger service ended) became the location of the major yard and shops in the Little Rock area after the Arkansas River Bridge was opened in 1899. *Rock Island Timetable No. 1*, dated March 18, 1979, provided a list of services available at Biddle Yard. These included general order boards and books, standard clock, train register station, and a train order station with train order signal. Biddle was also a fuel and water station, and there was a wayside radio. The turntable was available until the end of Rock Island service, and the entire area was protected by yard limits. Timetables also stated that "134 pole 32 to 136 pole 16, all tracks are yard tracks."

In 1979, the track from Memphis, Tennessee, to Biddle Yard in Little Rock, Arkansas, was Subdivision 29 of the Southern Division. This line had earlier been a part of the Arkansas Division, being assigned the name of Subdivision 52. The subdivision is the eastern end of the Choctaw Route, an almost direct line between Memphis and Amarillo, Texas, and on to Tucumcari, New Mexico. Heading west, the line to Booneville, Arkansas, was Subdivision 30 of the Southern Division. Biddle was also the north end of Subdivision 37 which headed south to Hot Springs, Arkansas, also a part of the Southern Division. Freight train crews changed at Biddle Yard while passenger train crews changed at the Choctaw Station in Little Rock.

Besides a crew change point and the dividing line between Subdivision 29 and Subdivision 30, it was also a dividing line between the freight volumes on the railroad. Heading east to Memphis, the line averaged about 14.0 million gross tons of traffic a year, thanks to the many grain elevators and the Cotton Belt traffic east of Brinkley. To the west, the line had 6.6 million gross tons. Much of this change was due to the eastward movement of the grain, and the traffic to and from south Arkansas and Louisiana.

Construction of Biddle Yard

There were reports by 1907 that the Rock Island was acquiring land in south Little Rock so that a rail yard could be built. The existing Argenta yards and shops were being overwhelmed, and the new Louisiana Division was pouring lumber and oil onto the Rock Island system here. The three-week-long 1907 Bankers' Panic slowed the economy and made money tight, but Biddle (MP 136.4) appeared in the railroad's timetable late in 1908.

An announcement in December 1908 stated that the yard that was being built in south Little Rock would be expanded, adding 15 tracks, a roundhouse, a coal chute, water tank, cinder pit, passing tracks, and repair tracks. The yard had been known as Hot Springs Junction Yard, but was renamed Biddle Yard. The name Biddle came from W. B. Biddle, the vice-president for traffic for the Rock Island. Biddle had come to the Rock Island from the Santa Fe in January 1905. He was at the Rock Island during its growth years, and then moved to the St. Louis - San Francisco Railway (Frisco) in 1910, where he later became president.

The first major challenge to build the yard was filling in the low marshy land. During December 1908, the Rock Island brought in a steam shovel and about 100 flat cars for hauling 135,000 cubic yards of dirt and distributing it to raise the area. Construction of the yard and shops was delayed until 1909-1910, when most of the buildings were erected. A front-page article in the April 15, 1910, *Arkansas Gazette*, provided information about the railroad's plans for the complex. The article stated that the company would spend $1,250,000 to build the yard, a 20-stall roundhouse with pits and turntable, plus other offices and shop buildings. It stated that when completed, the shops would be as large as those at Shawnee, Oklahoma. An interesting part of the construction of the roundhouse was the use of concrete piling to provide a stable foundation for the roundhouse, believed to be the first use of its kind in Arkansas.

The work at Biddle included a large roundhouse, office building, mechanical shop, storeroom, 300-ton capacity coal chute, 165,000-gallon water tower, and a cinder pit. Throughout the 1910s, Biddle obtained more assignments until all mainline trains and shop work were based at Biddle in 1918. Other facilities such as a re-icing station and a 40-foot, 100,000-pound capacity track scale were eventually added.

Biddle Yard was enough of a complete railroad facility that it was used to train the 743rd Railway Operating Battalion during 1944. This battalion was headquartered at Camp Joseph T. Robinson in North Little Rock, and was "made up of a Headquarters Company (operators, dispatchers, etc.); Company A (Maintenance of Way); Company B (Maintenance of Equipment); and Company C (Transportation)," according to a Rock Island story that year. Members of the battalion were put to work repairing track and railroad equipment, and also received training on railroad operations.

The facilities remained an important terminal for decades, and a portion of the roundhouse and the yard office continued in their original function until the end of the railroad. In 1968, the yard obtained a new cinder block building so that offices could be consolidated here from the Choctaw Station, freight house, and other locations. During the late 1970s, Biddle Yard was primarily a car shop, and a number of freight cars were rebuilt here.

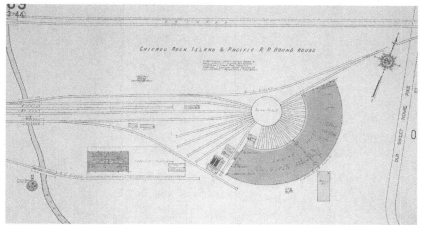

Sanborn Map of CRI&P Roundhouse at Little Rock – 1913. *Sanborn Fire Insurance Map from Little Rock, Pulaski County, Arkansas.* Sanborn Map Company, Vol.1, 1913. Map. Retrieved from the Library of Congress, https://www.loc.gov/item/sanborn00285_005/.

Biddle Yard After the Rock Island

After the Chicago, Rock Island & Pacific closed, Biddle Yard was used March 24 - May 31, 1980, by the St. Louis Southwestern as a part of their Memphis to Little Rock to Fordyce and Perry operations, changing the name to Little Rock Yard. On June 1, 1980, Missouri Pacific took over operations at Biddle. The final Rock Island action was an auction of passenger cars, freight cars, heavy equipment, buildings, a 190,000-gallon water tower, and lots of furniture and tools on October 14, 1981. The remains of the roundhouse were also sold, with Ace Brick and Stone paying $150 for more than 100,000 salvageable bricks. On November 17, 1983, Missouri Pacific bought Biddle Yard, but the Rock Island trustees continued to use part of it to store equipment and scrap freight cars. Union Pacific has since rebuilt the yard and uses it to serve area customers as part of their new route from North Little Rock to Pine Bluff. A few offices remain, plus the track material sorting operation of Rail Service Group, Inc. A few of the original CRI&P foundations can still be found in the brush at the east end of the complex.

This sign marks the street entrance to Union Pacific's Biddle Yard.

Like all of the track from Little Rock Junction to McGehee, Arkansas, the mileposts here have changed over the years. In 1984, when the line was reopened by Union Pacific, Biddle was at Union Pacific Milepost 347.2. When the mileposts were changed to avoid conflicts in South Arkansas around McGehee, Biddle became Milepost 308.6. Modern Union Pacific timetables show South (east) Biddle as Control Point A309, Milepost 309.0. North (west) Biddle is defined as Control Point A307 at Milepost 307.5.

Interstate 30

About the center of Biddle Yard, the tracks are crossed by Interstate 30. This highway is only about 370 miles long and connects I-40 at North Little Rock with I-20 on the west side of Fort Worth, Texas. Interstate 30 ends in zero, which normally indicates a nearly coast-to-coast interstate highway. However, I-30 is the shortest such Interstate in the country. I-30 was also one of the earliest built Interstates, with most of the route completed by 1965.

Further west is the Arch Street bridge, long a popular location to watch the west end of Biddle Yard.

136.4 HOT SPRINGS JUNCTION – Hot Springs Junction was for many years an important location on the Rock Island Railroad. The location basically split the traffic moving in and out of the west end of Biddle Yard, with traffic heading to South Arkansas and Louisiana turning off the Choctaw Route. This traffic served places like Hot Springs, Camden and Crossett, Arkansas, as well as Ruston, Alexandria and Eunice, Louisiana. Besides the timber, oil and agricultural products that came off of the route, Hot Springs was for many years an important passenger train destination. The thermal water spas, mountains and lakes, and horse racing attracted many vacationers, as did the illegal gambling, booze and dames controlled by the Chicago mob. Al Capone, Frank Costello, Bugs Moran, Lucky Luciano, Owney "The Killer" Madden, and other infamous mobsters came to rest and hide out at Hot Springs from the late 1800s until the mid-1900s. When finally stopped in the 1960s, Hot Springs was considered by the federal government to be "the site of the largest illegal gambling operation in the U.S."

Hot Springs Junction was created by the opening of the Little Rock & Hot Springs Western Railroad (LR&HSW) in April 1900. At the time, both the Choctaw, Oklahoma & Gulf and the Iron Mountain used the LR&HSW to reach Hot Springs. A year later, backers of the Iron Mountain acquired the LR&HSW, cutting off the Choctaw Route. In response, the CO&G bought the older Hot Springs Railroad. However, a connecting line from Little Rock to Benton and on to Malvern was needed, and the CO&G started surveys for the route. The Iron Mountain had their own mainline along the route, plus the northern end of the LR&HSW, and leased and then sold the Little Rock to Benton part of the line to the CO&G. Less than twenty miles of track were still required south of Benton to reach the Hot Springs Railroad, but the Rock Island soon had their own route into Hot Springs, in operation on May 13, 1902. An important station along this new track between Benton and Butterfield was Haskell, Arkansas. This is where the new route into South Arkansas and Louisiana began.

Union Pacific

When the Rock Island closed, the route was used for a few months by the Cotton Belt, but it was soon closed and much of it abandoned. Union Pacific records state that the remains of the line were "purchased from CRI&P Rwy 11-17-1983." In 1986, the former line toward Hot Springs was shown to be the Brittian Spur, with a length of 4.69 miles. The line served several customers in an industrial park, as well as the large Big Rock quarry, in existence since the 1870s and operated today by the 3M Company. At the time, Union Pacific showed that the mainline wye was still in existence at Milepost 346.24, or Milepost 0.0 on the Brittian Spur.

By 2012, Union Pacific timetables show that the wye was gone and the track connected to the White Bluff Subdivision at Milepost 307.4, known again as Hot Springs Junction, located just west of Biddle Yard. The line is still 4.7 miles long, but it now carries the name Hot Springs Industrial Lead.

Heading west from Hot Springs Junction, the Rock Island mainline curved back to the north, with Little Rock to the north and east, and woods to the south and west. Much of this is due to the Fourche Creek watershed to the south.

137.9 ROOSEVELT ROAD – The railroad again meets Roosevelt Road, this time passing under it. Here, Roosevelt Road is a more major roadway, serving as U.S. Highway 70B. For Union Pacific, it is Milepost 305.9 of the White Bluff Subdivision, and Milepost 344.7 of the older mileposts on the Pine Bluff Subdivision. For trains heading west, the grade has stiffened to 1.0%, sometimes requiring a Biddle switch engine to shove trains on their way westward.

Just compass-south, railroad-east, of Roosevelt Road is Barton Coliseum and the grounds of the Arkansas State Fair. There was a spur track here for years, allowing livestock to be moved to and from the site. The track was also used by circus trains when giving performances at Barton Coliseum. The coliseum was named for Thomas Harry Barton, founder of Lion Oil, and opened on September 29, 1952.

As the Rock Island grade passes under Roosevelt Road, the Missouri Pacific Texas to Little Rock mainline comes in from the west. The two lines parallel each other to near the Arkansas State Capital building, where the Rock Island once crossed the Missouri Pacific and headed west again.

Across the Missouri Pacific tracks to the west is Roselawn Memorial Park, also known as Roselawn Cemetery. The cemetery dates from May 25, 1919, when plans were created for the 100-acre facility. The first burial was on February 4, 1920, and more than 22,000 burials have taken place since. Roselawn was the first perpetual care cemetery in Arkansas, and is the burial site of governors, congressmen and senators, industrialists, Congressional Medal of Honor recipients, and major league baseball players. The original office, known as "The Gatehouse," is listed on the National Register of Historic Places.

138.4 ASHER AVENUE – The two railroads are in a trench, allowing city streets to pass overhead. This bridge, built in 1940, connects Wright Avenue to the east, and Asher Avenue to the west. The route was once the Military Road from Little Rock to the Red River at Fulton, a major route to Texas.

Wright Avenue causes a great deal of trouble for people who don't know Little Rock. The streets are numbered from north to south, with 18th Street north of Wright Avenue. However, 19th Street is south of Wright Avenue, adding an extra street and block to the city's street system. Wright Avenue was named for Dr. Weldon Edwards Wright, who platted the first addition south of Little Rock, naming the street bordering the original part of Little Rock after himself. Wright was also involved in the Brooks-Baxter War of 1874. This war was an open conflict between the supporters of the two candidates for governor of Arkansas. More than 200 were killed, and it took federal action to stop the fighting. The end of fighting put a Democrat in office, ending what was essentially Republican rule and the era of Reconstruction.

The Asher Avenue Bridge has several railroad mileposts. Besides the Rock Island milepost, there is the Union Pacific White Bluff Subdivision milepost of 305.4. The milepost on Union Pacific's Little Rock Subdivision is 347.5. At one time, the Rock Island had a short siding to the east here, with the south end just north of West 20th Street, and the north end at 15th Street. This siding was used to serve several warehouses and small factories to the east.

Further to the east at 15th Street is Little Rock Central High School. When built in 1927 at a cost of $1.5 million, Little Rock Central High School was the largest and most expensive high school in the United States. In 1957, the school was the center of the desegregation movement as the Little Rock Nine were denied entrance to the school. In 1954, a U.S. Supreme Court ruling had ordered integration of all public schools, leading to a political battle between Governor Orval Faubus and President Dwight D. Eisenhower. Using military and legal force, Eisenhower succeeded in admitting the nine black students over the objection of Faubus and many in the community. Little Rock Central High School is now listed on the U.S. National Register of Historic Places, and has been named as a U.S. National Historic Landmark and a National Historic Site.

138.7 LR JUNCTION – Also known as Little Rock Junction, this switch was installed to connect Union Pacific's Little Rock Subdivision to the former Rock Island mainline to create a new route for Valley trains toward New Orleans. It is located at Milepost 305.1 on the White Bluff Subdivision, and Milepost 347.2 on the Little Rock Subdivision.

Little Rock Junction (AR) to Gill Street (AR)
Abandoned

For several years after the railroad shut down, the Rock Island mainline remained in place, allowing trains to reach the Missouri Pacific yard by circling Little Rock. In 1984, Union Pacific installed LR Junction and started changes on how the line from the west connected to North Little Rock. A new track was built that turned the trains of the Little Rock & Western northward and then onto the Little Rock Subdivision. They then crossed the Baring Cross Bridge over the Arkansas River and did their interchange business in Union Pacific's North Little Rock yard. With the changes, almost two miles of former Rock Island mainline track were abandoned.

138.7 LR JUNCTION – Also known as Little Rock Junction, this switch was installed to connect Union Pacific's Little Rock Subdivision to the former Rock Island mainline to create a new route for Valley trains toward New Orleans. It is located at Milepost 305.1 on the White Bluff Subdivision, and Milepost 347.2 on the Little Rock Subdivision.

138.8 14TH STREET – The railroad passed under this street, still to the east of the Missouri Pacific line. 14th Street runs along the north side of Little Rock Central High School and has been renamed Daisy L. Gatson Bates Drive. Daisy Lee Gatson Bates played a leading role in the Little Rock Integration Crisis of 1957, covering the event and distributing information both locally and nationally. She is considered to be a leading Arkansas and American civil rights activist, and was also a publisher, journalist, and lecturer.

Heading on north (railroad-west), the railroad passed under 13th Street (Milepost 138.9) and 12th Street (Milepost 139.0). During the late 1930s, the railroads were lowered slightly and new street bridges built. The 14th Street and 12th Street bridges opened in 1936.

139.1 10TH STREET PASSENGER STATION – During the early 1900s, the Rock Island had a second passenger station in Little Rock, Arkansas. It was located here on the northeast corner of the 10th Street grade crossing. Timetables included this station, designated as the Tenth Street Station, as a Little Rock station along with the Choctaw Station and the station at Pulaski. This station was close to the Arkansas State Capital and the surrounding neighborhoods. The station was still listed in the January 12, 1936, passenger timetable, but was shown to have no agent and no trains were scheduled to stop. A 1939 Sanborn insurance map showed that the station was vacant.

Just north of the station, a short siding to the east began at 9th Street, also known as Maryland Avenue. During the first part of the Twentieth Century, the railroad served Central Mill and Lumber Company here. Just north of 9th Street, the grade passes under Interstate 630 at CRI&P Milepost 139.2. This roadway was conceived in the 1930s and was first planned by the Pulaski County Planning Board in their 1941 report. However, little construction took place until the 1960s when the 8th Street Expressway was started. During the 1970s, U.S. Representative Wilbur D. Mills arranged to have the highway added to the Interstate Highway system and it became Interstate 630. The 7.4-mile route was completed on September 30, 1985. Its east end is at Interstate 30, while its west end is at Interstate 430.

139.4 7TH STREET – The Rock Island bridged over 7th Street, and while the tracks are abandoned, the two-track-wide bridge remains. This highway underpass of both the Rock Island and Missouri Pacific lines has dates of 1936 and 1937 on it. There were several rail-served industries in this area. Just to the south was a spur to the east into the Southwestern Bell Telephone Company pole yard. To the north was a track into the City Machinery Shop, located at West 6th and Dennison. Further north was the end of the short siding to the east.

139.9 MOPAC CROSSING – Just south of 3rd Street, the Rock Island Railroad once turned to the northwest and crossed the Missouri Pacific to head to Oklahoma. To protect the diamond, there was FA switch tower to the east for many years. In the 1979 Rock Island timetable, the crossing was listed as an automatic interlocking. The abandoned grade west of the crossing can still be made out today, located on the west side of the small stream in this area. The line curved to the northwest, often in a narrow cut all the way to Cantrell Road.

This plate shows that Uvalde Construction built the 7th Street underpass for the Arkansas State Highway Commission and the United States Bureau of Public Roads.

The railroad from Little Rock south to Texarkana, now the Little Rock Subdivision of Union Pacific Railroad, was built by one of many railroads that eventually became part of Missouri Pacific Railroad. The route began as the Cairo & Fulton Railroad, which was chartered on February 9, 1853, to build a railroad line across Arkansas, from Missouri to Texas. However, the Civil War and then a shortage of cash prevented the line from being built. In 1872, the Cairo & Fulton became the Cairo, Arkansas & Texas Railroad (CA&T), which built seventy miles of track to Newport, Arkansas. The tracks reached Argenta on January 11, 1873. The original Baring Cross Bridge opened on December 20, 1873, and passenger service to St. Louis started two days later.

Union Pacific records show that the CA&T was already building south, even before the Arkansas River was bridged. UP states that the CA&T was built through here in 1873 using a track gauge of five feet. The track was completed to Texarkana on January 15, 1874, and it was leased to the St. Louis, Iron Mountain & Southern on May 6, 1874. Different parts of the Iron Mountain had been built to different track gauges, and the line was rebuilt to standard gauge on June 28, 1879. On May 12, 1917, the St. Louis, Iron Mountain & Southern merged into Missouri Pacific, which became a part of Union Pacific in 1982.

Just east of here is the Arkansas State Capital. Construction on the capital building started in 1899 and ended in 1915. A unique part of the construction was that prisoners from the state penitentiary helped build the capital, as it was located on the site of the existing state penitentiary. Because the building looks like a smaller U.S. Capital, it has been used in several movies and television shows to represent Washington, D.C.

140.3 GILL STREET – The original grade has a junction near here with tracks used by the Little Rock & Western, which operates the Rock Island west of Little Rock to Perry and beyond.

In this area during the early 1900s was Ferguson Spur Crossing, with what was shown to be a three-car spur track. Near here was Ferguson's Mill, where the Choctaw, Oklahoma & Gulf Railroad began building westward.

Gill Street (AR) to Danville (AR)
Little Rock & Western Railway

This track was originally built for the Choctaw, Oklahoma & Gulf Railroad, and in 1904 became part of the Memphis to Tucumcari Choctaw Route. The Cotton Belt and Missouri Pacific both provided service on the line for a few months in 1980 after the Rock Island shut down. On March 25, 1980, the Interstate Commerce Commission issued instructions to the Cotton Belt to serve the mill at Perry, and on March 28th the Cotton Belt assumed dispatching and operating responsibilities for the line as far as Perry. The line was handled by a Perry Turn from Biddle Yard, known as Little Rock Yard by the St. Louis Southwestern.

Later in 1980, the Arkansas Kraft Corporation leased the line from Pulaski to Perry. This rail service was important to the paper mill as it shipped an average of 21 cars per day, and the company was concerned about how long the Cotton Belt would operate the line, especially after the railroad announced its end of service east and south of Little Rock. To operate the line, the Little Rock & Western Railway (LRWN) was created, using a mix of locomotives over the years. However, the most famous were a pair of Alco C420 diesels which attracted railfans from across the country.

Rail Management Corporation, created by J. Earl Durden, was contracted to manage the railroad for Arkansas Kraft. The Little Rock & Western Railway began operations on June 1, 1980, running trains between Perry and Pulaski, where interchange was made with Missouri Pacific. The railroad also served a propane distributor at Perry and a cross tie manufacturer. The LRWN felt that it was essential to also interchange with the Cotton Belt, so during late summer of 1980, the railroad received rights to operate to the SSW at North Little Rock using the CRI&P mainline around Little Rock.

The railroad started operations using leased Missouri Pacific locomotives, and then leased Green Bay & Western RS-3 locomotives. 1982 was a big year for the railroad as it bought the Pulaski to Perry line for $2.7 million on May 5, 1982. The company also built a servicing and inspection pit at Perry as the start of today's shop complex, and then bought the C420s and had them rebuilt later in the year.

The Little Rock & Western Railway expanded their operation to Danville, Arkansas, when Continental Grain Company contracted with them to provide service to the Danville poultry feed mill in 1986. With more business running on the line, and the desire by Union Pacific to rebuild the Rock Island mainline east of LR Junction, a new line was built from near Gill Street that would allow

Little Rock & Western trains to turn north and get to North Little Rock via the Baring Cross Bridge. By this time, interchange between the LRWN and UP was being conducted in North Little Rock instead of at Pulaski, but UP still held onto ownership of the track as far west as Pulaski.

On June 28, 1991, the Interstate Commerce Commission approved the purchase of the Little Rock & Western Railway Corporation by LRW Ry. L.P. This was part of a plan to restructure the relationship between K. Earl Durden and Green Bay Packaging, as well as other subsidiaries of each company.

In June 2005, LRWN became the property of Genesee & Wyoming Inc., when Rail Management Corporation was acquired. The railroad is based in Perry, Arkansas, and handles products like wood and paper products, grain, limestone slurry, cornstarch, salt, LP gas, and pulp mill liquid. The railroad owns about 80 miles of track and uses trackage rights from Pulaski to the Union Pacific yard in North Little Rock where they interchange with both UP and BNSF.

In 2005, the Little Rock & Western became a part of the large system of Arkansas short-lines owned by Genesee & Wyoming, as shown by this sign at Perry, Arkansas.

Trains haven't run west of Ola in a number of years. Wayne Farms at Danville, Arkansas, relied upon the Rock Island to deliver grain, and when the railroad closed down, it acquired the tracks west of Perry and contracted with the Little Rock & Western to maintain the service. However, Wayne Farms later bought an idled poultry feed mill at Atkins, Arkansas. This mill is on the mainline of Union Pacific and was operated until 2004 by ConAgra, and then

Pilgrim's Pride. Union Pacific offered better rates at this Atkins mill and Wayne Farms now trucks feed to area poultry farms from this alternative facility. Thus, the tracks are no longer in regular use to Danville.

Service to Ola has also recently stopped as the low volume of lumber from the sawmill there hasn't justified the service, and much of the lumber is now trucked to a transload facility on the Dardanelle & Russellville Railroad to the north.

140.3   GILL STREET – The original grade has a junction near here with tracks used by the Little Rock & Western, which operates the Rock Island west of Little Rock to Perry and beyond. Union Pacific actually owns the track as far west as Milepost 141.0. The track is known as the Pulaski Spur, and it breaks off of the Little Rock Subdivision not far south of the Baring Cross Bridge over the Arkansas River, and west of the former Missouri Pacific Union Station, now used by Amtrak. The current route has been rebuilt and adjusted several times and now enters the Union Pacific mainline at Milepost 345.46, or what is shown to be the equivalent of Rock Island Milepost 139.74.

Before the CO&G built west of Little Rock, the St. Louis, Iron Mountain & Southern had a branch to the west to serve several industries. An 1897 Sanborn map showed that there was a switch in Little Rock, just north of the Iron Mountain Station, then shown as Pratt's Hotel. Pratt's Hotel had the passenger train station in the south end and the hotel in the north end of the building. The switch was west of Pulaski, just south of North Street, close to where the Little Rock & Western switch is today. The line curved immediately west and through the L. C. Gleason's Wheel Barrow factory (the former Choctaw & Memphis freight house), just south of North Street. The track continued west through what is today the north side of the large private school complex in this area.

By 1939, there was a full wye to connect to the line, and the route went by the Ozark Fruit Company vinegar works and Hudson & Dugger Company of Arkansas, a manufacturer of barrel heading. The Missouri Pacific line passed under Lincoln Avenue, today's Cantrell Road, to serve several additional shippers. The route can still be found under the Cantrell overpass. Meanwhile, the Rock Island mainline was just to the southwest and didn't serve any customers in this area.

In 1990, the latest change on the rail routes in this area took place. This was because of the development west of the Missouri Pacific Union Station. Developers Flake and Tabor were working to clean and develop the land that Wrape Mill once sat on. At the time, the Little Rock & Western used the Vinegar Spur route, named for the Ozark Fruit Company vinegar works, to interchange with Union Pacific. Union Pacific moved the line back to the Rock Island grade to loop south of the property now used by the Episcopal Collegiate School. The rail route was then turned northward alongside the west side of Union Pacific's mainline, where it connects at Control Point X345 – Arkansas River.

140.4 CANTRELL ROAD – The Rock Island mainline, as well as the Missouri Pacific industry line, passed under Cantrell Road, once known as Lincoln Avenue. After the Civil War, what was River Road was renamed Lincoln Avenue for President Abraham Lincoln. Later, it was renamed Cantrell Road for Deadrick Harrell Cantrell, president of the Little Rock Railway & Electric Company, the company that operated the trolley system in Little Rock.

Cantrell Road is a major route west out of Little Rock and becomes Arkansas Highway 10 to head further west. Starting at Perry, Arkansas, Highway 10 closely follows the Rock Island westward past Booneville.

141.0 PROPERTY LINE – This location is not far east of the grade crossing with Riverfront Drive. The track west of here is owned by the Little Rock & Western Railway. East of here, the track is owned by Union Pacific.

141.2 WEST END – During the early years of the railroad, West End was located here as both a 30-car siding and a 24-car industrial spur track. As the nearby Pulaski station developed, a new siding was built there about 1910 that replaced West End.

141.7 PULASKI – Look for the grade crossing with Riverdale Road, where the station once stood. The station name comes from the county's name, although some claim that it comes from nearby Pulaski Heights. Pulaski was another local passenger station that served the Little Rock area, this time the far west side and the prestigious Pulaski Heights area. This series of neighborhoods is located on hills west of town, with many houses looking down onto the Arkansas River. Even today, it is considered to be one of the most affluent neighborhoods in Little Rock, and is the home of the Country Club of Little Rock.

A 65-car siding was first built here about 1910, and it was expanded as trains increased in length since it was the last siding before reaching Biddle Yard for eastbound trains. In 1950, the siding to the north was listed as being 100 cars long. In 1979, it was listed as being 4609 feet long. Today, a crossover in the middle of the siding allows trains to be worked here. This was installed when Pulaski was the initial interchange location between the Little Rock & Western and Missouri Pacific. Additionally, there is a house track to the south that is used for transload operations for local truck delivery or pickup.

Besides the siding, there were tracks to two large shippers – Pulaski Stone Company and Southern Sand and Material. These two shippers moved about 300 cars a month, keeping the agent at Pulaski busy. This business was gone by World War II. A railroad section house and a bunk house lasted until the early 1950s, and a final tool and handcar house was here when the railroad shut down.

Heading west, the railroad generally runs along a bluff to the south, with a number of parks and golf courses to the north between the tracks and the Arkansas River.

Creation of the Pulaski Heights Depot

This is another passenger station that came about because of the demand of local residents. In March 1907, the town council of Pulaski Heights passed a resolution requesting that the Chicago, Rock Island & Pacific build a depot within the town limits. Residents were complaining that they had to travel seven miles to get to a railroad station, but the CRI&P argued that a street car ran from Pulaski Heights to their station in Little Rock, so a depot was not justified. Pulaski Heights next petitioned the Arkansas Railroad Commission for a depot. In October 1908, the Arkansas Railroad Commission reviewed the need for a station at Pulaski Heights as well as near West Tenth Street in Little Rock. At both locations, the CRI&P was ordered to build a passenger and freight depot.

Construction on a brick station for Pulaski Heights began on February 22, 1909, and the city began installing a park with trees and flowers nearby. Reports were that the station measured 44 feet by 90 feet, and there was a 300-foot-long concrete platform. The brick was manufactured by the Clark Pressed Brick Company of Malvern, Arkansas, which was experiencing a shortage of brick at the time. The station opened about July 1, 1909. There is some conflict in the information about who actually built the station. While most reports state that the Rock Island built the station, some report that Pulaski Heights built the station, or at least helped fund it, since the community wanted a better building than the railroad was willing to provide.

The station was impressive, being one of the first brick Rock Island stations in Arkansas. The station also had an outside architect, giving it a unique look. Charles L. Thompson, who had earlier designed the Little Rock City Hall, was selected by the residents of Pulaski Heights to do the work. The result was an impressive building that featured, from west to east, a "White Waiting Room" and a "Colored Waiting Room" separated by an "Agent's Office" with a bay window trackside. An open patio separated the passenger station from the attached freight and baggage room, located on the east end of the structure.

Initially, the station was listed as a continuous train order office, meaning that it was staffed 24 hours a day. However, by late 1912, it was down to two shifts a day for 18 hours. In 1919, there was a single agent handling the station from 7:15am until 4:15pm, daily except Sunday. The agency closed in 1932, and trains ended their service to Pulaski in 1941. The station was torn down in January 1946, but the foundation was used for a newer office building years later.

145.0 KEWITT-JOHNSON – A siding, shown as having a 76-car capacity in 1969, was once to the north, near the current Overlook Drive grade crossing. The west end still remains as a short spur track. The siding used the name of one of the contractors working on the construction of Murray Lock & Dam (Lock & Dam No. 7), built as part of the McClellan–Kerr Arkansas River Navigation System. The lock is along the south bank and is easily seen from the railroad.

In the 1960s and named for John C. (Jack) Murray, a traffic expert for the Little Rock Chamber of Commerce. He was a major advocate of the McClellan–Kerr river project.

On top of the dam is Big Dam Bridge, also known as the "Pulaski County Pedestrian and Bicycle Bridge," the "Murray Lock and Dam Bicycle Pedestrian Bridge," or "Buddy's Bridge." The bridge is the world's longest purpose-built pedestrian/bicycle bridge, spanning 3463 feet of the Arkansas River, and 4300 feet in total length. Supported by Pulaski County Judge Floyd G. "Buddy" Villines, the bridge connects a number of area trails located on both sides of the Arkansas River.

146.6 INTERSTATE 430 – Interstate 430 was a part of the original interstate highway design, providing a western bypass around Little Rock that connects Interstate 40 and Interstate 30. The thirteen miles of highway was opened in the early 1980s.

Just west of Interstate 430, the railroad passes the Two Rivers Park Bridge. This carries the Arkansas River Trail across the Little Maumelle River, which the railroad follows westward. There is plenty of parking here for watching rail and river traffic. For the next four miles, the railroad runs through woods without any grade crossings. To the south is Walton Heights, a ridge that towers more than 300 feet above the tracks. The housing development on the hill was developed by Gus B. Walton, president of Walton & Company, a Little Rock investment securities firm.

150.4 MAUMELLE – Maumelle was once a 36-car siding to the north that was turned into a 765-foot-long spur track at the Pinnacle Valley Road grade crossing. There was once a gravel pit here. The Little Maumelle River is still to the north of the tracks, and just west of here, the railroad bridges over several tributaries of the stream. Until recently, this area was rural western Pulaski County, but it has seen a great deal of development over the past decade.

The name Maumelle is used for several streams and a community in the area. According to a number of sources, this area was named "mamelle" by early French explorers for the shape of the mountain now known as Pinnacle. Mamelle means breast or teat.

Railroad Communications

A report in the *Arkansas Gazette* on August 27, 1905, leads to a good discussion about the technology being used soon after the railroad was built. During August 1905, a crew was installing a new quad-copper telegraph line that would provide five lines instead of two to communicate between Chicago and Little Rock. The route wasn't direct as it went from Little Rock to Topeka (Kansas) to Chicago. During late August of 1905, one of the crews installing the system was at Maumelle, Arkansas. The article also stated that a 32-wire switchboard was going to be installed at Little Rock during early September.

While the telegraph line is long gone, old communication poles can be found in a number of places along the railroad. These poles once held telegraph lines, and along parts of the railroad, lines for the signal systems.

Telegraphy had a long history with the Rock Island Railroad as the first union involving telegraphy was created on the railroad at La Porte, Iowa, in 1886. The Order of Railroad Telegraphers was created to control the skill, with the union demanding that members would not be required to teach telegraphy. The reason for this was they wanted to control who had the skill, essentially keeping the skill in the families of its members.

The Wreck of Passenger Train No. 112

On February 5, 1947, at 2:21am, "east-bound first-class passenger train" No. 112 derailed "0.68 miles east of the station at Maumelle," The train consisted of locomotive #4021 (4-8-2), one baggage car, one combination mail-baggage car, three coaches, one dining car and one sleeping car. The locomotive and first four cars derailed. The derailment resulted in the "death of one train-service employee, and the injury of two passengers, one dining-car employee and one train-service employee." The engineer and fireman were the train-service employees killed and injured as the steam locomotive fell against an embankment on the south side of the grade, demolishing the locomotive cab and breaking a number of steam pipes.

The investigation described the track as from the "west there are in succession, a tangent 1,156 feet in length, an 8 degree 40' curve to the left 829 feet, a tangent 43 feet and an 8 degree 40' curve to the right 409 feet to the point of accident and 436 feet eastward. The grade is level." The curve was super elevated (outside rail higher than the inside rail in a curve) 5¾ inches at the point of the full curvature, and the speed limit was 25mph.

During the investigation, it was found that the "flanges of the left No. 1 and right No. 2 wheels were considerably flange-worn," the "male and female center castings and their shims were not lubricated," and that there was a "lack of lubrication on moving parts of the pivoting assembly and the constant-resistance-rocker assembly." Basically, the derailment was caused by a lack of careful maintenance and lubrication on the locomotive which created a "defective engine truck."

152.9 PINNACLE – The community of Pinnacle is to the west less than a mile, and East Pinnacle Road connects it to the site of the former railroad station. The railroad was built through here during the late 1890s, using the name Little Maumelle in 1899. The name soon changed as a post office opened at Pinnacle during 1901, and closed in 1953. During 1912, the residents of Pinnacle, Arkansas, petitioned the Arkansas Railroad Commission for a station. Before the Commission met, the Chicago, Rock Island & Pacific had agreed to build a joint passenger and freight facility at Pinnacle.

At one time there was a 4753-foot (96-car) siding to the south, along with a 580-foot (14-car) house track. Pinnacle was also a water station for many years. During the early 1920s, the Rock Island also operated a three-pen stockyard here. Johnson Brothers Lumber Company was also operating a sawmill at Pinnacle at the same time.

153.6 LITTLE MAUMELLE RIVER BRIDGE – The railroad crosses the river that it has been following using three deck plate girder spans. The center span is 80 feet long, while the two end spans are each 61 feet long. Just to the east is a 60-foot deck plate girder span, which crosses an overflow channel.

There are two Maumelle Rivers in the area. The Maumelle River, often known as the Big Maumelle River, flows north of Pinnacle Mountain, while the Little Maumelle River flows south of Pinnacle Mountain. However, both are about thirty miles long, starting in the Ouachita Mountains to the southwest, and flow into the Arkansas River. The Little Maumelle River is free of rapids and is a designated Arkansas Water Trail. The river is often lined with cypress trees and is a favorite fishing river for largemouth and spotted bass, crappie and bream.

Pinnacle Mountain State Park

As the railroad continues west (compass-north), it enters Pinnacle Mountain State Park, and then squeezes between hillsides on the east side of Pinnacle Mountain, the tallest and westernmost of what is known as the Maumelle Pinnacles. The 2356-acre park is relatively new, created in 1973 by the Arkansas General Assembly. The park covers both Pinnacle Mountain and the lands down to the east toward the Arkansas River. When first seen, many people comment that Pinnacle Mountain looks like a volcano, but it is not one. It is simply a rock peak that has survived the erosion that is typical throughout the area. The hard rock has been used for area construction, including for the Lake Maumelle dam during the 1950s. At 1011 feet high, Pinnacle is the second highest natural point in Pulaski County. As previously stated, the name was originally Mamelle, the French name for a breast-shaped hill.

The park is extremely popular and is the current western end of the Arkansas River Trail and the eastern starting point for the Ouachita National Recreation Trail. This trail first covers 32 miles on private and other public lands, and then 192 miles through the Ouachita National Forest to the Talimena State Park in Oklahoma. It is the longest trail in the Ouachita National Forest, one of the largest and oldest national forests in the South. The national forest covers 1.8 million acres and was created through an executive order by President Theodore Roosevelt on December 18, 1907.

The Ouachita Mountains, generally just known as the Ouachitas, are a mountain range in western Arkansas and southeastern Oklahoma. Combined with the Ozark Mountains to the north of the Arkansas River, they form what is known as the Interior Highlands. Magazine Mountain, generally known as Mount Magazine, is the highest point at 2753 feet. The Ouachita name has some conflict in its meaning. Many sources state that it relates to an area of good hunting. For example, one source says that it is Choctaw for "big hunt far from home." Another says that it is a French version of a Caddo word that means "good hunting grounds." Another source states that it is a mix of Choctaw words that mean "country of large buffaloes" for the herds of buffalo that used to roam the valleys.

155.1 MAUMELLE RIVER – The railroad uses a bridge with two deck plate girder spans (38'-6" and 75'), plus about a half-dozen ballast deck timber pile spans on each end.

The Maumelle River forms in the Ouachita National Forest in Perry County and then flows eastward to the Arkansas River, looping around the north side of Pinnacle Mountain. The clear water became the target of the communities in Pulaski County when more drinking water was needed. During the late 1950s, a dam was built just west of here to form the 8900-acre Lake Maumelle, which now supplies drinking water for ninety-five percent of the residents of Pulaski County. The water is often rated as some of the best in the country, and the lake and watershed are managed by Central Arkansas Water to keep it that way. It should be noted that the Lake Maumelle dam is primarily made up of material from the eastern slope of Pinnacle Mountain.

155.9 NATURAL STEPS – Natural Steps is a small unincorporated community with a population of 426 in the 2010 census. The area economy is based upon farming and a bit of logging, and the town is scattered along Arkansas Highway 300. The town began as an Arkansas River port, identified by a series of large rocks that gave the impression of a stairway, thus Natural Steps. The Natural Steps were documented by many early explorers and used as a navigation guide on the Arkansas River. The formation has been described as "two perfectly parallel vertical walls of sandstone, twenty feet apart." Between the vertical walls are steps that ascend from the river level about fifty feet to the top of the bluff.

Archaeological research in the area has uncovered fifty-seven burials, as well as pottery from both the Quapaw and Caddo tribes, so the early settlers weren't the first to appreciate the area's river access. Spain issued a land grant at Natural Steps to Eli Stidwell, and John Standlee was living here by the late 1770s. Several conflicting land claims during the early 1800s caused some chaos, but the Sam Taylor sawmill opened during the 1820s to supply Little Rock with lumber. By 1822, Natural Steps was being used as a boat landing because of the easy river access to the banks. The landing was being used by people hiking to nearby Pinnacle Mountain, to load farm and lumber shipments, and to deliver supplies for area settlers. It became a popular picnic area with the *Arkansas Gazette* newspaper reporting as many as twenty steamboats a week using the landing in 1849. However, even with all of this activity, maps failed to show a town here before the Civil War.

Following the Civil War, settlement did begin at Natural Steps. In 1866, Bart Moreland and his family moved to the area and soon opened a general store. The location was documented on a series of maps drawn in 1870 for the effort to create a navigation map of the Arkansas River. In that year, Colonel John Navarre Macomb of the Army Corps of Engineers was assigned to lead a mapping effort along the Arkansas River that would show landings, gravel bars and shoals, and other major features of the river. This was not the first such mapping effort by Macomb, as in 1859, he led an expedition in search of the confluence of the Green and Colorado Rivers. During that exploration, he discovered and mapped what is today Canyonlands National Park.

On May 8, 1874, one of the battles of the Brooks-Baxter War took place here between the steamboat *Hallie*, carrying Baxter supporters, and a flatboat of Brooks supporters who were delivering guns to Little Rock. Additional Brooks loyalists on the river bank joined in and helped disable the steamboat.

About the same time, the Moreland family cleared land and began growing cotton. They built a cotton gin and cottonseed house, a blacksmith shop, a sawmill, and a commissary that helped support the community. A post office opened on September 6, 1880, at the commissary, but it closed on October 3, 1881.

In 1898, the railroad built through the community and erected a depot using the name Big Maumelle. This led to a new post office, which opened on March 15, 1901, as Natural Steps. The railroad followed suit in 1903, renaming the station Natural Steps. A general store, several small sawmills, two churches and a school also soon opened. Cotton, corn, railroad ties, lumber, and shingles were shipped using the railroad. However, a town never really developed and the depot closed, followed by the post office on August 31, 1925, with Bart Moreland the last postmaster. A dispatcher telephone was located here for many years.

Most of the Natural Steps still remain today, although several searches looking for legendary lost Confederate gold or Jesse James riches have damaged them. They are now on private land making them closed to the general public.

Not far south of Natural Steps on Arkansas Highway 300 is the Clay Baylor Cemetery. In 1887, Henry Clay Baylor and his wife Mary Jackson Baylor bought 40 acres here, and in 1896 donated one acre for a church and cemetery. The Baylors were leaders in the area's African-American community, and the St. Matthew Methodist Church and the cemetery served the needs of the Natural Steps, Roland and Monnie Springs residents.

The Railroad at Natural Steps

The Rock Island Railroad and its predecessors had significant plans for Natural Steps. The railroad built a depot at the Maple Avenue grade crossing, but it didn't last much past the early 1900s. There was also a 34-car siding to the south in the 1950 employee timetable. It was still shown in a 1973 track chart, but was not listed in the 1969 employee timetable. In 1921, the railroad had a livestock chute, and also served the L. B. Moreland cotton gin. Today, there are no reasons for the trains of the Little Rock & Western to stop.

At 9:44am on October 13, 1899, the Little Rock to Oklahoma mainline was completed near here, although the exact location wasn't provided in the reporting. Heading west from Natural Steps, Arkansas Highway 300 closely follows the railroad to Roland.

This marker stands beside Arkansas Highway 300 at the Clay Baylor Cemetery, located not far south of Natural Steps, Arkansas.

159.5 ROLAND – Roland is an unincorporated community with a population of 746 during the 2010 census. Roland was a typical farming community wedged between the Arkansas River and the Ouachita Mountains, but it was large enough for a post office to open in 1884. The Choctaw & Memphis Railroad built their Little Rock to Indian Territory (Oklahoma) line through Roland in 1899, helping the community to grow even more. Initially the railroad called the station Spring Hill, but it soon became Roland.

Cotton was an important crop during the early 1900s, and a 1903 Department of Agriculture report indicated that there were 462 rail shipments of cotton from Roland in 1902-1903. A state listing of industry showed that the Clay & Nowlin cotton gin was here in 1921. About the same time, Roland became the home of the St. Francis church cemetery, supporting a growing population of Italian immigrants. During the 1900s, Roland was able to retain its business importance, and its post office survived and handles the mail of other nearby communities such as Natural Steps.

A depot once stood here, located at the Henry Street, often shown as Green Street, grade crossing. By 1979, there was only a dispatcher telephone. Because of the business here, the railroad had a long siding to the north (4581 feet, or 100 railcars long), plus a short 29-car track to the south. Both tracks still exist and the siding is often used to store railcars while the house track is used to inspect and repair freight cars, especially box cars for the paper mill near Perry.

The sign for East Railroad and Beale streets stands at the northern-most crossing at Roland, Arkansas.

160.5 HALL'S – A station using this name was shown in the 1899 timetable of the Choctaw & Memphis. It was gone soon after. From this area south (railroad-east) to Natural Steps, Arkansas Highway 300 closely follows the railroad.

161.1 MONNIE SPRINGS – Monnie Springs was not listed as a station on the Rock Island, but it is a significant landmark for the railroad. Here, the railroad changes direction from heading northeast to northwest. In a short distance, the railroad rounds the end of Moss Mountain and turns west, running on a narrow ledge between Moss Mountain to the south, and the Arkansas River to the north.

Monnie Springs is a rural, unincorporated community that includes a dozen houses, a church, and the Kennerly Cemetery, named for the family of an early settler. To the east is farmland and the Arkansas River, while to the west are the woods of the Ouachita Mountains.

Moss Mountain

Moss Mountain is the eastern end of a long ridge that runs along the south bank of the Arkansas River. For eight miles, the railroad has this ridge to the south. It is likely that Moss Mountain is named for an early black settler named Moss. To the north and in the Arkansas River is Beaverdam Island, which forces the navigation channel close to the north bank of the river.

On top of the ridge to the south in Moss Mountain Farm, the home of P. Allen Smith, often described as one of America's most talented garden designers. Smith's home, also known as The Garden Home Retreat for some of his television work, is open for special events and includes his vegetable garden, rose garden, terraced gardens, Poultryville (a collection of historic poultry species), various animals, Garden Home, and the eHow Cottage. P. Allen Smith was educated at Hendrix College in nearby Conway, and also in England. His farm has been described as a center for promoting the local food movement, organic gardening and the preservation of heritage poultry breeds.

165.6 COUNTY LINE – The county line is located just west of Bridge 165.6, a 60-foot deck plate girder span over the stream that flows out of Ross Hollow, at the west end of Moss Mountain. The Ross Hollow area was considered to be one of the hardest locations to build a railroad. This was because it was squeezed between a mountain and the Arkansas River. In December 1898, 800 men were working in the area, blasting rock away to make a grade. As the railroad heads west, it leaves **Pulaski County** and enters **Perry County**.

Perry County was created from parts of Conway County on December 18, 1840, with Perryville eventually chosen as its county seat. The county is lightly populated with about 10,000 residents, the same as in 1920, and is the third-smallest Arkansas county by total area. Much of the county is included in the Ouachita National Forest, and it is the home of Heifer Ranch, part of Heifer International, a nonprofit organization which provides food and agricultural training for people all around the world. The county was named for Commodore Oliver Hazard Perry, naval hero in the War of 1812. Perry was known for his battle flag that read "Don't Give Up the Ship," and his battle report that started "We have met the enemy and they are ours..."

166.9 LEDWIDGE – Ledwidge is located in another short gap in the mountain to the south, with Kenney Mountain forming the western half of the ridge. This area was part of a series of mountain farming communities, many settled by Italian immigrants. The town had a general store, post office (1900-1929), school house, and a railroad depot (the community petitioned the Arkansas Railroad Commission for a depot on May 12, 1911). It was never the source of a great deal of freight, but 109 rail shipments of cotton moved from here in 1902-1903. The town was never large and was only a flag stop for the railroad. There is little here today as the community was destroyed by a flood during the 1950s. A few foundations remain, and there is a grade crossing with Perry County Road 298.

About the time that Ledwidge went away, the railroad had a 16-car siding to the south, plus a 5-car spur track. By 1979, there was only a dispatcher telephone and 275 feet of spur track at Ledwidge.

167.4 BRIDGE – This bridge is used to cross a small stream that flows out of Kenney Mountain just west of Ledwidge. The bridge consists of two deck plate girder spans. The east span, and the one that crosses the main channel, was built in 1912 by the American Bridge Company and measures 80 feet long. The western span measures 55 feet long and was built by Vierling Steel Works of Chicago in 1950. It is likely that this span was added after the flooding of the early 1950s.

Vierling Steel Works started as Paxton & Vierling Iron Works in 1885, created from a merger of Vierling Steel Company in Chicago, and the William Paxton Company in Omaha. The firm quickly produced the majority of the street lamps in Omaha, Nebraska, and many steel components for Midwest buildings and bridges. In 1937, the company was sold to Fred Owens, an employee, creating Owens Industries. The firm now has several plants across the Midwest and still works as an international structural fabricator.

169.3 KENNEY – This station was listed in the 1899 list of Choctaw & Memphis stations. It took its name from nearby Kenney Mountain, which was named for the Kenney family, who settled in the area after the Civil War. The station didn't last long, and a post office was here only from 1900 to 1905. The general area is still Kenney Township.

Kenny was located where the Fourche La Fave River flows into the Arkansas River. A small private road still provides access to the area.

170.4 FOURCHE LA FAVE RIVER BRIDGE – Just east of here, the railroad exited the narrow pathway between Kenney Mountain and the Arkansas River. In that area, the Fourche La Fave River, often shown as Fourche LaFave River, flows into the Arkansas River. The river starts in southern Scott County south of Waldron, Arkansas, and flows about 150 miles northeast to here. It drains much of the northern part of the Ouachita Mountains, historically flooding whenever a heavy rain fell in the mountains. To try to solve the problem, Lake Nimrod was created in 1942 to hold back much of the river's water. This was not the first federal government involvement with the Fourche La Fave. On March 3, 1879, Congress passed an act to improve the river, and work began to make it navigable to Perryville. This work included the dynamiting of shoals along the stream, and the project was considered finished in 1889. Because of this, when the Choctaw & Memphis Railroad built a bridge across the river, it was forced to include a turn span for navigation. The current bridge used by the Little Rock & Western includes 12 ballast deck pile trestle spans on each end with a 152-foot-long through truss span over the water. The former pier for the turn span sits in the middle of the river, under the through truss span.

The name Fourche La Fave has created some argument over its origin. It is agreed that Fourche is a French word that means "fork," especially of a stream or road, thus a fork of the Arkansas River. However, different sources create La Fave from different families or people. *The Origin of Certain Place Names in the United States* by Henry Gannett (1905), for example, states that La Fave could refer to a family that once lived along the river or to early settler Peter La Fave. Other sources credit Peter La Fave with being the first to explore the river, and with giving it its name. During the early 1800s, the Dunban and Hunter exploration reported that a family named LeFevre lived on the river, while other explorers spelled the name LeFeve. The name probably came from some part of this family, but the spelling has certainly changed.

What is known is that Aaron Price settled alongside the river in 1808, being the first settler in Perry County. He and other early settlers cleared land and grew crops, including cotton. After the Choctaw & Memphis Railroad arrived in 1898, the area boomed with logging and timber companies. One of these, the Fourche River Lumber Company, built a sawmill on the river near the railroad. Others built mills in Bigelow or the nearby logging community of Fourche. Most were gone by the 1930s.

171.2 FOURCHE – Researching this area can be confusing. Fourche, Esau, Bigelow and Graytown are all names for the area, and they were often used interchangeably. For example, the incorporation records of the Fourche River Valley & Indian Territory Railway listed Fourche as its headquarters, but it was actually Graytown, an unincorporated company town outside Bigelow, once known as Esau. The reason Fourche was cited at the incorporation is that Fourche was already in existence and had a post office. The other towns came about because of the lumber company.

Fourche, often called Fourche Station, is located on the north side of a low ridge that turns the Fourche La Fave River back to the southeast to flow into the Arkansas River. Today, Fourche is an area of several blocks of scattered houses to the railroad-north. Its population is about 60 residents, but it was larger during the lumbering boom days of the early 1900s. Records show a peak population of 164 in 1920, but the town had a far larger impact due to the sawmill and logging railroad that once operated here. The town of Fourche is located on the banks of the Fourche La Fave River, where the town's name came from. Early settlers were German farmers who created a number of small communities throughout the area. At the time there was a general store and a few other businesses required by local farmers.

Things changed greatly with the arrival of the Choctaw & Memphis Railroad. Soon, logging began to increase in the mountains and valleys to the south and west. With this growth in logging, a war began between Fourche and the nearby town of Esau, later named Bigelow. Each town was controlled by a competing lumber company that seemed to spend as much time trying to sabotage the other through lawsuits and actual violence as they did cutting their own lumber.

Postal records show the first Fourche post office in Perry County being open 1871-1874. This was about the time of the first arrival of a large number of German immigrants. Among them were the Faisst family, who soon operated a number of businesses at Fourche. This included a tomato cannery (the Central Arkansas Food Products Company), a wine saloon, a skating rink, and a pool hall. The family building also served as a community meeting hall for the German settlers. The Faisst family was also responsible for the Faisst Cemetery, located on top of the ridge to the south. This was the family cemetery for the Faisst family, but a number of other people with German names are also buried here. The earliest burial was in 1902, and there are about sixty marked graves.

Bryant Lumber Company

With the arrival of the railroad, Fourche was incorporated in 1906. A post office opened again in that year, reportedly obtained from Esau, but it lasted only until 1909, when it moved to Bigelow. The status of the post office seemed to have a lot to do with the status of the Bryant Lumber Company. The lumber company opened in 1900, slowly growing as it acquired timber in the area. A major challenge was that the Fourche River Valley & Indian Territory Railway actually built across some of their lands, and the Bryant Lumber Company used this railroad, owned by the competing Fourche River Lumber Company, to move much of its timber. Over the years, this resulted in several legal cases, generally about unfair or different rates charged by the railroad to the two different companies, seemingly always to the advantage of the Fourche River Lumber Company.

On April 4, 1909, the Bryant Lumber Company, which employed as many as 175 workers, suffered a fire that destroyed its mill and a great deal of the cut lumber that was ready to ship. According to *The Lumber World* of April 15, 1909, the damage was estimated at $60,000 to $75,000, and the fire started in the planing mill. The closure of the mill due to the fire greatly impacted Fourche as by that time, the town included a bank, cotton gin, the Fourche Inn, a CRI&P livestock chute at a local stockyard, and the Finkbeiner Meat Packing Company, but most residents worked for the lumber company. The railroad also had a depot here.

The Bryant Lumber Company reopened a year later, but it soon gained a bad reputation as violence and slavery seemed to be a part of its culture. A notorious story about the company stated that the firm once hired a dozen Hungarian immigrants from New York City who spoke no English. When they arrived at Fourche, their papers and possessions were taken from them and they were forced to work, living in what was essentially a prison. When some escaped, the local police arrested them and returned them to the lumber company, but the word was out about the work conditions.

A second story deals with the relationship between the Bryant Lumber Company and the Fourche River Lumber Company. When Fourche River Lumber was building their railroad, they avoided getting a charter, although they used railroad laws to get a right-of-way across some of the land of Bryant Lumber. The story goes that several people hired by Bryant Lumber blew up some track and a locomotive and threatened more action if Fourche River Lumber didn't comply with the law. Soon, Fourche River Lumber incorporated their railroad.

The Fourche post office opened again in 1913, supported by a new Bryant sawmill. Legal suits with Fourche River Lumber continued, but the mill continued to operate, often using African-American labor. A unique characteristic of the town was that both the churches and school were integrated, generally because there were insufficient numbers to have separate facilities. By late 1918, Bryant Lumber Company was in receivership, and the receiver sued Fourche River Lumber saying that the railroad was not being operated as a common carrier, putting Bryant Lumber at a disadvantage. The lumber company closed during the 1920s, and many of the residents moved away, enough that the post office closed in 1933. The Rock Island removed their industry tracks about the same time, and Fourche became a farm community reliant upon the larger Bigelow for its business needs. In 1975, a city hall was built, but the population continued to decline, down to 62 in the 2010 census.

172.3 BIGELOW (VN) ~ The history of Bigelow actually starts in Germany, when Gustave Klingelhoeffer and a group of immigrants organized to come to the United States during the 1830s. In 1833, they arrived in Little Rock and explored the mountains to the west, first settling several miles west of today's Perryville. There, Klingelhoeffer operated a ferry across the Fourche La Fave River. In 1856, he acquired land along a mountain several miles north of today's Bigelow, where he and his family started several businesses. By 1880, they were operating a cotton gin, shingle mill, and a store, and a post office opened that year. The town had taken the name Esau, in spite of an initial attempt to name it Cottonwood. There is no clear reason for the name, but Esau, according to the Hebrew Bible, was the eldest son of Isaac and Rebekah, and the grandson of Abraham and Sarah. Esau's brother was Jacob, the patriarch of the Israelites. The name seemed to be popular with a number of German groups coming to the United States for religious freedom.

In 1900, the Choctaw, Oklahoma & Gulf Railroad was operating to the south, and Prichard Niemeyer started up a small sawmill near the railroad and on the banks of the Fourche La Fave River. Bryant Lumber Company started up at nearby Fourche the same year, attracting more people to the area, even from Esau. In 1902, the Fourche River Lumber Company opened a mill along the Fourche La Fave River a mile upstream of Fourche, and about a half-mile from the railroad. Reports from the time state that the mill was equipped with two band saws and could produce 125,000 board feet of lumber a day. The new Fourche River Lumber town was a company town, with the office building, commissary, a 53-bed hotel, and all residences owned by the lumber company. They painted them all gray, soon giving the unincorporated community the name Graytown. Fourche River Lumber acquired the timber rights of Prichard Niemeyer and developed plans to reach far into the Ouachita Mountains.

As Graytown grew, an independent town also grew to its northeast along the railroad tracks. This town was named Esau as it was basically the older town that had moved to the Rock Island Railroad. In 1905, Esau was incorporated and included Graytown, to which it had earlier been connected by a number of board sidewalks. In 1909, the post office moved from Fourche to Esau, but it was named Bigelow after the lumber company's vice president, N. P. Bigelow, who was the Chicago representative of the company.

One of the major projects of the Fourche River Lumber Company was a railroad deep into the Ouachita Mountains. Known as the Fourche River Valley & Indian Territory Railway, it connected with the Rock Island Railroad at Bigelow, and the Bryant Lumber Company at nearby Fourche. The year 1910 was probably the peak of activity, and some claimed that Bigelow was the largest city between Little Rock and

267

Fort Smith. The estimated population of 10,000 at the time is certainly too large, but the city was a busy place. Besides the Fourche River Lumber Company, there were hardware and jewelry stores, a drug store, barber shop, two dry cleaning establishments, three general stores, an ice house, a baker, and a butcher shop. There was also a state bank, four hotels, and a large hall used for dances, fraternal meetings, and other public events. All of this was reported on by the *Citizen's Press*, the local newspaper.

In 1911, N. P. Bigelow built an elaborate white house of the best lumber on a hill above the town. He was elected mayor, and then campaigned to change the name of Esau to Bigelow. Later that year, the town officially changed its name to Bigelow, and an attempt was made to move the county seat to the lumber town. A 1915 vote approved the change, but the move was never made. The *Arkansas Marketing and Industrial Guide* of 1921 listed a number of businesses at Bigelow, including the Bigelow Canning Company, W. S. Brickley cotton gin, Hawkins & Gray, and the Fourche River Lumber Company, which produced both general lumber and hardwood flooring. About this time, the population was approximately 600, and the lumber boom was almost over as all of the nearby timber had been cut. In 1921, the Fourche River Lumber Company closed its mill and moved out of the community. Most of the residents quickly followed. Much of the remaining timber holdings were eventually acquired by Dierks, a major timber company in Arkansas and Oklahoma. There was a small economic boom from 1969 until the late 1990s as the Bigelow Manufacturing Company built mobile homes here, employing about 120 people. The population today is about 300, and Bigelow has a post office, a school system, and a few stores along Arkansas Highway 113.

Because of the lumber business here, the Rock Island had a number of tracks at Bigelow, even after the mills closed. In 1950, there was a 75-car siding to the south with a 16-car house track. In that same year, passenger trains No. 111 and No. 112 – both named *Cherokee* – were scheduled to meet at Bigelow at 1:45am. However, the railroad had office hours 8:30am-5:30pm at the station located near today's Arkansas Highway 113 grade crossing. At the end of the CRI&P's operations, the siding was shown to be 3408 feet long, and the house track was 430 feet long. The siding still exists and is used by the Little Rock & Western to store freight cars.

Rock Island Joint Facilities

Because of the volume of business at Bigelow, the CRI&P and the Fourche River Lumber Company (Fourche River Valley & Indian Territory Railway – FRV&IT) had a number of joint facility agreements because each company often used the facilities of the other. The June 15, 1915, joint facilities contract is a good example. This contract stated that the FRV&IT owned the depot at Bigelow, but that it was located on the property of the Chicago, Rock Island & Pacific. The CRI&P actually operated the depot and maintained it, with these expenses being shared equally between the two companies.

There were also a number of tracks that were jointly used for switching and interchanging freight cars. The agreement stated that the CRI&P paid two-thirds of the maintenance costs of the FRV&IT tracks used jointly, and paid all costs of the CRI&P-owned tracks used jointly.

Fourche River Valley & Indian Territory Railway

For a small railroad that was a mix of logging railroad and common carrier, and especially for one abandoned during the 1920s, there is a great deal of material about the Fourche River Valley & Indian Territory Railway. This information comes from many sources, including the Interstate Commerce Commission, court records, and company communications. The Fourche River Lumber Company cut timber from as much as twenty miles away from Bigelow, and used both logging lines and a common carrier railroad to move logs to its sawmill at Graytown. Some credit the Bigelow Brothers, who had just closed sawmills in Michigan and Wisconsin, with starting up the logging company and railroads, but it was far more complicated than that. Interstate Commerce Commission records show that the railroad operations began with the Arkansas River & Southern Railway. The June 2, 1904, issue of the *Manufacturers' Record* reported on the creation of the railroad. The short article stated that the Arkansas River & Southern "proposes to build a line 20 miles long from Redemption, in Perry county, Arkansas, to Maumelle, in Pulaski county." Redemption is now known as Toad Suck, Arkansas, and is located on the Arkansas River less than ten miles to the northeast.

From the beginning, the Rock Island provided a financial reward for delivering carloads of freight to their line at Bigelow. The Interstate Commerce Commission reported that "on August 9, 1904, a contract was entered into by the Rock Island lines with the Arkansas River & Southern Railroad, and this has been assigned to the Fourche River Valley & Indian Territory. It provides for the payment of divisions to the tap line, and requires that not less than 50 per cent of its traffic shall be given to the Rock Island."

Some sources state that the Arkansas River & Southern Railway was affiliated with the Fourche River Lumber Company. However, the directors listed for the railroad were "Gordon N. Peay, T. Guy Bragg and B. Thurston of Little Rock, R. B. Edgar and C. Ketcham of Perry county."

This compares with the directors of the Fourche River Valley & Indian Territory Railway, which in 1906 listed "F. H. Hartshorne, C. S. Sailor, Fourche, Ark.; Chas. Neimeyer, Little Rock, Ark.; L. T. Walker, N. P. Bigelow, Chicago, Ill." As can be seen, there are no common directors, so it appears that the companies were different. Researching the corporations, the Fourche River Lumber Company and the associated railroads were actually owned by the Bigelow Brothers & Walker Company, chartered on November 3, 1902. Based in Chicago, this firm was created to "deal generally in timber, goods, wares and merchandise."

While the incorporation announcement for the Arkansas River & Southern Railway was in 1904, there are some reports that tracks were installed before that. In the report on the "Tap Line Case", published in *Decisions of the Interstate Commerce Commission* (ICC), there was a great amount of detail about the railroad. It stated that the "mill is at a company town known as Graytown, less than a mile from the line of the Rock Island, and was erected in 1903. Before the machinery was installed a track was built from a point on the Rock Island then known as Esau, but now in the town of Bigelow. When the mill was opened this track was extended south and west for the purpose of reaching the timber, and in August, 1905, when the railroad corporation was formed, was about 9 miles in length."

Poor's Manual of the Railroads of the United States (1906) stated that the Fourche River Valley & Indian Territory (FRV&IT) was chartered on August 16, 1905, and had 11.5 miles of track completed from Fourche to Orchard by September 1, 1906, and an extension graded. It also reported that the railroad was chartered to build 45 miles of track from Fourche to Yell County, Arkansas. *The Railroad Gazette* of March 15, 1907, reported that the FRV&IT had let a contract to Robert G. Jenkins of Fourche, to build a railroad extension from Camp D to the west line of Perry County, a total of 38 miles.

The June 30, 1916, valuation by the Interstate Commerce Commission provided a detailed report from that year. It contained the following statement about the railroad's route and purpose.

> *[The railroad] is a single-track standard-gauge steam railroad located in Perry and Pulaski Counties, Ark. The owned mileage extends in a generally westerly direction from Bigelow to Thornburg, Ark., a distance of 18.649 miles. The carrier also owns yards and sidetracks totaling 2.882 miles. Its road thus embraces 21.531 miles of all tracks owned.*

*The carrier was incorporated on October 28, 1905, under
the general laws of Arkansas, for a term of 50 years. Its principal office is at Bigelow, Ark. The carrier was organized in
the interest of Fourche River Lumber Company, for the purpose of constructing, owning, and maintaining a railroad at
Bigelow, Ark., and proceeding westwardly on the south side
of the Fourche la Fave River to the county line separating
Perry and Yell Counties at a point 3 miles south of the post
office of Jennings Falls, all in Perry County, and to be 44
miles in length. The Fourche River Lumber Company controls the carrier through ownership of its entire capital stock.*

The Fourche River Valley & Indian Territory can generally be followed as much of the route is now county or farm and forestry roads.
From Bigelow, the railroad headed west, crossed the river where the
remains of its through truss bridge still stands, and turned to the southwest. It then went up Rankin Creek and Holmes Hollow to Wye. There,
the mainline turned almost due west. Near Thornburg, the former grade
is now Tram Road. The ICC provided a great deal of information about
the railroad and its operations, as stated here.

*The tap line, as described of record, is standard gauge,
laid with 56-pound steel and having substantial bridges. It
extends from Bigelow, a town on the Rock Island, to Bellev-
ue, a distance of 15 miles, with about 2 miles of side track.
At a switch known as Wye, about 9 miles from Bigelow, unincorporated logging tracks connect with the tap line and
reach out into the woods. The tap line has 1 locomotive, 1
combination passenger and baggage car, 1 tank car, and 61
freight and logging cars. The lumber company itself owns
two locomotives, which it operates on the logging tracks. The
tap line has a two-story building at Graytown, used as a station and office, with small sheds and a loading platform at
one or two other points. It apparently uses the Rock Island
station at Bigelow, and it weighs carload shipments on the
lumber company's track scale at Graytown.*

Over the years, the Fourche River Valley & Indian Territory was involved in two major legal cases. The first was the ICC Tap Line Case
where railroads owned by their primary shipper were examined to determine if they were really a common carrier, or simply a private railroad trying to claim a share of the freight and passenger tariff. The ICC
provided a great deal of information about the railroad's operation.

> *The tap line operates two logging trains daily in each direction with a coach, but its passenger revenues for the fiscal year 1910 were only $1,100. Its principal tonnage is forest products, amounting for the year 1910 to 142,359 tons, of which 31,176 tons was lumber. It moved during the same period 3,825 tons of miscellaneous freight, including nearly 2,000 tons of coal. The record indicates that 6,082 tons of freight moving outbound and 448 tons moving inbound were furnished by others than the proprietary company, or an aggregate of about 5 per cent of its traffic. It does not participate in through rates on articles other than forest products, and its local charges on merchandise are not filed with the Commission.*

Initially, the ICC considered the FRV&IT to be simply a logging railroad owned by the timber company. However, after a Supreme Court case involving such rulings, the ICC redefined what such lines are. For this railroad, the ICC allowed the Rock Island to credit the Fourche River Valley & Indian Territory a $1.50 switching charge for moving the products of the controlling mill at Graytown to the junction point at Bigelow, a distance of nearly 1 mile.

In a May 15, 1914, advertisement in *The St. Louis Lumberman*, the Fourche River Lumber Company promoted its "Arkansas Short Leaf Hill Pine" and listed its officers. In that year, Nelson P. Bigelow was president and Lyman T. Walker was vice-president, and both were shown as being based in Chicago. Frank H. Hartshorne was shown to be the secretary-treasurer and general manager and was based at Bigelow. The three officials were at the time the owners of the Bigelow Brothers & Walker Company, which owned the logging company and railroad.

About this time, the Bryant Lumber Company was in court charging that the FRV&IT was discriminating against what was essentially its owner's competitor. At the time, Bryant Lumber was shipping logs over the railroad to their mill at Fourche, and their claim was that the rates were higher than those charged to the railroad's owner for the same service. The service arrangements dated back to 1905 when the railroad built across land owned by Bryant Lumber. The agreement required the FRV&IT to install switches and build track as needed for Bryant Lumber in exchange for the use of the right-of-way. The agreement also stated that the railroad "shall be required to carry timber and other freight equally without discrimination for or against the Bryant Company." The argument was that the railroad received a rebate on all shipments, thus benefitting Fourche River Lumber and not Bryant Lumber. However, the courts ruled that the money went to the railroad and not the lumber company. This argument continued until both companies closed in the 1920s.

During World War I, the FRV&IT was placed under federal control January 1 - June 30, 1918. Indirect control lasted until February 20, 1920. This was caused by the *Federal Possession and Control Act*, creating the United States Railroad Administration (USRA) as part of an effort to coordinate railroad operations as part of the war effort. At the end of the control, it was determined that the federal government owed the Fourche River Valley & Indian Territory $73,332.16 due to the damage done to the railroad, and the restrictions on its operations. About that time, both logging companies had cut their timber and operations were being shut down. Although the 1921 *Arkansas Marketing and Industrial Guide* still listed the Fourche River Valley & Indian Territory Railway, the lumber company shut down that year. The railroad reportedly lasted until 1923 when the timberlands were sold to the Dierks Lumber & Coal Company. Several sources show that the railroad's incorporation ended on October 1, 1923.

Locomotives of the Fourche River Valley & Indian Territory Railway

Information about the railroad's locomotives should be included. Some of the locomotives and freight cars were rented from the Rock Island, especially those used to switch the mill and handle finished products. The company also bought secondhand equipment, such as Union Pacific #1289 (2-8-0) that became FRV&IT #2. The company also had at least five Shay locomotives used on the logging lines.

The first was Shay #1, built for the Bigelow Brothers & Walker Company and assigned immediately to the Fourche River Valley & Indian Territory in 1903. Built in December of that year as Shop Number 842, the 55-ton, 2-truck Shay was sold to the Tremont & Gulf Railway, becoming their second #21, in 1922. It was scrapped in 1927 at Rocheile, Louisiana.

Shay #3 was built for the Fourche River Lumber Company and assigned to the FRV&IT. This was a larger Shay, weighing 70 tons and having 3 trucks. Assigned Shop Number 1971, it had an August 1907 build date. It also went to the Tremont & Gulf Railway, becoming their #22. It was also later scrapped.

Shay #4 was Shop Number 896, built in July 1904 for the H. C. McDaniels Lumber Company in El Dorado, Arkansas. The 65-ton, 3-truck Shay was sold to several other companies before being acquired on August 6, 1912, and lasted on the FRV&IT until the end of the railroad. It became Trinity County Lumber Company #4 (Texas) in 1923, and was scrapped during the early 1930s.

Another Shay was FRV&IT #6. It was Shop Number 2507 and was built in February 1912, for the Champion Lumber Company of Crestmont, North Carolina. After going through several owners, the 70-ton, 3-truck Shay arrived at Bigelow during August 1919, and was sold two years later to the Gloster Lumber Company at Gloster, Arkansas. It was later scrapped.

Shay #7 was the last one acquired by the Fourche River Valley & Indian Territory. It was built in December 1901 for the James Strong Lumber Company of Bristol, Tennessee, as a 65-ton, 3-truck Shay with Shop Number 678. It was the oldest Shay owned by the railroad and logging company. The FRV&IT acquired it during June 1920 and had it for sale two years later as the railroad closed. It went to the Green River Lumber Company at McIntosh, Washington, in 1924, and it was later scrapped.

174.3 MILL CREEK BRIDGE – Look for the two 70-foot deck plate girder spans. Mill Creek forms near New Dixie on the south side of Toms Mountain, a major east-west running ridge that forces the Arkansas River to the north. Mill Creek flows southwest, under the tracks here, and then south into the Fourche La Fave River, not far west of Bigelow. The name of the creek comes from one of several sawmills that was once on the stream.

From Bigelow to Houston, the railroad cuts northwest through woods and fields, while Arkansas Highway 113 takes an indirect route, first heading north and then turning west. There are few places to reach the railroad in this area.

176.6 HOUSTON – During the late 1840s, John L. Houston was operating a ferry across the Fourche La Fave River, serving several places along the river. He had settled near the Arkansas River, creating a small community that used his name before he moved to Perryville. Nearby was Brown's Landing, named for Robert Brown, who led a group of settlers from Kentucky to this area in 1853. Brown's Landing grew near the Arkansas River until it included several stores, a blacksmith shop, a school, and a few houses. In 1878, a post office was authorized for the community, and Postmaster James W. Marshall tried to name it Jamesville after himself. However, there already was a Jamesville, so it became Houston, a name already used for the general area. At the time the community included two or three small stores, a church and school, a blacksmith shop, cemetery, and a few houses. The town's general area is today marked by the site of the Old Houston Cemetery, located on the south side of Toms Mountain to the northeast of today's Houston. Little remains as during the late 1890s, most of it moved to be near the new railroad.

The railroad at Houston was built from the west, and the Choctaw & Memphis had completed grading as far east as Houston by August 1899. Here, the railroad was built through the property of Margaret Long, who donated the right-of-way through her property, but with the requirement that a station stop be established. With a guaranteed stop, "New Houston" quickly developed alongside the railroad. Initially, the Choctaw & Memphis was involved with the creation of the Houston townsite. However, the railroad deeded all interest in the project to J. E. England, described as a "prominent capitalist" by local newspapers, during October 1899.

Unlike other towns in the area, Houston was based more upon farming than logging, and only hosted one small sawmill initially. In addition, there was a cotton gin, drugstore, millinery, butcher shop, shoe repair shop, movie theater, hotel, two saloons, and a bank. Both a Methodist and a Baptist church were built, as was a larger school in 1902. On June 21st of that year, Houston was officially incorporated.

By the early 1900s, several small timber companies operated at Houston, including the Ayer & Lord Tie Company and W. E. Edmondson, but they generally just bought wood and shipped it to other mills along the railroad. The Choctaw, Oklahoma & Gulf (Rock Island Railroad) owned a one-pen stockyard to handle what livestock moved in the area. A bit more growth at the time added a casket making shop, butcher shop, soda fountain, and a barber shop. On January 25, 1908, the town faced a challenge as much of the business district was burned by outlaws as a part of their effort to rob the Bank of Houston. The use of too much nitroglycerine to open the safe is the cited cause of the fire. With little standing besides the post office, one drug store and a barber shop, much of the downtown was rebuilt with brick.

Census records indicate that Houston's population peaked in 1920 at 403 residents, and the town has experienced a slow decline since. The Flood of 1927 greatly impacted the town as the railroad was flooded and the town isolated. In 1929, the Rock Island Railroad had a derailment in town. The train was carrying gasoline, crude oil, kerosene, and alcohol, and it caught fire, forcing residents to flee the community. The Great Depression greatly impacted local business, driving many families off of their nearby farms and closing what timber business was left. Since the 1940s, most new buildings at Houston have simply replaced older ones, like the new post office and city hall building that was built in 1972. The population was 173 at the 2010 census.

The station agency at Houston opened and closed during the late 1920s and early 1930s as business came and went. On February 15, 1928, the Arkansas Railroad Commission allowed the railroad to replace its agent with a caretaker. However, the petition to discontinue Houston as a regular stop was denied and the Rock Island was ordered to stop certain trains on a daily basis. In 1931, the CRI&P closed its agency at Houston due to a lack of business. A number of hearings by the Arkansas Railroad Commission followed. In 1932, the Arkansas Railroad Commission's work was transferred to the Arkansas Corporation Commission. Therefore, in 1933, the Chicago, Rock Island & Pacific petitioned the Arkansas Corporation Commission to close the station at Houston. An initial hearing resulted in permission on March 16, 1933, but an appeal required additional hearings. A final decision on August 17, 1933, again gave the railroad permission to close the station at Houston. In 1950, Houston was still the location of a railroad siding, measuring 34 cars long, and the station building stood near the Arkansas Highway 113 grade crossing. Additionally, there were several short spur tracks that had a combined capacity of 26 cars. By 1973, the siding was gone and one short 500-foot-long spur track remained at the abandoned grain silos at the northwest end of town.

178.6 COPPERAS GAP – Copperas Gap is the name of the gap between Perry Mountain to the west and Toms Mountain to the east. A small community was founded here, and the cemetery still remains, as do several houses. At one time, cotton was shipped from here, including a reported 406 rail shipments in 1902-1903. In 1950, there was a 41-car siding, but it was gone by the late 1960s. The siding was often used for doubling trains over the gap, and the Perry Switcher would sometimes be used to help trains make the grade, which was 1.0% each way. The 8-degree curve at the top of the grade makes it even harder for trains to negotiate the hill.

Copperas Gap was an important location for the Choctaw & Memphis. As the railroad was building east from Indian Territory, there was talk about the St. Louis, Iron Mountain & Southern building west from Little Rock to block the route. The pass at Copperas Gap was believed to be the only effective route for any railroad building west from Little Rock. To control the Gap, the Choctaw & Memphis had 55 men working at Copperas Gap by November 1898. The grade was built to here by August 1899, and the major trestle was almost completed.

Located not far west of Copperas Gap is the grade crossing with Copperas Gap Road.

Going through the pass, the railroad is against Perry Mountain while Arkansas Highway 113 is against Toms Mountain. Above the railroad is a steep hillside that is several hundred feet high. After heading north through Copperas Gap, the railroad loops around the end of Perry Mountain and turns to the southwest. A dispatcher telephone was located in this area for train crews to report their progress, or lack thereof.

A major wooden trestle once stood here, but now a large concrete culvert and a long fill mark the location. The worn date of 1918 can still be found on the culvert.

180.2 ARKANSAS KRAFT – This switch leads to a more than three-mile-long lead track to the Green Bay Packaging, Arkansas Kraft Division, board mill. Construction on this mill started in 1965, and on a 2½ mile rail spur on February 20, 1965. The mill began operating during October 1966, using both pulpwood and wood chips. Much of the inbound pulpwood came from Arkansas yards at Belleville, Booneville, Vick and Benton. Wood chips came from sawmills at Ola and Mansfield. The Rock Island handled most inbound and outbound shipments, although shortages of railcars was a constant issue forcing some moves by trucks. The March/April 1967 issue of *The Rocket* stated that "Arkansas Kraft will expand its plant capacity from a planned 250 tons per day to 350 tons per day over the next six months." To handle the switching at the mill, Arkansas Kraft bought CRI&P Alco S2 locomotive #721, which had just been retired as the Stuttgart switcher. In 1979, the Rock Island listed the spur track as having 18,630 feet of capacity.

Arkansas Kraft has always been owned by Green Bay Packaging. The mill, now known as the Arkansas Mill Division, uses a combination of virgin and recycled fiber to produce kraft linerboard and medium. The term kraft has a special meaning, and is a paper that is used to make cardboard boxes and heavy-duty wrapping paper. The mill is certified to the SFI® Certified Sourcing standard and the Chain of Custody standard. These standards require the tracking of forest fiber content during manufacturing of products. Today, Arkansas Kraft is an integrated, two machine, virgin mill that produces more than 400,000 tons of paper per year.

Between the Arkansas Kraft mill and Perry, the tracks can be followed using Bone Hollow Road. This Little Rock & Western grade crossing sign can be found along the route.

183.8 PERRY (RY) – Perry is the home of the Little Rock & Western Railway, and is where they have their office and shops. In 1950, Perry was a train order station with the office opened 6:00am-3:00pm. The station code at the time was "RY". There was a 100-car-long siding, plus several other tracks with a capacity of 62 cars. Perry was also the west end of automatic block signals (ABS) that had been installed from Biddle Yard to here in 1950. These signals were installed partly in response to a head-on collision between train No. 111 (westbound Memphis-Californian) and an eastbound local freight on January 15, 1948, that took place not far west of Pulaski.

In 1989, the former Rock Island depot at Perry, Arkansas, still stood next to the tracks in relatively fresh paint with its train order semaphore.

Perry started when the Choctaw & Memphis built a station here to serve the county seat of Perryville, which is located less than five miles to the south. The station was originally named North Perryville in 1898, but became simply Perry in 1899 when a post office opened. The residents of Perryville were not happy that the railroad built north of their town and campaigned to have a new route used. There were several articles complaining about the location of the Perry station, with at least one calling it an unhealthy location because of a nearby cypress swamp. The track reached here by late September, 1899, as by that time it was too late to change the route.

The town grew quickly and a saloon was open even before the tracks arrived. A school was built in 1900, and a 1901 story stated that there were several saloons, four hotels, several stores, a sawmill, a shingle mill, a bakery, a livery stable, a grist mill, and a millinery shop. From the start, Perry was a busy place for the railroad. The volume of freight traffic brought about a hearing by the Railroad Commission of Arkansas. In August 1905, the Commission reported that the railroad failed to furnish Reynold and Van Cleve with sufficient cars at Perry, Arkansas. An additional hearing in December 1906 commented on the same problem.

The Little Rock & Western has their locomotive shops at Perry. This view shows the new expansion that was made possible when the former Rock Island depot was moved a block away.

A 1914 Sanborn map showed that the railroad depot was on the north side of Front Street (today's Choctaw Avenue) and west of Main Street, on the south side of the mainline. There was a platform on the north side of the siding, which was north of the mainline. At the time, the Lakeside Hotel was across the street from the depot on Front Street. Perry incorporated in 1914.

1920 was an important year for Perry, Arkansas. It reached its peak population of 540 that year, and the town received electricity from W. A. Halbrook, making it the first community in Perry County to have electric street lights and power to individual houses. The electricity was reportedly available from 6:00am until 10:00pm. In 1921, Perry was shown to be a busy community with the B. E. Cragen cotton gin, St. Francis Valley Lumber Company, Perry Lumber & Shingle Company, W. B. Holbrook sawmill, Moseley Brothers sawmill, and R. Hayden & Son sawmill. The railroad had a one-pen stockyard. Perry was also an important water stop for the railroad as the water had a low mineral content.

As the timber business moved away, the population started a slow decline to today's 270. In 1949, the Perry school district consolidated with the Casa system. After the Rock Island shut down in 1980, the St. Louis Southwestern operated Little Rock to Perry for a few months to support the nearby paper mill. While there was some hope for service further west, it was soon clear that there was no interest by any company of operating the railroad west of here. This led to Perry becoming the home of the Little Rock & Western Railway later in 1980. The company initially used the old passenger depot as their office, then built a new office building. In 2018, the town of Perry acquired the old depot after it was included on Preserve Arkansas' Most Endangered Places list. The depot was built in 1918 and is the only remaining wood-frame depot from the Rock Island in Arkansas. The station was moved a short distance off railroad property in 2019 with plans for restoring the building and turning it into a museum.

This photo shows the track side of the Perry depot. In 2019, the depot was moved to the north side of the tracks and just west of Arkansas Highway 9. There are plans to restore the building and use it as a local museum.

This view of the Perry depot shows the back side of the building, a side hidden for several decades from public view.

Heading west, Arkansas Highway 10 closely follows the railroad almost all the way to Oklahoma.

Perry to Danville Operations

The Little Rock & Western acquired the rail line only to Perry, but during the summer of 1986 the railroad began operating westward to Danville, Arkansas. To save service to their feed mill at Danville, Wayne Farms and Continental Grain Company gained control of the 35 miles of track from Perry to Danville. The company contracted with the Little Rock & Western to provide the rail service as needed.

On May 22, 1986, the Interstate Commerce Commission approved the operation, and operations began in July. The Little Rock & Western would deliver carloads of feed for the feed mill, serve the sawmill at Ola, and store freight cars on the line for a number of years. Service to Danville ended soon after Wayne Farms bought a poultry feed mill at Atkins, Arkansas, in 2012, moving their feed operations to there. Service to Ola continued for a while to handle the business of the PotlatchDeltic mill at Ola.

186.8 BRYANT – This station was listed in the *Fifth Annual Report of the Railroad Commission of the State of Arkansas* (1904). A family by the name Bryant lived in the area. There is no sign of this station today.

189.7 ADONA – Adona is another Ouachita Mountain town created by the railroad, promoted by the Choctaw, Oklahoma and Memphis Town Site Company as "The Garden Spot." While the railroad and their land company located the townsite and initially promoted it, during October 1899, the deeds to the property were turned over to J. E. England. From 1900 until 1904, J. E. England was part of Cornish & England, a banking and real estate firm in Arkansas.

Adona is also another town whose population peaked in 1920, this one at 241 residents. Adona advertises itself as "the first city in Arkansas" due to its position in the state list of communities. The land Adona sits on was first owned by Franklin Russell, who claimed it in 1849. However, he never lived here, and instead sold it to John Howell. Howell started a small community using Cypress Creek for a water source, giving the town the name Cypress Valley. The name of the community became Adona by the time the post office opened in 1879, named for one of John Howell's descendants. A school opened by the 1880s.

A depot was built here in 1901, and a town was officially platted, with it being incorporated in 1903. Several sawmills operated in the area, and the Adona Gin Company was processing area cotton. A grist mill was also opened in the area to handle local corn production. In 1950, the railroad served the local shippers with a 31-car capacity house track. By the late 1960s, all tracks were gone except the mainline.

Today, Adona is a collection of houses, barns, and a post office scattered over about a dozen blocks, most located between the railroad and Arkansas Highway 10 to the south. John Howell is still memorialized by Howell Creek, which forms the west boundary of Adona. The population during the 2010 census was 209.

Adona, Arkansas, is another town that recognized the important of the railroad by naming a street for it.

Fowler Mill

About two miles west of Adona is the Fowler Cemetery. The cemetery was named for the Fowler family, and almost fifty family members are buried here. Nearby was the Fowler Mill, a sawmill owned and operated by the Fort Smith Lumber Company. The lumber company operated a number of sawmills in Perry, Yell and Sebastian counties, and even operated several logging railroads. This mill began operating soon after the Choctaw, Oklahoma & Gulf opened their railroad through here, and cut timber from as far away as Petit Jean Mountain, located a dozen miles to the north. Lumber was hauled to the mill using a 30-inch narrow gauge railroad. Some reports state that this was the narrowest logging railroad in Arkansas, and it had a mainline about 6.5 miles long. According to the Interstate Commerce Commission's *Twenty First Annual Report on the Statistics of Railways in the United States for the Year Ending June 30, 1908*, the line was the Rose Creek Railroad, a private railroad owned by the Fort Smith Lumber Company, but it was listed as being out of service. Earlier reports show that the line had one locomotive and thirty railcars. There are several reports that the mill experienced a fire about 1907, and it closed in 1909 when the last of the marketable timber in the area had been cut.

The work of Dr. T. W. Hardison is recognized by this statue at the new Petit Jean State Park visitor center.

Signs like this can be found at the various entrances to Petit Jean State Park.

Petit Jean State Park

The operations of the Fowler Mill, and the Fort Smith Lumber Company, helped to create Petit Jean State Park, a 3471-acre park atop Petit Jean Mountain. In 1907, a tour of the mill and the timber being cut led to a discussion about the difficulty in cutting much of the timber in the Seven Hollows area of the mountain, and the idea of donating it as a park. A leader of this suggestion was Dr. T. W. Hardison, the Fort Smith Lumber physician at the sawmill and nearby logging camps. Officials of the company approved of the idea and set the land aside and protected it from logging. Dr. Hardison was later the official who worked with the State in creating the state park, the first in Arkansas. Hardison lived on the mountain the rest of his life, providing medical care for area settlers.

While the Fowler Mill closed in 1909, some timbering continued in the area, and it wasn't until 1921 that the timber company was ready to hand over the property. At first, the plan was for the creation of a national park, and a bill to create Petit Jean National Park was introduced in the U.S. House of Representatives. A meeting between Dr. Hardison and Stephen Mather, director of the National Park Service, resulted in a decision that the property was too small to justify the cost of development and administration. Instead, it was recommended that it be turned into an Arkansas state park.

While the State of Arkansas considered the gift, and the Fort Smith Lumber Company altered its agreement from giving the land to the federal government and instead to the state government, a group of eight Arkansas residents donated eighty acres that included the Cedar Falls area. This eighty acres was the first state park land ever acquired by Arkansas, and it led to the creation of Petit Jean State Park in 1923. Not long after, Fort Smith Lumber donated the Seven Hollows area. Additional acquisitions, plus the work of the Civilian Conservation Corps, helped create one of the highest rated state parks in the country. Today, Seven Hollows is a popular hiking area, and a visit will easily demonstrate why it would have been hard to log this country.

This sign marks the start of the Seven Hollows Trail. The Seven Hollows area, once owned by the Fort Smith Lumber Company, was the inspiration for what became Petit Jean State Park.

The Petit Jean Name

The name Petit Jean is generally credited to the legend of a young French woman who posed as a man to follow her lover to America. Serving as a cabin boy, her small size earned her the name "Petit Jean" from the ship's crew. The story continues that she became ill after arriving near the mountain, her history became known, and she died and was buried on the eastern end of Petit Jean Mountain. The legend is popular and has been heavily researched without firm proof of the history, however the story continues to be told. An alternative source of the name comes from the explanation that the nearby river was named

"Little Yellow River" by the French, or "petit jaune" which became "Petty Jean" by the English settlers.

What may be the real story was collected by settler Marion McCabe and told to Dr. T. W. Hardison as efforts were underway to create the park. A Jean LaCaze fled France at the start of the French Revolution of the 1790s, taking with him his wife and son, Petit Jean. LaCaze sailed to New Orleans, and then up the Mississippi and Arkansas rivers to the base of today's Petit Jean Mountain. He located a site on the south brow of the mountain and built a cabin for his family, trading with members of local tribes. However, the death that he fled soon caught up with him as first his wife died during childbirth, and then Petit Jean passed away a few years later. In despair, Jean LaCaze became a hermit on the mountain which took his son's name. As other settlers began to arrive in the area, La Caze withdrew even more, disappearing for good. Legend has that he fell into one of the area caves, but his body was never found.

191.0 HOGUE SIDING – This siding was listed as being under construction in October 1899. This would have been near where the Fowler Mill once stood. Heading north from here on Arkansas Highway 324, and then Highway 155, takes you to Petit Jean State Park.

194.3 HOMEWOOD – Homewood is located at the grade crossing of County Road 217, also known as Dempsey Lane. Homewood Farms, with its large poultry barns, can be found alongside Arkansas Highway 10. Rock Island records show a siding here that was 3586 feet long, or 78 railcars. The siding is still here to the south of the mainline. During the early 1900s, the Fort Smith Lumber Company had a sawmill operating at Homewood.

The east switch of Homewood is at the top of the grade from Perry. The grade climbs from 294 feet at Perry to 439 feet at Homewood, with grades as stiff as 1.0% for westbound trains. Eastbound trains start climbing at Milepost 200 where the elevation is 320 feet. Grades for these trains are as much as 0.9%.

In a timetable from 1900, this station was shown as Beard, a siding. At the time, D. J. Beard was the principal assistant engineer of the Choctaw & Memphis. The railroad had a practice of naming new towns and stations after investors and company management.

Over the years, the Rock Island Railroad made a number of repairs and improvements along the line. This small timber trestle at Milepost 196.6 shows how the timber piles were replaced by a solid concrete pier.

198.4 CASA – Casa is a Spanish word for house, and this is considered to be one of the oldest communities in Perry County. It was first settled during the 1830s by the Grace and McGhee families, and then others from Georgia and South Carolina. The wide valley was perfect for farming, and the nearby timber was used for buildings. A general store opened in 1850, and the current post office opened in 1854. During the Civil War, much of the town was destroyed by guerrilla forces. The town recovered and grew more after the war, gaining a new school, several churches, and a number of small businesses. The railroad opened in 1899, and the Town of Casa was incorporated on May 10, 1900.

While Casa was already here when the railroad built through the area, the Choctaw, Oklahoma and Memphis Town Site Company did plat a community around the proposed station, promoting it as "Rich in Land and Timber." In October 1899, the land company transferred the deeds for the townsite to J. E. England, who was also in the land development and promotion business.

A small coal mine opened at Casa in 1900, but the coal seam soon played out. The timber lasted longer, and the Fort Smith Lumber Company and at least two other lumber companies opened sawmills here.

The new jobs attracted other businesses such as four saloons, two newspapers, a bank, and four physicians. Farming was also a major activity, and a 1903 Department of Agriculture report indicated that there were 1285 rail shipments of cotton from Casa in 1902-1903.

The Fort Smith Lumber Company mill closed about 1907, and its 3-mile-long, 36-inch gauge logging railroad was packed up and moved elsewhere. Records indicate that the logging company used one locomotive and eight log cars on the line. As the timber was cut, farming slowly took over, and Casa reached its peak population of 310 in 1910. A highlight for the community was the April 1912 visit by former President Theodore Roosevelt, who made a five-minute campaign stop in Casa. Roosevelt traveled much of the Choctaw Route, speaking as part of his election run as the Progressive Party ("Bull Moose") nominee.

A 1914 map shows Casa at probably what was its peak. The Rock Island Railroad tracks ran through the middle of town on Front Street, with North and South Front Streets designated. Today, South Front Street is Railroad Avenue and North Front Street is gone. Also gone are the many tracks and buildings that the railroad once had here. The depot was between the mainline (to south) and the siding (to north), located east of Broadway. To the east of the depot was a large cotton platform, and there were cotton shed houses to the west of the depot on the north side of the siding. The Commercial Hotel was convenient to the depot, being located to the north on North Front Street.

In 1921, the *Arkansas Marketing and Industrial Guide* listed a number of businesses at Casa, including the Kemper Brothers cotton gin (once owned by Horn & Knight), Robertson Brothers Lumber Company, H. C. McGhee lumber mill, and the J. O. Allen lumber mill. The Rock Island had a two-pen stockyard. Earlier, there had been a Farmers' Union Cotton Warehouse.

The Great Depression was hard on Casa as the last sawmill closed and the bank failed in 1929. In late 1932, the railroad petitioned the Arkansas Railroad Commission to discontinue its telegraph station at Casa. The farming and lumber economy became very bad, but electricity did reach Casa in 1937. A 1940 report showed that Casa still had three grocery stores, three general merchandise stores, a barber shop, a café, two garages, three gas stations, and a cotton gin. In 1950, the railroad had a short 34-car siding at Casa, plus industry tracks that could hold 20 more cars. In 1969, Casa was still listed as a train order station. By 1973, there was just a siding on the north side of the mainline, and in 1979, the railroad showed only 500 feet of house track and a dispatcher telephone. A switch and a few feet of track are east of Broadway today, and the 2010 census population was 171. Most of the town, and its post office, are now located to the south of the tracks and along Arkansas Highway 10.

Sanborn Map - Casa Downtown Area - 1914. *Sanborn Fire Insurance Map from Casa, Perry County, Arkansas.* Sanborn Map Company, Apr, 1914. Map. Retrieved from the Library of Congress, https://www.loc.gov/item/sanborn00216_001/.

199.5 DAMAN – This is another railroad station that no longer exists today. The station was located about at the Needmore Road grade crossing. The Daman family lived in the area. The W. P. Daman Lumber Company, based at nearby Danville, was incorporated on September 9, 1901.

201.9 COUNTY LINE – The county line is just west of Baskin Creek Road, with **Perry County** to the east and **Yell County** to the west. The location is clearly marked by signs on Highway 10, just south of the tracks. Even those who have never been to Yell County have probably heard of it. This is because Mattie Ross in the novel and movie *True Grit* was from near Dardanelle in Yell County, a statement that she made several times.

   Yell County was once the home of numerous Native American tribes, including the Osage, Caddo, and Cherokee. Many of these tribes came to the area during the late 1700s as they moved west to avoid white settlers. Earlier tribes had hunted and fished the area, mostly living along the Arkansas River. These tribes had in 1541 prevented Hernando de Soto's expedition from exploring the area after defeating the Spanish at what was known as Tula, believed to be located in southwestern Yell County.

In 1819, the first white settlement began in the area, and several Cherokee villages were documented at the time. As the population grew, Yell County was created on December 5, 1840, from portions of Scott and Pope counties. The first county seat was Monrovia, located about five miles northwest of Danville. It moved to Danville in 1844, and a new courthouse was built. In 1875, a second county seat was added at Dardanelle due to the nature of the country. Both county seats are still officially in use. The county's population peaked at 26,323 in 1910. It had dropped to 11,940 by 1960, and had increased back to 22,185 in 2010, thanks to strong growth around Dardanelle.

Yell County was named for Archibald Yell, who was the first member of the U.S. House of Representatives from Arkansas. He was also the second governor of Arkansas. Yell had earlier served with General Andrew Jackson at the Battle of New Orleans during the War of 1812, where he made many political connections. These included Jackson and James K. Polk, who sent him to Texas to campaign for annexation into the United States. While serving in Congress, Yell left to join the American forces in the Mexican War. He was made a Brigadier General of United States Volunteers and was killed at the Battle of Buena Vista on February 23, 1847.

203.5 BIRTA – Birta was another small logging town during the early 1900s that doesn't exist today. It was once located on both sides of the track at the Santa Fe Ridge Road grade crossing. The Fort Smith Lumber Company once had a sawmill here, about when the post office opened in 1904. In 1910, there were a series of hearings by the Arkansas Railroad Commission for the need of a train station and agent at Birta. The small town claimed that it originated more traffic than any other town its size between Little Rock and Amarillo, and therefore needed a station. In February, the railroad agreed to build a station, and construction began in April.

Despite the construction of the station, Birta was never large. In 1921, W. W. Gardner & Company, a lumber company, was the only industry operating. In 1950, the railroad had an 81-car siding. The post office closed in 1953, and by 1970, the railroad siding was gone. A dispatcher telephone was once located here.

208.6 OLA (AO) – From 1906 until the 1930s, Ola was an important junction location for the Rock Island Railroad. An article in the December 15, 1907, issue of the *Arkansas Gazette* reported that the Rock Island had interchanged 202 cars with other lines in November at Ola. Additionally, 50 cars of cotton and 37 cars of lumber were shipped out, and the railroad shipped in 15 cars of flour and feed during the same month.

The article also stated that the railroad employed seven men at Ola, five in the office and two in the yard.

To the north was the Dardanelle, Ola & Southern, while to the south was the Central Railway Company of Arkansas. Because of these other railroads, there were a number of facilities here, all at an elevation of 361 feet. A joint facilities agreement dated June 30, 1915, stated that the Central Railway Company used 1.16 miles of shared track, with expenses paid on a basis of the business handled. Additionally, the Central Railway of Arkansas paid 2½% of the terminal's $15,153 valuation. The Interstate Commerce Commission later reported that the Central Railway Company "uses, jointly with the Chicago, Rock Island & Pacific Railway Company, the latter's depot at Ola and about 1.165 miles of tracks at Ola."

The CRI&P facilities at Ola matched the business levels found there. In 1910, Ola was considered to be the most important yard between Booneville and Little Rock. Because of this, a new 130-ton coal chute was installed that year. Additionally, the 65-pound rail between Biddle and Ola was replaced with 85-pound rail at the time. In 1913, the CRI&P had a depot and a freight house west of the Main Street grade crossing. A siding ran south of these two buildings, and three tracks were to the north. The coal chute was to the east. Further east was the G. W. & I. Miks cotton gin and seed house, served from the south siding. The railroad also had three cotton seed houses and a cotton platform in town. None of these structures survive today.

By 1950, the only railroad at Ola was the Rock Island, but there was still a 100-car siding, plus other tracks with 41 cars of capacity. In that same year, the station was still a busy place. It was a train order station and was staffed 10:30am-6:00pm and 11:00pm-7:00am on weekdays, and 11:00pm-7:00am on weekends. Passenger trains No. 111 and No. 112 – the *Cherokee* – were night trains with eastbound No. 112 here at 12:40am, and westbound at 2:42am. The *Choctaw Rocket* passenger trains were daytime trains. Westbound No. 51 departed at 1:20pm and eastbound No. 52 departed at 2:17pm. The freight trains passed through Ola westbound early to mid-mornings, while the eastbound trains passed through late afternoon and early evenings.

In 1973, most of the tracks were still in place. There was a spur track to the south, located east of town. This track served the Midland Products site. There was a long siding to the north with a house track on the east end. There was a shorter siding to the south. The depot was north of the mainline and south of the siding, near the east end of the siding. At the end of operations, the railroad had a 4583-foot siding, plus 4175 feet of other tracks. Ola was still a train orders station and a water station.

In 1991, Little Rock & Western #103 is pulling a short cut of grain cars westward past the Ola, Arkansas, depot. The depot and the train order signals didn't have many more years, and neither did the rail service to Danville.

The railroad cuts across the northeast side of Ola. The siding remains in service and has been used for car storage and to allow locomotives to run around their trains when working the nearby lumber mill. Heading west, the railroad loops around the northeast end of Danville Mountain, and then turns west to arrive at Danville. Arkansas. Highway 10 follows the railroad closely along the entire route.

City of Ola

This area was already settled by 1840, known as Red Lick at the time. Postal service was established through the area in 1848 under the name Petit Jean, indicating a good-sized population. Many of the early settlers, both before and after the Civil War, were from North Carolina, South Carolina, Alabama, and Tennessee, often from places similar to the setting between mountains and a large river valley. Elisha Harrel built the first house at what became Ola in 1860. Little growth happened during the Civil War, but farmers moving west for new land were soon attracted to the area. In 1866, Red Lick was renamed Petit Jean to match the post office. About the same time, Confederate Captain John Mathias Harkey returned to his farm and built a sawmill, a flour and grist mill, and a cotton gin, attracting more settlers.

During 1870, a mercantile store was opened by Harkey. Although the community was growing, on September 27, 1875, the Petit Jean Post Office closed. A vocal protest followed, and the post office re-opened on

January 10, 1876. In 1880, there was a move to change the name of the town, and it was decided to honor Harkey by naming it after his oldest daughter, Ola. The post office changed its name at the same time.

In 1899, Harkey played another important role in Ola's development when he granted a right-of-way through the area to the Choctaw & Memphis Railroad. He had two conditions on the gift – that a station named Ola be opened, and that trains would stop at Ola for a guaranteed ninety-nine years. The railroad quickly got involved with selling the town, with their Choctaw, Oklahoma and Memphis Town Site Company promoting it as "The Cotton Metropolis." With the arrival of the railroad, businesses such as a livery stable, a blacksmith and wagon yard, three saloons, several cafes, three hotels, numerous retail businesses, a weekly newspaper, attorneys and doctors, and several sawmills soon opened. This led to Ola being incorporated on March 20, 1900.

The community grew and its economy became based upon timber products, wheat, fruit, and cotton production. Timber came from the south while farming took place to the north along the Petit Jean River. W. W. Gardner & Company and Fort Smith Lumber Company both had mills and operations here. The P. J. Burnett cotton gin was also located here, handling enough cotton that in 1903, the Department of Agriculture reported that 5635 rail shipments of cotton moved from here in 1902-1903. The railroad also operated a one-pen stockyard about the same time, and the Ola Electric Power Plant opened in 1912. The Ola Bottle Works manufactured glass bottles for soft-drink companies like NuGrape, Nehi, and Orange Soda from 1920 until 1928.

The 1930s were hard on Ola. The Central Railway Company of Arkansas, as well as the Rock Island & Dardanelle, were abandoned. A tornado damaged much of the town in 1930. A 1934 fire destroyed an entire city block, burning down a bank, the post office and almost a half-dozen stores. After World War II, agriculture and timber reduced in importance, but poultry production increased significantly. In 1979, Midland Products, a wood-preserving treatment plant, was still being served by the railroad east of town. The Environmental Protection Agency has been cleaning the site during the early 2000s, which is west of Rose Cut-Off Road. In their report, the EPA has stated that a sawmill and a creosote treatment plant operated on the property before Midland Products.

The discontinuance of rail service by the Rock Island Railway on March 24, 1980, ended more economic activity at Ola. The return of service by the Little Rock & Western had little impact, although PotlatchDeltic was served by the railroad. The Ola lumber sawmill started operations in 1971 and was spun off by the Murphy Corporation, becoming the Deltic Timber Corporation in 1996. In 2018, the firm merged with Potlatch, becoming the PotlatchDeltic Corporation.

In 2010, the population of Ola was 1281, making it the third-largest city in Yell County.

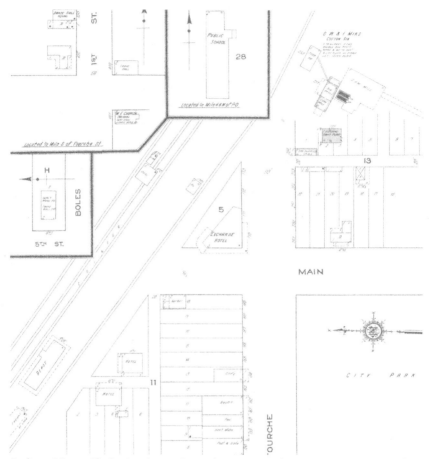

Sanborn Map – Ola Station Area – December 1913. *Sanborn Fire Insurance Map from Ola, Yell County, Arkansas.* Sanborn Map Company, De, 1913. Map. Retrieved from the Library of Congress, https://www.loc.gov/item/sanborn00318_001/.

295

The PotlatchDeltic sawmill at Ola is a modern facility, as shown in this picture from adjacent Arkansas Highway 10.

Central Railway Company of Arkansas

The busiest of the railroad connections at Ola was the Central Railway Company of Arkansas, often noted as the Central Railway of Arkansas. This line existed from 1906 until 1932 and was a common carrier railroad built to handle the needs of the Fort Smith Lumber Company. The lumber company started with a number of small sawmills built along the Choctaw, Oklahoma & Gulf between Perry, Arkansas, and Howe, Oklahoma. As the company acquired more timber rights across Yell and Sebastian counties, rail transportation was needed to reach the forests and move the cut lumber to market.

The company was first planned as the Central Railroad Company of Arkansas, established in 1903, but reorganized as the Central Railway Company of Arkansas on January 31, 1906. W. W. Gardner & Company received a contract to build the railroad on March 10, 1906, and the railroad opened Fall 1907. W. W. Gardner was associated with the Fort Smith Lumber Company, which paid for the railroad's construction and received all of its stock in return.

The Interstate Commerce Commission (ICC) produced two significant reports on the Central Railway Company of Arkansas. The first was information involving the Tap Line Case, published in *Decisions of the Interstate Commerce Commission.* The second report was the valuation report for the railroad found in the *Decisions of the Interstate Commerce Commission of the United States – July-November 1925.* The ICC stated that the "Central Railway Company of Arkansas was incorporated in January, 1906, with a capital stock of $2,600,000. Its charter describes a line 130 miles in length terminating at or near Hot Springs, Ark.; but as actually completed in 1907 it terminates at a point known as Brizi, Ark., about 13 miles from its other terminus at Ola, where it connects with the Rock Island." A more detailed route description for the planned railroad stated that it was "between Dardanelle, Yell County, and Hot Springs, Garland County, 70 miles and Plainview, Yell County, and Waldron, Scott County, 60 miles, or a total of 130 miles, all within the State of Arkansas."

As noted by the ICC, the "mill of the lumber company is at Plainview, on the tap line 7 miles from its junction with the Rock Island. The lumber company has an unincorporated logging track extending into its timber from a point intermediate between the mill and the junction point, but it has no engines or cars. The tap line has 5 locomotives, a combination passenger car, 3 box cars, and 16 flat cars. It also has three train crews, a number of track men, and a station agent at the mill point, Plainview, where there is a station building." As long as the railroad operated, Plainview was the center of operations. There was a depot and office building, hotel, coal chute, water tank, and a machine shop that was used by both the railroad and the lumber mill.

In 1910, the ICC stated that there were "three independent sawmills on the tap line and five or six other mills in that vicinity which haul their lumber to the tap line for shipment." However, this traffic was only about 80 carloads a year, and 90% of the traffic on the railroad came from the Fort Smith Lumber Company.

The ICC stated that the railroad had five steam locomotives in 1910, and two in 1916. Almost all of these were Shay locomotives in later years, and they seemed to have been owned by the lumber company and then used by the railroad. Fort Smith Lumber #3 was a 37-ton, 2-truck Shay obtained secondhand in August 1909. Originally built for the E. W. Gates Lumber Company in 1905 (Shop Number 1552), the Shay served both at Plainview and later at Abbot, Arkansas. It was for sale by late 1928, and then scrapped.

Central Railway Company of Arkansas #4 was built new for the railroad in 1912 (Shop Number 2612) and lasted until the end of operations. This was a 70-ton, 3-truck Shay and was for sale in late 1928 and then scrapped. Fort Smith Lumber #6 was also bought new, this one in 1920 (Shop Number 3083). It was another 70-ton, 3-truck Shay and was also for sale in late 1928. This Shay was sold to S.A. Compania Maderera de Durango, El Salto, Durango, Mexico by 1933, and was later scrapped.

297

Two other Shay locomotives came from the Caddo River Lumber Company and their Caddo & Choctaw Railroad. The first was acquired in 1919 and was former Caddo & Choctaw #3. This 42-ton, 2-truck Shay was built in 1910 (Shop Number 2318) but only lasted a year or two before being sold to the Trapp Mountain Railway at Malvern, Arkansas. It then went through several owners before being scrapped during the 1930s. The final known Shay was Fort Smith Lumber Company #1, former Caddo & Choctaw #1. It was a small 37-ton, 2-truck Shay built in 1906 (Shop Number 1765). It was scrapped when the logging company shut down in 1928.

The May 15, 1916, issue of *The Lumber Trade Journal* reported that the Fort Smith Lumber Company owned "100,000 acres of land in Yell county, and is negotiating for the purchase of 50,000 additional acres." This growth seemed to have had a positive impact on the railroad. Financial results for July 1, 1915 - June 30, 1916, showed freight revenues of $60,959.44, passenger revenues of $3202.09, express $849.99, mail $309.93, and other $91.25, for a total of $65,412.70. Because of the traffic volumes, of which about 40% was general freight, the ICC approved a "maximum of 1½ cents as the division of this tap line out of the rate on the products of the mill of the controlling company."

Fort Smith Lumber continued to cut timber in Yell and Sebastian counties in Arkansas, and in Oklahoma, until about 1928. By that time, most of the timber had been cut and the Great Depression was starting to be felt. The railroad remained in place until a decision about its abandonment was made on September 15, 1931. The track was reportedly removed by 1932.

Dardanelle, Ola & Southern

The Dardanelle, Ola & Southern was created to provide railroad competition for the Dardanelle area, and to reach the growing farm and timber areas south of the Arkansas River. After a number of years of promotion by local citizens, several railroads were chartered that resulted in no construction. These included the Dardanelle & Ola Railroad Company (February 28, 1899) and the Ola & Hot Springs Railroad Company (April 27, 1899). The first shovel of dirt was turned on March 12, 1906, by Mrs. C. C. Godman, the wife of the original promoter. With construction work already started, the Dardanelle, Ola & Southern Railway received a charter from the State of Arkansas on May 1, 1906.

The railroad was delayed by a lack of funds, wet weather, and poor soil for construction. While the projected completion date was November 1906, the contractors finally reached Ola during August 1907. Business was generally good and a number of trains ran daily, but the constant track repair left no money to pay off the construction debt. On December 9, 1910, the railroad filed for bankruptcy.

In the July 1911, issue of *The Official Guide of the Railways and Steam Navigation Lines of the United States,* the Dardanelle, Ola & Southern – the "Mount Nebo Route" – had a large listing that included a map of Arkansas and a full schedule of its trains. The timetable showed the importance of the Rock Island connection by stating that "No. 2 will always wait for Rock Island Train No. 42, at Ola when not over an hour late, and No. 4 will always wait for Rock Island Train No. 41, at Ola, when not over two hours late." The railroad's offices were in Dardanelle, and William C. Fordyce was receiver. It should be noted that William C. Fordyce was the son of Samuel W. Fordyce, who helped build the St. Louis Southwestern, which the Rock Island crossed at Brinkley, Arkansas. At the time, William C. Fordyce was vice president of the Commonwealth Trust Company of St. Louis, Missouri, which carried much of the railroad's debt.

The valuation report of the railroad, found in the *Decisions of the Interstate Commerce Commission of the United States January-March, 1929*, tells much of the next part of the railroad's history. It stated: "The Rock Island and Dardanelle was incorporated October 31, 1911, under the laws of Arkansas in the interest of the Commonwealth Trust Company of St Louis, Mo., for the purpose of acquiring the property of the Dardanelle, Ola and Southern Railway Company, which had been sold at foreclosure sale on July 7, 1911." At the time, the railroad was described as "a single track, standard gauge steam railroad, located entirely in Arkansas and extending from Ola to Dardanelle, 13.915 miles. It also owns 0.721 mile of other tracks. Its road thus embraces 14.636 miles of all tracks."

On December 31, 1911, the Rock Island & Dardanelle was leased to the Chicago, Rock Island & Pacific for 999 years, and efforts were made to rebuild the line. The Rock Island used the line as a feeder branch line, but traffic never grew to what the railroad hoped. On September 8, 1920, the line was leased to the Ft. Smith, Subiaco & Eastern, which connected to the Missouri Pacific Railroad at Paris, Arkansas. The new organization, given the name of the Fort Smith, Subiaco & Rock Island Railroad, again spent money to make the railroad reliable, and coordinated service all the way between Ola and Fort Smith. One modernization effort was the use of a 1923 J. G. Brill gasoline-powered motorcar, numbered A-1.

The Great Depression of the late 1920s and early 1930s eliminated much of the line's business, and trains and services were eliminated. The Interstate Commerce Commission approved the abandonment of the line between Ola and Dardanelle, and on west to Scranton, on September 22, 1937, and the tracks were removed in early 1938 by the Hyman-Michalls Company of Chicago.

213.8   MICKLES – This is reportedly the only location named Mickles in the United States. The lumber operations of L. E. Meadows were here in 1921, but little else. A county map from 1936 shows that Mickles (Mickle's in early timetables) was a few houses scattered alongside the tracks and highway, with a small downtown area north of the tracks. A few old buildings still stand in the woods in the area. In 1950, there was a 41-car siding, but it was gone by 1973.

Three Trains, Two Tracks, One Wreck

Mickles was the scene of a rear-end collision between a Rock Island freight and passenger train on July 29, 1915. The accident killed two railroad employees, and injured three employees and three passengers. The accident has an interesting story that is worth telling.

According to the accident investigation, eastbound freight train Extra 1776 with 41 cars and a caboose, received a train order at Blue Mountain that stated that eastbound passenger train No. 44 was 1 hour and 15 minutes late. At Waveland, the conductor moved to the locomotive to create a plan, but told the flagman to watch out for train No. 44. Extra 1776 planned to take the siding at Danville, and when it stopped, the flagman started walking to protect the train. However, Extra 1776 received a new order stating that No. 44 was now 90 minutes late, so the freight headed on east, without its flagman. According to the investigation, no whistle signal was made to recall the flagman and he couldn't catch the train as it started moving eastbound.

Extra 1776 came on to Mickles to clear, but found westbound Extra 1775 already in the siding, and there was not enough space for both trains. Extra 1776 went to the east switch with the plan that passenger train No. 44 would stop between the switches, Extra 1775 would head west and Extra 1776 would back into the siding to clear. The whistle was blown for the flagman to protect Extra 1776, but he was on passenger train No. 44, having been picked up after being left behind earlier. With no flagman to protect the train, No. 44 hit the caboose of Extra 1776 at 11:23pm while traveling at a speed of 45 miles per hour. Locomotive #1018 on train No. 44 turned over onto its side as it slid down the embankment, and ten freight cars and the caboose on Extra 1776 were destroyed.

Not far west of Mickles at Milepost 215.0 is this concrete culvert, dated 1929. This is the location of one of many timber trestles that were replaced with a more modern structure during the 1920s.

219.5 DANVILLE (DA) – Danville was here long before the railroad, having been selected in 1840 as the county seat for the new Yell County. The City of Danville, named for a steamboat that managed to navigate up the Petit Jean River, was laid out in December 1841. A post office opened in 1842. A log courthouse was constructed at Danville in 1844, and a newer frame building was erected in 1850. By this time Danville was large enough to support a Masonic lodge.

The Civil War had little direct impact on Danville, and a flour mill opened during the late 1860s, one of several mills built about that time on local creeks. By that time, Danville also had a ginning and wool-carding mill, a sawmill, general store and drug store. A brick courthouse was built in 1873. With Danville serving as the county seat, the town also had its share of lawyers, doctors, and other professionals. More business was attracted to the area when a bridge over the Petit Jean River opened in 1879.

The Choctaw & Memphis (Choctaw, Oklahoma & Gulf) was building their line through Danville by 1899, and the city incorporated on February 18, 1899. On July 31, 1899, a construction train crossed a temporary bridge over the Petit Jean River and entered Danville at 10am, becoming the first train in the city. The first train arrived from Little Rock on December 10, 1899. Unlike most towns along the new railroad, Danville did not grow much when the line opened. This was likely due to three reasons. The first was that Danville already had the basic facilities of a county seat and had little need to grow. Second, Danville was not a base for the lumber industry, so it didn't go through the boom and bust that many other Ouachita Mountain towns experienced. Finally, Danville was already developed, so the Choctaw, Oklahoma and Memphis Town Site Company didn't promote it heavily, instead focusing on the many new towns created by the railroad's arrival.

About 1900, there were a number of plans for railroads in this area. One of these was the Danville, Fourche Valley & Southern Railroad, incorporated in Arkansas to "construct a line from Danville to Cobb's Ferry, on the Arkansas River, about 15 miles." Although the charter, dated July 12, 1901, was announced in a number of magazines and newspapers, there was no further coverage or news.

While Danville was a government town, it did have other businesses. In 1902-1903, 4577 rail shipments of cotton moved from Danville. C. T. Meadows operated a lumber company that specialized in hardwood. The railroad also had a one-pen stockyard. In 1950, the Rock Island had a 38-car siding, and other tracks with a listed capacity of 51 cars. The tracks lasted until the end of the Rock Island, with the siding to the north and several house tracks to the south. As late as the 1979 timetable, Danville was still listed as a water station, a location where general order boards and books were kept, and as a train order station. After the railroad shut down in 1980, the tracks remained for several years as there were hopes that another railroad would buy the line, but eventually the tracks were taken up west of the Petit Jean River bridge. The siding remains to allow the railroad to switch the Wayne Farms facility, which only received eight cars a month during the last few years of CRI&P operation.

During the last quarter of the Twentieth Century, the poultry industry attracted Latino immigrants to Yell County. In the 2010 census, when Danville reached its peak population of 2409 residents, more than half were Hispanic.

During a 1986 tour of the line in western Arkansas, this photo was taken of the former Danville depot, at the time part of a feed and supply store.

Wayne Farms

Located on the east side of Danville at Milepost 218.4, Wayne Farms is the reason that the tracks still remain this far west from Little Rock. The Arkansas operations began in 1966 when Allied Mills purchased the operations of Joe Ray and his facilities located alongside the Petit Jean River. In 1970, the Allied Mills poultry division opened a feed mill here, and then a hatchery in 1972, followed by a 90,000 square-foot processing facility in 1979. In 1981, Allied Mills merged into Continental Grain Company. Continental Grain changed its name to ContiGroup Companies, Inc. in 1999, and then the Poultry Division was renamed Wayne Farms LLC in 2000. Wayne Farms is now based in Oakwood, Georgia, and is the sixth largest firm in the poultry industry with more than $2 billion in sales yearly.

The company relied upon the Rock Island Railroad to deliver various feed grains to the feed mill, which were then distributed to local farms where the poultry was being raised. When the railroad shut down, Wayne Farms had to haul grain in by truck at a higher expense. By 1986, Continental Grain had acquired 35 miles of track from Perry to Danville, and then authorized the Little Rock & Western (LRWN) to operate it. On July16, 1986, the LRWN operated its first train west of Perry, hauling feed grains to the mill at Danville.

The tracks west of Ola to Danville are currently overgrown as Wayne Farms now receives its poultry feed at a mill at Atkins, Arkansas, acquired in 2008. Union Pacific offered better rates to the mill on their mainline, and Wayne Farms now trucks feed to area poultry farms from this facility.

Danville (AR) to Howe (OK)
Abandoned

The line from Danville, Arkansas, west to Howe, Oklahoma, was scrapped in 1984-1985 by L. B. Foster and its subcontractors. L. B. Foster was started by Lee B. Foster in 1902 to buy and sell used rail. Over the years, the firm entered other businesses, handling materials and construction for many types of projects. However, for years, L. B. Foster was probably the biggest name in track removal and material salvage.

Besides the track materials, many of the bridges were removed and reused or scrapped. Others had the good timbers and easy pieces of steel salvaged. Some later reports indicate that much of the actual right-of-way was also sold, including parts to O. Taylor Enterprises of Guthrie, Oklahoma. There were advertisements and announcements that O. Taylor Enterprises was selling property and materials, such as the track ballast for $1900 a mile and land at $340 or more an acre.

Because it has been four decades since the railroad was abandoned, the grade can often be hard to follow between Danville and Howe. In a number of places, the grade has been removed, while in others, it has been converted into farm roads. Parts of a number of the bridges do remain, but only the burned shell of the Booneville depot remains of the many buildings that once stood next to the rails. Nevertheless, a drive along the route takes one through the beautiful Ouachita Mountains.

219.5 DANVILLE (DA) – The west end of the Little Rock & Western is located just east of the Petit Jean River, with the track west of here being removed by L. B. Foster. The tracks once curved northward, crossed the Petit Jean River, and then followed the south side of Belleville Ridge to Belleville.

219.6 PETIT JEAN RIVER BRIDGE – The Petit Jean River, also known in some sources as Petit Jean Creek, starts when several streams merge near Waldron, Arkansas. It flows east and north for about 120 miles before entering the Arkansas River north of Petit Jean Mountain. It forms part of the county line between Yell County and Conway County. The Petit Jean River Valley is some rare Ouachita Mountain flat land rich for farming. Native Americans have been here since 10,000 BC, and Indian mounds, pictographs and petroglyphs have been found along the river. Many of the first settlers in the area farmed the bottomlands along the stream, and cotton was a popular crop for decades. Because of this, ef-

305

forts were made to use the river for shipping, but only a few voyages were successful, using the small *Danville* steamship.

The Rock Island Railroad Bridge

The railroad crossed the Petit Jean River just downstream of Main Street, Arkansas Highway 10. The bridge is a 9-panel, 175-foot Parker through truss, built in 1899 by the Pennsylvania Steel Company of Steelton, Pennsylvania. Pennsylvania Steel established its first steel mill in 1867 on the banks of the Susquehanna River. Their plant included both a series of blast furnaces and a Bessemer process mill. The company stayed independent until being acquired by Bethlehem Steel in 1917. The plant has been rebuilt numerous times and now is part of ArcelorMittal.

Rock Island records from 1973 show that the steel through truss span had three timber spans on the east end and eighteen on the west end. This bridge is an original structure from the construction of the line for the Choctaw, Oklahoma & Gulf. When the line was acquired by Continental Grain, the rail was still on the bridge and railcars were often stored on it. However, concerns about the bridge's integrity has caused the line to now be blocked just east of the structure.

219.7 SPRING CREEK BRIDGE – Some sources show that this is the Petit Jean River Relief Bridge, but it is in fact a bridge over Spring Creek. Spring Creek forms in the Chickalah Mountain area of northern Yell County, and flows south through a narrow gap in South Bluff, where it is dammed to form Spring Lake, which is part of the Ozark National Forest Spring Lake Recreation Area. Heading south, Spring Creek enters the wide Petit Jean River Valley and flows to just north of Danville, where it passes by a series of ponds. The stream then passes under the railroad twice and enters the Petit Jean River to the north of the Milepost 219.6 bridge.

This bridge is a 74-foot through plate girder span, with 16 timber spans to the east and eight to the west. There is no builders plate on the steel span, but a concrete pier is clearly marked with the date of 1918.

220.3 SPRING CREEK BRIDGE – This was an eleven panel, ballast deck timber pile trestle. The bridge still remains, not far south (railroad-east) of where the railroad passes under Arkansas Highway 27. The Spring Creek bridge is at an elevation of 330 feet, and the railroad fought a 1.0% grade westward before reaching an elevation of 356 feet in less than a mile, where the grade slackened to 0.5% for the next mile or so.

223.7 FEW BRANCH BRIDGE – Look for this three-span I-beam and concrete slab bridge not far north of Arkansas Highway 10. Note the 1908 date built into the structure. Few Branch starts a few miles to the north on Jones Ridge, and flows south into Russell Branch not far south of here.

The Few Branch Bridge stands next to Arkansas Highway 10 just east of Belleville. Dated 1908, this is another bridge that was rebuilt by the railroad as traffic volumes grew.

223.8 BELLEVILLE (UN) – Approaching Belleville from the east, the railroad grade is now used as the Danville Municipal Airport, which is categorized as a general aviation facility. The airport runway is labeled 29 and is designated as runway 11-29, which means that it is angled at 290 degrees. The runway is 5325 feet in length. The land for the airport was acquired in 1987, shortly after the railroad track was removed by L. B. Foster.

At Belleville, the railroad passed through town north of Arkansas Highway 10. Several new buildings now sit on this right-of-way. A depot once sat on the south side of the tracks about the center of the siding. In 1950, there was a 100-car siding, plus a 24-car spur track. The siding was on the north side of the mainline, and there was a short industry track further west in 1973. The 1979 Rock Island employee timetable stated that there was a 4619-foot siding at Belleville, plus a 1045-foot industry track. All of these tracks are now gone, removed by 1986.

This beautiful stone sign, located downtown, welcomes you to Belleville, Arkansas.

This area was part of a region known as Monrovia, a collection of farms and settlements in Yell County. Because of its isolation, it was used as a temporary prison camp by the Union Army during the Civil War. The area remained generally empty after the war, but William Fergeson built a sawmill and store here in 1872. In 1873, a school was established by the Methodist church, attracting more settlers. In 1878, the Ferguson's Mill Post Office opened, as did the John Choate store. The post office and community was renamed Belleville in 1886. The change in name is not fully explained, but there are two stories about the source of the name. One states that the new town was named for the outlaw Belle Starr, who allegedly visited the area frequently. The more popular story is that it was named for all of the beautiful girls in town.

A report from 1889 stated that there were eight stores, a harness shop, a drugstore, a milliner's shop, a wagon maker, more than one blacksmith, a stave mill, and a hotel. In 1898, the Choctaw & Memphis built through the area, but passed about a mile south of town. A siding was initially installed here using the name Marvinville, with the name borrowed from another nearby community located about five miles to the west. Quickly, much of Ferguson Mill moved south to the tracks and incorporated as Belleville at the depot on April 25, 1899. The move became permanent as a new two-story school was built at the new site. The Choctaw, Oklahoma & Gulf renamed its station and siding Belleville by late 1899.

With the arrival of the railroad, farming and timber grew. Belleville had its peak population in 1900 at 552 residents. In 1902-1903, 421 rail shipments of cotton moved from Belleville, and Roy Howard and J. T. Walker were both in the cotton business running gins by 1920. J. H. Harris operated a sawmill at the time, and a theater, telephone office, a bank, and a weekly newspaper had also opened. During the early 1900s, the Rock Island Railroad had a 40-foot track scale with a capacity of 100,000 pounds here, the only one between Biddle and Booneville.

The population had dropped to 273 in the 1940 census, and the George Cline timber company was about the only major business in town. Since then, the poultry and cattle businesses have grown in the area, allowing the population to climb back to 441 by the 2010 census. Belleville still has a post office, elementary school, grocery store, restaurant, and a few other businesses. One claim-to-fame of the community is F. C. Jones, the great-grandfather of actress Carol Burnett. Jones once made his living in retailing and farming at Belleville.

Heading west from Belleville, the old grade stays north of Arkansas Highway 10, generally marked by a narrow tree-line. Hundreds of poultry houses line this route today.

The Wreck of Passenger Train No. 42

Railroading can be a risky business, and derailments can be caused by track and mechanical problems, as well as the failure of employees to properly do their job. They can also be caused by a bit of confusion between train service employees. An example of this happened on October 21, 1931, when two passenger trains (eastbound No. 42 and westbound No. 111) managed to hit each other at Belleville at 5:32am, where the two trains frequently met at the time.

Train No. 42 consisted of one combination baggage and mail car, two coaches, one Pullman sleeping car, and one dining car, all hauled by steam locomotive #853 (4-6-2). Train No. 42 had orders to meet train No. 111 at Belleville. Since No. 111 was to hold the main track, No. 42 was using the west switch to head into the siding (also called the team track and shown to be 1697 feet in length at the time) when No. 111 struck its second car. At the time, train No. 42 was a superior train by direction, but train No. 111 was the more important train and therefore the right to hold the main track was given to train No. 111 by the dispatcher.

There were several factors involved in the accident. First, No. 42 was running a few minutes late, and was delayed further by having to couple to four freight cars standing on the passing track, and then having to shove them eastward, The next issue was that the engineer and other crew members of No. 111 saw the brakeman of train No. 42 giving a "come-ahead" signal to his engineer, mistaking the signal as being for their train.

Westbound passenger train No. 111 consisted of a combination baggage and mail car, two coaches, and two Pullman sleeping cars, all pulled by steam locomotive #836 (4-6-2). Locomotive #836 made contact with "the right side of the second car in train No. 42 at a point about 15 feet from its front end, scraping it from that point back to the rear end and then striking the right front corner of the vestibule of the third car, considerably damaging this car. None of the equipment in train No. 42 was derailed, although the entire train was driven back a distance of about 70 feet by the force of the collision. Engine 836 turned over on its left side and was considerably damaged; the tender was leaning at an angle of about 45 degrees but remained coupled to the engine and the first car in the train. None of the remaining equipment in train No. 111 was derailed or damaged." No deaths occurred, but the engineer, fireman and head brakeman of train No. 111 were injured, as was a dining car employee and two passengers on train No. 42.

224.1 RUSSELL BRANCH BRIDGE – Hidden in the brush north of the highway is this 30-foot deck plate girder span. Russell Branch forms to the north along Jones Ridge, and then flows southward. It eventually joins several other streams before entering the Petit Jean River.

Heading west from Belleville, the railroad crossed a number of bridges, most rebuilt using concrete. This short bridge at Milepost 224.5 is an example.

A number of short deck plate girder bridges were used in west Arkansas. At Milepost 225.5, the concrete headwalls are all that remain of the 44-foot deck plate girder bridge.

227.2 CEDAR CREEK BRIDGE – Located in a patch of woods north of Arkansas Highway 10, currently surrounded by poultry houses, are the remains of a 20-span open deck timber trestle with several through plate girder spans. Cedar Creek forms a few miles to the north with much of its water flow coming from East Cedar Creek, which is dammed to create Cedar-Piney Lake. Cedar Creek flows several miles south of here into Big Piney Creek.

Located just north of this small natural gas compressor station are the remains of the Cedar Creek Bridge.

228.6 HAVANA – This area was originally known as Marvinville, but it moved a short distance and became Greenville when the railroad was built through the area. It later was renamed Havana. The August 1899, issue of *The Choctaw*, a newspaper "issued monthly by authority of the Choctaw, Oklahoma and Gulf, and the Choctaw and Memphis Railroads," had a story about Marvinville and how it became Greenville.

> *Marvinville, Yell County, one of the towns on the Choctaw, killed itself by its rapacity. They would not donate an acre of land for depot or other purposes, and asked exorbitant prices for the land. General B. W. Green, general town site agent, went a mile and a half east of the old town site and purchased 60 acres, where the town of Greenville, named in his honor, is now being laid out, and where the depot will be located. It is said the old town will practically be deserted.*

The area along the Petit Jean River was popular with early settlers. When the Military Road was built between Dardanelle and Booneville, a small town developed. The first name used was Marvinville, apparently named for an early settler. The Civil War had little impact on the community except the name Gardner Station began to be used for the area. The new name came from Richard H. Gardner, a doctor and Confederate veteran. No matter the name, the town grew until it included three doctors, several stores, a cotton gin, a sawmill, a blacksmith shop, and a post office, which opened as Marvinville in 1871.

1898 was an important year for Marvinville as the railroad was being built through the area. As reported by the Choctaw, Marvinville wasn't cooperative with the railroad, so a new town was created nearby. Green, who worked for the company, bought land from O. J. Fergeson and laid out the new town, promoted as a "Great Timber Center" by the Choctaw, Oklahoma and Memphis Town Site Company. In October 1899, the Town Site Company deeded its property to J. E. England and his land company and financial firm. The post office moved to the new town and became Greenville in 1900, and the town was incorporated on April 19, 1900.

For some reason, the town and post office were renamed Havana in 1902, possibly to avoid conflict with several other towns with the same Greenville name. The source of the name Havana is also not clear. While the railroad promoted the local timber, farming was also important. In 1902-1903, 623 rail shipments of cotton were made from Havana. Meanwhile, a number of timber companies opened at Havana, including the Valley Pine Lumber Company in 1905, which built several saw mills and a planing mill. All of the new businesses attracted new settlers, and the town peaked in population at 621 residents.

Early in the 1920s, Havana was at its peak of business activity. In 1921, the *Arkansas Marketing and Industrial Guide* listed the J. F. Oats broom factory, F. G. Turner & Son Gin Company, the milling firm of Berry Brothers, the Farmers Union Warehouse Company, and the coal dealership of Jennings & Ray. Also by that time, Havana had a number of general stores, two hotels, five doctors, a shingle mill, two cafes, a theater, and a school. There was also a service station for automobiles, a sign of changes to come. Tourism, cattle and poultry have replaced most of the timber and cotton businesses. In particular, nearby Mount Magazine and Blue Mountain Lake attract large numbers of visitors each year. However, the population of Havana was only 375 in the 2010 census.

Baseball and Havana

While small, Havana was the home of three major league baseball pitchers – James Elton Walkup, James Huey Walkup, and Johnny Sain. The two Walkups were actually cousins who both pitched for the Detroit Tigers. James Huey Walkup was born here in 1895 and pitched in only two games in 1927 for the Tigers. His younger cousin, James Elton

Walkup, was born here in 1909 and pitched for both the Detroit Tigers and St. Louis Browns 1934-1939. He died in nearby Danville in 1997.

The third pitcher, Johnny Sain, was much more successful as he was the runner-up for the National League's Most Valuable Player Award in 1948, the year that his team, the Boston Braves, won the pennant. In that year, while pitching with Warren Spahn, Sain led the National League in wins, complete games and innings pitched. During his career, Sain played for the Boston Braves, New York Yankees, and Kansas City Athletics. He also coached for six different major league teams, and won three World Series as a player and three as a coach, five with the Yankees. He is still regarded as one of the top pitching coaches in baseball.

The Railroad at Havana

The railroad once passed through the south side of Havana, just north of Arkansas Highway 10, which locally has the name Railroad Avenue. Its grade can be followed through town, including the drive-through window of the local bank. Looking around Havana, nothing more than the grade exists from the railroad's abandonment during the 1980s. Originally, there was a siding to the north of the mainline, with the depot located between the two tracks. In 1950, the siding was 32 cars long, while there was a 21-car spur track. By 1969, only a short spur track remained, and in 1979, only 620 feet of the siding was left. There was also a Rock Island dispatcher telephone here when the railroad closed down.

Heading west, the railroad passed the old location of Marvinville at the east end of a low ridge where the grade crosses County Road 533. From there, the grade loops around the north side of the ridge and heads west. For the first time since Perry, the railroad grade isn't next to Arkansas Highway 10. Instead, it follows a few smaller roads and is often isolated until it gets to Waveland.

Also heading west, the railroad starts a steady climb, with grades at 1.0%. The elevation of Havana is 365 feet, it is 457 feet at Waveland, and then it peaks at 588 feet at Milepost 237.5.

Nothing remains of the railroad at Havana except for this mowed grade, located just west of Main Street.

Mount Magazine State Park

At Havana, the railroad crosses Arkansas Highway 309, the Mount Magazine Scenic Byway. This road heads north to Mount Magazine, Arkansas's highest point at 2753 feet of elevation. Today, it is the home of the Mount Magazine State Park, but it once was a series of farms located in an area with cooler temperatures and great views. It is also the second state park along the Choctaw Route in western Arkansas that the railroad indirectly helped to create.

Mount Magazine, also known as Magazine Mountain, was created by a general uplift of the area, creating both the Ouachita and Ozark Mountains. Various streams wore down parts of these mountains as they flowed to the Arkansas River, leaving several tall mountains with hard capstone still standing.

In 1722, Bernard de la Harpe produced the first report about traveling the Arkansas River through western Arkansas. When French explorers and hunters explored the Arkansas River, they reported on a series of tall mountains to the south that they called the Magasin (Magazine) Mountains. This included just about all of the mountains between the Arkansas River and the Ouachita Mountains, and especially those along the Petit Jean River. The name came from their almost box-like shape, which the French felt looked like a barn, storehouse, or a military stores magazine. As the individual mountains were named, Mount Magazine became the mountain near Dardanelle, now known as Mount Nebo. Botanist Thomas Nuttall covered this naming issue in his reports from his 1819 trip through the area. Nuttall commented about one mountain that carried its own name. He wrote that "a lofty ridge appears to the south called by the French the Cassetete, or Tomahawk Mountain." The mountain later took the name Reveille or Revolee, named for an adjacent stream and community. The community of Reveille obtained a post office in 1848, located just off the west end of the mountain. When Mount Nebo finally received its name, the Magazine name was moved to the mountain that now carries it.

In 1853, Mount Magazine was covered by a land grant provided for a railroad building through the area. Land was also sold on the mountain, and later homestead laws made it easier to claim land. Few settlers moved to the top of the mountain until after the Civil War when families like Cameron, Benefield, Brown, Morsbach, Greenfield, and Buckman claimed property and built farms. Because of the cooler weather during summers, several of the settlers took in summer boarders, often building several extra cabins to rent out. This move toward tourism attracted the interest of those building the Choctaw, Oklahoma & Gulf.

In 1882, J. M. Birmingham acquired 120 acres on the west end of Mount Magazine. In 1900, O. M. Ellsworth, Secretary of the Choctaw, Oklahoma and Memphis Town Site Company (often incorrectly called Townsite Company), registered a plot for the Town of Mount Magazine on the western end of the mountain on Birmingham's property. Ellsworth was heavily involved with creating towns along the new railroad across western Arkansas, and in May of 1901, was promoted to commercial agent of the Choctaw, Oklahoma & Gulf at Kansas City, Missouri. Two signs in the lobby of the new conference center of the Mount Magazine State Park explain what happened next.

> *In 1900, the Choctaw, Oklahoma and Memphis Townsite Company platted the Town of Mount Magazine covering the western end of the mountain top. The plat included streets, parks and 439 lots.*

The Choctaw, Oklahoma and Memphis Townsite Company developed the west end of the mountain into a resort town called the "Town of Mount Magazine." In addition to the ten-room hotel, the town included streets, parks and a post office. A dance pavilion on the western tip of the summit was later converted into more hotel rooms.

This sign marks the entrance to Magazine Mountain State Park.

The hotel was the Skycrest Inn, noted as the mountain's first hotel. The hotel and community were not as successful as hoped for, and the hotel changed hands several times. Meanwhile, other hotels opened up on the mountain, including the Buckman Inn and the Greenfield log cabin camp. Captain Joseph Evans, a former steamship captain, bought most of the plat after he finished his development of nearby Mount Nebo. However, as the economy worsened during the late 1920s, some of the land was lost by their owners due to a failure to pay taxes. By the early 1930s, the U.S. Resettlement Administration was buying land on the mountain with plans to restore the land and use it as a demonstration farm to teach proper methods of land use. Some of the farmers were still successful, but the government forced the sale of the remaining land, with the last family, the Greenfields, being forced from their land in 1936. Despite the original plans, the land was transferred to the U.S. Forest Service's Ouachita National Forest in 1938. In 1936, the Works Progress Administration had begun work on a scenic road across the

317

mountain, and in 1939, work began on cabins and a 27-room lodge and restaurant. Tourism was again becoming a theme for the mountain.

The lodge opened in late June 1940, and the following year the mountain was assigned to the Ozark National Forest. The operations of the park and lodge on the mountain were contracted out to different companies and individuals over the years, until the lodge burned on February 3, 1971. Soon after, the State of Arkansas began looking at the mountain as a possible new state park. Several hearings were held and a number of committees met over the next few years. Negotiations began with the Forest Service in 1983 to lease the top of the mountain for the new park. Soon, a law was passed in Arkansas authorizing the park.

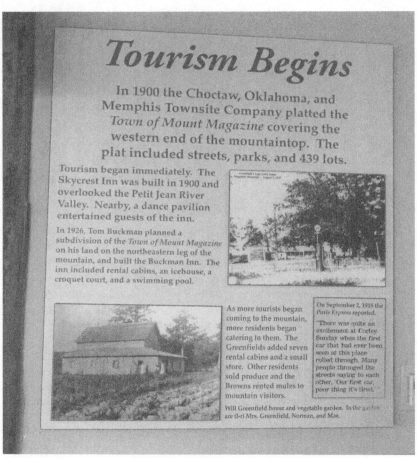

The new lodge at the Magazine Mountain State Park features a number of signs about the history of the mountain, including several about the involvement of the Choctaw, Oklahoma & Gulf and its Choctaw, Oklahoma and Memphis Town Site Company.

Sign advertising the Choctaw, Oklahoma & Gulf R.R. and its Choctaw, Oklahoma and Memphis Town Site Company at the Magazine Mountain State Park lodge.

Things don't always move quickly in government, and it wasn't until 1989 that a Special Use Permit was issued by the U.S. Forest Service to the Arkansas Department of Parks and Tourism. The next half-dozen years were spent conducting environmental impact reports and statements, and land was finally leased in 1998. Construction on the new park began in 1999, with investments in campgrounds, a visitor center, and a lodge, completed in 2006. The new Lodge at Mount Magazine features 60 guest rooms, a conference center, the Skycrest Restaurant, a number of cabins, and great views. It is also the home of the Mount Magazine hang glider launch site where Mark Stump once sailed 178 miles before landing. The State Park is certainly worth a visit.

229.9 BRIDGE – In this area, the railroad had a bridge consisting of a 50-foot through plate girder span, plus seven timber spans. Just to the west, the old grade is now Railroad Lane, used to reach several houses. Much of this area also includes tree farms with row after row of pine trees.

233.2 CLEAR CREEK BRIDGE – This was an 8-panel ballast deck pile trestle bridge. Clear Creek flows off the south side of Magazine Mountain, comes south and flows into the Petit Jean River, south of Waveland. To the north of the tracks is Shoot Cemetery.

234.5 WAVELAND – The railroad grade returns to Arkansas Highway 10 at Waveland, a small crossroads along the highway. The town features a gas and convenience store, several dozen houses, and lots of poultry

319

houses. There is also the access road to Waveland Park on Blue Mountain Lake, located to the south on the Petit Jean River. Waveland Park includes campsites with electrical and water hookups, restrooms with showers, a swim beach, boat ramps, and many other recreational facilities. Blue Mountain Lake is another lake created to reduce flooding in the Ouachita Mountains and along the streams as they flow into the Arkansas River Valley. The dam closed the waterway in 1947 and is now operated by the U.S. Corps of Engineers, providing flood control and outdoor recreation. Unfortunately, the lake is never visible from the railroad grade.

Waveland is not an incorporated community, but is actually a township in Yell County and has a reported population of 285. A Waveland post office opened during 1881, but it closed in 1997. Almost as soon as the railroad opened, lumber was shipped from here. During late 1910, there were several hearings of the Arkansas Railroad Commission to determine the need for a passenger and freight depot. In 1921, companies such as Rock Island Lumber Company, Morse Brothers Lumber Company, and Nelms & Son (milling) were operating in the area.

In 1950, Waveland was the scheduled meeting location for westbound passenger train No. 51, and eastbound No. 52, the two *Choctaw Rocket* trains, at 1:48pm. At the time, there was a 93-car siding, plus spur tracks that could hold 27 freight cars. In 1973, there was a siding on the north side of the mainline. It was shown as being 4585 feet long in 1979, when there was also a dispatcher telephone at Waveland.

The three miles of grade heading west provided a challenge for many trains as it was the longest one-percent westbound grade between Little Rock and Booneville. The route also featured a series of three degree curves and crossed a number of bridges, allowing water to flow off of the ridge to the north. Some of these bridges were updated during the 1940s to allow heavier locomotives that could pull larger trains up the hill.

235.1 FALLING ROCK ROAD BRIDGE – This 50-foot deck plate girder span crosses Falling Rock Road, which is also County Road 503, just north of Arkansas Highway 10. A small stream also flows under the very west end of the span.

West of Waveland, the railroad stayed on top of a low ridge while the highway followed the valley. This led to the need for several bridges to cross local roads and streams. This deck plate girder span crosses Fall Rock Road at Milepost 235.1.

235.2 SMALLWOOD CREEK BRIDGE – This is another 50-foot deck plate girder span. It crossed Smallwood Creek and Pettycord Road, officially County Road 575. There is a plate on this bridge that states it was manufactured in 1941 by the American Bridge Company of New York.

235.5 ARKANSAS HIGHWAY 10 VIADUCT – There used to be a 43'-9" deck plate girder span that crossed Highway 10 here, along with 11 ballast deck timber pile panels on the west end. This bridge was removed in September 1999 because of its low clearance of 14'-3". The removal also allowed the road to be widened.

Arkansas Highway 10 runs east-west from Little Rock to the Oklahoma border near Hackett. It is one of the original Arkansas State Highways designed in 1926, and still closely follows its original route. The highway is 135 miles long and generally follows the Rock Island Railroad's Choctaw Route across western Arkansas.

If you look carefully, some of the concrete footings for the former railroad overpass can still be found to the west of Arkansas Highway 10.

236.7 ROCK CREEK BRIDGE – After following Rock Creek up the grade since Waveland, the railroad crossed it here using a 75-foot through plate girder span. The span can be seen sitting in the woods not far south of Arkansas Highway 10, but it looks more like a bridge skeleton than a real bridge. This is because someone cut out the flat steel plate between the I-beam girders. The east end of the bridge is also now missing.

In this area, there are a number of natural gas wells, most from the recent boom that started about 2005 in the Fayetteville Shale formation in central Arkansas, and the Arkoma Basin Province in western Arkansas. In 2009, there were 5600 gas wells operating in Arkansas.

Not far west of here at Milepost 237.5 is the top of the grade at 588 feet above sea level. The grade then drops at 1.0% to Magazine, 150 feet lower in elevation.

239.2 COUNTY LINE – **Yell County** is to the east while **Logan County** is to the west. **Logan County** was founded on March 22, 1871, as Sarber County, named for a state senator from Yell County who had proposed the new county. However, on December 14, 1875, it became Logan County. The reason for the change was that the Democrat Party had taken control of the state government and considered Saber a carpet-bagger, so they renamed the county after James Logan, an early settler. The northern part of the county was located in the Arkansas Valley and was more developed, so a location in that area was chosen as the new county seat, eventually being named Paris.

Logan County grew quickly during the 1880s, going from 14,885 residents in 1880, to 20,774 in 1890. The Choctaw & Memphis built through southern Logan County, passing through the early trade town of Booneville. The sudden growth along the railroad encouraged the creation of the Southern Judicial District of Logan County in 1901, with a county seat in Booneville. Paris was left as the county seat for the Northern Judicial District. This makes Logan County one of ten counties in Arkansas with two county seats. With the division, the population also grew from 20,563 in 1900 to the county's peak population of 26,350 in 1910. The growth came about due to the opening of coal mines, sawmills, cotton gins, and many other industries. However, most closed during the 1950s and the population dropped to 15,957 by 1960. Tourism and bedroom communities have led to a population of 22,353 in 2010.

239.4 BLUE MOUNTAIN – Thomas Ryles was one of the first to acquire a land patent in the area when he settled here in 1860. Following the Civil War, several other families settled in the area and a Baptist congregation was formed during the late 1870s. The population grew enough that a post office opened in 1893, known as Maggie. The Choctaw, Oklahoma & Gulf Railroad started rail service through here in 1899 and the town began to grow even more as the railroad's land development company promoted the area. The railroad started calling the community Blue Mountain, named for a part of Mount Magazine, the highest point in the State of Arkansas. For example, the October 1899, issue of *The Choctaw*, a newspaper "issued monthly by authority of the Choctaw, Oklahoma and Gulf, and the Choctaw and Memphis Railroads," had a large advertisement by the Choctaw, Oklahoma and Memphis Town Site Company. Among the towns being promoted was Blue Mountain, called "The Scenic Gem" by the company.

Blue Mountain was incorporated on March 7, 1901, and the post office changed its name from Maggie to Blue Mountain that same year. The railroad planned for the town to be a resort community, but it never grew to be much more than a rural farming and lumbering community. At the time of incorporation, the town had about seventy-five homes, fifteen businesses, two blacksmith shops, a church, and a school. Even so, tourism did reach the town as Blue Mountain sits in a beautiful valley between Potts Ridge (860 feet high) to the south, and Mount Magazine (2753 feet high) to the north. The Rock Island did promote tours to the mountains that used Blue Mountain as the primary rail station.

Cotton was grown in the area, and 252 rail shipments were made in 1902-1903. Some lumber also moved from the town. Apparently, there was some political support for the town as Act 343 of the Arkansas General Assembly, passed on May 17, 1907, required that at least two passenger trains per day stop at Blue Mountain. Additionally, it required that the depot would be open every day from 6am to 6pm, staffed with a station agent, expressman and telegraph operator. The law did note that the three duties could be done by one person.

The title "The Scenic Gem" is no longer used for Blue Mountain, which instead labels itself as the "Gateway to Blue Mountain Lake."

A major challenge to the railroad occurred in 1926 when Arkansas Highway 10 was planned and built alongside the Rock Island, about a block to the north in this area. Soon after, the Great Depression led to the closure of most of the town's businesses. On June 30, 1931, the Arkansas Railroad Commission approved a plan to discontinue the regular agent and employ a caretaker to open and close the station as needed. By mid-1931, the railroad had closed its station at Blue Mountain, but a petition by local residents and a hearing on November 3rd resulted in an order to reopen the station. This didn't last long as the Arkansas Corporation Commission approved removing the agent at Blue Mountain on April 3, 1933. Things did improve some when Civilian Conservation Corps Camp No. 768 was established at Blue Mountain, with the men engaged in road building and forestry. In 1946, parts of the town burned and little was rebuilt.

Blue Mountain was located in a short sag between two ridges. These ridges were the ruling grade of the railroad in this area. These grades were 1.0% and helped to dictate the size of trains, and the locomotives required to move trains over the line.

In 1950, the railroad had a 71-car siding plus a 16-car spur track at Blue Mountain, located at today's Blue Mountain Park about two blocks south of Arkansas Highway 10. The siding was located on the north side of the mainline, but it was removed during the 1960s. In 1979, there was only a 340-foot spur track and a dispatcher telephone at Blue Mountain. The tracks were removed in 1986. The town still has its post office, but few other businesses. With a population of 124 in the 2010 census, Blue Mountain now relies upon area poultry producers for much of its economic activity.

The Depot of the Blue Mountain Extension Homemaker's Club

On March 29, 1939, the Rock Island sold off its depot at Blue Mountain, several years after it was closed. The depot was acquired by the Blue Mountain Extension Homemaker's Club, which moved it about a block away. During the move, the depot (which originally faced south) was turned to face north. For decades, the building was used as a community center, and during World War II the building was where bandages were folded for the war effort.

Despite being placed on the National Register of Historic Places in 1978, the former CRI&P depot at Blue Mountain was in bad shape in 1986, when this photo was taken.

As part of an effort to raise money to restore the depot, it was placed on the National Register of Historic Places in 1978. The application stated that the depot was built during the late 1890s and was a single-story rectangular wood frame structure, featuring ship-lap siding. It measured 40'-6" long, and 18'-6" wide. There was a freight and express room, two waiting rooms (black and white), and an office, which also provided Western Union telegraph service. Unfortunately, the fundraising failed and the depot was later demolished.

239.8 BRIAR CREEK BRIDGE – From Blue Mountain to Magazine, the railroad is located across the fields to the south of Arkansas Highway 10. This 45-foot deck plate girder span remains and is used as part of a private road into a poultry farm. The bridge was manufactured by the American Bridge Company in 1926. The cement piers are also marked 1926, apparently when the bridge was rebuilt. Heading west, the railroad stays about 500 feet south of Highway 10, forming a long tree line. The valley it runs through is south of Donathan Ridge and north of Potts Ridge, an area used for poultry and livestock production.

Heading west, trains faced a 1.0% grade for the next mile, and then headed down similar grades all the way to Magazine.

244.4 REVILEE CREEK BRIDGE – This stream forms south of Pleasant Hill, less than a dozen miles to the northeast. From here, it flows south for a few miles and enters the Petit Jean River. Some sources show this to be Prairie Branch, while others show it as Revilee Creek. Researching the history of the stream, spellings such as Reville and Reveille are also found. However, Revilee is probably the correct spelling as it was cited that way in early government reports.

The Revilee Creek Bridge can just be seen downstream from the Highway 10 bridge. The Rock Island Railroad 1973 track chart states that this bridge consisted of two 50-foot deck plate girder (DPG) spans, one 35-foot DPG, and a 30-foot I-beam span, all from east to west. The bridge was apparently manufactured by the American Bridge Company, with the deck plate girder spans set on large concrete piers. The west end of the I-beam span sits on a steel-pile bent with a concrete cap, looking like a replacement.

Just west of Revilee Creek, the railroad grade turns to the southwest to pass around the south end of the City of Magazine.

Almost hidden in the woods is the former Revilee Creek bridge, still featuring the deck plate girder spans used by the railroad.

245.1 MAGAZINE – By the 1860s, the area around Magazine was already being settled, and the Magazine Post Office opened in 1867, named for the nearby mountain. A store was opened here in 1870 after Eli D. Hooper, an Illinois storekeeper, moved to the area. The location attracted more merchants, and by the early 1880s, the town had five stores, a church, and 200 residents. By 1890, the town was up to 400 residents and had gained a cotton gin to process cotton from local farmers. On June 24, 1899, the track crews reached the Magazine area, and an announcement was made that the depot and switches were to be finished in a few days. Shortly thereafter, a planing mill and a big brick kiln opened. Reports from the time state that the railroad built about a mile north of Magazine's downtown, but the railroad made land available along the north side of the tracks, causing the town to spread out. This formed Old Magazine to the south and New Magazine to the north. Eventually the town was to the north of the tracks and industries were to the south.

The New Magazine maneuver seemed to be a common practice for the Choctaw Railroad, as it tended to just miss a number of existing communities. New towns were surveyed and platted, and then promoted by the Choctaw, Oklahoma and Memphis Town Site Company. In their advertisement, the land company promoted Magazine as "The Natural Mountain Resort." The town grew, adding a $10,000 brick high school in 1907. Banks, a private academy, more churches, a weekly newspaper, and more stores also arrived. While the railroad promoted Magazine as a resort town, manufacturers were also attracted by the Choctaw Route. These included the Magazine Gin Company, the Valentine Gin Company, the Petit Jean Canning Company, and the Magazine Marble Company. Agriculture was also important, especially cotton, corn and various hay crops. With this boom, the population peaked at 968 in 1910.

In February 1917, the residents of Magazine petitioned the Arkansas Railroad Commission for a newer and larger depot. However, the 1920s and 1930s saw Magazine's economy hurt as tourism stopped, the timber was cut, and crops failed. Some activity took place as the Works Progress Administration (WPA) and the Civilian Conservation Corps (CCC) built roads and buildings on Mount Magazine and in nearby National Forests, creating a series of parks. Livestock and poultry also started replacing cotton farming. During the latter part of the Twentieth Century, Magazine became the center of activity east of Booneville. The town still has a high school and post office, a number of stores and farm supply businesses, churches and homes. In 1992, an eighteen-hole golf course was opened at Magazine by the 1955 U.S. Open golf tournament champion – Jack Fleck. He reportedly used his champion's gold medal, won when he beat Ben Hogan in a playoff, to raise the funds needed to keep it operating. The course closed in 2003 and Fleck died in 2014. It is easy to see why a golf course might not survive as the population of Magazine in 2010 was just 847.

Magazine was never a major rail terminal for the railroad, especially with Booneville not far to the west. In 1950, there was a 34-car siding and a 21-car industry track. By 1973, all of the side tracks were gone. The grade can generally be found as it loops around the south end of Magazine. Some new construction has used the grade, such as the Magazine High School track and field facility, and the Magazine Ballpark west of town.

Heading west from Magazine, the railroad runs east-west on the north side of Potts Ridge, with the Petit Jean River just to the south, shown on many early maps as Petit Jean Creek. The rail route generally cuts straight toward Booneville, a short distance south of Arkansas Highway 10.

246.4 SCOTT CREEK BRIDGE – This deck plate girder span replaced a series of timber piles and frame sets, as can be seen by the concrete footing in the middle of Scott Creek, under the metal span. This is another girder span that has been cut up, with all of the plate panels now missing.

Scott Creek, often shown as Scotts Creek, starts north of the ridges to the north and flows south through Whiteoak Valley and a narrow divide in Turkey Ridge. It then flows through another low ridge to this point. Several miles south of here, Scott Creek flows into the Petit Jean River.

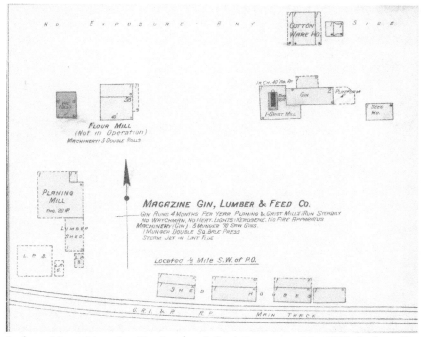

Sanborn Map – Magazine Gin, Lumber & Feed Company – May 1908. *Sanborn Fire Insurance Map from Magazine, Logan County, Arkansas.* Sanborn Map Company, May, 1908. Map. Retrieved from the Library of Congress, https://www.loc.gov/item/sanborn00293_002/.

249.2 WOLVERINE TOY COMPANY – After World War II, Booneville worked to attract manufacturing to replace the lost timber and farming income. One of the businesses that was brought to town was the Wolverine Toy Company. The firm was started by Benjamin Franklin Bain, who founded the Wolverine Supply and Manufacturing Company in 1903, created to manufacture metal kitchen tools and household supplies. The firm located in Pittsburgh, Pennsylvania, and acquired the Sand Toy Company in 1909. Over the years, the firm added more toys and they became the primary revenue producer for the company, so the firm was renamed the Wolverine Toy Company in 1962. In 1970, the company moved to Booneville and built the large factory to the north of the tracks, using a 3002-foot-long spur track for service that remained in the timetable until the end of the railroad. Since then, the firm has gone through several names and product lines.

The plant was important enough to be reported on in the September/October 1969 issue of *The Rocket*, a newsletter "published bimonthly in Chicago by the Public Relations department of the Rock Island Lines for and about its active and retired employees." It stated:

> At Booneville, Arkansas, the Wolverine Toy Company, of Pittsburgh, a subsidiary of Spang and Company, will begin construction this fall of a 400,000-square-foot, $3.5 million manufacturing plant and warehouse on a 400-acre tract two miles east of town.
>
> The new toy factory will employ between 350 and 400 persons and account for an annual payroll of nearly $1.5 million. The company produces a line of metal and plastic toys with the major emphasis on girls' housekeeping toys. Completion of the new facility is expected by July, 1970.

During the late 1970s, eighty percent of the goods made by the Wolverine Toy Company were shipped by rail. This equaled to about 400 carloads per month. Today, the facility is used by Rockline Industries, a leading manufacturer of wet wipes, coffee filters and baking cups. This is a wet wipe manufacturing and distribution facility. The grade of the Rock Island mainline has been turned into Arkansas Highway 197 as part of a plan to turn this area into an industrial park.

251.7 BOONEVILLE (BO) – Booneville was an important terminal on the Chicago, Rock Island & Pacific Railroad, located at an elevation of 490 feet. From the very beginning of the Choctaw & Memphis – Choctaw, Oklahoma & Gulf – Booneville has been a center of railroad activity. In 1899, the Choctaw, Oklahoma and Memphis Town Site Company was based in Booneville, and it advertised the city as "The Railroad Division Town." At the time, the railroad had just completed a line between McAlester, Oklahoma, and Little Rock, Arkansas, where it connected to a line on east to Memphis, Tennessee. As a part of the operating plan, Booneville was designated as a division point for crew changes.

In 1950, Booneville was the west end of the Arkansas Division, and it was still the west end of Subdivision 30 of the Southern Division in 1979. Subdivision 30 went as far east as Biddle Yard. Heading west was Subdivision 31, which was shown as part of the Arkansas Division in the 1973 track charts. Subdivision 31 went as far west as Hartshorne, Oklahoma.

The tracks were built to Booneville on June 17, 1899, and the line opened to regular traffic on October 1, 1899. In several sources, Booneville was called a Chicago, Rock Island & Pacific Railroad Roundhouse and Terminal. The Rock Island had a yard, roundhouse and shops here, located west of Owen Avenue. The roundhouse was significant enough to be reported on during 1908 by such magazines as *Railway Journal* and *Railway Master Mechanic*, a year after it was enlarged. In 1907, the CRI&P also installed a new wye on the north side of the shops and a new track at the depot for freight cars. The railroad also had a re-icing station; a stockyard consisting of four pens plus a cleaning pen; and a 40-foot, 100,000-pound capacity track scale.

For passengers, the railroad had a large wooden station that included, from east to west, a waiting room, office, baggage room, freight room, and dispatcher's office. To the east was a Spanish Mission-style building with stone columns, operated by the John J. Grier Hotel Company. Initially, the Rock Island Railroad bought and built restaurants along their lines so they could control the eating houses in towns where trains stopped for meal breaks. John J. Grier received the franchise to operate some of them starting in 1908, growing to 34 locations in eight states. In Arkansas, this included the restaurant and hotel at Forrest City, and the one here at Booneville. The stone building was built as the restaurant, with a small hotel to the east. In 1913, Sanborn labeled the building as the Greer Hotel Company with the Petit Jean Tavern, with a kitchen, lunch room and dining room.

In 1936, trains no longer stopped for meals at Booneville, instead serving them on the train, and the Grier restaurant closed. The Rock Island slowly started moving their facilities into the building, and by 1946, all railroad operations had been moved from the old wooden depot into the Grier Eating House. Passenger service ended in 1967 and the station continued in use as a railroad office, ending when the railroad closed in 1980. The building stood for years, owned by various local businesses and used for office space, but it burned down in 2001, leaving only the rock columns and one end wall. The remains still stand west of the new post office building.

The former Grier Eating House, later the Rock Island station, still stood during this December 1986 visit.

Little remains of the John J. Grier Restaurant, more commonly called the Grier Eating House, and later used as the Rock Island Railroad station. However, the remains can still be found behind the post office at Booneville, Arkansas.

In 1950, the railroad timetable showed that there was a 34-car siding at Booneville, plus yard tracks and several industry tracks that could hold another 515 freight cars. The yard was to the west of the station, and there was a spur that ran past the station and north of the yard that included a wye for turning locomotives and freight cars. In 1979, the railroad showed that there was a 4424-foot siding and a yard. *Rock Island Timetable No. 1*, dated March 18, 1979, also showed a number of facilities and services at Booneville. These included general order boards and books, a standard clock, train register station, a train order station with no train order signals, a wayside radio, water station, and wye, all protected by yard limits (Mileposts 247.5 to 254.0).

The City of Booneville

Booneville is an older city that existed for almost seventy years before the railroad arrived. A general store was opened alongside the Petit Jean River in 1828 by Walter Cauthron. The name Booneville resulted, although there is controversy about where the name came from. Some sources state that it is a misspelled version of Bonneville, named for the friend and traveling companion of Walter Cauthron – Captain Benjamin Bonneville. Other sources claim that the name came from Daniel Boone, a friend of James Logan, for whom the county is named.

It should be mentioned that James Logan once lived to the north of Booneville. There, he farmed and operated the Logan Post Office, but he moved closer to Booneville in 1833 to avoid a cholera outbreak after a series of floods along the Arkansas River and across its watershed. During the same year, Scott County was created from part of Crawford County, and Booneville became the county seat. In 1837, Walter Cauthron laid out a town of nine blocks on his property and a post office opened, first as Petit Jean, and then as Booneville. The population was 400 by the time of the Civil War, and it was the only trading center between Fort Smith and Dardanelle, two major Arkansas River port towns. The Civil War did not destroy Booneville, but many residents moved away to avoid the constant movement of troops and guerrilla forces. After the war, Booneville again grew and gained a number of stores, churches, a cotton gin, a drugstore, a blacksmith shop, and the *Booneville Enterprise* newspaper. However, it lost the title of county seat when Sarber/Logan County was created on March 22, 1871, and Paris became the county seat. Still, with continued growth, Booneville was incorporated in May 1878.

A major change happened on December 11, 1899, when the first through passenger train arrived. The major issue was that the existing Booneville was south of the tracks, and the Choctaw, Oklahoma and Memphis Town Site Company bought the farm of W. D. Sadler, which was located north of the tracks. A new Booneville was platted, featuring wide streets and alleys that were appropriate for a major city. To quickly develop the community, the land company offered lots in the new downtown to companies in the older town, and held its first townsite sales at Booneville on April 26, 1899. Newspaper reports indicate that the Town Site Company even helped to move the buildings owned by those that moved. In 1899, Booneville incorporated again to reflect the new design and location of the city. Much of this new downtown is now part of the Booneville Commercial Historic District.

The railroad also helped fill the town's new lots, and kept the local companies busy. The railroad hired the John J. Grier Hotel Company to run a restaurant and hotel, handling the daily passenger trains that made a 20 to 25-minute meal break here. There were also dozens of railroad employees working in the shops, operating and dispatching trains, maintaining the track and bridges, and managing the operations of the railroad. The railroad also had their own company doctor at Booneville. Booneville also gained when in 1901, the Southern Judicial District of Logan County was created with Booneville as its county seat.

Because of the railroad, Booneville became important enough to attract numerous events. On September 16, 1906, Williams Jennings Bryant stopped to make a presidential campaign speech. In September 1908, Booneville attracted people from miles around when it hosted two performances of the Ringling Brothers Circus. Another presidential campaign led President Franklin D. Roosevelt to stop for a talk to four thousand people on July 9, 1938. This was his only campaign stop in Arkansas.

Several sources provide different views of the development of Booneville during the early 1900s. Sanborn mapping showed that in 1908, the Robeca & Company cotton gin was located just north of the Rock Island tracks south of Railroad Street (today's 1st Street) and east of Grant Avenue. Across the street to the north was W. L. Shamblee's cotton gin. Additionally, the large Coleman & Yount Lumber Company was located south of Cooke Avenue (today's 2nd Street) and west of Kennedy Avenue. Just west of the sawmill was the Booneville Ice, Light & Cold Storage Company.

The October 1913 Sanborn map showed a number of changes. It still showed the Coleman & Yount Lumber Company and ice company, and also showed railroad section houses, an ice house, and a coal bin along the tracks just to the southeast. It noted that the Robeca & Company cotton gin was now Valentine's Gin, and that a grist mill had been built as a part of the complex. W. L. Shamblee's Gin still stood, and the Greenway & Harvey electric light and power plant was located just east of Valentine's complex. The December 1918 Sanborn map noted a few additional changes. Valentine's Gin had become Jones & Company, and W. L. Shamblee was the W. T. Roberts Cotton Gin. Finally, Coleman & Yount was shown to be Scott County Land & Lumber Company, a supplier of yellow pine lumber.

Farming and timber were obviously sources of business during the early 1900s. The U.S. Department of Agriculture reported that Booneville was the source of 4194 rail shipments of cotton in 1902-1903. The *Arkansas Marketing and Industrial Guide* of 1921 listed a number of other businesses. These included the Booneville Bottling Works, W. D.

Walker (brooms), Booneville Lumber & Timber Company, C. H. Hodges Lumber Company, Lick Creek Nursery, and M. S. Pierce (quarry). Another major activity near Booneville was the Arkansas State Tuberculosis Sanatorium, opened in 1910 and considered to be one of the most successful and modern hospitals for the treatment of tuberculosis of its day. By the time it closed in 1973, the sanatorium had treated over 70,000 patients.

Following World War II, Booneville began to lose much of its traditional industry, and the Booneville Industrial Development Commission was established to attract new industry. A few of the companies attracted include the Ace Comb Company, Baldwin Music, Arkansas Kraft Products, Waggoner Brothers, Simmons Lumber, Wolverine Toy Company, and Del Pero Monden (Cargill). Booneville was also a loading point for pulpwood heading to the paper mill near Perry. Not all of these companies are still in operation here, and the railroad is certainly also gone, with the last train leaving Booneville on March 30, 1980. Over the years, Booneville has been the home of the 1982 Miss America Elizabeth Ward Gracen, actress Kimberly Foster (*Dallas* and *All My Children*), and baseball players Jay Hanna "Dizzy" Dean and Paul Dee "Daffy" Dean. The city's population peaked at 4117 in the 2000 census, with a population of 3990 in 2010.

The John J. Grier Restaurant

Of all of the Chicago, Rock Island & Pacific facilities that once stood at Booneville, the remains of the John J. Grier Restaurant is about all that can still be found. An article in the September 3, 1910, issue of the *Arkansas Gazette* provided a lot of information about the restaurant. It stated that the Greer Hotel Company spent $50,000 on the new dining room at Booneville. This included $300 for kitchen equipment and $500 for artwork. The tables and other furnishings consisted of leather and Arkansas hardwoods.

When built, passenger trains stopped at Booneville for a 25-minute meal break since dining cars were not yet being used on the route. The company bragged that the menu was supervised by S. J. Jewell, who had managed western restaurants for a decade. The restaurant could handle 50 in the dining room and 50 more at the lunch counter. The cost of a typical meal was 75 cents.

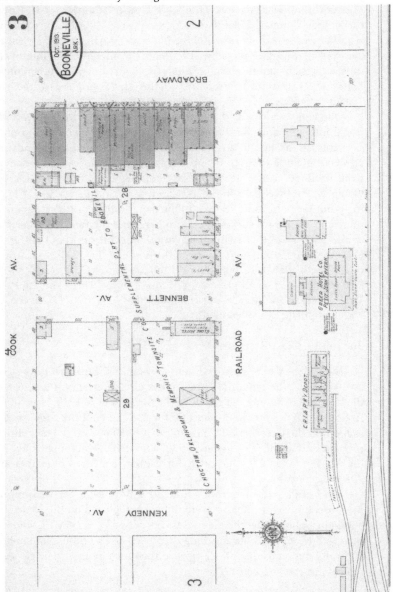

Sanborn Map of Booneville station area – October 1913. *Sanborn Fire Insurance Map from Booneville, Logan County, Arkansas.* Sanborn Map Company, Oct, 1913. Map. Retrieved from the Library of Congress, https://www.loc.gov/item/sanborn00207_002/.

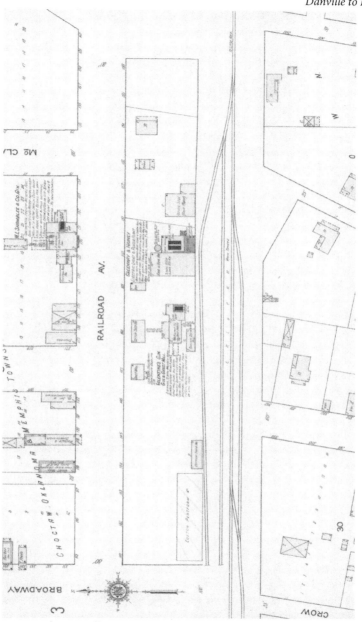

Sanborn Map of Booneville cotton gin to east of depot – October 1913. *Sanborn Fire Insurance Map from Booneville, Logan County, Arkansas.* Sanborn Map Company, Oct, 1913. Map. Retrieved from the Library of Congress, https://www.loc.gov/item/sanborn00207_002/.

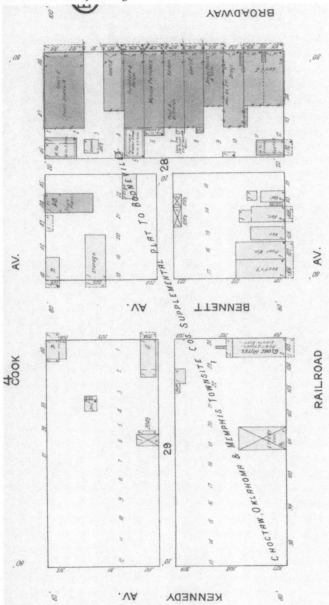

Sanborn Map – Choctaw, Oklahoma & Memphis Town Site Company – October 1913. *Sanborn Fire Insurance Map from Booneville, Logan County, Arkansas.* Sanborn Map Company, Oct, 1913. Map. Retrieved from the Library of Congress, https://www.loc.gov/item/sanborn00207_002/.

252.1 BOONEVILLE YARD – The Rock Island had a yard, roundhouse, and shops here, located west of Owen Avenue. The complex started small, built for the equipment used about 1900. As locomotives and freight cars got bigger, the Chicago, Rock Island & Pacific invested in its yards and shops across the system. In early 1910, the railroad announced plans to make improvements at Booneville. This included adding more yard tracks, a 165,000-gallon water station, and a 300-ton coal chute.

From 1902 until May 1, 1919, hostler service was provided to passenger trains at Booneville to swap locomotives on through trains. This changed because of a higher wage for hostler employees if they entered the mainline. A hearing by the Railroad Board of Adjustment described the changes required as part of an evaluation of the impact on the train crews, who felt that enginemen should be relieved of handling the engines to and from the yard. The Board agreed with the train crews in a 1920 hearing.

Before May 1, 1919, the eastbound trains pulled up in front of the depot and eating house on the main line when trains did not meet there, the engine was cut off from the train and the hostlers took charge. Now the following practice is followed:

On eastbound trains the train stops back from the depot 1,800 feet, heads in on south passing track, pulls down to the depot, stops and engine is cut off from the train, engine then runs out to main line 360 feet, engine is then backed by train between train depot and eating house to north yard 780 feet, then engine is backed in on lead onto either track 1, 2, or 3 to clear lead and the engineer is relieved. Then eastbound engine on outbound train pulls out on main line, goes ahead between train and depot 780 feet and backs in on train, requiring from 10 to 25 minutes time for west end men, and from 5 to 15 minutes for east end men.

The westbound trains make no change for the enginemen on the Arkansas division. On the westbound trains on the Indian Territory division makes very little difference from the former practice to the engine crews, as the engine is left just inside of the north yard on track 1 or 2 instead of being placed on the main line as was previously done by the hostler and instead of the outbound engineer getting engine on main line he gets it inside of yard and backs it onto the train, which is very little difference in the movement.

In 1950, timetables showed that the yard could handle about 500 cars. There was a track north of the yard that included a wye for turning locomotives and freight cars. In 1979, the railroad had a 4424-foot siding and a yard. *Rock Island Timetable No. 1*, dated March 18, 1979, also showed a number of facilities and services at Booneville. These included general order boards and books, a standard clock, train register station, a train order station with no train order signals, a wayside radio, water station, and wye. Many of these were based out of the yard since passenger service had ended on the line. Foundations remain where the shops once stood, but all of the tracks are gone.

Heading west, the railroad stays just north of Barber Ridge/Bassinger Mountain and Bear Mountain. It can be followed using Barber Road, which stays to the south of the abandoned railroad grade most of the way. The railroad grade is generally marked by a row of trees, making it easy to find as it crosses through fields and pastures.

253.2 ARKANSAS LIQUIFIED GAS – In 1979, this 250-foot industry track was listed as being here, explaining why the yard limits for Booneville went all the way to Milepost 254.0. The propane dealership can still be found at this location.

253.8 RACOON CREEK RAILROAD BRIDGE – This bridge is north of Barber Road and east of Roy Franks Lane on private property. This bridge consisted of a 60-foot through plate girder span, plus three timber pile spans on the east end. This is another plate girder span that has had the plates cut out.

Racoon Creek forms on the southeast side of Bonneville Mountain and flows to the southeast. It enters the Petit Jean River several miles south of here.

259.2 WASHBURN CREEK BRIDGE – Washburn Creek starts on the southeast side of the Washburn Mountains, flowing east and then south between White Oak Mountain and Bonneville Mountain. Heading south, it passes between Blythe Ridge and Mebane Ridge, where a dam forms Booneville Lake, used as a municipal water source for the City of Booneville. The lake also carries the name Upper Petit Jean Site Number Nine Reservoir. The water works and pumping station sit on top of Mebane Ridge.

In this area are the town of Washburn, Washburn Township, and Washburn Creek. All are named for Reverend Cephas Washburn. Washburn was a Presbyterian missionary who was involved with the founding of the Dwight Mission, built to bring Christianity and education to the Cherokee and other Native Americans in Arkansas and the Indian Territory. He conducted his work for four decades. One of his sons, Edward Payson Washburn, was an artist who is best known for his piece, the *Arkansas Traveler.*

Washburn Creek is fairly large in this area as it heads south another mile to the Petit Jean River. The railroad bridge consisted of two 160-foot pin-connected through truss spans. Also known as Barber Bridge, it was removed when the tracks were salvaged. The bridge location is at an elevation of 490 feet. Heading west, trains climbed a grade of 0.79%-1.0% all the way to Echo, which is at an elevation of 673 feet.

259.5 BARBER – Barber was a small community at the west end of Barber Ridge, located on the west bank of Washburn Creek. Early records show that a Barber family once owned land in the area and sold 480 acres that later resulted in a lawsuit over ownership, so the area is likely named after them. A post office opened here in 1878, but it closed in 1981, the year after the railroad was abandoned. Records indicate that the depot was on the north side of the mainline, and that it was never much more than a flag stop for the railroad.

During the early 1900s, the Arkansas General Assembly had passed legislation that required the Chicago, Rock Island & Pacific to open a station and agency at Barber. The railroad discontinued the agency on April 14, 1909, making the station a flag stop, handling only prepaid freight and express. A petition was soon filed with the Arkansas Railroad Commission to force the railroad to reopen the station. The railroad then re-established the agency, but applied in 1928 to close it for good. However, an Arkansas Railroad Commission ruling on May 8, 1928, denied the request to close the station, but did allow the agent to be replaced by a caretaker. By 1969, all of the side tracks had been removed.

Heading west, the railroad runs along the north side of Sand Ridge all the way to Echo. Parts of the grade are used as driveways leading to new houses, access to various pastures, or roads to natural gas wells.

264.1 ECHO – Look for the old grade crossing with Echo Road, now marked by an electric power transmission line. Echo was once located just east of here. Note that there are a number of shale pits in this area, which is at the southeast end of Black Jack Ridge.

Echo was another small flag stop community along the railroad, mostly located to the north of the tracks. While the Choctaw, Oklahoma and Memphis Town Site Company originally platted the community, like several other projects, it turned the deeds over to land developer J. E. England in late 1899. A post office opened here in 1886, but it closed in 1912. On July 2, 1913, the Arkansas Railroad Commission ordered the CRI&P to assign an agent to the town. Business at Echo didn't last long, and there were no tracks here by the 1970s. Today, the area is a series of natural gas wells and no sign of the community remains.

264.3 COUNTY LINE – The county line is where the Rock Island Railroad used to cross Echo Road, not far north of the intersection with Sand Ridge Mountain Road. To the east is **Logan County**, while to the west is **Scott County**.

Scott County was created as Arkansas' 28th county from parts of Crawford, Pope, and Pulaski counties on November 5, 1833. The county was named for Arkansas Territory Supreme Court Justice Andrew Horatio Scott, appointed by President James Monroe. The Arkansas Territory was created on March 2, 1819, and Scott was the first territorial official to arrive at the capitol at Arkansas Post, arriving on July 4, 1819.

The initial county seat was the residence of Walter Cauthron, located near what is now Booneville. In 1836, the county seat was moved to Cauthron, which is also now in Logan County. In 1840, the county seat moved to Winfield, and then to Waldron in 1845. Some of these moves were made due to poor roads, while others were made to locate the county seat in the center of the county. A significant issue is that Yell (1840), Sebastian (1851), and Logan (1871) counties were all created from parts of Scott County. The county's population was 14,302 in 1910 when coal mining, lumbering, and cotton production were at their peak. The population dropped to 7297 in the 1960 census, and then back up to 11,233 in the 2010 census. Poultry production is currently the largest employer in the county, especially due to Tyson Foods and O.K. Foods.

266.5 BRIDGE – This six-span ballast deck pile trestle was the site of a suspected arson attack against the Chicago, Rock Island & Pacific on September 3, 1979. There were a number of small timber bridges in this area to handle water flowing off of Black Jack Ridge to the north, but this was the largest within a number of miles.

The bridge fire essentially shut down the railroad west of Booneville. With the railroad under the control of the Interstate Commerce Commission, the Kansas City Terminal was ordered to make repairs, with work starting by November 5, 1979. While repairs were estimated to cost $10,300, the Interstate Commerce Commission actually provided $20,000 to make the repairs and get trains running again, although just for a brief period of time.

268.4 ABBOTT – The area where Abbott stands today was first known as Black Jack, named for a ridge northeast of the town. The black jack oak is a native and popular tree. There are some reports that state a Black

Jack Post Office was established in the area in 1851. Some of the early settlers were the Sorrels and Looper families, both remembered due to their family cemeteries. The town was renamed Farmer in 1885, and the post office also took the same name. When the railroad arrived in 1899, William R. Abbott (Fort Smith Lumber Company) bought much of the town and built a sawmill. Later that year, the post office and town were renamed Abbott. William R. Abbott was the first postmaster for the renamed community.

Abbott, also known as Abbott's, was for many years essentially a company town, being dominated by the Fort Smith Lumber Company and its offices and sawmill, which produced more than 20,000 board feet of lumber a day. Some of the log ponds can still be found near U.S. Highway 71. While the Fort Smith Lumber Company dominated the community, agriculture and mining were also important. Iron ore was mined for several years, but the quality was too poor to be profitable. Some coal mining also took place in the area. In 1902, the first commercial gas field was discovered near Abbott, with the Choctaw Oil and Gas Company doing the drilling. Today, Abbott is an unincorporated community and agriculture continues to be an important industry among residents, primarily revolving around cattle and poultry. There are also numerous active natural gas wells. The Abbott Post Office was closed in 1973 and the mail is now handled at Mansfield.

In 1917, Abbott was a flag stop on the railroad. When the sawmill closed, the Rock Island began removing tracks. By the 1970s, there was nothing here but the mainline. The elevation at Abbott is 626 feet as the railroad once climbed its way between a series of ridges.

William Richard Abbott

William Abbott had a relatively short history in the timber business, with the latter portion of his career involved with investing in companies in the Fort Smith, Arkansas, area. Abbott, who was born on July 3, 1868, started work in the industry in 1887 when he took a job in the yard of the Chicago Lumber Company at Wichita, Kansas. He soon moved to Ogden, Utah, to work for the Eccles Lumber Company. After less than a year, he went to work for the Kansas Grain & Elevator Company at Cherryvale, Kansas, and then Long-Bell in Indian Territory during September 1890.

In 1892, Abbott began his own operations when he borrowed $20,000 and organized the Fort Smith Lumber Company. Short of money, he tied in with William Blair, a banker of Fort Smith. After a few years of cutting timber from Indian Territory, he incorporated the Fort Smith Lumber Company, built a sizeable mill at the new town of Abbott, and acquired 76,400 acres of timber. Needing money to expand the operation, he sold part of the company to Alfred Toll, who was associated with the Badger Lumber Company of Kansas City.

In 1903, William Blair died and Abbott took his place as president of the American National Bank at Fort Smith. His position led him to other investments, becoming president of the Cameron Coal & Mercantile Company at Williams, Indian Territory; vice president of the Mansfield Pressed Brick & Terra Cotta Company; and a significant investor in the Fort Smith Refrigerator Works, the Fort Smith Ice and Storage Company, and the Fort Smith Hardwood Manufacturing Company. In June 1904, Abbott also bought the controlling interest in the Fort Smith Light & Traction Company.

William Richard Abbott died of a heart attack on June 25, 1907, leaving the company to be managed by his officers. After several years, his sisters, who lived across the country, sued the Fort Smith Lumber Company, the American National Bank, many of the lumber company's officers, and just about anyone who had worked with Abbott in his investments. Their charge was that these people had somehow robbed the sisters, operating the companies for their own benefit and not those of the sisters. After a long hearing, the lawsuits were thrown out.

268.6 U.S. HIGHWAY 71 UNDERPASS – When the railroad was in operation, there was a 157-foot highway underpass here. Heading toward Oklahoma, the railroad was straight until the west side of Mansfield.

271.2 COOP CREEK BRIDGE – The east switch of the Rock Island Railroad siding at Mansfield was just west of this bridge. Heading east, the old grade is used by Tiger Trail, a new road that serves a small housing area near Mansfield High School. To the west, the former railroad grade can still be followed, but there are a number of new buildings on the right-of-way.

Coop Creek forms to the south and flows north around the east and north side of Mansfield, where it enters Cherokee Creek. Where the stream flows through the ridge south of town, a dam has been built to create Mansfield Lake. The lake was created in 1934-1935 as a source for drinking water, but a park has been added on the west side of the lake.

Rock Island records show that the railroad bridge, which was just north of Center Street, was once a five-panel ballast deck pile trestle. However, today there are nine narrow concrete piers here, a replacement of the older design. This is a design that the Rock Island would sometimes use with small I-beam spans. In some cases, the railroad also used spans built of old rails, set on wood or concrete piers.

271.5 MANSFIELD (MF) – In 1899, Mansfield was advertised as "The Great Junction City of the Choctaw Route and the Frisco Route," and for several decades it was a busy railroad and mining town that may have justified the nickname. Mansfield was created by the Little Rock & Texas Railway Company, a subsidiary of the Frisco. As described in several articles, the town was founded in 1887 in the middle of nowhere. The railroad had originally ended at the coal mining town of Huntington, but then built further south to reach farmers who were reluctant to do business in a coal company town. One explanation of the name Mansfield comes from the town's location – "over in the man's field." While this is a popular story, it is more likely that the town was named for William W. Mansfield, an attorney who held many positions in Arkansas. In 1856, he was chosen to represent Franklin County in the General Assembly. He also served on the convention committee that debated secession before the Civil War, and was a member of the convention of 1874 which wrote a new Arkansas constitution. Mansfield also served as an elected judge of the Fifth Judicial Circuit, and then was asked to compile a digest of the statutes of Arkansas, what became known as *Mansfield's Digest* when it was published in 1884. He next served as reporter for the Arkansas Supreme Court, and then as an associate justice of the Arkansas Supreme Court 1891-1894.

The community of Mansfield was platted in 1887 on property between the communities of Coop Prairie and Chocoville. Coop Prairie was established in 1849 on the land of Martin T. Taylor. The town became big enough to include a trading post, church and cemetery. Chocoville and its post office opened in 1852. The post office was the first in the region, and opened and closed several times. The Mansfield post office, which is still open today, was created in 1887. The railroad encouraged the two nearby towns to consolidate around the tracks. On August 29, 1888, the towns merged and the City of Mansfield was incorporated. The new city soon bragged that it was surrounded by a magnificent country, with everything and more a new settler would need.

Between the railroad, coal mining, lumbering and farming, Mansfield boomed during the 1880s and 1890s, and grew more with the arrival of the Rock Island. During the construction of the railroad through west Arkansas, many of the supplies arrived here on the Frisco, making Mansfield a base for the Rock Island contractors. By May 1899, the Choctaw & Memphis had completed their line from Howe to Mansfield, and a yard and tracks to connect to the St. Louis & San Francisco were also in place. On May 25, 1899, the railroad's townsite company held a sale on lots owned by the Choctaw & Memphis.

The two railroads surrounded the town on two sides. The Frisco cut across the northeast side of town, with their tracks lined with warehouses just north of City Hall. The Rock Island passed through the southeast

345

side of Mansfield, having fewer industries since it was the second railroad built to the city. Cotton gins, grist mills, sawmills, and many other factories and businesses opened throughout the town. A 1903 Department of Agriculture report stated that there were 3341 rail shipments of cotton from Mansfield in 1902-1903. At the same time, the Choctaw Oil and Gas Company was drilling Arkansas' first commercial gas field south of Mansfield. Because of the activity, the population of Mansfield reached 368 in 1900, and 816 in 1910.

In 1913, a number of companies created jobs, including Mansfield Roller Mill Company, Choctaw Brick & Gas Company, Farmer's Union Warehouse Company (cotton warehouse, cotton gin and compress), Mansfield Lumber Company, and Hickerson Brothers (planing mill). Two additional industries were shown to exist in 1919, both on the Rock Island. One was the J. C. Brown Cotton Gin and Feed Mill, located just west of Coop Creek on the north side of the tracks. The second one was the J. M. Lile cotton gin, located west of Division on the north side of the Rock Island. The numbers had grown even more by 1921 when C. N. Clever's grist mill, C. H. Hodges Lumber Company sawmill, and Mansfield Ice & Cold Storage Company were added to the list of businesses.

The Great Depression and the end of coal mining impacted the economy. However, gas drilling, farming and poultry production helped to create jobs, and unlike many other communities, the population kept growing. Also unlike many other area communities, Mansfield didn't get a newspaper, the *Citizen*, until 1967. The timber industry also hasn't disappeared, with West Fraser still operating a lumber facility and being the largest employer in town. Just east of the West Fraser mill is the large Coop Prairie Cemetery. Note how U.S. Highway 71 goes through the middle of the cemetery, becoming the first such cemetery in the United States. Because of this, it has been reported on by both *Ripley's Believe It or Not* and the *Guinness Book of World Records*. Mansfield also features stores, banks, restaurants, gas stations, schools, churches, and almost everything else needed by its population of about 1200, its peak in the life of the city.

In 1973, the railroad had a siding to the north, and in 1979 the timetable showed only 1160 feet of other tracks. In 1979, the CRI&P had no offices here, but a dispatcher telephone was available to train crews.

Frisco Mansfield Branch

Mansfield was an interchange point between the Frisco and the Rock Island that at one time had some importance. During the early 1900s, the Reid-Moore Syndicate controlled both the Rock Island

and Frisco, so there was an effort to coordinate activities. This resulted in a Union Station at Mansfield, and for a few years, through Pullman service between Fort Smith and Little Rock via Mansfield. As many as three trains a day in each direction provided this service, creating a competing service to Missouri Pacific, which had its own route between the two cities. The service began on July 19, 1903, and ended on November 20, 1907. After almost two years, the service started again on September 12, 1909, but it ended for good on June 4, 1910, after there became separate ownership of the two railroads.

The Mansfield Branch was built by the Little Rock & Texas Railway Company, incorporated on March 28, 1887, to build a railroad from near Fort Smith toward Little Rock. Almost twenty miles of track were built and the line opened to Mansfield by October 1887. While the Little Rock & Texas Railway was the name used, the work was actually funded and supervised by the St. Louis & San Francisco Railway Co. (StL&SF, or SL-SF), better known as the Frisco. When completed, the Frisco also operated the line, even though no agreement technically existed. This was solved on April 30, 1907, when a 99-year lease agreement was made.

While the line was planned to go all the way to Little Rock, it never built past Mansfield. The line basically became a coal railroad, hauling coal from more than a half-dozen mines. Much of the coal was used by the Frisco in their steam locomotives, and even by other railroads. Reports from 1918 state that there were as many miles of yard and industry tracks as there were of main track.

In 1899, the Choctaw & Memphis built through Mansfield, providing an interchange opportunity, especially for the next decade as the two railroads had common ownership. Initially, the two railroads had separate operations at Mansfield, with the Frisco depot north of Olive and Howard between the siding and mainline. About 1903, the Frisco moved to the Rock Island station, located five blocks east of Division at the corner of Center and Caldwell, about where the Mansfield Water Department stands today. After the move, the Frisco station was used as a railroad and crew office, and wasn't torn down until the 1940s. A legal case heard by the Supreme Court of Arkansas in 1917 provided a description of the operations at Mansfield.

At the town of Mansfield, Arkansas, where the injury occurred, the St. Louis & San Francisco Railroad (commonly known as the Frisco) connects with the line of the Chicago, Rock Island & Pacific Railway Company, and the two companies maintain and use a joint station. The Rock Island runs nearly east and west through the town, and the Frisco comes in from the north and curves toward the west [sic – it should be east]. The connecting point of the two roads is

> *about 1,200 feet east of the depot. The Frisco trains, in order
> to reach the depot, leave the main line of that road at the
> point of connection with the Rock Island and back up to the
> depot over what is called the "run-around track," which is
> used by both roads for switching purposes.*

These joint tracks were covered by a series of agreements. For example, a June 30, 1915, agreement stated that all costs of the shared tracks were to be covered equally. Another characteristic of the joint trackage is that it was all operated as yard limits where all operations were to be conducted based upon visible clearance. This caused the death of two Frisco brakemen on May 5, 1914, when a train from each railroad tried to use the same tracks without providing proper flagging. The investigation by the Interstate Commerce Commission provided more information about the operations.

> *This yard is operated under a joint contract, both roads
> using any and all of the tracks within the yard limits, there
> being regular designated tracks for delivering cars to both
> lines. However each road has a separate track for entrance
> to the station, but it appeared to be customary for the Rock
> Island to use the track assigned to the Frisco while switching
> in this yard.*

The original joint station, often called Union Depot or Union Station, was replaced with a modern brick station during the late 1910s. The station was very similar to the brick stations at Argenta and Lonoke, and featured both passenger and freight sections. The Frisco had a stub track on the north side, ending just west of the station. To the south of the station was the mainline of the CRI&P. To the east were several transfer tracks and a stock pen. Along the Frisco was a wye track to the north of their mainline. Also located just east of the station was a mail crane. This station lasted until almost the end of the railroad, coming down during the early 1970s. Remains of the foundation are still just east of the Mansfield Water Department building at Center Street and Caldwell Avenue. The foundation is now used to store asphalt and other materials. A short distance further east is a culvert under the 95-foot-wide railroad right-of-way. The adjacent Center Street culvert is marked USA WPA 1941.

The foundation of the Mansfield station still remains, used by the Mansfield Water Department for storage of construction materials.

If you look carefully east of the former Mansfield station, this stone culvert can be found, built during the early days of the railroad.

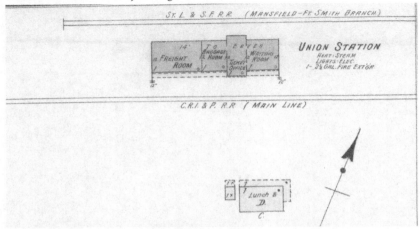

Sanborn Map of Union Station Area – January 1919. Sanborn Fire Insurance Map from Mansfield, Sebastian And Scott Counties, Arkansas. Sanborn Map Company, Jan, 1919. Map. Retrieved from the Library of Congress, https://www.loc.gov/item/sanborn00298_002/.

The Frisco started abandoning the Mansfield Branch in 1960, taking out the track from Mansfield north to the strip mine tipple near the former Central Coal Mine #24 at Huntington. The last miles were abandoned in December 1983 by Burlington Northern.

271.7 COUNTY LINE – Mansfield sits on the county line between **Scott County** (to the north, or railroad-east) and **Sebastian County** (to the south, or railroad-west). The county line is crossed at an angle and is approximately where several churches now stand on the old railroad grade, south of Center Street and east of Chestnut Avenue.

Sebastian County is the fourth-most populous county in Arkansas (125,744 residents in the 2010 census), thanks to Fort Smith, which is one of the two county seats – Greenwood is the other. Sebastian County was created from parts of Scott, Polk, and Crawford counties on January 6, 1851, making it the 56th of 75 counties created in Arkansas. The county was named for William King Sebastian, who was a U.S. Senator at the time. Sebastian was born in Tennessee and started practicing law at Helena, Arkansas, after he was admitted to the bar in 1835. He served as a U.S. Senator from 1848 until 1861, when he withdrew from the Senate after Arkansas seceded at the start of the Civil War. He never served in the Confederate government, and died in 1865 just days after the Civil War ended. In 1877, the United States Senate reinstated him by a posthumous resolution.

272.8 CHEROKEE CREEK BRIDGE – The railroad grade from Mansfield heads southwest, being used as a driveway and then as a farm road. At Cherokee Creek, the railroad's concrete bridge piers still stand, once used to support two 37'-6" wide-flanged beam spans. There were also six ballast deck pile trestle panels to the west, and seven to the east.

Cherokee Creek forms south of here near the Poteau Mountain Wilderness Area, and flows through Park Lake and Lake Number 2 on its way to the Mansfield area. It continues to flow north to Huntington, a route used by the Frisco's Mansfield Branch.

The railroad once continued to the southwest, with much of the grade serving as Railway Drive, and then turned west to cross the James Fork. From there, the railroad grade can be seen just south of Hartford-Mansfield Road, Arkansas Highway 96, all the way to Hartford.

276.6 JAMES FORK BRIDGE – The 100-foot through plate girder span that once stood here is long gone, but some of the headwalls can still be found, hidden in the woods about 750 feet south of Arkansas Highway 96.

The James Fork is considered to be part of the watershed of the Poteau River, which flows northward in Oklahoma, eventually entering the Arkansas River. The James Fork is about fifty miles long and forms on the northern slopes of Poteau Mountain, located in the Ouachita National Forest. As described by Goodspeed Publishing in 1889, in the book *History of Benton, Washington, Carroll, Madison, Crawford, Franklin, and Sebastian Counties, Arkansas*, "The James Fork of the latter [Poteau] river is formed by the conjunction of streams from the Poteau Mountains, and into it, from the extreme southwest portion of the county, flows West Creek, and from the valley north of Black Jack Ridge flows Prairie Creek. This fork then flows in a northwesterly direction, receiving the waters of many smaller streams, and finally leaves the county [Sebastian] near the center of its western boundary line."

Early reports about the James Fork almost always included statements about the coal found in the area, often calling it James Fork coal. A number of coal mines opened in the area during the late 1800s and early 1900s. The James Fork was also a favorite route through the hills in this area, and settlements like Hartford, Midland, and Hackett (originally named James Fork) developed alongside it. Both the Frisco's Mansfield Branch, and the Midland Valley Railroad's route to Hartford, were built alongside the stream. Today, the James Fork is a major source of drinking water for southern Sebastian County and much of Scott County. The James Fork Creek Reservoir was built in the hills to the south, and is now operated by the James Fork Regional Water District.

277.0 PEORIA – Peoria was shown on a county map from 1889, and later in 1903, as being about a mile south of the tracks just west of James Fork. The station was at a grade crossing, but was never more than a flag stop. Peoria had a post office from April 30, 1878, until December 31, 1915. After that, the mail was handled at Mansfield. The town was never large but did include the James Fork Church. The area was known for its strawberries and other farm crops. Today, the area is a collection of large farms, generally handling livestock and poultry.

277.8 PRAIRIE CREEK JUNCTION – Prairie Creek Junction, and the Rock Island branch line to Prairie Creek, are listed in the *Fifth Annual Report of the Railroad Commission of the State of Arkansas* (1904). It is also referred to in several financial reports about the railroad from that time, one of which states that the branch was 2.08 miles long to the Prairie Creek Mine.

The remains of a wye are barely visible north of a small bridge located just west of the junction between Arkansas Highway 96 and Center Point Road, County Road 19. The railroad once headed to the northeast to serve Prairie Creek Mines No. 3 and No. 4. In 1903, the Midland Valley Railroad acquired the branch line, as well as many of the coal mines in the area. The northern half of the branch was included in the new Midland Valley mainline, while the track below Prairie Creek Mine No. 3 was abandoned in 1904. Several articles state that the Midland Valley did not pay for the branch line, but instead promised to ship enough coal over the Rock Island to justify the ownership swap. In 1910, the wye was again installed on the Rock Island, and a new spur track was built to the northwest to serve the Mammoth Vein Mine. With this new track, Prairie Creek Junction was renamed Big Mammoth Wye.

One of the reasons that this area was important to the Choctaw, Oklahoma & Gulf and the Rock Island was coal. At one time, the mines in this area provided a large amount of the locomotive coal for the major railroads of the region. However, the actions here actually encouraged many of the railroads to start using oil fuel in their locomotives, because this was the site of the Sebastian County Union War of 1914. In that year, all of the mines were tied to a common union contract. The owner of many of the area coal mines, Bache-Denman Coal Company (Franklin Bache), attempted to get out of the contract by leasing several of his mines to a non-union coal company. Union members from around the region organized against Prairie Creek Mine No. 4, and after a rally on April 6, 1914, marched on the mine, overpowered the guards and non-union workers, and took over the mine. The striking miners shut down the pumps and destroyed some of the buildings and equipment. Open confrontation between the miners and the mine's guards resulted in a number of shootings over the next few months, and two guards were shot and killed while prisoners of the union. About the same time, other mines in the area were dynamited.

On July 25, 1914, Bache closed all of his area businesses and fired all of his employees, much to the pleasure of the union, who bragged about their success in running Bache out of the coal business. However, Bache, through his Coronado Coal Company, sued the United Mine Workers, local union members, and others who supported the union's strike and violence. In 1917, Bach won his suit and the union, members and supporters were ordered to pay $720,000. An appeal went to the Supreme Court and other courts, but the union eventually settled out of court for a much smaller sum.

While the United Mine Workers probably won the local battle, they have certainly suffered in the area since. First, the railroads stopped using coal from the area as they needed a reliable supply, and many even changed to fuel oils. An article in the January 6, 1923, issue of the *Arkansas Gazette* reported on this change. It stated that the Rock Island announced on January 5th that it would convert all of its remaining coal burning locomotives to oil, ending the need to buy 650,000 tons of coal per year from its own Oklahoma mines, as well as the Central Coal & Coke Company at Hartford, Arkansas. The article also stated that the St. Louis & San Francisco and the St. Louis Southwestern railroads were also converting more locomotives to oil.

A second result was that within a few years, there were no union coal mines in this part of Arkansas. The violence and job losses scared off many owners and workers, and the mines changed to being more automated with less labor. The third result is probably the most important as it set a precedent that unions could be held liable for the actions of their locals and members.

After the strike, the Prairie Creek Mine No. 4 became Central Coal & Coke Mine No. 11 in 1915. A great deal of money was spent to reopen the mine as much of the mine was burned and destroyed while the United Mine Workers held the complex. However, with the loss of coal orders from area railroads, the mine closed down for good during December 1920.

278.3 BRIDGE – Look into the pasture just south of Arkansas Highway 96 to see nine thin concrete piers, the remains of a small bridge that once stood here. CRI&P records show that this was once an eight-panel ballast deck pile trestle bridge, but the concrete piers show that it was replaced. Bridges like this were fairly common on the Rock Island and were used to cheaply replace timber pile trestles. A number of trestles in this area were replaced the same way.

A number of bridges in Western Arkansas had their old timber piles replaced by concrete piers, as shown by this pier that remains standing in a field alongside Arkansas Highway 96.

278.8 WEST CREEK BRIDGE – Just to the south of Arkansas Highway 96 are the remains of a 50-foot through plate girder span, which has had its panels cut out. The span still sits on its cut stone headwalls. To the west are several thin concrete piers and wooden timber pile bents. The concrete piers likely replaced some of the timber piles during one of the frequent floods in the area.

West Creek is a tributary of James Fork. By the late 1880s, local blacksmiths were using coal from along this stream in their forges. The ability to ford West Creek in this area helped lead to the development of nearby Hartford.

The West Creek Bridge still features the cut stone headwalls that were once typical on the railroad. Over the years,
many of them were repaired or replaced with concrete.

280.0 HARTFORD – Hartford was a town built on coal, with dozens of coal
mines in the area. However, it actually started as two nearby communities. The first was settled before the Civil War not far west of today's
Hartford, located between the Sugar Loaf and Poteau mountains. Because of this, many called it the Old Sugarloaf Valley Community. However, James and Betsy Hart lived near a crossing of West Creek which
took the name Hart's Ford, and later Hartford. A post office opened as
Hartford in 1874. The town wasn't large, but it had a store, school and
church. By 1889, the town had grown to include several stores, four
blacksmith shops, a boot and shoe shop, a grist mill, a cotton gin, several doctors, a school, and a union church used by Methodists, Baptists,
and Cumberland Presbyterians.

After the Civil War, a second community started nearby. This one
first used the name Center Point. However, it was soon changed to Gwyn
for Wylie P. Gwyn, who homesteaded there in 1868. A decade later, Wylie Gwyn (sometimes spelled Gwynn) began coal mining on his farm.
During the late 1890s, the Choctaw & Memphis bought a right-of-way
through Gwyn's property and a small town began to form, gaining a
post office named Gwynn in 1899. That same year, the railroad bought

355

more of Gwyn's land for coal mining and a new railroad town. The August 1899 issue of *The Choctaw* reported, "The new town of Hartford is being laid out in the southwest corner of Sebastian County, 3 miles east of the old town. The Choctaw and Memphis and the Kansas and Texas Coal Company are opening up coal mines in that section, and the results are very satisfactory." In the same issue, the Choctaw, Oklahoma and Memphis Town Site Company promoted Hartford as "The Big Coal Town."

The Choctaw & Memphis built the railroad through here for the Choctaw, Oklahoma & Gulf, and the combined town of Hartford was officially incorporated on March 5, 1900. With this, old Hartford started being called West Hartford or Old Hartford, while Gwynn was now Hartford. However, until 1905, the two post offices remained, but they were merged that year into a new Hartford post office. With area coal mining, and the railroad transportation available, workers were needed, and many arrived from Italy and other European countries. One part of Hartford even became known as "Little Italy" for the residents.

In 1900, Hartford had a population of 460, and it still relied upon agriculture for lots of its business. For example, in 1902-1903, 390 rail shipments of cotton were moved from Hartford. In 1908, the Sanborn Map Company documented the many area coal mines, as well as Hartford itself. It showed that there was a siding to the north of the Rock Island mainline, plus two tracks to the south. The Rock Island depot was located between the mainline and the siding, on Gwynn Street between Oak and Broadway. Across the street was the Grand View Hotel. Located south of the tracks and on the south side of West Creek near Elm Street, was the G. W. Wallace grist mill and cotton gin.

While coal mining was important in the area, mines were not in town, but instead spread over miles of territory in almost all directions from Hartford. One article about Hartford stated that there were sixteen coal mines operating within seven miles of Hartford, including three within the city limits. On April 2, 1912, Peter Stewart was elected mayor of Hartford, showing the influence that the mines and labor union had on the town. Stewart was a miner, and was the first socialist mayor elected in Arkansas.

A Sanborn map from the following year showed that the Rock Island Railroad had stock pens to the east of the depot, just east of Broadway on the north side of the siding. It also showed that the Grand View Hotel had competition, with the Hotel Anderson standing on the northwest corner of Gwynn and Oak, across from the station. Also in town was the cotton gin of Frazier & Smith, and the sawmills and lumberyards of G. W. Wallace and the Mansfield Lumber Company.

Hartford continued to grow, but the labor unrest and decreased demand for coal, plus several fires, soon led to people leaving the area.

The census population peaked at 2067 in 1920, and it had dropped to 1210 by 1930. One positive note from that time was the Hartford Music Company, which sold more than 100,000 books of gospel music per year. The firm remained in Hartford until it was sold and moved to Missouri in 1948.

Hartford is still the home of a few stores, a bank, a post office, restaurants and more. Its downtown business district was added to the National Register of Historic Places in 2009. The town is noted for its views of both the Sugarloaf and Poteau mountains, and is the home of the last working coal mine in the state of Arkansas. Hartford's population in the 2010 census was 642.

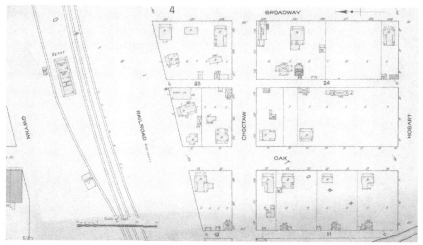

Sanborn Map – Depot at Hartford – October 1913. *Sanborn Fire Insurance Map from Hartford, Sebastian County, Arkansas.* Sanborn Map Company, Oct, 1913. Map. Retrieved from the Library of Congress, https://www.loc.gov/item/sanborn00261_002/.

The Rock Island at Hartford

The Rock Island never had a large number of shippers at Hartford as the coal mines were primarily on the Midland Valley's line that came in from the north. However, they did interchange cars on a regular basis. In fact, a search of Interstate Commerce Commission and Arkansas Railroad Commission records will uncover a number of requests and hearings about joint Rock Island-Midland Valley rates. The first series of requests involved coal in 1904. A more unusual request was made on February 14, 1908, by the Merchants Freight Bureau of Little Rock, Arkansas. This group was buying cotton seed from several gins in Oklahoma and wanted an alternative route. In the hearing, it was noted that many of the gins were on the Midland Valley, so a joint rate with the Chicago, Rock Island & Pacific made sense. A decision approving the rate was made on March 16, 1908.

At the west end of town, the Rock Island had spur tracks, one running north and one running south. The one to the south served the Central Coal & Coke Company Mine No. 4. The spur to the north served several mines, including the Smokeless Fuel Coal Company near 2nd and Oak streets, and the Bolen-Darnall Coal Company Mine No. 2, north of Broadway and 2nd.

To support the business, the railroad had a series of tracks near the station. These included a siding to the north of the mainline, plus two yard tracks to the south. The railroad also had a 40-foot, 100,000-pound capacity scale to weigh shipments moving over the line. The combination depot featured a waiting room in the east end of the building, with an office and telegrapher station in the middle. On the west end was the freight and express room. The railroad applied to shut down the freight agency in August of 1959 due to lack of business. By 1979, many of the tracks were gone, but there was still a 3683-foot siding, then located to the south. Additionally, there were about 1900 feet of other tracks to the north of the mainline.

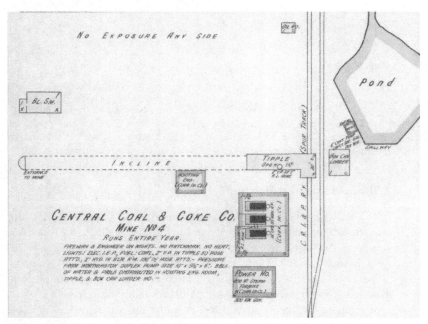

Sanborn Map – Central Coal & Coke #4 – October 1913. *Sanborn Fire Insurance Map from Hartford, Sebastian County, Arkansas.* Sanborn Map Company, Oct, 1913. Map. Retrieved from the Library of Congress, https://www.loc.gov/item/sanborn00261_002/.

The former Rock Island grade through Hartford is easy to find, especially the wide area between Gwynn and McLoud Streets. Gwynn Street was once the main street along the north side of the tracks. This open area east of Broadway was where many of the yard tracks once were located. The depot was just west of Broadway and south of Gwynn, where the new fire department building is located. Heading west, the railroad grade is often a tree line cutting across pastures.

280.8 WEST CREEK BRIDGE – The railroad again crosses West Creek. The stream forms in the hills to the north, flows south around the west side of Hartford, and then east and back north, circling Hartford. It then flows further northeast before entering the James Branch. The bridge, from west to east, included three timber panel spans, a 30-foot I-beam span, and then four timber panel spans. Heading west, the railroad looped to the north and then back to the southwest to get around the end of a ridge.

281.1 HARTFORD JUNCTION – Known as CRIP Crossing by the Midland Valley, this is where the Hartford Branch crossed the Rock Island on its way to Hoye. There was an interchange track in the northeast quadrant so that southbound Midland Valley trains could turn east into the Rock Island yards.

Construction of the Midland Valley actually began at Hartford since the supplies could be delivered by the Choctaw, Oklahoma & Gulf. Contracts for grading were awarded on June 11, 1903, and the Cherokee Construction Company, a subsidiary of the railroad, began construction. By fall, the railroad had reached a connection with the Frisco and was building even further north. The line that reached Hartford was known by several names, including the Hartford Branch and the Hoye & Excelsior District.

For several decades, the Midland Valley was tied closely to the coal mines, since many were located on railroad property, and some were even owned by the railroad's owners. As the mines closed during the late 1910s and early 1920s, the advantage of owning both ended. In 1923, the Midland Valley, along with the Kansas, Oklahoma & Gulf, and the Oklahoma City, Ada & Atoka, were bought by the Muskogee Roads of Philadelphia, creating a unified series of lines in Arkansas and Oklahoma. Eventually, the Muskogee Roads were purchased by the Texas & Pacific which was owned by the Missouri Pacific.

Midland Valley service to Hartford ended in 1943. To quote the National Railroad Adjustment Board, "On October 29, 1943, the Interstate Commerce Commission issued its Certificate of Public Convenience and Necessity in Finance Docket 14345, to become effective 15 days thereafter, authorizing the abandonment of the branch line of railroad extending from a connection with main line at Excelsior to Hartford Junction, approximately 16.7 miles, in Sebastian County, Arkansas." While it could be sooner, the Midland Valley set 12:01 AM, on November 26, 1943, as when operations on the line would be discontinued.

282.0 APEX – This location is in a cut through the north end of a ridge that is north of West Hartford. It is south of the farm on Arkansas Highway 96 that is east of Eagle Babb Road. Apex was the peak of the grade that started near Peoria to the east, and Monroe from the west. Apex is located at an elevation of 690 feet. This was not the only Apex, Arkansas, on the Rock Island. The second one was located south of El Dorado on the former Arkansas Southern Railway.

283.7 SUGARLOAF CREEK BRIDGE – This stream, often spelled Sugar Loaf Creek, forms in the Sugar Loaf Mountains, in the gap between Oklahoma Peak and Midland Peak. It flows south to near the railroad at Apex, and then turns to the southwest. Sugarloaf Creek then heads west through Monroe, Oklahoma, and into the Poteau River. The Choctaw & Memphis built their grade along the stream from Apex to near the Poteau River, providing a steady grade through these rolling hills.

Located just east of the intersection of West Hartford Road and Pitchford Road is where a 101-foot through plate girder span was once used by the railroad to cross the stream.

284.2 AR-OK STATE LINE – Heading west from Apex, the railroad grade is immediately to the north of Pitchford Road. The state line is easy to find as the vegetation changes greatly, with pasture to the east and woods to the west. The road name also changes from Pitchford to D1398. To the east is **Sebastian County** of Arkansas. Sebastian County was created from parts of Scott, Polk, and Crawford counties on January 6, 1851, making it the 56th of 75 counties created in Arkansas. It was named for U.S. Senator William King Sebastian.

The Territory of **Arkansas** was admitted to the Union as the 25th state on June 15, 1836. It is the 29th largest state, and the 32nd most populated. Little Rock is the capitol, and the most populated city. Arkansas can be flat or mountainous depending upon where you travel. The southeast half is lowlands and river delta, while the northwest includes the highlands of the Ouachita and Ozark Mountains – the only major mountainous region between the Rocky Mountains and the Appalachian Mountains. Arkansas is also the only state where diamonds are mined, and you can go mine them yourself at the Crater of Diamonds State Park.

To the west is **Oklahoma,** once known as Indian Territory (1834-1907), and later partly as Oklahoma Territory (1890-1907). Oklahoma means "red people" in the Choctaw language, and the name was decided during an 1866 meeting between federal officials and leaders of the five Indian nations who had been moved there. During the late 1800s, the western part of Oklahoma was the Oklahoma Territory, while the eastern part was Indian Territory. The two merged and became the 46th state on November 16, 1907. It is the 20th largest state and the 28th most populated, with about four million residents. Two-thirds of Oklahomans live in the Oklahoma City (the state capitol) and Tulsa metropolitan areas. The state is known as "The Sooner State" due to the number of white settlers who staked their land claims out before the official opening date in the western Oklahoma Territory. Heading west, the land steadily increases in elevation.

The Railroad Act of 1886 opened the way for railroad construction across Indian Territory. The builders of the various railroads took advantage of this Act to build across the state, in what was actually a relatively late burst of railroad activity.

This is **Le Flore County** Oklahoma. The land became owned by the Choctaw Nation after they ceded much of their homelands with the Treaty of Doak's Stand in 1820, and then the rest with the Treaty of Dancing Rabbit Creek in 1830. While this was Indian Territory, it was part of the Moshulatubbee and Apukshunnubbee districts of the Choctaw Nation. Coal and timber attracted settlers, industry and railroads to the region. The county has about 50,000 residents, and Poteau is the county seat.

The county is named for the LeFlore family, which dates back to Frenchman Louis LeFleur, who married the daughter of the renowned Choctaw warrior Pushmataha. LeFleur became a wealthy trader and fought with Andrew Jackson in the War of 1812. His son, Greenwood LeFlore, was a leader in education and Christianity for the Choctaws. He married Elizabeth Coodey, sister of Cherokee leader William Shorey Coodey and a niece of Chief John Ross. LeFlore later signed the Treaty of Dancing Rabbit Creek, thinking that moving west would enable the Choctaws to retain their sovereignty. The family continued to play a leading role in tribal matters, both in Indian Territory and in Mississippi.

The grade west to Howe, a bit more than eleven miles, was acquired in 2016 by the Arkansas-Oklahoma Railroad Company from the Oklahoma Department of Transportation, which bought it along with other parts of the Rock Island Railroad across the state.

286.3 SUGARLOAF CREEK BRIDGE – This area is called Trestle Ford, and is actually listed as a populated place in several federal records. At one time, both the railroad and road D1398 had bridges across Sugarloaf Creek here. Today, neither do, but D1398 does cross the stream by ford-ing it. Also, some of the concrete piers of the Rock Island bridge still remain.

Heading west, the railroad once closely followed Old Monroe Highway all the way to Monroe, Oklahoma, staying just south of the road's shoulder.

287.5 WILSON CREEK BRIDGE – The railroad once crossed Wilson Creek using two 40-foot deck plate girder spans. Wilson Creek starts to the south on the northern slopes of Cowskin Ridge. Just north of here, Wilson Creek flows into Sugarloaf Creek.

287.9 COWSKIN CREEK BRIDGE – Cowskin Creek forms from a number of small streams that flow off the west end of Cowskin Ridge, including some from the south side that flow around the west end of the ridge. The lower end of Cowskin Creek flows north past the east side of Monroe, eventually into Sugarloaf Creek.

The railroad bridge consisted of an 80-foot through plate girder span, with four timber panels to the east set on concrete piers. Only the concrete piers remain. The road bridge to the north has been washed out, and much of it now sits in the streambed.

288.3 MONROE – What was called Monroe Post Office opened on February 25, 1881, being named for the first postmaster, Simon Monroe Griffith. Monroe was never large, but it did have a few businesses, such as the W. R. Mabile & Company store. Today, the town is still a small, unincorporated community with a population of less than 200.

The Rock Island passed through Monroe not far north of Hickory Street, and then headed west just south of Oklahoma Highway 83. At one time, the railroad had a siding to the north, installed in May 1899, but it was gone by the 1979 employee timetable.

292.8 HORSEPEN CREEK BRIDGE – Horsepen Creek is located not far west of where the railroad turned to the southwest and Highway 83 turns west. Horsepen Creek is another stream that drains the mountains to the south and heads north to join Sugarloaf Creek. It forms on the northwest side of the Poteau Mountains, near Round Mountain.

The railroad used a 100-foot riveted Warren deck truss to cross Horsepen Creek. The bridge is still there, now surrounded by trees and brush east of Morris Creek Road.

295.4 MORRIS CREEK BRIDGE – Just a few feet east of the former diamond at Howe was a 12-panel timber pile trestle bridge over Morris Creek. The concrete footings can still be found in the stream. Morris Creek forms on the south side of Round Mountain and then flows to the west and north to here. It continues flowing to the north a few miles to enter the Poteau River.

While the Morris Creek Bridge is gone, the concrete footings remain in the stream, visible when water levels are low.

295.4 HOWE (BX) – Howe was a crossing and interchange connection with the Kansas City Southern Railway Company. The crossing was an automatic interlocking, and the connecting track was in the southwest quadrant, where it is still located. While the tracks east of here are abandoned, the tracks to the west are in place and operated by the Arkansas-Oklahoma Railroad Company.

Howe (OK) to McAlester (OK)
Arkansas-Oklahoma Railroad Company

The line from Howe to McAlester has been through a number of hands since the end of the Chicago, Rock Island & Pacific. The line at first sat unused, but in 1986, the State of Oklahoma purchased the line from near McAlester to Howe from L. B. Foster for $2,778,406. A contract was soon reached that had the Missouri-Kansas-Texas (MKT or Katy) operate the line, calling the track from Howe (MP 295.5) to the MKT at McAlester (MP 366.4) the Howe Subdivision. On August 12, 1988, Union Pacific (UP) acquired the Katy through its Missouri Pacific Railroad. UP took over operations of the line, but almost immediately began looking for someone to take over the railroad. On March 3, 1996, Union Pacific, with the approval of the State of Oklahoma, transferred all rights of the line to the Arkansas-Oklahoma Railroad Company (A-OK). Later, the A-OK Railroad also leased track in the McAlester, Oklahoma, area (August 1, 1997), as well as the track between Shawnee and Oklahoma City (July 7, 2000).

The Arkansas-Oklahoma Railroad Company is a Class III shortline railroad. When created, the railroad operated seventy miles of track and served two customers. Within a decade, the company operated almost 120 miles of track, serving twenty rail shippers. The company handles products like coal, aggregate, decorative stone, wheat, corn, oats, frac sand and drilling fluid products, pipe, lumber, plastic resin pellets, automobiles, and various chemicals. The company has their own fleet of freight cars and also handles car storage for a number of companies. Besides direct on-line customers, the A-OK also has several transload facilities that allow shippers without tracks to use the railroad.

During April 2016, the Arkansas-Oklahoma Railroad Company bought the Howe to McAlester line from the State of Oklahoma. However, due to an error, the sale was never formally approved by the Surface Transportation Board. Therefore, a new application with the Board was made, and as of October 19, 2019, the line was officially sold. The notice published on September 24, 2019, stated that the Surface Transportation Board "is granting an exemption under 49 U.S.C. 10502 from the prior approval requirements of 49 U.S.C. 10902 for Arkansas-Oklahoma Railroad Company (AOK), a Class III carrier, to acquire from the State of Oklahoma and operate approximately 69.60 miles of rail line extending from milepost 295.36 in Howe, Okla., to milepost 364.96 in McAlester, Okla."

Additionally, the Arkansas-Oklahoma Railroad leased the track between Milepost 364.96 and Milepost 370.5 on what became Union Pacific's Shawnee Branch, as well as "the Krebs Industrial Lead from the clearance point of the mainline switch on UP's Cherokee Subdivision at milepost 0.0 in McAlester to the end of the track at milepost 7.04 in Krebs."

The railroad provides regular service on parts of the lines, and operates as needed elsewhere. The firm is based in Wilburton, Oklahoma, and is known for its bright red and yellow locomotives painted to resemble those of the original Rock Island Railroad. The railroad is also known for allowing motorcar trips by groups such as the Oklahoma Railway Museum.

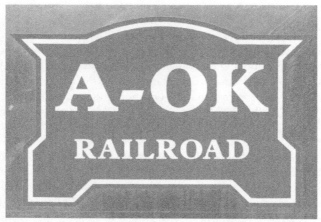

The emblem of the Arkansas-Oklahoma Railroad Company clearly displays its Rock Island heritage, as shown on this grade crossing signal box at Wister, Oklahoma.

295.4 HOWE (BX) – Howe started as the small Choctaw Nation town of Klondike. The town was based upon farming and served as a post village for the Nation. However, when the Kansas City, Pittsburgh & Gulf Railroad (KCP&G) built through the area in late 1895, the residents renamed it for Dr. Herbert M. Howe, a director of the railroad. In 1898, a post office opened using that name, and the Choctaw, Oklahoma & Gulf was building east. In 1900, the KCP&G became the Kansas City Southern Railroad. That same year, Howe had a population of 626, and business grew as coal was discovered.

The coal boom started in the late 1890s as several mines opened, and then the Mexican Gulf Coal and Transportation Company built one hundred coke ovens west of Howe. Soon the property was sold to the Degnan and McConnell Coal and Coke Company, which only operated the coal mines. However, after World War I, the coke ovens were reopened by the Howe-McCurtain Coal and Coke Company. Farming was also still important, and 784 shipments of cotton were shipped out from Howe in 1903-1904. All of this activity attracted a cotton gin, several general and grocery stores, a hotel, four doctors, four drugstores, and the *Howe Herald* newspaper.

Over the next several decades, the population went up and down based upon the activity at the coal mines. The Lincoln Coal Company was able to survive the Great Depression, but most other area mines closed, and by 1960, Howe was down to 390 residents. A contract to sell coal to Japanese steel mills starting in 1967 helped the Howe Coal Company and encouraged people to move back to Howe. Today, coal is no longer a force here, and agriculture is back to providing much of the purpose of Howe. Howe is also helped by having U.S. Highway 59 pass just to the east, the location of several gas stations and discount stores. The post office and the Howe School District are still here, and the town had a population of 802 in the 2010 census, the highest recorded in Howe's history.

Construction of the Railroad

Construction on the track in western Arkansas and very eastern Oklahoma initially began at Wister, Oklahoma, and worked eastward. *Poor's Manual* (1899) reported that the Choctaw, Oklahoma & Gulf Railroad completed its track from Wister to Howe by September 6, 1898. The distance cited was 6.4 miles. The *Arkansas Gazette* (October 6, 1898) quoted the *Mena Democrat* by reporting "The Choctaw, Oklahoma & Gulf railroad has completed its tracks to Howe, a new station about four miles south of Poteau, and is now making direct connection with the K.C.P.&G. at the latter place, thus saving those going that route from a trip to Poteau and thence to Wister Junction. This will be a great benefit to Mena people, many of whom make frequent trips through Oklahoma, having interest there."

Construction began at both Howe and Little Rock "with great earnestness" on December 1, 1898. Various 1899 issues of *The Choctaw* covered this construction, stating that grading was to be done by July 1899. One issue stated that track laying began at Howe on April 20, 1899, and that construction materials were being brought to Howe and Mansfield. It also stated that the parts for three steel bridges were at Howe and ready for assembly. There were also details about the construction. One detail was that the construction for the "100 miles east from Howe was under contract to the Choctaw Construction Company, sub-let to McCabe & Steen, and the contract for 66 miles west from Little Rock was held by McCarthy & Reichardt, of Little Rock, who sub-let 43 miles to McCabe & Steen." The report also stated that McCabe &

Steen was using a Roberts track-laying machine, getting as much as two miles a day of track built.

A Roberts track-laying machine was built by the Roberts Steam Track-Layer Company of Seattle, Washington. A track-laying machine included a pioneer (front) car with a conveyor belt that brought track materials to the point of construction. The Roberts machine featured a 20-horsepower steam engine on the lead car that drove the material conveyor belt to deliver the ties, and powered a derrick to pull the rails forward to the delivery booms. The steam engine was supplied steam from the locomotive through a series of pipes along the train. For those wanting more details, the July 1915 *Practical Track Work* issue of the *Railway Engineering and Maintenance of Way* journal included a full article on the machine.

The October 1899 issue of *The Choctaw* showed that the line west of Howe was complete and being operated by the Choctaw, Oklahoma & Gulf (Howe to Wister completed in 1898), while the Little Rock to Howe track was still shown as being "now under construction." However, at 9:44am on October 13, 1899, the railroad was completed about 22 miles west of Little Rock.

For years, there was a joint depot in the northwest quadrant of the diamond at Howe, built square to fit along the tracks of the two railroads. The building featured an eight-sided windowed tower at the corner of the building, overlooking both railroad's tracks in all directions. In 1910, the Corporation Commission of the State of Oklahoma had several hearings at Howe on the issue of John Begley requesting a depot from both the Kansas City Southern and the Chicago, Rock Island & Pacific. About the same time, the Commission ordered both railroads to improve the depot at Howe.

With the railroad completed to the east, Howe soon had a number of facilities for the Rock Island Railroad. A 1973 track chart showed that there was a long siding to the south of the mainline, just east of the diamond with Kansas City Southern. There was then a 12-panel ballast deck pile trestle over Morris Creek, and then the KCS Crossing. The 1979 employee timetable listed facilities like a fuel station, water station, and a train order station. In that year, there was a 3705-foot siding as well as other tracks measuring 1860 feet.

For years, the Rock Island had a track heading south to serve several coal mines. The track departed from the west side of Howe and went as far as the north side of Lost Mountain, about where U.S. Highway 59 loops around the hill today. Many maps note a number of strip mines along this route. A contract from December 1948 covered the use of a track by the Gaither Coal Company.

Today, everything is gone except for a siding and a connection to the Kansas City Southern. In November 1957, the railroad retired 314 feet of the Freight House Track. The train order office was gone soon after the railroad closed. All that can be found here now is an occasional A-OK locomotive, some interchange cars, and lots of Kansas City Southern freight trains heading north and south where the CRI&P diamond once was.

KCS Crossing

Located at an elevation of 475 feet, this was one of the few places that the Rock Island and KCS actually touched each other. For a number of years, there was a joint passenger station, and in 1979, it was an automatic interlocking. When the east-west railroad opened, it was the Choctaw, Oklahoma & Gulf Railroad, and became the Chicago, Rock Island & Pacific Railway in 1904.

The north-south railroad, a maverick just by its design, is the Kansas City Southern Railway. Similar to the Rock Island, the KCS was assembled from a number of railroads, some built by the primary company to connect the routes of the others. The KCS traces its history back to 1887 when the Kansas City Suburban Belt Railway was incorporated by Arthur Edward Stilwell and Edward L. Martin. The railroad was completed in 1890, and Arthur Stilwell began looking at a rail route to the Gulf Coast to provide farmers a new route to new markets. To do this he bought the Texarkana & Fort Smith Railroad in 1892, which already had a bridge across the Red River. Immediately reorganized as the Kansas City, Pittsburg & Gulf Railroad (KCP&G), Stilwell used his new purchase to acquire and build additional track.

Stilwell's next move was to buy Matthias Splitlog's Kansas City, Fort Smith & Southern in 1893. This railroad was already operating between Joplin, Missouri, and Sulphur Springs, Arkansas. With the Panic of 1893 ending sources of money in the States, Stilwell went to the Netherlands for more money, which explains the Dutch names used along the railroad. European funds allowed construction to begin again, with track reaching Siloam Springs, Arkansas, late in 1893, and Indian Territory the next year. The line was completed to Port Arthur, Texas, on September 11, 1897. Unfortunately, a financial deal with George Pullman wasn't completed before Pullman's death, and Stilwell lost control of the company. New owners purchased the railroad and reorganized it as the Kansas City Southern Railway Company in 1900. The investment paid off quickly thanks to an east Texas oil boom.

Over the next century, the railroad grew, adding the Louisiana & Arkansas Railway and other routes. Howe was never an important station on the railroad, as Heavener, Oklahoma, a shops and crew change point, is just five miles to the south. In 1966, Howe still had telegraph service 7:00am-4:00pm weekdays. It was also a flag stop for the railroad's premier train, the *Southern Belle*, whose last run took place on November 3, 1969. During the 1990s and later, KCS grew substantially by acquiring MidSouth Rail, Gateway Western Railway, and rail routes in Mexico. Even with this, it is still the smallest Class I freight railroad in the United States.

For years, Howe and the interlocking was listed as being at Milepost 333.0. Today, the diamond is gone, but the north end of two main tracks through Heavener is at North Howe, Milepost 333.1. To the west of the KCS mainline is a two-track yard known as Howe Storage, used to interchange traffic between KCS and the Arkansas-Oklahoma Railroad Company. The KCS timetable shows Howe Storage North Track as being at Milepost 333.1, and Howe Storage South Track as being at Milepost 333.5.

The east end of the Arkansas-Oklahoma Railroad is clearly marked by this barricade and stop sign at Howe, Oklahoma.

With the Howe diamond removed, the KCS extended its tracks northward, with the North Howe Control Point and switch located here now.

Despite the diamond being removed, this pair of signals still stands to direct eastbound train movements at Howe, Oklahoma.

The Arkansas-Oklahoma Railroad Company

Howe is an important center for the Arkansas-Oklahoma Railroad (AOK). There is an interchange to the south with Kansas City Southern. A stub track that was once the mainline across the KCS is now used to park locomotives and track equipment. Heading southwest (railroad-west), the tracks pass through Howe between North Railroad Street and South Railroad Street. In this area, the railroad has two sidings used for interchange, to switch trains, and to store cars. One siding is on each side of the mainline.

Heading west along Coal Creek, the railroad is now running through ranching country that is very different than the wooded mountains to the east. At Milepost 298.4 is a new siding to the south.

299.6 POTEAU RIVER BRIDGE – From east to west, this bridge consists of a 150-foot Warren through truss with all verticals, a 90-foot through plate girder, and a 30-foot concrete stringer span, which replaced a 16-panel ballast deck pile trestle. Less than a mile south of this bridge is Wister Dam, which creates Lake Wister on the Poteau River. The dam closed the river during December 1949. While the dam and lake were authorized to prevent flooding and improve area conservation by the Flood Control Act of 1938, much of the land around the reservoir is Lake Wister State Park.

Wister Dam forms Lake Wister about a mile south of the Poteau River Bridge at Milepost 299.6.

The Poteau River is unique as it is the only north-flowing river in Oklahoma, starting two miles south of Bee Mountain near Waldron, Arkansas, and heading almost 150 miles to the Arkansas River at Belle Point in Fort Smith, Arkansas. While a few miles of the start and end of the river are in Arkansas, the rest is in Oklahoma, making it the seventh largest river in the state.

The name Poteau is used for many things in this area, including the Poteau River, Poteau Mountains, and the City of Poteau. In the French language, poteau means post. There is a belief that early French explorers marked the river with a large post or stake to identify the river or to mark the territory.

301.4 CASTON CREEK BRIDGE – Caston Creek is a major tributary of the Poteau River. It forms to the northwest in Wildhorse Hollow, west of Wolf Mountain. It has historically been a source of flooding for the area.

There is a 100-foot through plate girder span over the creek's main channel, plus four 44-foot deck plate girder spans on the east end. Not far to the east is a 308-foot-long ballasted deck pile trestle, consisting of 22 panels. This trestle allows flood waters to take a shorter route to the Poteau River. This bridge has also been known as the Wister Bridge or the East Caston Creek Bridge.

In the *Engineering News* of May 20, 1897, and *The Railway and Engineering Review* of May 29, 1897, there were short announcements about this bridge and the nearby Poteau River Bridge. "Bids are asked until June 30 for constructing the superstructure of a 100-ft. riveted, lattice girder, through-span bridge over Caston Creek, with a 150-ft. through, pin connected, truss bridge, with supported floor system, over Poteau River, for the Choctaw, Oklahoma & Gulf R.R. Co."

The Caston Creek bridge was rebuilt and strengthened over the years. In the May-June 1962 issue of *The Rocket*, there was an article that provided some information about this bridge. The article reported on a bridge near Wichita, Kansas, that was replaced by culverts after a drainage project on the Cowskin Creek. A 100-foot-long through plate girder span from the Cowskin Creek bridge was shipped to Wister to replace a troublesome and lightweight 100-foot pony truss span, which at the time sat on timber falsework to support the heavy loads.

301.8 WISTER – Wister once included a diamond with the Frisco Railroad, shown as "not protected by interlocking" in the Rock Island timetable, and "protected by gate operated by trainman" and "normal position of gate against SLSF" by the Frisco. The two railroads arrived here within a few years of each other during the late 1880s, and in 1892, the Choctaw Coal & Railway Company (Choctaw, Oklahoma & Gulf) had 31 miles of track between Oklahoma City and El Reno, and 66 miles from

South McAlester to Wister. Construction on closing the gap began in 1894 and the 1899 *Poor's Manual* stated that the Choctaw, Oklahoma & Gulf Railroad had completed 216.1 miles of railroad from Fort Reno, in Oklahoma Territory, to Wister, in Indian Territory, on October 1, 1895.

The completion of the line attracted a great deal of attention, and was reported across the country. A special report in the September 26, 1895, issue of the *Arkansas Gazette* reported on the end of construction and the planning for train operations.

> *Yesterday about 4 o'clock p.m. the last spike was driven in the C.O. and G. Railway, which completes the connection between Wister, I.T., and El Reno, O.T., a distance of 240 miles. The first train to pass over the new line will be a coal train followed by 100 cars of lumber. Double passenger trains daily will be put on October 15.*

In 1897, the railroad was building east to reach Howe, and eventually Little Rock, Arkansas. When passenger service began, Wister was a 15-minute train stop for meals. A lunchroom was once located on the platform west of the joint passenger station at the diamond, providing this service. The railroad also had facilities for freight shippers, including a cotton platform and stock yards. With the railroad complete and passenger trains running, mail service began between Little Rock and Wister, connecting to service from Little Rock to Memphis, and west from Wister to Weatherford, Oklahoma Territory. The first load of mail reportedly moved on February 12, 1900.

From June 1, 1904, until December 1909, the Chicago, Rock Island & Pacific offered Fort Smith, Arkansas, to El Reno, Indian Territory, passenger service. As stated in several announcements, the train service used the St. Louis & San Francisco to make connections at Wister for the service. This service ended in late 1909 when the two railroads were separated from common ownership and operating control. With the breakup of the two railroads, the Rock Island ended its train service into Fort Smith and closed its Fort Smith office. However, a Fort Smith-Little Rock sleeping car continued to operate, and passengers could still change trains at Wister.

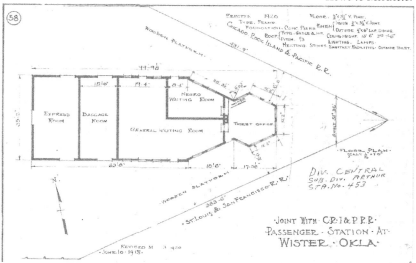

Wister Depot Drawing. This Frisco diagram shows the general design of the station at Wister, Oklahoma. Courtesy of Mike Condren.

The Rock Island once had a number of tracks here, including a transfer track that causes the curve in Pawnee Street. During the early 1970s, there was a siding and a long house track to the west of the transfer track. By 1979, the timetable indicated that there was a 3125-foot siding and 1320 feet of other tracks. Wister was also shown to be a water station and had a dispatcher telephone available to train crews. The Arkansas-Oklahoma Railroad still has two sidings to the north at Wister. The shorter north track is used by the Rail Import Propane Terminal of Westchase Power Corporation.

During November 2019, AOK locomotives #2504 and #2511 were stationed at Wister to handle the propane business at the Rail Import Propane Terminal of Westchase Power Corporation. Both GP35 locomotives were built for the Atchison, Topeka & Santa Fe in 1964 as #2804 and #2811, were renumbered by BNSF, sold to LTEX, and then obtained by the Arkansas-Oklahoma.

SL-SF Crossing

Wister was once the junction between the St. Louis to Texas main-line of the St. Louis & San Francisco Railway Company (Frisco), and the Memphis to Oklahoma mainline of the Choctaw, Oklahoma & Gulf. Today, the Frisco line is gone and the grade is used by the Old Frisco Trail for about seven miles between Wister and Poteau. As justified by such a connection, there was a station in the southwest quadrant of the diamond, serving both lines. The original station was replaced in 1920 with a building similar to the one at nearby Howe, featuring waiting rooms, a ticket office near the diamond, a baggage room and an express room. To the northwest was a transfer track with a freight warehouse toward the diamond. This freight house had platforms that served all three tracks. There was also a plank platform to the south to connect with the business district of Wister, and J. F. Kennady's Cotton Gin was on the Frisco to the east of downtown.

The Frisco built their line between St. Louis and Texas by buying several railroads and creating a number of new ones. The start of the company was the Atlantic & Pacific Railroad (A&P), created by the U.S. Congress in 1866 as a transcontinental railroad. On October 23, 1875, a suit was filed against the A&P due to unpaid interest on certain Missouri Division bonds, and receivers were soon assigned. The Missouri Division was sold by auction on September 8, 1876, to a representative of the St. Louis & San Francisco Railway Company (Frisco, StL&SF, or SL-SF).

The Frisco's first route toward Texas came south from Monett, Missouri. As was typical at the time, the construction involved a number of paper companies coming together to build and initially operate the railroad. The first of these companies was the St. Louis, Arkansas & Texas Railway Company of Missouri, incorporated June 4, 1880. By summer 1881, the company owned and operated 32 miles of track from Monett to the Missouri-Arkansas state line. The second company involved was incorporated on July 17, 1880. This company, the St. Louis, Arkansas & Texas Railway Company of Arkansas, built approximately 37 miles of track from the Missouri-Arkansas state line to near Fayetteville, Arkansas. In September 1880, the Frisco created a third railroad subsidiary, the Missouri, Arkansas & Southern Railway of Arkansas. The new subsidiary was authorized "to build in a southerly direction" – likely from Fayetteville (Washington County) – "to some point on the Little Rock and Fort Smith Railway, not east of Clarksville, with total mileage of about 55 miles." Within a year, the railroad had 63 miles of track under construction between Fayetteville and Fort Smith.

On June 28, 1881, these three railroads were merged to create the St. Louis, Arkansas & Texas Railway Company. Seven months later, the St. Louis, Arkansas & Texas Railway Company was sold to the St. Louis & San Francisco Railway Company on January 21, 1882. The line from Fort Smith south to the Arkansas-Oklahoma state line was built by the Ft. Smith & Southern Railway Company, incorporated in 1886 and absorbed by the Frisco in 1887. An important part of this plan was the incorporation of the Fort Smith & Van Buren Bridge Company in March, 1885, capitalized by the Frisco to build a bridge over the Arkansas River at Van Buren. From the state line through Wister to Paris, Texas, the line was built by the St. Louis & San Francisco Railway Company and the Paris & Great Northern Railroad Company. The Monett to Paris line was completed on July 1, 1887, connecting with the Texas & Pacific Railway to Dallas and Fort Worth. On June 30, 1896, the railroad was sold to the St. Louis & San Francisco Railroad Company, which was sold to the St. Louis-San Francisco Railway Company (Frisco) on September 15, 1916.

After the Frisco's improved mainline was built to the west across Oklahoma during the late 1890s and early 1900s, the line between Monett, Missouri, and Paris, Texas, took on the role of a secondary line mostly serving local businesses. By 1926, six passenger trains headed west out of Springfield (MO) on a daily basis, but only two turned south at Monett to cover this route, although the Fort Smith route was still part of Table 1 in the *Official Guide*. By 1934, Table 1 was the route through Tulsa, with the route to Paris now on Table 1a. In 1949, the Fort Smith route had fallen to Table 5.

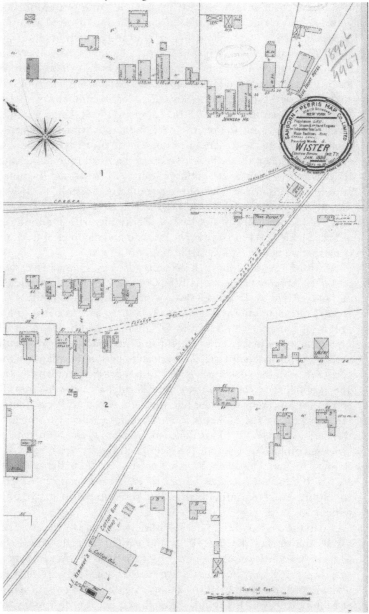

Sanborn-Perris Map Company – Wister Junction Area – January 1899. *Sanborn Fire Insurance Map from Wister, Le Flore County, Oklahoma.* Sanborn Map Company, Jan, 1899. Map. Retrieved from the Library of Congress, https://www.loc.gov/item/sanborn07306_001/.

In 1961, the line from Fort Smith to Paris was the Arthur Subdivision, Central Division, of the St. Louis-San Francisco Railway Company. The Frisco became a part of the Burlington Northern Railroad (BN) on November 21, 1980, and the abandonment of the line soon began. During 1983, BN abandoned the line south of Wister all the way to Antlers, Oklahoma, making the line north of here the 6th Subdivision – a branch line of the Springfield Division. On March 15, 1984, BN abandoned the line northward from Wister to Poteau. The line south of Antlers is now the Kiamichi Railroad, while the track from Poteau to Fort Smith is owned by the Kansas City Southern. Fort Smith to Monett is the Arkansas & Missouri Railroad.

The Town of Wister

The Wister area was settled by members of the Choctaw Nation who were moved west during the 1830s, but no real town existed where Wister now stands. After the Civil War, the Choctaws saw the business potential of their land and signed a treaty in 1866 that would allow the construction of railroads through their territory. Access to railroads would allow the Choctaw to move and sell livestock, farm products, timber and coal, all found in eastern Oklahoma.

As noted in several sources, the arrival of the Frisco, and the construction of the Choctaw Coal & Railway Company westward to McAlester in 1886, led to a major increase in coal and timber production in the area. This expanded even more when the Frisco built to Texas, and the Choctaw, Oklahoma & Gulf expanded east into Arkansas. What became Wister was being built by the mid-1880s, and there was a hotel, store and a few other buildings here alongside the tracks. On June 30, 1890, the Wister post office opened, named for Gutman G. Wister, who was associated with the Choctaw Coal & Railway Company. While few records about G. G. Wister exist, the same is not true for his son, Owen Wister. Owen is credited with being the "Father of Western Fiction" due to his book *The Virginian*. Considered both a writer and historian, he also wrote a biography of Ulysses S. Grant.

Timetables of the Choctaw, Oklahoma & Gulf often used the name Wister Junction during the late 1890s. By 1900, the population of Wister was 313, and due to the Wister cotton gin there were 1130 rail shipments of cotton from Wister during 1903-1904. By this time, cotton was an important business for the railroad. In a report about the business activity on the railroad, J. F. Holden, traffic manager, stated that the railroad moved 65,384 bales of cotton from stations in Oklahoma from September 1900 to June 1901, and 65,515 bales from September 1901 to June 1902.

379

The town kept growing, with about 500 residents, several stores, a bank, hotel, cotton gin, gristmill, sawmill, and a newspaper. There were also several coal mines in the area. Today, Wister has a post office, banks, stores, schools, gas stations, the Le Flore County Livestock Auction facility, and about 1200 residents.

While Wister was once a busy town, today its downtown mainly features empty buildings such as these just north of the tracks.

Wister Wildlife Management Area

South of Wister is the 35,500-acre Wister Wildlife Management Area, located around the 7000-acre Wister Reservoir. The site includes bottomland hardwoods, small fields of native grasses, and some foothills featuring post oak, hickory and pine. The area is home to deer, bobcats, coyotes, foxes, river otter, bear, rabbit, squirrel, turkey, and many other local species. Bald and golden eagles are also often spotted.

The Wister Wildlife Management Area (WMA) is managed by the Oklahoma Department of Wildlife Conservation. The Wister Reservoir is the center of the property and camping and boating are allowed.

This sign alongside the tracks west of Wister directs visitors to the nearby Wister Wildlife Management Area.

302.5 MOUNTAIN CREEK BRIDGE – Just west of Wister, the railroad crosses three deck plate girder (DPG) bridges. The first is just west of Mills Street and is a 50-foot DPG over an unnamed stream (Milepost 302.3). The second is an 84-foot DPG over Mountain Creek. The third is a 40-foot DPG that allows water to flow between two pastures (Milepost 302.7). The west switch of Wister siding is just east of the Mountain Creek bridge.

Mountain Creek forms from several small streams between Deer Ridge and Potato Peaks, about ten miles to the north. It flows south to here, and then into Caston Creek a short distance to the south.

305.3 NEVADA RAILROAD MATERIALS – To the south of the tracks are generally large piles of used railroad ties at the rail tie refurbishment plant, also known as the Oklahoma Plant of Nevada Railroad Materials. The company acquires carloads of ties from track retirements and tie replacement projects, and then refurbishes them so they can be reused in various track projects, or for other purposes. What is unique about the Nevada Railroad Materials site is that it is served using the mainline of the Arkansas-Oklahoma Railroad. Gondolas are simply parked on the mainline for loading and unloading.

381

This sign marks the entrance to the Nevada Railroad Materials facility west of Wister, Oklahoma.

At one time, the railroad had a station in this area named Victor. Some maps show the station to be just west of Nevada Railroad Materials at the grade crossing with road N4630. There was a post office here from May 1, 1901, to October 15, 1925. In the 1922 *Bullinger's Postal and Shippers Guide,* Victor was shown to be a station on the Booneville District of the Indian Territory Division of the CRI&P.

307.3 CASTON CREEK BRIDGE – Located just south of U.S. Highway 270/271 is a 100-foot-long Warren deck truss bridge, the second crossing of Caston Creek.

308.8 CASTON – This was once the site of two towns with very similar names, as well as several coal mines operated by the Kansas and Texas Coal Company. The first town in the area started under the name of Maxey. Maxey and its post office were established on June 4, 1884. The name Maxey, sometimes spelled Maxie, came from Napoleon Bonaparte Maxey, who was an area attorney and judge. On November 5, 1887, Maxey was renamed Caston, but the town almost disappeared and the post office closed in 1891.

The Arkansas-Oklahoma Railroad makes much of its money from storing railcars, like these autoracks that were parked on the mainline just west of the Caston Creek Bridge in early 2020.

The second town dates back to about the same era, with a post office opening with the name Braidwood on July 11, 1891. The town became Pocahontas on May 11, 1895, and then Caston Switch on April 18, 1898. The name Caston Switch came about because it was the closest switch on the railroad to the coal mining town of Caston. Later in 1898, Caston and Caston Switch merged to form one town and one new post office. However, the town was soon abandoned and the post office closed late in 1898. Nevertheless, the railroad kept a Caston here for decades. On the south side of the mainline was a 4510-foot siding.

For employees of the Rock Island, Caston was better known for many years as the location of an October 30, 1931, derailment which took place under mysterious circumstances. The Interstate Commerce Commission (ICC) described the railroad in the area as "a single-track line over which trains are operated by time-table, train orders, and a manual block-signal system. The track is laid with 90-pound rails, 39 feet in length, with an average of 22 ties to the rail-length, single-spiked, and ballasted with crushed limestone to a depth of about 12 inches; the track is well maintained. The speed limit for passenger trains in the vicinity of the point of accident is 50 miles per hour."

Shortly after midnight, westbound passenger train No. 41 derailed at the east siding switch of Caston. The train was running a few minutes late and consisted of steam locomotive #853 (4-6-2), a combination mail and baggage car, two coaches, and one Pullman sleeping car. All but the last car of the train derailed, with the locomotive "in an upright position south of the main track with its front end 360 feet west of the switch and 55 feet from the main track. The tender cistern was torn from its frame and came to rest, upright, between the engine and the passing track; the frame was on its right side but remained coupled to the engine. The baggage car stopped north of the main track and was leaning to the right at an angle of about 45 degrees, and the two coaches were upright and on the roadbed practically in line with the track. The engine and first car were badly damaged, the second car had its front vestibule crushed, and the third car sustained only slight damage."

During the inspection of the scene, it was determined that the switch stand was showing a green light from its switch lamp. However, it was found that the south switch point was "lying almost in the center of the track, with both bridle rods disconnected from it, and the switch lock hasp on the switch stand broken off, the switch lock still being in locked position and hanging to its chain." Additionally, the "bolts, nuts and cotter keys of the bridle rod which held the point to the stock rail had been removed and were lying between the ties, while the bolts on the other tie rods showed marks indicating that they had been tampered with, although the rods were not damaged." Basically, the south rail had been removed at the switch, leaving nothing for the train to run on. Yes – there had been sabotage ("malicious tampering" in the words of the ICC) on the railroad that led to the derailment.

312.6 FANSHAWE – The town of Fanshawe was named for John Richardson Fanshawe, secretary of the Lehigh Valley Railroad and the Lehigh Valley Coal Company for thirty-one years (1871-1902). It might seem confusing to some why an executive of a railroad in Pennsylvania was honored with the name of a town in Oklahoma. However, the Lehigh Valley Railroad was involved with the creation of the Choctaw Coal & Railway Company, which built the railroad from Wister west to South McAlester. There is a story that when the railroad was built, a number of the executives and investors rode across the line in a private business car, inspecting the track. At each location designated to be a station, the names of those on the trip were placed in a hat, with one name drawn that would be the station's new name.

Fanshawe Post Office opened during 1891, with a focus on coal, lumber, livestock and farming. As the community grew, there was a decision to formalize the town, and it was surveyed and then platted on August 29, 1902. Besides several general stores, two groceries, two saw mills and one sorghum mill, the railroad had a section gang based at Fanshawe during the early 1900s, when the population was about 100.

As the old growth timber was cut, the railroad began to haul pulpwood from the area, using a short spur track. Landscape stone has also been sold from here. Meanwhile, farming was impacted by the creation of Wister Lake, which flooded much of the nearby pasture and farmland. However, Fanshawe is still the home of a school, post office, numerous broiler chicken houses, and about 400 residents, located both north and south of the tracks.

For many miles west of here, the railroad and U.S. Highway 270 stay side-by-side.

313.8 COUNTY LINE – To the east is **Le Flore County**, while to the west is **Latimer County**. **Latimer County** was named for James L. Latimer, a delegate from Wilburton to the 1906 Oklahoma State Constitutional Convention. Wilburton is the county seat, and in 2010, the population was just under 11,000.

The organization of the Latimer County area dates back to 1831 when the Choctaw Nation created their own government. The Choctaws created their counties using natural landmarks, such as ridges, rivers and peaks. Because of this, all three of the Choctaw Nation Districts – Apukshunubbee, Moshulatubbee, and Pushmataha, met here. With Oklahoma statehood on November 16, 1907, counties were redrawn and created using almost straight township and range lines.

314.6 CEDAR CREEK BRIDGE – Just south of the highway are two 50-foot deck plate girder spans. The eastern-most is over the main channel of Cedar Creek, while the western one is over Cedar Creek's floodplain. Cedar Creek forms just a few miles north of here on Red Oak Mountain, and flows south into the Fourche Maline and Wister Lake.

315.0 BARTON – Barton was a small independent community during the early 1900s, located just west of Cedar Creek. The Barton family lived in this area soon after the railroad was built, with the most prominent member of the family probably being Dr. Albert Huston Barton.

316.0 HUGHES – Near here was Edwards' Station, a stage stop on the Butterfield Overland Mail route that was established in 1858. During the late 1890s, coal mining began in this area and the Hughes post office opened on May 17, 1900, named for local coal operator Joe Hughes. The town soon became the headquarters of the Le Bosquet Coal and Mining Company, which had a company town a short distance to the south. This allowed Hughes to grow with several independent stores and businesses, and the railroad had a depot. Topographical maps from

September 1909 show that there was a rail line that looped south and then turned east along the ridge to reach Le Bosquet.

The coal seam that Le Bosquet was mining began to play out by the late 1910s, but the Turkey Creek Mining Company continued to operate in the area, using mule teams to mine and giving the station the name Turkey Creek for a few years. When the coal ran out, the mine owners and workers left, and the post office closed on July 15, 1931. Not long after, the tracks for the mines were torn out. A Union Pacific condensed profile from 1988 showed a wye and a track to the south known as the Turkey Creek Spur. About all that remains today are a few foundations.

317.1 TURKEY CREEK BRIDGE – Look for the 84-foot deck plate girder span, located just south of U.S. Highway 270. Turkey Creek is another stream that drains off of the south side of Red Oak Mountain. It flows south from here into Red Oak Creek, a short distance before that stream flows into Fourche Maline.

319.4 DENMAN SWITCH – Located just east of N4490 Road was once a switch to a track that went a mile south to the Bache & Denman Coal Company, located in the Bull Hill area. This mine started operating about 1905 and was related to the coal operations that also were around Hartford, Arkansas. This mine was one of those reported on in the *Seventy-Eighth Annual Report of the Commissioner of Indian Affairs* (1909) as it was on lands assigned to the Choctaw Nation. The mine was not a large producer for long, and by the fiscal year July 1, 1913, to June 30, 1914, produced only 34,958 tons of coal. 1914 was the year that the United Mine Workers went on strike against the various Bache-Denman coal companies, so the output might have been reduced by this action. Additionally, on July 25, 1914, all ten of the companies operated by Bache and Denman were placed in receivership.

The small town that grew up around the mine used the name Denman, named for Franklin Bache's partner in many Arkansas and Oklahoma coal mining operations, Heber Denman. Denman was a trained mining engineer, having graduated from Lehigh University in 1882. He was credited with surveying and platting the mining town of Windber, Pennsylvania, for the Berwind-White Company, where he worked for many years. In the late 1890s, Denman partnered with Bache on almost a dozen different coal mining companies in Arkansas and Oklahoma, before returning to the Berwind-White Company in early 1914 as their Assistant General Manager. In September 1916, Denman acquired the property of the Scranton Anthracite Coal Mining Company near Spadra, Arkansas.

At Milepost 320.0 is a small bridge that shows some of the engineering practices of the Rock Island Railroad. The bridge headwalls were built using cut stone, but later they were strengthened with concrete. The bridge span was built using timber, creating a solid ballast deck that was almost invisible from a train.

The mines near Red Oak eventually became the property of the Ka-li-Inla Coal Company. For a number of years, the coal company had their own private telephone line to serve the mine and office.

321.1 COAL LOADER – East of Red Oak is a traditional ramp coal loader, used by coal trucks to pour coal into railcars. Arkoma Basin has had a number of coal leases in the area since the mid-1990s, but all are now inactive. Bache and Denman operated an underground coal mine here from approximately 1907 to at least 1925. The slope mine used a room-and-pillar method of mining and covered about 47 acres.

This photo shows part of the coal loader, as well as a front end loader, located at Milepost 321.1.

322.3 RED OAK (RO) – Red Oak (Redoak in some documents) is an easy town to find as it straddles U.S. Highway 270 and the railroad, which is still located just south of the highway. The town supports the local area with a post office, bank, convenience store and gas station, retail and hardware stores, restaurants, schools, and other such businesses. In 2010, the population of Red Oak was 549.

This is not the original Red Oak. Nearby were several settlements, including a council house that was used by the Choctaw government and leadership. About eight miles to the northeast, a settlement began using the name Red Oak, probably for the trees in the area. The town was along the Fort Smith-Boggy Depot Road and Thomas Edwards opened a trading post there in 1850 on the property of his wife, Nancy Hardaway, a Choctaw native. Edwards' store became a stop on the Butterfield Overland Mail route in 1858, and it started informally handling mail and express shipments. After the Civil War, Edwards' store became an official post office during March 1868, with the official designation of Red Oak, Skullyville County, Choctaw Nation.

Meanwhile, another stage was operating between Fort Smith and Texas, and a stage stop started southwest of Edwards' store. The Choctaw Coal & Railway built their line west from Wister near this stage route, and the stage stop became a natural railroad stop. With the railroad running, much of the original Red Oak and its post office moved southwest to the rail line, creating a new Red Oak community.

The town quickly grew and featured a sawmill, a lumberyard, a general merchandise store with a Masonic Hall above, a livery, wagonyard, grocery, doctors, and the Miners' and Merchants' Bank. For some years, Red Oak was also the home of U.S. Marshal Seaton Thomas and his family. Reports from the time indicate that the business district was just south of the tracks along Main and Market streets. During this time, the Edwards' Store closed, but it still stands and is listed in the National Register of Historic Places. With the growth along the railroad, Red Oak was officially incorporated in 1900.

Agriculture and coal mining were the two largest activities in the Red Oak area. Cotton was a popular crop, and 1251 rail shipments of cotton were made from here in 1903-1904. Coal was initially used locally, but the railroad allowed commercial mining, and the Bache & Denman Coal Company operated a few miles to the east of town. *The Coal Catalog* of 1920 stated that the Oak Ridge Coal Company – Oak Ridge Mine No. 2 was located at Red Oak. *The Coal Catalog* listed the coal produced as being bituminous coal from the Hartshorne Lower seam, making it "Suitable for Cement Burning, Domestic, Railway, Producer Gas, Smithing, Melting, Powdered Coal, Tile and Pottery Burning and Steam Uses."

Because of the business activity, schools were built at Red Oak, including the Alice Savage Elementary School which was built in 1938 by the Works Progress Administration. However, the Depression forced some farmers and most of the miners to leave the area, and Red Oak's population dropped to 484 in 1940, from a peak of 593 in 1920.

The improvements on U.S. Highway 270, and the activities of the Sinclair Coal Company, encouraged the growth of the business district. Immediately after World War II, the Sinclair Coal Company opened a coal mine at Red Oak. In 1946, the Rock Island Railroad announced that "necessary trackage was recently built to serve the seven to ten million ton coal mine of the Sinclair Coal Company at Red Oak, Oklahoma. This firm supplies high grade coal to the Central States." The coal company leased tracks from the railroad in 1947 for coal loading. In 1961, the Central States Coal Company also leased a track at Red Oak from the railroad. Another railroad lease was made in 1966 to the Arkoma Liquid Company. With this area activity, the population peaked at 676 in 1980, but has dropped again to today's estimate of 550 as coal mining has ended in the area. However, drilling for natural gas has grown, creating some new jobs.

The railroad once had a passing siding at Red Oak, located to the north of the tracks. In 1899, the railroad depot was south of the mainline with a cotton platform to the north, across the mainline and siding. To serve several local companies, a short siding to the south was built through town, passing south of the depot at the Main Street grade crossing. By 1979, all that was left was the house track to the south, shown as being 1080 feet long. This track remains in place.

Heading west, the tracks stay just south of Highway 270 and a long series of mountains as far as Wilburton. To the northeast of Red Oak is Red Oak Peak (1469 feet), and to the north is Red Oak Mountain (1312 feet). To the west is Second Mountain (1655 feet) and First Mountain (1097 feet). Together, they form the south edge of the San Bois Mountains. To the south are lower ridges and valleys that feature a number of large ponds that used to be coal and shale strip mines.

Nothing remains of the railroad at Red Oak except for a few tracks and several foundations, like this one just west of Main Street.

329.5 LITTLE FOURCHE MALINE BRIDGE – The railroad crosses this stream using two deck plate girder spans, each slightly more than 100 feet long. Little Fourche Maline forms at an elevation of 1500 feet in the Sans Bois Mountains to the north. Sans Bois is a French term that means "without forest" or "without wood." The mountains are a frontal belt of the Ouachita Mountains. The stream flows to the southwest through a reservoir at an elevation of 680 feet, and then south to here. It then turns east and south through Red Oak Ridge, and enters the Fourche Maline.

Just west of this bridge is the east switch of the Panola siding. The west switch is now gone, but the track is often used for storing cars, or by regional shippers needing access to a track.

The Little Fourche Maline Bridge still features Rock Island Lines lettering, although today heavily faded. The tank cars on the bridge were parked here in May 2020 for storage.

330.0 PANOLA – Today, Panola at best can be described as a small unincorporated community in Latimer County, but it is still home to the Panola Bearcats. The Panola High School, located south of the tracks, has embraced online education and its students can take four online classes, along with two on campus, each semester. The high school and gymnasium, which were built by the Works Progress Administration, are both on the National Register of Historic Places. The post office that opened on March 18, 1911, is also still open along U.S. Highway 270.

Panola is a Choctaw word that originally meant filament or thread, but has been altered to mean cotton. Other related words include ponola anihechi (cotton gin) and ponola nihi (cotton seed). At one time there was Panola kaunti, or Panola County (Cotton County) in the southeastern corner of the Chickasaw District of the Choctaw Nation in 1850. The county was noted for its large slave-owning plantations and its large cotton production that was often shipped out on the Red River. This Panola is some distance from the Panola County, but it once was an important center for the Choctaw Nation. While the area was mostly pastureland, there was the county seat of Gaines Courthouse near here.

The railroad had a number of tracks in the area to serve several early coal mines. There was also a siding with a house track to the north here. By 1979, the Rock Island showed that there was only a 545-foot industry track and a dispatcher telephone. Today much of the siding is back in place but without its west switch, making it a long house track.

332.3 FOURCHE MALINE BRIDGE – Depending upon the source, this is Fourche Maline River, Fourche Maline Creek, or simply Fourche Maline. The meaning has as many choices – Wicked Fork, Bad Fork, or Treacherous Fork. No matter, the stream seemed to be named for the way it wanders, changes channels, and is just plain hard to float. The Fourche Maline forms in the Sans Bois Mountains, flows to the southwest and through Robbers Cave State Park, and then turns southeastward to near Wilburton. It then turns east and flows to the Poteau River, staying north of Limestone Ridge. Because of the creation of Lake Wister, the Fourche Maline now enters the lake instead of directly into the Poteau River, cutting about six miles off of its original forty-mile route.

The Fourche Maline is a popular fishing stream. Some of the most common fish caught are walleye, bream, bluegill, catfish, smallmouth bass, and carp. Every winter from November 1st until March 15th, the State of Oklahoma stocks the stream with rainbow trout, and a section just below Carlton Lake Dam is well-known for trout fishing.

This bridge is easy to see from U.S. Highway 70 as the track is just to the south, but curves away just west of here. This bridge is a 151-foot-long, 6-panel pin connected Pratt through truss. The Pratt through truss span features a triangular truss design whose diagonal members slope toward the center of the bridge. The design was created in 1844 by Thomas Willis Pratt and his father Caleb Pratt. The bridge design was one of the first that could span distances up to 250 feet.

Soon after the Choctaw, Oklahoma & Gulf acquired the railroad, there was a station shown to be here using the name La Fourche Maline. Just west of the Fourche Maline, the railroad curves away from Highway 270. At one time, the highway continued to closely follow the tracks on to Wilburton. However, the newer highway stays about a block to the north.

332.7 LUTIE – In 1858, the Butterfield Overland Mail stage company established a route through the Indian Territory and had a stage stop near here at what was called Riddle's Station. A small community grew up nearby. It became Ola about the time the railroad built through here, and it received a post office in 1886. The name came from Ola Baird, the daughter of William and Mary Baird. William, who operated a business here, became the first postmaster when the post office opened, thus he had the power to name the location.

This was a coal mine town, dating from its earliest days. How it was operated changed in 1898 when Congress ended control of the coal mines by the various tribes and turned it over to the Secretary of the Interior. The change allowed parties in possession of mines who had made improvements and produced coal in substantial quantities to have preference in taking new leases. However, if no investments had been made, then the coal leases would go away and there could be competition for the coal.

One of the people who took advantage of this change was Dr. Daniel Morris Hailey. Hailey had been involved with the Oklahoma coal fields since the 1870s when he and William Pusley introduced Jay Gould to the coal fields there. Hailey stayed involved with various coal operations and acquired the Osage Trading Company in 1887. His interest in both industries allowed him to take advantage of the change, creating the Hailey-Ola Coal Company to mine coal at Haileyville and Ola. At the two coal mines, Hailey also opened his own stores, and the workers were paid at least partly in Hailey-Ola Coal Company script, good only at his stores. Because of the power of the coal company, on October 4, 1901, the Ola post office and community was renamed Lutie, for Lutie Hailey Walcott, daughter of Dr. D. M. Hailey. The post office later closed on January 31, 1942.

On November 29, 1930, the Hailey-Ola Coal Company made news across the country when a gas explosion at their Lutie No. 5 mine killed thirteen miners and injured four more. Covered by newspapers as far away as the *New York Times*, the details vary some in different reports. Apparently the coal company, spelled as Hali-Ola Coal Company in come reports, was now owned by the McAlester Fuel Company. The reports stated that about sixty workers were in the mine early in the afternoon, but that seventeen men were working 1700 feet underground where the explosion took place. Rescue workers from McAlester and Pittsburgh joined those from the mine, and many had just recently participated in training for just such a disaster. For those who want the full story, check out the Lutie Coal Miners Museum.

This street sign alongside the tracks marks the general route to the site of the Lutie No. 5 mine, which suffered a deadly explosion on November 29, 1930.

335.6 WILBURTON (WN) – Wilburton, with a population of 2843 in 2010, is the largest city along the Rock Island route since Little Rock, Arkansas. This may help explain some of the challenges with the economics of the rail line. Located at 655 feet of elevation, Wilburton is big enough to host hotels, restaurants, gas stations, schools, a casino, and all types of stores and businesses. There are a number of government offices here since Wilburton is the county seat of Latimer County. It is also the home of Eastern Oklahoma State College, and the headquarters of the Arkansas-Oklahoma Railroad Company. The AOK headquarters is easy to find thanks to the train order semaphore signals, a reminder of when Wilburton was a train order station on the railroad. Locomotives and the railroad's business railcar can generally be found in the rail yard to the south of the headquarters building.

Wilburton has always been an important location on the railroad, thanks to all of the area coal mines and the need for a rail yard to handle the business. In 1979, the Rock Island showed that there was a 3273-foot siding, plus 3885 feet of other tracks. Probably most of these still exist, as even today, there is a mainline through Wilburton with two sidings to the south and a spur track to the north for Anchor Drilling Fluids USA. The south sidings are now used as yard and engine service tracks.

This sign marks the corporate office of the Arkansas-Oklahoma Railroad Company at Wilburton, Oklahoma.

Records of the railroad show that other industries were once served by the railroad, including Thomas Brothers Lumber & Supply (1948-1973) and the Atlas Mud Company. Cotton was important during the first part of the Twentieth Century (150 rail shipments of cotton in fiscal year 1903-1904), and coal was a significant source of jobs and freight business. The *Seventy-Eighth Annual Report of the Commissioner of Indian Affairs* for July 1, 1908 - June 30, 1909, listed the Eastern Coal and Mining Company, Great Western Coal & Coke Company, Hailey-Ola Coal Company, and McAlester Coal and Mineral Company as operating in Wilburton. A report for 1913-1914 stated that Eastern Coal & Mining produced 79,660 tons of coal, Great Western Coal & Coke produced 50,303 tons, MK&T Coal 127,114 tons, and Degnan-McConnell 32,756 tons, all from Wilburton area mines.

To handle all of these shippers, there were a number of tracks throughout the Wiburton area. Just to the east of downtown Wilburton, a track headed to the southeast to serve a coal mine. The railroad once had a wye to the south, located about two blocks east of Central Avenue. Also to the south was a spur track that left the mainline east of downtown. It then looped to the west to serve a coal mine located along Central Avenue, about four blocks south of the railroad's mainline. Many tracks like these came and went as mines opened and closed.

The Creation of Wilburton

The settlement of the Wiburton area began with the movement of the Choctaw Nation to Oklahoma, and was pushed by the presence of the Butterfield Overland Mail stagecoach stop at nearby Riddle's Station. Wilburton itself began with the Choctaw Coal & Railway Company, and later the platting of the town by railroad contractor and surveyor, Will Burton. While many sources state that the city was named after Will Burton, some also credit Elisha Wilbur, who was the president of the Lehigh Valley Railroad. The town was a livestock center for the large cattle ranches in the area, and a post office opened in 1891. Coal mining soon surpassed the cattle. The mining activity encouraged Oklahoma to create the Oklahoma School of Mines and Metallurgy in Wilburton, which later became Eastern Oklahoma A&M College, and then Eastern Oklahoma State College.

The initial public schools were built by mine owners James Degnan and James McConnell, but they were replaced as Wilburton grew. Also as the town grew, the county acquired the former Great Western Coal and Coke Mining Company's general merchandise store, located on East Main Street, as a courthouse. It was finally replaced in 1941 by a new building, built with the help of the Works Projects Administration. After World War II, strip mining replaced underground coal mining, and then natural gas and oil production helped Wilburton grow. Although several fires and a 1960 tornado damaged parts of town, Wilburton still features everything needed by residents and visitors. Visitors are common thanks to nearby Robbers Cave State Park and the annual Robbers Cave Fall Festival. Robbers Cave adds stories to the local legends, and outlaw names like the Younger Brothers and Belle Starr are often tied to the area.

The MKT's Wilburton Branch

The Missouri, Kansas & Texas Railway Company once had a branch from North McAlester to Wilburton, passing through Krebs Junction, Carbon, Drumb, and Patterson. The line was built in many parts by many companies. In 1872, the Osage Coal and Mining Company built 3.4 miles of track from North McAlester to Krebs Junction, creating what was called the Krebs Branch. A line was also built southward from Krebs Junction to the large coal mine at Krebs.

As more mines opened, the line was extended to the east. The line was extended to Milepost 7 by the Missouri, Kansas & Texas Railroad Company in 1898-1899. The next expansion was to Milepost 18 in 1902-1904, built by the Missouri, Kansas & Texas Railway Company. In 1906 (some sources state 1904), the MKT extended the line another

10.4 miles, reaching Wilburton from the northwest. A later legal case about the ownership of the abandoned right-of-way provided information about the line's construction. "The M.K. T. Railway acquired the right of way in 1906 from the Choctaw Indian Tribe under Section 13 of the Enid-Anadarko Act of February 28, 1902 (32 Stat. 43), which authorized railroads to condemn rights of way for railroad purposes across Indian Territory."

As long as the coal supply at the mines held out, there was a great deal of traffic on the Wilburton Branch. In 1909, the Missouri, Kansas & Texas Railway operated two roundtrip passenger trains daily, one during the morning (No. 122 eastbound and then No. 121 westbound) and the second during the late afternoon (No. 124 eastbound and then No. 123 westbound). At the time the line was known as the Wilburton Division by the railroad.

However, the mines started closing by the 1920s, and traffic quickly dropped. By 1939, the Wilburton Branch was served by two scheduled mixed trains, plus what extra coal trains were required. Mixed train No. 93 operated eastbound from North McAlester to Wilburton on Mondays, Wednesdays and Fridays, with a scheduled travel time of 2 hours and 15 minutes. On Tuesdays, Thursdays and Saturdays, mixed train No. 92 operated westbound, scheduled for a 2-hour trip. The interchange work between the two railroads at Wilburton was never what was hoped for, and most of the line was officially abandoned on April 1, 1950, leaving just a few miles of track near North McAlester.

Osage Coal and Mining Company

The Osage Coal and Mining Company (Osage Company) was the first commercial mining company in Indian Territory, also one of the last to operate, and was owned by the Missouri, Kansas & Texas (Katy). The coal company started in 1872 when Joshua Pulsey leased a coal mine to the Osage Company. At the time, there was no clear process for such an action, but Choctaw law stated that the discoverer of minerals controlled that resource for one mile in each direction, and they also could lease the rights to the minerals to another party. However, the Choctaw and Chickasaw nations wanted royalties from the mines. A change was made that allowed such leases, but that the nations would receive part of the lease's royalties.

The first two large coal mines, the Osage Coal and Mining Company, and the Atoka Coal and Mining Company, were subsidiaries of the Missouri Pacific Railroad. Most of this coal was used by the railroad, or sold to customers in Texas and Mexico. In 1886, the Katy acquired the Osage Coal and Mining Company and mined approximately one-quarter of a million tons of coal each year from mines at Krebs and McAlester. This made the company about the same size as the mines of the Choctaw, Oklahoma & Gulf Railway Company. As mining grew, the mining company's superintendent, William Cameron, became known for his efforts to increase both safety and production. One of the practices that he began was the long-wall system of mining. This process uses equipment to take a long single cut of coal from a side of a mine wall. The process has one of the highest coal recovery rates at 80% and also reduces the exposure of workers to roof-fall, or the collapse and cave-in of a mine.

The firm stayed active, surviving several major mine explosions and a labor strike, until the Great Depression. By the late 1920s and early 1930s, the demand and prices for coal were down, the railroads were making the change to using oil instead of coal, and the coal that was easiest to mine had all been used up. As stated by the Oklahoma Historical Society, the economy "caused the company to shut down the mines at Krebs and auction its equipment."

Major Coal Mine Disasters at Wilburton

While a number of workers lost their lives working in the mines, and roof failures and explosions did happen, two major explosions made national headlines. The first was in what was called Missouri, Kansas and Texas Coal Company Mine No. 19. An explosion happened on April 30, 1905, near the bottom of a 350-foot shaft. *The Lowell Sun* of Lowell, Massachusetts, reported that thirteen miners on the midnight shift were entombed and probably killed by an explosion. While some suspected a gas explosion, workers on the previous shift stated that there was no gas issue in the mine. It was believed that explosives being used to break up the coal by the earlier shift may have been accidently set off by the midnight shift. Mine No. 19 was opened in 1904 and located along the MKT's Wilburton Branch.

The largest and most noted of the Wilburton mine disasters occurred on January 13, 1926. A reported 91 coal miners and mine engineers were killed in this explosion which impacted a shift of 105 workers at the Eastern Coal and Mining Company Mine No. 21. This explosion was covered in newspapers from *The New York Times* to the *Waterloo Evening Courier* (Waterloo, Iowa), and they described the stories of the surviving miners as they climbed over bodies trying to reach a way out of the mine.

Because of the size of the explosion and the news it made, the mine immediately became a tourist attraction with thousands of visitors trying to watch the rescue operations. The traffic from visitors and the miner's families blocked many of the rescuers and equipment trying to reach the scene. Rescue teams from a number of surrounding mines responded to the disaster, as did groups like the Red Cross, which established a temporary hospital and served hot coffee and doughnuts to the workers.

The Eastern Coal and Mining Company was based in Wilburton, and had operated a number of area mines served by the Chicago, Rock Island & Pacific Railroad. About 1907, the company opened Mine No. 21, located on both the CRI&P and the Katy. All of the company's mines were located northwest of Wilburton.

Wilburton to Haileyville – The Rock Island's North Line

Heading west from Wilburton, the Choctaw, Oklahoma & Gulf/Chicago, Rock Island & Pacific once had two rail lines that could be followed, known as the North Line and the South Line. The North Line headed west from a connection just west of today's 3rd Street grade crossing. It curved northwest and followed the north side of the low ridge, passing by a number of underground coal mines, some of which were later strip mines. The railroad curved west through Patterson (known as Thurston before October 31, 1906) and then to the southwest before turning back to the west to cross the Missouri, Kansas & Texas Wilburton Branch at Boiling, shown as Chilli on some maps. The North Line then headed west on a grade just north of the Katy's Wilburton Branch, passing through Drumb. Just west of Adamson (a post office opened on March 1, 1906, named for mine owner Peter Adamson), the North Line turned south, crossed the MKT and then headed to Haileyville.

The *First Annual Report of the Rock Island Company For the Fiscal Year Ending June 30, 1903*, stated that the Rock Island System was in the process of building 16.79 miles of track between Wilburton and Haileyville. It should be noted that according to *The Railway Age* (March 20, 1903), in 1902, the Indian Territory had 541 miles of new track built, the most of any state or territory in the United States. Oklahoma Territory was second with 532 miles. *The Chronicle* of October 22, 1904, reported on the progress of the construction on the North Line.

> *HAILEYVILLE, I. T., TO WILBURTON, I. T. – Of the line from Haileyville to Wilburton, I. T., five and one-half miles at the easterly end and one and six-tenths miles at the westerly end have been completed and included in the mileage under operation. Work on the balance of the line is under progress, the track having been laid and, as soon as the work of surfacing and ballasting is completed, will be ready for operation. This line follows along the coal outcrop, parallel with and north of the main line.*

The June 30, 1904, *Annual Report of the Rock Island Company*, stated that The Chicago, Rock Island & Pacific Railway was operating 7.16 miles of track from "Haileyville, I. T., toward Wilburton, I. T." This distance was up to 10.17 miles by the June 30, 1905, report. This line was built to serve a number of coal mines north of the original mainline, some of which the Missouri, Kansas & Texas would also soon serve. Known for a while as the Coal Branch, the line was mentioned in some newspaper articles as being the new mainline between Wilburton and Haileyville. However, parts of the North Line were quickly abandoned, with a company statement to "deduct 8.57 miles of track from Haileyville toward Wilburton, classified as side track, effective July 1, 1908." Another report from about the same time stated that the Coal Branch was 8.85 miles long. The remains of the Coal Branch lasted only as long as the coal mines, and it was basically gone by the late 1920s.

Wilburton to Haileyville – The South Line

The South Line is the original line built by the Choctaw Coal & Railway Company, and is today's mainline. It leaves Wilburton heading southwest to follow a valley between ridges north of Blue Mountain. The route was 16 miles long, slightly shorter than the North Line, but it didn't directly connect with the coal mines in the area. Instead, it passes through pasture and farmland, generally following the valley of Gaines Creek. Customers along the route moved agricultural and lime products.

336.7 BANDY CREEK BRIDGE – This 30-foot deck plate girder span, with several pile trestle spans off each end, is located southwest of Wilburton. Bandy Creek forms in the hills to the west, and flows east and enters the Fource Maline south of Lutie.

Just west of the Bandy Creek Bridge is the Wilburton Cemetery, located to the north of the tracks. To the south is Franklin Electric, a part of their water systems business. FranklinTECH holds training courses that are open to professional water systems distributors, contractors, and installers. CRI&P timetables show that Congoleum Industry once had a 580-foot spur track here. Congoleum, a flooring company, moved into a new Wilburton plant in 1970. The company went through several ownership changes, leading to the building's use by Franklin Electric.

338.1 TRANSLOAD TERMINAL – A two-track transload terminal, built for the movement of frac sand, is located to the south. Recently, the terminal has been used for other purposes such as car storage, as the base of track maintenance, and for contractor work by Donoley Construction.

This view looking northward (railroad-east) shows the jointed rails west of Wilburton. The former frac sand facility near Limestone can be seen in the distance.

340.0 LIMESTONE – At the end of the operations of the Rock Island, there was a 7558-foot siding to the north here, as well as a dispatcher telephone for train crews. The siding is still in place and is generally used for car storage.

Not far west of the siding is a grade crossing with Limestone Road. This area is at the west end of Limestone Ridge, named for the thick seams of limestone that are in this area. For a number of years, limestone was burned here to manufacture lime for various purposes. A small community using the name Limestone grew up around the limestone kilns and along the tracks.

342.7 HOLSON – What is left of Holson can be found where Holson Road crosses the railroad at grade. The Holson family had land in this area, and a small community briefly grew up alongside the railroad on their property. Some reports show that the name Vista was also once used for the railroad station location.

401

347.0 GAINES CREEK – The community of Gaines Creek started when S. M. Chesterford, Choctaw Agent, authorized Henry Harder to open a trading post at Gaines Creek on December 22, 1848. The trading post grew enough that a Gaines Creek, Choctaw Nation, post office opened on January 7, 1850, with Harder as postmaster. However, it appears that the trading post and post office wasn't worth the effort as the post office closed on December 26, 1850, and in early 1851, Harder moved east to near Hartford, Arkansas.

Any tracks that were once at Gaines Creek have been gone for years, and were certainly not in the 1969 employee timetable.

347.1 GAINES CREEK BRIDGE – The name Gaines is common throughout the former Choctaw Nation area, with courthouses and counties using the name. While there is no clear explanation, many stories state that the name Gaines came from a man on the Mississippi River who was a good friend of the Choctaw. Some sources specifically mention U.S. Army Colonel George S. Gaines. Gaines was reportedly a licensed trader who explored Indian Territory along with a Choctaw party in 1830, preparing for the movement of the tribe from Mississippi. Records state that George Gaines was appointed by Secretary of War Lewis Coss to be the general supervisor of the tribe's movement, and it was Gaines that proposed moving one-third of the Choctaws per year during the early 1830s. However, Gaines can also be held responsible for much of the poor planning and the lack of proper food and transportation involved with the move.

This Gaines Creek has its headwaters on the south side of Blue Mountain. It flows west around the mountain and turns north and then northeast to get around another series of ridges. It eventually turns west and flows into Lake Eufaula, Oklahoma's largest-capacity lake, opened in 1964 on the Canadian River.

The railroad has a 150-foot Pratt through truss bridge over Gaines Creek. Just to the east is a 20-panel ballast deck pile trestle, used to allow flood waters to move under the track. Heading west, the railroad makes a large S-curve using two three-degree curves to pass through a ridge that is more than 100 feet higher than the grade that the railroad is on. A stream also flows through this gap, and the railroad has a number of thirty and forty-foot deck plate girder bridge spans along the route.

349.2 COUNTY LINE – Look for the 20-foot-long reinforced concrete box culvert. This is the county line between **Latimer County**, located to the east, and **Pittsburg County** to the west. **Pittsburg County** was named for Pittsburg, Pennsylvania, thinking that the new county would boom with the coal mining, and possible steel production that would follow. Note that there is no "H" in the spelling. The federal spelling of the Pennsylvania city's name was Pittsburg from 1891 until 1911, when a local campaign changed it back to Pittsburgh. Pittsburg County was formed on July 16, 1907, so the spelling used the practice that was current at the time.

Pittsburg County was created from parts of five counties found within the Moshulatubbee District and Pushmataha District of the Choctaw Nation. The county was created at the crossroads of the Texas Road, one of several branches of the California Trail and the Butterfield Overland Mail route. It was also the home of the Osage Coal and Mining Company, the first major coal company in the Indian Territory, and later the largest. World War II produced an economic boom as a U.S. Navy ammunition depot was built at McAlester. It became an Army facility in 1977. Agriculture is also important, with corn and cotton initially major area crops. Sorghum was popular by the 1960s, and wheat became the most important crop by the year 2000. The county seat is McAlester, the largest city in the county. The population of the county is approximately 45,000.

349.7 GOWEN SWITCH – Gowen Switch was once just west of today's Phillips Road grade crossing, and connected to two different coal mine tracks. The eastern track went to Gowen and then on to Dwight, while the western track went to Centerville. Number 10 Mountain stands between the former coal-mine towns. *Poor's Manual* (1897) stated that the Choctaw, Oklahoma & Gulf had a Gowen Branch located between Hartshone and Gowen, 3.10 miles long. Union Pacific track charts from 1988 show the line was a "Spur to Shaft No. 3."

Gowen was the location of a Choctaw, Oklahoma & Gulf Railway coal mine, in operation by 1895. The mine was later operated by the Kali-Inla Coal Company (from about 1904), one of several coal mine companies controlled by the Choctaw, Oklahoma & Gulf. News reports from June 1900 stated that there were rumors that the Choctaw, Oklahoma & Gulf was going to lease its coal properties in the Indian Territory to the Kali-Inla Coal Company. The firm controlled a major part of the coal industry in southeastern Oklahoma for almost half a century, with mines in 1900 listed as being at Hartshorne, Gowen, Alderson, and Wilburton in Oklahoma, and at Hartford in Arkansas.

A post office opened in 1894 as the mine began production, and it is still open today. Gowen was once the home of Lincoln Theodore Monroe Andrew Perry, the first black actor to earn a million dollars and to receive featured screen credit in a film. He started by working medicine shows, then vaudeville, and finally movies. One of his popular characters was Stepin Fetchit, billed as "The Laziest Man in the World."

Centerville is located between Number 10 Mountain and Belle Starr Mountain, both of which are northeast of Hartshorne. Centerville was never a major coal town and the tracks didn't last long.

350.5 U.S. HIGHWAY 270 – The railroad passes under this highway, and just west of the overpass is where the tracks once crossed over the road. Highway 270 is slightly less than 650 miles long, starting at Liberal, Kansas, and ending at White Hall, Arkansas. Between its end points, it passes through Oklahoma City and McAlester in Oklahoma, and Hot Springs in Arkansas.

Just east of this bridge at Mile 350 Pole 10 was once the east end of the Yard Limits for Hartshorne and Haileyville. The west end of the Yard Limits were at Milepost 354.0.

351.5 HARTSHORNE (HN) – Hartshorne is the eastern city of the Hartshorne-Haileyville twin cities. Both towns were established on the Choctaw Coal & Railway Company about 1890 as coal mining communities. Hartshorne actually dates to about 1850 when coal was first mined here. The community started as a company town with company housing, a company store and office, and a post office which opened on March 5, 1850. The town was eventually named for Dr. Charles Hartshorne, described as being a wealthy investor from Philadelphia, Pennsylvania. His funding allowed the commercial coal mining operations to develop. Charles Hartshorne was later a member of the board of directors of the Choctaw & Memphis Railroad.

After the Choctaw Coal & Railway Company reached Hartshorne in 1890, the town began to grow with new businesses. The growth was somewhat caused by plans of the Choctaw Coal & Railway Company to build south from here to Denison, Texas (a line was actually built in that direction from nearby Haileyville). *The Hartshorne Sun* newspaper opened in 1895, and as the town grew, a four-room school opened in 1897. Soon, four banks, an ice plant, saw mill, cotton gin, opera house, three hotels, and a telephone company were in business at Hartshorne. The town incorporated on March 1, 1900, when the population was 2352 and eighty businesses were listed as operating. There were also two United Mine Workers of America locals within a few years as coal mining expanded.

With the growth of mining in the area, agriculture was not a major activity. A 1903 Department of Agriculture report indicated that there were only 185 rail shipments of cotton from Hartshorne in 1902-1903. The *Seventy-eighth Annual Report of the Commissioner of Indian Affairs* (July 1, 1908 - June 30, 1909) stated that the Rock Island Coal and Mining Company and the Kali-Inla Coal Company were both at Hartshorne. The Rock Island Coal and Mining Company output during the fiscal year July 1, 1913 - June 30 1914, was 601,409 net tons of coal. The Choctaw Portland Cement Company was also located at Hartshorne. The facility crushed local Wapanucka limestone, something several plants in the region did to produce lime for Portland cement.

The Kali-Inla Coal Company, located in the McAlester mining district near Hartshorne, was created when Sam Mitchell, Gerald S. Riedt, and G.A. Riedt acquired a number of coal companies, including the Bache-Denman Company. Kali-Inla controlled a major part of the coal industry in southeastern Oklahoma until the 1950s.

The population of Hartshorne peaked in the 1930 census with 3587 residents. With the Great Depression and the loss of coal mining, Hartshorne saw the Works Progress Administration (WPA) and other government agencies locate in the area to handle the unemployment and economic issues. Several local schools were built by the WPA, now listed on the National Register of Historic Places. The population dropped to 1903 in the 1960 census, and has recovered enough to stay at just about 2000 residents ever since. It is now the second largest city in Pittsburg County.

Warren Spahn, Hall of Fame baseball player, once was a resident of the Hartshorne area. Spahn was the 1957 Cy Young Award winner and won 20 games or more in 13 of his 21 major league seasons. He won 363 games, the most by a left-handed pitcher. It was claimed that Spahn was one of the smartest pitchers in history, and he had the slogan of "Hitting is timing. Pitching is upsetting timing." Spahn served in the military during World War II and was awarded a Purple Heart. He owned a ranch at Hartshorne, and although he died in 2003 at his home in Broken Arrow, he was buried in Elmwood Cemetery at Hartshorne. A 9-foot-tall statue of Warren Spahn was installed at the event center of the Hartshorne Public Schools complex in 2018.

The Railroad at Hartshorne

At first, Hartshorne was simply a junction with several lines that served area coal mines. This activity required a small yard and several tracks. During the late 1890s, Choctaw Coal & Railway Company Shaft No. 1 was located at the west end of town. It was on the south side of the mainline, located north of Pennsylvania Avenue and east of 2nd Street. To the east of the coal mine was a baled hay warehouse and an ice house. The hay warehouse was later converted into a lumber warehouse.

Much of the coal business went away during the mid-1920s. On January 5, 1923, the Chicago, Rock Island & Pacific announced that it would convert all of its remaining coal burning locomotives to oil. The railroad had been buying 650,000 tons of coal per year from several company mines, and the company would close its coal mines at Alderson and Hartshorne.

Hartshorne was always a scheduled stop for passenger trains, and the town saw an increase in importance on April 15, 1958, when the crew change terminal at Haileyville was moved here. This move resulted in a hearing by the National Railroad Adjustment Board (Docket No CL-10794) which examined the impact of the move on the clerk and staff at Haileyville. At Hartshorne, the agent and two operators called both the train and engine crews, instead of a designated crew caller at Haileyville. It was also noted that some of the crews at Hartshorne were staying at a motel, and the hotel manager was being contacted to call the crews.

The move of the terminal was eventually approved and Hartshorne became the west end of Subdivision 31 (Booneville to Hartshorne), and the east end of Subdivision 32, which went west to Shawnee. Located at an elevation of 704 feet, a track chart from 1973 shows that there was a siding to the south, and then a spur track to the west, also to the south. The train order station, located near North 11th Street, was shown to be between the mainline and siding. By the 1979 timetable, there were only 1080 feet of "other tracks." The timetable also showed that Hartshorne was a train order station with no train order signals, since crews changed at the station and checked the general order boards and books that were maintained there. The station was also protected by yard limit signs. The Rock Island noted that Hartshorne had a wayside radio and standard clock, and was also a water station.

This building alongside the tracks serves as the local office for the railroad.

During 1975, the railroad business in eastern Oklahoma was still important enough that the Interstate Commerce Commission assigned carriers to provide service should the Chicago, Rock Island & Pacific close down. The *April 1975 Takeover List* assigned the St. Louis-San Francisco (Frisco) to the Booneville-Hartshorne line, and the Missouri-Kansas-Texas to the line from Harsthorne west to Oklahoma City.

This sign marks the Hartshorne office of the Arkansas-Oklahoma Railroad.

Pittsburg County Railway

From Hartshorne west to South McAlester, the Pittsburg County Railway Company, an electric interurban line, once paralleled the CO&G/CRI&P, never being more than 1½ miles away. The railroad operated 1903-1947, with a city system connecting South McAlester and McAlester. A report dated March 26, 1947, which approved the line's abandonment, stated that the railroad was 18.44 miles long, and had 4.85 miles of sidings or other tracks.

The Pittsburg County Railway Company dates back to December 10th, 1901, when the Indian Territory Traction Company was chartered for 40 years. A map of the proposed line was officially accepted by the Secretary of the Interior on July 25, 1903. The second part of the company was the light and power company for McAlester, a franchise issued to W. J. Wade on January 14, 1901. Wade sold the franchise to Donald Grant and Lawrence Boyle, who then sold it to the Choctaw Electric Company.

407

The interurban and city railroads began operating on September 15, 1903. The May 25, 1907, issue of the *Street Railway Journal* had an article about the interurban. It provided details about some of the operations and construction. The line was heavily used by miners, and the interurban rail line was crossed by several mine leads from the CO&G and MKT. Some of the coal was moved by the electric line to customers and the company's own power plant. The route also had one mainline crossing with a steam railroad, and there were interchange connections at Bache and Krebs. The line had a number of deep rock cuts and also had a large wooden trestle and wood truss bridge at Brushy Creek near Dow Lake. The article also discussed the brick Hartshorne station, which included a material storage yard behind the building.

The electric railroad, from the west, was located on the north side of the Rock Island mainline, crossed west of Hartshorne and then turned back north to downtown Hartshorne. The Indian Territory Traction Company carried passengers, mail, and freight, and also furnished power for lighting around McAlester. The company had a power house and repair shop at South McAlester, used to support the ten operating cars. The general office of the railroad was in McAlester, but much of the upper management was in Chicago. These included Lawrence P. Boyle (President) and A. W. Underwood (2nd Vice President).

On February 1, 1908, the Indian Territory Traction Company and the Choctaw Electric Company merged to form the Choctaw Railway & Lighting Company. As payments for the construction came due, the company entered receivership in 1915. In 1916, the interurban railway was reorganized as the Pittsburg County Railway Company. The company later became a subsidiary of the Public Service Company of Oklahoma, and closed in 1947.

One interurban car used by the Indian Territory Traction Company/Pittsburg County Railway still exists, on display at 21 East Monroe Avenue in McAlester. The car (#32) was built by Niles Car & Manufacturing in 1907, and is on display with other rail equipment.

352.7 EQUATION – During the early 1960s, the Chicago, Rock Island & Pacific was forced to build several miles of new track due to the federal government's Eufala Reservoir project. This project included a 3200-foot-long dam across the South Canadian River, creating a 102,500-acre lake. Although the dam was almost 30 miles away, the lake was designed to back up into Brushy Creek, requiring the new railroad alignment. This new alignment was 2.2 miles long as compared to the older route of 2.6 miles, creating an equation of **352.68 = 353.09**.

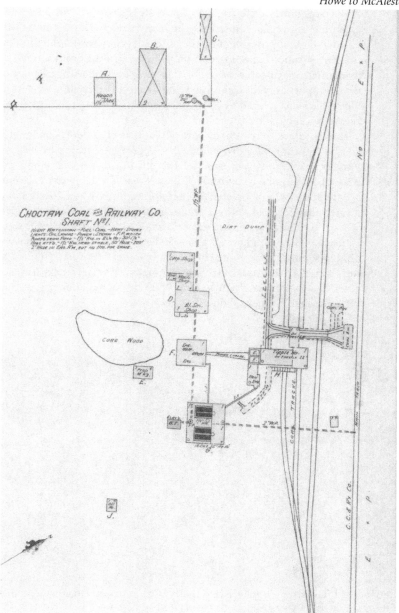

Sanborn Map Company – Choctaw Coal & Railway Company Shaft No. 1 – February 1894. *Sanborn Fire Insurance Map from Hartshorne, Pittsburg County, Oklahoma.* Sanborn Map Company, Feb, 1894. Map. Retrieved from the Library of Congress, https://www.loc.gov/item/sanborn07117_001/.

The September-October 1963 issue of *The Rocket* had an article explaining the work required for the line change. The new route was considered an improvement by the railroad as it was straighter and at a higher elevation. The line had only "three shallow curves, none of which is over one degree" as opposed to the older line with five sharper curves. Importantly for train crews, the sharp curve heading west from Haileyville was replaced by a straighter track, allowing trains to climb the westbound grade easier.

Three bridges were built as part of the new alignment. The longest was the 260-foot-long Brushy Creek bridge, followed by the 92-foot concrete span over Craig Avenue. The third bridge was a temporary 135-foot-long timber pile trestle, built to cross U.S. Highway 270 until its new grade was completed. When the highway was relocated and elevated along the old railroad grade, the timber trestle was to be filled in, but still stands today. Besides the bridges, five cuts and five fills were required, with the highest fill about 30 feet tall. Most of the cuts were through sandstone, with the largest cut being 55 feet deep. One of the cuts created a great deal of trouble as quicksand was hit near its base, requiring a significant drain system. Work began in October 1962 and was completed by the end of 1963.

The concrete bridge over Craig Avenue at Haileyville is unique on the line, a product of the new line built west of Haileyville during the early 1960s.

353.1 HAILEYVILLE – Haileyville was once an important coal mining and railroad town. The Oklahoma Historical Society states that the area was first mapped in 1719 when French explorer Jean Baptiste Bénard de La Harpe was exploring the Arkansas River. The next major historical character in the area was Dr. David Morris Hailey, a Confederate veteran who left Louisiana after the Civil War and moved to Oklahoma. Here, he practiced medicine and got involved with several businesses. While doing this, he began to note the many coal seams found in the area.

In 1889, Dr. Hailey and James Elliot created the Hailey-Ola Mining Company, leased land from the Choctaw Coal & Railway Company, and opened the Number One Slope mine on St. Patrick's Day. This was the first coal mine shaft in the McAlester district of the Pittsburg County coal field. The mine started a thirty-year coal boom, earning Dr. Hailey a portrait in the State Confederate Memorial Hall of the Oklahoma Historical Society Building in Oklahoma City.

To support the mine, the company town of Haileyville was created. Although in the Choctaw Nation, Haileyville housed a big mix of miners, including Italians, Native Americans, Russians, and Americans. A post office opened at Haileyville on April 20, 1901. As the Choctaw, Oklahoma & Gulf built across Arkansas and Oklahoma, Haileyville became a crew change point for the railroad, adding to the town's prosperity. By 1910, there were more than 2000 residents, a bank, newspaper, five hotels, three doctors, several retail stores, and other typical businesses, ending the "Company Town" label for the community. Haileyville became the western "Twin City" of the area, and officially became a first-class city on February 12, 1912. The *Seventy-eighth Annual Report of the Commissioner of Indian Affairs* (June 30, 1909) showed that the Hailey-Ola Coal Company dominated local mining, and records show that the company mined 178,575 tons of coal July 1, 1913 - June 30, 1914.

However, as the coal mining began to slow and even end, the population peaked at 2067 residents in 1920, and then dropped to 1183 in 1940, when the city was down to one coal company, a bank, an ice plant, several gas stations, grocery stores, and a hardware store. During the late 1950s, the railroad moved their offices to nearby Hartshorne, and the population was down to 922 residents in the 1960 census. Today, the population hovers at about 900, but Haileyville still has its own high school and small downtown business area, although Hartshorne certainly has a larger business district and population.

The Railroad at Haileyville

Haileyville was once the home of freight and passenger offices of the Choctaw, Oklahoma, & Gulf, and later Chicago, Rock Island & Pacific. It was a junction town with a connection to the North Line, the branch-line to Ardmore, and a number of coal leads. Crews and locomotives were changed at Haileyville, requiring a rail yard, roundhouse, and other facilities. For a number of years, the Indian Territory Division, covering Booneville to Shawnee, had its offices at Haileyville.

In 1904, the shops at Haileyville were expanded, using equipment from the machine shop at Argenta, creating more rumors that the Argenta shops would be closed. However, all wasn't good as the North Line to Wilburton, built less than a decade before, was already being abandoned by 1908. But Haileyville remained important and was the subject of a significant article in the July 1916 issue of the *Rock Island Employes' Magazine*. The article included a number of photos of the station area, which featured a two-story brick station and a one-story brick freight house. It also reported on the Railroad Y.M.C.A., a three-story brick building with a large covered front porch, which had been dedicated on March 8, 1913.

> *Upon the hill the Railroad Y.M.C.A. stands proudly, a monument that marks the very foundation of welfare work in that terminal. From this splendid "home" Old Glory waves proudly and upon certain occasions other flags appear, always under that "Emblem of the Home of the Brave and the Land of the Free." Not content with the building alone, with its comfortable appointments, its splendid dining room and kitchen facilities, evidenced best by a meal taken there, its genial and well liked, yea, well loved Secretary and his able and painstaking assistants, the "boys" wanted the grounds beautified. The campaign started, efforts proved availing, until today Haileyville's Rock Island Lines Park and walks, together with tastefully arranged flagpole, fountain and relics of earlier days of the railroad man, displayed therein, make one of the most attractive spots for the eye to behold, not alone in that part of the country, but a credit to any place along OUR RAILROAD.*

In 1922, Haileyville was part of the work of modernizing the Pan Handle-Indian Territory Division of the Rock Island. Larger steam locomotives were being used on the line, and four stalls of the roundhouse were extended to handle these new locomotives. Additionally, the 70-foot turntable was replaced by a 100-foot turntable.

The decrease in local trains serving the area coal mines reduced the need for the railroad yard and roundhouse. In 1939, positions such as the roundhouse clerk were eliminated. As steam was replaced by diesel power, the shop facilities at Haileyville were further reduced. The construction of a freight car repair facility at the U.S. Navy ammunition depot near McAlester also reduced the mechanical work at Haileyville.

During 1957-1958, the Rock Island Railroad moved its offices, crew change activities, and other tasks from Haileyville to nearby Hartshorne, Oklahoma. A series of hearings by the National Railroad Adjustment Board dealt with complaints by clerical staff and others who fought the move and the changes in assignments. The reports involving Docket No. CL-10794 provided a great deal of information about the operations of the railroad at the time.

On November 7, 1957, the railroad started the process of closing Haileyville when it "abolished the full-time clerical position and assigned calling of train and engine crews, checking train yard, checking trains, supplying cabooses, and making of general yard reports to the Telegraphers." On April 15, 1958, Haileyville was discontinued as a terminal, and the crew change was moved to Hartshorne, 1.8 miles from Haileyville. Prior to the change, Haileyville was the home point for train and engine crews working to and from Booneville, Arkansas, and was the away-from-home terminal for train and engine crews operating from Shawnee, Oklahoma. At the time, approximately 25 freight men worked Haileyville to Booneville, and ten worked Haileyville to Shawnee. An average of four freight crews were called daily. Freight train No. 991 was scheduled to depart Haileyville at 10:45am, while freight train No. 994 was scheduled to leave at 12:45pm. There were also two locals that departed at various times. A daytime switch engine was operated at the Haileyville yard, switching the four trains and weighing about 15 cars every other day. Four passenger trains stopped at Haileyville in 1958. These were No. 15 (4:15am), No. 52 (10:10am), No. 51 (6:04pm) and No. 14 (10:00pm). With the move to Hartshorne, the same crews were still involved, but instead did their job about two miles away.

Nothing remains of the railroad at Haileyville but the mainline of the Arkansas-Oklahoma Railroad Company. It is further complicated by the fact that the mainline was moved several blocks to the north in 1963. The original mainline was replaced by today's U.S. Highway 270, and the remains of the station gardens can be found at the Veterans Memorial Park between Main Street and Highway 270. The location of the roundhouse is along Highway 270, and has been cleaned up as part of an Environmental Protection Agency project.

354.6 BRUSHY CREEK BRIDGE – This bridge was built as part of the line realignment in 1963. It consists of three 56-foot-long deck plate girder spans, as well as one 90-foot deck plate girder span, all covered with a concrete ballasted deck.

Brushy Creek is a major creek that feeds into Eufaula Lake. Brushy Creek originates on the south side of Pine Mountain, west of Brushy Narrows, near the small community of Union Chapel. It generally flows to the northeast to here, and then less than ten miles on north to Eufaula Lake. The valley created by Brushy Creek was used for the north end of the Ardmore Branch.

Heading west, the railroad climbs up grades as much as 1.68% as far as Milepost 358.

354.8 ARDMORE JUNCTION – Note that Ardmore Junction was located on the original line just west of the Brushy Creek Bridge. When the new route was built in 1963, no new junction was needed. However, the new 1963 route did cross the grade of the old CO&G North Line, not far west of the new Brushy Creek Bridge.

Also known as Branch Junction or Haileyville Junction, there was once a wye here that connected to the Ardmore Branch. The branch was built by 1902 from here to Ardmore, Oklahoma, almost 120 miles away. At the time, both the Rock Island and the Frisco were controlled by the same stockholders, so the branch was built in coordination between the two railroads. The lower 14 miles was jointly used between Ardmore and Frisco Junction. The Frisco line was the St. Louis, San Francisco & New Orleans Railroad Company, designed to connect Colorado and western Oklahoma with New Orleans. Instead, the line was only built from Hope, Arkansas, to Ardmore, Oklahoma. Today, most of this line is operated by the Kiamichi Railroad.

At Ardmore, the Rock Island combined with the Atchison, Topeka & Santa Fe to build a new passenger station in 1916. The station was built of brick with stucco walls, and featured the names of both railroads. In 1998, the Ardmore Main Street Authority acquired the station and the adjacent Railway Express Agency building. Both were restored by 2001. Amtrak's *Heartland Flyer* still uses the station.

The Ardmore Branch didn't last long. The first part abandoned was Frisco Junction to a connection with the Missouri-Kansas-Texas at Pittsburg, Oklahoma, 20 miles from Haileyville. This abandonment in 1938 saw the Frisco Junction to Ardmore track leased to the Frisco, which already had half-interest in the 14 miles. Records of the two railroads indicate that the discussion about this lease and abandonment started as early as September 1935. In 1940, the Frisco acquired full ownership of that part of the line. The last of the Rock Island branch was abandoned from Pittsburg to Branch Junction in 1950.

355.4 DOW – Dow was another town that became a company town to support the local coal mines. In 1909, the company was the Milby & Dow Coal & Mining Company, which produced 161,580 tons of coal July 1, 1913 - June 30, 1914. Just east of Dow was M&D Shaft No. 1, while Shaft No. 9 was just west (railroad-south) of the tracks and town. To the north of town was Shaft No. 2. Much of this development was covered in the article "The McAlester Coal Field in Oklahoma" in the August 2, 1913, issue of *Coal Age*. During June 1914, Mine No. 9 caught on fire, and despite efforts to extinguish the flames, the shaft was sealed as an attempt to put the fire out.

As with many of the coal towns in the area, Dow was named after the owner or operator of the local mine. A post office opened at Dow in 1898, and it stayed open until 1964. About the same time, the railroad abandoned its facilities at Dow, and nothing remained there when the CRI&P shut down.

358.4 BACHE – The coal mine town of Bache was actually located north of the railroad, which passed through the middle of Shaft No. 6 on lands leased by the Rock Island Improvement Company. Named for coal company operator Franklin Bache, there was a post office here from February 26, 1903, until July 29, 1995. The name Franklin Bache should be familiar as he and his partners were involved with a number of coal mines near Hartford, Arkansas, which were part of the Sebastian County Union War of 1914. Franklin Bache was the receiver of the Mexican Gulf Coal & Transportation Company (Alderson) in 1901, president of Bache-Denman Coal Company, and president of the Kali-Inla Coal Company. All of these companies were tied together in different ways, a common situation since the Missouri, Kansas & Texas and the Chicago, Rock Island & Pacific controlled much of the coal lands and many of the coal companies in the McAlester Coal District.

Today, Bache is an unincorporated community in Pittsburg County, located alongside U.S. Highway 270. The community is big enough to have a gas station and convenience store.

360.9 ALDERSON – Alderson is another community that started as a coal mining town. The local history states that it was named for W. C. Alderson, an employee of the Choctaw, Oklahoma & Gulf Railroad. However, Alderson was listed as being in the management of the Lehigh Valley Railroad by 1901. A post office opened using the name Alderson in 1890. In late 1898, there were two major coal operations at Alderson. One was the Mexican Gulf Coal & Transportation Company, located less than a mile southwest of the railroad's depot. This company had fifty or more coke ovens operating, with three railroad tracks being used to serve the loading bins. The October 1899 issue of *The Choctaw* stated that the "coke ovens at Alderson are sending large quantities of their output to the Republic of Mexico." The 1897 issue of *Poor's Manual* stated that there was a 0.80-mile-long Alderson Branch from "Alderson to Mine."

The second coal operation at Alderson in late 1898 was the Kali-In-la Mining Company Shaft No. 7, located less than a mile west of the depot and served by four tracks under the main tipple. This coal company mined a number of coal properties in the Indian Territory that it had leased from the Choctaw, Oklahoma & Gulf. To serve the miners and their families, the Choctaw Railway & Lighting Company operated down Main Street, today's U.S. Highway 270.

The *Seventy-eighth Annual Report of the Commissioner of Indian Affairs* (June 30, 1909) stated that the Rock Island Coal & Mining Company was operating at Alderson. Historical reports state that in 1910, Rock Island Coal Mining Company Mine No. 5, and McAlester Coal & Coke Company Mine No. 6, were both operating at Alderson. The population had grown to 786 residents, most of them mine workers and their families from Italy and Poland. In that year, a bond was approved to build a new brick school. By the time the school opened, seven teachers were required to handle the three hundred students.

Alderson soon had four general stores, nine grocers, three physicians, one hotel, one livery, one blacksmith, one drugstore, and one lumberyard. Alderson's population peaked at 855 in the 1920 census, just as mining began to decline. Things got worse in 1923 when the Chicago, Rock Island & Pacific announced that it would soon stop buying coal and convert its remaining coal burning locomotives to oil. By this time, McAlester coal was largely purchased and used by railroads, and Alderson was one of two Oklahoma mines still owned by the Rock Island. Other railroads such as the St. Louis Southwestern and the St. Louis & San Francisco were doing the same thing, leaving little market for the coal.

By 1930, the population was down to 421. A 1935 map of the McAlester Coal District showed that the lands in the area were still under the control of the Rock Island Improvement Company. With the loss of demand for coal, and few other businesses in the area, Alderson never recovered from the end of mining. The town's schools closed in the 1980s and the population was down to 304 in the 2010 census. The post office is still open.

Besides the coal tracks, the Rock Island Railroad had several other tracks at Alderson. In 1973, there was a siding to the south of the mainline. A 1979 employee timetable showed that there were 3604 feet of other tracks, as well as a dispatcher telephone. Some of the station foundations can still be found. The siding is still in place for the Arkansas-Oklahoma Railroad, and it has been used for car storage or to serve the Halliburton Energy Services facility.

On May 28, 2020, AOK locomotive #4098 was found parked at Alderson, actually surrounded by stored freight cars. This U23B locomotive was built by GE as Western Pacific #2260 in 1972. It went to the Monongahela Railway (#2308) where it was rebuilt by GE as a B23 "Super 7" in 1990. It went to Conrail and then became the property of Norfolk Southern (#4098).

The 1894 Miner Strike

The 1890s saw several financial challenges where coal prices swung wildly, and firms gained or lost investor confidence. Because of this, the mines at Alderson cut wages in 1894 in an attempt to stay profitable. The miners went out on strike, closing the primary coal mine.

At the time, the Choctaw Nation was due a royalty on all coal mined. They had also levied a monthly tax for each employee, something the mining corporations stopped paying. With this tax not being paid, anyone who was not Choctaw was now on the property illegally. The Choctaw Nation then requested their removal as intruders. The request was heard by the Commissioner of Indian Affairs, then the Secretary of the Interior, and finally President Cleveland. The request to remove the striking miners was approved and three companies of infantry and two companies of cavalry were sent to Alderson to protect the Choctaw Nation. Using Alderson as a base of operations, the military loaded approximately two hundred workers and their families into boxcars and had them shipped to Jenson, Arkansas, just off the Indian Territory.

Despite protests by the governor of Arkansas, and the representatives of Italy and Great Britain, the moves were made and the workers were kept out of the Indian Territory and the lands of the Choctaw Nation. Shortly after, the strike ended, the mines reopened and started shipping coal. The Choctaw Nation was again receiving coal royalties and employee tax payments, and the coal miners and their families were again welcomed in the community.

363.6 KREBS – Welcome to Krebs – Oklahoma's Little Italy. Krebs was founded in the late 1800s as coal mining began, and many of its first residents were Italian miners. In 1872, the Osage Coal & Mining Company built 3.4 miles of track from North McAlester to Krebs Junction, and on southward to the large coal mine at Krebs. Osage Coal was the first major coal company in Indian Territory, and its success attracted numerous others to the Territory. A town grew quickly and the first post office was established in 1886. While many area coal towns were named for the mine owner or mine company, Krebs was named for Judge Edmond Folsom Krebs. Judge Krebs had a mix of German and Choctaw ancestry, was born in Mississippi, and served the Choctaw Nation as a judge in McAlester, Indian Territory.

On January 7, 1892, Mine No. 11 of the Osage Coal & Mining Company experienced an explosion that killed about 100 workers and injured another 150. Despite this, there were as many as 15 coal mines operating in the area, and the United Mine Workers started their first local in Indian Territory at Krebs in 1898. The October 1899 issue of *The Choctaw* reported that there were 2000 miners working in the mines at Krebs.

The early 1900s saw many improvements to the town. Krebs was incorporated in 1903. During the same year, St. Joseph's Catholic Church and the city Opera House were built, becoming the first two brick buildings in town. The Choctaw Railway & Lighting Company also started operating their interurban railroad through Krebs in 1903. A public school system opened in 1907, about the same time as the creation of the State of Oklahoma. The peak of Krebs' population was in 1910 with 2884 residents.

The population dropped as the mines closed, and was down to 1375 by 1930. After that, the population slowly grew as it became a bedroom community for nearby McAlester. The population reached 2053 in the 2010 census. Besides the popular Italian restaurants, Krebs is also known as an infamous speed trap.

The Railroads of Krebs

As previously stated, the Osage Coal & Mining Company built a railroad from North McAlester to Krebs in 1872. This line became part of the Missouri, Kansas & Texas Railroad's Wilburton Branch, and the Katy had a train station located in downtown Krebs. The Choctaw Coal & Railway Company built its east-west line south of Krebs, with a station to the southwest of downtown.

As the mines closed, the Rock Island also closed its facilities at Krebs. By 1973, the Rock Island track chart no longer showed any facilities here. Heading west, the railroad is climbing a 1.0% grade, which peaks at an elevation of 750 feet at Milepost 365.5. Just as in the 1979 Rock Island timetable, the current Arkansas-Oklahoma Railroad has no station at Krebs on the Choctaw Route. However, the Arkansas-Oklahoma Railroad does reach Krebs as it has leased the Krebs Industrial Lead from Union Pacific. This line is the old Katy Krebs Branch, and the Arkansas-Oklahoma Railroad operates it all the way from McAlester to Krebs, a distance of 7.04 miles.

364.8 U.S. HIGHWAY 69 – Entering the McAlester area, the railroad passes under Highway 69, also known as the George Nigh Expressway. George Nigh served as the 17th and the 22nd Governor of Oklahoma. U.S. Highway 69 is about 1140 miles long and extends from Albert Lea, Minnesota, to Port Arthur, Texas.

365.0 PROPERTY LINE – This location marks the border between the Arkansas-Oklahoma Railroad Company (AOK) to the east, and Union Pacific to the west. The Surface Transportation Board approved the AOK purchase of the line from the State of Oklahoma between Howe (Milepost 295.36) and McAlester (Milepost 364.96) in 2019.

Since 1997, the Arkansas-Oklahoma Railroad has leased 5.54 miles of track west from here, all the way to Milepost 370.5, just west of the Indian Nation Turnpike underpass. The lease agreement includes a financial incentive to interchange traffic with Union Pacific rather than with Kansas City Southern.

365.1 U.S. HIGHWAY 270 – The railroad passes under U.S. Highway 270, which in the McAlester area is known as the Carl Albert Parkway. Albert, known as the "Little Giant from Little Dixie," was Speaker of the United States House of Representatives from 1971 to 1977. This made him the holder of the highest political office of any Oklahoman in history.

Just to the west of the underpass, the railroad served a series of agricultural businesses to the north.

The McAlester Feed Mill complex still stands next to the tracks on the east side of McAlester, Oklahoma.

365.8 U.S. HIGHWAY 270 – The railroad turns back to the southwest and again passes under Highway 270. The railroad grade peaks near here at an elevation of 750 feet.

366.4 MCALESTER (MA) – This location, which once had a yard, is centered around 2nd Street. In 1979, the Rock Island still had a number of facilities at McAlester, including a standard clock, a wayside radio, and a water station. McAlester also served as a train register station and a train orders station. Yard limits, located between Milepost 365.0 and 368.6, were here to protect the small yard and interchange work. During the 1970s, the subdivision change at Hartshorne had been moved to here. This made McAlester the subdivision limits between Subdivision 31 (east to Booneville) and Subdivision 32 (west to Shawnee), both part of the Southern Division at the time. In 1988, the Missouri-Kansas-Texas had the Howe Subdivision to the east, and the Oklahoma Subdivision to Harter to the west.

The railroad once had a number of structures at McAlester, including a water station, stockyards, a freight and passenger station, and others. Maps from 1898 show that the Missouri, Kansas & Texas Railway had a dining hall on the southeast corner of the diamond, used to serve meals to passengers on their trains. On the northeast side of the diamond was a station used by both railroads. There was also an interchange track in this quadrant. The Pittsburg County Farmers Market now uses this area.

The Choctaw, Oklahoma & Gulf once had their own station, located north of the tracks and east of 2nd Street. It was being used as general offices by the late 1890s. Further east was the Choctaw Ice Company, the LaFlore Milling Company, and the Cooper Lumber Company. West of the station was the Choctaw Compress Company and the National Manufacturing Company's planing mill. Other businesses that were once served by the railroad included Sheffield Steel, LoneStar Steel, Southeastern Iron & Metal, and the Pittsburgh County Cooperative. None of these are there now. The rail yard to the east of the diamond is gone, replaced by a larger yard and siding to the west, still used by Union Pacific and the Arkansas-Oklahoma Railroad Company.

While Wilburton is the corporate office of the Arkansas-Oklahoma Railroad, McAlester is probably the center of freight operations. Because of this, locomotives are often found parked in the area. Here, AOK #536, originally Rock Island #536, sits near the office building at McAlester. This SW1 was built in 1942 and returned to the red and yellow paint in 2009.

Van Noy Brothers Eating Houses

McAlester, or what was known as South McAlester during the late 1800s and early 1900s, was an important stop for passenger trains on the Choctaw Route. The purpose was generally to providing dining service at an eating house operated by the Van Noy Brothers. In 1902, the Van Noy Brothers had a number of eating houses along the railroad which served the various trains. Westbound Choctaw, Oklahoma & Gulf Train No. 1 showed stopping for lunch (called dinner at the time) at Little Rock; supper at Booneville, Arkansas; and breakfast at Sayre, Oklahoma. Westbound Train No. 3 stopped for breakfast at South McAlester and lunch at Oklahoma City. Eastbound CO&G No. 2 stopped for supper at Amarillo; breakfast at South McAlester; and lunch at Little Rock. Finally, eastbound Train No. 4 had lunch at Oklahoma City; supper at South McAlester; and breakfast at Memphis.

The company started in Kansas City, Missouri, in 1893 when Ira Clinton Van Noy formed a retail cigar and news business. The Van Noy Railroad News Company was created on July 26, 1897, when several more brothers and an outside investor joined the company. The firm operated a chain of railroad station newsstands and on-train news butch salesmen. Besides the Choctaw Route, the company had contracts with Missouri Pacific Railway and its subsidiary, the St. Louis, Iron Mountain & Southern Railway, and even operated train crew hotels. By 1910, the company reportedly had 52 hotels and restaurants, 20 concession stores, and 21 distribution offices. The company changed its name to the Van Noy Railway Hotel and News Company in 1912 to reflect its entire market.

The company acquired other similar firms, and then merged with the Interstate News Company, creating the Van Noy Interstate News Company in 1917. As dining cars and sleepers were added to trains, the company moved away from contracts with railroads, but still operated restaurants in train and bus stations. The firm expanded its hotel holdings, even adding the Beverly Hills Hotel. By the 1950s, the company operated airport restaurants. In 1959, the company became Interstate HOSTS, and then Host International in 1968. It was acquired by the Marriott Corporation in 1982, becoming the Host Marriott Corporation.

On March 22, 2002, Autogrill S.p.A. purchased Host Marriott Services from the Marriott Corporation. This gave the company contracts in 18 of the 20 largest United States airports, plus franchises of Pizza Hut, Burger King, Sbarro, and Starbucks. The firm moved back into the railroad industry, gaining contracts with European railroads. The company became HMSHost, and then Host Hotels and Resorts.

Van Noy Brothers is known for its association with Walt Disney. In 1916, Disney worked for the company as a summer news butch. He was based in Kansas City and sold merchandise on various routes out of the city, but never on the Choctaw Route.

The City of McAlester

McAlester started about two miles to the north. It wasn't the first town in the area, as Perryville once was located nearby. For a number of years, Perryville was the capital of the Choctaw Nation and County Seat of Tobucksy County. During the Civil War, it was used as a

Confederate supply depot by the Choctaw Nation. The entire town was burned by Union forces during August 1863. After the war, Confederate Captain James Jackson McAlester got involved with the Reynolds and Hannaford trading company and operated several trading posts for them. McAlester knew about the coal in the area and was allowed to explore the region because he was a citizen of the Chickasaw Nation through his marriage to Rebecca Burney, a full-blood Chickasaw. He soon acquired mining rights from the Choctaw Nation.

When the Missouri, Kansas & Texas Railway built through the area, it passed by a trading post created by J. J. McAlester called Bucklucksy. A railroad station was created at Bucklucksy, named McAlister by the railroad. J. J. McAlester was able to sell coal to the railroad, making the stop an important one. The McAlister post office opened in 1873, but the spelling was corrected to McAlester in 1885. Soon, the remaining residents of Perryville moved to McAlester, and the town quickly grew, especially after area coal mining picked up in volume. In 1875, the Osage Coal & Mining Company introduced more modern mining methods when it leased coal lands from J. J. McAlester and others.

When the Choctaw Coal & Railway Company built through the area, land costs forced it to locate about two miles south of the existing McAlester. A town known as South McAlester grew up at the junction between the two railroads, quickly becoming the larger of the two communities. The 1900 census showed this as it reported a population of 642 for McAlester and 3470 for South McAlester. The town of McAlester incorporated during January 1899, while South McAlester was incorporated during November of the same year. Many of the residents at the time were there for mining, with many foreign-born or from other mining states like Pennsylvania. McAlester was broken up into a number of small communities due to these miners, with many from places like Germany, France, Lithuania, Poland, Russia, Mexico, and the Slavic countries. At least 25 percent of the residents were foreign-born.

Because of their presence in the Indian Territory, federal action was required for many of the changes in government. South McAlester continued to grow, and in 1907, the United States Congress passed an act to merge the two communities as the new McAlester. Since South McAlester was far larger, its government took over control of the new McAlester, with parts of the old McAlester being called North McAlester. With a population of 8144 at statehood that year, the post office moved to the South McAlester area, but still with the McAlester name. Today, downtown McAlester sits where South McAlester once stood, showing that two railroads can be better than one when it comes to city development.

MINE DISASTER'S
SOUTHEASTERN OKLAHOMA
1885 TO 1945

KREBS	1885	JUMBO	1910
SAVANNA	1887	LEHIGH	1912
KREBS	1892	McCURTAIN	1912
ALDERSON	1893	ADAMSON	1914
ALDERSON	1897	ALDERSON	1919
ALDERSON	1901	WILBURTON	1920
HARTSHORNE	1901	McCURTAIN	1922
DOW	1902	WILBURTON	1926
CARBON	1903	TAHONA	1926
WILBURTON	1905	TAHONA	1929
WITTEVILLE	1906	McALESTER	1929
HAILEYVILLE	1908	McALESTER	1930
HARTSHORNE	1909	LUTIE	1930
WILBURTON	1910	CRAIG	1945

A half-dozen blocks south of the tracks on Third Street is the Pioneer Coal Miner Memorial Park, which features this list of mine disasters in southeastern Oklahoma.

Coal mining dominated the local economy for many years, and the Pioneer Coal Miner Memorial documents this history. Located just south of downtown at Third and Kiowa, the park includes a wall that memorializes the major coal mining disasters of Southeastern Oklahoma. Other industries such as agriculture were also important. While the Department of Agriculture reported only 13 rail shipments of cotton from McAlester in 1902-1903, there were three cotton gins and one cotton compress in town. The compress was capable of processing twelve hundred bales per day and was soon producing forty thousand bales per year. The population grew to 12,954 by 1910, but the reduction of coal mining, a boll weevil attack on the cotton crop, and the Great Depression forced a number of major changes. The population dropped, but World War II and the opening of a number of government offices and the Naval Ammunition Depot suddenly increased the population, with 17,878 residents by 1950. The Naval Ammunition Depot eventually became the McAlester Army Ammunition Plant, which manufactures almost all of the bombs used by the United States military. The U.S. Defense Ammunition Center moved to the plant in 1998.

Today, McAlester has a population of just under 20,000, making it the largest city in the Oklahoma Choctaw Nation. Besides the ammunition plant, McAlester is also the home of the Oklahoma State Penitentiary. McAlester was also the location of the Oklahoma state trial for Terry Nichols, involved in the 1995 Oklahoma City bombing. The town is a regional business center and features many businesses and the primary area hospital. Most of downtown was rebuilt as an urban renewal project, so much of the historic look is gone.

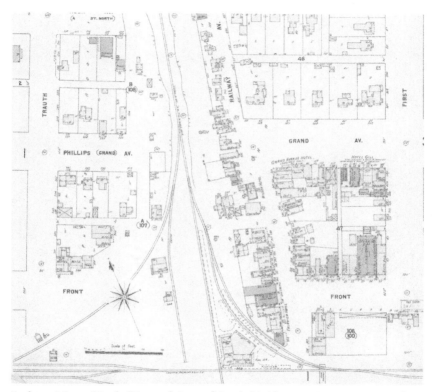

Sanborn Map – North Diamond Area of South McAlester – August 1897. *Sanborn Fire Insurance Map from South McAlester, Pittsburg County, Oklahoma.* Sanborn Map Company, Aug, 1897. Map. Retrieved from the Library of Congress, https://www.loc.gov/item/sanborn07254_002/.

425

Sanborn Map – South Diamond Area of South McAlester – August 1897. *Sanborn Fire Insurance Map from South McAlester, Pittsburg County, Oklahoma.* Sanborn Map Company, Aug, 1897. Map. Retrieved from the Library of Congress, https://www.loc.gov/item/sanborn07254_002/.

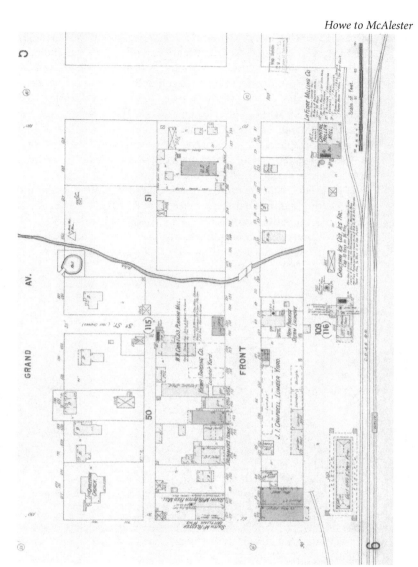

Sanborn Map – Old Depot Location of South McAlester – August 1897. *Sanborn Fire Insurance Map from South McAlester, Pittsburg County, Oklahoma.* Sanborn Map Company, Aug, 1897. Map. Retrieved from the Library of Congress, https://www.loc.gov/item/sanborn07254_002/.

366.4 MKT CROSSING – The diamond is located just south of U.S. Highway 270, and west of South Main Street. Currently, there are interchange tracks between the Arkansas-Oklahoma Railroad Company and Union Pacific in the southwest and northwest quadrants. In the 1979 employee timetable, this was shown to be an automatic interlocking, basically controlled by whichever railroad reached the crossing first. At the time, the crossing was with the Missouri-Kansas-Texas Railroad. MKT System Timetable No. 7, dated May 15, 1988, showed that the line was the Choctaw Subdivision, stretching from Muskogee to the yard at Ray, near Denison, Texas. The MKT milepost was 565.9.

During late 1988, the railroad was acquired by Union Pacific and assigned to the Texoma Division Service Unit. By 2012, McAlester was the dividing point between the Kansas City Area and the Dallas/Ft. Worth Area on Union Pacific. Heading north was Union Pacific's Cherokee Subdivision, while to the south was UP's Choctaw Subdivision.

The Arkansas-Oklahoma Railroad has this office located just west of the MKT Crossing at McAlester.

South McAlester

This was one of several connections between the Missouri-Kansas-Texas and the Chicago, Rock Island & Pacific. Because both railroads were heavily involved in the coal market, these connections were important. When the railroad was built, the Choctaw Coal & Railway Company aimed to connect in downtown McAlester. However, the owner of much of the land, J. J. McAlester, reportedly demanded four thousand dollars.

The Choctaw Coal & Railway Company then contacted Fritz Sittel (also shown as Sittle in some reports), who owned a large ranch just south of McAlester. Sittel agreed to allow the railroad to cross his ranch, and soon laid out a community around the new junction. The community took the name South McAlester, and a number of businesses moved several miles south from McAlester to be near two railroads. The Choctaw Coal & Railway Company located its headquarters here, and today the downtown business district of McAlester is in this area.

It was reported in late 1899, "The Choctaw railroad office forces have been consolidated, the headquarters having been removed from South McAlester, I. T., to Little Rock, and other departments also centered there." The move was reported by a number of newspapers, including the *South McAlester Capital*, which published the following.

> *Preparations are going on down at the general offices for the removal to Little Rock. The traffic department is topsy turvy, and by tomorrow everything will be in readiness. The boys are bidding farewell to their best girls, and otherwise getting in shape for the change. They say the change will do them good, but the boys, and also some of the girls, are very skeptical on this point. Anyway, they are getting ready, and will leave Sunday morning at 3 o'clock on a special train. The boys will leave very pleasant memories behind — in fact, it is believed that several of them will return in a very short time and take their pleasant memories away with them. But, be that as it may, all the young men connected with the department are nice, gentlemanly fellows, and will be missed in South McAlester.*

The *Arkansas Democrat* reported on the amount of work required to make the move, and the volume of the materials, furniture, books, and other materials that were hauled from South McAlester to Little Rock.

> *Six car loads of office furniture and records have arrived over the Choctaw and Memphis from South McAlester, I. T. These are the effects of S. J. Haydon, auditor of the Choctaw, Oklahoma and Gulf, whose office is consolidated with that of F. E. Hastings, who has been auditor of the Little Rock road. Mr. Haydon will be auditor. All of his staff, also the staff of Traffic Manager Holden, arrived. There are about thirty employees in the party, all of whom are now established at the general headquarters in the city. There was one*

> *car load of General Solicitor McLoud's library. All the staff*
> *of the Choctaw, Oklahoma and Gulf passenger depot, ex-*
> *cept General Superintendent J. H. Harris, came with the*
> *party. There was a whole train load, one reclining chair car*
> *being set apart for the employees. All the general offices of*
> *the Choctaw and Memphis are now located here.*

The Missouri-Kansas-Texas Railroad

The north-south railroad is the former Missouri-Kansas-Texas Railroad, known as "The Katy" for its early stock exchange symbol "KT". The rail line was one of the earliest built by the company, which started as the Union Pacific Railway Southern Branch, incorporated in Kansas on September 25, 1865. Construction started near Fort Riley in Kansas, and headed west. At the time, the federal government wanted a railroad built across the region to connect various military posts. To do this, it offered land grants and the exclusive right to build through the Indian territories to whichever railroad first reached the southern Kansas border at a point in the Neosho Valley.

As construction was nearing the border, the railroad changed its name to the Missouri, Kansas & Texas Railway Company on May 14, 1870. The next day, the MK&T Railway consolidated with the Labette & Sedalia Railway Company and the Neosho Valley & Holden Railway Company to create the Missouri, Kansas & Texas Railroad Company. The new MK&T Railroad reached the border south of Chetopa, Kansas, on July 12, 1870. The land grants through Indian Territory were never awarded, but investors jumped on the company's stock because of its ability to build into the eastern Oklahoma coal fields. This led to a name change to the Missouri, Kansas & Texas Railway Company on December 12, 1870. Yes, that is three name changes in one year.

Construction proceeded quickly, reaching Muskogee early in 1872, McAlester by mid-year, and the Red River was crossed by the end of 1872. Denison, Texas, was created as the southern headquarters in 1873. However, the construction created a great deal of debt, and The Panic of 1873 caused the railroad to enter receivership. The company was reorganized under its own name and was leased to the Missouri Pacific from 1880 until 1888. During this time, coal mines were developed by the railroad, which later became the property of the Missouri, Kansas & Texas. On November 24, 1899, the Missouri, Kansas & Texas Railway Company consolidated with The Kansas City & Pacific Railroad Company (incorporated in Kansas on July 24, 1886) to form the new Missouri, Kansas & Texas Railway Company. The new company again started building lines, including one to Oklahoma City in 1903, and leasing others such as the Wichita Falls & Northwestern (leased in 1914 and acquired in 1922).

The railroad was again in trouble by the 1910s, and entered receivership. In 1923, the railroad was again reorganized, becoming the Missouri-Kansas-Texas Railroad Company. The new company cut costs and survived the Great Depression, but became one of the weaker granger railroads serving the region. When the Rock Island folded, the Missouri-Kansas-Texas acquired several Rock Island lines through purchase and lease, often using the Oklahoma-Kansas-Texas as the company. On August 12, 1988, Union Pacific acquired The Katy through its Missouri Pacific subsidiary. It was formally merged into the Missouri Pacific on December 1, 1989, and now is simply a part of Union Pacific.

368.0 WEST END MCALESTER SIDING – The Rock Island showed that this siding was 6538 feet long in 1979, one of the longest on the entire line.

369.7 TAYLOR INDUSTRIAL PARK – The shippers to the south explain why the Arkansas-Oklahoma Railroad has leased 5.54 miles of Union Pacific (former Rock Island) track west to Milepost 370.5. Shippers include the Berry Plastics Corporation and Dura-Line. Berry Plastics started as Imperial Plastics in 1967, and became Berry Plastics in 1983. The firm started in the injection molding industry, and has expanded into many product lines under the name Berry Global. The plant is normally full of large covered hoppers handling plastic pellets.

Dura-Line also receives specialty plastics, as it manufactures various types of High Density Polyethylene (HDPE) conduits and pipes. The firm was founded in 1971 in Middlesboro, Kentucky, manufacturing water and gas products. It produced the first conduit for the telecom industry, especially fiber optic subduct. By 2012, the firm had twenty manufacturing facilities worldwide.

This industrial park sits on Union Pacific track, but is served by
the Arkansas-Oklahoma Railroad through a lease agreement.

370.5 END OF ARKANSAS-OKLAHOMA RAILROAD – Since 1997, the
Arkansas-Oklahoma Railroad has leased the former Choctaw Route
this far to provide service to the Taylor Industrial Park. In 1992, Union
Pacific obtained authority to abandon the Shawnee branch between
McAlester and Wewoka, Oklahoma, after several potential operators
inspected the line. However, the tracks were never removed, and in
2011, Union Pacific requested approval to keep the line in place but not
operate over it.

Milepost 370.5 is not far west of the Indian Nation Turnpike overpass, and the Oklahoma Highway 31 grade crossing.

McAlester (OK) to Tecumseh Junction (OK)
Union Pacific Railroad – Out of Service

Not long after the Rock Island Railroad shut down, parts of the railroad across Oklahoma were sold. The tracks from McAlester west to El Reno, Oklahoma, were acquired by the Missouri-Kansas-Texas System, which consisted of the original Missouri-Kansas-Texas and its Oklahoma, Kansas & Texas. Until 1988, the line from McAlester to Shawnee and on to Harter was operated as the Oklahoma Subdivision. On August 12, 1988, Union Pacific acquired The Katy through its Missouri Pacific subsidiary. It was formally merged into the Missouri Pacific on December 1, 1989, and now is simply a part of Union Pacific.

Union Pacific operated the line west from McAlester for a few years, calling it the Shawnee Subdivision, and then the Shawnee Branch. In 1992, Union Pacific obtained authority to abandon the Shawnee branch between McAlester (MP 370.5) and Wewoka (MP 418.7), Oklahoma, after several potential operators inspected the line. However, the tracks were never removed, and in 2011, Union Pacific requested approval to keep the line in place but not operate over it between McAlester (MP 370.5) and Seminole (MP 428.0). The notice was published in the January 12, 2012, *Federal Register*.

370.5 END OF ARKANSAS-OKLAHOMA RAILROAD – Since 1997, the Arkansas-Oklahoma Railroad has leased the former Choctaw Route this far to provide service to the Taylor Industrial Park. In 1992, Union Pacific obtained authority to abandon the Shawnee branch between McAlester and Wewoka, Oklahoma. The tracks were never removed and in 2011, Union Pacific requested approval to keep the line in place but not operate over it. Some of this track is now operated by the Arkansas-Oklahoma Railroad.

Milepost 370.5 is not far west of the Indian Nation Turnpike overpass, and the Oklahoma Highway 31 grade crossing. Heading west, the railroad generally follows Oklahoma Highway 31 to Haywood. This area features a mix of rolling pasture and woods. There are a number of small deck plate girder spans over a series of wandering streams. In places, there are stored cars along the line, but the route has become heavily overgrown due to the lack of operating trains.

374.7 HIGHWAY 31 – This grade crossing is where the railroad exits the woods and returns to the shoulder of the highway. At one time, there was a siding east of here, located on the south side of the mainline. A station was once located at the Meredith Road grade crossing.

376.4 BARNETT – This station was listed in several 1899 timetables of the Choctaw, Oklahoma & Gulf. In 1906, a topography map of the area showed this to be Barnett Station. The railroad has been following Deer Creek through this area.

377.4 HAYWOOD – Haywood is a small unincorporated community just north of the McAlester Army Ammunition Plant, near the north entrance. The town was located at the west end of the McAlester Coal District. As with many of the coal towns, it was created as the mines opened. A post office opened on September 20, 1904, but it closed in 1995. Unique for the area, the town was not named for a mine owner or operator. Instead, it was named for William D. "Big Bill" Haywood, a prominent socialist and labor leader during the early 1900s.

Big Bill Haywood was the founding member and leader of the Industrial Workers of the World (IWW), and he also served on the executive committee of the Socialist Party of America. He participated in a number of labor strikes and government movements, even calling for a violent overthrow of the United States government. He regularly called for one union that represented all workers, no matter their craft or race. Many of his actions were so far out of the norm that Haywood was often rejected by union leadership. His call for violence even led him to be recalled from the Socialist Party executive committee in 1913.

Big Bill faced several trials for murder, assault and property destruction, but he was finally found guilty of violating the Espionage Act of 1917. After several appeals, he was released on bail and fled to Russia to serve as labor advisor to Lenin's Bolshevik government. After two years, he was removed from that position and was involved with creating industrial colonies, many of which were failures. He died of alcoholism and diabetes in Russia in 1928, after several years of reported depression and loneliness.

The railroad has a wye to the south that connects with the government railroad in the ammunition plant, allowing rail service from either direction on the Rock Island. A rail connection was also built to the Missouri-Kansas-Texas line to provide multiple options for rail shipments. However, when Union Pacific gained control of both lines, the MKT route became the preferred route and the Rock Island line was closed. Besides the wye, a small yard was located south of the mainline, now hidden by heavy brush. For the train crews, the railroad had a dispatcher telephone at Haywood.

Haywood itself now consists of several blocks of scattered houses, the Haywood Public School, and Haywood Baptist Church. Just to the south are thousands of bunkers (igloos) that are used to hold the munitions manufactured and stored by the McAlester Army Ammunition Plant.

Heading west, the railroad curves through woods and a number of new natural gas wells.

McAlester Army Ammunition Plant

To the south of the tracks, and clearly marked by fencing and warnings about trespassing, is the McAlester Army Ammunition Plant (MCAAP). This facility is known as the premier bomb-loading and warhead-loading facility for the U.S. Department of Defense. It is one of fourteen installations that are part of the Joint Munitions Command (JMC). Besides manufacturing, MCAAP also receives, demilitarizes, and disposes of conventional ammunition components. It is the largest such facility in terms of storage, and it holds almost one-third of the Department of Defense's munitions stockpile. The property includes 44,964 acres, 2891 buildings, 2426 munition igloos, and a total storage capacity of 8,840,559 square feet.

Haywood is probably best known today as an entrance to the McAlester Army Ammunition Plant. The fence around the facility is covered with warning signs, such as this one at Haywood.

For the rail enthusiast, the MCAAP has 223 miles of track. This is 25 percent of the total of the Joint Munitions Command, or almost ten percent of the total owned by the Army. The McAlester facility is also the home of the Army Center of Excellence for Railroad Infrastructure Repair. The track crews based here handle projects for facilities from across the country.

The plant began as the McAlester Naval Depot on May 20, 1943, as a part of adding weapons capacity during World War II. On October 1, 1977, the facility was assigned to the U.S. Army. In 1998, the U.S. Army Defense Ammunition Center (DAC) was moved to McAlester from the closed Savanna Army Depot. The next year, the Red River Munitions Center in northeastern Texas became the responsibility of the MCAAP. Since then, other facilities from across the country have moved to McAlester.

380.5 COAL CREEK BRIDGE – This bridge consists of a 100-foot through plate girder span over the water, with about 100 feet of timber pile trestle off each end. From here, Coal Creek flows to the northeast, merges with a number of other streams, and eventually flows into Eufaula Lake. Heading west, the railroad follows the grade created by Coal Creek to near Stuart, where the stream forms from the merger of a number of small streams.

383.2 COAL CREEK BRIDGE – This is a 100-foot deck plate girder span with almost 150 feet of timber pile trestle off each end.

384.5 COAL CREEK BRIDGE – This is another 100-foot deck plate girder span with almost 150 feet of timber pile trestle off each end.

385.5 COAL CREEK BRIDGE – This is a 100-foot through plate girder span over the water, with about 60 feet of timber pile trestle off each end.

386.1 COUNTY LINE – A small farm crossing is located at the county line. To the east is **Pittsburg County**, while to the west is **Hughes County**. **Hughes County** was created at the same time as the State of Oklahoma. The northern half of the county came from the Wewoka District of the Creek Nation, while the southern part included land from the Moshulatubbee District of the Choctaw Nation. The county, created in 1907, had a population of 19,945 residents when formed. It was named for W. C. Hughes, a practicing attorney from Oklahoma City who was a member of the Oklahoma Constitutional Convention. Because of the number of streams in the area, evidence of settlement dates back to at least 6000 B.C. Some of the sandstone overhangs in the area feature pictographs.

The original tribes moved out, and the Creek arrived during the late 1820s, and the Choctaw during the early 1830s. Coal mining has never been of any significance, but oil and natural gas wells can be found throughout the county, with drilling starting in the 1920s. Farming is a major activity, with cotton, corn, sorghum, and wheat being the primary crops. Timber farming has also become popular.

386.5 STUART – The Stuart area was once the Choctaw village of Hoyuby, and a Hoyuby post office opened on June 23, 1892. In 1895, the Choctaw, Oklahoma & Gulf Railroad built through the area and a stop was planned. In 1896, the station was named Stuart for Judge Charles Bingley Stuart of McAlester, who at the time was an attorney for the railway company. On April 14, 1896, the post office was also renamed to honor Stuart.

Stuart had practiced law in Texas, and was appointed to the United States Court for the Indian Territory in 1893 by President Grover Cleveland. Stuart stepped down in 1895 to enter private practice and to represent the railroad. He later was president of the Indian Territory Bar Association and the Oklahoma Bar Association.

Standing a block south of the Rock Island railroad grade is the Stuart Hotel, restored and now serving as the Stuart town hall.

The town grew quickly with access to the railroad, and the Stuart Hotel soon opened. There was little industry in the region, and farming was the major source of revenue for most settlers. Cotton was important, and 91 rail shipments of cotton were moved in 1902-1903. By 1909, the town had a bank, five general stores, two blacksmith shops, two lumberyards, a cotton gin, and several livery stables. Stuart was also big enough to support Baptist, Christian, and Methodist churches. The son of Judge Stuart, Royal C. Stuart, started his banking career as a cashier at the Bank of Stuart, and worked much of his life in the banking and investment industries. By 1920, the Town of Stuart also featured a gristmill and the Choctaw Cotton Oil Company.

The 1930s were not kind, but the town still had two cotton gins, a blacksmith, and to serve the local oil industry, the Texas Pipe Line Company. However, the two banks in town closed and the population dropped to only several hundred. The school system is still open, and there is still a post office, a farm and ranch supply store, and a gasoline and convenience store at Stuart. The population remains about two hundred residents.

Two noted structures at Stuart are the Stuart Hotel and the 1918 jail. Located south of the tracks, the Stuart Hotel was built in 1903 to serve the growing community. It closed in 1968, was placed on the National Register of Historic Places in 1982, and restored 1989-1991. Much of the interior is original, including furniture and fixtures, and the building now serves as the Town Hall. Further south is the small stone jail that was built in 1918 by Monroe and Raymond Elms.

Stuart has long had a siding and several industry tracks. There was a water tower here until the end of steam. A 4080-foot siding was to the north of the mainline, and a short 560-foot track was to the south, wrapping around the depot. After the station was gone, train crews still had access to a dispatcher telephone at Stuart. The grade is to the north of town and a few of the old railroad building foundations can still be found west of Roosevelt Avenue.

While the tracks have been removed from the Roosevelt Avenue grade crossing, this station sign still stands in the brush to the east.

Heading west, the railroad is almost impossible to follow as it passes through woods that have overgrown the right-of-way. The line crosses Coal Creek again, makes an S-curve, and climbs grades averaging one percent, topping off at 901 feet of elevation just east of the appropriately named Hilltop station.

386.8 COAL CREEK BRIDGE – This bridge consists of two 50-foot deck plate girder spans, with 40 feet or more of timber pile trestle off each end.

391.1 HILLTOP – Hilltop is just west of the top of grade, located at an elevation of about 885 feet. The grades from each direction were shown to be 1.0% and were the ruling grades between Booneville and Shawnee. Hidden in the brush at South 3845 Road is the mainline and a 2239-foot siding, located on the south side of the mainline. A dispatcher telephone was here in 1979. Little else was here at the time, but today several gas and oil wells have been drilled next to the tracks.

Heading west, the grade now drops at an average of 1.0% for the next four miles.

393.4 U.S. HIGHWAY 270 BRIDGE – The railroad bridges over Highway 270 using three ballast deck beam spans. Although it has been forty years since the Rock Island operated the railroad, the bridge is still clearly marked "Rock Island Lines."

Along the Choctaw Route, a number of bridges were lettered with "Rock Island Lines." The bridge over U.S. Highway 270 east of Calvin still carries these words.

394.4 **SALT CREEK BRIDGE** – Deck plate and through plate girder bridges were popular with the Rock Island Railroad. This is another 100-foot deck plate girder span. Off each end are more than 60 feet of timber pile trestles.

Salt Creek flows north from here and enters the Canadian River in about a mile. The stream forms near Gerty, Oklahoma, making it about 15 miles long. The name Salt Creek comes from several salt licks once found along the stream.

396.3 **KO&G CROSSING** – The location of the CRI&P-KO&G diamond was just north of the Hughes County District 3 Barn, east of Calvin.

The Kansas, Oklahoma & Gulf Railway (KO&G) actually started as the Missouri, Oklahoma & Gulf Railway (MO&G), incorporated on October 24, 1904. The railroad was backed by European money, which had made profits from several lines built through the coal country of Indian Territory (Eastern Oklahoma). The MO&G started construction at Muskogee, first building north. In 1905, the railroad expanded to the southwest, reaching Henryetta and Dustin, about thirty miles to the northeast from here. Construction proceeded slowly, with grading often ahead of the track laying. By 1909, the railroad had reached Calvin, and then a burst of energy had the railroad reach the Red River by 1910. A few other small additions were made over the next several years. Connections in Texas provided traffic from the south end of the railroad at Denison. Because of laws in Texas, a subsidiary, the Missouri, Oklahoma & Gulf Railway Company of Texas, was chartered on March 28, 1910, to handle the trackage in that state. The north end of the railroad was at Baxter Springs, Kansas, plus trackage rights over the Frisco to Joplin, Missouri, providing a large number of connections. However, the traffic wasn't enough to cover expenses, and the MO&G went bankrupt in 1913.

On July 31, 1919, the railroad was finally sold to the Kansas, Oklahoma & Gulf Railway (KO&G), and the Kansas, Oklahoma & Gulf Railway Company of Texas. Things didn't get better, and the KO&G entered receivership in 1924. By late 1925, the KO&G had been acquired by the Muskogee Company, which later also controlled the Midland Valley Railroad and the Oklahoma City-Ada-Atoka Railway. The Muskogee Roads, or Muskogee Lines, survived by being efficient, keeping costs low to match the freight and passenger volumes.

One major source of revenue for the railroad was bridge traffic between the Missouri Pacific at Okay, Oklahoma, and the Missouri Pacific-controlled Texas & Pacific Railway at Denison, Texas. In 1964, the railroad became the property of the Texas & Pacific Railway Company. The track in Texas was abandoned as duplicate mileage, and the KO&G quickly disappeared into the Texas & Pacific, and then Missouri Pacific. After Union Pacific and Missouri Pacific merged, much of the KO&G was rebuilt. However, the acquisition of the Missouri-Kansas-Texas resulted in Union Pacific owning too many north-south lines across Oklahoma.

The KO&G could at best be called curvy and circuitous, and very successful at avoiding major towns and online shippers. It was the obvious choice for elimination, and an application to abandon all but a few miles of the former KO&G was filed in 1987.

In 1979, the Rock Island Railroad showed that the crossing had automatic interlocking, as well as a dispatcher telephone. In 1986, Union Pacific showed that the KO&G line was their Oklahoma Subdivision of the Kansas Division. It was shown as a crossing with the Missouri-Kansas-Texas and that it was still an automatic interlocking.

397.2 CALVIN (CA) – For many years, Calvin was a railroad junction town between the Chicago, Rock Island & Pacific, and the Kansas, Oklahoma & Gulf Railway. Both railroads had a siding at Calvin, located on the north side of town. The KO&G siding was 4303 feet long, while the Rock Island siding was 4486 feet long. The Rock Island also had 2320 feet of other tracks, as well as a dispatcher telephone, in 1979. There was also an interchange track at the east end of the tracks that connected the two railroads together.

Railroads led to the creation of Calvin when the Choctaw, Oklahoma & Gulf built through the area in 1895. The town was initially called Riverview, and a Riverview post office opened on March 21, 1895. The name Riverview came about because the community was located on the hillside along the south bank of the Canadian River. The name didn't last long, and the station and post office changed to Calvin during June 1895.

The name Calvin came from landowner Calvin Perry. Perry's land was surveyed in 1895 by the Choctaw Nation Town Site Commission, and 350 lots were created and sold. While Perry was honored, J. W. Hundley was primarily responsible for the town's development. Hundley was a trader and banker who over the next several decades continued to invest in the town and built the largest mercantile establishment in Hughes County. Much of the business at Calvin was aimed at farming, especially cotton. In 1902-1903, there were 2935 rail shipments of cotton from Calvin.

A 1904 fire set the town back, but led to the construction of a number of more substantial brick buildings. The population passed 300 residents in 1905, and in 1910, the population was reported to be 570. With a ferry crossing the Canadian River that funneled traffic to Calvin, the town had four cotton gins, eight general stores, two hotels, and the other traditional businesses. Some unique industries at Calvin included peanuts and peanut-processing, and the Calvin Pickle Company, which was a curing station for cucumber pickle processors in Alabama and Texas. Cattle and hogs also moved by rail from Calvin, and the population peaked at 700 residents in 1920.

Although farming is still important in the area, Calvin has lost much of its importance, with most business moving to nearby Holdenville. The population dropped steadily after 1920, reaching 589 in 1940, 315 in 1980, and less than 300 today. Both railroads are closed, with one abandoned and gone. The Calvin Peanut Company still operates north of the remains of the tracks, which are covered with brush and trees on the north side of town.

397.8 CANADIAN RIVER BRIDGE – The Canadian River has long been an important river in Colorado, New Mexico, Texas and Oklahoma. It has served as part or all of the border of the United States, several Indian Nations, Oklahoma and Indian Territory, and many land grants and homesteader claims. The river is more than 900 miles long, making it the longest tributary of the Arkansas River. The river flows east from here, through Eufaula Lake, and into the Arkansas River west of Sallisaw, Oklahoma. There are actually two Canadian Rivers in Oklahoma. The other one is known as the North Canadian River, and the river this bridge crosses is sometimes called the South Canadian River to avoid confusion.

The former CRI&P bridge across the Canadian River has had a number of names over the years. These include the South Canadian River Bridge, the Calvin Railroad Bridge, and CRI&P Bridge #3978. The bridge is 830 feet long and consists of two 310-foot pin-connected Parker through truss spans over the river, and a single 210-foot pin-connected Parker through truss span on the east end.

Looking upstream from the U.S. Highway 270 Canadian River Bridge at Calvin, the former Rock Island bridge can be clearly seen. Looking downstream from the same location, the Kansas, Oklahoma & Gulf Railway can also be seen.

401.0 CINDY CREEK BRIDGE – This 116-foot-long bridge was rebuilt with three spans using welded flange beams. This type of bridge design was fairly common as a replacement along the Rock Island Railroad. For the next two miles, the track has been realigned by the railroad, and this bridge was likely part of the line change.

Cindy Creek forms in the hills to the north and flows about seven miles to the south to here, and then a few feet further to enter the Canadian River.

401.8 AGUA – During the early 1900s, this location was a flagstop for the daily McAlester-El Reno local (No. 47 and No. 48), but there was no agent assigned to Agua. The passenger service allowed riders to get on the train before 8:00am and travel west to Holdenville, Shawnee and Oklahoma City. They could spend a day conducting business, shopping, or seeing family. They could then catch early morning eastbound local No. 48, arriving back at 4:15am. This was probably not the most convenient schedule, but the station of Agua didn't last long.

402.8 EQUATION – In 1923 and 1927, track from Milepost 401.0 to 402.8 was moved to the north to avoid flooding from the Canadian River. This move increased the length of the line by about 0.20 miles, creating an equation of **402.78 = 402.59**.

Not far west of here at Milepost 403.1, the railroad passes under the Canadian River bridge of Oklahoma Highway 48. It then squeezes between the river and a hillside to the north before turning north-northwest for Holdenville.

405.2 BILBY – Bilby was also a flag stop, but it had more passenger train choices as No. 43 and No. 44 (*Fast Mail*) would also stop here. The stop had no agent and was located near the intersection of Ew 139 Road and Ns 373 Road.

Bilby was a confusing location that actually carried two names. The name Wecharty was used for the stop when the Choctaw, Oklahoma & Gulf built through here. However, Nicholas Bilby had settled on the high ground to the north and had opened a cattle ranch, farm and store. Soon, Bilby built stockyards, a lumber mill, a store, and his home near the tracks, attracting a few other settlers. Bilby's store was known to mint its own tokens, generally stating that the coins were good for merchandise at the N. V. Bilby store at Wecharty, Indian Territory. Bilby also built a two-room brick schoolhouse.

The community he created attracted a post office which opened on August 2, 1904, as Wecharty. For many years, his stockyards shipped cattle, hogs and sheep, and his warehouse shipped a number of crops out and farm needs in. Because of this, the railroad station was renamed

Bilby, but the post office remained Wecharty until it closed on January 15, 1912.

The different names for the railroad station and the post office resulted in several cases of confusion. One of these was when a family tried to visit sick relatives at Wecharty, but kept missing the Bilby station. The family was apparently confused about which trains stopped at Bilby (Wecharty) despite several railroad employees providing directions about which connecting trains to use. A family member passed away before they arrived and a lawsuit was later filed against the railroad. The legal case went through several levels of the courts, including the United States Circuit Court of Appeals, with the claim denied. The case was reported on in several magazines, and an article in *The Federal Reporter* (1911) also provided a description of the town. "Bilby is a small station with only a post office, one store, a small cotton gin, and three or four families."

405.7 SAND PIT – This station was listed in an 1899 timetable of the Choctaw, Oklahoma & Gulf. Several small ponds in the area show where the sand was acquired.

406.0 BRIDGE – This bridge features a 60-foot deck plate girder span, with almost 80 feet of timber pile trestle off each end. This unnamed stream drains the hills to the north and flows south under the railroad and into the Little River.

Just to the east (railroad-north) is the Holdenville State Fish Hatchery, located below Holdenville Dam. The fish hatchery is one of more than 300 fish hatcheries that were built or enlarged by the WPA (Works Progress Administration). About the same time (1932-1933), Holdenville Lake was built as a reservoir to provide drinking water for much of Hughes County. The WPA also built a caretaker cottage and office building here. Today, the fish hatchery and lake are operated together, with the hatchery involved with producing bass, and the lake managed to produce trophy-sized bass.

The Holdenville State Fish Hatchery stands just northeast of the Chicago, Rock Island & Pacific mainline near Holdenville, Oklahoma.

410.7 HOLDENVILLE (HD) – Holdenville is another city that was built as a result of the railroad. In 1895, the Choctaw, Oklahoma & Gulf Railroad built a line from McAlester to Oklahoma City, passing through what became Holdenville. Although a community already existed in the area, the new town of Holdenville was surveyed on September 19, 1895. Today, the Chicago, Rock Island & Pacific's mainline passes through downtown Holdenville, located between Choctaw and Oklahoma Avenue, heading southeast to northwest. It can easily be found as a large block-wide right-of-way through town with the remains of several grain elevators and warehouses.

Just as there are a number of changes with the railroad, there have been a number of changes with the city. Streets have had their names changed, and some routes which were once closed at the tracks are now open. Three significant streets have had their names changed over the years. Today's Broadway was Cedar Street in 1898. Oklahoma Street, which now runs along the north side of the railroad was once Choctaw Street. The road to the south was Railroad Street in 1898, but today uses the name Choctaw Street.

In 1898, the Choctaw, Oklahoma & Gulf was the only railroad at Holdenville, and there was a depot on the north side of the tracks in the middle of Creek Street, two blocks east of the Frisco, which built through the area a few years after the CO&G. On the south side of the CRI&P tracks at Cedar Street was the railroad's stock yards. There were also two cotton gins at Holdenville in 1898. One was the Owens Cotton Gin, located south of the tracks between Creek and Cedar streets. The other was the Red & Johnston's Cotton Gin, located several blocks to the east of the station. Over the years, other shippers also had tracks such as the Continental Baking Company and the Holdenville Water Works.

Today, the diamond between the Rock Island and the Frisco is gone, but the remains of the interchange tracks in the northwest quadrant remain. The one in the northeast quadrant is gone, although parts of the grade are still visible. About where the old express building once stood, there is a small white building. This building was used as a ticket office and train order station by the Rock Island after the joint station was torn down in the early 1960s. Next to the station is Missouri Pacific caboose #13062, disguised as Rock Island caboose #74848. This is one of the short cabooses that the Missouri Pacific built at their DeSoto and Sedalia shops in Missouri during 1981 and 1982. The cabooses were later assigned Union Pacific Class CA-34, and were the newest cabooses on the railroad. The caboose was retired on January 17, 1991, and eventually donated to Holdenville.

The depot built after the Rock Island moved out of the joint Rock Island-Frisco station still stands, used as a local museum.

The small depot at Holdenville carries these old-style Rock Island markings.

The City of Holdenville

> *I grew up in Holdenville, Oklahoma, where they liked to say "the pavement ends, the West begins, and the Rock Island crosses the Frisco."*

> T. Boone Pickens

The first town in the Holdenville area was Edwards's, located on the Little River near Bilby. Edwards's developed around Edwards's Store, opened by James Edwards during the early 1830s. The temporary Camp Holmes was named for Lieutenant Theophilus Hunter Holmes, an officer of the United States Army in the Seminole and Mexican–American wars. Later, he was appointed commander of the Confederate Trans-Mississippi Department during the Civil War.

Also in the area was the village of Echo (Creek for deer). Planning for the construction of the Choctaw, Oklahoma & Gulf Railroad, Echo was renamed Fentress and a post office opened using that name on May 24, 1895. The CO&G missed all of the existing settlements and the new town of Holdenville was located on the property of Frank Jacobs, John Jacobs, and Charlie Grayson. The name Holdenville came from J. F. Holden, Traffic Manager for the Choctaw & Memphis and the Choctaw,

447

Oklahoma & Gulf railroads. Holden led the driving of the last spike event of the Choctaw & Memphis in western Arkansas in 1899.

Holdenville began to take shape when the Fentress post office became the Holdenville post office on November 15, 1895. A private school opened in 1896, followed by a public school in 1904. The Town of Holdenville was incorporated on November 14, 1898, elections were held on December 27, 1898, and the first city council meeting was held on January 4, 1899. The population was 749 in the 1900 census, but another boom happened at Holdenville in 1901 as the St. Louis, Oklahoma & Southern Railway built through town. On September 10, 1908, Holdenville won a runoff election to become the county seat of Hughes County, leading to more development of the community.

Holdenville was initially a farm town, moving farm products like cotton (3227 rail shipments in 1902-1903), livestock and hides, peanuts, pecans, corn, hay, oats, sweet and Irish potatoes, and orchard fruits. By 1910, the city had three newspapers, five banks, three cotton gins, four lumberyards, a cottonseed oil mill, and numerous stores, restaurants and hotels. The population hit 2296 residents that year. Unlike many towns in rural Oklahoma, the Dust Bowl and Great Depression didn't impact the town greatly. The discovery of oil and the businesses associated with it actually led to another community boom. In 1930, the population peaked at 7268, there were five cotton gins and two grain elevators, as well as numerous oil companies at Holdenville.

During the 1920s and 1930s, Thomas Boone Sibley Pickens was working at Holdenville as an oil and mineral landman, obtaining mineral rights and leases for drillers. On May 22, 1928, his son Thomas Boone Pickens Jr. became the first child ever born via Caesarean section at the Holdenville hospital. T. Boone Pickens later worked in the oil and gas industry, becoming one of the leading supporters of the use of natural gas. During his life, Pickens donated more than $700 million to various charities and universities, including for the expansion of Holdenville's Grace M. Pickens Public Library, named for his mother.

The population slowly dropped to 4732 by the year 2000, mainly due to a reduction in agriculture and related industries, and the maturity of the oil business. The population has grown since, and companies such as plastics manufacturer Covey Corporation, lingerie manufacturer Seamprufe Corporation, fishing tackle manufacturer F. B. Fly Company, and the hog breeding operations of Tyson Foods have located at Holdenville. The city is back up to about 6000 residents and a number of retail stores can be found along U.S. Highway 270 on the north side of town. Many of the original brick and stone buildings still stand in downtown Holdenville, just a block or two north of the CRI&P tracks.

SL-SF Crossing

The milepost for Holdenville is also the milepost for the crossing diamond between the Rock Island and the Frisco. For years, it was an automatic interlocking. A joint CRI&P-Frisco passenger station was built in the northeast quadrant of the diamond. The office was at the diamond, with the general waiting room alongside the Rock Island. The baggage room was at the north end of the station alongside the Frisco. A separate express building stood east of the passenger station.

A National Railroad Adjustment Board report stated that up to 1952, "each road maintained an exclusive Freight Agent and staff at its respective office. The passenger station, separate and apart from either freight office, is situated at the immediate intersection of the two main lines, and is jointly operated by the two roads." At the time, the two railroads shared in staffing the passenger station. The Ticket Agent-Telegrapher was a Rock Island employee, while the second trick (shift) telegrapher worked for the Frisco. A third trick telegrapher also worked the station. This position swapped every three years between being assigned to a Frisco employee and a Rock Island employee. The reason for the report of the National Railroad Adjustment Board was that by 1952, business had slowed and the Rock Island Railroad wanted the Ticket Agent-Telegrapher to also do some of the work of the Freight Agent, such as signing reports and station drafts.

One interesting part of the National Railroad Adjustment Board hearing was a report on the tasks of the Holdenville Ticket Agent-Telegrapher. These duties were:

- *Handle all train orders during assigned hours for both Rock Island and Frisco.*

- *Handle all telegraphing during assigned hours for both Rock Island and Frisco.*

- *Handle the electrically locked interlocker for each freight or passenger train (Rock Island and Frisco) using the crossing.*

- *Assist in handling baggage and mail to and from trains of both roads.*

- *Sell tickets for both roads.*

- *Check baggage for both roads.*

- *Handle all inquiries from the public as to train fares, routes, reservations, etc., for both roads.*

- *Make station record of all tickets sold, both roads.*

- *Make separate ticket accounts for both roads.*

- *Make remittances for funds collected at passenger station, both roads.*

- *Supervise and make reports for station gum machines.*

- *Sell and make reports for traveler's insurance sold.*

- *Make all monthly ticket reports for both roads.*

- *Supervision of the Passenger Station.*

The station was a train orders station per Rule 221 for the Rock Island. The Rock Island had a 7215-foot siding that extended through town and across the SL-SF Crossing. The railroad was also shown to have a yard, with a number of tracks both east and west of the station. Holdenville was also a water station.

The Frisco Railroad

When the Choctaw, Oklahoma & Gulf arrived at Holdenville, it was the first railroad in town. On August 13, 1895, the St. Louis, Oklahoma & Southern Railway Company was incorporated under the laws of the Territory of Oklahoma. The company received the "right of locating, constructing, owning, equipping and operating, using and maintaining a railway and telegraph and telephone line through the Indian and Oklahoma Territories" from the United States Congress. The railroad was initially slow to build, having a line opened from Sapulpa to Okmulgee in the Indian Territory by the end of 1900. The next year, the railroad built on south through Holdenville and on to the north bank of the Red River, near Denison, Texas.

On June 22, 1901, the 193-mile railroad was sold to the St. Louis & San Francisco Railroad Company. The line quickly became important for the Frisco Railroad as it provided a route to the Dallas-Fort Worth area. The St. Louis & San Francisco Railroad was sold to the St. Louis-San Francisco Railway Company (Frisco) on September 15, 1916. Holdenville became Milepost 519.6 of the Creek Subdivision, a part of the Southwestern Division.

This route was a heavy freight route due to the connection to Texas. It was also a popular passenger train route, with *The Black Gold* operating between Tulsa and Dallas/Fort Worth. The train operated overnight, and in October 1959, southbound No. 517 left Holdenville at 12:36am, while northbound No. 518 was scheduled to depart at 4:00am.

The Frisco became a part of Burlington Northern Railroad (BN) on November 21, 1980. When the BN merged with the Atchison, Topeka & Santa Fe on December 31, 1996, the railroad became Burlington Northern Santa Fe, now known simply as the BNSF Railway Company. The line is now the Creek Subdivision of the Texas Division, and the Holdenville milepost is still 519.6.

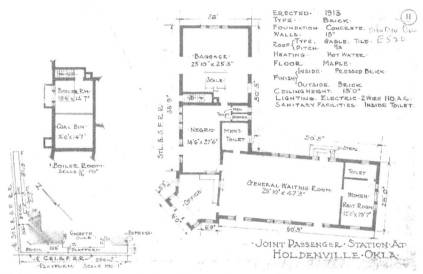

Holdenville Joint Passenger Station Diagram. Courtesy of Mike Condren.

411.8 U.S. HIGHWAY 270 – The railroad and U.S. Highway 270 again meet, this time with the railroad passing under the highway. Heading railroad-west from Holdenville, the tracks actually are going north-north-west until the county line, and then they turn to the northwest and eventually west as they near Oklahoma City.

414.7 COUNTY LINE – The county line is just west of the Jacobs Creek bridge, made up of three deck plate girder bridge spans (30-foot, 50-foot and 59-foot), creating a 139-foot-long bridge. Jacobs Creeks forms about ten miles to the south and flows north under the railroad and into Wewoka Creek to the north. To the east is **Hughes County**, while to the west is **Seminole County**. The railroad has been passing through rolling pastureland and soon begins following Wewoka Creek.

The name **Seminole County** comes about from the resettlement of the area by the Seminoles. During the 1830s, the area was assigned to the Creek and Seminole tribes. In 1856, the Seminoles were moved east, and then back to the area after several agreements, including the Re-

451

construction Treaties of 1866. Wewoka became the capitol of the Seminoles after they bought additional land from the Creek Nation and the federal government. In 1905, the Seminole participated in the Sequoyah Convention, which attempted to make Indian Territory its own state. When Indian Territory and Oklahoma Territory were combined and the State of Oklahoma was created in 1907, Seminole County was also created. The first courthouse was the old Seminole National Capitol building. While Seminole County often had its economy based on farming, its lands were much less suited for farming than those to the south and east. Crop failures were common, but oil discoveries in the 1920s helped the local economy, although when drilling ended, almost 20,000 residents left the county. This may seem large, but the county grew from 23,808 residents in 1920 to 79,621 in 1930.

Seminole County stretches from the Canadian River northward to the North Canadian River, about fifty miles east of Oklahoma City. Interstate 40 passes through the north end of the county, and its county seat is still Wewoka. The population is down to about 25,000, with about 70% of the residents being white and 20% being American Indian.

417.4 NU METALS – In 1969, this was the Phillips Spur with a four-car capacity. In 1979, this location was listed as part of the "industrial or spur tracks between stations" in the Rock Island employee timetable. The timetable showed it to be at mile 417 pole 27, and the track was 564 feet long. Later, Missouri-Kansas-Texas and Union Pacific records show it at Milepost 417.4.

Nothing remains here today but an abandoned grade to the south, located just east of a 150-foot-long timber pile trestle.

418.7 WEWOKA (WA) – Wewoka is an unusual place along the railroad as the railroad station still stands. The wooden station is where it once stood, but at one time it had been moved to Bowlegs, about ten miles to the west of Wewoka. However, in 2002, the building was moved back to here and restored. It is now used by the local Chamber of Commerce. Next to the station is Missouri Pacific caboose #13082, relettered for the Rock Island Railroad. Like the caboose at Holdenville, this is one of the short cabooses that the Missouri Pacific built at their DeSoto and Sedalia shops in Missouri during 1981 and 1982. The cabooses were later assigned Union Pacific Class CA-34, and were the newest cabooses on the railroad. The caboose was one of the last retired and was still in service in May 1995.

The station and railroad are at the very north end of Wewoka. The station handled train orders per Rule 221. Rule 221 was part of the railroad industry's Standard Code, and allowed the use of train order signals at stations. The version that the Rock Island used was technically Rule 221(A), which provided for the signal to stand normally in the "stop" position, and could only be cleared to allow a train to proceed or when there was no operator on duty. Generally, the railroad used the three-position semaphore as the standard train order signal. Basically, this allowed the trains to be told to stop and sign for orders (Form #31), to pick up orders while moving (Form #19), or to proceed without picking up any orders.

Besides the station, Wewoka was also declared a water station. In 1979, the railroad had a 2400-foot siding on the north side of the mainline, along with several spur tracks. To the south was a short industrial siding, with the non-siding tracks totaling 2950 feet of capacity. The small yard was probably large for a community the size of Wewoka, but several histories of Wewoka claim that it "was the largest such system of Rock Island's west of the Mississippi," certainly a great exaggeration. However, Wewoka was a busy station, handling a large area of demand. The oil boom of the 1920s overwhelmed the station, and soon there were more freight cars than tracks. This led to the inability to unload freight cars even when they were at Wewoka, and the name of the station became a cuss word in the region. Phrases such as "Worse than a Wewoka Switch", "Lost in Wewoka Switch", and "I'm caught in a Wewoka Switch" became common statements of frustration and futility.

The Wewoka station has been restored and now houses the Wewoka Chamber of Business & Industry.

Wewoka and the National Register of Historic Places

What is called the "Wewoka Switch and Side Tracks" is listed on the National Register of Historic Places. The location was identified in 1985 in its application as follows.

> *The Wewoka Switch and Side Tracks consist of four switch stands and approximately .56 mile of tracks. There are two switch stands at the east end of the system and two at the west end.*

However, there are clearly a number of errors in the application. One of these states that "during the pre-statehood railroad era in Indian Territory, it was the only side track between Oklahoma City and Little Rock." It also stated that "[e]ven though other side tracks were soon built, it has remained the longest side track system on the Rock Island route from Oklahoma City to Little Rock." This statement obviously overlooks places like Booneville (AR), Haileyville (OK), and Shawnee (OK), which once had large yard complexes. The application also states that "the depot was destroyed by fire in the 1930s."

City of Wewoka

Wewoka, or as often promoted, Wewoka Switch, is one of the oldest communities in Oklahoma, with a community started in the area by John Horse and a number of Black Seminoles in January 1849. The city was officially founded in 1866 by Elijah Brown as part of the Reconstruction Treaties of 1866, which allowed the Seminoles to return to this part of Oklahoma, where they had first moved during the 1830s.

After the Civil War, Wewoka was chosen as the capitol of the Seminoles, and a capitol building and several other government structures were erected. A post office opened at Wewoka on May 13, 1867, with the official document stating We-Wo-Ka, Seminole Nation, State of Arkansas. The town remained a Seminole community until the 1890s when the Choctaw, Oklahoma & Gulf built their railroad through the community. This led more merchants and traders to open stores at Wewoka, and a number of warehouses were soon erected to handle goods for nearby communities. Farming and ranching were also popular in the area, and in 1903 the Department of Agriculture reported 1936 rail shipments of cotton from Wewoka during the 1902-1903 reporting season.

During November 1902, the town was expanded with business and house lots being sold by a raffle, part of a city reorganization approved by Congress. At the time, the area was still basically its own country.

The Wewoka Trading Company took advantage of this, becoming the largest general store in the southwest, and even printing its own money known as Choka Sodka. In 1905, the Seminole participated in the Sequoyah Convention, which attempted to make Indian Territory its own state. When Indian Territory and Oklahoma Territory were combined and the State of Oklahoma was created in 1907, Wewoka was made the county seat of the new Seminole County. The first courthouse was the old Seminole National Capitol building.

An oil boom started in March 1923, causing the population of Wewoka to jump from 2500 to nearly 12,000 (20,000 in some histories) in just a few months. The boom created a great deal of local trouble as the community couldn't handle all of the new residents, with many sleeping in tents. Businesses and drillers couldn't get enough supplies moved to Wewoka, and there are numerous stories about food prices and other basic supplies suddenly doubling in price. By 1930, the official population was 10,401, where it stayed for the decade. However, it dropped to about 6000 by 1960.

Wewoka developed a reputation of being very insular, and outsiders, including businesses, were not welcomed. Stores like Walmart were turned away because they could compete against the businesses of the city leaders. This led to a further loss of population with 40% of the residents leaving over the next two decades. Efforts over the past several decades have attempted to reverse this trend and bring jobs to the area. The Seminole National Museum is located in a building built by the Works Progress Administration (WPA) in 1934. Just north of the train station is the factory of Expanded Solutions, a firm formed in December 2002 from Acker Industries. The company manufactures expanded metals, security mesh, mini-mesh and expanded grating. Wewoka is still the capitol of the Seminole Nation of Oklahoma, but has only about 3200 residents today. The entire town is to the south of the tracks, stretched all the way to U.S. Highway 270, where many of the Seminole Nation offices are located.

Finally – the name Wewoka deserves an explanation. Most sources state that the word means Barking Water in the Seminole language. Wewoka was located in a bend in the nearby Wewoka Creek, and the stream has several small rapids in the area. However, several historians have made the claim that the town was actually named Wewokea after Osceola's second wife. Osceola was actually a mix of Creek, Scottish, English and African-American, but he joined the Seminole when his family fled to Florida after the Creek Wars. Osceola was one of the last military leaders of the Seminole before he was captured in 1837. He died in captivity in 1838, having never been to Oklahoma.

419.9 WEWOKA CREEK BRIDGE – This bridge is a total of 134 feet long, consisting of seven beam spans, all open deck. Wewoka Creek is about fifty miles long, with its headwaters near Earlsboro, Oklahoma. The creek then heads southeast to Wewoka, where it flows east into the North Canadian River east of Wetumka, Oklahoma.

With the railroad closely following Wewoka Creek, the railroad has to cross a number of small streams as they flow into the larger creek. Because of this, there are several dozen small timber pile trestles over the next several miles.

422.0 WEWOKA BRICK – The Rock Island Railroad showed that there was a small spur track here in 1979, located just east of where Old Highway 270 bridges over the railroad. Later, both the Missouri-Kansas-Texas and Union Pacific showed the station as Brick. To the north is the Commercial Brick Corporation. While once a noted railroad user, rail service is no longer provided to the brick plant, or anyone in this area.

This brick plant, and the large associated clay quarry, was started in 1925 by the Wewoka Brick & Tile Company. In 1975, the plant and quarry became the Commercial Brick Corporation, a family-owned company. It initially produced about 25 million king-size face brick per year using a Lingl kiln, serving the Oklahoma market. It has expanded to serve neighboring states like Arkansas and Texas by adding a second Lingl kiln and automating many of the brick handling processes. The firm is now the largest employer in the rural Wewoka area.

Old Highway 270 essentially passes through the middle of the Commercial Brick plant, once a significant customer for the Rock Island Railroad.

In 2011, the firm looked to cut the costs of the natural gas-fired kilns. The WCA Waste Corporation was using part of the old quarry as a landfill, and was able to supply biogas methane from the decomposing matter in the facility. With methane often considered as a waste gas, finding a use for it had benefits for both companies. WCA installed vertical gas wells in the landfill, connecting them to a central blower. The methane is then pushed through a half-mile pipeline to the brick kilns.

424.1 U.S. HIGHWAY 270 – The railroad again passes under U.S. Highway 270, which is a two-lane highway through this area.

425.0 LIMA – Lima is considered to be one of the surviving historically All-Black Towns in Oklahoma, although the latest census showed that almost 45% of the residents were white and 35% were African-American. The town was founded about 1900 by Seminoles and Seminole Freedmen. Seminole Freedmen, also known as Black Seminoles, were slaves that had fled to the protection of the Seminole tribe. This started in the late 1600s when Spain offered freedom to fugitives who came to Spanish Florida and agreed to defend the Spanish crown. Another migration of escaped slaves came to Florida during the American Revolution, attracted by promises of freedom if they supported the British army. As described by the Seminole Nation Museum, these "black fugitives were forming strategic alliances with another set of newcomers to Florida, Seminole Indians, who migrated from Georgia and Alabama" by the 1780s. Many of the Seminole Freedmen moved to Indian Territory during the 1840s, but some fled to Mexico to escape possible re-enslavement. Some became members of the Seminole Negro Indian Scouts and helped to pacify the Texas frontier during the 1870s. A number remained or returned to the Seminole lands in Indian Territory. "Today, the Seminole Nation of Oklahoma has two Freedman Bands, the Cesar Bruner Band and Doser Barkus Band. Each band has its own form of tribal leadership and three General Council Representatives."

Reports claim that the name Lima came from the local limestone quarries. A post office opened in 1907, and the *Lima Observer* newspaper was publishing by the mid-1910s. Lima was incorporated in 1913, and over the next decade, the Mount Zion Methodist Church and the brick Rosenwald Hall were built. Rosenwald Hall served as the public school with classes up to the eighth grade, and it was placed on the National Register of Historic Places in 1984.

The 1920 census showed 146 residents, about the same time that the Farmers' Union organized many of the workers at Lima, forming the first black affiliation in the country – Local Number One. An interesting legal case was settled by the Oklahoma Supreme Court in 1925 when it declared that the white school would be the racially separate school since there were 232 black students to 16 white students in the school system.

The discovery of oil in 1926 brought new residents to the area, and the population reached 239 in the 1930 census. Most of the oil workers and other newcomers settled just east of Lima, forming what was called New Lima. The new town opened its own school system, a post office in 1929, and a number of businesses. However, it never incorporated and census reports have always combined the two communities. The population dropped to 99 in 1950 and stayed at that level for several decades. The Lima post office closed in 1957, leaving the two communities with just the New Lima post office. The two school systems also merged in that year. The combined towns started growing again, reaching 256 residents by 1980. The New Lima post office closed in 1978 and the population has dropped sharply, down to 53 in 2010. The New Lima School is still used, but few other businesses exist in this very rural community.

The Choctaw, Oklahoma & Gulf built along the south side of Lima, and the New Lima High School and the remains of the town are to the north of the tracks. The railroad had a siding here until the end of the Rock Island, and then the Missouri-Kansas-Texas and Union Pacific also kept it in service. The siding is to the south of the mainline and measured 5635 feet. A dispatcher telephone also stood here in 1979.

427.7 HALLIBURTON OIL WELL CEMENTING COMPANY – Shown as being at Mile 427 Pole 31 in 1979, this was a short 340-foot-long spur track to the north of the mainline.

Halliburton started as an oil well cementing business in Duncan, Oklahoma, in 1919. During the 1930s, the firm tested a number of cement mixes, and then got involved with offshore drilling in the Creole Field in the Gulf of Mexico. The company was heavily involved in the oil fields in this area, sealing off wells after their drilling to increase pumping efficiency. Nothing remains here except a small clearing in the woods off Northsouth 3590 Road.

428.0 DISCONTINUANCES OF SERVICE LIMITS – As stated elsewhere, on January 12, 2012, a notice was published in the *Federal Register* about the use of the former Choctaw Route between McAlester and Seminole.

> *Union Pacific Railroad Company (UP) has filed a verified notice of exemption under 49 CFR pt. 1152 subpart F – Exempt Abandonments and Discontinuances of Service to discontinue service over a portion of a line of railroad known as the Shawnee Branch Line, between milepost 428.00, near Seminole, and milepost 370.5, near McAlester,*

*a distance of 57.69 miles, in Pittsburg, Hughes, and Semi-
nole Counties, Okla.*

*UP has certified that: (1) No local traffic has moved over
the line for at least 2 years; (2) there is no overhead traffic on
the line; and (3) no formal complaint filed by a user of rail
service on the line (or by a state or local government entity
acting on behalf of such user) regarding cessation of service
over the line either is pending with the Surface Transportation Board (Board) or with any U.S. District Court or has
been decided in favor of complainant within the 2-year period.*

Although this notice only covered the track between mileposts 370.5
and 428.0, the track is actually out of service further west.

429.4 FERTIG YARD – This yard is generally just referred to as Seminole
Yard, but some documents call it Fertig Yard. It is likely that it was
named after Clarence C. Fertig, who spent most of his career with the
Rock Island Railroad on the Oklahoma Division. He began his railroad
career as yardmaster at Shawnee, Oklahoma, in 1911, and worked his
way up to superintendent of the Oklahoma Division by the 1940s.

Fertig Yard included about a dozen yard tracks. Among them were
some facilities for the neighboring oil companies. Many of these companies had loading racks to ship oil to refineries around North America.
One that lasted long enough to be listed on the National Register of Historic Places was the Sinclair Loading Rack. The National Register stated
that Sinclair used the loading rack from the time of its construction in
1928 until the 1950s to transport crude oil to distant refineries. After
oil shipments peaked and began to decline, Sinclair began to also ship
natural gas byproducts from the facility.

The loading rack was used until 1970. The facility has now been demolished, but the foundations remain. The National Register described
the facility as follows.

*The Sinclair Loading Rack is an industrial structure con-
sisting of an elevated walkway, approximately 1500' long
and 5' wide, and a series of vertical standpipes (filling lines),
valves, and loading arms attached to both sides of the walkway. The loading rack complex, located between two side
tracks of the Chicago, Rock Island and Pacific Railroad, is
used for filling railroad tank cars from the top.*

459

This Russell Lee photo from August 1939 shows a typical tank car loading rack at Seminole, Oklahoma. Lee, Russell, photographer. *Loading platform for tank cars, Seminole oil field, Oklahoma.* Seminole, Oklahoma, Aug. 1939. Photograph. Retrieved from the Library of Congress, https://www.loc.gov/item/2017740726/.

This photo by Russell Lee shows a railroad tank car being loaded at Seminole, Oklahoma, during August 1939. Lee, Russell, photographer. *Tankcar loader, Seminole oil field, Oklahoma.* Seminola, Oklahoma, Aug. 1939. Photograph. Retrieved from the Library of Congress, https://www.loc.gov/item/2017740728/.

431.2 SEMINOLE (DM) – Welcome to the original home of the founder of Sonic Drive-In, that national chain of hamburger restaurants with speakers for drive-up orders. This is also the home of the Seminole Oil Field, one of the largest discovered in Oklahoma.

Seminole wasn't the first community here, and as with many places along the route of the Choctaw, Oklahoma & Gulf, the railroad somehow bypassed the earlier village. The town of Tidmore was once located about two miles west of today's Seminole, located "on low-lying and often muddy land near Wewoka Creek" according to a report by The Great Seminole Nation of Oklahoma. Tidmore began during the early 1890s as "the service center for the Seminole Indians, Seminole freedmen, and whites living nearby." About the same time, a contractor by the name Tidmore was assigned the job of building the Mekasukey Academy, a Seminole Nation school for boys that opened in 1893. This activity led to the town obtaining a few stores, a lumberyard, a bank, and a few other businesses. A post office opened on May 17, 1902.

When the Choctaw, Oklahoma & Gulf built through the area, the railroad stayed on the north side of Wewoka Creek on higher ground, missing Tidmore. Initially, no new railroad town was built. However, in 1906, a new town named Seminole was platted on the railroad, and the residents of Tidmore quickly moved east to the higher ground. On February 6, 1907, the Tidmore post office closed and one opened at Seminole. Due to the success of Seminole, nothing remains at Tidmore, and the Mekasukey Academy closed in 1930 and was eventually torn down.

Although a new community when the State of Oklahoma was created in 1907, the 206 residents of Seminole entered the campaign to be the new county seat of Seminole County, but lost to the larger and existing city of Wewoka. With no government activity, and an economy based upon local farming and ranching, the town grew slowly to 476 residents in 1910, and 854 in 1920.

The Seminole Oil Field

Things were generally quiet in Seminole until the mid-1920s. There were those who felt that the ground around Seminole contained great deposits of oil, and a number of oil companies located in town. The increase in population led to the incorporation of the City of Seminole on December 26, 1924. A report by the United States Department of the Interior, National Park Service, explains what happened next.

On July 17, 1926, the Fixico No. 1 oil well, located half a mile east of Seminole, was brought in as a gusher flowing 10,000 barrels of high grade crude every 24 hours. Drilled at a depth of 4,073', it had penetrated the true Wilcox zone,

461

> which was to become the most prolific oil bearing forma-
> tion in the Seminole Oil Field. With the discovery of Fixico
> No. 1, the Seminole Oil Field, one of the most important
> fields in American petroleum history, was opened.

Overnight, Seminole went from being a small farm community to a town hosting 25,000 – 30,000 – 40,000 workers, with numbers ranging wildly. Tent and shack cities sprang up, streets and roads quickly became mud pits, and claims were made that the "railway business in and out of the town soon was the third highest in the nation." Whatever the real numbers were, it was obvious that Seminole was overwhelmed by the sudden oil boom. New hotels, restaurants, and businesses of all kinds opened at Seminole and many nearby communities.

The 1930 census showed 11,459 residents, and it stayed about that number through the 1960 census. Many companies located here with plans to stay, resulting in structures like the Strother Memorial Chapel at the Maple Grove Cemetery, the W. E. Grisso Mansion, and the Home Stake Oil and Gas Company Building, all listed on the National Register of Historic Places. The Strother Memorial Chapel was built in 1928 to honor O. D. Strother, a founding father of the local oil industry. Strother had created the Home Stake Oil and Gas Company in 1917, and drilled a number of dry wells. It turns out that he was always on the oil; he just didn't drill deep enough to reach it. He died exactly four months before the Fixico No. 1 oil well hit the crude.

"The Home Stake Oil and Gas Company Building is significant because it is the only remaining historic resource in Seminole associated with the first petroleum company to explore, sell leases, and drill wells in the Greater Seminole Oil Field, a field which produced 702,157,800 barrels of oil from 1926 to 1936." This is how the National Register of Historic Places describes the importance of the building. After O. D. Strother's death, his son-in-law, J. R. Simpson, took over the company and built this building at 315 East Broadway in 1927, after the Strother A Lease became the richest quarter section of the Seminole Oil Field.

In downtown Seminole at 315 East Broadway is the Home Stake Oil and Gas Company Building, a reminder of the oil boom that essentially created the city.

Just east of the Home Stake Building is what was once a major competitor to the Rock Island Railroad – the Union Bus Station.

The W. E. Grisso Mansion is another sign of the wealth created by the oil boom. William Edward Grisso moved from Arkansas to the Seminole area about when the town was created. He planned to be a doctor, but didn't complete his training. Instead, he opened the Seminole Drug Store and made and lost money. However, he invested in the oil industry before the boom and became president of the Grisso Oil Company. He built the Spanish-style Grisso Mansion in 1926, which featured a large courtyard, accessed by eleven doors, making it a center of entertainment. Reportedly, every governor and major politician of Oklahoma attended an event at the mansion during the life of W. E. Grisso.

The oil boom ended by the 1940s, but other oil-based and natural gas products replaced much of the lost activity. Other businesses such as clothing (Wrangler Jeans) and boat manufacturing (Blue Wave Boats) have created jobs. Seminole State College and the Gordon Cooper Technology Center provide advanced education, and museums like the Seminole Historical and Oil Museum, and the Jasmine Moran Children's Museum, add to that effort. Seminole also hosts the typical hotels and chain restaurants found at almost any major transportation hub, being located on U.S. Highway 377 less than ten miles south of Interstate 40. The population of Seminole has been steady at slightly more than 7000 and the city remains one of the most prosperous in the region.

Troy N. Smith and Sonic Drive-In

Troy N. Smith was born in Seminole on May 26, 1922. He initially did things like drive a milk truck, and served in the United States Army Air Forces during World War II. After the war, he opened and operated several restaurants, including steakhouses and regular diners. His most famous was initially in nearby Shawnee, a hamburger stand called the Top Hat, which had the Log House restaurant in the rear of the complex. While traveling, he saw several diners with intercoms at parking spots. He quickly obtained the design of the intercom system, sold his restaurants to his partner, and opened his first drive-up restaurant on Harrison Street in Shawnee. He promoted that a customer could drive up, place an order through the intercom, and have the food delivered to the customer's car within three minutes by carhops on roller skates. He also added angled parking for more privacy and popular music on the speakers.

The second restaurant opened at Stillwater, Oklahoma, using the name Sonic. The slogan "Service with the Speed of Sound" was used, and franchises began to open across the country, with the company eventually based in Oklahoma City. For health reasons, Troy N. Smith stepped down from daily management in 1983, but remained on the board. Smith donated to numerous causes across the region, including education. When Smith died in 2009, Sonic Drive-In had 3600 restaurants in 42 states.

The Rock Island Railroad at Seminole

Initially, Seminole was little more than a flag stop for the railroad. In fact, Seminole wasn't even listed in the January 1910 *Official Guide*. This changed in 1926 with the oil boom. Suddenly, tracks were needed at multiple towns along the railroad, and the Rock Island couldn't keep up with the demand. A number of tracks were built near the station area, located around today's 1st Street at the south end of town.

Unfortunately, the railroad was already squeezed between the Wewoka River to the south and the town of Seminole to the north. Since much of the oil product activity was just east of Seminole, a yard was built about a mile to the east and used to handle the large volumes of freight that were moved during the 1920s and 1930s. A report available through the Oklahoma Historical Society describes the volumes of freight moved at the time.

> *The Rock Island worked around the clock to cooperate with the oil companies in handling shipments of oil field equipment, supplies, parts, pipes, and crude oil. Ten freight trains carried material in and out of Seminole daily. Not only did the depot handle oil field supplies, it was responsible for lumber to build houses and goods necessary for daily consumption by workers. During the peak production years, 500 carloads of lumber and 25 cars of fresh meat were shipped into Seminole on a monthly basis.*
>
> *In one month 5,000 carloads of high gravity oil or gasoline rolled out of Seminole along with a turnover of 16,000 cars of freight. From 1928 to 1935, Amerada Petroleum sent 40 tank cars each week to Imperial Refineries at Regina, Saskatchewan, Canada. Tankcars also hauled Seminole crude oil to refineries in Texas, Kansas, and other parts of Oklahoma.*

While the railroad was much less busy at Seminole after World War II, there were still a number of tracks being used by customers. Rock Island property leases during the 1950s and 1960s included Steelman Construction, Halliburton Oil, St. Louis Iron and Metal, Oklahoma Gas and Electric, Clausing's Feeders Supply, Noble Petroleum, and the Frito Lay Company.

In 1979, Seminole was still shown as a water station, and the depot was listed as a train orders station per Rule 221. There was a 2692-foot siding to the south, and a yard. A number of industry tracks were also still in place, located both east and west of the station.

What little track exists today is almost invisible, covered with years of vegetation growth. Located to the south of the intersection between Main Street and Osage Avenue is the former CRI&P station, now used as a restaurant. The building features the Spanish Colonial Revival architectural style popular with the railroad. The building is a one-story rectangular (24' x 95') building, with a gabled roof. The outside is a combination of red brick and white stucco.

Still with its Seminole lettering, the former Rock Island station still stands. It is currently used as a Mexican Restaurant, appropriate for its Spanish Colonial Revival design. Unfortunately, parts of the building have been modified and the building is normally surrounded by cars, making photography difficult.

432.9 TIDMORE – Initially, this station was known as Mekusukey for the Mekusukey Mission that is located several miles to the south. The Mekusukey Mission was built by the Seminole Tribe in 1891 as a school for boys. It closed about 1930. There was a Mekusukey post office 1894-1915. Today, the mission property houses tribal offices, a community center, recreational areas, industrial and commercial areas, and a cultural area.

The railroad later used the name Tidmore for this location. Tidmore was founded during the early 1890s as the service center for the Seminole Nation. The name Tidmore reportedly came from the contractor who received construction materials for the Mission. The village was originally located on low-lying ground that was flooded by Wewoka Creek. The railroad chose higher ground, so the town moved closer to the tracks a few years after the railroad was built. A bank, general store and lumberyard were here first, with a post office 1902-1907, but nothing remains today as the town moved east to Seminole when it developed.

435.8 TRACY – Tracy is a 4050-foot siding to the south, and the Rock Island had a dispatcher telephone here in 1979. The remains of the mainline and siding can be seen at the grade crossing with Northsouth 3520. Rock Island Railroad documents show that the elevation here is 905 feet, while Union Pacific listed it as being at 855 feet. The grade is uphill to near King at Milepost 441, at an elevation of 1103 feet.

Tracy was once a fairly busy location, as can be seen by some of the buildings in the area. During the 1950s-1960s, the Mid Continent Warehouse & Storage Company was located here. Today, to the south is Goff Inc. The company manufactures a complete line of abrasive shot blast cleaning equipment and hot water degreasing equipment.

437.4 WEWOKA CREEK BRIDGE – Heading west, this is the last time that the railroad crosses Wewoka Creek. Unlike the other bridges, this one is a 104-foot timber pile trestle.

437.8 COUNTY LINE – The county line can be found where a powerline comes in from the north, and then turns to the southeast to follow the tracks. To the east is **Seminole County**, while to the west is **Pottawatomie County**.

This land has a confusing history involving Indian settlement. Initially, the land was assigned to the Creek and Seminole after their forced removal from Georgia and Florida. Both the Creek and Seminole generally fought on the side of the Confederacy, and after the Civil War, much of their land was taken back by the federal government to be settled by tribes like the Iowa, Sac and Fox, Absentee Shawnee, Potawatomi and Kickapoo. In 1891, the land was moved from tribal control to individual ownership, and white settlement began in the area.

With the increase in population, a county was created in this area called County B, using Tecumseh as the county seat. In 1892, the county was renamed **Pottawatomie County** after the Potawatomi Indians. The Potawatomi (also Pottawatomi or Pottawatomie) lived in the Great Plains, upper Mississippi River, and western Great Lakes region. They were part of the Council of Three Fires, but most of the tribe moved west to avoid Europeans, and then were resettled in Nebraska, Kansas, and Indian Territory. A final big land run happened in 1895 after the Kickapoo Tribe gave up much of their land. Tecumseh remained the county seat until 1930 when the much larger town of Shawnee won an election to become the new county seat. The Works Progress Administration built the new Pottawatomie County Court House in 1934. Today, Shawnee is still the county seat, the county's population is about 70,000, and it is part of the Oklahoma City-Shawnee Combined Statistical Area.

439.1 U.S. HIGHWAY 270 BRIDGE – This 3-span-beam railroad bridge, crosses over Highway 270.

439.6 EARLSBORO – Earlsborough, as spelled originally, or Earlsboro, is a town of about 600. The town began in 1891 with the construction of the Choctaw Coal & Railway Company. It was strategically located about one-half mile west of the border between Oklahoma Territory (to the west) and Indian Territory (to the east). Because Indian Territory was legally dry, where liquor was not allowed to be sold, and Oklahoma Territory was about as wet as it could get, Earlsborough became known as "the town that whisky built and oil broke."

The name Earlsborough came from James Earls, the former orderly for Confederate General Joseph Wheeler during the Civil War. This made the town somewhat unique because Earls was black, a rare choice for the source of a town's name at the time. However, Earls was a successful local farmer and businessman. When created, the first three businesses were saloons, and even as general stores, liveries, butchers, and other businesses opened, reports said that 90 percent of the merchants were engaged in liquor sales. On June 12, 1895, the spelling became Earlsboro thanks to the post office that opened that day. The population passed 500 in 1905, but more than twice that many were often in town, visitors from Indian Territory.

In 1907, Earlsboro became dry when the State of Oklahoma was created. The population and trade activity immediately dropped, and agriculture took over. Cotton was an early crop, but shipments never approached those of neighboring towns. The oil boom of the late 1920s led to a large increase in population, The town quickly built things like a water and sewer system. A $100,000 hotel was built. Schools and a large number of new businesses opened. However, the oil field around Earlsboro was a bust, and production dropped quickly after 1930, as did Earlsboro's population. With all of the abandoned homes and businesses, and a fortune in unpaid taxes, the town went into bankruptcy, explaining the second part of the town's catchy reputation.

The final claim-to-fame of Earlsboro is baseball. Wilver "Willie" Dornell Stargell was born in Earlsboro, Oklahoma on March 6, 1940. Willie, also known as Pops, played 21 seasons for the Pittsburgh Pirates (1962-1982), covering left field and first base. Early in his career, he hit the first home run at Shea Stadium (April 17, 1964). Later, Stargell was a seven-time All-Star and two-time National League home run leader. In 1979, he won three of the most prestigious awards in baseball. These included the National League Most Valuable Player (MVP) Award, the National League Championship Series MVP Award, and the World Series MVP Award.

For the railroad, there was once a short siding to the north, and an industrial siding to the south at Earlsboro. Unlike many towns in the area, the railroad passes through the center of Earlsboro, not along the very edge of the community. Here, the railroad is also actually heading north-south on its west-east route. North of town, the railroad curves to the west around the Earlsboro Cemetery.

442.1 KING – King was once a siding south of the mainline, with a spur track to the north. It was located about where the Benson Park Road grade crossing is now. This area was known as the King Oil Field, mainly located to the north.

445.0 EAST END OF ARKANSAS-OKLAHOMA RAILROAD TRACK-AGE RIGHTS – The track east of here is basically abandoned, but left in place in case there is ever a need. The tracks to the west of Brangus Road are in service and operated by the Arkansas-Oklahoma Railroad (AOK). The tracks are owned by Union Pacific in both directions, but leased by the AOK to the west.

Tecumseh Junction (OK) to Goodner (OK)
Arkansas-Oklahoma Railroad Company

The operator of this part of the Choctaw Route is the same Arkansas-Oklahoma Railroad Company that operates from Howe to west of McAlester, Oklahoma. On August 12, 1988, Union Pacific (UP) acquired the Katy through its Missouri Pacific Railroad. UP took over operations of the line, but almost immediately began looking for someone to take over the railroad. The track from near Shawnee, and then west to near Oklahoma City, was leased to the Arkansas-Oklahoma Railroad Company in two parts. Most of the track was leased in July 2000. Information about the lease was published in the July 21, 2000, issue of the *Federal Register*.

> *Arkansas-Oklahoma Railroad Company, a Class III rail carrier, has filed a verified notice of exemption under 49 CFR 1150.41 to lease and operate 35.5 miles of rail line from Union Pacific Railroad Company between milepost 446.5, near Shawnee, OK, and milepost 482.0, near Oklahoma City, OK.*
>
> *The transaction was scheduled to be consummated within seven days following the July 7, 2000 effective date of the exemption.*

The second part of the lease came about in August 2012. This additional property was designed to reach a bit to the east of the North Canadian River where a new industrial park is being developed by the Citizen Potawatomi Nation. Information about this lease was published in the August 22, 2012, issue of the *Federal Register*.

> *Arkansas-Oklahoma Railroad, Inc. (AOK), a Class III rail carrier, has filed a verified notice of exemption under 49 CFR 1150.41 to lease from Union Pacific Railroad Company and to operate approximately 1.5 miles of rail line between milepost 446.5, at/near Shawnee, and milepost 445.0, east of Shawnee at Brangus Road, in Pottawatomie County, Okla.*
>
> *AOK states that consummation of the transaction will occur on or about September 4, 2012. The earliest the transaction can be consummated, however, is September 5, 2012, the effective date of the exemption (30 days after the exemption was filed).*

In addition to the track from Tecumseh Junction to near Oklahoma City, the Arkansas-Oklahoma Railroad also switches the Midwest City Automobile Logistics Facility. The Arkansas-Oklahoma Railroad Company is a Class III shortline railroad, based in Wilburton, Oklahoma. When created, the railroad operated seventy miles of track and served two customers between McAlester and Howe, Oklahoma. Within a decade, the company operated almost 120 miles of track, serving twenty rail shippers. The company handles products like coal, aggregate, decorative stone, wheat, corn, oats, frac sand and drilling fluid products, pipe, lumber, plastic resin pellets, automobiles, and various chemicals. The company has their own fleet of freight cars and also handles car storage for a number of companies. Besides direct on-line customers, the A-OK also has several transload facilities that allow shippers without tracks to use the railroad.

The track west of Milepost 445, owned by Union Pacific, has been leased by the Arkansas-Oklahoma Railroad Company.

445.0 EAST END OF ARKANSAS-OKLAHOMA RAILROAD TRACK-AGE RIGHTS – The track east of here is basically abandoned, but left in place in case there is ever a need. The tracks to the west of Brangus Road are in service and operated by the Arkansas-Oklahoma Railroad (AOK). The tracks are owned by Union Pacific in both directions, but leased by the AOK to the west.

The grade crossing signs west of Milepost 445.0 indicate the lease, showing the Arkansas-Oklahoma Railroad as the operating company.

445.4 IRON HORSE INDUSTRIAL PARK – Located between Brangus Road (Milepost 445.4) and the North Canadian River Bridge (Milepost 446.0) is the Iron Horse Industrial Park, a 400-acre plot of Native American trust land owned by the Citizen Potawatomi Nation. This ownership provides various tax incentives and other legal practices that can reduce lease rates.

The Iron Horse Industrial Park is a newly developed, general-use industrial park. Construction started in 2016, and the park includes 7000 feet of internal rail lines. The industrial park is also designated as a Foreign-Trade Zone, a magnet site of the Port of Greater Oklahoma City's Foreign-Trade Zone #106.

Ownership of the new Iron Horse Industrial Park
is made clear by this no trespassing sign.

Ground was broken on October 18, 2019, for the park's first tenant. The company is Pro Pipe USA, a manufacturer of high density polyethylene pipe for the oil and gas, mining, irrigation, sewer, telecommunications, geothermal and municipal water markets. The company will locate on 25 acres and build a 50,000-square-foot production facility. For the Arkansas-Oklahoma Railroad, high density polyethylene will likely be shipped by rail.

Just west of here is the traditional location of the start of the Shawnee Yard Limits for westbound trains. In 1979, this was located at 445 Pole 25, or about Milepost 445.6.

445.7 TECUMSEH JUNCTION – Where the Iron Horse Industrial Park was built was once Tecumseh Junction. A railroad branchline went south through Tecumseh and on to Asher, near the Canadian River. When the Choctaw Coal & Railway/Choctaw, Oklahoma & Gulf was building across this part of Oklahoma, the railroad was sued in 1895 to force it to built a line to Tecumseh. At the time, Tecumseh was the county seat of Pottawatomie County, and the railroad was building about five miles to the north. Tecumseh remained the county seat until 1930 when Shawnee was selected as the new county seat.

On August 20, 1896, the Tecumseh Railway Company was incorporated in the Territory of Oklahoma. It built 5.21 miles of track from Tecumseh Junction to Tecumseh. On October 12, 1900, the Tecumseh Railway Company was purchased by the Choctaw, Oklahoma & Gulf for $12,000. By the end of 1902, the CO&G had extended the railroad 20 miles to Asher, located on the north bank of the Canadian River. The railroad also built a depot at Romulus on the line. Cost for the line and its structures was reported as $422,873. On March 24, 1904, the Rock Island took over the operations of the Choctaw, Oklahoma & Gulf, including those on the Tecumseh Branch, also known as the Asher Branch.

The railroad operated the branch daily during the oil boom of the late 1920s and early 1930s, with crews and trains operating between the roundhouse and yards at Shawnee, east on the mainline to Tecumseh Junction and then south to Asher. By the late 1930s, the oil boom was over and train operations were down to a single weekly trip, or even just when enough freight was available to justify a run. Approval to abandon the line was received in late 1941, and service ended on February 10, 1942. The line was quickly abandoned for the track materials, which were used elsewhere during World War II.

The railroad once had a wye at Tecumseh Junction. Early maps show that the east leg of the wye crossed Brangus Road. About a half-mile south of Tecumseh Junction, the Asher Branch crossed the Shawnee Branch of the Missouri, Kansas & Texas, later the Oklahoma City-Ada-Atoka Railway (OCAA).

445.9 OCA JUNCTION – This was a relatively new junction on the line, created after the Atchison, Topeka & Santa Fe abandoned the route from near here on west to Oklahoma City.

The line started as the Denison & Washita Valley Railway Company, which built ten miles of track from Atoka to Lehigh, both in Oklahoma, in 1882. In 1886, the line was extended six more miles to Coalgate, Oklahoma. This track was soon sold to the Texas & Oklahoma Railroad Company when it was created on May 15, 1902. Immediately, the Texas & Oklahoma Railroad Company built forty miles of track northwest from Coalgate. On December 12, 1903, the Texas & Oklahoma Railroad and the Missouri, Kansas & Oklahoma Railroad Company (of 1901) consolidated to form the Missouri, Kansas & Oklahoma Railroad Company (of 1903). This new company extended the line on through Shawnee to Oklahoma City by 1904. This line stayed a part of the Missouri, Kansas & Texas until the railroad was reorganized in 1923. The new company decided that the line wasn't needed, and it was sold to the new Oklahoma City-Ada-Atoka Railway (OCAA). At first, the company was successful and it was acquired by the Muskogee Company in 1929.

The Muskogee Company was incorporated in Delaware, but was based in Philadelphia. Many of the founders invested in coal and railroads, including the Choctaw, Oklahoma & Gulf Railroad, and coal mines in Northeastern Indian Territory and Arkansas. When the company sold its stock in the CO&G, they built the Midland Valley Railroad from Fort Smith, Arkansas, to Wichita, Kansas. This allowed the railroad to serve many of their mines. The discovery of oil also landed in the lap of the company, and the owners looked to expand their rail network. Eventually, the Muskogee Company owned the Midland Valley Railroad; Kansas, Oklahoma & Gulf Railway; and the Oklahoma City-Ada-Atoka Railway. The OCAA operated a fourth railroad, the Oklahoma City-Shawnee Interurban Electric Railway, from 1924 until its final abandonment in 1930.

The Muskogee Company assets were sold to the Missouri Pacific Railroad in 1964, and the Oklahoma City-Ada-Atoka Railway became part of the Texas & Pacific Railway. Traffic quickly died, and the line was sold (almost given) to the Atchison, Topeka & Santa Fe Railway on December 1, 1967. This provided a route between Oklahoma City and Shawnee for the ATSF, allowing much of the former Eastern Oklahoma Railway route to be abandoned. Trackage rights were soon obtained over the Rock Island between here and Oklahoma City, allowing the OCAA line to be abandoned.

As a part of this agreement, a new junction was built just east of the North Canadian River bridge. This allowed the ATSF to abandon the former Oklahoma City-Ada-Atoka Railway bridge over the North Canadian River. The line to Ada was kept because it served a power plant just north of Konawa. The line from Ada to Shawnee was abandoned in 1982, caused by the loss of a bridge near Konawa that was damaged in a flood. By 1985, basically the entire OCAA was abandoned. Today, no sign of this junction can be found thanks to the grading of the new Iron Horse Industrial Park.

446.0 NORTH CANADIAN RIVER BRIDGE – The primary span of the bridge is a 150-foot riveted Warren through truss span. This type of bridge is fairly typical on the line. The through truss is on the east end of the structure, and a number of timber pile trestle spans are located on the west end, making the bridge 225 feet long. The bridge was rehabilitated as part of the development of the Iron Horse Industrial Park. When the work was completed, the Citizen Potawatomi Nation participated in a dedication of what was called the Iron Horse Bridge.

What is or is not the North Canadian River has changed a number of times, with the latest in 2004. From 1914 until 1970, the United States considered the North Canadian to also include the Beaver River, and tributary Corrumpa Creek, as part of the river. This extended it into New Mexico and Texas. This definition was supported by a 1914 decision by the U.S. Board on Geographic Names. However, in 1970, the U.S. Board on Geographic Names changed its ruling and determined that the North Canadian River began at the confluence of the Beaver River and Wolf Creek. This makes the river 440 miles long, all in Oklahoma. It is considered to be a tributary of the larger Canadian River, which is sometimes known as the South Canadian River, as they join as part of Eufaula Lake.

In 2004, part of the North Canadian River was renamed the Oklahoma River. This part was seven miles of river that flows through Oklahoma City. The renaming was part of the development of the river for recreation and competition. A series of small dams and locks were built in the river, creating a series of small lakes for rowing, kayaking and canoeing. A number of competitive events have been held on this stretch of the river, including at night thanks to a lighting system. It also includes a series of popular parks.

Further confusion about the name of the river is due to the number of names used by early explorers and settlers. Other names that have been used include Honih'hiyo'he (used by the Cheyenne); Branche Nord de la Riviere Canadienne; Beaver Creek; Beaver River; North Fork Canadian River; and North Fork of Canadian River. Another confusing element is that the origin of the name is not clear, but believed to be the Spanish word cañada which means glen. This term could have come from the broad canyons that the river flows through.

447.6 BRIDGE OVER BNSF – This is a 36-foot deck plate girder span that crosses a former Atchison, Topeka & Santa Fe line. The track below is the final remains of the Gulf, Colorado & Santa Fe Railroad that was built through Shawnee. Once a mainline, it is now the BNSF Shawnee Industrial Spur. The line is in service southward for about 1.5 miles to the north side of Firelake Golf Course to serve a scrap yard. Northward, the tracks go seven miles to an industrial area north of Interstate 40. Approximately one-half mile north of here is the former ATSF train station. The station is a unique Romanesque Revival structure with a dome over the circular ticket office and what looks to be a medieval watch tower. The building was constructed in 1902-1903 using cut red sandstone. It is now listed on the National Register of Historic Places and is the home of the Pottawatomie County Museum.

The Santa Fe station at Shawnee has got to be one of the more unique stations built in the country. It still stands not far north of the Rock Island and houses the Pottawatomie County Museum.

This line was built by The Eastern Oklahoma Railway Company, chartered on July 24, 1899. The company built a 180-mile rail line from Newkirk to Pauls Valley, both in Oklahoma. The line was essentially an alternative north-south main line, located east of the primary Atchison, Topeka & Santa Fe route, and connecting with it at both ends. The Eastern Oklahoma Railway Company was always a paper company, and the track was leased by the Atchison, Topeka & Santa Fe Railway Company as soon as it was completed, with the first track in operation on January 1, 1900. On June 20, 1907, The Eastern Oklahoma Railway was sold to the ATSF.

The line was obviously the secondary line when compared to the line through Oklahoma City, and the track from Shawnee south to Byars, northeast of Pauls Valley, was abandoned during the early 1960s. The line on to Pauls Valley was abandoned in 1971. An application to abandon northward from the Shawnee area to near Cushing was made on December 22, 1975. This left about eight miles of industry track in the Shawnee area. When the Atchison, Topeka & Santa Fe merged with Burlington Northern on December 31, 1996, the railroad became Burlington Northern Santa Fe, now known simply as the BNSF Railway Company.

447.8 ATSF JUNCTION – Now known as BNSF Junction, this connection is with the BNSF Shawnee Industrial Spur, once ATSF's Newkirk to Pauls Valley line built by The Eastern Oklahoma Railway Company. This junction is important for BNSF as the ATSF abandoned their line from Oklahoma City to Shawnee on December 20, 1971, and obtained trackage rights on the Chicago, Rock Island & Pacific. Today, BNSF trains use the line, now owned by Union Pacific, between Shawnee and the Harter Yard area in Oklahoma City.

These two signs mark the location of ATSF Junction.

For years, the Rock Island Railroad employee timetable noted the trackage rights and stated "ATSF trains and MKT trains will register at Shawnee by ticket Form 1339."

During September 2021, the AOK filed a notice to lease the Shawnee Industrial Spur from BNSF.

Shawnee Milling Company

To the south is a spur track into Shawnee Milling. Shawnee Milling is a significant industry that has been here since about the time that the railroad arrived. A historical marker stands next to the mill that explains its history. The original wooden mill was built in 1891, located south of

479

the North Canadian River. It was moved to its current location in 1895. As the company states in its history, "The original wooden mill...was dragged across the North Canadian River using horses, ropes and skids during a drought in 1895 to its current location."

The Shawnee Milling facility is almost impossible to miss as it is the large white complex on the south end of town, still standing next to, and served by, the railroad.

The Shawnee Roller Mills was bought by J. Lloyd Ford on April 20, 1906, and renamed the Shawnee Milling Company. The complex was soon expanded and Shawnee Chief Flour became a noted product of the mill. Another brand was called Climax, and it was renamed Shawnee's Best Flour when it became the best-selling product. J. Lloyd Ford acquired nine more milling companies across Oklahoma, using them to jointly market products. On August 11, 1934, the Shawnee Milling Company burned, and was rebuilt with a more modern concrete complex. It has continued to expand and modernize.

448.9 SHAWNEE (JE) – Shawnee is a land-rush town, created during the Land Run of 1891. The first land run had taken place in 1889, going after what was known as the Unassigned Land. For the Land Run of 1891, potential settlers lined up on the border of the Kickapoo Tribe for a chance at surplus lands of the Sac and Fox, Citizen Pottawatomie and Shawnee. Shawnee got its start when four people each staked a quarter section here, located just west of the line that would later become Kickapoo Street.

The four were John T. Beard, James T. Farrall, Elijah A. Alley, and Etta B. Ray. A month later, Etta Ray married Henry Beard, the brother of John T. Beard, and built the first cabin at Shawnee (listed on the National Register of Historic Places). James Farrall built the first street, which was named Farrall Street. With a town developing, a number of suggestions like Brockway, Forest City and Shawneetown came up for the town's name. Eventually, the name Shawnee was chosen to honor the tribe that had been living here.

Soon, lots were sold, a post office opened, and the population hit 250 in 1892. Records show that three streets had become the business district – Farrall, Beard and Broadway. They featured a number of stores and banks, two newspapers, two brickyards, a livery stable, three flour mills, and seven cotton gins. Much of this development was based on the speculation that the Choctaw, Oklahoma & Gulf would build through the area. To ensure this, Etta and Henry Beard gave the CO&G one-half of their claim of one hundred and sixty acres. With the arrival of the railroad, the City of Shawnee was founded on July 4, 1895. Within a year, the population passed 2500.

Things continued to grow as the Atchison, Topeka & Santa Fe Railway, and the Missouri, Kansas & Texas Railway, built through town by 1904. Again, the Beard family, as well as James Farrall, provided land incentives to the railroads, and businesses and industry developed on their city lots. The railroads also opened up markets to the local farms and ranches. Cotton, potatoes, and peaches began to be shipped, and warehouses and cotton gins and compresses were built. According to several sources, by 1902, there were seven cotton gins and two cotton compresses at Shawnee. They shipped 150,000 bales of cotton and 375 railcars of cotton products between March 1901 and March 1902. For 1903-1904, the Department of Agriculture reported that there were 26,147 rail shipments of cotton from Shawnee, and that it was a concentrating point for other local communities. Because of his, one of the largest cottonseed oil mills in the Southwest was built at Shawnee, and later the operation processed peanuts.

In 1903, another tradition of Shawnee began when Round House Manufacturing began producing ROUND HOUSE® workwear. The firm, which claims to be the oldest operating manufacturing company in Oklahoma, produced denim jeans and overalls based upon the needs of local rail workers. Round House now claims to be the largest manufacturer of American-made jeans and overalls, and is sold under its own name and under numerous private names through hundreds of stores.

The railroads were a great incentive for the jeans. They employed hundreds of workers at Shawnee, especially with the large Rock Island shops. According to the Chamber of Commerce, in 1907, more than one hundred trains passed through Shawnee daily, many crewed by residents of Shawnee. Shawnee had great plans, but was third in the 1910 election to determine the new state capital. It also lost out on campaigns to attract some other railroads and industries, but was successful in growing. The late 1920s saw the regional oil boom. Little oil was found at Shawnee, but a number of companies located here to be in a bigger city with better rail service. The population hit 23,283 in the 1930 census, and a campaign continued to move the county seat of Pottawatomie County from Tecumseh to the larger Shawnee. On December 19, 1930, a county-wide vote approved the change, and a new courthouse opened on July 6, 1935, built by the Works Progress Administration as part of its mission to employ workers and help local economies during the Great Depression.

Despite the Great Depression, World War II, and the loss of the railroad shops and many of the older industries, Shawnee never went through the bust cycle that was typical of many other Oklahoma towns and cities. The population slowly grew to 26,017 in the 1990 census. A number of small industries have moved in, many near Interstate 40. Additionally, retail stores, restaurants, and other such businesses can be found throughout town, especially along Harrison and Kickapoo Avenues. Much of the old downtown still stands, with many of the traditional brick buildings in use. As a part of creating a historical feel for the area, many of the streets are paved with bricks, or at least concrete stamped with brick designs. The population has hit approximately 30,000, and is still growing.

Shawnee has a long list of residents that can easily be identified. Actor Brad Pitt was born in Shawnee, while Robert Reed (Mike Brady of *The Brady Bunch*) attended high school here. Less famous might be Brewster Higley, but he wrote the poem that became the song *Home on the Range*. Leroy Gordon Cooper was born in Shawnee in 1927. Cooper was one of the original Mercury Seven astronauts, and in 1963, piloted the last of the Mercury missions. While on *Mercury-Atlas 9*, he became the first American to spend an entire day in space, the first to sleep in space, and the last American launched on an entirely solo orbital mission.

Another famous person who claimed Shawnee as home was Jim Thorpe. Actually born elsewhere and having spent much of his life traveling, Thorpe still considered Shawnee to be his hometown. Jim Thorpe, a member of the Sac and Fox Nation, was the first Native American to win an Olympic gold medal for the United States when he won the pentathlon and decathlon in 1912. He also played college and professional football, and professional baseball and basketball. Thorpe was inducted in the inaugural class (1963) of the Pro Football Hall of Fame. He was also voted as the Greatest Athlete of the Twentieth Century by an ABC Sports fan poll.

The Rock Island Railroad and Shawnee

> *Shawnee is in the geographical center of the state with*
> *railroads radiating in seven directions and within a day's*
> *ride of the farthest point in the state. There are three rail-*
> *road lines serving Shawnee. The Chicago, Rock Island and*
> *Pacific, the Atchison, Topeka and Santa Fe and The Mis-*
> *souri, Kansas and Texas. Division points are maintained*
> *for both the Rock Island and Santa Fe, approximately 1500*
> *men being employed in the shops and on the trains, all of*
> *whom make their home in Shawnee.*

This was how the November 1921 issue of the *Rock Island Magazine* described Shawnee. The issue had a short article about the community and many of the employees and managers who worked there. The City of Shawnee was greatly impacted by the construction of the three railroads through the area, with the large Rock Island shops on the southwest side of town, and the Santa Fe shops to the south, located between the North Canadian River and Squirrel Creek.

Based upon early information, it is obvious that the Choctaw, Oklahoma & Gulf and the City of Shawnee both benefitted from the other. By March 1898, the railroad had numerous facilities and served a number of customers. A station complex stood at Union Avenue, and Shawnee was the headquarters of the Indian Territory Division for many years. There were three buildings, with the station in the center, a baggage and express office to the west, and a lunch house to the east, all connected by a single platform. The mainline and a second track were to the south of these buildings, with a siding to the north, which served the Anheuser Busch beer and ice house and a cotton storage shed.

Heading west, there were two cotton platforms to the north of the tracks, located east of Bell Avenue. The 150-foot freight house was located west of Kickapoo Street, again to the north of the tracks. South of the tracks and west of Broadway was the Shawnee Cotton Oil Company. The railroad also had a track down Oakland Street, with the remains now being used to serve Shawnee Milling. Just east of Bell Avenue, the railroad delivered coal to the Shawnee Electric Company. Just west of Beard, where a small rail yard was built, the railroad also served Shawnee Ice & Cold Storage and the Oklahoma Round Bale Cotton Gin.

The volume of traffic grew, and investments were required. As part of the improvements at Shawnee, the communications system was also being modernized. A telephone dispatching system was placed in operation during the summer of 1910 to control trains between Booneville and Shawnee. In 1909, construction began on a new Rock Island station. Using Southwest Spanish Heritage architecture, common along the Choctaw Route, the station opened in May 1910, as one of the largest stations on the line. It included a large passenger section, room for offices, and a multi-room baggage and express area. The station saw its last passenger train in 1967 and it was torn down during the early 1970s.

At the time, there were three passenger stations in Shawnee, and there was never a union station for the railroads. The January 1910 *Official Guide* provided information about the distances between the stations for those changing trains. It stated that the ATSF and CRI&P stations were "about 1/4 mile apart" while the ATSF and and MKT stations were "about 7/8 mile apart." The two closest stations were those of the CRI&P and MKT, which were shown to be "300 yards apart."

In 1922, the roundhouse at Shawnee received a number of improvements so it could handle the larger locomotives then being acquired by the railroad. Four new stalls were added to the structure, and thirteen stalls were extended. The 75-foot turntable was replaced by a 100-foot turntable, the final project needed for the new steam locomotives.

The Rock Island and its shop complex west of Beard Street kept the railroad a major employer until about 1939, when most of the shops were closed and moved to El Reno. Even with this move, train crews still changed at Shawnee. A sizeable yard remained west of Kickapoo Street. At the end of the Rock Island in 1979, the yard still included a fueling and water station, and there was a 3700-foot siding. The yard office hosted a standard clock, general order boards and books, and a wayside radio. It also served as a train register station and train order station. Because crews changed at Shawnee, the yard office did not feature a train order signal.

Today, a few of the yard tracks remain, and much of the property is used as a transload facility. The Arkansas-Oklahoma Railroad bases one or more train crews out of the Shawnee Yard office, and their locomotives can frequently be found here.

The Shawnee Shops of the Rock Island

As the railroad built across Oklahoma, it began locating crew change stops. At the time, steam locomotives and cabooses were generally changed with each crew, requiring at least a small shop complex to make inspections and conduct simple repairs. Larger shops would then be built every few crew districts that could do more major work. Additional shops were also needed to repair or build freight and passenger cars. In 1896, it was decided that a series of major repair shops would be built at Shawnee. As the Chicago, Rock Island & Pacific became involved with the Choctaw, Oklahoma & Gulf, more financing for the shops became available.

Located in southwest Shawnee is the former Rock Island Railroad yard, now used by the Arkansas-Oklahoma Railroad. The company has a small office here, identified by this sign.

With that, *The Railway Age* (September 6, 1901) announced that the Choctaw, Oklahoma & Gulf had issued contracts for "improvements and extensions to shops at Shawnee, Okla. The work will include four buildings, all of brick, with stone trimmings: blacksmith shop, 91 by 101 feet; an extension to the erecting shop, 60 by 91 feet; an additional story and extension to the woodworking shop, 91 by 119 feet; and a storehouse, 52 by 122 feet, containing a fireproof oil room. An office for the master mechanic at Shawnee will be fitted up in the new portion of the woodworking shop."

The shops at Shawnee were located about the center of the Choctaw Route, and were designed to handle all of the major work that couldn't be done by the smaller shops at Argenta, Arkansas. Different comparisons were used by different sources, but in 1908, the Shawnee Chamber of Commerce stated that these railway shops were the largest in the Southwest. Within a decade, the locomotive repair facility had twelve tracks and handled steam locomotives from the Panhandle, Indian and Southern Divisions. The freight car shops could handle 150 cars at a time, and repaired everything from flat cars to boxcars. The passenger car shop had twelve tracks. There was also a two-car paint shop.

All of these shops were located west of South Beard Street, and reports state that at least a dozen shop tracks crossed Beard Street, and the switching often tied up the street for hours. Additionally, a 10-track rail yard (later enlarged to 22 tracks) was located to the north and next to the mainline. One of the dominant buildings at Shawnee was the roundhouse, located at the south end of the shop complex and accessed from the west. Various Rock Island documents state that the Shawnee Roundhouse had 16 bays. Nine of these were 92 feet deep, while seven were 102 feet deep. The turntable was 100 feet long, making it one of the five largest on the Rock Island during the late 1920s.

The 1922 National Shopmen Railroad Strike led to changes, and eventually the closing of most of the shops at Shawnee. At the time, there were major shops at El Reno, Shawnee and Chickasha, and improvements in equipment and the maintenance processes required fewer shops. Changes at Shawnee were sped up by an evening fire on July 7, 1924, which burned the coach shop, car shed, master mechanic offices, storekeeper offices, the district accounting office, and a number of freight and passenger cars. A new 124' by 240' coach shop with offices on the upper floor was built, as well as several other support buildings.

The *Rock Island Employees Magazine* (August 1924) had an article about the shops, and stated that there were 985 employees at the shops, and the annual payroll was $1,316.111.28. The plans to move some of the shops away from Shawnee were put on hold due to the discovery of the Seminole Oil Field. Thousands of freight cars were suddenly needed to move the freight and oil associated with the oil boom, and the shops were overwhelmed. More employees were hired, a dozen more tracks were added to the Shawnee rail yard, and the mainline was double-tracked through town.

In 1927, a new car repair facility was built at El Reno, where the Choctaw Route met the Rock Island's Minnesota-Houston north-south line across Oklahoma. The end of the oil boom and the Great Depression allowed the Rock Island to start consolidating its facilities. At first, all of the back shops (locomotive heavy repair facilities) across the railroad were closed down except for Shawnee and Silvis, Illinois. In Oklahoma, the Shawnee shops were closed during 1939 and the work was moved to the improved shops at El Reno. When the round-house closed, the turntable was moved to Burr Oak, Illinois.

Most of the shop buildings that once stood at Shawnee are now gone. However, a few still stand, marking the location. The most obvious is the large car repair shop, clearly visible from South Beard Street. The engine repair facility has been rebuilt and is used as a garage for the City of Shawnee Public Works vehicles. A small oil house and a handful of other sheds also still stand, some occupied by companies that now use the property. A number of foundations and a few tracks are still scattered across the property, and there are efforts to find new uses for the site.

Lots of foundations and the former car repair shop mark the location of the once enormous Shawnee shop complex of the Rock Island Railroad.

The 1922 Shopmen Strike

During World War I, the United States government experimented with nationalizing industries, and the railroad industry was a victim of this practice. The United States Railroad Administration (USRA) took over most of the national railroad system starting on December 28, 1917. The government consolidated services between competing railroads, designed generic rail equipment, and even eliminated some railroads. To prevent any labor issues during World War I, the wage scales for most rail workers were raised by the USRA. Additionally, the federal government negotiated new labor contracts without the input of the railroads involved, leading to changes in work assignments, work schedules, and crew assignments.

The United States Railroad Administration returned the railroads to their owners starting on February 28, 1920. With an economic recession starting, most railroads cut wages back to what they were before government control, lengthened crew assignments, and made other changes that conflicted with the labor contracts created by the unions and the federal government. By 1922, there were strikes across the county where railroaders were demanding higher wages and guaranteed employment. Unfortunately, the timing could hardly be worse as many of the railroads had suffered greatly under government control, and few had the money to pay bills. Additionally, some of the loudest voices associated with the strikers were also tied to various socialist and communist groups who were calling for the overthrow of the United States government. This quickly cost some of the strikers the support of local governments and businesses.

The strike at the Chicago, Rock Island & Pacific shops started about July 1, 1922. At first, the strike was peaceful, and most of the residents of Shawnee supported the employees. The railroad responded by hiring some new workers and staffing the shops at much lower levels. On August 18th, there were reports of strikers shooting into the shops and rail yards to scare off these new workers. The railroad immediately complained to the federal government, over the objections of the local police. Federal troops and U.S. Marshals were sent to Shawnee to keep the peace and to investigate the shootings.

Up until that time, the strikers had been careful to not delay the U.S. Mail or other federal activities, trying to keep the strike a local matter. However, once federal troops and U.S. Marshals arrived, the strike started getting more violent. Shootings became more common, and one or more management homes were actually dynamited. This led to two meetings. The first meeting involved federal, county and city officials to trade information about the violence. As stated by a number of sources, the result of the meeting "was a proclamation issued and signed by the city, county, and federal law officers, declaring that all meeting of striking shopmen and their congregation upon the streets of the city must cease." The second was of 250 of the town's businessmen, who pledged their financial and physical support to bring the perpetrators "of the recent outrages in Shawnee" to justice. With the loss of local support, the strike didn't last much longer.

Newspapers from early 1923 were full of reports about the arrest and trials of numerous strikers and outside union representatives. These individual workers were convicted of such crimes as robbing non-union workers of their paychecks, shooting at railroad workers and the shops, theft and sabotage of railroad property, and the dynamiting of six different houses and structures. U.S. Marshal Alva McDonald, who was in charge of the investigations, was often quoted about the evidence found in the houses and barns of strikers, and the testimony provided by other strikers. The arrests essentially ended the strike and some of the workers were allowed to return to the shops.

Shawnee's Interurban Railroads and Street Cars

Shawnee once had their own streetcar system which expanded into a short interurban line that connected to nearby Tecumseh. The company started as the Shawnee Traction Company, incorporated on December 3, 1903. The firm built 6.5 miles of track through the streets of Shawnee by 1904. The company operated on many of the primary streets in town. The *Visit Shawnee* website provides the following description of the route.

> *Tracks stretched from St. Benedict's on Kickapoo up to Broadway at Main. Tracks also ran down the middle of Broadway and turned left on Georgia to make a stop near Oklahoma Baptist University. Another line went east on Main to Pesotum and on to turn around at the country club.*

The company was acquired by the Shawnee-Tecumseh Traction Company, called the Shawnee-Tecumseh Street Car Company in some newspaper reports, on July 1, 1906. The new firm quickly built a six-mile interurban line south to Tecumseh. The company was part of a much larger company, controlled by New York interests, that also owned the Market Street Railway in San Francisco. The Shawnee company began with 11 electric cars, which included three interurbans, four closed city cars and four open city cars. The line soon had 15 cars and one motor.

The interurban line headed south, just east of the ATSF mainline. The Rock Island bridge over Harrison Street shows where the line once was. To stimulate business on the line, the interurban railway built Benson Park in 1907. On July 17, 1907, twenty acres of land was bought by the Deka Development Company from Thomas Wildcat Alford's Indian allotment. The property was located just east of the ATSF mainline along what is today Benson Park Road. Newspaper reports stated that construction of Benson Park began just three days after the land was acquired, and it opened on September 1, 1907, at a cost of $85,000 to the traction company.

The Shawnee-Tecumseh Traction Company built a covered depot where the interurban passed the front entrance to the park. The park featured picnic grounds, a bandstand, a lake and botanical garden, baseball fields, and an opera house. The expansion of the facilities featured a roller coaster, and then the most popular attraction, an indoor swimming pool. The interurban handled as many as 20,000 riders to the park in a single year. However, this wasn't enough, and in 1921, the track along South Broadway was removed as street paving was underway. It took an order of the Corporate Commission of Oklahoma to have the tracks replaced by the traction company. The company gave up on its trolley and interurban operations on January 9, 1927, using buses instead. Even these were stopped on January 21, 1931. Benson Park also closed after the 1932 season, a victim of the Great Depression and the end of passenger service.

Reports also show the Oklahoma City-Shawnee Interurban Railway Company as serving Shawnee. This was actually a proposed interurban railroad that had acquired the former Missouri, Kansas & Texas Railway branch from Shawnee to Oklahoma City. The Oklahoma City-Shawnee Interurban Railway Company was incorporated on October 1, 1923, with plans to convert the line into an interurban railway. The electrification did not take place, and the Oklahoma City-Ada-Atoka Railway Company operated the line under contract starting May 1, 1924. On May 1, 1930, the property was sold to the OCAA, and the Oklahoma City-Shawnee Interurban Railway Company was dissolved on December 18. 1930, without ever being an interurban railroad.

449.6 U.S. HIGHWAY 270 – This bridge carries U.S. Highway 270, and U.S. Highway 177, over the tracks. Highway 270 is slightly less than 650 miles long, starting at Liberal, Kansas, and ending at White Hall, Arkansas. Between its end points, it passes through Oklahoma City and McAlester in Oklahoma, and Hot Springs in Arkansas.

U.S. Highway 177 initially functioned as a shortcut for Wichita to Oklahoma City traffic. Technically a spur of U.S. Highway 77, the road is a bit more than 230 miles long. Its north end is at South Haven, Kansas, while its south end is at Madill, Oklahoma.

The west end of the Shawnee yard complex is west of here, but east of the North Leo Street grade crossing. Heading west, the railroad passes through a mix of pasture and farmland, and a few clusters of homes and businesses.

450.9 DIVISION LIMITS – For many years, Milepost 450.87 was the limits between the Arkansas Division and Subdivision 32 to the east, and the Southern Division and Subdivision 33 to the west. Subdivision 32 covered the track from Hartshorne to here. Subdivision 33 went west to the important terminal at El Reno.

This location was also the west end of the Shawnee Yard Limits, identified in the 1979 employee timetable as being at Mile 450 Pole 30. It is located just west of West Independence Street.

453.0 GRAHAM SIDING – This station is shown on a January 1909 topography map. It was located about where the railroad crosses McArthur Street.

490

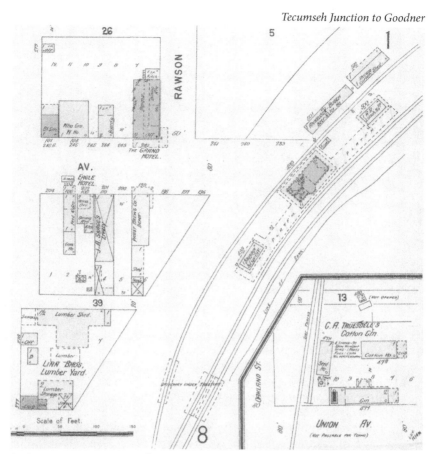

Sanborn Map Company – Shawnee Railroad Station – March 1898. *Sanborn Fire Insurance Map from Shawnee, Pottawatomie County, Oklahoma.* Sanborn Map Company, March 1898. Map. Retrieved from the Library of Congress, https://www.loc.gov/item/sanborn07248_002/.

455.3 NORTH CANADIAN RIVER BRIDGE – Coming from the east, the railroad passes under Interstate 40 and then bridges over the North Canadian River. Interstate 40 stretches from Barstow, California, to Wilmington, North Carolina. Sources say that the Interstate Highway is 2555 miles long.

The river bridge consists of two 60-foot deck plate girder spans over the river, plus 42-foot timber pile trestles off each end. Note the long timber pile trestles either side of the main bridge. The North Canadian River is known for its flooding, often damaging the railroad, and these extra trestles still exist to allow for the movement of flood waters.

491

Viewed from the tight shoulder of Interstate 40, the North Canadian River bridge west of Shawnee still stands, although often filled with debris washed downstream.

457.0 DALE – A small community located near here started about 1890 as a stagecoach relay station on the Oklahoma City to Fort Smith route. There was a saloon, hotel, blacksmith shop, general store and doctor by April 25, 1891, when a post office opened in R. B. Kennedy's general store. The community was named for John King, one of the first young men of the Shawnee Tribe to be sent to a white school, in this case, the Hampton Institute in 1879. King came back and helped to handle much of the tribe's business. He had been issued a land allotment in this area, and later served as the second postmaster. The town didn't grow much, and the post office closed on October 26, 1893.

After the Choctaw, Oklahoma & Gulf built their line, the town of King moved closer to the railroad. Enough of the town had moved that the Dale post office opened on October 26, 1893. In 1885, the town changed its name to Dale. The name Dale came from Frank Dale, the second Chief Justice of the Territorial Supreme Court (1893-1898). Today, the town is unincorporated, has a population of less than 200, and lies alongside the North Canadian River at an elevation of 1044 feet. The 4588-foot siding can still be found north of Westech Road on the north side of Dale. A dispatcher telephone was here in 1979.

Heading railroad-west to McLoud, the tracks actually head straight to the northwest for almost four miles. The track is closely followed by Oklahoma Highway 270 as it passes through farmland.

459.0 SUNNYSIDE – In 1914, Sunnyside was shown as a flag stop for trains No. 47 (9:55am) and No. 48 (1:45am), but it had no station agent. It was gone by the late 1920s.

461.0 MCLOUD – Into the 1970s, McLoud was still a short siding to the south, located at North Main Street, also known as Oklahoma Highway 102. McLoud was named for John W. McLoud, the general solicitor and later trustee for the Choctaw, Oklahoma & Gulf. McLoud was based in South McAlester and was part of the major corporate move to Little Rock in 1899. It was claimed that his professional library required an entire railroad car to move. McLoud later worked for the Midland Valley and the Central Railway Company of Arkansas.

The town of McLoud was important enough in 1899 that it was a scheduled stop for all passenger trains. The community began when the railroad was built through the area. A post office opened during June 1895, but the name was misspelled as McCloud. In October, the post office corrected the spelling to McLoud. The town quickly became a trade center for both white settlers and the Indian Territory to the east. This meant that liquor was an important early product, and McLoud developed a reputation for excellent whiskey. McLoud was incorporated on July 7, 1896, and the population was 498 in the 1900 census. It climbed to more than 600 over the next several decades, experienced a flood and moved to slightly higher ground to the south, and developed several agricultural businesses.

Besides the typical cotton, McLoud also grew blackberries. In a smart move, a case of McLoud blackberries was sent to President Harry S. Truman in 1949. The result was a proclamation declaring McLoud to be the "Blackberry Capital of the World." About the same time, the annual Blackberry Festival was founded, now held the first weekend in July. The festival has continued, even as agriculture has diminished and blackberry production is no longer conducted on a large scale.

McLoud never went through the boom and bust of the oil industry, and stayed as a small rural community until the suburban growth of nearby Oklahoma City turned it into a bedroom community. The population began to grow in the 1960s, and today it has almost 5000 residents, as well as its own school system. Downtown McLoud is located several blocks to the south of the tracks, still featuring some of the original brick and stone buildings.

463.6 COUNTY LINE – The county line is just east of a 58-foot timber pile trestle over a small stream that flows into the nearby North Canadian River. The county line is actually Reno Avenue, which ends just west of here. To the railroad-east (compass-south) is **Pottawatomie County**. To the north (railroad-west) is **Lincoln County**. In this area, the railroad is

running southeast-northwest and is squeezed between the North Canadian River to the north, and the rolling hills to the south. The railroad passes through the very southwest corner of Lincoln County.

Lincoln County was named for President Abraham Lincoln. The
area was originally hunted by the Osage, and then assigned to the Creek
and the Seminoles during the early 1830s. The tribes lost this land in
1866 due to the Reconstruction Treaties, punishment for fighting with
the Confederacy during the Civil War. Other tribes such as the Sac and
Fox, Potawatomi, Kickapoo and Ioway were then assigned to the land.
The Land Run of 1891 allowed settlers to claim unused land, followed
by the Land Run of 1895. When Oklahoma became a state, the county
was officially organized as Lincoln County.

Today, Chandler is the county seat and the county's population is
about 35,000. The county was once one of the top two cotton producing counties in Oklahoma, but its thin soil didn't last and the Dust
Bowl saw almost 75,000 acres abandoned. Lincoln County can claim to
be the center of Oklahoma as of 2010, at least based upon population.

464.3 COUNTY LINE – The county line runs north-south here, and is in
line with North Pottawatomie Road. To the east is **Lincoln County**,
while **Oklahoma County** is to the west.

Oklahoma County, like many of the counties in this part of Oklahoma, was created from a combination of unassigned lands. It became
County Two in 1890, thanks to the Organic Act of 1890, which established seven counties. The county was already well-settled with 11,742
residents in 1890. In 1907, the county was renamed Oklahoma County.
Since Oklahoma City came first, most reports state that the county was
named after what became the county seat, and in 1910, the state capitol.
During the early 1900s, Oklahoma County was a mix of government
city and rural agriculture. The primary crops that were grown and sold
for cash included cotton, wheat, corn, oats, Kaffir corn, potatoes, alfalfa, hay, and sorghum. Livestock such as cattle, hogs and chickens
was also important to the county. While farming and ranching are still
important, Oklahoma County is now dominated by Oklahoma City.

466.1 HARRAH (RH) – The history of Harrah is based upon the ability to
cross the North Canadian River, located along the north side of the
town. To the north of the river was the Kickapoo Reservation, and to
the south was the Potawatomi Reservation. The area had plenty of fish
and game, orchards did well, and the tribes were able to grow plenty of
crops, so there was a great deal of food to trade with area settlers. To
help with the trade, E. W. Sweeney opened a ferry across the river in
1891, and then built a toll bridge. The community that developed was

known as Sweeney, the name used for a post office June 22, 1896 - December 22, 1898.

After the railroad was built, Frank Harrah purchased eighty acres in April 1898 and laid out a townsite on forty of them. He heavily promoted the local farms and the ability to ship by rail, and officially changed the name of the community and its post office to Harrah on December 22, 1898. Cotton was an early product moved on the railroad, with the Department of Agriculture reporting 686 rail shipments of cotton in 1903-1904. Harrah was incorporated in 1908, and the town grew to about 350 residents and stayed that way for several decades. The construction of an Oklahoma Gas & Electric Company (OG&E) generating plant helped Harrah survive the Great Depression and Dust Bowl years. Cotton also held on, and Harrah was a center of cotton ginning. The production of various grains also continued, and the Jorski Mill & Elevator Company had a track here for many years.

The N&R Feed and Supply elevator marks the industrial area of Harrah, Oklahoma, where there were once a number of rail shippers.

Like nearby McLoud, the growth of Oklahoma City led to a change in Harrah, moving from agriculture to being a residential suburb for those looking for a more rural environment. The town reached 1931 residents in 1970, 4206 in 1990, and 5095 in 2010. The public school system has an excellent reputation, drawing even more residents and more than 2000 students. However, the land north of the North Canadian River has remained farmland. This farming has helped to create a farm recreation industry around Harrah, with orchards and farm stands allowing the town to claim that it is the "Heart of the Heartland."

Because of the farm business at Harrah, there were once several industry tracks that served grain elevators, cotton platforms, and other businesses. In 1979, 1540 feet of these tracks still existed on the south side of the mainline, used to serve a feed store. A 4613-foot siding was located to the north. These tracks are all gone today. Harrah is located at an elevation of 1070 feet, and there is a steady climb to the west.

Even though the side tracks are gone, there are still reminders about the Rock Island Railroad at Harrah. On Main Street at the mainline is the Harrah Historical Society, which includes the restored CRI&P depot. Also on display are two ex-OG&E side-dump cars, once used at the Horseshoe Lake Power Plant. A third railcar at the museum is Atchison, Topeka & Santa Fe caboose #999211. While the Santa Fe didn't have their own track through Harrah, they did have trackage rights over the Rock Island. This caboose was built as #2096 by the Santa Fe in 1942. It was rebuilt in 1968 as Class Ce-1 with cushion underframes and sealed windows as part of an upgrade of the fleet as changes were made in the use of cabooses on the railroads. Until the early 1960s, cabooses had been assigned to specific crews. With the new contract, cabooses could stay on the train whenever crews changed. This run-through practice required fewer cabooses and saved time, but the contract required certain upgrades to the equipment.

Harrah was the birthplace of actor Dale Robertson. Robertson was on television shows like *Tales of Wells Fargo*, *Death Valley Days*, and *Dynasty*. He performed in a number of other television shows and movies, and was described by *Time* magazine in 1959 as "probably the best horseman on television." He didn't really fit in to the Hollywood scene and won the press' *Sour Apple Award* for three years in a row for his lack of cooperation with reporters, finally beaten by Frank Sinatra. Robertson seemed to have taken it in good fun, stating "that dang Sinatra had to hit some photographer in the nose and stop me from getting my fourth."

Surrounded by displays of the Harrah Historical Society, the small wooden Rock Island depot still stands in Harrah, Oklahoma.

This sign points the way to the Depot Museum of the Harrah Historical Society.

467.3 HUEY – Huey was shown as a 5825-foot industry lead to the north that served the Horseshoe Lake Power Plant of Oklahoma Gas & Electric (OG&E). When the plant was built during the early 1920s, it burned coal delivered by the Rock Island Railroad. The Huey switch was designed to allow trains from the east to head north to the plant. The plant was modernized in 1963 to burn natural gas, and the Rock Island still provided service. The industry lead crossed the North Canadian River using a 450-foot steel bridge, which included a through truss span over the river.

OG&E, Oklahoma's largest electric company by the 1920s, explains that the Horseshoe Lake Power Plant, which is still operating, was the "world's largest combined-cycle power plant...more than tripling the power generated by other plants." So what is a combined-cycle power plant? These plants use gas turbines combined with steam turbines to generate electricity. And what is the source of the name Huey for the mainline switch? It comes from Arthur S. Huey, once the president of Oklahoma Gas & Electric.

While this area appears rural, the tracks are less than a mile from a number of growing suburbs connected to Oklahoma City. Heading west, there are several places where it is easy to see where the North Canadian River has changed its channel, sometimes attacking the railroad grade. Large piles of rip-rap stone have been used to try to stabilize the areas.

The Rock Island Railroad station sign for Huey is now located at the nearby Harrah Historical Society.

471.1 CHANDLER SPUR – Track charts of the Rock Island Railroad with dates from the 1960s and early 1970s show a Chandler Spur on the north side of the tracks, located about where the Indian Meridan Road grade crossing is now.

Chandler Spur served the Haydite clay pits of the Chandler Materials Company. This was their Choctaw Division, and the company was based in Tulsa, Oklahoma. Haydite is a lightweight aggregate made up of clay, shale and slate, about 40 percent lighter than typical aggregate used in concrete.

472.2 U.S. HIGHWAY 62 – The railroad passes under this four-lane highway as it approaches Choctaw. U.S. Highway 62 is a 2250-mile east-west federal highway, yet it connects Niagara Falls, New York, with El Paso, Texas. This makes it the only east-west highway to connect Canada and Mexico. At Choctaw, the highway separates the tracks, which are to the south, from the city, which is to the north.

472.6 CHOCTAW – Little exists of the many railroad facilities that once were at Choctaw. Today, only a 530-foot spur track remains on the north side of the tracks, just east of the Harper Road grade crossing. While this was all that was there in 1979, before that there was a siding to the north of the mainline, serving the railroad station. To the east at the Henny Road grade crossing (Milepost 473.3) is a reminder of the railroad's history. Located north of the tracks and east of the roadway is a small park that houses Chicago, Rock Island & Pacific caboose #17725. This caboose is typical of those that operated throughout the region after World War II. These wooden, outside-braced cabooses were rebuilt from 1938 until 1944, using much older single-sheathed outside-braced wooden boxcars. The work added end platforms, a steel cupola, and windows. The interior was fixed up and included a conductor's desk, stove and ice box, tool locker, toilet, and crew bunks.

Choctaw claims to be the oldest chartered town from the Oklahoma Territory. However, it didn't start as a town, instead it was part of the 7C Ranch of William McClure. The ranch included a trading post in this area, making it a popular stop for travelers. Land was claimed by John S. Muzzy during the 1889 Land Run into the Unassigned Lands, much of which included the McClure ranch. Muzzy quickly laid out a townsite, and the Choctaw City post office opened in early 1890. The town became official in 1893 when the newly appointed territorial governor approved the application. By this time, almost twenty businesses operated at Choctaw City. It should be noted that the Choctaw City name actually has nothing to do with the Choctaw Nation, which is based in southeastern Oklahoma. However, the name could have been used to encourage the Choctaw, Oklahoma & Gulf Railroad to build through the community.

While Muzzy started the town, the Choctaw, Oklahoma & Gulf played its normal trick and bought land just west of the existing Choctaw City to create the new Railroad Addition to Choctaw City, also known as West Choctaw. The town began in 1894, and when the railroad arrived in 1895, the CO&G built tracks, a freight house and a depot in their part of the community. Most businesses soon moved west, and in 1896, the Choctaw City post office moved and became simply the Choctaw post office. With the growth, Choctaw incorporated during April 1904.

Beautifully restored, CRI&P wooden caboose #17725 stands preserved at Choctaw, Oklahoma.

Choctaw didn't grow fast, with many blaming the short distance to Oklahoma City. The town only had 230 residents in 1907, supporting a bank, several stores, three cotton gins, a newspaper, schools, and four churches. The population didn't change much, and it reached 355 in the 1950 census. However, by the 1950s, the proximity of Oklahoma City started to cause growth at Choctaw. A General Motors assembly plant was built nearby, and along with Tinker Air Force Base, caused development on the east side of Oklahoma City. The town became more of a bedroom community, and almost 5000 people lived here by

1970. Several industries located in the area, but none used the railroad. By 2010, the population was well over 11,000 and still growing.

Heading west and starting about Milepost 474, the railroad makes a steady climb of 1.0%, going from 1128 feet to 1258 feet of elevation at Milepost 476.6.

Louis L'Amour

Louis L'Amour (Louis Dearborn LaMoore) moved and traveled all around the world, but he considered Choctaw, Oklahoma, to be home. Louis was born in Jamestown, North Dakota, in 1908. His family moved around to handle various jobs, and he moved with his parents to Choctaw, Oklahoma, in the early 1930s. By this time, he had worked as a mine assessment worker, professional boxer and merchant seaman, having visited places like England, Japan, China, Borneo, the Dutch East Indies, Arabia, Egypt, and Panama.

Louis had a desire to be a writer, and he changed his name to Louis L'Amour at Choctaw and began writing. At first his works were rejected, but he kept busy writing and editing sections of the *WPA Guide Book to Oklahoma*, articles on boxing, and poems. After dozens of his short stories were rejected, he finally sold one and then hit the big time. While most people think of Louis L'Amour as a writer of westerns, he also wrote historical and science fiction, non-fiction, a series of sea adventures and crime stories, and poetry. Much of his work was published initially in pulp magazines. It wasn't until after World War II that he began writing westerns, and he also got involved with numerous films made from his works. His first published novel was *Hondo*, and a movie was soon made starring John Wayne. Until his death, he released three novels a year. During his life he wrote 89 novels, 14 short-story collections, and two full-length works of nonfiction. He died in Los Angeles, California, and is buried there.

475.6 NICOMA PARK ~ Nicoma Park was a late addition to the communities along the Chicago, Rock Island & Pacific Railroad. It was actually not started until 1926, when Dr. G. A. Nichols established a townsite to be used by a group of poultry farmers. The name Nicoma came from the first three letters of Nichols and the last three letters of Oklahoma. By 1928, a number of poultry production facilities had already located here along with almost 100 settlers. The Nicoma Park Cooperative was established to represent the growers, and it processed, packaged and shipped eggs from coast to coast.

For the railroad, the movement of chicks by train, as well as the large volumes of feed grain, produced nice revenues during the late 1920s. With the growth of the community, a post office opened on February 7,

1929. However, during the early 1930s, a truck load of diseased chickens arrived from California, and the disease hit every producer in the Nicoma Park area. Most of the residents lost everything, and with the Great Depression underway, few could recover.

After World War II, Nicoma Park became a bedroom community for Oklahoma City. The population grew enough for the community to be incorporated as the Town of Nicoma Park in 1959. In 1960, the first shopping center in Eastern Oklahoma County was built here. Soon, the town featured the world's largest Western Auto Store. The tracks are now surrounded by houses, many on larger lots, and the population was 2393 at the 2010 census.

478.9 DICKSON – Dickson was a small town that started due to the railroad, and is today another one of the string of suburbs that now serve Oklahoma City. Unlike many of the other towns, Dickson no longer exists as it was absorbed by Midwest City. To find its location, look for the grade crossing with Spencer Road.

Chaddick started during the late 1880s as plans were being made for the railroad. A post office opened on April 16, 1890. The area history states that the town was named for a railroad official. If that is true, then the town's name was incorrectly spelled as the receiver for the Choctaw Coal & Railway Company as of December 1890 was Edwin D. Chadick. After the Choctaw Coal & Railway was acquired by the Choctaw, Oklahoma & Gulf, Edwin D. Chadick served as the agent and general manager of the coal and railway company.

The Chaddick post office was renamed Dickson on July 17, 1896. No clear reason has been found for the new name, but it didn't seem to help as the Dickson post office closed on August 15, 1906. To the west at Midwest Boulevard, the railroad once had a spur track to the north to serve several pits, once used to mine clays, sand and gravel.

481.0 MIDWEST CITY AUTO FACILITY – Located between Air Depot Boulevard (Milepost 480.5) and NE 10th Street (Milepost 481.4) are three tracks, used as a yard to serve the Union Pacific Midwest City Auto Facility, also known as the Midwest City Automobile Logistics Facility, to the north. The facility serves as a mixing system where cars and trucks are delivered for distribution to area dealerships, and vehicles can be reloaded for shipment elsewhere. As a part of the lease of the tracks in this area, the Arkansas-Oklahoma Railroad Company switches the facility, generally their main business on the line. As a part of the agreement, Union Pacific supplies and delivers autorack cars to this location. The Arkansas-Oklahoma Railroad handles the switching required for loading and unloading, and then the cars are switched back to Union Pacific. The Arkansas-Oklahoma Railroad normally keeps several locomotives here to handle switching of the auto facility, which has been inactive as of late.

For a number of years, the Midwest City Auto Facility was a major source of business on the line. For the past few years, business has been slow, but the facility remains.

The development of the facility has led to additional development in the area, with petroleum tank farms and other businesses located nearby.

481.5 GOODNER – Goodner was located about where the Sooner Road grade crossing is now. There was an industrial siding to the south, used by the Horton Grain Company for many years. In 1979, the siding was shown to be 1125 feet long.

482.0 END OF ARKANSAS-OKLAHOMA RAILROAD TRACKAGE RIGHTS – This location is at the Vickie Drive grade crossing. Just west of the crossing is the milepost sign, a yard limits sign for westbound trains, and a sign reminding train crews to use Channel 24.

The tracks through here were built by the Choctaw, Oklahoma & Gulf, and became the Chicago, Rock Island & Pacific in 1904. Over the years, the Atchison, Topeka & Santa Fe (ATSF) and the Missouri-Kansas-Texas (MKT) also used the line via trackage rights. When the Rock Island Railroad shut down in 1980, the MKT purchased the line from the railroad's trustee. It became part of Union Pacific when it acquired the MKT. The Arkansas-Oklahoma eventually leased the track from Shawnee to this point. BNSF also has trackage rights over the same track so they can reach their industry tracks at Shawnee.

The tracks west of here through Oklahoma City and all the way to west of El Reno, Oklahoma, is Union Pacific's Oklahoma City Subdivision, part of the Dallas/Ft. Worth Area in 2012.

Goodner (OK) to El Reno (OK)
Union Pacific Railroad

The track from near Oklahoma City west to the El Reno area was built 1890-1892 by the Choctaw Coal & Railway Company. In 1894, the line was acquired by the Choctaw, Oklahoma & Gulf Railroad which completed the line eastward to Wister, Indian Territory, on October 1, 1895. After the Chicago, Rock Island & Pacific took over the line, it went through a number of different districts and divisions. Traffic was generally heavy as it connected the oil fields in Oklahoma and Texas, handled cotton and other farm products, and moved a number of passenger trains. The line was important enough for the Rock Island that it received Automatic Block System (ABS) signals to help control the train traffic.

After the Rock Island's closure in 1980, the line from Harter to El Reno became the Yukon Subdivision of the Oklahoma, Kansas & Texas Railroad Company (reporting mark OKKT), eventually operating without the ABS signal system. The OKKT was created by the Missouri-Kansas-Texas Railroad on May 29, 1980, to operate parts of the Rock Island Railroad until permanent plans were made by the trustee. Besides the El Reno line, the OKKT also operated the Mid-Continent Route (often shown as Midcontinent Route) between Herington, Kansas, and Fort Worth, Texas. Due to a disagreement over rental charges between the railroad and the trustee, service ended on December 31, 1981, and negotiations began on buying the line, with the State of Oklahoma and the Oklahoma, Kansas and Texas Rail Users' Association heavily involved.

During the time of the negotiations, other small railroads operated parts of the line. On October 20, 1982, an agreement was reached for the Oklahoma, Kansas & Texas Railroad to acquire the Mid-Continent Route, as well as some of the branch lines. On November 1, 1982, the OKKT again began operating the Herrinton-Fort Worth line, as well as the Chickasha to Lawton branch, the Waurika to Walters branch, Herington to Abilene branch, and the El Reno to Oklahoma City secondary main. The El Reno-Oklahoma City line was known as the Yukon Subdivision.

On August 12, 1988, Union Pacific (UP) acquired the Katy through its Missouri Pacific Railroad. Initially, this line was nothing more than a branch line for Union Pacific, with slow speeds and infrequent service. Unit stone and sand trains to the Dolese Brothers cement plant were the only major business on the line. However, when the Midwest City Automobile Logistics Facility opened, the line was improved to move vehicles to and from the Mid-Continent Route at El Reno. Several frac sand facilities also located on the line, although at least one closed in late 2019.

Today, this is Union Pacific's Oklahoma City Subdivision, covering the line from Milepost 482.0 to Milepost 515.0. Few signs of the old Rock Island can be found as the line is now welded rail with many of the sidings and industry tracks removed, with the subdivision basically designed to move freight from one end of the line to the other.

482.0 END UNION PACIFIC MAIN TRACK – This location is at the Vickie Drive grade crossing. Just west of the crossing is the milepost sign, a yard limits sign for westbound trains, and a sign reminding train crews to use Channel 24. To the east, the track is used by the Arkansas-Oklahoma Railroad and BNSF. To the west is the Oklahoma City Subdivision of Union Pacific.

Just west of here there is a Buzzi Unicem USA facility to the south. This is one of 34 cement terminals that the firm has across the country. Cement is delivered here by rail from one of its seven cement plants (Greencastle, IN; Cape Girardeau and Festus, MO; Pryor, OK; Stockertown, PA; Chattanooga, TN; and Maryneal, TX), and then delivered by truck to local customers.

482.5 SL-SF CROSSING – This is a sharp diamond, shown as 20 degrees 51 minutes by Union Pacific. The Rock Island showed that in 1979 this was an automatic interlocking. The Missouri-Kansas-Texas listed this as BN Crossing in 1988, also an automatic interlocking. During the 2000s, Union Pacific showed this to be Stillwater Crossing, and that it was still an automatic interlocking, with the signals controlled by the first train that approached.

The Choctaw Route, now owned by Union Pacific, once crossed the St. Louis-San Francisco Railway here. Later it was Burlington Northern, and is today the Stillwater Central Railroad. Just to the west are a series of tracks used to hold and interchange cars and trains. To the north on the Stillwater Central is a large sand facility, while to the south is a connection to their branch to Tinker Air Force Base, the former Oklahoma City-Ada-Atoka Railway line. Further to the south is the large Watco transload terminal, operated by the Stillwater Central.

The Frisco built their line between St. Louis and Texas by buying several railroads and creating a number of new ones. The start of the company was the Atlantic & Pacific Railroad (A&P), created by the U.S. Congress in 1866 as a transcontinental railroad. On October 23, 1875, a suit was filed against the A&P due to unpaid interest on certain Missouri Division bonds, and receivers were assigned. The Missouri Division was sold by auction on September 8, 1876, to a representative of the St. Louis & San Francisco Railway Company (Frisco, StL&SF, or SL-SF). When the Frisco originally built from St. Louis to Texas, it turned south at Monett, Missouri, and took a route through northwest Arkansas that is now the Arkansas & Missouri Railroad.

As it became possible to build across Indian Territory, the Frisco built an improved mainline to the west across Oklahoma during the late 1890s and early 1900s. This left the line from Monett to Fort Smith, and on south to Paris, Texas, as a secondary line mostly serving local businesses.

The St. Louis & San Francisco Railroad Company was sold to the St. Louis-San Francisco Railway Company (Frisco) on September 15, 1916. Eventually, the Frisco merged into the Burlington Northern Railroad (BN) on November 21, 1980. When BN merged with the Atchison, Topeka & Santa Fe on December 31, 1996, the railroad became Burlington Northern Santa Fe, now known simply as the BNSF Railway Company.

The history of this line dates to 1895 when the Saint Louis & Oklahoma City Railroad (SL&OC) was incorporated on November 20, 1895, to extend the Atlantic & Pacific Railroad's route at Sapulpa on to Oklahoma City. As planning was taking place, the Atlantic & Pacific was sold at foreclosure to the Frisco in 1897. With help from the Frisco, the SL&OC built 103.2 miles of track from Sapulpa to Oklahoma City in 1898, which was acquired by the Saint Louis & San Francisco Railroad Company on March 28, 1899.

This route soon became a major passenger and freight route, and in the early 1920s, was the home of passenger trains like *The Meteor*, *The Southwest Limited*, and *The Texan*. Even in 1959, toward the end of the passenger train era, the route was still the home of *The Will Rogers* and *The Meteor*. Despite the importance of the line, as Burlington Northern looked at its system, and then merged with the Atchison, Topeka & Santa Fe, the railroad had duplicate routes and began attempts to abandon some of them. To protect rail service in Oklahoma, the Oklahoma Department of Transportation bought some of these lines, including 97.5 miles of track east of Oklahoma City to the western edge of Sapulpa, acquired in February 1998.

The Stillwater Central Railroad Company (SLWC), a shortline railroad owned by Watco Companies, was chosen to operate the line in July 1998. Eventually, the SLWC obtained the right to operate on other BNSF lines, for a total of more than 275 miles. The railroad has responsibility for the track from Sapulpa to Oklahoma City and on to Lawton and Snyder. The railroad also has trackage rights from Sapulpa to Tulsa, and from Snyder to Long. There is also a branchline from Stillwater to Pawnee. During the summer of 2014, the Oklahoma Department of Transportation sold the Sapulpa-Oklahoma City line to the Stillwater Central Railroad for $75 million. As part of this sale, there have been plans to evaluate the return of passenger service on the line to add Tulsa to the national Amtrak network. With the sale, Oklahoma retained the right to acquire a passenger rail easement along the route should the company decide not to operate its own passenger service.

482.7 DEL CITY – Del City is located to the south and east of this location. Eagle Lake and the Eagle Lake Park are to the south of the tracks not far east of the North Canadian River Bridge.

Del City was planned and built as a bedroom community, founded by George Epperly and incorporated in 1948. The townsite was created in a 160-acre wheat field, owned by the Pybas family since the Land Run of 1889, and bought in 1946. Epperly, who named the town after his eldest daughter – Delaphene – planned to build fifty houses, but 582 stood by the end of 1948. To gain more land, Carter Park (1954) and Midway Village (1963) were annexed. Land between Del City and Tinker Air Force Base was also acquired after winning a court case against Oklahoma City, which also wanted to annex the land.

During the 2010 census, the population of Del City was 21,332. The town covers 7.5-square miles and is surrounded by Oklahoma City to the north, west, and south. Sooner Road forms the eastern boundary. Besides a few retail stores, there is little to no industry, and Del City is still simply a suburb of the larger Oklahoma City.

483.0 MIDWEST – Midwest was shown as a yard in the 1979 timetable of the Chicago, Rock Island & Pacific. However, it wasn't shown on a 1973 track chart. A five-track yard is here today, used for interchange between several railroads in the area. It is also used by locals to switch nearby shippers.

Midwest is named for nearby Midwest City, which was created in response to the development of the Midwest Air Depot, later Tinker Air Force Base. For those who are interested, the name Tinker came from Major General Clarence L. Tinker of Pawhuska, Oklahoma. Tinker was the first Native-American to reach the rank of major general. In 1942, he was made the Commander of the Seventh Air Force in Hawaii. On June 7, 1942, he was flying to Midway to lead the air resistance as part of the Battle of Midway. His plane crashed before he got there, becoming the first U.S. Army general officer to be killed in World War II.

483.4 NORTH CANADIAN RIVER – The railroad again crosses the North Canadian River. In this area, the river has been contained in a large ditch. To cross the stream, the railroad uses nine 90-foot deck plate girder spans, plus one 55-foot deck plate girder span. To the south, the remains of the piles of the bridge used by the Missouri, Kansas & Texas, later the Oklahoma City-Ada-Atoka Railway (OCAA), can be seen.

Viewed from NE Fourth Street, the Rock Island Railroad's bridge across the North Canadian River shows its simple deck plate girder design. The view also shows the remains of the bridge once used by the Missouri, Kansas & Texas on its route east to Shawnee.

A dam further south of here at Eastern Avenue backs up the North Canadian River to the west, an area that is now called the Oklahoma River. In 2004, seven miles of the North Canadian River that passes through Oklahoma City were renamed the Oklahoma River. The re-naming was part as the development of the river for recreation and competition. A series of small dams and locks was built in the river, creating a series of small lakes for rowing, kayaking and canoeing. A number of competitive events have been held on this stretch of the riv-er, including at night thanks to a lighting system, and it also includes a series of popular parks.

484.1 U.S. INTERSTATE 35 – The railroad passes under I-35, the ninth-lon-gest of all Interstate Highways and the third-longest north-south Inter-state Highway. It stretches 1568 miles from Laredo, Texas, to Duluth, Minnesota. This is the north end of the large interchange between I-35 and Interstate 40, which creates a complex network of elevated roads on the north bank of the North Canadian River.

484.1 MKT CROSSING – There was once a railroad crossing on the west side of Interstate 35. As stated in the Rock Island employee timetable, the railroad crossing was not protected by an automatic interlocking. Instead, it was protected by a gate operated by trainman, with the normal position of the gate against the Missouri-Kansas-Texas. There was also a dispatcher telephone here.

This crossing no longer exists, but it once was on a Katy line that connected the Oklahoma City – Bartlesville line to the east end of Harter Yard. The grade north of here is now abandoned, removed in 1977 after the Missouri-Kansas-Texas acquired trackage rights over the Rock Island to access Oklahoma City. Several miles of track to the north, between Simmons Boulevard and NE 50th Street, are now used by the Oklahoma Railway Museum. The museum is based at the shops accessible from NE 34th Street. Some of the old grade is also used by the Katy Trail, a 7.5-mile hiking and biking route that connects many of the area attractions such as the Oklahoma Railway Museum, the Zoo, the Firefighter Museum, the Science Museum, and Remington Park.

The railroad north from here was built over several years as a number of different projects. In 1902-1903, the Missouri, Kansas & Oklahoma Railroad Company (incorporated December 23, 1901) built 53.8 miles of track from Oklahoma City to near Agra, Oklahoma. At the same time, the railroad built 9.6 miles of track from Osage to Hominy, both in Oklahoma. On December 12, 1903, the original Missouri, Kansas & Oklahoma Railroad consolidated with the Texas & Oklahoma Railroad Company to create the new Missouri, Kansas & Oklahoma Railroad Company.

This Missouri, Kansas & Oklahoma Railroad Company then built two lines over the next year that completed the Oklahoma City-Bartlesville line. 40.0 miles of track were built Agra to Osage, and 42.3 miles of track from Hominy to Bartlesville. The company property was sold to the Missouri, Kansas & Texas Railway Company on June 30, 1904. During December 1922, this railroad was consolidated with the Wichita Falls & Northwestern Railway Company to create the Missouri-Kansas-Texas Railroad Company.

On September 6, 1977, the Missouri-Kansas-Texas abandoned the Oklahoma City to Bartlesville line, leaving only a few miles of track in Oklahoma City that are used by Union Pacific at the west end of Harter Yard, and the Oklahoma Railway Museum.

484.5 FRANKLIN – Franklin wasn't shown in the 1979 employee timetable, but it was shown in the 1973 track chart. It was located at the east end of the Rock Island's Harter Yard.

485.5 ATSF JUNCTION – This location was included in Timetable No. 1, dated March 18, 1979. This location comes from the use of the Rock Island mainline to Shawnee by the Santa Fe to reach their industrial track, started when the company abandoned its north-south line through Shawnee, and the former Oklahoma City-Ada-Atoka Railway line which once closely followed the Rock Island eastward from here.

485.6 MKT CROSSING – This diamond is now gone, replaced by several switches. This was the mainline of what was once the Oklahoma City to Bartlesville line. Like the crossing further east, this railroad crossing was not protected by an automatic interlocking. Instead, it was protected by a gate operated by a trainman, with the normal position of the gate against the Missouri-Kansas-Texas.

485.6 HARTER (KX) – During the peak of activity for the Rock Island Railroad at Oklahoma City, they had three areas that they called yards – East Yard, Middle Yard, and West Yard. Middle Yard and West Yard were small clusters of tracks that were used to handle local industrial areas. However, East Yard, what was later renamed Harter Yard, was actually a rail yard and is still one today.

This photo by John Vachon, taken at Oklahoma City in November 1942, explains much of the business on the railroad before World War II. Behind the Chickasaw Cotton Oil Company tank car are a number of oil wells, a common sight at the time. Vachon, John, photographer. *Oklahoma City, Oklahoma. Oil wells adjoining the railroad yards.* Oklahoma City, Oklahoma, Nov 1942. Photograph. Retrieved from the Library of Congress, https://www.loc.gov/item/2017839588/.

While Harter Yard wasn't a crew change point for mainline trains, a number of locals were based here, so the yard did provide some services. *Rock Island Timetable No. 1*, dated March 18, 1979, listed these as follows: general order boards and books; train orders station per Rule 221; standard clock; fuel station; water station; and wayside radio. At the time, all of Oklahoma City was included in yard limits, which were from Mile 482 pole 0 to Mile 495 pole 20.

In a 1964 article about Oklahoma City, *The Rocket* (March-April) noted that Harter Yard was one of the busiest small yards on the system, and that Oklahoma City was second only to Chicago for forwarded business. Three shippers at Harter Yard were clearly noted in the 1979 employee timetable because each had their own track scales that locomotives were not supposed to cross. These were Hammonds Mills, Ralston Purina, and Eckroat Grain.

First the Missouri-Kansas-Texas, and then Union Pacific, adopted the yard after the closing of the Rock Island Railroad. While the MKT called the yard Harter, Union Pacific timetables simply note it as Oklahoma City. Union Pacific has rebuilt the yard, with the mainline to the south, then five long yard tracks, and then five more shorter tracks on the north side of the yard. Toward the west end, UP has a single track locomotive servicing shed and a small yard office. Today the yard is mostly surrounded by industry, except around the yard office where there are blocks of abandoned home lots. The primary access road to the yard office comes south off of Kelley Avenue. Where it crosses the yard, the Federal Railroad Administration shows the milepost to be 485.77.

On the morning of May 29, 2020, Union Pacific #1416 was busy switching Harter Yard, known as Oklahoma City by the current owner.

The large white yard office at what was Rock Island Railroad's Harter Yard now carries the name Oklahoma City for its current owner Union Pacific Railroad.

The Original Route Through Oklahoma City

When the Choctaw, Oklahoma & Gulf built through the Oklahoma City area, it passed just north of what was essentially downtown. From the west end of Harter Yard, it continued straight and crossed the Santa Fe about a block north of Main Street, about where Park Avenue now is. The line continued west to about where the Civic Center Music Hall now stands, and then curved to the northwest. At North Western Avenue, the track once joined what is now the end of an industrial lead, where Purina Mills is now located. This industry lead is about three miles long and now connects with the mainline near Reno Avenue at Milepost 489.3.

West of Villa Avenue, where the industrial lead curves to the south, the mainline used to continue to the west. It did this to stay north of a series of large bends in the North Canadian River, which made the largest bend about where Villa Avenue is today. The original mainline grade connected with the new mainline about where the wye now is west of North Portland Avenue. At this location, the Milepost of the original line was 491.2, while the new line that opened in 1930 was slightly longer, with the location being at Milepost 491.6. Information about the change in the tracks through Oklahoma City follows.

The Oklahoma City Track Realignment

As each railroad arrived at Oklahoma City, it received a right-of-way into the heart of the growing city, an attempt to bring more commerce to downtown. The *Report of the Corporation Commission of Oklahoma For the Year Ending June 30, 1923*, provided a description of the railroads that had reached Oklahoma City. Parts of this description are printed here.

> *Oklahoma City is at the intersection of the Santa Fe line from Newton, Kansas, to Galveston, Texas, and the Rock Island line from Memphis to Amarillo. The city is the terminus of a line of the Katy railway running northwest to Parsons, Kansas, there branching to Kansas City and St. Louis, and of another line of the same railway connecting at Atoka, Oklahoma, with the Parsons-Denison (Texas) line of the Katy. Oklahoma City is also served by the St Louis-San Francisco Railway. The Frisco division passing through Oklahoma City brings traffic from St. Louis and Kansas City through northeastern Oklahoma, passing through Tulsa and Sapulpa, and continues through Oklahoma City southwest to Quanah, Texas. The Ft. Smith and Western Railway traverses the eastern one-half of the State of Oklahoma, its trains running from Ft. Smith, Arkansas, to Oklahoma City, entering the latter point over the Katy tracks and using the Katy passenger facilities. The Oklahoma Railway Company operates a local electric street car system within the city of Oklahoma City, and an interurban electric railway system competing with the Santa Fe from Oklahoma City to Guthrie, and from Oklahoma City to Norman, and with the Rock Island from Oklahoma City to El Reno. The Rock Island and Katy Railways have parallel lines between Oklahoma City and Shawnee.*
>
> *The intersection of the Rock Island and Santa Fe in Oklahoma City is one block east of Broadway, one of the main business streets of the city and one block north of Main street, the city's principal retail thoroughfare. The business development on Broadway is both north and south of the Rock Island Railroad and the retail shopping section on Main street, one and one-half blocks south of the Rock Island Railway, parallels that line for one-half mile or more.*

The Frisco railroad passes through the city from east to west, crossing the Santa Fe a little more than one-half mile south of the Rock Island intersection and continues west through the city at approximately that distance from the Rock Island. The Frisco has a track extending from its main line to a proposed passenger terminal site adjacent to the Rock Island right-of-way, said track extending northward from the Frisco main line a little more than one-half mile west of the Santa Fe. The said track turns east upon reaching a point adjacent to the Rock Island right-of-way and extends parallel thereto approximately one-half mile, or to a point within one block of the heart of the retail shopping section of Oklahoma City. There is, therefore, a section of Oklahoma City somewhat greater in area than one-half mile square, bounded on the east by the Santa Fe, on the south and west by the Frisco, and on the north by the Rock Island, containing in its northeast quarter the principal retail and commercial office business section of the city.

The present passenger facilities for the various roads are located as follows:

The Santa Fe station is two blocks south of the Rock Island intersection, or within three blocks of the heart of the retail district and is used by the Santa Fe and Frisco lines, the latter being a tenant.

The Katy station is one block south and one and one-half blocks east of the Santa Fe station, or from five to six blocks from the most active business locality and is used by the Katy and Ft. Smith and Western, the latter being a tenant.

The Rock Island station is at Broadway, one block west of the Santa Fe intersection. It is in the shadow at noonday of one of the city's largest hotels and its trains must be broken at Broadway to avoid a prohibitive interruption of street railway and other traffic on the busiest north and south street of Oklahoma City.

The Frisco erected a passenger station at the uptown end of the loop line and used said station until approximately five years ago when the arrangement with the Santa Fe, now in effect, was made and the Frisco station removed.

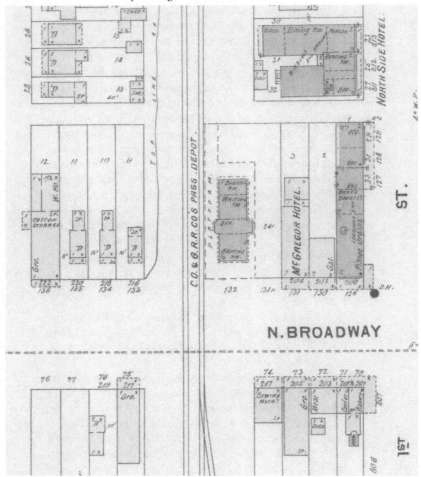

Sanborn Map Company – Oklahoma City CO&G Station – September 1898. *Sanborn Fire Insurance Map from Oklahoma City, Oklahoma County, Oklahoma.* Sanborn Map Company, Sep, 1898. Map. Retrieved from the Library of Congress, https://www.loc.gov/item/sanborn07202_003/.

By the 1920s, all of these lines, located at grade with the downtown streets, were blocking street traffic much of the day. The city developed plans to grade-separate many of the lines, and to consolidate the Rock Island and Frisco lines on the same route south of downtown. After several years of campaigning, a bond issue was approved that provided $10,329,000 for moving tracks, building overpasses and underpasses, paving streets, and basically straightening out many of the traffic problems of downtown Oklahoma City. About $4 million was used to buy a new railroad right-of-way around the south side of downtown. The east-west lines of the Rock Island and the Frisco used this line, while an elevated Santa Fe line was built through downtown on a north-south alignment.

For the Rock Island, the mainline was changed to turn to the southwest as it headed west from Harter Yard. About SW 8th Street, the Rock Island and the Frisco lines came together and turned west to pass south of downtown. Between Robinson and Walker, the new line passed the new Oklahoma City Union Station, built as part of the project to consolidate several passenger stations. Not far west of the station, the Frisco line turned to the southwest while the Rock Island route turned slightly to the west-northwest to return to the original grade west of downtown.

The Frisco and Rock Island railroads used their old stations for the last time on November 30, 1930, and the old routes were abandoned almost immediately. Until the new Union Station opened on July 15, 1931, the two railroads used a temporary station at the foot of South Hudson Street, less than a block west of the new station. While the Rock Island and Frisco used the new station, the Santa Fe and Missouri-Kansas-Texas each continued to use their old stations.

The Twenty-First Century Changes

While Union Pacific still follows this route built in 1930, a number of changes have taken place, many related to the construction of Interstate Highway 40. For years, Interstate 40 was an elevated six-lane path through Oklahoma City, located about SW 3rd Street. While sufficient when it was built, the freeway could no longer handle the traffic volumes or the tonnages. About 2002, planning started on a new highway. The solution eventually was a new route south of downtown along the Rock Island-Frisco right-of-way. While the route was controversial and resulted in almost 200 houses and businesses being torn down, as well as the removal of the Union Station rail yard and passenger tracks, it allowed the highway to be greatly widened and placed in a deep cut.

Eastbound traffic started using the new highway on January 5, 2012, and westbound traffic on February 19, 2012. The original Oklahoma City Crosstown Expressway was soon torn down, and a new street is being built through the area. The land alongside the old expressway is also being developed into parks, shopping, and other entertainment opportunities.

Several changes were made with the railroads. The official contract included four new railroad bridges, the relocation of two mainlines, and several new line connections. The BNSF line, formerly the ATSF, received a new bridge over Interstate 40. All of the local streets were also raised over both Interstate 40 and the railroads. This created a major change for the Rock Island-Frisco route as the line used to go over the highways on very decorative bridges, with both railroad's emblems cast into the concrete. Unfortunately, these designs were destroyed as the roads were raised as part of the project.

This route guide follows the current route around the south side of downtown Oklahoma City.

485.9 MKT CROSSING – In 1979, this was a "railroad crossing not protected by interlocking" that was "protected by gate operated by trainman, normal position of gate against MKT." Today, the railroad passes under Interstate 235 at this location. I-235 is a short 5.4-mile highway that connects Interstate 40 (to the south) with Interstate 44 (to the north). Completed in 1989, I-235 passes just east of the downtown business district.

During the 1930s, this could be a busy crossing as it led to the Missouri-Kansas-Texas passenger station, once located at 200 East Reno Street. Besides the Missouri-Kansas-Texas, the Fort Smith & Western Railway and the Oklahoma City-Ada-Atoka Railway also used the station over the years. Nothing remains of this track or of the station, but the station area is now a popular part of the Bricktown entertainment district. In this area is a Bass Pro Shop, several hotels, and more restaurants and bars than you could hope to visit. The station once stood south of the Chickasaw Bricktown Ballpark and west of the corporate headquarters of Sonic Drive In.

Note that in this area, Reno Avenue has been renamed Johnny Bench Drive. Johnny Bench was born in Oklahoma City, and is one-eighth Choctaw. Bench was a major league baseball catcher for the Cincinnati Reds from 1967 to 1983. He career is full of awards, things like being the 1968 National League Rookie of the Year, a 14-time All-Star selection, a two-time National League Most Valuable Player, and a member of the National Baseball Hall of Fame.

In this area is also the Centennial Land Run Monument, a large collection of bronze statues built to commemorate the opening of the Unassigned Land in Oklahoma Territory with the Land Run of 1889. These statues include wagons, horses and riders, and many other items that would have been found at the start of a land rush.

Northwest of the tracks near Reno Avenue is the Bricktown River Walk Park and the Centennial Land Run Monument, one of the world's largest collection of bronze sculptures. It features 45 figures of land run participants as they race to claim new homesteads.

486.5 SL-SF CROSSING – This is another diamond that existed in 1979, and until the construction of the new Interstate 40. This line came north from the west end of Frisco's Oklahoma Yard to serve several shippers that were located just south of the original Interstate 40. It was another non-interlocked diamond, "protected by gate operated by trainman, normal position of gate against SLSF."

According to *Union Pacific Dallas/Ft. Worth Area Timetable #4*, dated March 26, 2012, this location is also the west end of Yard Limits for the Harter Yard area of the Oklahoma City Subdivision.

486.8 SL-SF CROSSING – This crossing with the Frisco was another line used to serve local shippers. Like the diamond just to the east, this one was a non-interlocked diamond, "protected by gate operated by trainman, normal position of gate against SLSF."

486.9 UNDER ATSF/BNSF – Overhead is a new bridge built to not only cross the Frisco and Rock Island line, but also the new Interstate 40. This is the Red Rock Subdivision (Arkansas City, Kansas, to Gainesville, Texas) of BNSF. The line hosts Amtrak's *Heartland Flyer*, an Oklahoma and Texas funded train that operates between Oklahoma City and Fort Worth.

This rail line was the first one to reach the Oklahoma City area. During 1886-1887, a line was built south from the Kansas-Oklahoma State Line to Purcell, passing through what became Oklahoma City. The builder was The Southern Kansas Railway Company, incorporated in Kansas on April 16, 1885. This company was sold to The Atchison, Topeka & Santa Fe Railway Company on February 15, 1899. Also in 1887, The Gulf, Colorado & Santa Fe Railway Company (incorporated May 28, 1873, in Texas) built a line from the Texas-Oklahoma State Line northward to Purcell, completing the line across what became Oklahoma. Even before the line was completed, The Gulf, Colorado & Santa Fe Railway Company (GC&SF) fell under the control of The Atchison, Topeka & Santa Fe Railway Company (March 3, 1886). For a number of reasons, the GC&SF remained a separate company, but was essentially invisible. It wasn't until August 1, 1965, that the GC&SF was merged into the ATSF. When Burlington Northern merged with the Atchison, Topeka & Santa Fe on December 31, 1996, the railroad became Burlington Northern Santa Fe, now known simply as the BNSF Railway Company.

The Southern Kansas Railway created a watering stop at Oklahoma Station. This stop quickly attracted residents, especially when the Oklahoma City area was officially opened for homesteading on April 22, 1889. Stories state that the water stop went from a railroad station and seven buildings to about 10,000 homesteaders on the land rush day.

The Santa Fe Station

North of here at 100 South E. K. Gaylord Boulevard (historically South Santa Fe Street) is the Santa Fe station. This is actually the third Santa Fe station here. The first wooden station was replaced in 1901 by an expanded stone depot. The founding of Oklahoma City established the Santa Fe station grounds between Grand (now Sheridan) Avenue and Reno Avenue.

Starting in 1911, talk began about elevating the rail lines in Oklahoma City, and in consolidating the many passenger stations. At first, the cost was a hindrance, and then concern came up that if all the lines were elevated, then downtown would be surrounded by high walls like a fort. In 1922, the Santa Fe and Rock Island proposed a union station at the intersection of their tracks. Hearings at the Interstate Commerce Commission followed, and then there was a proposal for two stations: a Santa Fe-Katy station and a Rock Island-Frisco station. Eventually, a new Union Station was built as a joint Rock Island-Frisco station, and the Katy station was left untouched. This left the Santa Fe with their old downtown station.

By 1927, the Santa Fe had plans to elevate its route through town and build a new station. The track was elevated over a several year period, starting at the North Canadian River. Starting in 1932, construction on the station began with the express room, followed by the passenger and baggage section. The station opened during September 1934, and a formal dedication took place on November 8th, featuring Samuel Thomas Bledsoe, president of the Santa Fe.

The Santa Fe station in Oklahoma City still stands, and is used by Amtrak as the terminus of the Heartland Flyer from Fort Worth, Texas.

From north the south, the Art Deco station features a large passenger section, a slightly narrower center baggage and mail room area, and then a relatively narrow express and freight section with a freight loading dock. The passenger services area featured many of the typical facilities of the time. Off the main concourse was a newsstand to the north and the ticket office to the south. As reported in the National Register application, the "ticket office features a full-width wooden counter with a granite top. The floor in the ticket office is plain gray tile with cream colored plaster walls. To the west of the ticket office is a large entryway to the main waiting room....to the east of the ticket office is the smaller, rectangular space that was originally the Colored Waiting Room...a baggage checking lobby, red cap office and janitor room were located between the historic men's rooms and women's rooms on the south end of the passenger section."

521

The Santa Fe operated passenger service out of this station until Amtrak took over on May 1, 1971. After that, Amtrak operated passenger service until October 2, 1979. Thanks to local funding, the *Heartland Flyer* starting operating south to Fort Worth on June 14, 1999. Since then, there have been efforts to connect the train with local passenger services, and the station is officially known as the Santa Fe Transit Hub, although "Santa Fe Station" is probably the most commonly used name. The building was placed on the National Register of Historic Places in 2015, and a great history of the efforts to consolidate the stations and raise the tracks at Oklahoma City can be found in the application.

Hell's Half Acre

The area around the original Santa Fe station quickly took on the name Hell's Half Acre when Oklahoma City was settled as part of the Land Run of 1889. The area was immediately packed with tents and prefab buildings, housing businesses such as Two Johns Saloon, the Turf Club, the Vendome (the plushest bawdy house in town), the First National Bank, and the Lee Hotel. Two well-known businesses were the Black and Rogers Saloon, with the city council chambers and police court on the second floor, and Big Anne Wynn's bordello, the first and largest source of female companionship for the overwhelmingly male population. By August, there were nine billiard halls and 18 club houses in the area.

The area was notorious, and Broadway was nicknamed Battle Row. Other streets had similar nicknames that described the environment, such as Alabaster Row, Hop Boulevard, and Bunco Alley. The owners of the saloons, gambling houses and bordellos like Big Anne Wynn held a great deal of power as they were a major source of license fees for the new city.

Another issue was that the new settlers butted their claims tight up against each other, leaving no room for streets. Within a few days of the Land Run, a mass meeting was called which elected a committee to bring order with a new survey. A fourteen member committee was elected to straighten out the land claims and lay out a town. Not surprisingly, the already organized Seminole Town and Improvement Company gained control of the committee and their plan for the city was soon enforced, including the businesses in Hell's Half Acre.

487.2 OKLAHOMA CITY UNION STATION – This station, and the yard that was once to the south, was built as part of the effort to eliminate the many grade crossings in downtown Oklahoma City. Located between South Robinson Avenue and South Walker Avenue, this station replaced those of the Rock Island (on North Broadway between West

1st and West 2nd Streets) and the Frisco (on North Hudson Street between West Main and West 1st Streets). The old stations were closed on November 30, 1930, as part of the change to the new rail routing. A temporary station was used until the new Union station opened on July 15, 1931. Several newspaper and magazine articles from the time, including one in *The Frisco Employes' Magazine* (February 1931), described the building.

Union Station was built in the California Spanish Mission Revival style, and had 55,000 square feet of space on the main floor level. Approaching the building from the front was a circular concrete driveway, with a fountain surrounded by lawns and colorful lights along its route. The Frisco's architectural department was involved with creating the design, which featured a 70-foot by 70-foot main lobby with a vaulted ceiling 20 feet high, marble walls and marble floor. As was common at the time, there were two waiting rooms with the ticket office in between.

The north end of the west wing featured wash and locker rooms for the trainmen. The west and south part of the west wing handled mail and baggage. The Railway Express Agency filled the east wing of the station. A tower, several courtyards, and a series of fountains and gardens surrounded the station building.

The Oklahoma City Union Station is a classic station. Thankfully it still stands, housing the main office of the Central Oklahoma Transportation & Parking Authority.

Twelve tracks handled the station's traffic. The tracks were accessed via ramps from the waiting room, while baggage and mail was moved underground and by elevators to track level. The tracks and platforms were protected by open-type butterfly sheds, approximately 1500 feet long. The Frisco bragged that the sheds were "constructed on steel column supports and electrically lighted and provided with telephone service for private cars." A small part of one of these platform canopies still stands on display at the Oklahoma Railway Museum.

The station construction also impacted area streets. Hudson and Harvey streets were left at-grade so that passengers, mail and express could easily be moved between train and highway vehicles. Robinson and Walker streets were built as underpasses, designed to improve the flow of traffic in the area. These underpasses featured the heralds of the two railroads that used the station, with the Robinson Street heralds later saved and relocated to the Oklahoma Railway Museum in Oklahoma City. The station served trains like the *Firefly* and *Meteor* (Frisco) and *Choctaw Rocket* and *Cherokee* (Rock Island). The peak of train volume was about when the station opened, thanks to the Great Depression and the end of passenger service. The last passenger train, the Rock Island's *Cherokee*, used Union Station during November 1967 (the last Frisco train was in May 1967).

The station sat mostly unused until it was acquired by the city of Oklahoma City during the 1980s. By that time, it had been added to the National Register of Historic Places (1979). The city planned to use the building as a multimodal transportation center. With the construction of Interstate 40, most of the tracks were removed, but space for two were left just in case they are needed in the future. The building now houses the main office of the Central Oklahoma Transportation & Parking Authority.

After the station closed, there was little said about the building in railroad timetables except that snow plows would not clear the concrete platform.

Oklahoma City Streetcar

Just west of the Union Station is the streetcar maintenance facility of the Oklahoma City Streetcar. This system has two loops – a Downtown Loop and a Bricktown Loop. The Downtown Loop operates daily, while the Bricktown Loop operates Friday, Saturday and Sunday. The route is about five miles long and is operated using "Liberty" model streetcars built by the Brookville Equipment Corporation of Pennsylvania. The cars use a unique mix of overhead wires for electric power, and battery power for about 40% of the route.

This Russell Lee photo from February 1940 shows two track workers at the east end of the Oklahoma City Union Station. Several of the platform canopies that are seen on the left have been preserved at the Oklahoma Railway Museum. Lee, Russell, photographer. *Railway workmen with hand car.* Oklahoma City, Oklahoma. Oklahoma City, Oklahoma, Oklahoma County, Feb 1940. Photograph. Retrieved from the Library of Congress, https://www.loc.gov/item/2017785269/.

This is not the first streetcar system using the streets of Oklahoma City. The early days of streetcar planning included names like Shartel, Berry, Classen, Harn and Patterson; most of them were land developers needing access to their property. John Shartel started the process in 1901 with his Metropolitan Railway Company. Meanwhile, Harold Berry formed his own company, which was acquired by Anton Classen in February 1902. Classen then gave his franchise to Shartel in return for a guarantee that a line would be built to Classen's property in the northwest part of the city. Shartel would also use Classen's company to build the railroad.

The 1915 *Poor's Manual of Public Utilities* provided more detail of the construction and consolidation of the streetcar and interurban system around Oklahoma City. It stated that the Oklahoma City Railway Company was incorporated on June 15, 1904, and acquired "the street railway system and franchise of the Metropolitan Railway Company of Oklahoma City" on July 1, 1904. On September 21, 1907, the company changed its name to the Oklahoma Railway Company. On April 1, 1910,

525

the company purchased the line of the Oklahoma City & Suburban Railway. On August 1, 1911, the El Reno Interurban Railway Company was purchased, including its street trackage in El Reno. This was followed by the lease of the Oklahoma Electric Terminal Company, and then the purchase of its terminal tracks and station on October 1, 1913.

This created a large network of tracks, including 59.71 miles of track within Oklahoma City; a 15.32-mile line to Norman; 10.69-mile line to Edmond; and a 26.53-mile line to El Reno. There was also additional street trackage in Guthrie and the short route of the North Canadian Valley Railroad. In total, there were 123.14 miles of standard gauge streetcar and interurban track. The Citizens Traction Company also operated a 5-mile streetcar line from "North East Park to Capitol" and had plans to connect Oklahoma City with Tecumseh and Shawnee. Additional lines were built and even more were planned, but eventually they were organized and based out of a central terminal at what is now Sheridan and Hudson in downtown Oklahoma City. Operations ended by 1947, and the routes were all removed.

Oklahoma City

Oklahoma City began when the Southern Kansas Railway (Santa Fe) built through the area in 1887 and created a watering stop here. Located on the North Canadian River, it was assigned the name Oklahoma Station in February 1887. The location received a post office with that name on December 30, 1887. The community wasn't big, just a few buildings and a train station, but it served a few ranches in what was called the Unassigned Lands. The post office was renamed Oklahoma on December 18, 1888.

A land run was planned for April 22, 1889, and several companies were organized to plat and sell townsites. One of these was the Seminole Town and Improvement Company, which after more than five thousand settlers had claimed land around the railroad watering station during the Land Run of 1889, somehow gained control of much of the area. The town was located west of the railroad tracks, and from April 22, 1889, until May 2, 1890, the land stayed under federal control.

Passage of the Organic Act on May 2, 1890, stated that Nebraska law applied to the Oklahoma Territory until it could organize its own laws. The legal system created County Two, one of seven counties established at the time, and soon Oklahoma City became the county seat. On July 15, 1890, Oklahoma City was incorporated with William L. Couch, of the Seminole Town and Improvement Company, as acting mayor. A census taken in 1890 showed that the town already had a population of 4151, and it reached 10,037 in 1900 as the town grew as a major business center in the middle of Oklahoma. Railroads were attracted to the location, bringing even more business to the city.

While business helped to create the Oklahoma City boom, agriculture was its base. A promotional pamphlet from the Oklahoma City Club (1899) stated that five to ten thousand bales of cotton were marketed, and seventy-five thousand bales were compressed at Oklahoma City. Cattle was a big business, and after shipping the livestock for many years, two meat-packing plants were built near the stockyards. Other businesses such as a corn mill, a grain elevator, a cotton gin, canning plant, and several grain mills opened.

By 1908, the population of Oklahoma City reached 64,205, and the state capital moved to Oklahoma City the same year. Transportation, warehousing and retail businesses helped the city keep growing, but the Oklahoma oil boom kept it going. The United States Post Office gave up and changed its name from Oklahoma to Oklahoma City on July 1, 1923. The population hit 185,389 residents in 1930. The Dust Bowl and Great Depression did slow the growth, but World War II brought workers and their families to the area thanks to the Midwest City Douglas Aircraft Company Plant and Tinker Air Force Base, and the population hit 243,504 in 1950.

Oklahoma City has continued to grow, still having a mix of government, urban business and agriculture as its economic base. Since about 2000, the city has been involved with turning much of downtown into a tourist and recreation attraction, with water activities along the North Canadian River (renamed the Oklahoma River through downtown), entertainment in Bricktown, and the removal of Interstate 40 from downtown. The population in the 2010 census was 579,999.

487.7 SL-SF CROSSING – This crossing was to allow the St. Louis-San Francisco Railway to turn to the southwest and leave Oklahoma City. This line, known as the Chickasha Subdivision, passed the National Stockyards, went through Chickasha, and on to Quanah, Texas. As part of the Interstate 40 project, the line was abandoned between the Union Station area to near the National Stockyards, and trains diverted onto the former Oklahoma City Junction Railway.

In 1979, this crossing was protected by a gate, with its normal position against the Frisco. The gate was operated by trainmen when needed.

489.1 OKLAHOMA CITY BOULEVARD – The railroad passes under the Interstate 40 on and off ramps that connect with Oklahoma City Boulevard, a new roadway using the right-of-way of the old I-40.

Just east of here at Milepost 488.9 was the eastern limits of the Automatic Block System (ABS) signals for the Rock Island Railroad. This system went as far west as Milepost 510.8. Union Pacific uses Track Warrant Control over the same basic stretch of track between Mileposts 486.5 and 512.3.

Not far west of here is the Reno Avenue grade crossing. This is where the industrial lead curves to the north to use some of the original Choctaw, Oklahoma & Gulf grade that once ran through downtown Oklahoma City.

489.4 LAKEVIEW – This station was listed in the 1896 Official Guide. It was gone not long after the area was absorbed by the growing Oklahoma City.

489.9 MARTIN – A small yard was once here that was used to serve local shippers.

490.8 INTERSTATE 44 – This freeway starts at St. Louis, Missouri, and heads to the southwest through Oklahoma City and on to Wichita Falls, Texas. Much of the eastern end of the interstate was once U.S. Highway 66. The highway is about 635 miles long and passes around the north and west sides of Oklahoma City.

The railroad passes under I-44. Just to the northeast is the Jim Norick Arena and the Oklahoma State Fairgrounds. At one time, the railroad had several spur tracks to the south.

The Jim Norick Arena stands tall just north of the Delmar Gardens grade crossing at Milepost 490.4.

491.1 WYE TRACK – This wye track to the south is relatively new and does not show on a 1973 Rock Island track chart.

491.5 EQUATION – The original mainline of the Choctaw, Oklahoma & Gulf was built from Oklahoma City to Fort Reno during 1890-1892. Eventually, four railroads – CRI&P, ATSF, MKT and Frisco – all had lines through downtown Oklahoma City. Plans were worked on for several decades to end the congestion caused by this. During the late 1920s, work was conducted to move the lines to just a few elevated routes. The Rock Island was looped around the south side of Oklahoma City, adding 0.4 miles to the distance and creating a milepost equation of **491.54 = 491.16**.

492.2 CAIN-ROCK ISLAND INDUSTRIAL DISTRICT – There are a number of rail shippers in this area, including warehouses and lumberyards. This was a planned industrial area created by the Chicago, Rock Island & Pacific in 1955. The Chamber of Commerce owned 225 acres in the area, and the railroad bought 88 acres to develop a railroad industrial park. Initially known as the Rock Island Industrial Park, a grain storage warehouse and an International Harvester distribution center opened there by the end of the decade. In 1959, Morgan Cain, founder of the Cain Coffee Company, bought 50 acres of adjacent land for further development. Since then, the area has been known as the Cain-Rock Island Industrial District, a name still used on property descriptions and re-zoning requests.

494.5 COUNCIL – Council was named for the Council Grove trading post and community, established in 1858 by Jesse Chisholm, the same Chisholm that has a famous cattle trail named after him. Council Grove became a significant trading center for area ranchers and the various Native-American tribes in the area. Before the Civil War, is was the location of a planned treaty negotiation with the Comanche, but the presence of too many troops ended the meeting early. During the Civil War, it was the base of one of the Confederate Indian agents, and the planned location of the surrender of the tribes who had fought with the Confederacy. However, Union forces threatened the tribes if they met here, and they were forced to surrender at Camp Napoleon on May 24, 1865.

Technically, Council Grove was in the Unassigned Lands, but the good grass, trees and water made it a popular meeting location, and it was also in the Creek Nation for their potential use. During the 1870s and 1880s, Montford T. Johnson operated a ranch at Council Grove, but was removed when President Hayes sent the calvary to remove settlers from the Unassigned Lands. The 1889 Land Run specifically excluded the Council Grove area as the timber was important to nearby Fort

Reno, but settlement took place all around it. A Council Grove post office opened on June 11, 1892. On December 7, 1894, the name of the post office was changed to Council. With the arrival of the railroad, cut timber could be shipped in and the land at Council Grove was sold starting on December 1, 1896.

A copy of the government plats from the original Government Survey Lot Report in 1905 shows that the Council railroad station and post office were on the north end of the Melrose property. I. F. Melrose was one of the first to buy land at Council, buying forty acres on December 1, 1896. The title to his land was signed by President Grover Cleveland, something that Melrose bragged about all his life. Despite the land sale, the Council post office was discontinued on August 15, 1906. The railroad depot was closed and removed in 1934, and Council is now a part of Oklahoma City.

As late as the 1970s, the Rock Island had an industry siding and several spur tracks on the south side of the mainline, located east of the grade crossing with Council Road. Records show that a magnesium plant once was nearby. These tracks are now gone.

495.6 COUNTY LINE – The county line runs straight north and south through this area, but generally follows the North Canadian River. At this location, the county line is just a short distance east of the river. **Oklahoma County** is to the east while **Canadian County** is to the west.

Canadian County, named for the Canadian River, is another county that was created through a series of Indian lands and land runs. The area was primarily plains – the Red Bed Plains – and the edge of the Gypsum Hills. Because of this, the area was mainly used by roaming tribes with little long-term settlement until the tribal land assignments began. This county area was where the last great battle between the Cheyenne, Arapaho and the United States Army took place. The first tribe assigned the area by the United States government was the Caddo of Louisiana, moved here in 1859. The first credited settler was Showetat, the last hereditary chief of the Caddos. The next tribe was the Wichita tribe, moved here in 1861. During the late 1860s, the land just west of the Caddos and Wichitas was given to the Cheyenne and Arapaho tribes by the Treaty of Medicine Lodge.

The first land run to allow non-Indian settlement in Canadian County was the Land Run of 1889. This run created El Reno and Reno City as major towns. County Four, which included the eastern half of the present Canadian County, was created when the Organic Act of 1890 created the Oklahoma Territory. Additional land runs brought more settlers, and El Reno was chosen as the county seat. The county grew quickly thanks to it being a railroad terminal and crossing of several major rail and highway routes. In the 2010 census, it had a population of 115,541, making it the fifth-most populous county in Oklahoma.

495.7 NORTH CANADIAN RIVER – This bridge, from east to west, features several modern concrete ballast deck spans, two 150-foot through truss spans, two 60-foot deck plate girder spans, and three modern concrete ballast deck spans.

This bridge crosses the North Canadian River in the middle of the Oklahoma Gas & Electric Mustang Power Plant. The West River Trail follows the east bank of North Canadian River, heading north from a parking lot along Reno Avenue, and passing under the bridge. Nice photos of the bridge are available from the trail.

A short walk on the West River Trail will take you to the former CRI&P North Canadian River bridge.

Heading west, the railroad makes a slow but steady climb from an elevation of 1235 feet at the North Canadian River, to 1311 feet at Milepost 500.

At the west end of the North Canadian River bridge is the Oklahoma Gas & Electric's Mustang Power Plant, as viewed from the West River Trail.

496.0 OG&E – The railroad passes along the south side of the Oklahoma Gas & Electric's Mustang Power Plant. This plant initially opened on May 5, 1950, using four natural gas-fired boilers to power the four 56,000 kilowatt generators. Recently, the older system was replaced with seven gas-fired simple-cycle combustion turbines. The work was completed by early 2018, and the site includes Oklahoma's first universal solar farm.

   In 1979, the Rock Island listed two tracks here measuring a total of 2385 feet. The tracks are still in the plant, but their mainline switch has been removed.

497.8 LACEY – Shown as being at Mile 497 Pole 33 in 1979, Lacey was a small 585-foot industrial siding to the north. Today, Union Pacific shows the track to be at Milepost 498.0, basically under the John Kilpatrick Turnpike (toll road) overpass.

   Lacey is used by a busy shipper on the railroad, the Dolese Brothers. The firm has been here a long time, and in 1973, the Rock Island track charts noted that there was a "Dolose Brothers Spur" at Lacey. The firm started before Oklahoma was a state, and its first purpose was to furnish quarried rock for railroad construction by operating railroad-owned ballast plants and quarries in Kansas, Oklahoma, and New Mexico. The firm has a number of plants and facilities across the region, producing concrete, crushed stone, sand and gravel, brick, and other construction materials. This one receives materials by rail and produces concrete for local construction projects.

500.8 OKRY CROSSING – From about 1909 until 1947, there was a competing electric interurban railroad that served the Oklahoma City to El Reno market. The line was built in two parts by the El Reno Interurban Railway Company and the Oklahoma Railway Company. The El Reno Interurban Railway Company was incorporated in Oklahoma on July 2, 1908, to construct an interurban railroad between El Reno and Oklahoma City. By the end of 1909, the company had a line built from Oklahoma City as far west as Yukon. The firm temporarily ran out of funding, but started building westward again in 1911. On August 1, 1911, the El Reno Interurban Railway Company was purchased by the Oklahoma Railway Company, and the line opened to El Reno on December 3, 1911. Combined with the street trackage in El Reno, there were 26.53 miles of track on the El Reno line.

As with many of the interurban lines, the Oklahoma Railway Company hit its peak in the late 1910s and the 1920s, and by the late 1930s was in trouble. World War II gave the line a boost of ridership, but after the war, trains were down to every 90 minutes on the El Reno line due to the drop in demand. To raise money, the interurban sold its freight trackage and rights over other lines to the Rock Island and the Santa Fe for $525,000 in 1943. The Oklahoma Railway Company entered receivership in 1946 and ceased operations on April 27, 1947.

East of Yukon, the right-of-way of the Oklahoma Railway Company is now used by what is called the 39th Expressway, also identified as Route 66. The road was originally built on either side of the interurban, leaving a large median after the tracks were removed.

500.9 YUKON (KU) – Welcome to the Czech Capital of Oklahoma, the home of the Millers, and the place where Garth Brooks grew up. While Yukon was once a major center of grain milling and a supply center for area farms and ranches, today it is primarily a bedroom community for Oklahoma City.

The town of Yukon was created by A.N. Spencer, a grading contractor for the Choctaw Coal & Railway Company. As he was clearing a right-of-way, he filed the plat on the townsite of Yukon on February 14, 1891. In return for establishing the town and grading the railroad through the property of Minnie Taylor and Luther S. Morrison, he received half of the town's lots. Taylor and Morrison had acquired the land in the Land Run of 1889 and had hoped to locate along the planned railroad. Spencer also bought land from Joseph Carson and his sister, Josephine, providing plenty of room for a large city.

The name Yukon has several conflicting sources, but they all relate to the Yukon Gold Rush which was in the news at the time. Some sources state that the name came from the Yukon River, others say it was from the Yukon Territory of Canada, while others say it came from the gold rush. Whatever the source, the name Yukon seems somewhat unique for the region.

It should be noted that A.N. Spencer was later one of the causes of the end of the Choctaw Coal & Railway Company. On August 13, 1891, Spencer was one of several contractors who filed suit against the railroad for non-payment of bills. At the time, Spencer was owed $34,000 for grading work. About the same time, a federal court ordered the railroad to complete its El Reno to Oklahoma City line as required by the Congressional Act allowing construction of the line. The result of the additional construction and the unpaid bills was foreclosure on September 9, 1894.

The town of Yukon grew quickly and newspapers reported that by early Spring 1891, the town had 25 homes, one bank, two real estate offices, two restaurants, a lumber yard, a hardware store, a grocery, a livery stable, two saloons, a blacksmith shop, a printing office, and a barber shop. The Yukon post office also opened in 1891, and the town was incorporated the same year. With railroad service extending all the way to Memphis, farmers began using Yukon as their point of sales, and the residents and businesses of other area towns like Frisco soon moved to here. The Yukon Mill & Grain Company, jointly owned by the Kroutil and Dobry families, opened in 1893, adding more agricultural business to the town.

By World War I, Yukon featured a library, city water and sewer, electricity, and the interurban railroad between Oklahoma City and El Reno. With land available, a large number of immigrants from eastern Europe moved to the area, especially from Bohemia (Czechoslovakia). Milling expanded during the 1930s when the partnership between the Kroutil and Dobry families split up, with the Dobry family building their own mill. The Kroutil's Yukon Mill & Grain Company was eventually sold to Shawnee Mills, and the Dobry Mill was acquired by Mid-Continent. With these large mills towering over the city, and the history of grain milling, the Yukon High School uses the nickname of the Millers.

The two large grain mills and elevators still stand at Yukon, although not served by the railroad. The MFC Farmers Co-op is to the north of the tracks at Main Street, while the Yukon Mill & Grain Company is to the south. The Yukon Mill is noted for its large painted "Yukon's Best Flour" sign and the lit sign on its roof. Other claims to fame for

Yukon include being the home town of Garth Brooks, the birthplace of Joe Albertson (founder of the Albertsons grocery store chain), and the Annual Czech Festival. The population of Yukon is about 25,000.

The MFC Farmers Co-op elevator complex towers over Route 66 on the east side of Yukon, Oklahoma.

Not far away is the more famous elevator of Yukon's Best Flour, which features this large advertisement.

The Railroads

In 1895, the Choctaw, Oklahoma & Gulf had their passenger depot on the south side of the tracks, located just north of Spencer Avenue (today's Main Street). Just south of Spencer Avenue and on the north side of the tracks were the railroad's stockyards. Maps show that there were three elevators south of Spencer Avenue and on the south side of the tracks. These were the J. H. Kuhlmans Elevator; the Sheldon & Newland Elevator; and the Yukon Mill & Elevator Company. By 1898, the two elevators had been acquired by Shields & Doyles.

Yukon was a water stop for the railroad during the early 1900s. In 1909, a new water treatment plant was installed at Yukon. In 1979, the Rock Island reported that Yukon was a train orders station per Rule 221, and that there was a 7668-foot siding to the north. Additionally, there were a number of industry tracks into the grain mills and elevators, totaling 6850 feet. Besides the elevators, Brooks & McConnell, Inc., a construction and asphalt firm, also leased a track during the 1960s.

Hidden away on the north side of Main Street between 3rd and 4th Streets is the wooden Oklahoma Railway Company station, and a metal transformer station. Just to the north, located on the spur track that once went east to the MFC Farmers Co-op mill and elevator, is the Yukon's Best Railroad Museum. The museum is in a converted plug-door box-car. Also at the museum is a former Union Pacific maintenance-of-way passenger car with Baltimore & Ohio trucks. Union Pacific Class CA-11 caboose #25865 is also located here. The caboose was one of 100 bay window-equipped compact-body cabooses that were received in 1979. This caboose was built in July 1979, and retired on March 13, 1992. It should be noted that the museum is generally open by appointment only.

A unique railroad heritage item at Yukon is the former Oklahoma Railway Company wood train station, hidden behind several businesses along Route 66.

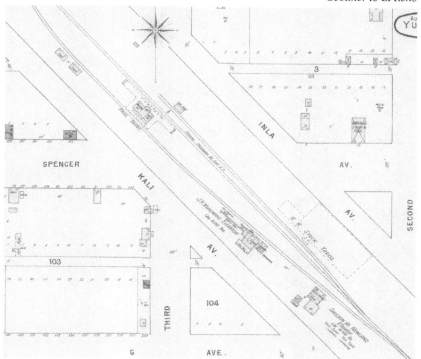

Sanborn Map Company – Depot and Elevators – August 1895. *Sanborn Fire Insurance Map from Yukon, Canadian County, Oklahoma.* Sanborn Map Company, Aug 1895. Map. Retrieved from the Library of Congress, https://www.loc.gov/item/sanborn07311_002/.

The core of the Yukon's Best Railroad Museum is this boxcar, located next to the former Rock Island Railroad tracks on the north side of Yukon, Oklahoma.

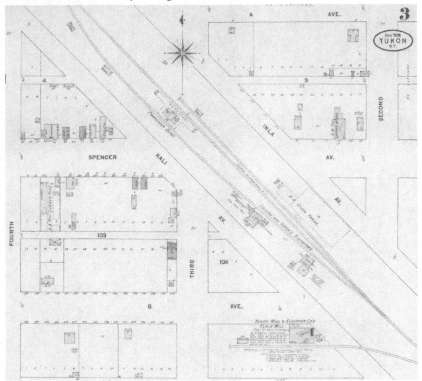

Sanborn Map Company – Depot and Elevators – August 1898. *Sanborn Fire Insurance Map from Yukon, Canadian County, Oklahoma.* Sanborn Map Company, Aug 1898. Map. Retrieved from the Library of Congress, https://www.loc.gov/item/sanborn07311_003/.

503.5 CIMARRON ELECTRIC – To the south was a 650-foot spur track into a large electric substation. In Rock Island documents, this location was shown as being at Mile 503 Pole 19. Missouri-Kansas-Texas and Union Pacific designated this track simply as Cimarron. The mainline switch was removed a number of years ago as part of the rebuild of the line by Union Pacific.

503.7 NATIONAL FEED LOT – To the north was once a 400-foot spur track that served a cattle feedmill. National Feed Lots was a subsidiary of the Oklahoma Livestock Marketing Association, which provided a cooperative feeding plan for its members. National Feed Lots operated the feedlot for the Marketing Association. This feedlot opened in 1960, but the remains of the facility are to the north, and the tracks have been completely removed. Even further north, the large feedlot is gone.

This location was shown as Mile 503 Pole 24 in the last Rock Island employee timetable. Union Pacific records show that both Cimarron Electric and National Feed Lot were included as Cimarron.

505.3 VIRGINIA – A station by this name was shown in an early Official Guide, but the name didn't last long and the station wasn't shown on early maps.

Not far to the west is a bridge at Milepost 505.7. This bridge consisted of a 40-foot I-beam span with several timber spans off each end. The 40-foot I-beam span was moved here in 1962 from Cowskin Creek near Wichita, Kansas. The Cowskin Creek bridge was replaced when the stream was diverted by a drainage project.

506.7 BANNER – The *American Co-operative Manager* of May 10, 1920, reported that the "Banner Co-operative Elevator Association has been incorporated for $50,000." This elevator association still exists and is located south of the mainline. The facility includes several older concrete elevators, a scale house, and several modern steel bins. The firm has locations here and at Union City and Tuttle. It supplies its members everything from bagged and bulk feed to fertilizers to diesel fuel. At one time, there was a 5420-foot elevator siding, but it has now been shortened and is simply a spur track with the switch on the east end.

The concrete elevator at Banner, Oklahoma, still carries the Banner Co-op name on its elevator tower.

The community was first known as Cereal, and it was the site of one of the Canadian Mill and Elevator operations, which was sold to James and John Maney in August 1905. A 1911 Rand McNally map showed the location to be "Banner or Cereal P.O." which implies the town was already known as Banner, but the post office was known as Cereal. Records of the post office show the station to be Cereal (1900-1911) and then Banner (1911-1954).

508.0 HALIBURTON SAND PLANT – To the south of the mainline is a large unit train loop track that is used to serve the El Reno sand plant of Haliburton Energy Solutions. The facility includes ten 90-foot sand silos and 16,267 feet of double loop railroad track. The facility was closed in December 2019 due to the reduction of drilling in the region.

These tall towers were built to handle frac sand during the peak of the oil and natural gas boom in western Oklahoma. By May 2020, they were closed due to a slowdown in drilling.

509.9 SIXMILE CREEK BRIDGE – This stream forms near Mustang Field, south of El Reno, and heads northeast to here. It turns east just north of the bridge and flows into the North Canadian River about four miles east of here. The railroad uses a 60-foot through plate girder span to cross the creek.

510.8 GULF JUNCTION – Today, this location is at the grade crossing with Alfadale Road. However, this was once the junction between the original Choctaw Coal & Railway Company's Fort Reno-Oklahoma City mainline and the El Reno Passenger Cut-Off that opened during November 1903.

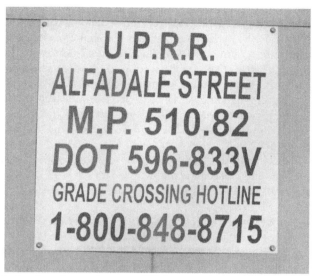

The Alfadale Road grade crossing east of El Reno marks the one-time location of Gulf Junction, the connection to the El Reno Passenger Cut-Off. The line opened in November 1903 to allow the use of a single Rock Island passenger station at El Reno.

Heading west, the original route, built by the Choctaw Coal & Railway Company as part of their Fort Reno to Oklahoma City railroad, continues straight from here, and then curves around El Reno. Maps from 1895 clearly show the track curving around the northeast side of town, following the route used by today's Union Pacific Oklahoma City Subdivision. This route passes Belt Junction, the El Reno rail yards, and then heads on west toward Amarillo, Texas.

Curving to the south was once the El Reno Passenger Cut-Off. This 2.4-mile line was built in 1903 to allow the consolidation of passenger services in downtown El Reno. The line connected with the north-south Rock Island mainline at Pacific Junction, providing access to the line in either direction. In addition, there was the freight bypass line that looped around the east side of town, making the area very busy. An Interstate Commerce Commission report described the location, but they used railroad directions, so the Kansas-Texas mainline was shown as running east-west, but was actually compass north-south. "There is a wye at Pacific Junction, the passenger cut-off forming the east leg, a wye track the west leg, and two tracks designated as the new main and the old main forming the north leg. The latter two tracks converge into the single-track main line a short distance west of the wye track. At a point 124.5 feet east of the main track or junction switch another track, known as the freight belt track, leads off the old main, while 151 feet farther east the wye track leads off the freight belt track to the right," and then connected with the line from Oklahoma City at Gulf Junction.

This complexity led to a collision between a passenger train and a freight train on June 11, 1934. On that date, a northbound freight was taking the "freight belt track" around El Reno. Meanwhile, passenger train No. 44 (one combination passenger coach and one baggage car) was being shoved southward by gas-electric motor #9000, with the crew planning to head east around the wye and then to Oklahoma City. The freight train was sideswiped by train No. 44, with the cause placed upon the conductor of the passenger train.

A labor complaint from the 1930s explains the operations from just a few years later. The complaint involved train No. 43, the Shawnee to El Reno local, and train No. 44, the El Reno to Shawnee local.

> *Beginning November 22, 1936, Train No. 44 secured its entire train of freight and passenger cars in the North Junction freight yard, proceeded south 1½ miles to the passenger station at El Reno, where mail, baggage, express and passengers were loaded, then continued on to the passenger main line, then northeast to the freight line at Gulf Junction, thence easterly to Shawnee. Beginning December 10, 1936, Train No. 43 made the return trip to El Reno passenger station by the same route where mail, baggage, express and passengers were unloaded and the crew thereafter required to take the freight cars and dead passenger equipment 1½ miles north to North Junction where it was backed into the far end of the freight yard from the east.*

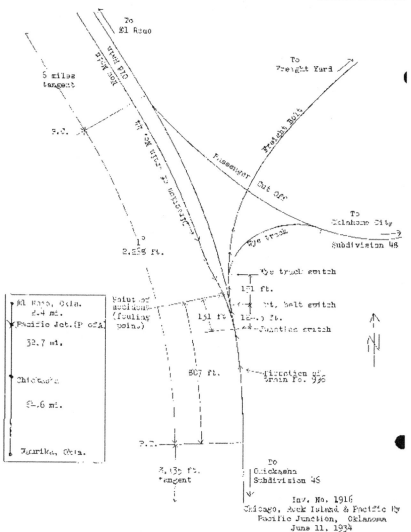

Diagram of Pacific Junction. *Report of the Director of the Bureau of Safety Concerning an Accident on the Chicago, Rock Island & Pacific Railway at Pacific Junction, Okla., on June 11, 1934.* Interstate Commerce Commission.

A westbound Choctaw Route passenger train would turn southwest at Gulf Junction and travel 2.4 miles on the El Reno Passenger Cut-Off to Pacific Junction (Milepost 403.6 on the north-south line). There, the train would turn north on the Mid-Continent Route, a Rock Island rail route that connected the Minneapolis-St. Paul area with the Fort Worth-Dallas region. A passenger train would travel one mile to the El Reno passenger station (Milepost 402.6), and then north to Rock Island Junction (Milepost 401.0) where the westbound passenger train would turn back onto the Choctaw Route. Meanwhile, westbound freight trains would typically remain on the Choctaw Route and enter the El Reno yard and shop complex, located on the northeast side of town. Eastbound trains would reverse these routes.

Gulf Junction was no longer in Rock Island timetables by 1969. After passenger service ended, the line wasn't needed and was abandoned in 1968. The grade can still be seen as it passes around the southeast side of El Reno. In 1979, this was the west end of the Automatic Block System of signals that started at Milepost 488.9 at Oklahoma City.

512.3 BELT JUNCTION – Belt Junction, located between East Woodson and East Rogers streets, is another junction created by the need to have joint facilities for the north-south Chicago, Kansas & Nebraska Railroad (CK&N) line, and the east-west Choctaw Coal & Railway Company line. The Belt Line started south of El Reno and curved to the northeast to connect to the Choctaw Route here. This 1.6-mile line allowed trains on the CK&N line to reach the Rock Island's yard and shops, located on the Choctaw Coal & Railway line on the northeast side of El Reno. The line was built in 1910 by the Chicago, Rock Island & Pacific Railway and still serves the same purpose for which it was created.

512.6 ST. LOUIS, EL RENO & WESTERN RAILWAY CROSSING – For about twenty years, the Rock Island Railroad had a crossing with the St. Louis, El Reno & Western Railway (SLER&W) north (railroad-west) of Belt Junction. The railroad diamond was on the north side of the Rogers grade crossing, where the SLER&W came south along Williams Avenue, once located a block west of Roberts Avenue. Just to the east was the El Reno Gas & Electric Company.

This railroad was built to benefit what was at the time the Territorial Capital of Oklahoma – Guthrie. The city already had several connections to the east, and the SLER&W planned to build to the southwest to reach the Rock Island terminal at El Reno, about 40 miles away. The railroad was incorporated in the Oklahoma Territory on January 5, 1903, and the railroad opened for operation during June 1904.

Belt Junction connects the Choctaw Route with a freight bypass from the Mid-Continent Route, which runs from Fort Worth to Minneapolis-St. Paul. The track to the left is the Choctaw Route mainline, although it looks like some kind of industry spur as it climbs up to the junction.

Initially the railroad benefitted from serving a number of oil boom towns, and the Fort Smith & Western Railroad Company bought 51% of the stock in 1906. This was probably the high point of the SLER&W as the capitol moved to Oklahoma City, and the oil boom in the Cushion Pool quickly came to an end, taking much of the freight and passenger business with it. Receivers were appointed in October 1915, and the line suffered through a 1920 flood.

A 1923 report by the Interstate Commerce Commission stated that "[i]n no year prior to the receivership (except possibly one) were the operating revenues sufficient to meet operating expenses and taxes. No interest has ever been paid on the company's funded debt and no part of the principal thereof has ever been paid." Service was stopped over the North Canadian River bridge due to damage, and all operations ended in late 1922-early 1923, with abandonment approved on March 27, 1923. The railroad was abandoned in 1924, but there are reports that a few trains ran as late as 1926 to move grain for some farmers and elevators. Finally, the track was gone by the end of 1927, except for part of the

545

El Reno terminal which was sold to the Oklahoma Railway Company in 1926.

Sanborn maps (1908) show that the St. Louis, El Reno & Western Railway once had a one-story wooden depot with a water tower nearby to the east of downtown El Reno, located on the northeast corner of the intersection of Woodson and Roberts. Their freight house was to the south. Some reports state that there was also a station near the First National Bank Building at 100 South Bickford Street. The January 1910 *Official Guide* stated that the CRI&P and the SLER&W stations were about ¼-mile apart.

513.3 EL RENO YARD (FO) – The El Reno Yard complex was a major terminal on the Chicago, Rock Island & Pacific, and in 1960 it contained 35 tracks and handled as many as 60,000 cars a month. The facilities handled not only the Choctaw Route traffic, but also the Mid-Continent Route that ran from Minneapolis-St. Paul to Fort Worth. Over the years, this facility has featured a large freight yard, a roundhouse, a backshop, diesel shop, car shops, wood mill, equipment paint shops, and numerous mechanical department offices. By the 1920s, more than 1200 of El Reno's 15,500 residents worked for the railroad.

In 1920, there were three shop complexes in the area – Shawnee, Chickasha and El Reno. At the time, Shawnee had a freight car repair shop with a capacity of 150 cars, El Reno with 100 cars, and Chickasha at 70 cars. In addition, all three locations had roundhouses and engine facilities. In 1927, a large car repair facility was constructed in El Reno not far north of the 23-stall roundhouse. With the Great Depression of 1929, there were two backshops located at Chickasha and Shawnee. Chickasha's backshop was closed and the work was moved to Shawnee. In 1939, the Shawnee shops were closed and transferred to El Reno.

During the 1950s, there was additional consolidation of shops at El Reno. The car repair shops were modernized, the capacity to build new cars was added, and a reported 1300 workers were employed by the Rock Island at El Reno. Until the end of the railroad, improvements were still made. For example, in 1978, a $1 million freight car painting facility was built. Track charts from the time show that there was an 8-track yard to the north of the mainline, and a 5-track yard to the south, plus a yard used by the car shops. When the railroad shut down, there was hope that the shops would be acquired by another railroad or by a freight car maintenance company. However, the yard and shops remained generally vacant for years.

To reach the shops area, there was a lead just north of the Foreman Drive overpass (Milepost 512.7) that passed the roundhouse and into the car shop yard. The overpass for North Choctaw (Milepost 513.3), also known as U.S. Highway 81, basically separated the shop area to the east from the freight yard to the west. The yard goes all the way to the diamond at CRI&P Crossing at Milepost 514.3. Today, the shops are all gone, but the foundations remain, and the rail yard has been rebuilt to mainly serve as a transload facility for sand. Much of the eight-track downtown yard remains to handle local switching.

During the operations by the Chicago, Rock Island & Pacific, there was a short stretch of Absolute Block System from Milepost 513.4 to Milepost 514.4 to allow trains in and out of the yard, through the junctions, and across the diamond known then as CRI&P Crossing.

Railroad Services at El Reno

The Rock Island Railroad was important to El Reno, and El Reno was important to the railroad. For the city, they went as far as renaming Main Street to Rock Island Street to honor the railroad that helped to create the city. Just as the shops were eventually consolidated at El Reno, management of the railroad also moved here, requiring the large office building downtown.

One of the earliest records of this consolidation was in February 1908 when W. S. Tinsman was named the manager of both the Southern and Choctaw districts, and was based at El Reno. In March 1910, the Southern and Choctaw districts were consolidated into a new Southern District, with T. H. Beacon as its head and based in El Reno. About the same time, the Rock Island's Southern District supervisor of water supply was moved from Little Rock to El Reno. During February of 1911, the freight office for the District was also moved from Little Rock to El Reno.

In 1979, El Reno was still a crew change point on the Choctaw Route, serving as the dividing line between Subdivision 33 to the east to Shawnee, and Subdivision 34 to the west to Sayre, Oklahoma. Because of this, there were a number of services provided at El Reno. General order boards and books, a train register station, a standard clock, wayside radio, and train orders (with no train order signal) were available at El Reno. For the trains, El Reno had a fuel and water station, plus a turntable. The area was protected by yard limits which stretched from Mile 510 Pole 9 to Mile 512 Pole 12.

Where Rock Island trains once operated, today Union Pacific handles the business. On this day in May 2020, Union Pacific #2691 is switching the grain elevator just south of the former Rock Island station on the Mid-Continent Route between Fort Worth to Minneapolis-St. Paul.

The City of El Reno

The City of El Reno had a fairly typical start for the area, but with a few twists thrown in. The land that the city sits on is actually divided by the 98th Meridian, so the land on the east side of town was settled as part of the Land Run of 1889. The land on the west side was in the lands of the Cheyenne and Arapaho that were part of the Land Run of April 1892. Two competing towns were settled in the 1889 land run – El Reno and Reno City – both named for the nearby Fort Reno. Both towns received a post office in 1889, causing some confusion with the mail. However, several floods along the North Canadian River and the construction of the railroads determined the winner, and the post office at Reno City closed in 1899.

However, El Reno almost didn't happen. John Foreman, Thomas Jensen and James Thompson all claimed acreage in the area, land that was used by the Oklahoma Homestead and Town Company to plat the townsite of El Reno. In 1890, the Village of El Reno was incorporated, but questions soon came up about how Foreman, Jensen and Thompson got the land. The U.S. Department of the Interior threw out the claims of the three men, leading to questions about the legality of El Reno. Eventually, the land became available again and legal title to the lots in El Reno became clear.

El Reno greatly benefitted from the arrival of the railroads. The Chicago, Kansas & Nebraska Railroad (CK&N) built from the Kansas-Oklahoma border southward through El Reno and on to Minco in 1889-1890. In 1891, the CK&N was sold to the Chicago, Rock Island & Pacific Railway Company, and the line was extended on to Texas the following year. From 1890 until 1892, the Choctaw Coal & Railway Company built east-west between Fort Reno and Oklahoma City. The two lines crossed at El Reno, making the town an important rail center.

In 1890, El Reno had a population of 285 and was growing quickly. By 1895, the El Reno Ice and Coal Company was located just north of Foreman Street on the Choctaw, Oklahoma & Gulf, former Choctaw Coal & Railway. Downtown on the Chicago, Rock Island & Pacific were two El Reno Mill & Elevator Company facilities, a Pabst Brewing Company's warehouse and ice house, railroad stockyards, and the Canadian County Mill & Elevator Company. With this growth in industry, the town reached 3383 residents by 1900. Agriculture and the railroad yards and shops supported the local economy, which was assisted even more by a number of government offices. With the population move to El Reno, it was chosen as the site for the district land offices for the 1901 land lottery drawings.

Despite the beginning of the Great Depression and the Dust Bowl, the population of El Reno reached 9384 in the 1930 census. This was helped even more when the fifth-largest prison in the United States was built west of town in 1934. Named the Southwestern Federal Reformatory, and later the Federal Correctional Institution of El Reno, it has remained a major employer, and the population of El Reno hit 10,078 in 1940. The City of El Reno was also far enough west of Oklahoma City that it was the center of business for the region, and featured a reported "twenty-four grocery stores, thirty-eight filling stations, twenty-four restaurants, ten hotels, eight tourist camps, twenty-seven barber and beauty shops, and sixty-three insurance companies, amid a host of other small businesses," according to the Oklahoma Historical Society.

El Reno continued a slow growth until it reached a population of 16,749 in the 2010 census. Much of this growth has been due to the construction of first U.S. Highway 66, and then Interstate 40, through the town. The City of El Reno is the county seat of Canadian County, and also the largest city in the county. Because of Interstate 40 passing along the south side of town, a number of new residential areas and businesses are located here, leaving the traditional downtown area at the far north end of the city limits. The area around Interstate 40 also features a number of hotels, restaurants, and gas stations.

The biggest event each year at El Reno is probably the annual Fried Onion Burger Day Festival, held the first Saturday in May. The event started with the Great Depression idea of stretching the meat supply using onions from local gardens. Each year, the event includes the cooking of the world's largest fried onion hamburger, weighing over 850 pounds. Other attractions include the Canadian County Historical Museum and the El Reno Heritage Express Trolley, both located downtown at the former Rock Island Railroad passenger station.

Rock Island Station and Canadian County Historical Museum

Located downtown on Grand Avenue is the Rock Island Depot (RF), a one-story brick structure built in 1907. Although not on the Choctaw Route, the station served trains using the passenger cut-off, providing connections from the east-west and north-south trains of the railroad. Because of the volume of passengers, baggage, express and mail, the station was 176 feet long, much longer than normal for this design. The station was built in the typical Mission or Spanish Colonial Style with red brick and a red tile roof.

The Rock Island brick station at El Reno still stands, but is hard to photograph as it is surrounded by other structures. Note that the building still features a pair of train order semaphores.

At the north end of the station was the baggage and express room, and the building was only 22 feet wide. The passenger part of the station was to the south and was 28 feet wide. Restrooms and a bay-window ticket office were in the center of the station, and two waiting rooms were to the south. The station stayed in use until the early 1970s.

After the station closed, the Canadian County Historical Society took ownership of the building. The complex now houses the Canadian County Historical Museum and its collection of buildings and artifacts. The buildings include the Rock Island station (1907), the El Reno Hotel (1892), Mennoville Mennonite Church (1893, the first Mennonite Church in the Oklahoma Territory), Red Cross Canteen (1918), Possum Holler School (1910), and General Sheridan's Headquarters (1876, Canadian County's oldest standing structure).

At the Rock Island station in El Reno, Oklahoma, a number of historic buildings have been preserved by the Canadian County Historical Society and its Canadian County Museum.

In addition to the buildings, the museum features former Rock Island #17209, a caboose built by the International Car Company in November 1971. The caboose was unique as it was one of the few that was painted blue and white as part of the last attempt to reorganize the railroad. During April 1980, the caboose became Union Pacific #24627, designated as a Class CA-13-4 caboose. The caboose was again chosen to be unique as it was equipped with Rockwell express trucks, which it retained in its service on UP. The caboose was finally retired on September 12, 1985, and donated to the Canadian County Historical Society during November 1988.

CRI&P caboose #24627 is located at the Canadian County Museum in El Reno, Oklahoma. The easily visible side carries Rock Island lettering, while the track side is painted for its Union Pacific days.

Besides the caboose, there is a former Rock Island Railroad steam locomotive tender. The tender is #2636, which makes it belong to a 2-8-2 built by the American Locomotive Company in early 1923. Tenders like this were often saved after the steam locomotive was scrapped as they were good for being a water car for maintenance-of-way use. This tender was donated to the museum in 1974.

A block south of the museum is the former Rock Island office building, often known as the Second District, or Southern Division, headquarters. The brick three-story (plus a basement) office building often housed as many as two District or Division offices. As late as April 1975, the Rock Island was still reorganizing its management units, with El Reno being impacted. An article in the April 23, 1975, *Arkansas Democrat*, stated that the Arkansas Division was being combined with the division at El Reno, Oklahoma, creating the large Southern Division. The Rock Island offices officially closed on March 31, 1980, and the building was soon owned by the El Reno Public Schools and used as their offices. Later, the building was used as the Heritage Park Apartments, a low-income housing facility. However, during May 2020, the building was closed due to several structural concerns and its future is unknown.

The former Rock Island Railroad office building still stands as of 2020, but its future is uncertain.

Forty years after the railroad closed, the Rock Island lettering in still barely visible above the entrance to the Rock Island Railroad office building at El Reno, Oklahoma.

In downtown El Reno is another remembrance of the Rock Island Railroad era – caboose #17145. This caboose was built in November 1967 by the International Car Company for the Rock Island Railroad. It became Union Pacific #24564 (Class CA-13-2) in April 1980. It was retired on September 12, 1985, and donated to Quinter, Kansas, a year later. It was eventually sold to a private individual at Yocemento, Kansas, and then moved to El Reno. This caboose is on display just south of the intersection of Choctaw Avenue and Wade Street.

CRI&P caboose #17145 sits in downtown El Reno. Unfortunately, a large box has been added to one side to protect the added heating and air conditioning.

Close to caboose #17145 is the Rock Island Diner, another indication of how important the railroad was to the community.

El Reno Heritage Express Trolley

Since August 2001, the Heritage Express Trolley has operated on 0.9 miles of track through downtown El Reno. The trolley barn was built just north of the former Chicago, Rock Island & Pacific Railroad station, and it operates from there to the downtown shopping district along Bickford Avenue.

The trolley is a double-ended car built by J. G. Brill in 1924. The car was first Philadelphia & Western Railway #60, known as a Strafford car for the route it ran. The car was rebuilt as #165 in 1931, and operated for SEPTA (Southeastern Pennsylvania Transportation Authority) until 1986. The trolley car then went to the Keokuk Junction Railway in 1991 and was used to move workers on the Mississippi River's Keokuk Dam. It was sold to El Reno during the late 1990s, and has operated here since. The car was rebuilt to use propane gas for power instead of overhead electric wires and renumbered to #145.

The El Reno Interurban Railway Company, and later the Oklahoma Railway Company, operated a suburban service in El Reno, and an interurban line east to Oklahoma City. This service ended in 1946-1947, and most of the track was removed from the streets. The former interurban building still stands, located just east of the Rock Island station.

The building is unique as it housed a hotel on the south end and the interurban station and offices on the north end. Today, one end is used as a senior citizens home while the other is used to house youth who have been removed from their homes for various reasons.

The south end of the interurban building at El Reno is certainly fancy compared to the north end, showing that this was the hotel end of the building. The building is still used for housing.

514.2 ROCK ISLAND JUNCTION – This was the switch that allowed west-bound trains on the Choctaw Route, and those from the El Reno yard and shops, to turn north onto the Mid-Continent Route toward Kansas, Iowa and Minnesota. A new connection has been built by Union Pacific that allows trains to now also turn south onto the Mid-Continent Route toward Texas.

514.3 CRIP CROSSING – This location, once known as Reno Junction, is the actual crossing of the Mid-Continent Route and the Choctaw Route, both of the Chicago, Rock Island & Pacific. Today it is known as El Reno Junction or UPRR Crossing, and is the diamond for the north-south Enid Subdivision and the east-west Oklahoma City Subdivision. His-torically, there have been connecting tracks in the northeast and south-west quadrants of the diamond, allowing trains to head to or from the nearby El Reno yard or the El Reno passenger train station downtown.

This diamond came about due to the construction by the Chicago, Kansas & Nebraska Railroad and the Choctaw Coal & Railway Com-pany. On June 29, 1888, the Chicago, Kansas & Nebraska Railroad was incorporated in Kansas (July 2, 1888, in Colorado), and over the next two years the railroad built south from Kansas and through El Reno to Minco, a total of 121 miles. The line soon entered foreclosure and was sold to the Chicago, Rock Island & Pacific Railway Company on June 10, 1891. The CRI&P extended the line on to Texas in 1892, making the line a through route across Oklahoma.

Running east-west was of course the Choctaw Coal & Railway Company, which surveyed a line from Fort Reno to about Oklahoma City. After several battles over the use of a right-of-way, the line opened during February 1892. The line became the property of the Choctaw, Oklahoma & Gulf Railroad in 1894, which continued construction of the line, completing it from Fort Reno, Oklahoma Territory, to Wister, Indian Territory, on October 1, 1895. Reportedly, the first train over the entire line was a coal train, followed by 100 cars of lumber. The line was built westward also, being completed from Fort Reno to Weatherford, Oklahoma Territory, in November 1898.

514.4 PANHANDLE JUNCTION – This switch just west of the diamond allows trains heading north from the El Reno passenger station to turn west toward Amarillo. There is also a storage track located north of the mainline at this location.

515.0 END OF UNION PACIFIC TRACKS – This is the west end of the Oklahoma City Subdivision, and the west end of El Reno Yard Limits. West of here, the track is owned by the State of Oklahoma and operated by the AT&L Railroad.

In this area the North Canadian River is often immediately adjacent to the north side of the tracks, often causing damage to the railroad during times of flooding.

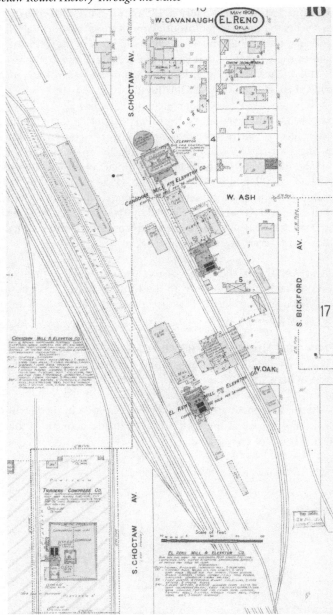

Sanborn Map – CRI&P Freight House and Elevators at El Reno – May 1908. *Sanborn Fire Insurance Map from El Reno, Canadian County, Oklahoma.* Sanborn Map Company, May, 1908. Map. Retrieved from the Library of Congress, https://www.loc.gov/item/sanborn07077_006/.

El Reno (OK) to Bridgeport (OK)
AT&L Railroad

The track west from near El Reno to the Texas-Oklahoma State Line near Erick is one of several major stretches of the Chicago, Rock Island & Pacific that was acquired by the Oklahoma Department of Transportation. These acquisitions were designed to protect existing industry and the vitality of a number of the towns and cities in Oklahoma, and to allow the continued economic development along the routes. The Oklahoma Rail Plan explains some of this activity.

> With major rail abandonments in the late 1970s and early 1980s, the State recognized the need to preserve as many of these abandoned lines as were feasible and economically possible. To accomplish this the State initially made available $22 million for the acquisition of abandoned rail freight lines. With these funds and appropriate studies the State acquired over 600 miles of rail lines with access to major rail carriers and expanded markets, replenishing a vital rail network to Oklahoma communities. As revenues developed from earlier rail line purchases the State made additional acquisitions with a final total of 867 miles of rail lines. In 2011 and 2012, as the individual agreements matured, two rail segments totaling 369 miles were returned to private companies. In accordance with the Department's long term plan of saving abandoned railroad lines they are eventually being returned to the private sector. The State's eight year maintenance plan assists short line operators with track maintenance.

By 1982, the trustee of the Chicago, Rock Island & Pacific was selling main-line routes at $50,000 a mile, and branch lines at $35,000 a mile. The Oklahoma Department of Transportation (ODOT) bought the Hydro to Elk City part of the line on November 19, 1981. Then, according to the ODOT, in July 1983, the Department acquired 37.6 miles between El Reno and Hydro from the former CRI&P Railroad for $1,700,000. Even as the purchase was underway, the North Central Oklahoma Railway (NCOK) started operating the line from El Reno to Geary on March 1, 1983. The NCOK also operated the Homestead Branch, which headed northwest from Geary. The track westward from Geary to Bridgeport and Hydro was used for car storage.

The NCOK was part of a company that owned several railroads operating parts of the CRI&P system. These included the North Central Texas Railway (NCTR – Dallas to Chico, Texas) and the Enid Central Railway (ENIC – Enid to El Reno, Oklahoma). The North Central Oklahoma Railway also operated Chickasha to El Reno, and Chickasha to Anadarko. The North Central Oklahoma Railway operated the El Reno-west line until late 1984 (some sources incorrectly say 1985), The Railroad Retirement Board (RRB) stated that the NCOK "ceased to be an employer under the jurisdiction of the Railroad Retirement and Railroad Unemployment Insurance Acts on October 1, 1984. The corporation was not dissolved but is defunct and non-operational." The RRB also shows that the AT&L Railroad Company started on May 12, 1985, founded by the Wheeler Brothers Grain Company as a way to protect the rail service. The company operated the line under a lease-purchase agreement with the State of Oklahoma.

Wheeler Brothers Grain was started in 1917 by brothers Frank and William "Bill" Wheeler. Frank's son, Gene, bought the company at the start of World War II and began building modern concrete grain elevators. The company also built a dry bulk fertilizer blending plant in Watonga, believed to be the second oldest in the state. Until 2014, the firm also operated cattle feedlots with a capacity of 27,000 head. The firm continued to expand, selling their feedlots but adding grain elevators for a total of 19, with a capacity of more than 20 million bushels. The firm is also heavily involved with the fertilizer, feed and seed industries.

The AT&L Railroad, named for Austin, Todd and Ladd Lafferty, grandsons of E. O. (Gene) Wheeler, who founded the railroad, operates former Rock Island track from Watonga to El Reno. It also operates 9.6 miles of the former mainline track from Geary to Bridgeport, Oklahoma. Finally, the AT&L also has overhead trackage rights on Union Pacific from El Reno to Oklahoma City.

According to the Oklahoma Department of Transportation, in 2013, "the AT&L completed an ongoing lease-purchase agreement for the 20 miles between El Reno and Geary and will continue to operate the 9.5 miles between Geary and Bridgeport under a lease operating agreement."

515.0 END OF UNION PACIFIC TRACKS – This is the west end of Union Pacific's Oklahoma City Subdivision. It is also the west end of the El Reno Yard Limits. West of here, the Choctaw Route tracks were bought by the State of Oklahoma and leased to the AT&L Railroad, which has since purchased them.

In this area to the south are several old gravel pits, and to the north is the North Canadian River. Heading west, the railroad slowly climbs through farms and pastureland.

516.8 TARGET CREEK BRIDGE – This six-span timber pile trestle crosses a small stream that drains the lands on the east side of Fort Reno. From this bridge, it flows northward for less than a mile before entering the North Canadian River.

Some legends state that Target Creek was where the name El Reno came from for the nearby city. Because of Fort Reno and nearby Reno City, the name Reno had been rejected by the post office. One of the town developers reportedly came up with "The Reno" for the name while crossing the stream, thus Elreno, and then El Reno as the name.

Heading west, the railroad passes through almost treeless country that is now used as pasture and farm fields. The railroad also faces an almost steady grade of 0.3% or more to Milepost 535.

517.5 FORT RENO – Fort Reno was the western end of the line built by the Choctaw Coal & Railway Company in 1890-1892. The line went as far as Oklahoma City before the Choctaw, Oklahoma & Gulf Railroad bought the railroad and extended it on east, completing the line from Fort Reno, Oklahoma Territory, to Wister, Indian Territory, on October 1, 1895. The CO&G built westward almost fifty miles to Weatherford, Oklahoma Territory, by late 1898.

Fort Reno was once a station that served Darlington to the north and Fort Reno to the southwest, located at what is today a farm road grade crossing. In 1914, Fort Reno was served by six passenger trains, although several would stop only for passengers going to or coming from specific stations. Two of the trains were locals – No. 725 and No. 726. The others were Trains No. 41 and No. 42, the *Western Express*, and No. 43 and No. 44, the *Fast Mail*. Westbound No. 43 was scheduled to meet eastbound local No. 726 here each evening at 8:39pm. The service didn't last and Fort Reno became a flag stop with limited service.

Because of the volume of freight moving on the railroad during World War II, a telegraph agency was established at Fort Reno on February 1, 1943. The station was opened as a freight agency and telegraph station only, and was closed soon after the war. By the 1970s, all of the side tracks and railroad facilities were gone.

Fort Reno has a long history, opening as a military post in 1876 and closing in 1948. The facility is today a Department of Agriculture research facility. The first settlement in this area was the Cheyenne and Arapaho Agency, located on the north bank of the North Canadian River and operated by Quaker Agent Brinton Darlington starting in 1869. In 1874, Indian Agent John Miles, stationed at the Darlington Indian Agency, demanded military protection after several uprisings took place in the area. Several different encampments were established, but after the Sand Hill battle in 1875, Fort Reno was authorized and built in 1875-1876.

The first activity was the location of a site on the south side of the North Canadian River, and the construction of corrals, a wagon yard, water wells, and a sawmill. A post was soon established, named Fort Reno at the order of General Phil Sheridan in February 1876. Major General Jesse L. Reno was an early friend of Sheridan, and he had been killed leading his troops in 1862 at the Battle of South Mountain in Maryland. Reno was a career officer, and had served in the Mexican-American War, the Utah War, several Indian Wars, and in the Civil War. A number of places have been named for him, including Reno, Nevada; Reno County, Kansas; and Fort Reno Park in Washington, D.C.

By the time Fort Reno had been built, most of the area fighting was over, and the fort was used to hold some of the most dangerous tribal leaders. In 1878, one of these, Dull Knife, attempted to escape with his North Cheyenne tribe members and fight their way north, but they were stopped. Fort Reno was also the home of the Cheyenne and Arapaho Indian Scouts, several units of the Buffalo Soldiers (Black calvary and infantry units), and U.S. Marshals. One of the jobs of the Fort was to manage the release of longhorn cattle for the Tribes to hunt for meat, an activity known as the beef issue. Fort Reno had a telegraph line installed to Fort Sill in 1879, and it was converted to a telephone line in 1884, making it the first one in Oklahoma. In 1898, the fort became a regimental headquarters for the Spanish-American War.

In 1909, the Darlington Agency closed and moved to Concho, Oklahoma. The next year, a Masonic Home was established at Darlington. During World War I, Fort Reno was used to train horses as cavalry mounts and to move supplies and artillery. In 1922, the Masonic Home closed. World War II had Fort Reno again handling horses and mules, this time as a purchasing depot. However, by 1943, the need for horses and mules had ended, and the 3000 horses at the fort were sold at auction over a three-day period. Fort Reno was also used as a prisoner-of-war camp for German and Italian prisoners. The Fort Reno Chapel was built during this time by members of the German Afrika Korps.

West of the main fort is the Fort Reno Cemetery, which includes graves for officers and enlisted men, wives and children, civilians, and even German and Italian Prisoners of War. The cedar tree-lined cemetery is worth a visit and tells its own story about the hardship involved at Fort Reno.

This special memorial at the Fort Reno Cemetery honors Corporal Patrick Lynch, killed in a battle against the Northern Cheyenne Indians on September 13, 1878. The unique stone was erected "by his comrades."

Just across a low wall from the calvary graves at the Fort Reno Cemetery is the grave of Bruno Stang, a German Luftwaffe unter offizier (junior non-commissioned officer) who died at Fort Reno as a POW on January 12, 1944.

In 1948-1949, Fort Reno was closed and the property transferred to the U.S. Department of Agriculture, which now operates it as the Southwestern Livestock and Forage Research Station. The mission of the center "is to develop and deliver improved technologies, management strategies, and strategic and tactical planning tools which help evaluate and manage economic and environmental risks, opportunities, and tradeoffs, for integrated crop, forage, and livestock systems under variable climate, energy and market conditions."

This water tower looks down upon the original Fort Reno, and makes it clear what the current purpose of the facility is.

Nearby El Reno took its name from Fort Reno, as did the failed town of Reno City. However, the fort has also been the center of several modern controversies. The combined Cheyenne-Arapaho Tribes claim the site and have been trying to re-acquire the lands the fort and research facility occupies. They claim that the fort was built illegally and the land is theirs according to various treaties and laws. The primary one is an 1883 executive order that stated that the 9493 acres was for "military purposes exclusively." However, an April 12, 1892, presidential proclamation ended tribal claims on the property as a part of making land available to individual tribal members.

A major issue with the attempt to claim the land was a $107,000 donation to the Democratic National Committee in 1997 which included a note about obtaining Fort Reno, along with a request to President Clinton. The immediate action by several Democratic politicians raised concern about what the campaign donation had been for. Things became worse when tribal leaders refused to answer questions without a grant of immunity. Although several attempts to give the land to the combined Cheyenne-Arapaho Tribes have been made, none have been successful.

Today, Fort Reno is open to the public. There is a visitor's center with fort memorabilia and exhibits, and many of the buildings still stand. Because of the history here, Fort Reno was added to the National Register of Historic Places in 1970.

This relatively modern building contains the official Fort Reno visitor's center, but a walk around the facility may be the best explanation of Fort Reno's history.

The Chisholm Trail

The Chisholm Trail passed through the Fort Reno area, but the Choctaw Route never benefitted from the cattle that were moved along it as the trail was in use from 1867 to the mid-1880s. The trail came about because of the large cattle herds in Texas that were left after the Civil War. Neither the Confederate or Union armies could reach the herds, so they grew and grew during the war. After the Civil War, there were large markets for the beef in the north and east, but there was no transportation to get them there.

Before the war, cattle had been driven through Missouri on the Sedalia Trail, but farmers had taken over the route and built fences to protect their crops. Additionally, the Texas longhorn cattle brought a tick disease which they were immune to, known as Texas Fever, which was fatal to the Missouri cattle. To protect their herds, Missouri farmers often attacked the Texas herds, stampeding them and running off their drovers. With cattle worth $4 in Texas and more than $40 in the eastern markets, a new route had to be found. Railroads to the north of Texas were the answer.

A new route was proposed by Joseph G. McCoy, an Illinois cattle feeder and broker. He determined that Texas cattle could be driven north during the grassy season to the Kansas Pacific Railway in Kansas. This would move the cattle to the railroad for shipping to eastern markets, and the grassy route would help to fatten them up. The route McCoy chose was being used by Jesse Chisholm, a mixed-blood Cherokee trader who worked with many of the area tribes. Earlier used by Federal troops to evacuate area forts during the Civil War, Chisholm used the route to move in supplies and goods.

Known initially as Jesse Chisholm's Trail, the cattle trail consisted of a number of smaller trails in Texas, and then several closely linked routes north from the Red River and across Oklahoma to Abilene, Kansas, where McCoy built stockyards. While the trails used moved about between Yukon and El Reno, the general route was always known as the Chisholm Trail. The first cattle drive was made in the spring and summer of 1867, moving 2400 head of cattle, part of the 35,000 head that were shipped from Abilene that year. The profits were large and 75,000 head moved in 1868, then 150,000 in 1869, and 300,000 in 1870. Soon, about one-half million cows and tens of thousands of mustang horses were moved north along the route each year.

One branch of the Chisholm Trail passed by Fort Reno, as it was a potential market for the beef, as well as being a resupply point. However, this route lasted less than twenty years. In 1885, Kansas passed a quarantine law to prevent Texas Fever from spreading through local cattle herds. Additionally, large ranches were forming and using barbed wire to control their grassy ranges, and railroads were spreading across Texas, ending the need for the long drives.

517.7 **BEEF CREEK BRIDGE** – A map from 1893 uses the name Beef Creek for this stream, while later maps have no name assigned to the creek. This 11-span timber pile trestle, and a 12-span timber pile trestle just to the west, cross this stream that drains the west side of Fort Reno. It flows about a mile to the north and into the North Canadian River.

521.5 **SIXMILE CREEK BRIDGE** – Look for the six-span timber pile trestle. This stream was known as Red Rock Creek in 1893, and it forms from Red Rock Spring in the hills to the south. The stream is much longer than six miles, as it turns to the northeast near here and winds through a number of fields before flowing into the North Canadian River north of Fort Reno.

523.2 CALUMET (UT) – This is the second location of the town of Calumet. Originally, the town was about a mile to the southwest, where a post office opened in 1893 using the name Calumet following the Land Run of 1892. The word calumet has an American Indian reputation because it was a word that was used for the peace pipe used by a number of tribes. However, the word is actually Norman, adopted by the French, who brought it to North America. In French, the word is "chalumeau" which means reeds or straw. The term came about because many of the pipes used a reed for the stem.

The tall, white elevator complex of Coffey Grain stands next to the former Rock Island mainline at Calumet, Oklahoma.

In 1898, the Choctaw, Oklahoma & Gulf Railroad began building west from Fort Reno and passed about a mile north of Calumet. As happened at a number of places, the nearby town moved lock, stock, and barrel to a new location around the railroad. During the move, Reuben G. Shirk laid out the new town on the property of William Tyler. The name officially became Calumet when the post office arrived from its old location. Calumet was a farming facility with up to three grain elevators and mills, several general stores, a hardware store, a farm supply store, and a few other businesses. Some additional businesses opened up after the new Route 66 was built through town in 1926, but an improved road was built five miles to the south in 1932, a route known as the El Reno Cutoff.

In an effort to get funding to build a community water system, Calumet incorporated in 1942. Calumet is still based upon farming, with the Coffey Grain elevator complex along the railroad. Records show that the elevator complex has a capacity of about 555,000 bushels and is served by the railroad. Another business in the area is the Canadian Valley Gas Plant, located several miles to the southwest. In the 2010 census, Calumet had a population of 507, but it has grown back to almost 600, the largest in the town's history. Much of this is due to Calumet having its own school system, elementary through high school.

For the railroad, in 1979, the Rock Island had a 5162-foot siding to the south of the mainline, and a 1649-foot elevator siding to the north. Both of these tracks are now used by the grain elevator.

In May 2020, the AT&L Railroad had locomotives #3001 (GP40, ex-MKT #227), #8102 (GP9, ex-IC #9254 rebuilt as a GP10, wearing McCoy Elkhorn Coal Corporation paint), and #5088 (GP38-2, ex-Southern #5088) parked at Calumet.

Heading west, U.S. Highway 270 closely follows the railroad to the south until near Geary. The track is also straight from Milepost 522.0 to Milepost 532.5.

529.4 KARNS – Shown sometimes as being Karns Spur, this was the only railroad spur between Geary and Calumet in the 1910s. In early 1917, the Corporation Commission of the State of Oklahoma held a hearing about Karns Spur and the complaints by approximately seventy-five area residents about the need for more services at the location. At the time, there was a small stockyard that had just been built "under a contract with a committee of certain shippers and stock men" who were to use the facility. A study of September-November 1916 showed that in those three months, 6 carloads of sheep, 3 carloads of corn, 2 carloads of hogs, 1 carload of cattle, and 1 carload of coal were shipped from the station.

The hearing led to a requirement that the railroad stop on flag one passenger train each way daily to take on and let off passengers and express, and to unload prepaid freight at Karns Spur for local customers. It also provided information about the location. One of the most interesting statements in the report described Karns by saying "that there is at Karns Spur but one building and this building is occupied as a general merchandise store...the store carried about a $2,500 stock of goods." It was also clear that there was only a short spur track at Karns, with no station or platform.

532.5 COYOTE HILL – The railroad passes around the north end of Coyote Hill and turns from heading northwest to heading southwest. This is the first curve on the railroad since east of Calumet. Coyote Hill exists because it is made of white dolomite, a material that is a harder and more resistant substance than sandstone; thus, it has survived the erosion so typical of the area.

The workers of the Writers Program of the Works Projects Administration (renamed from Work Progress Administration in 1939) reported on Coyote Hill in their book *Oklahoma: A Guide to the Sooner State*. The book stated that Coyote Hill was a favorite meeting place for the Cheyenne and Arapaho Indians, especially during the "Ghost Dance" or "Messiah" craze of 1890. This was a movement that was waiting for an Indian Messiah to lead the local tribes to triumph over the white settlers. Here, the attendees would reportedly bring food, blankets and a bed for the Indian Messiah.

According to the Works Projects Administration, there was a simple explanation for the supplies. "When the white man's God came to visit His children, He was a poor man. He had no house. He had no bed. He had no money. The little bird had a nest in the tree, the coyote had a hole under a rock, but white man's God had no place to sleep. We are better than white man. When our God comes He will find that we, His people, have bed ready for Him."

534.7 COUNTY LINE – The county line is at the County Line Road grade crossing with **Canadian County** to the east, while to the west is **Blaine County**. **Blaine County** started as County C after the Land Run of 1892. The county was named for James G. Blaine, a Republican who held many different positions in Washington, D.C. He represented Maine in the U.S. House of Representatives (1863-1876) and served as Speaker of the House (1869-1875), and then represented the state in the Senate (1876-1881). He was one of only two people to be Secretary of State under three separate presidents, and narrowly lost the 1884 presidential election to Grover Cleveland.

The Canadian-Blaine county line is easy to find at Geary, thanks to County Line Road.

The county is rural and farming, ranching and petroleum dominate. Blaine County may best be known for being the birthplace of Clarence Nash, the voice of Donald Duck and his three nephews Huey, Dewey and Louie. He performed the voices for 51 years and in more than 120 shorts and films. Nash was born in Watonga, the county seat of Blaine County. In the 2010 census, the county's population was 9785.

534.8 GEARY (GY) – Geary, despite its small size, was a fairly important railroad town. Running east-west was the mainline of the Choctaw, Oklahoma & Gulf Railroad Company. Heading north from the wye at the east end of town in 1969 was what was called the Geary Branch to Homestead, known as Subdivision 34A in 1979. The Geary Branch, also known as the Northern Branch, dates back to the Watonga & Northwestern Railroad Company, which was incorporated in the Territory of Oklahoma on May 19, 1900. Before work began, the company changed its charter and name and became the Choctaw Northern

Railroad Company on March 22, 1901. In 1902, the railroad built a 137-mile railroad northward from Geary to a connection with the Santa Fe Railroad at Anthony, Kansas. During this construction, the railroad was sold to the Choctaw, Oklahoma & Gulf Railroad Company on May 3, 1902. The route of the Choctaw Northern was described as having light grades and curves, and it was built by McGhee, Kahmann & Co. of Kansas City, Missouri, using 65-pound rail. C. E. Ingersoll of Philadelphia was the company president and the project was based out of the Choctaw's Little Rock office.

This tall elevator still stands on the former Choctaw Northern Railroad route at Geary. It is now operated by Wheeler Brothers Grain Company, founder of the AT&L Railroad.

The Chicago, Rock Island & Pacific Railway Company also acquired a second rail route north of Geary. This one was built by the Enid & Anadarko Railway Company (E&A), which was incorporated under the laws of the Territory of Oklahoma on March 8, 1901. The railroad built several sections of track, plus received permission to build a line east to Fort Smith, Arkansas, through Indian Territory. However, when the Rock Island acquired the railroad on October 21, 1903, the E&A had built only 65 miles of track from Enid west to Ringwood and then south

571

to Watonga, and on to Greenfield Junction, six miles further. In 1902, the company built almost forty more miles of track from Bridgeport to Anadarko, Oklahoma, and also from near Geary south to near Bridgeport, passing around the west side of Geary.

The year 1902 was a busy one for the Choctaw, Oklahoma & Gulf at Geary. The railroad served more and more shippers, including Kroutil Brothers (40,000-bushel grain elevator), a stockyard, the Clair Cotton & Grain Company, the Geary Milling and Elevator Company (50,000 and 10,000-bushel elevators, plus a 150-barrel-per-day milling operation), the Choctaw Mill and Elevator Company (8000-bushel elevator), and R. H. Harsh and Company (5000-bushel elevator). The railroad's depot stood on the north side of the tracks at the south end of Broadway. A report by the Governor of the Oklahoma Territory stated that by 1904, the Chicago, Rock Island & Pacific had already "established a terminal and freight division with roundhouse and other conveniences employing now sufficient men so that over 50 families are living here supported from that source alone...[t]he railroad's business now uses over 5 miles of side track here."

Initially, the general manager of the Choctaw Northern Railroad was based at Geary, and the offices stayed here for a few years after the line was acquired by the Rock Island. On January 15, 1907, the Rock Island Lines reorganized a number of its divisions as new track was being built. The Pan-Handle (Panhandle) Division included the Geary to Texola mainline, the Enid to Anadarko line (Enid & Anadarko Railway), Geary north to Anthony in Kansas, and Ingersoll to Alva (both Choctaw Northern Railroad). The division offices were at Geary, Oklahoma Territory. However, the headquarters was moved to El Reno on July 1, 1908. As the shops expanded at El Reno, and the trains on the branches began to coordinate with mainline trains, few divisional facilities were left at Geary.

Because of the various railroads that built to Geary, there were once a number of tracks scattered through the community. Many of these tracks are now gone. There was a Rock Island rail line that looped around the northwest side of Geary, just west of Galena Avenue. This part of town was the Rock Island Addition, a part of Geary created by the railroad. Even today, some of the railroad grade of the Enid & Anadarko Railway is still visible for several miles southwest of Geary as it follows the current rail line.

The Choctaw Northern Versus the Enid & Anadarko

While these two small railroads may seem to be insignificant in the big picture of the Rock Island Railroad, they were actually a part of a larger battle between the owners of the Chicago, Rock Island & Pacific and the Choctaw, Oklahoma & Gulf. A number of newspaper reports covered the issue that the Enid & Anadarko Railway was supported by the Rock Island, while the Choctaw Northern Railroad was backed by the Choctaw Route. At the same time, the Rock Island had announced some plans to build other lines parallel to the CO&G. With many of the stockholders of the Choctaw being more interested in turning a profit than in fighting a railroad war, the railroad was reorganized for sale to the Rock Island on May 6, 1902, and then fully acquired on March 24, 1904. Therefore, the two railroads were initially built as competing lines, but they soon fell under common ownership and their lines were consolidated where appropriate.

Geary Passenger Train Service

In late 1909, Geary was a center of passenger service. The east-west Choctaw Route had three trains operating in each direction at the time. Westbound No. 45-41, *Western Express*, was here at 8:40am. This allowed passengers to get off at Geary and catch No. 770 north to Watonga and Alva. The second westbound was No. 769, a local that was operating from Oklahoma City to Geary and that was scheduled to arrive at 9:20am, where it turned north and became train No. 770 on the Northern Branch. The final westbound was No. 47 at 2:50pm. This was a McAlester to Sayre all-stop train.

Eastbound, the Sayre-McAlester No. 48 departed at 11:43am. The second passenger train that headed east was No. 770, which was No. 769 on the Northern Branch. It was scheduled to depart Geary at 8:30pm. The final Choctaw Route eastbound was No. 42-46, which left here at 9:50pm.

The Northern Branch – Geary to Caldwell – had a daily passenger train (No. 770) that departed Geary at 9:30am and arrived at Alva at 2:00pm. It then returned as train No. 769, departing Alva at 3:15pm and arriving at Geary at 8:15pm. Both trains were actually part of an Oklahoma City-Geary-Alva service. The complication of the operation was that the trains changed numbers on the branch from what they were on the mainline.

Train No. 753 operated southbound from Enid to Waurika on what was shown as the Enid and Waurika Line. It was scheduled to depart Geary at 1:50pm. Northbound No. 754 operated over the same route and departed Geary at 11:43am. Both of these trains operated on the Choctaw Route between Geary and Bridgeport.

Today's Railroad at Geary

The Choctaw Northern Railroad route wasn't very successful, and the track north of Watonga was abandoned on October 31, 1926. For a number of years, the Enid & Anadarko Railway also served as branches off the Choctaw Route. The first abandonment was the duplicate trackage between Watonga and Greenfield (six miles abandoned on March 1, 1920). The track from Bridgeport to Anadarko was abandoned in 1939. By the 1960s, only the track between Geary and Homestead remained.

For the Choctaw Route mainline, there were several yard tracks between the legs of the wye to the north. To the south was a siding plus a house track. In 1979, the siding was 4354 feet long, and the other tracks had 5762 feet of capacity. Geary was also a train orders station per Rule 221, a train register station, and it housed a standard clock. For the locomotives, Geary was a water station. Now, the locomotives of the AT&L Railroad Company are often found here in the small yard that remains.

AT&L Railroad #2165, former AT&SF #2877 (GP7, rebuilt and renumbered by the Santa Fe as a GP7u), has been a constant on the railroad for almost two decades. Here, it is parked at Geary in 2020.

Heading west from Geary, the railroad tops the grade at Milepost 535.0 at an elevation of 1553 feet. It then starts down Lumpmouth Creek as it heads to the crossing of the Canadian River near Bridgeport. The bottom of the 1% grade is near Milepost 539 and is at an elevation of 1415 feet.

On May 14, 1986, the Oklahoma Department of Transportation and the AT&L Railroad reached an agreement to have the AT&L provide operations on the 9.5 miles of track between Geary and Bridgeport. Oklahoma DOT records state that while the lease is for 9.5 miles, only about five miles are actually used due to a washout. However, several freight cars have been spotted at Bridgeport, indicating that track repairs were made. Small amounts of traffic have moved over this route and it has often been used for car storage. However, by 2020, the line west of Geary was overgrown with trees and vegetation, and the grade crossings show that no trains have passed in years.

This grade crossing at Milepost 538.6 shows the lack of use of the tracks west of Geary, Oklahoma.

City of Geary

Geary is another community created by the Land Run of April 1892 on land that was previously part of the Cheyenne-Arapaho reservation. S. E. Huff and his son William filed claim on land to the northwest of today's Geary, and a townsite company acquired two quarter sections from the Huffs for a new town. Edmund Guerriere, a former Army scout and interpreter of French-Cheyenne ancestry, claimed land near-by, and his name was used for the new town. However, the difficult spelling and pronunciation of his name led to the use of Geary as the name. The Geary post office opened on October 12, 1892.

When the Choctaw, Oklahoma & Gulf Railroad started building west in 1898, it was obvious that the town was several miles to the north of where the track would be located. Even before the track was built, residents began moving south to create a new Geary, with the town officially established on May 3, 1898. By the time the railroad arrived on July 4, 1898, the population was already approaching 700 residents.

With the arrival of the railroad, Geary became a farm trading center and was established as a first-class city in 1902 with a population of 2561. While the area was prairie, there were 26 rail shipments of cotton in 1903-1904. Churches were built, and there was a dry goods store, several grocery and hardware stores, three lumberyards, three banks, two bakeries, a rooming house, ice plant, and eleven saloons. Industry included a 300-barrel flour mill, a canning factory, a broom factory, a bottling works, several cotton gins, and at least two grain elevators. Some of the major rail shippers during the 1910s included the Curtis Brothers Light & Ice Company, the W. H. Morrison Mill & Elevator (built 1909 with a capacity of 10,000 bushels), and the Geary Milling & Elevator Company.

At the same time that the town was growing, Geary experienced five major fires in 1903-1904 leading to more brick buildings. Until that time, the town used a series of public wells and water troughs, one of which remains and is listed on the National Register of Historic Places. Shortly thereafter, a city water system was installed. By the time of statehood (1907), the Special Census for Oklahoma found 1438 residents at Geary. The population experienced a boom with almost 1900 residents in the 1930 census, by which time Route 66 had been built through the town and several new businesses had started up to serve the traveling public.

This Route 66 mural covers the side of the Geary city hall.

Until the 1970s, Geary saw a slow decline in population until the drilling boom started in the area and the population bounced back to 1700 in 1970. Since then it has dropped to about 1300. Geary hosts several stores, restaurants, banks, and a full school system. Several grain elevators (2,230,000 and 240,000-bushel capacities) remain at Geary, although not served by the railroad. There is also a large fertilizer facility in the center of the wye that is served by the railroad.

Located downtown at Broadway and Main Street is the Gillespie Building, built by G. F. Gillespie in 1903 for his Bank of Commerce. The building is now listed in the National Register of Historic Places and houses the Canadian Rivers Historical Museum. The building is on the southeast corner of the intersection. Across Main Street is CRI&P caboose #17043. This caboose was built as a wide-vision model by the International Car Company in 1958. When the Rock Island Railroad shut down, it became Oklahoma, Kansas & Texas Railroad #43.

AT&L Railroad #2491 (ex-AT&SF CF7 built from F7A #37C) is parked at the Wheeler Brothers fertilizer plant at Geary on May 30, 2020.

After bouncing around several times, Rock Island caboose #17043 is now on display at the Canadian Rivers Historical Museum in downtown Geary, Oklahoma.

539.2 LUMPMOUTH CREEK BRIDGE – This bridge includes an 80-foot deck plate girder span, plus three timber pile trestles. The name Lumpmouth comes from the Arapaho tribe. Just south of the bridge, the railroad turns back to the west.

542.1 CANADIAN RIVER BRIDGE – The 900-foot-long bridge across the Canadian River is a mix of a number of different types of spans. There are two 200-foot riveted Warren through truss spans, a 250-foot pin-connected Parker through truss span, two 42-foot deck plate girder spans, a 44-foot and a 50-foot deck plate girder span, and about five timber pile trestle spans.

Several reports state that this is not the original bridge. In 1907, the bridge was apparently destroyed by a train that derailed on it. Legend has it that the train was full of German emigrants along with their livestock and other possessions. Several stories say that some of the cars are still buried in the river's quicksand, full of their clothes and furniture. Another report states that the bridge washed out in 1914 during a major flood.

This view of the northern end of the Canadian River bridge near Bridgeport, Oklahoma, gives an idea of what a locomotive engineer saw on the approach to the Canadian River.

579

Off the north end of this bridge, the railroad makes a nine-degree turn, sharp for a mainline. This area is known as Fire Canyon, and can be reached on East 1000 Road, found west of U.S. Highway 281 not far north of the Canadian River. Remains of the old toll bridge can be found alongside the river at Fire Canyon. Both were once part of Route 66.

The Chicago, Rock Island & Pacific showed that this was the South Canadian River. The railroad last crossed the Canadian River at Calvin, where it is much larger. In this area, the river can either be shallow after a dry spell or high and fast after a heavy rain. The river is more than 900 miles long, making it the longest tributary of the Arkansas River.

542.8 ENID & ANADARKO RAILWAY JUNCTION – From 1902 until 1939, this was a junction with the Enid & Anadarko Railway Company. This company built several sections of track in the area and used part of the Geary Branch and the Rock Island mainline to bridge them together. The Enid & Anadarko Railway Company was incorporated in Oklahoma on March 8, 1901. It first built about sixty miles from Enid, Oklahoma, to Watonga, Oklahoma, and on to Greenfield Junction, six miles further. In 1902, the company built almost forty more miles of track from Bridgeport to Anadarko, Oklahoma. In 1903, the company was sold to the Chicago, Rock Island & Pacific Railway Company.

For a number of years, the railroad basically served as branches off the Choctaw Route. The first abandonment was the duplicate trackage between Watonga and Greenfield (six miles abandoned on March 1, 1920). The track from Bridgeport to Anadarko was abandoned in 1939. The grade of the Enid & Anadarko Railway can still be found as it curves east and the Choctaw mainline curves west, located north of what remains of the town of Bridgeport.

543.0 COUNTY LINE – The railroad is running north-south here as it passes from **Blaine County** to the north, and into **Caddo County** to the south. **Caddo County** is named for the Caddo Tribe, which was moved to a reservation in this area during the 1870s. Later, the Kiowa, Comanche and Arapaho were also moved to the region. On August 6, 1901, the county was organized, and with statehood in 1907, part of the county was used to create Grady County. While oil has been important to the local economy, agriculture still rules. Products such as cotton, corn, wheat, alfalfa, broom and kaffir corn, poultry and livestock lead the list of agricultural products produced. During the 1960s and later, Caddo County led the state in producing peanuts, hogs and poultry. The county has about 30,000 residents and the county seat is Anadarko.

543.4 BRIDGEPORT – A quick look at Bridgeport today, with its population of about 100 residents scattered over more than a dozen blocks, fails to show what this town once was. The town started as an informal community in 1895, and then was officially created as a federal townsite in 1901 after the railroad was built through the area. The town was incorporated as Bridgeport in 1902.

The name Bridgeport, and its location, had a complex history tied to the Canadian River. At first, the area north of town was where stagecoaches and wagons could ford the river when water levels were low, or where a ferry operated when they were high. A toll bridge was built in 1893, and a store and post office opened in 1895 to serve those using the bridge. A small community began to grow around the store and the road to the south.

This sign welcomes visitors to Bridgeport, Oklahoma, and shows the early suspension bridge used by Route 66 to cross the Canadian River.

The original Bridgeport was to the east on the old road, but much of the town moved west about one-half mile to be where the railroad built several side tracks. Wheat and cotton (70 rail shipments during July 1903 - July 1904) were the primary agricultural products that moved by the railroad. When the State of Oklahoma was formed in 1907, the population was 462 and the town had a number of stores, a grain and cotton warehouse, and three banks. The 1910 census showed that the population had dropped some to 428, a trend that the town has had ever since.

As the area developed, the toll bridge was replaced by a free bridge in 1915, but it was soon damaged by a flood. What was known as the Key Bridge, a long cable bridge, replaced the free bridge, charging a toll for several years before becoming free. A small boom took place in 1926 when Route 66 was built so that it would use the Key Bridge north of town and pass through Bridgeport. This led the town to grow again, and the Oklahoma Historical Society reports that in the mid-1930s, the town had "twenty-five commercial enterprises, including a large cotton gin, two grain elevators, two hotels, a bank, and a lumberyard."

The Great Depression led to a steady decrease in population (302 in 1940, 199 in 1950, and 139 in 1960), and it didn't help when Route 66 moved. This route change came about in 1934 when a new bridge was built across the Canadian River to the east of Bridgeport, now used by U.S. Highway 281. This put Route 66 passing about a mile south of Bridgeport, where its remains can still be followed as a part of the National Register of Historic Places. Interstate 40 is in the same area, and the exit doesn't even list Bridgeport, but there is a truck stop and several casinos.

The Key Bridge burned in 1948 as part of a grass fire and was removed. The population stayed in the lower 100s, and the Bridgeport post office closed during 1976. The population was 116 in the 2010 census. The railroad's 1969 employee timetable showed that there was just a spur track left, capable of holding only eighteen freight cars. In 1979, the track was shown to be 1050 feet long. There was also a dispatcher telephone here for the use of train crews and track workers. The foundation of the depot and the shell of a grain elevator can still be found alongside the tracks of this community, which is approaching ghost town status. Much of the area around the tracks is now gated and fenced. From the brush along the railroad, it is clear that the railroad has not been used to Bridgeport for a number of years.

Heading west from Bridgeport, several washouts and heavy vegetation clearly indicate that the track is unused. To Weatherford, the line can be found as it passes through communities, but much of the rest now passes through private property or is washed out.

The Bridgeport post office closed in 1976, but the shell of the building still stood in early 2020.

Bridgeport (OK) to Weatherford (OK)
Oklahoma Department of Transportation – Out of Service

This track was built in the late 1890s by the Choctaw, Oklahoma & Gulf, and eventually became part of the Southern Division of the Chicago, Rock Island & Pacific. In July 1983, the Oklahoma Department of Transportation acquired 37.6 miles of track between El Reno and Hydro from the former CRI&P Railroad for $1,700,000. Before that, during November 1981, the Department acquired 62.4 miles of Rock Island track between Hydro and Elk City for $3,100,000. The track east of Bridgeport has been leased or sold to the AT&L Railroad Company, while the track west of Weatherford is leased and operated by the Farmrail Corporation. The track between Bridgeport and Weatherford is still owned by the Oklahoma DOT and is preserved should it be needed. At the moment, the track would need large investments to repair bridges and washouts, to install ties and cut brush, and to basically clean up and replace much of the railroad.

A 2018 report by the Oklahoma Department of Transportation explains the condition of the line between Bridgeport and Weatherford. "Currently a segment of this line from Hydro east to the Canadian River, in addition to the previously noted segment from Weatherford to Hydro, is not in operation because of structural damage, most of which occurred in 1987. This segment is presently the longest segment of state-owned property that is not operable. The rehabilitation of this route has been postponed pending additional economic and engineering evaluation."

543.4 BRIDGEPORT – Bridgeport, approaching ghost town status but just a few miles north of Interstate 40, is the west end of potential operations by the AT&L Railroad. Heading west from Bridgeport, several washouts and heavy vegetation clearly indicate that the track is unused.

544.5 BRIDGE – This bridge is essentially the west end of the AT&L Railroad lease, but the track east to Bridgeport is out of service. The bridge consists of a 61-foot deck plate girder span with about five timber pile spans off each end. This bridge, and a number of others in this area, cross streams that drain the hills to the south and flow northward into the Canadian River.

545.9 WHITE CANYON BRIDGE – This is another stream that drains the hills to the south. It is named for the white rock and soil found along its route. This bridge has been washed out several times, and the last bridge was built using three 45-foot welded flange beam spans.

In this area, the railroad passes through patches of woods with the Canadian River not far to the north. The county line between Caddo and Blaine counties is also just to the north, generally between the tracks and the river.

546.9 BRIDGE – This is another un-named stream that drains the hills to the south. While this stream has no publicly used name, there is a gravel pit along it, as well as several recent oil wells. The bridge consists of three deck plate girder spans that measure 32 feet, 35 feet and 60 feet.

This photo of Route 66, located not far south of the tracks, may help to explain all of the bridges in this area. Numerous streams flow north to the Canadian River, creating low ridge after low ridge.

548.5 DEER CREEK BRIDGE – Heading west, the railroad follows Deer Creek uphill as far as Weatherford, producing grades of less than 1.0% as it winds back and forth across the stream. This is what some sources call Deer Creek Bridge #1, or Rock Island Bridge No. 5485.

Deer Creek has flooded heavily in this area, destroying the approaches on each end of the bridge. New fill has been built, replacing the open panel timber pile trestles off each end. The bridge was once 542 feet long, but all that is left are the two 124-foot through truss spans over the main channel of the stream. In this area, Deer Creek is heavily impacted by flooding on the Canadian River, which the creek flows into less than a mile to the north.

548.7 MCCOOL – An early U.S. Coast and Geodetic Survey called McCool a "temporary station of the Chicago Rock Island & Pacific Railway." There were a number of gravel pits in this area, some used for track ballast. It is likely that the station was named for the McCool family who owned land in the area.

Not far west of McCool, the railroad has been washed out as a bend in the stream moved northward. Some of the rail still can be found in the streambed.

551.6 DEER CREEK BRIDGE – This is Deer Creek Bridge #2, or Rock Island Bridge No. 5516. The bridge consists of a number of different types of spans. From east to west, there are two timber pile trestle spans, a 50-foot deck plate girder span, a 124-foot through truss span, a 50-foot deck plate girder span, and eight timber pile trestle spans. While most of this bridge survived the 1987 flooding, there is some damage on the ends.

This bridge has long been an issue for the railroad, with large amounts of drift timber being left against the structure by Deer Creek. The bridge was rebuilt with three 50-foot girders on timber piers that had been reinforced with steel pilings, with timber trestle approaches. However, this was not enough as the piers blocked the flow of the stream during high water conditions. In 1961-1962, the bridge was replaced to provide a wider river channel. The work was the subject of an article in the March-April 1962 issue of *The Rocket*, the railroad's company magazine.

The reason for the article was the unique manner in which the bridge was replaced. Initially, the existing bridge was raised to provide additional clearance. At the same time, a spur track was built to the west of the bridge to store work equipment. The engineers on the project decided to also use the spur track as the construction site for the new bridge. "The new span was constructed over the spur track. When completed the span was raised onto a flat car and rolled into place above the new piers. After it was in place and the floor system installed, the three old timber piers, in the center of the picture, were razed, creating a new and larger opening for the stream. After the span was installed, the old deck-plate girders were removed and a new floor system installed in the truss spans. With the floor system in place, new rails were put into position."

The through truss span was set on a 60-foot flatcar, and bolted to the deck. Two bridge cranes were involved with the project, and one of the bridge cranes towed the car from the spur track onto the mainline while the second crane held the bridge steady on the flat car. The two cranes placed the bridge on the new piers as part of the plan. This was not the first use of this through truss span, as it had originally been used to cross Soldier Creek near Topeka, Kansas, replaced due to a flood control project.

With the 125-foot through truss span in place, most of the timber trestle to the west was replaced by one of the 50-foot-long girder spans, with the same work conducted to the east. As described by *The Rocket* article, the "new bridge consists of a 125-foot-long truss span, two of the old 50-foot girder spans and pile trestle approaches. The truss span and both girders rest on new concrete-capped steel pile piers. Steel sheathing has been applied to the piers to prevent debris from catching in the piling when it comes floating downstream."

552.6   DEER CREEK BRIDGE – This is Deer Creek Bridge #3, or Rock Island Bridge No. 5526. This bridge consisted of a 58-foot through plate girder span, with four timber pile trestle spans to the east, and five timber pile trestle spans to the west. The west end of this bridge is gone, washed out when Deer Creek flooded and widened the channel.

553.6   CADDO – About 1900, a station with this name was here. It was gone by the 1910 timetable and there was never a post office here. Caddo moved about a mile to the west and was renamed Hydro. This may be because there is another Caddo in Bryan County, located southeast of Oklahoma City.

554.6   HYDRO (CO) – Hydro was founded in 1901 as Caddo, located alongside the Choctaw, Oklahoma & Gulf Railroad. The official founding date was August 6, 1901, but when the post office opened during September, it used the name Hydro. The name Hydro came about as an effort to promote the town's plentiful well water, unusual for the area. The town of Hydro started late when compared to some of the towns to the east, but it couldn't be settled until the Wichita and Caddo Reservation was opened for settlement in 1901.

A school, several churches, and a newspaper (*The Hydro Review*) opened before the end of the year. Like many of the towns in western Oklahoma, farming and ranching were the primary businesses. Corn and cotton were the major crops grown, with 136 rail shipments of cotton from Hydro in 1903-1904. Livestock was probably more important, with cattle, hogs, sheep, horses and mules being shipped from the railroad stockyards. To celebrate the early good crops, the first Hydro Harvest Festival was held in September 1904. The fair, now known as the Hydro Free Fair, is reportedly Oklahoma's longest running free fair.

Located at the southwest corner of Hydro is the Hydro City Park, also known as the Hydro Fairgrounds. At the park is a small wooden

Rock Island depot. This is not the original Hydro station, as initially the station was larger, with one end being two stories to provide housing for the station agent and his family.

This small wooden depot is squeezed between several other buildings at the Hydro City Park. It has been greatly altered for other uses.

When Oklahoma became a state, Hydro's population was 524. By 1930, the presence of Route 66 just south of town had helped to grow the population to 948, but the Great Depression and the Dust Bowl ran people off from the community. South of Hydro on the old Route 66 is Lucille's Gas Station, listed on the National Register of Historic Places. Lucille was Lucille Arthurs Hamons, known as "The Mother of the Mother Road." She and her husband Carl operated the gas station and the Hamons Tourist Courts. The restored gas station remains, and the Hamons Tourist Court sign has been displayed at the Smithsonian Institution.

An oil boom during the 1980s brought some population back to Hydro, which surpassed 1000 residents. Downtown Hydro and its several blocks of original business district is about four blocks north of the tracks. The county line between Caddo and Blaine counties is a few blocks further north, leaving the north end of town in Blaine County while downtown and the tracks are in Caddo County. Around the Arapaho Avenue grade crossing, where the railroad station once stood, is the Hydro Co-Op Association, which uses several of the old concrete grain elevators that stand alongside the tracks. The railroad had a 3847-foot siding to the south, while there were several elevator tracks on the north side of the mainline, providing 2670 feet of track for grain loading.

589

South of Hydro, Oklahoma, is the early roadway of Route 66 and Lucille's Gas Station. Throughout western Oklahoma, Route 66 and the Rock Island Railroad followed each other closely, helping to make or break many of the communities that they passed through.

To find Hydro, Oklahoma, simply look for the large white Hydro Co-op elevator.

One of the things that Hydro is known for is a series of mounds south of town. They have many names, including Caddo Mounds, Antelope Buttes, and Hydro Mounds. Additionally, some were named individually by Route 66 travelers. Located about a mile north of Interstate 40, about 1000 residents still live at Hydro and the post office is still open.

556.2 **WASHOUT** – This is another area where Deer Creek has changed its channel and washed out the railroad. In this location, the stream created a new bend north of its original channel, washing out the railroad twice.

556.8 **DEER CREEK BRIDGE** – This is Deer Creek Bridge #4, or Rock Island Bridge No. 5568. This bridge included one 80-foot through plate girder span, and two 50-foot deck plate girder spans. The bridge still stands, but normally over dry land, as Deer Creek changed its channel and washed out the grade at the west end of the bridge.

557.1 **COUNTY LINE** – To the east is **Caddo County**, while to the west is **Custer County**. There is only one Caddo County in the United States, but six states have a Custer County – Colorado, Idaho, Montana, Nebraska, Oklahoma and South Dakota.

Custer County started as County G when the land was opened for settlement on April 19, 1892, and was part of the Oklahoma Territory. The land had previously been assigned to the Cheyenne and Arapaho tribes. During November 1896, the county was renamed Custer by a vote of the settlers in the county. The name Custer, naturally, came from General George Armstrong Custer. Custer is an agricultural county with a population of less than 30,000. Being in a higher and drier environment, the major crops grown in this area include wheat, alfalfa, and broomcorn.

The county seat of Custer County is Arapaho. The town was created by a federal government survey and plat that was made before the county was created so that there would be a county seat for the new Custer County government.

Custer County was once the home of three significant groups of traditional farmers – the Amish, the Dunkards, and the River Brethren. All three were basically Swiss/German religious groups with similar practices. The Amish are well-known, being a group of traditionalist Christian church fellowships that trace back to Swiss/German Anabaptist origins.

Dunkards, also known as Dunkers and Tunkers, are similar but with a belief in baptism by dunking, or full immersion. Properly known as the Schwarzenau Brethren, they wore plain clothing, coats with standing collars for the men, plain bonnets and hoods for the women. Beards were encouraged, but a solo mustache could not be worn. They spoke German, didn't celebrate holidays such as Thanksgiving or Christmas, didn't participate in politics, and did not use instruments of music in the house of God.

The third group was the River Brethren, basically a similar group that developed about 1770 along the east bank of the Susquehanna River in Pennsylvania. The group had similar requirements about plain dress and an opposition to war, alcohol, tobacco, and worldly pleasures. While the three groups can be confused by outsiders, the details of their faith led to separate leaderships and often a community separation. However, all three groups spread west as farmland became available.

558.0 LITTLE DEEP CREEK BRIDGE – Little Deep Creek forms west of Weatherford, flows around the south side of town, and then turns northeast to flow into Deer Creek not far north of here. This bridge is an 80-foot deck plate girder with five timber pile trestle spans off each end. The bridge was shown to be a total of 220 feet long at one time.

The name Deep Creek reportedly comes from the deep channels that the stream flows through, making cross country travel difficult for explorers and early settlers.

This highway sign for Little Deep Creek is not far from the Rock Island's own bridge across the stream.

558.4 INTERSTATE 40 – The tracks cross Route 66 using a seven I-beam span that measures 32 feet long. It still carries faded Rock Island lettering. Just to the south (railroad-west) the tracks go under Interstate 40. The railroad follows Little Deep Creek as it loops around the east and south sides of Weatherford.

Despite forty years of inactivity, the bridge over Route 66 near Weatherford still carries Rock Island lettering.

560.0 FARMRAIL LIMITS – This is the east end of the switching limits of the Farmrail Sunbelt Division. While the track east of here is out of service, heading west it can be used by Farmrail.

Weatherford (OK) to Erick (OK)
Farmrail Corporation

The August 16, 1901, issue of *The Railway Age* reported on the construction of the Choctaw, Oklahoma & Gulf west from Weatherford.

> *The extension from Weatherford, Okla., west to Amarillo, Tex., 203 miles, is being built under the charter of the Western Oklahoma Railroad Company. The entire line has been surveyed and grading will be completed from Weatherford to the Texas State line, 84 miles by October 1. Tracklaying is being pushed, and already 35 miles of rail are down from Weatherford to a point west of Foss. The contractors are Johnson Bros. & Faught of Saint Elmo, Ill. The maximum grade is 1 per cent for 64 miles and six-tenths per cent for the remainder of the line. This extension is being laid with 70 pound steel rails. The Texas portion of the line is being built under the charter of the Choctaw, Oklahoma & Texas, of which S. M. Ramsdell of Amarillo, Tex., is chief engineer.*

In November 1981, the Oklahoma Department of Transportation acquired 62.4 miles of Chicago, Rock Island & Pacific Railroad track between Hydro and Elk City for $3,100,000. In 1981, Farmrail Corporation (FMRC) was created and started operation of 82 miles of track between Weatherford (Milepost 560.0) and Erick (Milepost 642.0) for the Oklahoma Department of Transportation and the Interstate Commerce Commission. This is part of the famous Choctaw Route, also called the Choctaw District, running across Oklahoma on the Chicago, Rock Island & Pacific's Memphis to Tucumcari route. Most of this route was built by the Choctaw, Oklahoma & Gulf, which reached Clinton and Elk City in 1901, and further west by 1904. This track is operated as the Sunbelt Division of Farmrail.

This is not the only route operated by the railroad. Farmrail purchased 89 miles of former Kansas City, Mexico & Orient Railway (later ATSF) track between Westhom and Elmer, also in Oklahoma, in 2013, after operating it for several decades. The Grainbelt Corporation (GNBC) was created in 1987 to purchase 178 miles of track from Burlington Northern, located between Enid and Frederick, again all in Oklahoma.

This sign at Elk City – "Operator for Oklahoma Department of Transportation" – says much about the relationship between Farmrail and Oklahoma.

Farmrail is one of two railroads that is part of the Farmrail System, an employee-owned holding company that advertises itself as "Western Oklahoma's Regional Railroad." The two railroads, Farmrail Corporation and Grainbelt Corporation, are operated as one large railroad that serves 29 communities in 12 rural Oklahoma counties, using almost 350 miles of track that once were operated by the St. Louis-San Francisco (Frisco); Atchison, Topeka & Santa Fe (Santa Fe); and the Chicago, Rock Island & Pacific (Rock Island).

The railroad serves more than sixty shippers, many of them major farm and energy companies. The region is considered to be one of the premium producers of hard red winter wheat, has some of the highest-quality gypsum deposits in the country, and includes the Anadarko Basin, the largest source of natural gas in the United States. According to the railroad, the principal commodities handled include "frac sand, drilling fluids, winter wheat, feed ingredients, crushed stone, gypsum products, agricultural chemicals, cotton seed, and farm machinery."

Farmrail (FMRC) and Grainbelt (GNBC) not only operate miles of former Rock Island track, they also operate a number of former Rock Island covered hoppers in grain service, as demonstrated by GNBC #753606.

Farmrail and Grainbelt are hard to tell apart, but they clearly have different track ownerships and leases. Based in Clinton, Oklahoma, this sign points the way.

560.0 FARMRAIL LIMITS – This is the east end of the switching limits of the Farmrail Sunbelt Division. It is located just west of Airport Road at Weatherford. The tracks east of here are heavily overgrown, and the track and bridges have been damaged from several floods.

Just east of here is the large and modern Wanderlust Crossing RV Park. To the north, Airport Road is on the east side of the Weatherford Airport and its Stafford Air & Space Museum. The museum is named for test pilot and astronaut, Lieutenant General Thomas P. Stafford, a native of Weatherford. Stafford flew on four space missions – Gemini 6, Gemini 9, Apollo 10, and Apollo-Soyuz. The museum has more than an acre of display space under one roof, with more than 3500 artifacts on display.

561.7 INTERSTATE 40 – The railroad again passes under I-40, also now designated as Route 66 in this area. Interstate 40, which stretches from Barstow, California, to Wilmington, North Carolina, is 2555 miles long, making it the third-longest Interstate Highway in the United States. I-40 connects Memphis and Little Rock, crossing east to west across the center of Arkansas, and then on across Oklahoma, the panhandle of Texas, and through New Mexico. The Interstate is seldom very far from the Choctaw Route. The construction of I-40 started in 1957 just as the Rock Island was starting to suffer economic issues. The number of times that the tracks and highway come together shows how the more modern highway was built to directly compete with the railroad.

In the 875 miles between Memphis and Tucumcari, the railroad and Interstate 40 cross each other fourteen times, with all but one of these being in the 400 miles west of Oklahoma City. The highway was noted several times as having taken business off of the railroad, leading to less rail service and financial losses.

562.6 WEATHERFORD (WF) – Until the end of the Rock Island, Weatherford was still a train order station and a water station. In the 1979 timetable, there was a 2491-foot siding, plus 5810 feet of other tracks at Weatherford. An interesting timetable note for years was that snow plows would not clear the station platform at Weatherford and that they were to use the siding when passing through town.

The city started in 1898 as the community of Dewey, named after Admiral George Dewey. Dewey had just won the Battle of Manila Bay on May 1, 1898, and his fame quickly spread across the country. The Dewey post office opened on August 10, 1898. The fame was short-lived as on October 28, 1898, the town changed its name to Weatherford, taking the name of the nearby post office named Weatherford that had recently closed. Don't worry about Dewey, a small town near Bartlesville took the name during the spring of 1899.

The original Weatherford post office is connected to William J. Weatherford and his family. In April 1892, the third of Oklahoma's great land runs took place, and William J. Weatherford selected a quarter section of land in the area he called Jordan Flats. He and his family, plus several hired hands, soon built a number of buildings and dug a well, becoming a center of the newly settled lands. On August 25, 1893, a post office opened in his home with his wife Lorinda, who had been a postmistress in Arkansas, holding the same title here. The main road in the area passed their home, making it a logical stop. The family also opened a school and held some church services in their home, essentially making their home a community center. William J. Weatherford was described as being influential in the community and county, and he served as one of the first county commissioners. He was also a constable and received a commission as deputy U.S. Marshal in August 1893.

In 1898, the Choctaw, Oklahoma & Gulf Railroad was building west from El Reno, but there were plans to halt construction in the area. The county seat of County G, the name at the time, was Arapaho, and it expected to be the terminal point. Because of this, Arapaho refused to make any payments to the railroad, and the Choctaw Townsite and Improvement Company located a new townsite, about two miles south of the original Weatherford.

At the time, Beeks Erick was president of the Choctaw Townsite and Improvement Company, and he held an election in early 1898 that resulted in him being named mayor of the new town. After the election, he completed his purchase of area land on July 16, 1898, immediately had it surveyed, and lots were sold. The first tent went up on July 18th, the town was incorporated on August 3rd, and the townsite was platted and filed on August 6, 1898. Beeks Erick was involved with a number of communities along the railroad, and Erick, Oklahoma, was named for him.

The first wood building was a bank that opened on August 3rd, even before the town was official. A number of other businesses quickly pitched their own tents, and Dewey was created. However, there was one issue as there was already a Dewey in Indian Territory, so the name could not be used. On September 26, 1898, the original Weatherford post office closed, and soon reopened at the new Weatherford. The railroad opened to this new Weatherford on November 14, 1898, after building 46 miles of track from Fort Reno, and the town boomed. Saloons and stockyards quickly opened, and the town was called "wild and wooly" in a number of sources. By 1900, the population was 1017.

Much of the boom ended during the summer of 1901 when the railroad built westward. However, farming and ranching grew because of the railroad station. Farm products like cotton, corn and maize were shipped out by the railroad. A 1904 Department of Agriculture report indicated that there were 906 rail shipments of cotton from Weatherford in 1903-1904. Soon there was also a brick plant, a cement plant, and a broom factory at Weatherford. Southwestern Normal School, now Southwestern Oklahoma State University, was also created at Weatherford in 1901. Records of the Rock Island Railroad indicate that a number of companies once had rail service, and even leased tracks or property. These include the Park-Ward Company, E. A. Hadley, William E. Tindel, and the Elk Supply Company.

The population of Weatherford stayed between 2000 and 3000 for the next several decades, even with the construction of Route 66 down Main Street. Oil and natural gas companies moved to Weatherford during the 1970s, and the town has become a major stop for travelers on Interstate 40, with numerous service stations, hotels and restaurants. The main route through town is lined with Route 66 signs. The population in the 2010 census was 10,833.

Route 66 and the Rock Island Railroad are tied together in many towns along the route, and Weatherford has lined its main street with these signs throughout town.

Farmrail at Weatherford

The railroad has a sizeable yard at Weatherford. It stretches for about five blocks between the south side of town and Interstate 40. The tall Farmers Co-Op Exchange elevator is at the east end of the yard. The five tracks cross a number of streets, making switching and car storage complicated. There are several shippers here that are related to the oil and gas exploration and drilling industry; therefore, the yard can either be very busy or very quiet depending upon the volume of local drilling.

Five signs on one grade crossing post at Weatherford, Oklahoma. Note the Farmrail sign about remote control locomotive operations.

For Farmrail, there is a Fairmount Santrol "Oil & Gas – Proppant Solutions Terminal" used for the movement of their materials. For those unclear on the term proppant, it is a solid material, typically sand, treated sand or man-made ceramic materials, designed to keep an induced hydraulic fracture open, during or following a fracturing treatment. In other words, it handles frac sand. Wildcat Minerals is also here, competing in the same product market. There are also a number of tracks in the area used for storing railcars.

Across much of the Midwest and West, the tallest buildings are the grain elevators. Here, the Farmers Co-op Exchange elevator towers over a cut of stored frac sand cars at Weatherford, Oklahoma, in 2020.

Besides oil and gas, Weatherford also is an important base for the wind turbine industry. The Wind Energy Park along SW Main has displays and information about the industry. Farmrail has moved wind turbine parts for several projects along its lines.

This windmill blade is on display in Wind Energy Park at Weatherford, Oklahoma. Farmrail has been involved with moving parts for several area wind energy projects.

565.0 BRIDGE – This creek drains the hillside to the north, and then flows south into Little Deep Creek, just south of here. The bridge consists of three deck plate girder spans, measuring 35 feet, 60 feet and 50 feet long, from east to west.

565.8 LITTLE DEEP CREEK BRIDGE – Starting in 1849, thousands of gold seekers headed south across this region on their way to California. Using the Santa Fe trail that headed west from Fort Smith, Arkansas, many tried to take shorter routes, but ran into a series of deep creeks that made travel difficult. This stream was one of them.

Little Deep Creek begins about three miles west-northwest of Weatherford, flows around the south side of town, and then turns to the northeast and empties into Deer Creek about four miles east-northeast of town. It has been a source of flooding, and is described by the Oklahoma Conservation Commission as having "a good variety of deep and shallow pools connected by a few rocky runs and riffles."

This railroad bridge consists of an 80-foot deck plate girder span with two pile trestle panels on each end.

566.2 LITTLE DEEP CREEK BRIDGE – The railroad crosses the upper end of the stream using a single 80-foot deck plate girder span. The railroad peaks just west of here at an elevation of 1795 feet and then starts downhill at grades of 1.0% all the way to Clinton, Oklahoma.

573.0 INDIANAPOLIS – This area was first settled about 1890, and the area became known as Bear Siding when the railroad built through here in 1901. On February 7, 1902, a post office opened using the name Indianapolis, borrowed from Indianapolis, Indiana. The town was never large, and the post office closed on August 15, 1949. Today, Indianapolis is still unincorporated and is a collection of a few farmhouses and one property with abandoned cars and mobile homes.

The long siding to the south is still in place, and is generally used for car storage. In 1979, the siding was 5160 feet long, and there was also a short house track off of the siding. The west switch of the siding is just west of Custer City Road. Heading west, the railroad winds and continues to drop as it follows Turtle Creek, passing through farmland and pasture until it reaches Clinton. It also crosses a number of small streams using multiple-span timber pile trestles.

580.1 WASHITA RIVER BRIDGE – This bridge is located in the middle of the Riverside Golf Course and is a 100-foot Warren pony truss bridge. A pony bridge is one without a top over the structure – it consists only of a bottom and sides. The bridge is unique for the Rock Island in that it was built by the Milliken Brothers Company of New York City. Mil-

603

liken Brothers traces its history to 1857 when Samuel Milliken started a construction company. He retired in 1883 and left his business to his sons, Edward and Foster. In 1887, the Milliken Brothers Company was created, soon becoming one of the first multi-national American construction companies, and one of the world's largest steel structure manufacturers. Besides the United States, the company built structures in places like Cuba, South Africa, Guam, Taiwan and Costa Rica. One of its most famous structures was the Singer Building of New York City, the world's tallest building when it was completed in 1908. The firm filed for bankruptcy in 1907, due to the financial panic that year, and slowly sold off its assets. The company built steel ship hulls during World War I, using a process that became a standard during World War II.

The international nature of Milliken Brothers is clear from the builder's plate located on the Washita River bridge. It is marked in both English and Spanish, and has a 1901 build date.

The Washita River bridge near Clinton, Oklahoma, is a Warren pony truss span. Note that there is no top span across the tracks, making it a pony-style bridge.

This plate on the Washita River bridge is surprisingly in Spanish, possibly indicating that it was initially manufactured for an overseas contract.

The Washita River is a 300-mile stream that starts in the Texas Panhandle in Roberts County, and it flows east and south before entering the Lake Texoma part of the Red River on the Oklahoma-Texas border. The river was first documented by Europeans when French explorers were traveling the Red River during the 1700s. Choctaw tribesmen had described an area river they called the Ouachita River, and the French initially used that name. However, an exploration of the river found it to be very different from what had been described by the Choctaw. Because of this, the river was named Faux Ouachita, or False Ouachita. English settlers took up the name False Ouachita, which became False Washita, and then simply Washita. The lower part of the river once hosted Fort Washita, established in 1842 at the orders of President Zachary Taylor to protect resettled citizens of the Choctaw and Chickasaw nations.

Not far to the northwest of here is the site of the Battle of Washita River, also known as the Washita River Massacre. On November 27, 1868, Lieutenant Colonel George Armstrong Custer and his 7th U.S. Cavalry attacked the encampment of Cheyenne Chief Black Kettle. The attack resulted in the death of a number of warriors, as well as women and children, although a firm count is not known. Additionally, many others were taken prisoner as an effort to force the end of the fighting. At the time, a number of tribal groups were in winter encampment along the river and in the area, but a war party which had just raided several white settlements passed through the camp of Black Kettle. Custer and his troops were in the area due to major fighting during the summer of 1868 that had involved warriors from the Southern and Northern

Cheyenne, Arapaho, Kiowa, Comanche, Cheyenne, Brulé, Oglala, and Pawnee tribes. This area is today the Town of Cheyenne and the Black Kettle National Grassland.

580.5 SL-SF CROSSING – The north-south line was once part of the St. Louis-San Francisco (Frisco), but it was built by the Blackwell, Enid & Southwestern Railway (BE&S). The railroad was built after the Kiowa-Comanche-Apache Indian Reservation was opened for settlement, and the BE&S was organized in March 1900 to build a 250-mile railroad from Vernon, Texas, north to Enid in Indian Territory. The line was built by the Choctaw Construction Company, later part of the Bee Line Construction Company, and opened in 1903. On July 20, 1907, the railroad was purchased by the Frisco, which operated it until the larger railroad was merged into Burlington Northern (BN) on November 21, 1980. In 1983, the line between Enid and Davidson was the Third Subdivision of the Tulsa Division, part of the Springfield Region of Burlington Northern. In 1987, BN sold 178 miles of track between Enid and Frederick, all in Oklahoma, to the Grainbelt Corporation.

To tie together the various lines of the Farmrail System, there are connecting tracks in the northwest and southwest quadrants of this diamond. These tracks were shown in a 1918 Sanborn map, indicating that they were a regular part of rail operations and the interchange business for more than a century. For example, according to a 1916 report of the Corporation Commission of Oklahoma, the Chicago, Rock Island & Pacific Railway Company and the St Louis & San Francisco Railroad Company had a joint depot in Clinton.

Both railroads – the Frisco and the Rock Island – showed this diamond to be a manual interlocking. The BN simply labeled it as a manual interlocking at Milepost 679.7. The Rock Island provided more detail, stating that the "railroad crossing not protected by interlocking" and that it was "protected by gate operated by trainman, normal position of gate against SLSF." The location has also used different names – SL-SF Crossing on the Rock Island, simply CRI&P on the Frisco, and East Junction and Clinton Junction in other documents.

The Frisco had their station, shared with the Rock Island for decades, south of Frisco Avenue and on the west side of the tracks. The south end of the station was for freight, the middle was for express and baggage, and passengers used the north end. By 1975, Frisco had a typical metal prefab building here. Today, Farmrail has their locomotive and freight car shops here, using many of the station tracks. At one time, this was the center of much of the rail business at Clinton. For example, the Chickasaw Cotton Oil Mill, Nelson Grain Company, Magnolia Petroleum, and the Western Oklahoma Gin (cotton) were all located east of the Frisco in this area. Cotton wasn't a huge business, but the Department of Agriculture stated that there were 228 rail shipments of cotton from Clinton in 1903-1904.

Looking east from U.S. Highway 183 north of Clinton, the many tracks in place in 2020 at the former SL-SF Crossing can be clearly seen.

580.6 KCMO CROSSING – This crossing no longer exists, but it once was where the Kansas City, Mexico & Orient Railway (KCM&O) bridged across the Rock Island Railroad. A government survey reported on a marker that was placed "on the face of the north concrete abutment of the plate-girder bridge on which the Kansas City, Mexico & Orient Railway crosses the Chicago, Rock Island & Pacific Railway." Not far south of the bridge, the KCM&O had a wye north of town the led to a line down 1st Street to their freight depot, which was on the west side of 1st Street and south of Choctaw Avenue. Some of this track is still used by Farmrail as a part of their shop facility.

The KCM&O was the second railroad created by Arthur Edward Stilwell. The first was the Kansas City Southern, which aimed to provide a Gulf of Mexico outlet for Kansas City. This line was built to provide the shortest distance to a Pacific Ocean port (Topolobampo, Mexico). It was reorganized as the Kansas City, Mexico & Orient Railroad in 1914, and then back to Railway in 1925. The line benefitted from the discovery of oil, which led to acquisition by the Atchison, Topeka & Santa Fe Railway in 1928.

According to a 1927 Interstate Commerce Commission report, the KCM&O had "trackage rights over the road of the St. Louis-San Francisco Railway Company from Foley to Ewing, Okla., 12.73 miles." Just north of the Rock Island, the line returned to its own track, then crossed the Rock Island and headed southwest. The route is now reached by a connecting switch in the small rail yard just west of here.

580.7 CLINTON JUNCTION (JN) – At first, the Rock Island only had freight facilities on its mainline, with passenger business conducted downtown at the Frisco station. For a few years during the first part of the 1900s, both railroads were jointly owned, so they coordinated a number of projects and facilities. The use of a common station near downtown Clinton was an example. To reach the Frisco station, trains would use the Frisco tracks, located just east of here. To coordinate these moves, and to handle those trains that bypassed the town, a station and agency named Clinton Junction was built at this location, just east of U.S. Highway 183 and on the north side of the Rock Island tracks.

However, not all Rock Island passenger trains used the Frisco Station. In 1926, trains No. 111 and No. 112 stopped at Clinton Junction, while trains No. 41 and No. 42 served the downtown Frisco station, known as Clinton and located 0.8 miles away. In 1934, the *Official Guide* showed that the Frisco and CRI&P still shared a downtown station, located 150 yards from the Santa Fe station. In that year, trains No. 111 and No. 112 stopped at Clinton Junction and Clinton, while trains No. 51 and No. 52 only served Clinton Junction. By 1941, all passenger trains stopped at Clinton Junction, which was renamed Clinton soon after World War II.

During 1928, the Chicago, Rock Island & Pacific announced plans to "substitute oil-burning locomotives for coal-burning locomotives on more than 1,500 miles of lines in Kansas, Texas and Oklahoma." This required the conversion of 125 steam locomotives, and the construction of oil stations at a number of locations. Clinton Junction was one of the locations where a new oil facility was placed, supplied by the Phillips Petroleum Company.

Until almost the end of the Rock Island, Clinton and Clinton Junction were still noted in official company records. The *Rock Island Station Book* (December 15, 1974) showed both Clinton (Milepost 581.3) and Clinton Junction (Milepost 582.6) with car accounting or blocking numbers 33582 and 33583. However, Clinton Jct was not assigned a revenue station audit number or an accounting billing station number. Additionally, an agent was shown as being at Clinton, but not one at Clinton Junction.

In 1979, the CRI&P stated that there was a 5085-foot siding here, 970 feet of other tracks, and a wye. Today, Farmrail has a long siding to the south of the mainline, a short siding to the north that serves as a yard track, and a crossover between the siding and mainline that allows the east end of the siding to also be used as a yard track. Several companies, such as Clinton Elevators and the Farmers Cooperative Elevator, once leased property and tracks from the Rock Island at Clinton.

National Railroad Adjustment Board and Clinton Junction

Clinton Junction and the operations downtown created several problems for the railroad and its employees. The location was a dividing line for a number of crafts, including the Roadmaster territories to the east and west. Other employees had assignments clearly defined by union agreements and company assignments. Some of these issues resulted in outside government agencies getting involved, including the National Railroad Adjustment Board (NRAB). One benefit of having organizations like the NRAB involved are the detailed reports created. One of these reports from 1940 provides a great deal of detail about some of the operations from the time.

The report stated that Clinton was an intermediate yard between the Divisional freight terminal yards at El Reno and Sayre. The railroad had a yard engine that worked the area 8:30am-4:30pm. The tracks "from Clinton Jct., to and including Clinton are Frisco ownership, but are joint with Rock Island and yard engine referred to performs both Rock Island and Frisco switching under joint arrangement." Since the local crew was only on duty during the daytime, it was the practice for local crews arriving at Clinton with cars to be placed or picked up "at Clinton proper, to leave their train at Clinton Junction, go with their engine to Clinton and set out or pick up, returning to Clinton Junction and proceed on their trip." An additional payment of two miles was paid to the crew.

An issue arose in 1938 when larger Mikado-type (2-8-2) locomotives began to be assigned to freight trains. The locomotives were too heavy to move over a bridge on the Frisco, and some crews began to use the smaller switch engine to make the move. One of these crews then filed a claim for 100 miles in addition to their regular pay, stating that they were working as a local yard crew, handling the move without the assistance of a station operator, and that they had "a good chance of getting into serious trouble." Later, the claim was changed from pay of 100 miles, to that of a minimum yard day. The NRAB denied the claim, stating that the practice of having local crews do this type of switching had existed for several decades, and it was not a new requirement that would result in new pay.

Another hearing, this one in 1946, dealt with the issue of only having a telegraph position at Clinton Junction from 6:00pm to 3:00am, seven days per week, with one hour allowed for meals. Several times, train orders were sent to nearby stations, and they were moved to Clinton Junction by other train crews or track employees. Because this was work that the assigned telegrapher could have performed, the railroad was ordered to make overtime payments to the Clinton Junction telegrapher.

Clinton, Oklahoma

Clinton is the home of the Farmrail System, with its old offices on the west side of town in the former ATSF yard, and the shops on the east side of town on the Frisco. The railroad office for many years was in the modern ATSF yard office, which replaced the original KCM&O depot. On October 22, 2019, a new office on the east side of Clinton was dedicated as Betke Station, named for George and Mary Ann Betke. George C. Betke, Jr., founded Farmrail in 1981, and now serves as chairman of Farmrail System. Betke has been involved with shortline railroads in Colorado, Michigan, Oklahoma and New York, and was awarded the Thomas L. Schlosser Distinguished Service Award by the American Short Line and Regional Railroad Association in 2016.

This marker on the new Farmrail office building at Clinton honors George and Mary Ann Betke.

The town of Clinton began in 1899 when J. L. Avant and E. E. Blake developed plans to create a townsite in the Washita River Valley. At the time, laws prevented "Indians" from selling more than half of their 160-acre allotment, so they bought connecting land from four "Indians" and created Washita Junction. The sale and purchase of the land was finally approved by Congress in 1902, and promotion of the new town could begin. The first businesses were the *Custer County Chronicle* newspaper and the First National Bank.

A post office was proposed with the name Washita Junction, but it was rejected because it was too similar to other Oklahoma towns. A new name of Clinton was proposed, and accepted, with the Clinton post office opening on May 22, 1903. The name Clinton came from Judge Clinton F. Irwin, an Associate Justice of the Oklahoma Territorial Supreme Court who had been appointed on February 21, 1889, by President William McKinley. When Oklahoma Territory was divided into seven Judicial Districts on June 4, 1902, Irwin was assigned District 2, which included Custer County. He retired from the court in 1907 and returned to his home in Illinois in 1908, where he practiced law and then served as a circuit judge until his death in late 1923.

The town grew with the presence of the Rock Island, and on October 1, 1906, the Kansas City, Mexico & Orient reached Clinton, helping the town to grow even more. By this time, the Mohawk Lodge Indian Store had been operating for over a decade, and would soon become a major tourist attraction along the new Route 66. Over the next two decades, two more railroads arrived at Clinton and Route 66 was becoming the primary coast-to-coast highway, giving Clinton the name "The Hub City of Western Oklahoma." The original U.S. Highway 66 Association shut down during World War II, but was restarted in 1947, based in Clinton.

Clinton was also a significant grain and livestock terminal, and flour milling and food processing also grew here. The population reached 7000 during the 1940s due to the construction of nearby Naval Air Station Clinton. This airport was closed in 1949, then reopened and enlarged as the Clinton-Sherman Air Force Base, the home of the 4123rd Strategic Wing, then the 70th Bombardment Wing. This made the airport home of aircraft such as B-52 Stratofortress and KC-135 Stratotanker aircraft. It was closed in 1971 and now is the Clinton-Sherman Industrial Airpark.

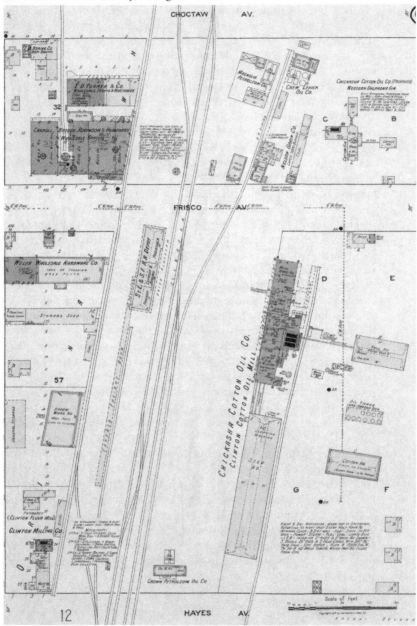

Sanborn Maps – Frisco-CRI&P Station – 1918. *Sanborn Fire Insurance Map from Clinton, Custer County, Oklahoma.* Sanborn Map Company, Nov, 1918. Map. Retrieved from the Library of Congress, https://www.loc.gov/item/sanborn07043_003/.

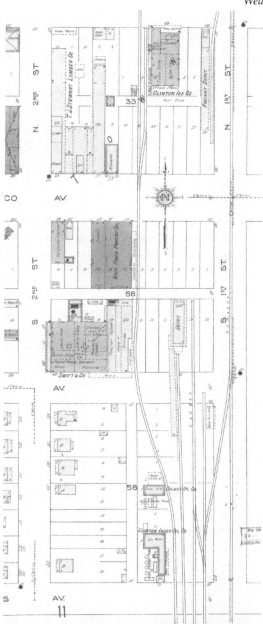

Sanborn Maps – Other Station – 1926. *Sanborn Fire Insurance Map from Clinton, Custer County, Oklahoma.* Sanborn Map Company, Apr, 1926. Map. Retrieved from the Library of Congress, https://www.loc.gov/item/sanborn07043_004/.

Clinton still has the Farmers Co-op Association elevator, Midwest Farmers, and several other agricultural companies. There are also a number of small manufacturing firms. Tourism still plays a major role at Clinton, with hotels and restaurants along I-40. Also, Clinton features the Oklahoma Route 66 Museum, the first state-sponsored Route 66 Museum in the nation. The population of Clinton was 9033 in the 2010 census.

The Electric Railroads of Clinton

Like many communities across the country, Clinton was the target of several proposed electric railroads, some built and some that only existed in the minds of their backers. The first was the Clinton, Cheyenne & Canadian Interurban Railway Company, incorporated on June 25, 1906. The announced plan was for a railroad 225 miles long from Clinton, Oklahoma, to Canadian, Texas, plus a branch line from Cheyenne to Mangum, both in Oklahoma. The announced cost to build the railroad was $1 million, and the backers stated that "it is expected to have the line in operation in one year."

Details and plans about the interurban railway were reported in a number of magazines such as *Street Railway Journal, Electric Railway Review, Electrical Review, Manufacturer's Record, Western Electrician* and *Engineering World*. A common theme was that the interurban railroad would "open up entirely new country not now reached by any steam or electric line and should it be successfully pushed to completion, will be of great value to the farmers and merchants of this section and also a profitable investment for the stockholders." While the news was heavy during June and July 1906, reporting on the line soon disappeared.

Nevertheless, maps showed an electric railway line beginning at Clinton, then extending west and north about 20 miles. By 1913, the Rand McNally map deleted the Clinton electric line and showed a steam railway on that route. This new steam railroad was the Clinton & Oklahoma Western. A search of the two companies showed that there was no common management or directors between the electric and steam railroads.

A second electric railroad was eventually built at Clinton, but it was less than two miles long and lasted only until Fall 1914. According to the *Municipal Journal and Engineer* (April 28, 1909), the Clinton Street Railway Company was chartered by a number of Clinton business leaders with the capital of $50,000. Several of those involved were also investors with the Clinton & Oklahoma Western. The railway started operating in 1909 using gasoline cars to shuttle people between the Frisco depot and the Kansas City, Mexico & Orient depot (located on the west side of the tracks at the west end of Frisco Street). The line was listed as being 1.25 miles long in 1910, and had an assessed value of $2500. Service with the gasoline cars ended in 1911 and electric streetcars were introduced in 1912. Their success was very short-lived as the service was discontinued on August 27, 1914. However, the firm was in existence several years later (1916) as it was still being sued for an earlier collision between a locomotive of the Kansas City, Mexico & Orient and a motor car of the Clinton Street Railway Company at a street crossing in the city of Clinton.

583.2 P&SF CROSSING – This is another rail crossing on the Rock Island that was "not protected by interlocking," but was instead "protected by gate operated by trainman, normal position of gate against P&SF." This was the former Clinton & Oklahoma Western Railway Company, incorporated in Oklahoma on November 10, 1908 (some sources state October 28, 1908). By the end of 1910, the railroad had built 21.5 miles of track from Clinton westward to Butler City, Oklahoma. On June 10, 1912, Congress passed *An Act To authorize the Clinton and Oklahoma Western Railway Company to construct and operate a railway through certain public lands, and for other purposes.* The Act stated that "the Clinton and Oklahoma Western Railway Company, a corporation created under and by virtue of the laws of the State of Oklahoma, be, and the same is hereby, empowered to survey, locate, construct, maintain, and operate a railway, telegraph and telephone lines." With that permission, the company built thirty more miles of track westward from Butler City to Strong City, Oklahoma.

The 21.52 miles of track between Clinton and Butler was turned over by the construction company for operation on March 21, 1910. By 1917, the railroad had 53.28 miles of track from Clinton to Strong City, Oklahoma. The company, with milling and railroad magnate Franklin Marian Frank Kell as president, owned five locomotives, four passenger cars, and 33 freight cars. Kell was heavily involved with a number of area railroads, and he either owned or was a partner in six railroads with more than 1300 miles of track: the Wichita Falls & Northwestern; the Wichita Falls & Southern; the Wichita Falls Railway; the Clinton & Oklahoma Western; the San Antonio, Uvalde and Gulf; and the Missouri & North Arkansas. Frank Kell was also a director of the Eleventh District Federal Reserve Bank from 1914 to 1927, chairman of the feed and food division of the Texas Advisory Council during World War I, chairman of the milling division of Texas and New Mexico under Herbert Hoover as national food administrator, and a director in the United States Chamber of Commerce in 1920.

Over the next decade, the Clinton & Oklahoma Western Railway (C&OW) joined with several other railroads to form a network as far west as Pampa, Texas. Later, the Atchison, Topeka & Santa Fe Railway acquired the railroad through their Panhandle subsidiary. "By our report and order in this proceeding, made after hearing and dated June 2, 1928, we authorized the Panhandle and Santa Fe Railway Company to acquire control by lease of the railroad of the Clinton and Oklahoma Western Railroad Company, extending from Clinton, Custer County, Okla., westward through Cheyenne to the Oklahoma-Texas State line, about 83.99 miles."

Starting in the 1960s, service on the line was reduced, and then abandoned. Into the 1980s, part of the line at Clinton was preserved as the Clinton Industrial Spur. One rail shipper still remains here, at a location shown as Ralph in some sources, served from the CRI&P line.

The Clinton & Oklahoma Western had their stations and engine facilities in downtown Clinton near the Frisco facilities. Their wooden passenger and freight station was located west of 1st Street and south of Frisco Street. It still stands, but is unused. The C&OW's engine house was south of Hayes Avenue and east of 2nd Street. The original C&OW mainline ran down the center of Frisco Street, turned south alongside the KCM&O, and then turned west south of Modelle Avenue. The track is still used as far as 28th Street.

The only passenger train station that still stands at Clinton once belonged to the Clinton & Oklahoma Western Railway, and is located just west of the Farmrail shops along 1st Street.

583.9 RALPH – Ralph was a station on the Rock Island that came into existence when the Clinton & Oklahoma Western (C&OW) route was abandoned west of Clinton. Located near Oklahoma Highway 73, the station served a former customer of the C&OW near where the diamond was once located. AES Drilling Fluids is still served by the railroad in the area.

585.3 PARKERSBURG – Only the railroad knows this location as Parkersburg, the local post office (open April 24, 1901-April 30, 1906) was named Parker. According to the book *Oklahoma Place Names*, the town was named for the townsite owner, J. N. Parker. However, other organizations used the name Parkersburg. The *Annual Report of the Governor of Oklahoma to the Secretary of the Interior for the Fiscal Year Ended June 30, 1902*, stated that a depot had just been built at Parkersburg.

The station was not listed in railroad documents from the 1960s. Today, there is nothing but a Farmrail mainline, pasture and fields here. Just to the west, the railroad briefly comes alongside Interstate 40.

592.9 COUNTY LINE – Heading west, the Rock Island was actually heading to the southwest, and passed from **Custer County** to the north (railroad-east), and into **Washita County** to the south (railroad-west). The railroad goes through the very northwest corner of Washita County.

Although this area was assigned to the Cheyenne and Arapaho, John Miles was able to lease three million acres of prairie to seven cattlemen. The leases were voided in 1885 by the Federal government, but some settlement took place the next year. The first significant settlement took place at Seger's Colony, one of the former ranch headquarters. John Seger was a teacher who encouraged Cheyenne and Arapaho tribesmen to settle at the colony to learn farming and ranching. There was some success, and the community is now Colony, Oklahoma.

On April 19, 1892, much of the unused Cheyenne and Arapaho Indian Reservation land was made available for homesteading, creating the Land Run of 1892. As part of the organization of the area, County H was created in the Territory of Oklahoma. In 1900, Cordell became the county seat due to its location in the center of the county. However, several court challenges led to an Oklahoma Territorial Supreme Court ruling that the county seat couldn't be moved without Federal approval, but Congress moved it to Cordell in 1906. A few changes led to the creation of New Cordell, which was made official on November 16, 1907, when Oklahoma became a state. At the same time, much of County H became **Washita County**.

The county was named for the nearby Washita River. One of the early flood control efforts in the area, funded by the Flood Control Act of 1944, was on the Cloud Creek Watershed in Washita County, completed in 1948. Washita County was also the inspiration of the song *Wichita Lineman*. The story goes that the writer was driving into the sun across Washita County, watching a long line of telephone poles. There was a worker on one of the poles, inspiring the lineman and loneliness concept of the song.

593.0 TURKEY CREEK BRIDGE – This 60-foot through plate girder span, plus three spans of a ballast deck pile trestle, are used to cross the major stream that has long been an attraction to the area. The Rock Island used the Turkey Creek valley as a route to climb grades to the west.

Turkey Creek is also a key part of the legend about Cascorillo, an old Mexican mining town on the banks of Turkey Creek. The town was reportedly the source of gold and silver for many years. However, no actual evidence of the town or mines have ever been found.

594.3 FOSS – When originally built, the railroad had a few facilities here. These included a station (built by June 30, 1902), stock yards that were retired in 1956, and a water tank that was leased to R. B. Hoover after it was no longer needed by the railroad. In the early 1970s, there was a 5180-foot siding to the south at Foss. Today, the siding has been broken up into two parts, split by Oklahoma Highway 44. To the east, a switch was added to keep a shorter siding. To the west, the siding now forms a long spur track that is generally used for car storage.

The first town in the area was Wilson, located about four miles to the south. As talk about the railroad started, much of the town moved north and settled along Turkey Creek, with plans to call the community Graham, taken from the postmaster's last name. Unfortunately, there was already a town by that name and the post office turned the name down. Spelling Graham backwards gave the name Maharg, and a post office opened with that name in 1898. After a flood, the town moved to higher ground and changed the name of the post office and town to Foss, honoring an early Cordell postmaster, J. M. Foss. The new post office officially opened on September 15, 1900.

Initially, Foss was a farm town, with four cotton gins, two grain elevators, a flour mill, two banks, two hotels, and an opera house. There were also several manufacturing plants that made hay balers, baby carriages, and brooms. Cotton was an important area farm product for a number of years, and the U.S. Department of Agriculture reported that 878 rail shipments of cotton moved out of Foss in 1903-1904. For a while, Foss had a population of about 500 as it served the region, but the population began to drop as transportation improved and larger towns like Clinton and Elk City got within reach with more services available.

Some growth did take place during and after World War II due to the nearby military bases, and Route 66 created the need for a service station and café. However, the new Interstate 40 missed Foss and the town lost a number of residents, with the last bank closing in 1977. By the 2000 census, the population was down to 127, but it grew back to

151 residents by the 2010 census as Foss became more of a bedroom community for Clinton and Elk City. The post office still remains, but few other businesses still operate at Foss.

Heading west, the railroad faces the ruling grade on this part of the line. Grades of as much as 1.0% are common, and the ruling grade is 0.82% for more than four miles. The top of the grade is at an elevation of 1990 feet at Milepost 603.5. Foss is at an elevation of 1634 feet.

There is something about a town where the first thing you see is the old jail cell, as happens here at Foss, Oklahoma.

601.6 INTERSTATE 40 BRIDGE – This modern steel-beam and concrete bridge crosses the Interstate just north of Canute, Oklahoma.

The Great Western Cattle Trail

In this area was once the Great Western Cattle Trail, a route between Southern Texas and Nebraska, and even as far north as Canada. It basically replaced the Chisholm Trail during the mid-1870s. The Great Western Cattle Trail was first used by Captain John T. Lytle in 1874. Lytle moved about 3500 longhorn cattle to Nebraska, where the prices paid for cattle were higher and the railroad rates to the eastern markets lower. The trail had different names such as the Western Trail, Fort Griffin Trail, Dodge City Trail, Northern Trail and Texas Trail, and it lasted until 1893 when the last major cattle drive used it to move stock to Deadwood, South Dakota. Like other trails, it was negatively impacted by barbed wire fences and concerns about the "Texas Fever" illness that was carried by some of the longhorns. During its years of use, an estimated six to seven million cattle and one million horses were moved along the route, which generally took almost one hundred days.

601.7 CANUTE – During the last decade of the Rock Island Railroad, there was nothing more than a 702-foot spur track and a dispatcher telephone at Canute. However, the town of Canute owes its existence to the railroad. In 1902, the Great Southwest Townsite Company surveyed the land, platted a town, and sold lots along the newly completed Choctaw, Oklahoma & Gulf Railroad. To sell and assign the lots, the Great Southwest Townsite Company sold lottery rights for ten dollars, and names were drawn from a box and given a random lot location.

The Land Run of 1892 led to the first settlement in the area, but at the end of the year, barely 20% of the 3.5 million acres of land opened for settlement was claimed, and by only 7600 people. The first community near Canute was about four miles to the northwest, known as Keen for the local general store operator, Robert Keene (some sources spell it Keen). In 1898, the St. Francis of Assisi Catholic Church opened about three miles to the southeast of what is now Canute.

The construction of railroads across Oklahoma organized much of the chaos, and the CO&G did much the same thing in this area. Speculation led to several towns being planned, leading to stores, post offices, and families moving to what was considered to be the next great railroad town. Robert Keene moved to Oak in 1898, and then the Canute area in 1899, where the Canute post office opened on February 24, 1899. Keene guessed correctly as the CO&G built through the area and the Great Southwest Townsite Company platted a town in 1902. By the end of the year, Canute featured a bank, a cotton gin, and a general merchandise store. The First State Bank of Canute was chartered in 1902, and is acknowledged as being the oldest Oklahoma chartered bank still in operation.

1917 saw the first oil well in Western Oklahoma, also reported to be the deepest well in the world at the time, drilled at Canute. History articles about Canute state that oil, farming and livestock led Canute to grow, and some of the businesses that developed included two newspapers, two hotels, three doctors, a buggy works, a carpenter shop, a lumberyard, two cotton gins, two hardware and implement dealers, two livery stables, a drugstore, two saloons, a blacksmith shop, three general merchandise and grocery stores, two furniture stores with funeral supplies, and a music store as well as several attorneys, real estate businesses, two banks, a photographer, and an auctioneer. The population grew to 366 in the 1930 census, and then remained stable until about 1970.

In 1926, U.S. Highway 66 was built through Canute, leading to some new businesses, but few new residents. This business was basically lost in 1970 when Interstate 40 was built around the north side of town. Other businesses were lost when the nearby Clinton-Sherman Air Force Base closed, and Canute's population peaked at 676 in 1980.

The remains of one of the cotton gins still stand at Canute, Oklahoma.

Canute Today

In the 2010 census, Canute had a population of 541. Canute still has a bank, several gas stations, a few farm-related businesses, and some new housing. Canute also still has an elementary and high school. There are also some remnants of the Route 66 days, including the Canute Service Station and Cotton Boll Motel, both standing but not open. There is also the 1918 Canute Jail and the Canute Cemetery with its grotto and life-size crucifixion.

Of these, the Canute Service Station, located on the southwest corner of Main and Highway 66, is listed on the National Register of Historic Places. In its application, the station is described as being "architecturally significant as an outstanding local example of the Pueblo Deco style, a style of architecture popular in the southwest, and especially on Route 66." The station was built in two stages, in 1936 and 1939. It features three bays, with the east and center bay used for the service station, with the west bay used as a roadhouse and dance hall. The station is now closed.

The Name Canute

Canute is somewhat of a unique town along the railroad as it wasn't named for an investor or manager of the railroad, a store or land owner, or the first postmaster. Instead, it was named for an early King of England (1016-1035). Canute, also known as "Cnut the Great," was a Viking who was born in Denmark and obtained the title of King of Denmark as he grew up. He led a campaign that captured England and Scotland, and then used his power (some sources say sheer brutality) and promises of wealth to combine the Danes and English under a common trade system. He also captured Norway, adding a fourth country to his kingdom, and then parts of Sweden where he also declared himself king. Canute died at Shaftesbury, United Kingdom, in 1035, and his heirs quickly let the empire fall apart, making him look even more powerful. Since many of the early settlers of the area were Danish, the town was named to honor one of their heroes.

601.9 OLD U.S. HIGHWAY 66 BRIDGE – This is a through plate girder bridge that was installed during the mid-1950s as part of an improvement project on Route 66. The highway passes through the very north side of Canute, and this bridge is at the west end of the road through town.

This bridge crosses the old Route 66 highway on the west side of Canute, Oklahoma.

606.7 COUNTY LINE – This is the county line between **Washita County** and **Beckham County**, located at North 2030 Road. East of here to Canute, the railroad has passed though large fields and pasture. West of here for the next few miles, the railroad passed through a number of industries.

Before the Civil War, **Beckham County** was part of the lands re-served for the Choctaw and Chickasaw Nations. However, they lost part of these lands as punishment for fighting for the Confederacy. Besides losing these lands, both tribes were required to free their slaves and make them citizens of their nations. The Dawes Act of 1891 further split up the land, providing land directly to the members of the tribes. Any land left over was made available for settlement. For a number of years, even the Native American-owned land was leased to cattlemen as graz-ing land.

As the territory was organized, this became County F, and then named Roger Mills County. In 1907, when Oklahoma became a state, land from Roger Mills and Greer counties were merged to create Beck-ham County. Sayre became the county seat by election in 1908. The county changed its size a few times due to survey changes, but it re-mains a county on the western border of the state with a population of about 22,000.

Beckham County was named for John Crepps Wickliffe Beckham, the 35th Governor of Kentucky and the Kentucky's first popularly-elect-ed senator after the passage of the Seventeenth Amendment. A former Kentuckian, who was serving as a delegate to the Oklahoma constitu-tional convention in 1907, suggested the name.

Industry

Approaching Elk City and just west of North 2030 Road is a switch to several tracks to the south to serve the Unimin Elk City unloading fa-cility. According to their website, "Unimin is one of the largest produc-ers of quartz proppants for oil and natural gas stimulation and recovery and is a leading supplier of multi-mineral product offerings to indus-trial customers in glass, construction, ceramics, coatings, polymers and foundry markets." During 2018, Fairmount Santrol and Unimin Corpo-ration merged to form Covia Holdings Corporation. Then to the north is the large two-track Santrol Elk City, once part of Fairmount Santrol. This is now the primary facility for the merged company.

The sand facilities go as far west as Eastern Avenue. Just west of East-ern is the Elk City Rock Yard, a distributor of various rock products for regional construction. Farmrail brings unit trains of stone to here, where it is unloaded and transferred to trucks for final delivery. The delivery of these trains generally results in several Farmrail locomotives being parked nearby, waiting for the cars to be emptied.

This sign on Eastern Avenue marks the entrance to the Santrol Elk City Terminal.

This sign marks the entrance to the Elk City Rock Yard, an important rail customer for Farmrail.

This red Shuttlewagon is used by the Elk City Rock Yard to switch the facility.

On May 31, 2020, Farmrail #2304 (actually lettered GNBC, former C&NW GP38-2 #4604) along with locomotives #627 and #626 (former Iowa Interstate and originally GM&O GP38AC locomotives #729 and #725) are parked outside Elk City waiting for rock cars to be unloaded at the Elk City Rock Yard.

608.3 INTERSTATE 40 – The railroad again passes under this highway as the road curves around the south side of Elk City. There are several industries just to the west, including M-I Swaco, a well drilling contractor, and the Farmrail railroad car repair shop.

To the south of the tracks (compass-west) is the Farmrail railcar-repair facility. This small facility was built in 1998 to repair and maintain the cars of American Milling. The facility also did repair work on other equipment for Farmrail. In late 2006, the Farmrail Corporation bought the railcar-repair facility and started using it to make running and heavy repairs on railcars, in a region described as being "without ready access to other shops."

608.8 MKT CROSSING – This crossing was located just east of the 55-foot through plate girder span over Elk Creek, and west of the eleven-span timber pile trestle, which also crosses a channel of Elk Creek. This was originally a diamond with the Wichita Falls & Northwestern Railway (WF&NW), chartered during September 1906. This railroad was one of several built by sponsors in the Wichita Falls, Texas area, and was the most important and successful of them. The WF&NW was designed to build north to Englewood, Kansas, providing new outside rail connections and potential new business that would flow through Wichita Falls.

The line never got to Englewood, but it did build through Frederick, Altus, and Elk City, to reach Forgan, Oklahoma, on November 1, 1912. At its peak, the railroad was 360 miles long. As traffic increased, the larger Missouri, Kansas & Texas Railway Company acquired the stock of the WF&NW and its affiliates by late 1911. However, the WF&NW was kept as a separate company until April 1, 1923, when most of the railroads were merged to create the new Missouri-Kansas-Texas Railroad Company. This part of the railroad was heavily based upon the grain and agricultural business, plus some peaks due to various oil booms. In 1973, the line from Altus north through Elk City and on to Forgan was abandoned.

609.1 ELK CREEK BRIDGE – This is the West Fork of Elk Creek. There are a number of small reservoirs upstream on this branch, built to reduce flooding and to ensure a steady supply of water.

This bridge consists of ten timber pile spans. Just west of the bridge is the east switch of the old north siding. This siding once looped around the north side of the Elk City passenger and freight stations, but it is now just a short house track.

609.3 ELK CITY (KC) – Today known as "The Shopping Center of Western Oklahoma," Elk City existed before the railroad arrived, but the transportation that the railroad provided is what made the town boom more than other communities in the area. Train service on the Choctaw Route started here on August 20, 1901 (a depot was built by June 30, 1902), and the Wichita Falls & Northwestern Railway arrived in 1910. Both railroads had significant facilities here that included a number of tracks and brick stations, representing the importance of this wheat and livestock town. The Wichita Falls & Northwestern became a part of the Missouri–Kansas–Texas and was abandoned through Elk City in 1973. However, the Rock Island Railroad lasted until 1980.

The lettering on the end of the Rock Island depot makes it clear that this is Elk City, Oklahoma.

Elk City was a legal dividing line on the Choctaw Route for a number of years. This was because the track from Weatherford to Elk City was completed by the Choctaw, Oklahoma & Gulf in October 1901. Meanwhile, the track to the west from Elk City to the Oklahoma-Texas State Line was built by the Western Oklahoma Railroad Company in 1901-1902. The Western Oklahoma Railroad was a Choctaw, Oklahoma & Gulf subsidiary established to build track in several places in Oklahoma. According to Rock Island Railroad records, the line was "practically completed by May 1, 1902."

The *Annual Report of the Governor of Oklahoma to the Secretary of the Interior for the Fiscal Year Ended June 30, 1902,* reported that by that time, the Western Oklahoma Railroad had built 39.4 miles of mainline, and 6.1 miles of sidings, on their Elk City to the Texas State Line railroad. The Interstate Commerce Commission later stated in their valuation report on the railroad that the Western Oklahoma Railroad Company's 40 miles of mainline had been purchased by the Choctaw, Oklahoma & Gulf.

The facilities and even the operations of a number of the Elk City agricultural firms remain, including this one near the depot.

In 1910, the Rock Island served a number of large shippers at Elk City, Oklahoma. These included grain firms like the Weatherford Milling Company (7000 bushel grain elevator built in 1901), the Elk City Mill & Elevator Company (built in 1907), and the D. G. Mosley Corn Mill. The Elk City Cotton Oil Company and Harris & Erby's Cotton Gin handled the local cotton business. Finally, the Elk City Fuel & Ice Company, and the Roger Mills County Cooperative Association (building materials) supported other needs of the community.

By 1923, the railroad was serving a number of new or expanded customers. The Roger Mills County Cooperative Association had added a creamery and a 9000-bushel elevator, and the Elk City Ice, Light & Fuel Company had expanded its services to the community and expanded its name. Weatherford Milling was now the American Milling Company. Cotton was handled by the Williams & Miller Gin Company (which also manufactured cotton gin machinery), the Planters Gin Company, and the Elk City Cotton Oil Company. The Farmers Mill & Supply Company built a 15,000-bushel grain elevator in 1922. Finally, a number of independent bulk oil stations had been built along the railroad.

Remains of the initial oil boom can still be found at Elk City, including this former oil and machinery supply company structure near the Rock Island passenger station.

The Railroad at Elk City

During the final years of the Rock Island, the railroad still had an agency and train order station here. Elk City was also shown to be a water station for watering diesel locomotives, livestock cars, and for other needs. The 1979 employee timetable stated that there was a 3816-foot siding, plus 8210 feet of other tracks. Diagrams from the 1970s show a long siding to the north that wrapped around the brick passenger station and brick freight house. There were also several short house tracks to the north, plus three to the south. After the Rock Island shut down, there was enough business to keep rail service this far west. The line was acquired by the State of Oklahoma, and this part operated by Farmrail starting in 1981. Initially, the railroad served the 35 miles linking Clinton and Elk City, but it soon grew. The *Federal Register*, dated October 4, 1983, contained a list of Rock Island routes "Authorized To Be Operated by Interim Operators." The listing stated that Farmrail Corporation could operate from "west of Elk City (milepost 615.0) to west of Erick, Oklahoma (milepost 642.0), a distance of approximately 27 miles." Today, Farmrail still operates to here and serves a number of shippers, as well as operates its own car shop at Elk City. Most of the tracks still exist, and a few new ones have been built. Heading west from here, Farmrail has posted that the "stations of Sayre, OK, and Erick, OK, are served by contract only."

According to the railroad, Elk City has been the center of a lot of the recent growth on the Farmrail System. In 2003, the railroad built a new 1500-foot spur to a "new stone-distribution terminal being built by Elk City Industrial Authority on a 160-acre industrial tract in that community." The plan was for granite aggregates to be shipped from the Martin Marietta quarry at Long, Oklahoma, to here for use in paving projects throughout western Oklahoma and the Texas Panhandle. In 2006, Farmrail bought the assets of American Milling's railcar-repair facility at Elk City, with plans that this would reduce the time and costs to repair rail equipment on the railroad.

In 2011, a sand-distribution facility was built for oilfield supplier Frac Tech Services. The facility included a new passing siding and double-ended spur for unloading different grades of product. This facility is located just east of Interstate 40 at the Santrol Elk City facility. About the same time, Illinois frac-sand producer Manley Brothers also established a facility at Elk City. Because of the growth in the area, Elk City purchased a 130-acre trackside parcel west of town in 2013 to develop as the rail-served Big Elk Industrial Park. Much of the use of the facility was planned to be oil related.

Besides the old Rock Island tracks, there are several historic railroad buildings that still stand at Elk City. Probably the most significant, and the one that relates most to the Chicago, Rock Island & Pacific, is the brick passenger station. Located on the northeast corner of 7th and Main, the train order semaphore signal and the city name built into the end walls make the station a classic *Choctaw Rocket* artifact. The station, very similar to the one in Argenta, Arkansas, features two waiting rooms due to Oklahoma segregation laws. The last passenger train stopped here on August 8, 1964, and the station is now owned by the State of Oklahoma, but used by Farmrail. Just northeast of the former Rock Island passenger station is the former freight house, built in a very similar style. This brick building was used for many years by the Elk City Street Maintenance Department, but was occupied by The Scissortail Co. Hair and Tanning Salon in 2020.

The former Wichita Falls & Northwestern brick depot also still stands in Elk City. One of the restaurants that has used the station building stated that it was built in 1901, but the company wasn't even organized until 1906, and the line didn't reach here until after 1910. However, the building is well preserved and is located on the northeast corner of 8th and Main. The MKT also once had a freight house, a small yard, and a locomotive fueling facility at Elk City.

This evening photograph shows that the Rock Island station at Elk City, Oklahoma, has been well taken care of and still stands next to the former mainline.

This morning photograph shows the track side of the Elk City depot, including the train order semaphore that still stands tall above the building.

Just east of the Elk City depot is the former freight house, used for years by the city, but more recently by a hair and tanning salon.

The Early Years of Elk City

It is known that Francisco Vásquez de Coronado passed through the region in 1541 while looking for the fabled city of Quivira, one of the mythical Seven Cities of Gold that he never found. Some have promoted the idea that he passed through what is today Elk City, but there is little to prove what route he actually took.

After land in the area became available, a small community grew up calling itself Crowe, located on the Great Western Cattle Trail from Texas to Dodge City, Kansas. A post office opened there on May 10, 1899. In 1901, the town moved a short distance from Beaver County to Roger Mills County, forming Busch on March 18, 1901. After Oklahoma became a state on November 16, 1907, Busch, which had been renamed Elk City on July 20, 1907, was suddenly in Beckham County.

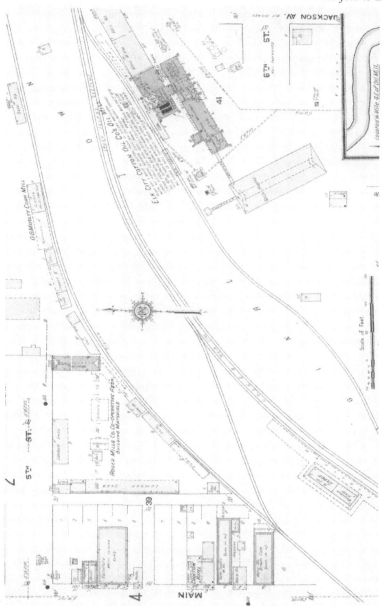

Sanborn Map – Elk City Rock Island Station Area – April 1910. *Sanborn Fire Insurance Map from Elk City, Beckham County, Oklahoma.* Sanborn Map Company, Apr 1910. Map. Retrieved from the Library of Congress, https://www.loc.gov/item/sanborn07079_003/.

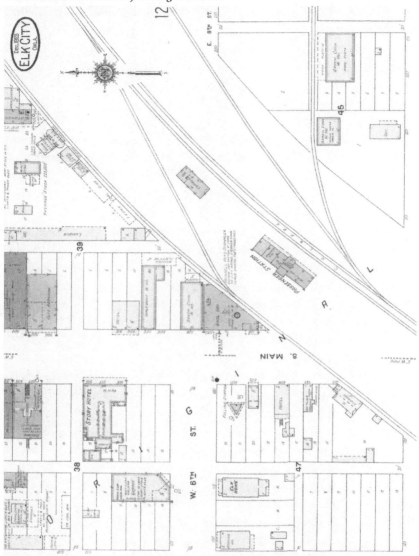

Sanborn Map – New CRI&P Depot, Elk City – December 1923. *Sanborn Fire Insurance Map from Elk City, Beckham County, Oklahoma.* Sanborn Map Company, Dec 1923. Map. Retrieved from the Library of Congress, https://www.loc.gov/item/sanborn07079_005/.

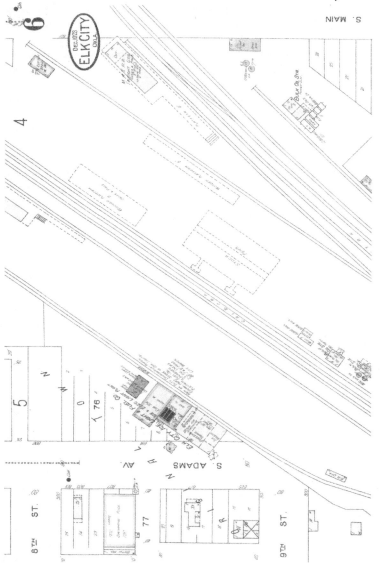

Sanborn Map – MKT Freight House and Rock Island Stockyards, Elk City – December 1923. *Sanborn Fire Insurance Map from Elk City, Beckham County, Oklahoma.* Sanborn Map Company, De, 1923. Map. Retrieved from the Library of Congress, https://www. loc.gov/item/sanborn07079_005/.

When the Choctaw, Oklahoma & Gulf Railroad reached Weatherford, construction halted for a time, but efforts were made to survey the route extension and to plat towns along it. One of these efforts was made by the Choctaw Townsite and Development Company, managed by Elva C. Barrows. Barrows was later involved with real estate in Oklahoma City and Tulsa, and then the oil and natural gas business. Among the several townsites he planned was Elk City, and the townsite company bought land from the early homesteaders along Elk Creek to accomplish this. Even before the town was platted and lots sold, a tent city had grown up with a population of several hundred residents.

On March 20, 1901, the first lots were sold, and on August 20, 1901, regular train service started on the Choctaw Route. By the end of the year, the population of Elk City had passed 1000 with more than sixty businesses up and running, making it one of the largest towns in western Oklahoma after less than a year. Fires in 1903 and 1906 led to the construction of more permanent buildings. Cotton and corn were early crops for farmers, and a 1904 Department of Agriculture report indicated that there were 8 rail shipments of cotton from Elk City in 1903-1904. By 1910, the town was a mix of agriculture, ranching and manufacturing, with four banks, four cotton gins, a cotton oil mill, and more than 2000 residents. A Carnegie Library opened on October 11, 1915, and the town added a cotton compress, an ice plant, two broom factories, and two flour mills soon after.

Naming Elk City

There are several stories about the source of the name Elk City, especially since the town started as Crowe, and then as Busch. The best explanation is that the name Elk City comes from nearby Elk Creek. Elk Creek received its name in 1852 when U.S. Army Captain Randolph B. Marcy was exploring the area. In his report, he wrote: "From the circumstance of having seen elk tracks upon the stream we passed in our march today, I have called it 'Elk Creek'. I am informed by our guide that five years since, elk were frequently seen in the Wichita Mountains; but now they are seldom met with in this part of the country."

An elk, also known as a wapiti, is a large member of the North American deer family. The town celebrates its name with a statue of a bull elk on the corner of 3rd and Washington.

Modern Elk City

Even during the hard years of the 1930s, Elk City held on to much of its industry, supporting the regional farm and livestock businesses. For example, there were nine cotton gins, six machine shops, a creamery, two ice plants, a meat packing plant, and a mattress factory. A cooperative hospital opened in 1931, with annual memberships in return for free medical treatment. The same year, thirty thousand people attended the annual U.S. Highway 66 Association Convention in Elk City.

Retail stores and businesses related to Route 66 opened during this time. The population reached 5666 in 1930, and then dropped down a bit to 5021 in 1940. Shell Oil Company brought in a producing oil well on November 24, 1947, and the town grew again, adding city parks, golf courses and a swimming pool. The population reached 7962 residents in 1950, and Elk City began promoting itself as the "Natural Gas Capital of the World." Various leases that involved the Chicago, Rock Island & Pacific demonstrate some of the companies that operated at Elk City over the years. These included Harold's Concrete Supplies, Elk City Gins, B. F. Allee (natural gas production), and W. R. Grace & Company.

In 2010, the population of Elk City reached 11,693, the largest in its history, and it has continued to grow with current estimates of about 13,000. The town features many gas stations, retail stores, hotels and restaurants since it is about half-way between Oklahoma City and Amarillo. Elk City also features several sites listed on the National Register of Historic Places, including the Casa Grande Hotel, Hedlund Motor Company Building, Storm House and the Whited Grist Mill. There is also the National Route 66 and Transportation Museum, and the Old Town Museum, located on Route 66 – West 3rd Street. At the museum is a replica depot and a Colorado & Southern caboose, lettered Choctaw, Oklahoma & Gulf. There is also the Anadarko Basin Museum of Natural History in town, and the annual Rodeo of Champions, held every September.

Elk City is also the home of Ackley Park, a 220-acre park with a carousel, softball complex, picnic shelters, a seasonal pool, and other activities. One of these facilities is the Centennial Carousel which features 36 hand-carved wooden horses, two bench seats, and one wheelchair spot. The carousel is modern, costing the city $450,000, and has been described as "the most elaborate all-wood carousel built since the 1930s."

Another park attraction is the Choctaw Express Miniature Train, described as an Ottaway 14-inch gauge "Rocketliner" train, considered to be a rarity in the miniature train world. These trains were built at Wichita, Kansas, both before and after WWII, by the Ottaway Amusement Company. The firm was basically a family-run operation that also built some children's rides. Ottaway Amusement eventually became a part of Chance Manufacturing, which was helping to build some of the trains. This firm still manufactures roller coasters and amusement rides.

611.9 WEST ELK CREEK BRIDGE – Leaving Elk City, the railroad loops around the south side of town, where there is a new siding at Milepost 610.4, west of the Randall Street grade crossing. At the Pioneer Street grade crossing are several rail shippers, including Haliburton, M2W Energy Services, and WestOK Logistics. The tracks then cross West Elk Creek.

Elk Creek flows around the east side of Elk City, and West Elk Creek goes around the west side. The stream forms in the hills to the northwest and flows south to here, where the railroad crosses it using an 80-foot deck plate girder span, with a 40-foot wide-flanged beam span off each end. The stream turns south and passes under Interstate 40, and flows into Elk City Lake, described as a 750-acre park with a 250-acre lake that is regularly stocked with fish. The park features free RV camping, boating and fishing, a swimming beach area, picnic pavilions, horse and bike trails, and other outdoor activities. The lake is also designated as the Elk City Reservoir.

613.1 INTERSTATE 40 – The railroad again passes under Interstate 40. It then curves to the southwest, generally passing through fields and pastureland south of I-40.

616.3 MERRITT – Some records show that the name Indian Creek was once used for this location. This town, once located east of the Oklahoma Highway 34 overpass, was named after Lafe Merritt, publisher of the *El Reno Globe*. There was a post office here from August 9, 1901, until July 15, 1908. For many years there was a siding on the north side of the railroad's mainline because this was the top of a five-mile eastbound ruling grade of 0.97%. Almost nothing of the town exists today except for the Merritt Community Cemetery and the Merritt Public School (K-12), "Home of the Oilers."

621.8 TIMBER CREEK BRIDGE – Timber Creek forms in the hills in the southwestern part of Rogers Mills County, and it flows south to here. It continues south before flowing into the North Fork of the Red River.

Timber Creek is considered to be one of the primary tributaries of the river.

This bridge features two 51-foot deck plate girder spans with seven-panel timber trestles off each end.

621.9 DOXEY – This town was originally named Pior for local resident John B. Pior. A post office was established here on March 3, 1900. The history of the name Doxey requires telling the story of the original Doxey, located to the northwest. The previous town was founded by the early 1890s as Doxey, named for cattle rancher Sam Doxie. On September 2, 1896, the Berlin Post Office opened at what had been the first Doxey. The Berlin post office lasted for almost seventy years, and closed on May 5, 1967.

Six years after the original Doxey became Berlin, the town of Pior, which in the meantime had become located on the railroad, changed its name to Doxey on December 5, 1902. The Western Oklahoma Railroad Company had completed their line through the area during early 1902, and the *Annual Report of the Governor of Oklahoma to the Secretary of the Interior for the Fiscal Year Ended June 30, 1902*, reported that a depot was built at Doxey during this time. There was also a water tank for the steam locomotives.

While the name of Doxey came from a rancher, some of the early shipments were farm products. A 1904 Department of Agriculture report stated that 42 rail shipments of cotton were made from Doxey in 1903-1904. Wheat, oats, cattle and calves were also shipped from this area.

In 1905, Berlin re-entered the story about Doxey. In that year, the Oklahoma & Northwestern Railroad Company was chartered with a capital stock of $1,875,000, to build a railroad from Doxey. The November 18, 1905, issue of *The Railway and Engineering Review* reported the following.

> *Mr. G. B. Sutton, Berlin, Okla., is superintendent of construction of the Oklahoma & Northwestern Railroad Co., which is to build a line from Doxey, O.T., to a point in Beaver county, with a branch to Sayre, 75 miles. Grading is reported under way from Doxey to Berlin, 12 miles. E. E. Reiss is president, with office at 171 La Salle street, Chicago. H. Jarvis & Co., 1749 Railway Exchange building, Chicago, are the engineers. The company is doing its own construction.*

Despite the news, it appears that the railroad was never built. A lot of other plans never materialized, and the Doxey post office closed on May 29, 1931. Nothing really remains alongside the tracks at Doxey except for the grade crossing with North 1910 Road, also known as BK25. To the north is the Doxey Cemetery, opened even before the railroad arrived.

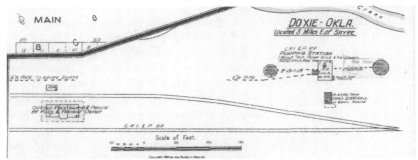

Sanborn Map – Doxey Depot and Water Station – January 1924. *Sanborn Fire Insurance Map from Sayre, Beckham County, Oklahoma.* Sanborn Map Company, Jan, 1924. Map. Retrieved from the Library of Congress, https://www.loc.gov/item/sanborn07243_004/.

The Passenger Trains at Doxey

Doxey was a fairly important station during the 1910s for the railroad, at least at 1:15am each early morning. At that time, trains No. 43 and No. 44 – both named the *Fast Mail* – were scheduled to meet here. The September 1914 timetable showed that four passenger trains a day served Doxey. They were No. 43 and No. 44, plus No. 41 and No. 42, the *Western Express.* In the timetables, it showed that Doxey was a flag stop for all of the trains except No. 44, which apparently arrived at Doxey and waited for No. 43 to pass.

In 1914, the four passenger trains that operated through Doxey had a somewhat complex schedule. At that time, trains No. 42 and No. 43 operated Memphis-Amarillo, while trains No. 41 and No. 44 operated Memphis-Tucumcari. This meant that cars and passengers were often swapped between trains. This process was made even more complicated by the way some trains were split or combined at Little Rock, Arkansas, and El Reno, Oklahoma. For the cars that passed through Doxey, they still had some complex details.

For the trains No. 41 (actually No. 45-41 in the timetable because of changes further east) and No. 42 (No. 42-46), known as the *Western Express*, the cars included everything from coaches to sleepers and dining cars. The following is from the September 1914 public timetable.

Electric-lighted drawing-room sleeping car, Memphis to Tucumcari on No. 45-41 (returning on No. 44). Twelve-section drawing-room sleeping car Amarillo to Memphis on No. 42-46. Chair car and partitioned coach between Memphis and Tucumcari. Dining car service between Tucumcari and El Reno.

For trains No. 43 and No. 44, the *Fast Mail*, the information about the cars that passed through Doxey was similar.

Drawing-room sleeper, Tucumcari to Memphis on No. 44, (returning on Nos. 45-41). Twelve-section drawing-room sleeping car Memphis to Amarillo on No. 43. Chair car, coach and partitioned coach between Memphis and Amarillo.

623.4 SAYRE-DOXEY CEMETERY – Located to the south of the tracks is one of the largest cemeteries in the region, easily seen in this treeless prairie. Several pipeline stations are located adjacent to the cemetery.

The entrance to the Sayre-Doxey Cemetery is marked by this sign and large American flag.

624.5 DEEP CREEK BRIDGE – Look for the 75-foot deck plate girder with a 3-panel timber pile trestle on each end. Deep Creek is somewhat of a common name in this region, and this one forms in the gas and oil fields about ten miles north of Sayre. It flows south, passes under this bridge, and then into the North Fork of the Red River several miles south of here.

625.3 INTERSTATE 40 BRIDGE – The CRI&P crossed over the freeway at this location on a five-span bridge. Just to the east is the North Fork Correctional Center. This facility was built by the Corrections Corporation of America in 1998 as a private prison to house inmates from across the country, mostly from California. The original facility housed 1440 inmates, and then in 2007 it was expanded by another 960 beds. The facility closed in 2015 and then reopened as an Oklahoma Department of Corrections facility.

626.3 SAYRE (SA) – Sayre was a division point for the Rock Island Railroad, with Subdivision 34 to the east and Subdivision 35 to the west, all part of the Southern Division at the end of the railroad's life. This need to change crews, and steam locomotives and cabooses during the first days of the railroad, led to the construction of a number of railroad facilities at Sayre. One of the first built was a depot, opened by June 30, 1902, according to the *Annual Report of the Governor of Oklahoma to the Secretary of the Interior*. Many of these tracks and facilities lasted only until World War II, and just the depot and a few yard tracks remain today.

When the railroad built through Sayre, the town's layout wasn't completed, so the railroad built where they needed to. This development took place to the west of today's downtown in an area that was quickly known as Railroad Hill. Initially, this put the yards, train station, and other railroad facilities outside of the city limits of Sayre, and about a mile to the west of the new downtown. The first passenger train arrived in Sayre on September 25, 1901, setting the stage for several decades of conflict between the railroad and the citizens of Sayre.

A small rail yard and a combination passenger-freight station was built by the end of 1901. The station was a wooden building with a one-story freight section to the west and a two-story passenger section to the east, providing housing for the station's agent. Facilities for steam locomotives were also built that year, including an engine house, coal chute, and turntable. A section house was built for the track forces, and several bunk houses were built for train crews and track forces. Several tool houses were also built for the track gangs and the mechanical forces.

In 1902, a Van Noy Brothers Eating House (some histories state that it was a Harvey House) was built to the west of the depot. This facility was required to feed not only train crews, but passengers who had a short stop here for meals. The building was two-story to provide housing for the workers, but the need to feed passengers soon ended as dining cars were added to the trains on the route. As the number of freight train crews assigned to Sayre decreased, the Eating House was closed and then sold in 1935. The buyer of the building reportedly moved it to town and used it as a house for many years.

An updated roundhouse was built at Sayre in 1908, along with a boiler house to provide steam for the shop and yard facilities. More facilities were added over the next few years as the facility was modernized, including a chemical house, water treatment facility, and hose house (1909), track scale (1911), and stock pens (1913). In 1915, the railroad expanded a number of locomotive facilities, adding a modern cinder pit, sand house, and a new 24' x 28' water tower. The track forces were issued motorcars about the same time, and the railroad reported the construction of a motorcar house. Also, for years, boxcars sat on the ground around the yard, being used as tool houses, warehouses, and bunk houses.

Improvements were halted when the federal government nationalized the country's railroads during World War I, but the mid-1920s saw a redesign of the rail yard to handle more traffic, and a new station was built downtown. Reports from the 1920s seem to show that this was the peak of traffic on the line. A report from September 1926 stated that passenger traffic through Sayre was "by far the heaviest this line has ever enjoyed," and that trains were running full. Freight trains were also busy and running in extra sections due to the discovery of oil and the increased production of wheat. The railroad tripled the size of the rail yard to hold as many as 600 freight cars, a new water tank was built that was connected to a series of stand pipes around the yard and along the mainline, and the shops received some new tools and equipment. All of this work led Sayre to be declared one of the largest freight terminals in Western Oklahoma, and the largest west of El Reno, Oklahoma. However, this was about the peak of demand and most of these facilities were gone by the 1960s.

Rock Island Timetable No. 1, dated March 18, 1979, provided a list of the services and facilities that remained at Sayre during the last year the railroad operated. These included general order boards and books, a standard clock, a train register station, a train order station, and a wayside radio. All of these were very logical since Sayre was still a crew change location. For the trains, there was a fuel and water station, and a wye to turn locomotives. The timetable also stated that there was a 4158-foot siding, plus a yard. To protect the yard operations, the railroad had yard limits from Milepost 624 pole 24 near Deep Creek Bridge, to Milepost 629.0.

Sayre marked another change in the traffic on the railroad. To the east, the traffic was almost seven million gross tons of freight per year during the Rock Island's last days. However, to the west towards Amarillo it was only three million gross tons. Most grain moved east, so the traffic west of here generally was local business or came from interchange traffic at Amarillo.

For Farmrail, there is still a yard at Sayre, plus several customers, although service west of Elk City is provided by contract only. Across from the Rock Island depot is a collection of old grain elevators, now the Sayre Grain and Farm Supply. West of the Main Street grade crossing is the east end of the Sayre yard, which has three long tracks and one short track. To the north of the yard is the Hampel Oil Distributors facility.

Sayre Rock Island Depot

Located on the north side of the tracks on Poplar Street, and just west of Broadway, is the former Rock Island passenger train station. This beautiful station was built in 1927 to handle the increased passenger business at Sayre. It also was located near the downtown business district, as the original 1901 station was on the edge of town at the railroad yards. The "new" station has a wide roof overhang to provide shade and protection from rain on all sides of the building, and has a design that has been described as Italian Renaissance Revival. The one-story depot is a combination of brick and stucco. The brick is along the lower portion of the walls, and the stucco is along the upper walls, with a stone stringcourse separating the brick from the stucco. The roof uses a gable-on-hipped design with red ceramic tile. The design was fairly common on the railroad, and is similar to the stations at Hobart and Walters, Oklahoma.

The depot also featured the required design of two waiting rooms, divided by a ticket office. At the time, Oklahoma was one of a number of states with laws that segregated railroad passengers by their race, so the station had separate white and black waiting rooms and ticket windows. The White Waiting Room was on the east end of the building, and featured both men's (northwest side) and women's (east side) restrooms. The ticket office and agent's office featured a bay window, and was located immediately west of the White Waiting Room, with ticket windows on both sides. On the west side of the ticket office was the Black Waiting Room, smaller but still with men's and women's restrooms. On the very west end of the station was the Baggage and Express Room, with a single freight door on the front and back sides of the station. In this area was a set of stairs to the basement where a furnace was located, used to heat the entire building.

This trackside view of the Sayre passenger station shows the general design of the building.

As stated, this is the second station built at Sayre. The original station was west of downtown about a mile, and during rains, people had to often deal with flooding from Short Creek. Complaints began from the start of the community, and by 1913, there were proposals to build a new station closer to downtown. In 1914, it was announced that the station would be built on Main Street at the west end of downtown, but that was still some distance from town, and Short Creek was still a concern. The actual announced plan for the station stated that it would be "directly in the middle" of Main Street, and that an underground crossing would be built under the tracks to "eliminate all possible danger to Main Street traffic at that point." Complaints about the location continued, but the forced sale of the railroad on October 19, 1914, ended all hope for an immediate solution.

1917 saw the railroad again promise a new station if a location could be agreed upon, and the City of Sayre filed a complaint against the railroad with the Oklahoma Corporation Commission (OCC). A hearing was held on June 23, 1917, where a number of presentations were made about the inadequacies of the current station and location. Within a month, the OCC ordered the railroad to build a new fire-proof depot in Sayre. The railroad designed a new station and eating house, but World War I and the nationalization of the railroads ended all new station construction.

After the war, a campaign to build a new station finally resulted in a plan being announced, but only if an appropriate location could be found. In early April of 1927, the railroad stated that they would like to build the station on the north side of the tracks between Broadway and Fourth Street. However, the City of Sayre owned the lot and had recently built the Sayre Community Hall there. A quick vote by the residents resulted in an agreement on the location, and construction began. At the same time, the Rock Island cut their depot in two and moved the passenger section to the southwest corner of South Ninth Street and West Main. The freight section was converted to an eating house for the freight and yard crews.

The first passenger train to use the new station arrived at 9:45am on Sunday, January 15, 1928. The event attracted a crowd and the Sayre High School band, which played for the crew and passengers. This station was for passengers only, and the old station was used as part of a new freight house. Passenger service declined after World War II, and it ended on August 8, 1964. Railroad offices remained in the station for a few years, but eventually moved to the yard. In 1972, the station was donated to the City of Sayre, and the Shortgrass Country Museum took over the building in 1992. The Sayre Rock Island Depot was placed on the National Register of Historic Places on June 9, 2000.

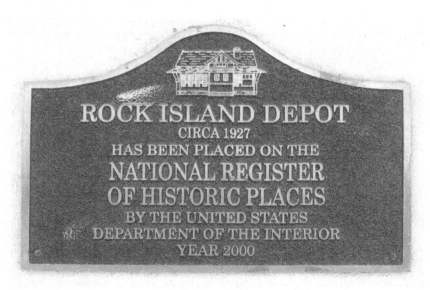

This marker on the Rock Island passenger station at Sayre, Oklahoma, states that the building has been placed on the National Register of Historic Places.

The City of Sayre

As McCabe & Steen Contractors built the railroad west in 1901, a number of companies were attempting to create new towns along the new tracks. At what became Sayre, the Choctaw Townsite and Improvement Company acquired land on the north side of the North Fork of the Red River, platted a town, and began selling lots. The town was named Sayre, after another Lehigh Valley Railroad manager and railroad developer, Robert H. Sayre. The Lehigh Valley Railroad had gotten involved with the railroad when they funded the Choctaw Coal & Railway Company in 1887, which built much of the east end of the railroad in Oklahoma. With the relationship established, a number of Lehigh Valley Railroad managers acquired stock and helped with the construction, including Robert Heysham Sayre. Sayre was a civil engineer who had first been involved with the Morris Canal in New Jersey, and the Mauch Chunk Switchback Railway. At age 29 (1854), Sayre was named Chief Engineer of the Lehigh Valley Railroad, and he was responsible for much of the expansion of the railroad. He later became vice president of the Lehigh Valley Railroad. He also was one of the founders, and then vice president, of the Bethlehem Iron Company, later the Bethlehem Steel Corporation. Finally, Sayre was a stockholder of the Choctaw, Oklahoma & Gulf, and he donated to the construction of the new Presbyterian Church at Sayre. Besides Sayre, Oklahoma, the town of Sayre, Pennsylvania, was named in his honor.

Oklahoma was not yet a state when the City of Sayre was founded in 1901, and it was located in Roger Mills County in Oklahoma Territory. Being a major railroad terminal, Sayre grew quickly and had more than 1000 residents by the following year. When Beckham County was organized as Oklahoma became a state in 1907, Sayre was made the temporary county seat until a 1908 election made it permanent. The county courthouse opened in 1911, and the building is now on the National Register of Historic Places.

Farming and ranching were the initial industries at Sayre, with 2559 rail shipments of cotton in 1903-1904. Wheat really took off during the 1920s. Oil and natural gas discoveries during the 1920s also attracted a number of residents. Major rail shippers at Sayre during the mid-1920s included the Planters Gin Company (cotton), Chickasaw Cotton Oil Company, Farmers Co-op Grain and Elevator Company, Oscar Ewton (5000-bushel grain elevator built in 1921), Sayre Ice Company, and The Western Lumber & Hardware Company.

Across the tracks from the passenger station was once a series of grain elevators, with these remaining at Sayre, Oklahoma.

Like many other towns along the route, the construction of Route 66 led to the expansion of the travel industry in Sayre. The highway was a major route during the 1920s and the Great Depression, and John Ford's movie *The Grapes of Wrath* used Sayre for several scenes. After World War II, Route 66 hit its peak with tourism. Another boom in the oil and natural gas industry took placed starting in the 1970s, and Sayre kept growing.

Today, the Sayre Downtown Historic District is listed on the National Register. The town is the host of a number of local festivals, including the Route 66 Hoot'n Scoot & Poker Run & Antique Car Show; the Sayre Championship Rodeo; and others. The population also reached a new high of 4375 in the 2010 census.

626.8 SHORT CREEK BRIDGE – Near Main Street is a 10-panel timber pile trestle bridge over Short Creek. This stream is much shorter than nearby Long Creek, forming to the northwest of Sayre, and flowing around the west and south side of the city before flowing into the North Fork of the Red River near East Main Street.

Just south of Main Street is the east switch of the remains of the Sayre railyard. It was in this area that the railroad had their shops and first railroad depot. There was also a car and locomotive repair shop, a coal tipple, a cinder pit, and a roundhouse.

In 2020, the Sayre yard was packed full of stored frac sand railcars.

627.8 LONG CREEK BRIDGE – This bridge consists of a 60-foot deck plate girder span with three panels of a ballast deck timber trestle off each end. Long Creek forms northwest of Berlin, Oklahoma, and heads south around the west side of Sayre and into the North Fork of the Red River just south of here.

Just south of the Long Creek Bridge, the railroad turns almost directly south to cross the North Fork of the Red River.

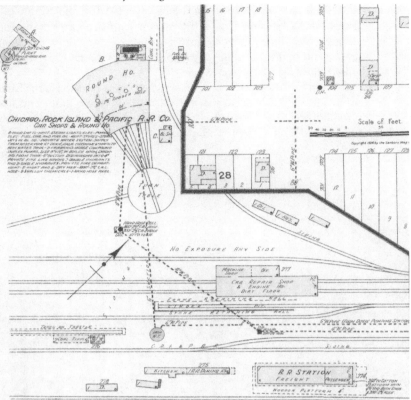

Sanborn Map Company – CRI&P Roundhouse, Shops and Station at Sayre – January 1924. *Sanborn Fire Insurance Map from Sayre, Beckham County, Oklahoma.* Sanborn Map Company, Jan, 1924. Map. Retrieved from the Library of Congress, https://www.loc.gov/item/sanborn07243_004/.

628.2 NORTH FORK RED RIVER BRIDGE – The North Fork Red River is often known simply as the North Fork, and was believed to be the main fork of the Red River for more than thirty years after the 1819 Adams-Onis Treaty defined the border between the United States and New Spain. The Treaty stated that the main channel of the Red River was the border, but in 1852, the Marcy Expedition discovered that the South Fork, also known as the Prairie Dog Town Fork, was the main channel. This change created first a problem with New Spain (Mexico), and then the Republic of Texas when it joined the United States. The land between the two river branches was claimed by both governments, and the United States Supreme Court finally settled the matter in 1896 and made the land part of Oklahoma Territory.

The North Fork forms in Gray County, Texas, and is slightly more than 270 miles long. From here, it turns south and eventually enters the South Fork to the southwest of Frederick, Oklahoma. The upper end of the river was the scene of a number of battles during the Indian Wars of the 1870s, as it was a primary water source and obstacle to travel. Today, it is the source of water for a number of communities along its route.

The river is normally narrow, but it has a wide and wandering channel to handle its flood waters. Because of this, the railroad bridge is 750 feet long. Rock Island Railroad documents from 1973 state that the bridge consisted of 30 pile trestle spans, five 30-foot deck plate girder spans, six 32-foot deck plate girder spans, one 34-foot deck plate girder span, and three 74-foot deck plate girder spans. The three longest spans are located directly over the main channel of the river, set on large concrete piers at an elevation of 1821 feet.

South of the bridge, the railroad curves to the southwest and then stays just north of Interstate 40. Throughout this area, the railroad passes dry pasture, often with a thin line of trees at the fence line.

632.2 BIG TURKEY CREEK BRIDGE – Big Turkey Creek was one of the main targets for settlers in the Land Rush of 1889. On April 22, 1889, large numbers of people headed for this stream as it was only ten miles west of the starting line, and the stream was known for its water, good pasture, and plentiful timber.

From east to west, this bridge is made up of a 54-foot deck plate girder span, a 60-foot deck plate girder span, and a 41-foot deck plate girder span. Old Route 66 is immediately to the south. Heading west, the grade stiffens to about 0.8% and climbs until Erick, Oklahoma.

634.6 HEXT RANCH – Named for William Hext, a prominent local resident and rancher, there was a post office here starting on June 4, 1901, and ending on November 29, 1902. Hext Ranch, or just Hext, was created when the railroad built through here. During the early 1900s, there were a few houses, a store or two, and a cotton gin.

In 1929, Route 66 was aligned through Hext on its 5th Street and was paved, the first street in town to have modern pavement. The 1946 book *A Guide Book to Highway 66* by Jack DeVere Rittenhouse, described Hext as "Not a community – just a gas station." During the 1950s, Route 66 received two more lanes for the traffic. When Interstate 40 was built just south of town, the original road finally lost its designation as U.S. Highway 66, the last section in Oklahoma to lose that designation to I-40.

Today, Hext is an unincorporated community with a few houses, barns and the remains of Route 66, centered around County Road East

1220. The north lanes, the original road, are now unused. The south lanes are still used as a local road.

Throughout this area, and heading west, are a number of round irrigated fields. These fields are watered using what is called center-pivot irrigation, a system invented in 1940 by farmer Frank Zybach of Strasburg, Colorado. Also known as central pivot irrigation, water-wheel irrigation, and circle irrigation, the field is watered using sprinklers that are attached to a central pivot. The pivot generally houses the water well, or at least a connection to a water line. The pivots and sprinkler system are powered either by the water pressure, or by electric motors.

This area is drier than average for the United States, with only 26 inches of rain and 7 inches of snow per year, with 253 sunny days per year, far above average. Wheat and alfalfa hay are the main crops grown in the area, but others such as cotton, kafir corn, milo maize, and broomcorn are also popular. Oklahoma ranks third in the country in the production of winter wheat, producing approximately 140 million bushels each year. Oklahoma also produces about six million tons of hay each year (sixth in the nation), most for its local livestock industry, which ranks fifth in the nation for cattle and calf production. It also ranks third in the production of meat goats. Overall, the state ranks fourth in the number of farms, which employ about 325,000 people.

636.8 INTERSTATE 40 – The railroad passes under I-40, just east of the Oklahoma Tourist Information Center on the highway. The railroad has been heading to the southwest, and turns more to the west to enter Erick.

640.9 ERICK (RI) – The town of Erick – Home of the Bobcats – was named for Beeks Erick, president of the Choctaw Townsite and Improvement Company, which platted a number of towns along the railroad. In his obituary in the July 26, 1914, issue of the *Indianapolis Star*, it stated that he was one of the wealthiest men in Fort Wayne, Indiana. It also stated that "he made his money building railroads in Oklahoma and financing banks in the West. At one time he was the sole owner of fourteen banks in Oklahoma."

Erick was established in 1901 as an agricultural community, originally named Dennis when a post office opened during February 1900. There is no clear source of the name Dennis, but it could have been music composer J. W. Dennis, who lived in the area. Dennis was a respected teacher and writer of music who was able to put out a new book of music each year. He co-wrote at least one song with L. H. Matthews of Erick. On November 16, 1901, the post office and town changed its name to Erick, and it was soon incorporated using the same name.

Erick quickly became known for its cotton and cotton gins, cattle, and salt that was extracted from nearby salt springs. The U.S. Department of Agriculture reported that there were 175 rail shipments of cotton from Erick in 1903-1904. When Oklahoma became a state in 1907, the population of Erick was recorded as being 686, and then 915 in the 1910 census. In 1924, the Sanborn Map Company showed a number of businesses along the railroad at Erick. These included East Erick Gin (cotton – operated by Western Oklahoma Gins), G. E. Harris (7500-bushel grain elevator built in 1912), and Flours & Forbes (1500-bushel capacity grain loading elevator).

The discovery of natural gas in the area during the 1920s, and the construction of Route 66, got Erick's population to peak at 2231 in the 1930 census. However, the Great Depression and the Dust Bowl ran many settlers off of their land. As jobs went away, there were several reports of racial fighting and great resentment towards some of those who traveled through the area looking for work or a handout.

Following World War II, there was again some development in Erick due to Route 66. The DeLuxe Courts was an early lodging establishment, and there are claims that it was the first area lodging to appear in the *AAA Directory of Motor Courts and Cottages*. Soon, other motels, trailer parks, cafes, and service stations also opened. In 1946, Jack Rittenhouse described Erick by writing that it is "the first town you encounter, going west, which has any of the true 'western' look, with its wide, sunbaked streets, frequent horsemen, occasional side-walk awnings, and similar touches."

Even with this development, the population of Erick dropped to 1285 in 1970. It temporarily increased as another oil and gas drilling boom took place, and construction on Interstate 40 and other local roads were underway. The four-lane highway of Route 66 between Erick and Sayre was the last part replaced by Interstate 40 in Oklahoma, meaning that the tourist businesses in Erick were some of the last to hold on. Most are now used for other purposes, closed, or completely gone. The population as of the 2010 census was 1052. The Erick Schools, a post office, and a few businesses still remain. Erick is also the home of the 100th Meridian Museum, located in the First National Bank building, which is listed in the National Register of Historic Places. The museum is: "Dedicated to the presentation of 100th Meridian Line, which has served as an often disputed international and, later, state boundary for the past 166 years. Special emphasis is placed on the many surveys that were made on the line, and the land disputes arising from them. Exhibits depict life along the 100th Meridian from prehistoric time through early day Erick."

The Railroads at Erick

During the 1920s, Erick had a train order office ("RI" – staffed 8am-midnight) and a water station for steam locomotives. There was a 30-car siding, and other tracks with a total capacity of 64 cars. The town was important enough for passenger trains Nos. 41 and 42 (*Choctaw Limited*) to be scheduled to stop, but Nos. 111 and 112 (*Memphis Californian*) stopped only when flagged.

A report about the staffing at the Erick station, located east of Main Street (Oklahoma Highway 30), stated that in January 1937, there were two shifts that were covered. The daytime shift (8:00am-5:00pm with one hour off for lunch) was handled by an agent-operator. This person handled both freight and passenger needs. During the night shift (11:30pm-8:30am with one hour off for lunch), a clerk handled the business, which featured two of the four passenger trains. The reason for the study was an effort by the railroad to replace the night clerk with a "caretaker" who would simply open the station and help distribute any luggage. It was denied by the federal government at the time. Erick was still a train order office in 1967, but that service soon ended.

Because of the number of cotton gins and grain elevators at Erick, there have always been a plenty of industry tracks here. One of these was the Farmers Union Co-op and their cotton gin, which had a lease dated September 1965 to use land and tracks owned by the Rock Island Railroad. Even during the 1970s, track charts showed four industry sidings. The 1979 employee timetable stated that there was no siding, but that there were 4573 feet of industry tracks.

When the Rock Island closed down in 1980, Farmrail soon started to provide service to Erick, but the business slowly went away and the last freight train served Erick in 2001. Until 2015, the tracks remained but no trains ran. In 2013, it was announced that the Oklahoma Department of Transportation was receiving funding to rehabilitate the "Sunbelt Line" track westward to Erick to serve new businesses moving into the Anadarko Basin. The first plan was to serve a new 65-acre coated-sand distribution center opened by Atlas Resin Proppants. The work necessary was reported to include 19,500 ties, 20,000 tons of ballast, a 1,500-foot side track, 17 road crossings, two bridge upgrades, and extensive brush-cutting.

On the east side of Erick, a cut of sand cars was parked near the Erick water tower in early 2020.

As the work progressed, a second frac-sand facility was planned for Erick – a 140-acre facility to be operated by Wisconsin-based Badger Mining. This facility included 3200 feet of siding and 7400 feet of industry tracks, capable of holding 160 railcars. During October 2015, Farmrail operated a passenger train to Erick as part of the line's dedication. Since then, Great Basin Brine has also opened at Erick. The new siding and major sand facility is located at Milepost 640.0. However, with the slowdown in drilling, the facility was generally used for car storage by 2020.

The streets in Erick have been paved over the tracks, and all in-service rail is on the east side of town. Heading west from Erick, the railroad grade drops from an elevation of 2075 feet to 2017 feet over the three miles to the Little Turkey Creek Bridge.

Near downtown Erick, Oklahoma, is this facility that was built using an old railroad covered hopper.

642.0 PROPERTY LIMITS – The *Federal Register*, dated October 4, 1983, contained a list of Rock Island routes "Authorized To Be Operated by Interim Operators." The listing stated that Farmrail Corporation could operate from "west of Elk City (milepost 615.0) to west of Erick, Oklahoma (milepost 642.0), a distance of approximately 27 miles." Today, Farmrail still operates the line as far west as Erick. Farmrail has posted that the "stations of Sayre, OK, and Erick, OK, are served by contract only."

Milepost 642.0 is just west of Highland Drive, also known as North 1740 Road. However, the tracks are actually gone starting a few blocks to the east. The State of Oklahoma didn't save the tracks west of here as there were no communities and nearby Texas did not participate in preserving the rail line on to Amarillo.

Heading west from Erick, Oklahoma, the track is not maintained or used, and is actually gone, as demonstrated by this grade crossing on the west side of town.

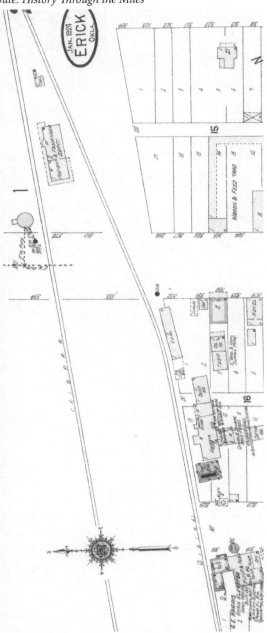

Sanborn Map – Erick Depot – January 1924. *Sanborn Fire Insurance Map from Erick, Beckham County, Oklahoma.* Sanborn Map Company, Jan, 1924. Map. Retrieved from the Library of Congress, https://www.loc.gov/item/sanborn07082_001/.

Erick (OK) to Pullman (TX)
Abandoned

The track from Elk City through Erick to the Oklahoma-Texas State Line was built by the Western Oklahoma Railroad Company, which was incorporated in the Territory of Oklahoma on December 11, 1900. West of the state line to Amarillo was built by the Choctaw, Oklahoma & Texas Railroad Company, incorporated on June 22, 1901. Both railroads were created for the Choctaw, Oklahoma & Gulf to build several lines in Oklahoma and Texas.

The State of Oklahoma Department of Transportation acquired the track between El Reno and Erick. The track west of there through Texas and New Mexico was not acquired by any state or railroad, but a few miles of track were saved in the Amarillo, Texas, area. Therefore, almost all of this track has been removed, but the right-of-way is generally easy to follow.

642.0 PROPERTY LIMITS – The Federal Register, dated October 4, 1983, contained a list of Rock Island routes "Authorized To Be Operated by Interim Operators." The listing stated that Farmrail Corporation could operate from "west of Elk City (milepost 615.0) to west of Erick, Oklahoma (milepost 642.0), a distance of approximately 27 miles." Today, Farmrail still operates the line as far west as Erick. Farmrail has posted that the "stations of Sayre, OK, and Erick, OK, are served by contract only."

Heading west, the old grade was just north of the original Route 66.

643.2 LITTLE TURKEY CREEK BRIDGE – The 12-panel timber pile trestle is now gone. This was the bottom of grades in each direction for the railroad. Little Turkey Creek is another stream that drains the surrounding hills, especially after a rain, and then takes the water to the North Fork of the Red River. The stream is easy to find as it is lined with trees. The railroad loops to the north to almost the location of Interstate 40, and then loops back to the southwest to Route 66 at Texola.

648.5 TEXOLA – Texola was once a fairly large town with more than twenty blocks of businesses and houses. However, today it is essentially a ghost town with many empty and abandoned buildings and a few houses. The official population was 36 in the 2010 census, and the town has almost as many mottos and nicknames, which include "Beerola" and "There is No Place Like Texola." The best might be the one on a bar which states

"There's no other place like this place anywhere near this place so this must be the place."

This is another town that was built to capitalize on the railroad being built through the area. A number of names were suggested and used, including Texoma and Texokla, playing on the two states that had their border here. A legal issue also developed as some of the town was in each state. The name Texola became official when a post office opened in 1901. The next year, the railroad arrived and a depot was built by June 30, 1902. The first major shipments from the area included cotton and other farm products. Cotton gins were quickly built, and 4 rail shipments of cotton were moved in 1903-1904. A newspaper opened in 1902, but it closed in 1921.

Route 66 arrived at Texola in 1926, being built down 5th Street following Oklahoma State Highway 3. The population of Texola peaked at 581 residents in 1930, but then it began a long slide until there were fewer than 100 residents in 1980. A highlight of the town today is the one-room jail built in 1910, using iron bars for door and windows. This small building can be found just south of where the tracks used to cross Main Avenue.

The railroad once angled southeast to northwest through Texola, and it still had a 454-foot spur track here in 1979 to serve the cotton gin, whose remains still stand.

This cotton gin at Texola, Oklahoma, is about the only reminder of the shippers that the railroad once served here.

649.0 OK-TX STATE LINE – The county line, located at an elevation of 2152 feet, separates Beckham County, **Oklahoma**, located to the east, with Wheeler County in **Texas**, located to the west. **Texas** is the second largest state, and the second most populated with almost 29 million residents. The word Texas is a version of the word taysha, which means "friends" in the Caddo language. Texas was part of Mexico until it gained independence in 1836, becoming the Republic of Texas. It joined the United States as the 28th state on December 29, 1845. The state is known as "The Lone Star State" for its one-time status as an independent republic. A single star is used on the Texas state flag and on the Texas state seal. The term Six Flags is also popular due to the number of flags that have flown over the state. Independently, Texas is the 10th largest economy in the world, and its capitol is Austin.

Near Texola, the grade of the Chicago, Rock Island & Pacific passes from Oklahoma and into Texas. This sign stands on Route 66 not far south of the railroad grade.

      Wheeler County, like many of the Panhandle counties, was created in 1876. It took several years to organize the county, and it wasn't until 1879 that a county seat was made official. The first county seat was Sweetwater, which soon was renamed Mobeetie. A stone courthouse was quickly built, but it was replaced by a larger wooden courthouse in 1888. Due to several challenges, the county seat was moved to Wheeler in 1908. As a part of the move, the wooden courthouse was also moved.

A newer courthouse was authorized in 1925, and the old wooden building was torn down and its material was used to build several barns on the ranch of Sheriff Riley Price. In 2010, the county had a population of 5410.

Wheeler County, and the county seat of Wheeler, were both named after Texas Supreme Court Chief Justice Royall Tyler Wheeler. Wheeler was born in Virginia and practiced law in Fayetteville, Arkansas, before moving to Texas to practice law. He advanced from district attorney to district judge to associate judge on the Supreme Court of the Republic of Texas. He remained on the court after Texas became a state, and eventually served as Chief Justice. In 1857, he left the Texas Supreme Court to be the founding head of the first iteration of the Baylor Law School.

Just west of the Oklahoma-Texas state line, the Rock Island grade curves back north to come alongside the south side of Interstate 40, which it once crossed to loop away to the north. At Milepost 649.5 was the property limits between the Chicago, Rock Island & Pacific to the east, and the Chicago, Rock Island & Gulf to the west.

649.7 INTERSTATE 40 – The railroad passed under I-40 as it heads northwest to Benonine. Nothing remains of the railroad grade as I-40 has been worked on and improved in the area.

649.9 BENONINE (BO) – Benonine was once located to the north of Interstate 40, about Milepost 176 of the highway. Benonine was one of a number of stations and communities platted in 1909 as the railroad was built. G. W. Burrow had started homesteading here about 1900, and C. B. Harbert platted Benonine in 1909. A post office using the name Benonine opened during October 1909. The town's name came from the Benonine Oil and Gas Company, which operated in the area but was based in Oklahoma City. The firm apparently gave up its charter in 1912.

Initially, Benonine was a significant community that featured a general store, bank, printing office, and a few more businesses and houses. It even competed with Shamrock for being the dominant trade center, but soon lost the battle and its post office in 1918. By 1920, the bank and other businesses were closed, and about all that was left were the railroad stock pens. One famous feature of Benonine was the nearby bison herd on the Brooks Ranch. The town never incorporated and today is just a few farm buildings.

In 1929, there was a 35-car siding at Benonine, as well as an agent and telegrapher, working the weekday 8:30am-5:30pm shift. Within a few years, the station no longer appeared in timetables or other Rock

Island documents. Heading west, the next several miles of the railroad grade are used as farm roads.

653.9 FULLER – Fuller was never a community, but there was a 51-car siding here in 1929. The railroad also had a section house at Fuller. The siding lasted until the end of the railroad, when it was 3700 feet long and located on the south side of the mainline. Heading west, trains once faced a five-mile-long, 0.8% grade.

The name Fuller was common in the area, and the siding was once located just west of Wheeler County Road 26. Not far west of Fuller, the railroad grade turns to the southwest.

655.9 INTERSTATE 40 – The railroad once passed under I-40 about Mile 171 on the highway. There are fewer miles of Interstate 40 in Texas than any other state. Track charts from the early 1970s show that there was a short spur track located just north of I-40. The grade can be seen to the south of I-40, but the underpass has been sealed off, leaving just the bridge on the south-side frontage road. This former Route 66 bridge is now listed on the National Register of Historic Places.

This lone pole is about all that marks the location of the old railroad grade where it once passed under Interstate 40, abandoned roughly four decades ago.

657.9 NORRICK – Norrick was not a community, but it was a United Carbon Company carbon black plant. Carbon black is a product produced from natural gas that is used in pigments and to help harden rubber so it can be used in tires. A report from 1965 about the carbon black industry stated that the Norrick plant used oil furnaces to produce 105 million pounds of carbon black a year.

This use of natural gas was an issue when the carbon black industry started in Texas during the 1910s. At the time, natural gas was hard to find and collect, and in 1920, the Texas Railroad Commission ruled that use of natural gas to produce carbon black was a direct violation of state laws concerning the conservation of oil and gas. A series of lawsuits and state campaigns led to a 1923 law that allowed the limited use of natural gas to manufacture carbon black in Texas. As plants were built, more natural gas was found, and in 1937, there were 40 carbon black plants in Texas that were producing 82 percent of the nation's carbon black. Most of these plants were in the Panhandle area and produced 90 percent of the output of Texas.

During the late 1950s and early 1960s, the Norrick plant was handled by the Rock Island agent at nearby Shamrock. A 1961 report by the Third Division of the National Railroad Adjustment Board explained how the plant was being handled at the time by the railroad.

> *This plant handles a large number of carloads and switching is required daily by Train No. 32, usually about 11:00 PM, but sometimes later at night. The waybilling, accounting, etc., for this plant is done by the agent-telegrapher at Shamrock....the Carrier commenced requiring the agent-telegrapher at Shamrock to drive to Norrick daily to check the cars on the track there and leave the waybills for the cars to be moved that night, together with a switch list in the bill box for Train No. 32. There are two advantages to this method of operation. First, it enables the Carrier to maintain an accurate record of cars on hand, loading, empty, etc., for demurrage records, and second, it saves Train No. 32 the inconvenience of stopping at Shamrock to pick up the switch list and waybills.*

This method, although it was used for several years and the agent-telegrapher made an hour of overtime pay for the work, was found to not comply with the union contract and the employee was no longer allowed to provide the switch list and waybills at Norrick.

In 1979, the plant was shown to have 1925 feet of track capacity. The plant is now abandoned, once located about a mile south of Exit 169 on Interstate 40. The September/October 1969 issue of *The Rocket*, a newsletter "published bimonthly in Chicago by the Public Relations department of the Rock Island Lines for and about its active and retired employees," had a large article about the Southern Division, which at the time included the Memphis to Tucumcari mainline. The article mentioned the carbon black plant, but also stated that from "Norrick to Amarillo the countryside is all wheat and milo." The railroad wandered westward before passing through the south side of Shamrock, Texas.

664.5 SHAMROCK (SK) – Settlement in this area actually pre-dates the railroad, with homesteaders staking out claims by the 1880s. The first town was about six miles north of today's Shamrock. The community needed a post office, and sheep rancher George Nickel, an Irish immigrant, volunteered to have the post office in his dugout, a basic cabin built into the side of a hillside. Needing a name, he wanted to honor his mother and remembered that she had told him to always depend on a shamrock to bring him good luck. From this, he named the post office Shamrock, and it was approved in 1890. The post office never opened, however, as Nickel's dugout soon burned, but Mary R. Jones operated one nearby for several years.

In the summer of 1902, the Chicago, Rock Island & Texas Railroad built through the area, creating a station here using the name Wheeler. By August, town lots were being sold, and Frank Exum opened a general store. He also applied for a post office, named after himself. The next year, the station was renamed Shamrock and the Shamrock post office opened. For the next few years, area towns like Story and Benonine competed with Shamrock to control the region's trade, but by 1906, businesses were moving to Shamrock and the battle had been won. In 1908, two banks were chartered at Shamrock, and the Shamrock Cotton Oil Mill (later the West Texas Cotton Oil Company) was in production. Shamrock was incorporated in 1911, and a water main was built in 1923, later supported by several water wells.

As a part of the creation of a community water system, $15,000 of bonds were sold. In 1915, the Chicago Bridge & Iron Company was hired to build a water tower for the community. When finished, the 75,000-gallon water tank stood 176 feet high. Records indicate that this was the tallest tower of this style ever built by the company. Today, the tower is a Texas Historical Landmark, and a downtown park has a number of historical markers that tell the story of the water tower.

The mid-1920s was probably the peak of Shamrock's activities. The population was 2500 in 1925, with almost 3800 in 1930 at its peak. In 1926, Shamrock was a busy regional town with lots of rail shippers. On the east side of town was the Shamrock Cotton Oil Company, located on the south side of the tracks. The Rock Island depot was on the north side of the tracks, and the wooden station still stands at its original location at the end of Texas Street. Further west, the A. G. York cotton gin and W. P. Dial Wholesale Feed & Grain were both on the south side of the tracks between Main and Wall streets. A block west and on the north side of the tracks was a row of oil companies, including Gulf Refining, Texas Oil, Pierce Petroleum, and Magnolia Petroleum. Across the tracks in this area was the Shamrock Mill & Ice Company plant. Finally, the Texas Compress & Warehouse Company was west of Arkansas Street, located north of the tracks.

Like many towns along the line, Shamrock, Texas, is still marked by a grain elevator and other agricultural businesses.

Oil and natural gas were discovered near Shamrock in 1926 by the Shamrock Gas Company, and the boom lasted until the 1940s. About the same time, the opening of Route 66 led to the construction of several hotels, service stations and restaurants. The first of these, the U-Drop Inn, opened in 1936 and was promoted as the only café within 100 miles of Shamrock. The U-Drop Inn was a noted stop along the route, and the Texas Historical Commission has called it one of the most impressive examples of Route 66 architecture. After I-40 was built around Shamrock, the café fell into disrepair. Efforts were made to save the structure, first by placing it on the National Register of Historic Places in 1997. Next, the First National Bank of Shamrock purchased the closed café and donated it to the community in May 1999. It has since been rebuilt and is used as a museum, visitors' center, gift shop, and the city's chamber of commerce. The building's style made it the model for Ramone's body shop in the animated movie *Cars*.

Along Route 66, just a few blocks north of the Rock Island Railroad grade at Shamrock, Texas, is the restored U-Drop Inn and Conoco Gas Station, a model for Ramone's body shop in the animated movie *Cars*.

Another historic building is the 1920s Reynolds Hotel, also saved from demolition, and converted into the Pioneer West Museum by local residents. All 25 rooms are used to display pioneer and Native American artifacts, historical information, and even a space exhibit. Since the 1980s, Shamrock has supported area farming and ranching, a chemical plant, and oil and gas processing plants. The town has its own school system and hospital. Within the city limits of Shamrock is the only place to purchase liquor in Wheeler County. However, many of the downtown businesses moved north to Interstate 40 when it was built.

Shamrock is known for its St. Patrick's Day celebration, held since 1938. The event includes a parade, banquet, food and entertainment, all surrounding a pillar in Elmore Park where a fragment of the genuine Blarney Stone, obtained from Blarney Castle in County Cork, Ireland, is mounted. Shamrock is also the home of the Eastern Panhandle Livestock Show and the High Cotton Gin Days festival, a series of events held the second weekend of each month from March through November.

Shamrock is also known for several movies filmed in the area. One of these was the 1999 film *Shadows of the Past*, originally named *Abilene*, that starred Ernest Borgnine. Another was *Cast Away* starring Tom Hanks. The closing scene occurs on U.S. Route 83 close to I-40, in Shamrock. Despite the activities and films, Shamrock had only 1910 residents in the 2010 census, the lowest recorded level since 1930.

In downtown Shamrock, Texas, near the old railroad grade, a large mural has been painted on a store building. Among the scenes included is one showing a Rock Island train and the city's water tower, a noted structure for decades.

The Rock Island Railroad

Once Shamrock began to grow, it became a major station on the railroad. It was busy enough that the station and agency were staffed day and night, seven days a week. In 1929, the first trick (shift) was staffed from 8:00am until 4:00pm Monday through Friday, while the second trick operated 10:45pm until 6:45am seven days a week. The first trick operated only 8:00am-10:00am on weekends. These hours were due to most trains operating through Shamrock at night, with only the eastbound No. 112 *Memphis Californian* stopping during daylight, at 9:07am daily.

The original wooden station had a second floor on the east end, used to house the station agent and his family. It was a typical design for the line. After World War II, the Rock Island updated a number of their stations, and Shamrock was one of them. The January 1946 issue of the *Rock Island Lines News Digest* had an article about rebuilding the station.

Work on the remodeling of the Rock Island depot at Shamrock, Texas, was begun this month. The outside of the present building will be torn down and the roof removed. The new building will be finished with asbestos roofing and siding, in a color scheme of gray and maroon.

Modern plumbing and a new heating system will be installed, as well as completely new furniture and office equipment. The building will be illuminated with fluorescent lights, and a concrete station platform is to be constructed.

In 1929, the railroad had a 61-car siding, plus a small yard and industry tracks with another 200 cars of capacity. It was a water stop and a train order station. The yard tracks remained here until the end of the railroad, with a 2740-foot siding and other tracks measuring 5800 feet long in 1979. The Rock Island station still stands at Shamrock, as it was active as a train order station until the railroad closed.

Although greatly changed since its original construction, with some changes after the railroad closed, the Rock Island depot at Shamrock, Texas, still stands.

665.0 TOWER 179 – This diamond was once located south of Railroad Avenue and west of Arkansas Street, and was the crossing of the Rock Island Railroad and the Fort Worth & Denver Northern Railway Company (FW&DN). The Fort Worth & Denver Northern was chartered on May 20, 1929, as a part of the Burlington system. The plan for the line was to build 110 miles of track from Childress north to Shamrock, and then to the northwest to Pampa, all in Texas. The railroad opened on July 15, 1932, serving as a shortcut and handling loads of oil products from the region. This line was the last major Texas railroad route built, with none more recent being more than 55 miles long.

There are some reports that the Rock Island once planned to buy half interest in the line to the south as part of an effort to connect to a proposed Frisco line at Wellington. This connection would have provided a direct route between the Texas Panhandle and Fort Worth. However, the Rock Island never took advantage of the option due to the economic situation at the time.

As soon as the FW&DN opened, Tower 179 was established as a cabin interlocker to control the interlocking. As described by the *Texas Railroad Interlocking Tower Website*: "An interlocker is a mechanical system used to protect trains from collisions where two railroads cross at grade. Many of the interlocking plants were located in two-story towers manned by railroad employees. Others were in cabins or huts, with controls operated as needed by train crews." As part of this interlocking, there was a connecting track in the southeast quadrant.

Hidden in the woods where Tower 179 once was is the former cabin interlocker building, used to protect the diamond between the Fort Worth & Denver Northern Railway and the Chicago, Rock Island & Pacific.

Also in the area of Tower 179 at Shamrock, Texas, are several concrete bases that once supported signals for the diamond.

The former Fort Worth & Denver Northern train station still stands at Shamrock, Texas, now used as a residence.

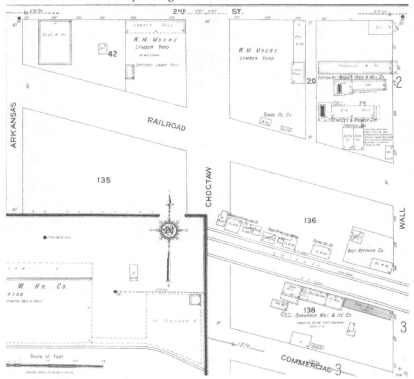

Sanborn Map – Businesses at Shamrock, Texas – January 1926. *Sanborn Fire Insurance Map from Shamrock, Texas.* Sanborn Map Company, Jan 1926. Map. Retrieved from the University of Texas, https://legacy.lib.utexas.edu/maps/sanborn/s-u/txu-sanborn-shamrock-1926-1.jpg.

666.2 GASPER – This was an 11-car spur in 1929, but the tracks and station were gone several decades later. Gasper is a family name that is common in the area. Heading west, the railroad stays south of Interstate 40, generally following Long Dry Creek and County Road SB.

670.5 LELA – At Exit 157 on Interstate 40 are the remains of Lela, which once had the station code of "RS". Today, Lela is a collection of homes near I-40, but it once was to the south along the railroad. Lela started as a railroad station named Story that was established in 1902. Quickly, the town had several businesses, a school, and the *Wheeler County Texan* newspaper. The same year, a post office opened, and the postmaster named it after his wife's sister, Lela. Soon, the railroad station and community also began to use the name Lela.

One advantage of Lela was water, and it served as a water station for the passenger and freight trains. The railroad was located beside Long Dry Creek, which generally was wet, and wells found shallow water. The abundance of water was actually a problem, as flooding forced the town to relocate to higher ground. By 1906, the effort to create a large town at Lela was over, and many of the businesses and the newspaper moved to Shamrock. The post office closed in 1917 as the town continued to shrink.

During the 1920s and 1930s, oil and natural gas were found in the area, a carbon black plant operated nearby, and the community once again began to grow. By 1926, an oil loading rack was built here, the first on the Rock Island in this area, providing the first competition to the Santa Fe for the movement of the region's oil. Travel on Route 66 also gave the town a boost, and several attractions developed in the area. One of these was the Regal Reptile Ranch, which operated like a chain store along Route 66 in Oklahoma and Texas. The final snake attraction was part of a service station at the Lela exit of I-40.

A new school was built in 1927 after the original building burned, but high school students started attending school in Shamrock during the 1930s. At the time, the Chicago, Rock Island & Gulf had a 50-car siding and a 33-car spur track at Lela, plus there was a water tower for the steam locomotives. After World War II, Lela still had four businesses, an elementary school, a church, and about fifty residents. By 1969, the only railroad track at Lela was the mainline, and the post office closed in 1973, despite the population growing to more than 100. In 1992, the local school closed and was merged with the Shamrock schools. Today, the community is simply a collection of houses and deteriorating buildings along I-40.

Heading west, the railroad begins a long climb from 2421 feet at Lela, to 3170 feet at Rockledge. This 30-mile grade averages more than 0.5%.

671.2 COLUMBIAN SPUR – In 1929, this location was listed as a 10-car spur track. There is conflicting information about who operated this carbon black plant. Reports on the industry stated that in 1931, this was a Magnolia Petroleum Company. Another report from 1938 stated that this was the Columbian Carbon Lela No. 55 carbon black plant. The tracks were gone for decades before the railroad was abandoned.

672.5 FAULKNER – The name Faulkner seems to have come from the Faulkner family. In 1936, a report stated that there was a Magnolia Petroleum Company carbon black plant at Faulkner, likely the plant also shown as being at what became Columbian Spur. In 1929, the railroad reported that there was a 24-car spur track here. Only a few scars on the land still mark this location.

677.0 RAMSDELL – Welcome to Ramsdell, the site of first area telephone system with 16 members. Ramsdell started as a station on the Chicago, Rock Island & Gulf Railway. It sits on property once owned by Reverend Ed R. Wallace, a Methodist circuit rider who started buying acreage in the area, eventually owning a dozen sections of land. When the railroad created a livestock station here, he plotted the town of Ramsdell along Sand Creek. The stockyards were used by area ranches, and eventually a depot and freight house were built to handle the passengers and freight shipments.

The Ramsdell post office was established on April 29, 1903, and then twice shut down until it became permanent in November 1904. The town had a few stores, a school, two hotels, a lumber yard, and about fifty buildings at its peak. The railroad handled livestock; farm products such as watermelons, eggs and cream; and cement sand from Sand Creek. With Reverend Wallace in charge, Ramsdell was a dry town, but weekly dances were held at the depot and the freight loading docks.

A combination of bad water and the move of many businesses to nearby Shamrock caused the post office to close in 1926. The construction of Route 66, which helped so many other towns, missed Ramsdell, and pulled even more people away. For the railroad, there was a 46-car siding and a 5-car spur track in 1929, with the station code of "MS", but no side tracks by the 1970s. Today, heading south from Exit 152 on Interstate 40 will get you to the site of Ramsdell, which is only marked by a few grades and foundations.

Ramsdell is at the bottom of a 16-mile westbound grade that averages 0.535%. The Ramsdell depot was at an elevation of 2556 feet, and the top of the 86,000-foot grade is 3032 feet. Heading west, the former railroad grade passes just south of Lake Loraine and Sandspur Lake, generally following South Long Dry Creek. Sandspur Lake is managed by the Sandspur Lake Club, and the lake is surrounded by boat docks and cabins. The line then curved to the northwest, coming next to Interstate 40 at McLean.

682.6 COUNTY LINE – The railroad crossed from **Wheeler County**, to the east, into **Gray County** to the west, as it crosses the appropriately named County Line Road, located south of Exit 146 on Interstate 40. Much of Gray County was part of the Francklyn Land and Cattle Company, chartered in 1881 to buy cattle land in the Panhandle of Texas. The firm bought 631,000 acres of land, and was led by Charles G. Francklyn, a son-in-law of E. G. Cunard, owner of the Cunard Steamship Line. Bad weather and high spending led to the bankruptcy of the ranch in 1886. It was reorganized as the White Deer Lands Trust, which soon became the White Deer Land Company. The firm continued operations until

1957, and the story of the venture is told at the White Deer Land Museum.

Gray County was created in 1876, but it wasn't fully organized until the railroad arrived in 1902. The county was named for Peter W. Gray, who held many political offices across Texas. In 1841, he became Houston's District Attorney, and in 1846 was elected to the House of Representatives in the first Texas state legislature. One of his first major tasks was to write the first procedural code in Texas. Two years later, he founded the Houston Lyceum, which later became the Houston Public Library. He represented Texas in the Confederate House of Representatives, and then he was appointed as an Associate Justice of the Texas Supreme Court in 1874, just months before his death.

682.7 WHITED – Whited, located at an elevation of 2740 feet, was an important siding during the early days of the railroad, and it was likely named for the Whited family who lived in the area. In 1929, Whited was a 55-car siding that was used for a scheduled three-train meet each evening at 10:55pm.

The first train to arrive was likely freight No. 992 – the eastbound *California-Memphis Gold Ball Freight*. Almost immediately, westbound freight No. 991 – the *California-Oklahoma-Louisiana Gold and Red Ball*, would arrive. Both trains would clear the mainline so eastbound passenger No. 52 – the *Oil Special*, could move through, passing freight No. 992. With the changes in train schedules and the elimination of most passenger trains, the siding at Whited was not needed and was removed about World War II.

687.0 INTERSTATE 40 – The railroad grade once passed under Interstate 40 just east of McLean where the I-40 Business Loop passes under the freeway.

687.2 MCLEAN (YD) – As the construction of the railroad continued west, the Choctaw, Oklahoma & Gulf Railroad chartered the Choctaw, Oklahoma & Texas Railroad (CO&T) in 1901 to handle the construction across the Texas Panhandle. Late in 1901, the CO&T built the mainline here, then added a switch, water well, water station, section house and stockyards. The station of McLean once handled train orders and used the station code of "YD", also used by West Memphis, Arkansas. A benchmark that was once on the station foundation stated that the elevation was 2868 feet. McLean was located between a series of curves used to help climb the grade.

Soon after the railroad was built, English rancher Alfred Rowe donated land next to the switch for the town of McLean. Alfred Rowe was the son of a British merchant, and was born in Lima, Peru. He obtained a ranch in Texas and regularly traveled between his holdings in England and the United States. On his trip in 1912, he was aboard the *Titanic* when it sank, and he perished. The name McLean also was important. It came from Judge William P. McLean, who was elected several times to the Texas House of Representatives, and later the U.S. House of Representatives. He served as a member of the Texas Constitutional Convention in 1875, a judge of the fifth judicial district, and a member of the first Texas Railroad Commission in 1891.

McLean grew quickly, and it had three general stores, a bank, two wagon yards and livery stables, a lumberyard, and a newspaper (*The McLean News*) by 1904. A post office opened in 1902, and remains open today. With more growth, McLean incorporated in 1909, and there was a population of 633 in 1910. There were several attempts to make McLean the county seat of Gray County, but all failed. Hogs, cattle, and farm products like watermelons were shipped regularly on the railroad, and the oil and gas industry, as well as the tourist industry brought on by Route 66, caused the town to grow to a population of 1521 by 1930, the largest McLean would ever have.

In 1933, the railroad went between Railroad Street, to the north, and South First Street. Railroad Street is now the I-40 Business Loop, while First Street is Graham Street. South of the tracks and east of Main was the W. P. Dial Elevator Company, where a shell of a wooden elevator still stands. On the south side of the tracks and west of Main Street was a row of petroleum company facilities, including The Texas Company, Magnolia Petroleum Company, and the Continental Oil Company. Across the tracks to the north was the Rock Island station, with three tracks to the south and two to the north of the building. The east end of the station was a freight house, with an office in the middle and a waiting room to the west.

In 1942, a prisoner of war camp for German prisoners was built northeast of town. Construction started in September, and the first group of prisoners arrived in July 1943. These first prisoners were members of the famed Afrika Korps, commanded by General Erwin Rommel. The camp quickly exceeded its official capacity of 3000 prisoners, but closed in July 1945, after the war was over and POWs were moved back to Europe.

This bulk fuel facility dates back to the Rock Island era at McLean, Texas.

This old grain elevator also dates from the early years of rail service at McLean, Texas,

By this time, Shamrock and Amarillo had become the major cities in the area, and McLean was left to serve the local farmers and ranchers. The population has dropped ever since, with 778 residents in 2010, but McLean is still the second largest town in Gray County. Because of the lack of change, the downtown has been preserved and the McLean Commercial District was placed on the National Register of Historic Places on December 20, 2006. Also in McLean, located at the intersection of First Street and Gray Street, is the restored Phillips 66 Gas Station, the first Phillips 66 station in Texas. In 1929, this station was built and leased to the oil company, and it has been restored, with claims made that it was the first restored gas station along Historic Route 66.

Along Route 66 through McLean, Texas, is a small restored Phillips 66 gas station, another reminder of the boom that the highway created.

About 1930, at the peak of industry at McLean, the Rock Island Railroad had a 51-car siding and other tracks that could hold 96 freight cars. It was also a fuel station, water station, and had a wye to turn locomotives. The location was so busy that an agent-telegrapher was on duty twenty-four hours a day, seven days a week. The rail facilities lasted until the end of the company, and there was a 2680-foot siding to the south, plus industry tracks to the north and south that totaled 1700 feet.

688.5 INTERSTATE 40 – The railroad, at an elevation of 2900 feet, once passed under Interstate 40, just west of Exit 142. The grade can easily be seen as it passes under the highway, but the grade has grown up towards McLean.

Heading west, the railroad winds its way uphill toward Alanreed, staying south of I-40. The grade can often be found, but it is seldom easily accessible as it works its way across private pastures. Bb Road, located south of Exit 135 on Interstate 40, follows the grade for several miles.

696.0 ALANREED – Alanreed was a typical railroad station (station code "A" during the early 1900s) for the Rock Island Railroad in the Texas Panhandle. It started as a significant shipping point with much promise, was used as a freight and train order station, but shrank and eventually lost those roles as business moved to trucks and the railroad modernized. During the 1920s, Alanreed featured a siding that was 56 cars long, plus a 28-car house track. It was a train order station, with an agent-telegrapher working the weekday 8:30am-5:30pm shift. By the 1960s, the tracks to the south had been combined to form a long house track, but they were gone by the late 1960s.

As this area was broken up into farms and large ranches, a small community developed about six miles north of here on the stagecoach route between Mobeetie and Clarendon. The land was timbered and along McClellan Creek, providing the wood and water that farmers and a town would need. As settlement began during the early 1880s, the Clarendon Land and Cattle Company began to sell lots at a townsite. According to a number of sources about Route 66, the community had a number of early informal names, including "Prairie Dog Town (for a prairie dog town that was nearby), Spring Town or Spring Tank (for a large spring fed pond, which Texas ranchers would call a tank) and Gouge Eye (for a bar room fight)." In 1886, a post office opened at the community using the name Eldridge.

As the Choctaw, Oklahoma & Texas Railroad built westward, the grade was south of Eldridge, and a new townsite was platted alongside the railroad. A school opened in 1901 to serve the settlers in the area, and in 1902, the town of Alanreed became official, and the post office moved from Eldridge to the railroad town. While it is not clear, many sources say that the name Alanreed was created from the names of the partners (Alan and Reed) of the contracting firm that was helping to build the railroad, and who laid out the townsite.

Alanreed grew quickly, and was a shipping station for cattle from surrounding ranches, and crops from area farms. By 1904, Alanreed was the largest town in Gray County, and soon featured a bank, two grocery stores, a hotel, a saloon, a hardware store, a livery stable, a blacksmith shop, and several churches. Farmers also benefited from the railroad, and more than 500 cars of watermelons were shipped from Alanreed annually. Telephone service began in 1917 and the population reached 250. Oil and tourism boomed during the 1920s, and the community made an attempt to become the county seat, but failed.

Nothing remains of the Rock Island Railroad at Alanreed, Texas, except for a few grades and foundations, and this milepost sign, still attached to a former railroad telegraph pole.

The Great Depression hurt Alanreed, and it lost its bank, hotel, and many other businesses. The population dropped from about 500 residents to about 200. Since then, the Alanreed schools moved to nearby McLean, a few businesses have held on at Alanreed, and fewer than 100 residents remain. Today, the unincorporated community is located between Interstate 40 to the north, and the old railroad grade to the south.

The post office, and just about every community business, is located inside the truck stop at the west end of town. At Main Street and Third Avenue is the original 66 Super Service Station, built in 1930 by Bradley Kiser. The station is closed and surrounded by trees, but it is maintained by the Texas Historic Route 66 Association. Also in Alanreed is what is claimed to be the oldest church on Texas Route 66, Alanreed Baptist Church, and the oldest cemetery, Alanreed Cemetery.

Alanreed was just west of the top of the grade that started at Ramsdell. The grade peaked at 3032 feet, dropped to 3011 feet, and then began to climb again. At Alanreed, the elevation is 3049 feet, and the grade continued to Rockledge at an elevation of 3172 feet. Heading west, the railroad continued looping to ease the climb, generally following the south side of Interstate 40. A number of large and small fills can be seen from the highway as the numerous small timber pile bridges were filled through this area. Parts of this grade are used as farm roads, or run immediately adjacent to farm roads which once were the original road through this area.

In the area around Milepost 700, the railroad worked its way through some very rough terrain, as shown here at the Gray County Rest Area on Interstate 40.

701.7 COUNTY LINE – The railroad is heading southwest at this point, and passes from **Gray County**, to the north (railroad-east), into **Donley County**. Donley was another county created in 1876 from parts of the Bexar District. Like many of these counties, the population was too light to actually create the county's government, and Donley County was finally organized on March 22, 1882. **Donley County** was named for Stockton P. Donley, an attorney and a one-time associate justice of the Supreme Court of Texas. Donley was born in Missouri, practiced law in Kentucky, and then moved to Texas where he was elected district attorney of the Sixth Judicial District in 1853. He served in the Seventh Regiment of Texas Volunteers during the Civil War, and was captured at Fort Donelson in 1862. After the war, Donley was elected to the Supreme Court of Texas in 1866, but was removed for political reasons during the Reconstruction era. The county seat of Donley County is Clarendon, and the county's population was 3677 in the 2010 census.

702.4 ROCKLEDGE – Rockledge has never been a town, instead, it has been the home of railroad track workers and employees who worked at a pumping station of a petroleum pipe line. The location was created by the railroad and the name apparently came from either a land survey known as Rockwall School Land, the steep rocky walls of a nearby canyon, or a combination of both. There was some livestock business at Rockledge as the surrounding grasslands were parts of the Red River Cattle Company, but there was apparently never a railroad agent.

The railroad did build a 51-car siding, plus a house track that could hold 32 more cars. There was a two-room clapboard section house for the track gang foreman. The railroad also had a sod-roof storage shed built from old ties, and a cistern that was filled from railroad tank cars when needed.

Things got busier at Rockledge in 1926 when a 10-inch petroleum pipe line was built from northern Panhandle to south Texas. To help move the oil, a pump station, two large storage tanks, and six homes were built nearby. As the pipeline went into operation, it was discovered that much of the route was downhill, so half of the pumping capacity was moved elsewhere. Three of the worker houses were also removed.

In 1922, the siding at Rockledge was the scheduled meeting point between trains No. 111 and No. 992. Each evening at 9:11pm, the eastbound *California-Memphis Gold Ball Freight*, train No. 992, would enter the siding to allow westbound passenger train No. 111, the *Memphis Californian*, to pass. Even after the passenger train operations ended, Rockledge siding remained, shown as being located to the south of the mainline and measuring 2700 feet in 1979.

Today, Rockledge is the site of a rest area on east bound I-40, oil pipeline pumping equipment, and a police radio tower. The last families were moved out shortly after the railroad was abandoned when automatic pump equipment was installed. Now, only a few foundations and the remains of the gardens and trees around the houses mark the location.

For a place that barely existed, there are several crime stories about Rockledge. The first involved a double-murder in 1905, reported by the railroad section crew who watched the shooting. The story goes that an Amarillo real estate agent was meeting with a local rancher and his son. After the real estate agent got off a train, he got in an argument with the rancher over some sort of financial issue. The real estate agent then pulled a gun and shot the rancher. The rancher's son then shot the real estate agent, who was fleeing to the safety of the railroad gang. Both bodies were shipped east on the next train.

The second major crime took place in 1939, when two young boys robbed the bank in Alanreed. They fled to here with $3000, but their car broke down and they ran into nearby Rockwell Canyon. A posse surrounded the boys, and they were captured within three hours, but half the money was never recovered.

708.0 JERICHO – A stagecoach stop here predated the railroad. Reportedly the stop was named Jericho because it was a place to change horses and rest, using a reference to the biblical city in Palestine. The original Jericho was a Canaanite town located near Jordan, and was considered to be the gateway to the Promised Land. A cemetery opened at Jericho, Texas, in 1895 when there was a need to start burying people who had died in an outbreak of malaria.

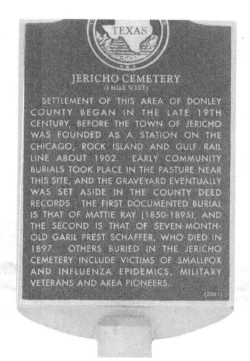

This historical marker at Jericho, Texas, explains some of the area's history.

The Chicago, Rock Island & Gulf Railway established a station here in 1902, using the existing name and the station code of "CH". A townsite was created and a post office opened in 1902. For the railroad, a depot, water tower and stockyards for cattle loading were built. Jericho

683

peaked about 1930 when there was a tourist court motel, three stores, a garage and filling station, a grain elevator, and about 100 residents. The railroad had a 51-car siding, plus a 12-car house track serving the elevator and stockyard. The railroad station was also busy since there was an agent-telegrapher working the weekday 8:30am-5:30pm shift, issuing train orders when needed.

Because of the number of washes in this area, the railroad often required large fills and culverts. This concrete culvert is located near Milepost 712 on the railroad and is visible from the frontage road of Interstate 40.

While some tourists stopped at Jericho, and grain continued to move through the elevator, the town was down to less than 50 residents by the 1940s, and the post office closed in 1955. The siding was gone by the 1970s, and the last few residents moved away during the 1980s. Today, little remains but a few building shells along County Road B, just west of Highway 70, about a mile south of Interstate 40 at Exit 124.

In this area also are some short stretches of the original Route 66, known as Jericho Gap. This was, until the 1930s, an unpaved stretch of the road that ran on muddy black soil. The road would develop deep ruts, and when wet, cars became easily stuck. A number of Jericho residents made a living pulling cars from the mud, and there were even accusations that locals watered the road to make more money.

Heading west, the grade continues to slowly climb, with almost no curves until near Amarillo. Parts of this grade have been removed to make large irrigated circle fields, while other parts run immediately beside large windmills. The railroad comes back to Interstate 40 just west of Exit 121.

713.7 COUNTY LINE – The railroad is heading northwest at this point, and passes from **Donley County** back into **Gray County**.

713.8 BOYDSTON – The remains of Boydston are marked by the two old grain elevators along the south side of Interstate 40, just west of where Boydston Road bridges over the highway. Boydston was started during the late 1880s and early 1890s when Henry Sanford Boydston, credited as the first settler in the area, donated land for a cemetery. The original Boydston was located just south of the county line in Donley County, and a post office opened in 1891 using the name Boydston. This fact disproves one theory that the town was named for H. S. Boyd, an official of the railroad that arrived a decade later.

The railroad built through Boydston in 1902, and a siding was built just across the county line in Gray County. The town and post office naturally moved the short distance to be at the station. The town didn't grow much, but it did have a general store by 1910, a store and ten residents by 1930, and then two businesses and forty residents by 1941. This was the peak of the community and the post office closed in 1940, with residents getting their mail through Groom. The town was gone by the 1960s, but two grain elevators remained until the railroad shut down in 1980. The two abandoned grain elevators still mark the spot where the Rock Island once operated.

In 1929, the railroad reported that there was only an 8-car spur track at Boydston. At the end of the railroad, there was a 1740-foot house track to the south that was used to serve the grain elevators. There was also a telephone here so that train crews could get information and talk to the railroad's dispatcher.

The location of Boydston, Texas, is still marked by these two old grain elevators, long out of business.

718.1 COUNTY LINE – Heading west, the railroad passed from **Gray County** and into **Carson County**, at the Interstate 40 Exit 114. This area was ranching country when Carson County was created in 1876 from parts of Bexar County. Among the largest were the Turkey Track Ranch of Richard E. McNalty, Charles G. Francklyn's 637,440-acre Francklyn Land and Cattle Company, and the one-million-plus-acre JA Ranch. The very rural nature of the area delayed the organization of the county until 1888, when the only town, Panhandle, was made the county seat. The county's population was still only 6182 in the 2010 census.

    Carson County was named for Samuel Price Carson, a politician who served in both North Carolina and Texas. He served four terms as a representative from North Carolina (1825-1833), and then served in the state senate, and on the North Carolina constitutional convention in 1835. Carson actually killed his political opponent in a dual during the 1827 campaign. Carson moved to Texas by 1836 and was almost immediately elected to the Convention of 1836 where he signed both the Texas Declaration of Independence and the Constitution of the Republic of Texas. He later served as Secretary of State for the Republic of Texas.

    Throughout this area, note the highway overpasses that once passed over Interstate 40 and the railroad. They all have extra bridge spans where the railroad once operated.

This overpass, located not far west of Groom, Texas, demonstrates the extra spans that still exist on many highways, once used to cross the Rock Island Railroad.

719.3 GROOM (GR) – Driving on Interstate 40, there are three items that will let you know that you are at Groom. The first is the 190-foot-tall cross, surrounded by life-sized statues of the 14 Stations of the Cross, located on the northwest side of town. On the northeast side of town is The Leaning Tower of Texas, also known as The Leaning Tower of Britten. This is a former water tower that was retired and then moved and installed at an angle to attract people to a truck stop and tourist information center. The truck stop is gone, but the leaning water tower is a popular tourist attraction that is lit for Christmas. The third item is the tall white elevator with the Groom Wheat Growers markings. Wheeler-Evans (formerly Wheeler Brothers) still has an operation here.

For the railroad, there was a 51-car siding, several house tracks with a total capacity of 40 cars, and a wye to the south. In 1929, this was the meeting point of westbound passenger train No. 111 – the *Memphis Californian*, and eastbound passenger train No. 52 – the *Oil Special*. At that time, the first trick (shift) was staffed from 6:15am until 2:15pm Monday through Friday, while the second trick operated 2:15pm until 10:15pm weekdays. On weekends, the first trick operated only 6:15am-8:15am, and the second trick 8:15pm-10:15pm. These times allowed all of the passenger trains to be handled by the agent-telegrapher. Unlike many other stations along this route, few of the tracks were ever retired before the end of the railroad. In 1979, there was a 4450-foot siding to the south, with a wye heading south off of it. To the north was a 3884-foot track that served several grain elevators, and the depot once stood between the mainline and this track. Groom was also a water station and a source of train orders, with an agent maintained to handle all of the grain business.

687

If you are following the old Rock Island Railroad grade on Interstate 40, this leaning water tower tells you that you have reached Groom, Texas.

Groom was another town that developed along the Rock Island Railroad on land that once was the grass prairies claimed by one of several large ranches. To get the name Groom, two different people were involved. The first was Colonel B. B. Groom, who helped with the creation of the Francklyn Land and Cattle Company. He was the one responsible for creating the Diamond F brand used on their cattle. He also acquired shorthorns from Kentucky, Angus from Scotland, and local longhorns as a part of his breeding operation at the ranch. However, because of a hard winter and unpaid bills, the Francklyn Land and Cattle Company failed by 1886. Some of the firm's land, much of it known as Groom's pasture, then became available to farmers and other ranchers, and a number of towns were created.

The second Groom was Harrison Groom, the Colonel's son. While he wasn't directly responsible for this town, he did establish several camps in the area that attracted more settlers. One of these was W. S. Wilkerson, who laid out a townsite alongside the railroad in 1902, naming it Groom after Colonel B. B. Groom. A post office opened in 1903, and a depot, bank, hotel, barbershop, general store, school, lumberyard, and a few other businesses soon followed. In 1911, Groom was incorporated with a population of 250, but there were major fires in 1912 and 1915. However, wheat, cattle, oil, and tourism kept the town growing.

Because of job opportunities in nearby Amarillo, Groom has survived. Its population peaked at about 800 in 1970, and dropped to 574 in the 2010 census. The post office and school are still open, and the former Groom Wheat Growers Cooperative elevator still stands along the abandoned railroad right-of-way, at the south edge of town.

A series of elevators, some still clearly marked for Groom Wheat Growers, still stand on the south side of Groom, Texas, along the abandoned grade of the Chicago, Rock Island & Pacific Railroad.

726.7 LARK – Lark was another Texas Panhandle town that was created by the arrival of the Chicago, Rock Island & Gulf. A station was located here in 1903 and was named for Lark Stangler, a local rancher. A store operated by the Krizan brothers soon opened, and a post office opened in 1909. However, the population remained less than a dozen and the post office closed in 1915, with mail handled through Conway, located less than ten miles away. The population grew a bit and the post office reopened in 1925.

Even for the CRI&G/CRI&P, Lark was not a major station, but during the 1920s it did have a 55-car siding as well as a 21-car track that served a local grain elevator. There was a water station and a section house at Lark, but the depot was not staffed. In 1929, Lark got to be a busy place every morning at 7:00am. Westbound passenger train No. 51, the *Oil Special*, would meet eastbound No. 112, the *Memphis Californian*. For No. 51, Lark was only a flag stop. For train No. 112, it was more complicated. According to the employee timetable, "No. 112 will stop at any station east of Amarillo to discharge revenue passengers from stations west of Amarillo."

While Lark wasn't a major station on the railroad, there are still a number of things to explore today. One of them is this former Texas & Pacific boxcar (#80463) that was turned into a storage shed and office. This car was originally built 1924-1925 by Pullman-Standard as a double sheathed auto car in the 60000-60999 series. During the late 1930s, more than five hundred of them were rebuilt with eight panel steel sides by the railroad's Marshall (Texas) Shops. These rebuilt cars were numbered in the 80000-80553 series.

Just before World War II, Lark had doubled in size with twenty residents, a church, school, and one business. This was about the peak, and the post office closed for good in 1957 and mail service moved to Groom. By the 1970s, the railroad was down to a long, 2489-foot elevator track on the south side of the mainline. At the time, there were two grain elevators at Lark, and their shells can still be seen just south of Interstate 40 at Exit 105. Throughout this area, the Rock Island grade is immediately south of the freeway, and there are a number of irrigated round fields. Anyone driving on Interstate 40 in this area knows that the highway can be straight, but the Rock Island had no curves between Mileposts 722 and 739.

Lark, Texas, is another former railroad station that still has its tall concrete grain elevator, painted white.

The elevator office and scale house still stands at Lark, Texas, but barely.

733.0 BRIDGE – Located at an elevation of 3437 feet, this small four panel timber pile trestle was one of several in the area that crossed wet-weather streams. The railroad fill is still in place today, but the trestle has been removed to provide access to the pastureland to the south.

While the trestle is gone at Milepost 733.0, some of the former pile bents remain.

735.2 CONWAY – The remains of Conway are less than a mile south of Exit 98 on Interstate 40. In this area, the highway curves to the north while the railroad continues heading directly west. For many years, Conway was a small sheep and cattle ranching community, but the opening of the Lone Star School in 1892 put it on the map. A number of reports state that it was the first permanent school in the Texas Panhandle, created to educate the children of area ranchers and homesteaders.

The railroad arrived in 1903, and a post office and town were started that were named for former Carson County Commissioner H. B. Conway. In 1905, Conway was officially platted by the Fisherin brothers, and Edward S. Carr opened the first store, where the post office moved in 1907. A grocery store, a blacksmith shop, and a church also opened, and a community steam-operated threshing machine was acquired and used on a number of area wheat farms. During the 1920s, Conway was large enough that a community club opened. However, reports state that the population was less than thirty, and the growth stopped about that time.

For the railroad, Conway was the first staffed station east of Amarillo during the first half of the Twentieth Century, using the station code of "CU". An agent-telegrapher was on duty weekdays from 8:00am until 5:00pm in 1929, when there was a 50-car siding, plus a 35-car track that served the grain elevators. At the same time, Route 66 was being planned and built through the region. However, the route near Conway was not agreed upon until 1930, when it was finally decided to build the route westward from Conway on the north side of the Chicago, Rock Island & Pacific Railroad. The ten miles of roadway was quickly graded, paved, and opened during late 1930. As with many area communities, many Conway residents felt that they would get rich off of the road and tourist courts, restaurants and service stations opened quickly. A new school also opened and the population reached 125 in 1939. However, during World War II, the school was closed and students were bused to Panhandle, and by 1970, the population was down to 50. At this time, there were two grain elevators, four service stations, three cafes, and a general store. A short population boom came about as I-40 was being built, but when it looped north of Conway, the remaining businesses moved to the exit north of town, and the post office closed in 1976. For the railroad, there was a 2120-foot elevator track to the south serving the grain industry.

Probably the most famous business and attraction that moved to the Interstate was the Longhorn Trading Post, operated by the Crutchfield family. In 1967, the family opened a complex that included a service station, curio shop, and a Rattlesnake Ranch. In 2002, they added the VW Bug Ranch, five Volkswagen Beetles that were buried nose down. The following year, the entire complex closed, but the buildings and the bugs remain.

Today, Conway is an unincorporated community with a population of less than a dozen. There is a truck stop and several hotels north of old Conway, located on Interstate 40. The old town site consists of the abandoned railroad grade, several houses, two concrete elevators labeled Robinson Grain Company, and lots of foundations. Heading west from Conway on road FM 2161 is what is described as the longest and best-preserved section of Route 66 in Texas. The 7.2 miles of roadway has been listed on the National Register of Historic Places since 2007.

The VW Bug Ranch at Conway, Texas, is one of many somewhat weird attractions that were created along Route 66 that can still be explored. Today, many seem to require group participation with spray paint.

Conway, Texas, was another grain terminal along the railroad, and two tall concrete elevators still stand.

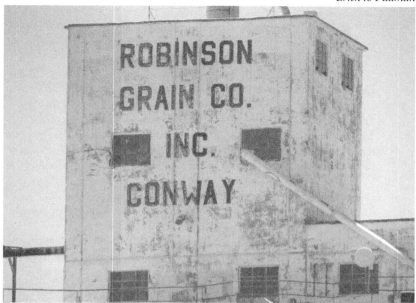

No question about who once owned this tall grain elevator at Conway, Texas.

743.7 YARNALL – Yarnall was never a town, it was simply a siding on the CRI&P, and for a few years, the location of Tower 48 and a Rock Island section house. The source of the name is unknown, and some documents had it spelled "Yarnell." Today, it is simply a grade and a farmhouse or two south of Exit 87 on Interstate 40, and east of Ranch Road 2373.

The first railroad here was the Panhandle Railway, but an explanation of the Southern Kansas Railroad is necessary. The Southern Kansas Railroad was a subsidiary of the Atchison, Topeka & Santa Fe that was incorporated to build 200 miles of new track from Kiowa, Kansas, southwest through Indian Territory to Panhandle City. There were two goals to the plan. The first was to develop farm and livestock business that could be hauled east. The second purpose of the line was to block the expansion of the Fort Worth & Denver City Railway (FW&DC) into areas served by the ATSF.

As a part of the plan, an Act of Congress was approved on July 4, 1884, that "gave the railroad company the right to locate, construct, own, equip and operate a railway-telegraph and telephone line through the Indian Territory. The company was given the privilege to construct its line, with a right-of-way 100 feet in width and with an additional strip 200 feet long and 3000 feet in length every ten miles for stations."

The Southern Kansas Railroad stopped at Panhandle as it was felt that this was where the FW&DC would build to, since it was the largest town in the Texas Panhandle. However, the FW&DC built further to the south and west, helping to create Amarillo, Texas.

To connect the Southern Kansas with the Fort Worth & Denver City, the Panhandle Railway Company was chartered on December 10, 1887, by a group of Fort Worth citizens. The plan was to build a line between Panhandle and Washburn, passing through what became Yarnall. The fifteen-mile railroad opened during April 1888, but the business couldn't pay the bills, and the receivers leased the Panhandle Railway to the FW&DC until April 20, 1898, when it was leased to the Southern Kansas. On December 5, 1898, the Panhandle Railway was sold to Edward Wilder, treasurer of the Santa Fe. The lease continued until the rail line was transferred to the Southern Kansas on January 1, 1900.

On July 6, 1902, the Choctaw, Oklahoma & Texas (CO&T) completed its own line to Yarnall, and a connection was built to allow trains to head south to Washburn, and then on to Amarillo over the Fort Worth & Denver City. Construction stopped at Yarnall until 1903, when the CO&T was fully acquired by the Chicago, Rock Island & Gulf Railway and the line was extended west to Amarillo at a reported cost of $108,615.64. A note in *The Chronicle* (October 22, 1904) reported on the Yarnall-Amarillo construction. "In November 1903, the line of The Chicago, Rock Island and Gulf Railway Company was completed between these points and the use of the lines of the Santa Fe and the Fort Worth and Denver City companies was discontinued." This construction required a diamond at Yarnall, and Tower 48 was established on July 13, 1904, to control the crossing.

It soon became obvious that Panhandle was not going to be the center of railroading in the Texas Panhandle, and that Amarillo was taking on that role. To get there, the Southern Kansas first obtained trackage rights over the FW&DC from Washburn to Amarillo, but then built its own 25-mile line from Panhandle City to Amarillo. This allowed the abandonment of the former Panhandle Railway, and the 1909 Railroad Commission Annual Report stated that the line was "abandoned March 28, 1908 and crossing removed."

In 1929, Yarnall was shown to have a 49-car siding on the south side of the Rock Island mainline, located just east of where the diamond once was. There was also a water tower and station for steam locomotives. Yarnall was also listed as a water stop for steam locomotives. When the Rock Island Railroad shut down, there was still a 2290-foot siding, as well as a dispatcher telephone.

747.5 JUNCTION WITH OLD MAIN – In 1955, the Rock Island changed its eastward route into Amarillo because of an expansion at the Amarillo Air Force Base. The start of the new grade can be seen just west of Mile 84.3 on Interstate 40. The original mainline went straight while the new main curved to the southwest.

The expansion of the Amarillo Air Force Base, now the Rick Husband Amarillo International Airport, was caused by the need to expand the runways to handle B-52 bombers for Strategic Air Command (SAC). At the time, the Rock Island mainline was a quarter mile south of the airport, and it was in the way of a new runway. The new line headed southwest until it came beside the Fort Worth & Denver (FW&D – today's BNSF) line, then it paralleled the FW&D for two miles heading west before angling back to the northwest to rejoin the original mainline at Milepost 758.3. Parts of this new line have been preserved to allow local shippers to be served by BNSF.

The original mainline once headed almost due west. Signs of the old grade can be found as Runway 31 passes through it. SAC Access Road uses the grade from the runway to near the terminal at the Rick Husband Amarillo International Airport. The Chicago, Rock Island & Gulf continued through the airport property and on west until it turned southwest to follow the south side of the former Panhandle & Santa Fe, the ATSF route that was built to extend the Southern Kansas Railroad to Amarillo and replace the Panhandle Railway. The pre-1955 mainline continued to the southwest until it rejoined the new line at Milepost 758.6, the old Milepost 758.3.

On this original mainline was the station of Royal, located at Milepost 752.2. In 1929, there was a 55-car siding at Royal that was the scheduled meet point between No. 51 – westbound passenger train *Oil Special*, and eastbound third-class local freight No. 88. The meet was scheduled to occur at 7:52am. A section house was also once located here.

In the 1979 employee timetable, the Rock Island showed that Royal was at "MP 748 Pole 3" with the note that there was 19,624 feet of capacity. Maps show that the original Royal was about where Runway 31 is now located, and that there were several shippers in the area that were served from the remains of the original mainline.

Carnegie Hero Fund Commission and Royal

The November 1915 issue of the *Rock Island Employee's Magazine* had an article entitled "Carnegie Medal and $1,000 to Rock Island Hero" about an incident near Royal.

> On April 29th, last [1914], as train 41, running thir-
> ty-five miles per hour, got within about six hundred feet of
> a highway crossing one mile west of Royal, Texas, on the
> Amarillo Division, a child, two years old, toddled on the
> crossing, stopped, gazed in wonderment at the approach-
> ing train, seemingly unmindful of its perilous position. En-
> gineer B. Bowen applied the emergency air and Fireman
> Charles A. Perkins, whose attention was attracted by the
> quick application of the air, took in the situation and with-
> out speaking, climbed swiftly through the cab window, out
> onto the running board, down on the pilot, and bracing
> himself, grasped the child and lifted it from the track, the
> engine moving slowly over the spot where the little tres-
> passer had stood.

The next year, Charles A. Perkins was awarded a bronze medal and the sum of $1000 by the Carnegie Hero Fund Commission.

747.9 COUNTY LINE – Located on the new line built in 1955, to the east is **Carson County**, while to the west is **Potter County**. **Potter County**, with the county seat of Amarillo, is another Panhandle county created in 1876, and like most of the others, it wasn't organized for many years, in 1887 for this county. However, it is now the most populated of these counties with more than 120,000 residents.

Potter County was named for Robert Potter, a politician who was a lawyer first in North Carolina, and then in Texas. Potter served as a midshipman in the United States Navy from 1815 to 1821, and then as a U.S. Representative from North Carolina. He came to Texas in 1835 and was a signer of the Texas Declaration of Independence. He also served as the Secretary of the Navy during the Texas Revolution. Robert Potter was killed at his home on March 2, 1842, as a part of the Regulator-Moderator War, also known as the Shelby County War, This battle between rival factions lasted from 1839 until 1844, and was a fight over land ownership and control of the local economy and government.

The Potter County area is well-known for its helium supply, the largest in the world. In 1968, the helium industry declared Potter County to be the "Helium Capital of the World."

751.3 JACKRABBIT ROAD BRIDGE – This location is just north of Exit 80 on Interstate 40. East of here, the track has been abandoned. West of here, it is owned and operated by BNSF.

Pullman (TX) to Amarillo (TX)
BNSF Railroad

After the Chicago, Rock Island & Pacific shut down, Burlington Northern (BN) took over the operations of some of the track to serve a number of shippers in the Amarillo area. Records show that CRI&P was authorized to be operated by the Fort Worth & Denver Railway Company (FW&D) "from Amarillo to Bushland, Texas, including terminal trackage at Amarillo, and approximately three miles northerly along the old Liberal Line." These announcements were routinely made in the *Federal Register* until the October 4, 1983, issue which stated that the Amarillo to Bushland track had been acquired by BN. Another document stated that BN acquired the track on the east side of Amarillo in 1982.

The track to Bushland was kept in place to serve the Southwest Portland Cement plant just west of Bushland, Texas. The line was shut down west of Amarillo Yard during the 1990s and the track materials were sold to TrackTech of Calvert City, Kentucky. TrackTech is a railroad construction contractor offering services such as 24-hour emergency response, new track construction, track maintenance, tie and rail renewal, and track removal.

751.3 JACKRABBIT ROAD BRIDGE – This location is just north of Exit 80 on Interstate 40. When Burlington Northern acquired some of the terminal operations of the Chicago, Rock Island & Pacific, the tracks were kept to this area to serve several shippers. The former mainline is now used for car storage for the nearby Progress Rail tank car facility. Documents of the Federal Railroad Administration show that this is part of the Kansas Division of BNSF.

752.3 PROGRESS RAIL – This facility wasn't here during the days of the Rock Island Railroad, but it is now reached by a wye to the south. The Progress Rail tank car facility covers 154 acres and has 133,000 square feet of shop space that can handle cleaning, painting, wheel replacement, and almost any other work necessary on a freight car. The facility also connects to the former Fort Worth & Denver, now BNSF line, to the south.

Progress Rail is a Caterpillar company, and produces rail cars, locomotives, infrastructure solutions, and technologies for the railroad industry. It also operates a number of freight car repair and maintenance facilities across the country. The firm was acquired by Caterpillar in 2006 and is based in Albertville, Alabama.

This is just a small part of the Progress Rail tank car facility east of Amarillo, Texas.

753.2 PULLMAN ROAD – Pullman was never a station of the Rock Island, but the rail line does cross Pullman Road at this location. Less than a quarter of a mile south was the station of Pullman that developed on the Fort Worth & Denver City. The community that grew up around the switch, which reportedly was named for a Pullman-built railcar that was part of the construction train, never incorporated and never grew to more than about thirty residents and a store or two. Pullman never had its own post office and is now within the city limits of Amarillo.

754.2 AIRPORT BOULEVARD – The railroad passes under this road, which connects Interstate 40 to the Amarillo airport. This area has changed greatly since when the Rock Island Railroad operated through here.

Just east of this overpass is a switch identified in the BNSF Texas Division employee timetable as the east end of two main tracks, CP 3294. This switch is at Milepost 329.4 on BNSF, and the Airport Boulevard overpass is Milepost 329.6. Heading west, BNSF uses the former Rock Island mainline as their Mainline #1, and the former Fort Worth & Denver City line as Mainline #2, until BNSF Milepost 334.6.

The former Rock Island Railroad grade crossing at Pullman Road, east of Amarillo, Texas, now carries a BNSF sign.

For years, the Rock Island Railroad passed next to this Producers Grain elevator at Milepost 754.4, located just south of the Amarillo, Texas, airport.

755.6 FW&D CROSSING – This location came about because of the expansion of the Amarillo Air Force Base and the new route that the CRI&P used to get into downtown Amarillo. Here, the Rock Island had to cross an existing FW&D spur that served several industries to the north. Because of the nature of the two tracks, there was the need to provide some sort of protection for all train movements.

On September 10, 1958, an "Electric Locked Crossing Gate" was placed in service, which when lined for the Fort Worth & Denver, turned distant signals on the Rock Island red. As described in Rock Island timetables, the crossing was not protected by interlocking, but instead was "protected by gate operated by trainman, normal position of gate against FW&D." The location was soon assigned the designation of Tower 209.

Today, the spur track to the north is served using a wye off of the CRI&P line. On this line are still several shippers such as Grupo Cementos de Chihuahua, a manufacturer "of gray Portland cement, mortar, premixed concrete, concrete blocks, plaster, aggregates and other construction materials." Valley Proteins, one of the largest rendering companies in the United States, also is on this line, as is a large grain elevator

Just south of the wye is the four-track fueling facility that was installed a number of years ago by BNSF. This facility was located here to fuel coal trains coming from the Powder River area in Wyoming, and to conduct the required 1000-mile train inspection. Just west of the fuel racks, the CRI&P line curves to the northwest to return to its original grade.

757.6 BC JUNCTION – On BNSF, this location is Milepost 332.8. This junction is located just before the new CRI&P line turns west to return to the original grade. The junction was part of a mile of new railroad built by BNSF to connect the Boise City Subdivision with the Red River Valley Subdivision. This connection allows BNSF to do directional running between Amarillo and Pueblo. Loads move south on the former Santa Fe through Boise City, and empties return north on the Fort Worth & Denver (BN) line through Dalhart.

758.4 GRAND STREET – The railroad passes under this highway overpass about where the Rock Island's new line connects back to the original alignment. Because of the slightly different distances, Rock Island documents showed that this was Milepost 758.57 on the new line, and Milepost 758.34 on the old main line.

For BNSF, this bridge is at Milepost 333.8. Just to the west is the Cargill Animal Nutrition elevator. This plant provides the materials for livestock feed for the Amarillo area. To the north are more grain elevators and warehouses that are served by BNSF. Next to Cargill is Amarillo Livestock Auction, which has a livestock auction every Monday at 11:00am. This was once the Western Stockyards facility. A historical marker at the site states that Amarillo was the largest rural cattle shipping point in the nation from 1892 until 1897, and this auction yard is "famed for handling more cattle than any other commission auction company in the United States." The facility was founded as Western Stockyards in 1904, and became the Amarillo Livestock Auction Company in 1945.

759.3 P&SF CROSSING – In 1979, this crossing was still shown as the P&SF – Panhandle & Santa Fe – although the railroad was merged into the Atchison, Topeka & Santa Fe Railway on August 1, 1965, after the Interstate Commerce Commission ruled that the Texas laws that required railroads operating within Texas to have headquarters inside the state were illegal. The P&SF started as the Southern Kansas Railway Company on November 2, 1886, and built as far west as Panhandle City, Texas. On June 5, 1914, the railroad became the Panhandle & Santa Fe and track was built throughout the region, making it one of the two major operating subsidiaries of the Atchison, Topeka & Santa Fe Railway Company in Texas. On January 1, 1931, many of the smaller Texas railroads and construction projects of the ATSF were leased to the P&SF. This lasted until 1965 when the need for a Texas subsidiary ended.

East Tower/Tower 75

When the Southern Kansas extended their line on to Amarillo, it crossed the Fort Worth & Denver City here. Soon, the Chicago, Rock Island & Gulf also built through the area. On July 6, 1908, the Railroad Commission of Texas approved Tower 75, the first interlocking in Amarillo. The original interlocking tower was described as a 27-function mechanical plant, but it was replaced with a new concrete tower in 1927, built with a 54-lever General Railway Signal (GRS) model 2 interlocking machine. When completed, the new Tower 75 included the work previously performed by Tower 177 at Dumas Junction.

The new three-story, concrete tower was responsible for the crossing that involved the ATSF/P&SF, Fort Worth & Denver, and the Rock Island, as well as the ATSF's line to Las Animas, Colorado. The tower was quickly named East Tower, and was one of the busiest railroad locations in Amarillo. Even during the Great Depression, train traffic through the Tower 75 area could be heavy. Fourteen passenger trains (four on each of the three railroads plus an ATSF mixed train on the branch north to La Junta), 25 to 35 freight trains (ATSF – 14 to 18; CRI&P – 6 to 9; and FW&D – 5 to 8), and 50 to 60 switching moves (ATSF – 15 to 20;

CRI&P – 5; and FW&D – 30 to 40) passed through the tower limits daily at the time. A further complication was that the Fort Worth & Denver had their yard to the west, but their roundhouse and coal chute were located to the east.

The former Fort Worth & Denver roundhouse can still be found off of Philadelphia Street, just east of Tower 75 at Amarillo, Texas.

The activity dropped when the Rock Island shut down, and the tower was closed in April 1986. As the Burlington Northern and the ATSF worked on their merger plans, the location was altered and the tower was torn down during the mid-1990s. In 1998, the interlocking was improved and enlarged to handle more train traffic with fewer delays. A second location known as West Tower was added, and then about 2005, a control point with the name 8th Street was added that provided a new connection between different subdivisions in the area. A fourth main track was added about 2018 and the connection between the former Rock Island part of the Red River Valley Subdivision and the Hereford Subdivision was improved.

Today, the diamonds are gone, replaced by turnouts, and the connections are for the Hereford Subdivision and the Red River Valley Subdivision, both part of BNSF. The Hereford Subdivision is part of the main Chicago to Los Angeles route that was built to bypass Raton Pass. The Red River Valley Subdivision is the primary route for coal and grain trains between Wyoming and the Northwest, and central and lower Texas. The interlocking also has connections on the southeast and northwest quadrants allowing trains to head in almost every direction on almost every line that touches Amarillo. East Tower, located at BNSF Milepost 334.7, is shown as the west end of multiple main tracks on the Red River Valley Subdivision.

760.4 BUCHANAN STREET – This highway underpass dates from 1936, and also hosts U.S. Highways 60 and 287. The underpass is clearly marked with Rock Island lettering, as well as a warning sign about a grade crossing in 790 feet. These markings are only on the northern-most steel span once used by the Rock Island, not found on the rest of the spans. The CRI&P yard was mainly east of here, but the open and closed nature of the subway clearly shows where tracks once were located.

These Rock Island signs can be found on the Buchannan Street underpass in Amarillo, Texas.

Just west of this highway underpass is the Bushland Pocket Switch. This switch allows trains to take the original CRI&P line to the west for a short distance, or to cross over to the Fort Worth & Denver City route towards Denver, Colorado. Further west is the 1931 Fillmore Street/U.S. Highway 87 underpass. These concrete spans have Burlington Route markings on the south span, and Rock Island markings on the north span.

The Fillmore Street underpass featured concrete spans cast with Rock Island Railroad emblems, as shown here in early June 2020.

760.6 AMARILLO (VN) – The Chicago, Rock Island & Gulf was the last major railroad to build into Amarillo. Therefore, it had to build around the existing facilities of the other railroads. For the Rock Island Railroad, there were two major facilities in Amarillo: the yard and the passenger station. Between the two, freight and passenger crews were exchanged, train orders delivered, and trains registered. For years, the route to the east as far as Sayre was Subdivision 3 of the El Paso-Amarillo Division, and to the west to Tucumcari was Subdivision 4. The line to Sayre later became Subdivision 3 of the Oklahoma Division, and then Subdivision 3 of the Southern Division. By the end of the railroad, it had been renumbered as Subdivision 35.

The article "Amarillo Shows Growth" in the March 1921 *Rock Island Magazine* had an interesting statement about the Amarillo area. "In writing a history of the Rock Island Lines in Amarillo and the Panhandle of Texas, we have been somewhat handicapped in securing full data on account of all the records being destroyed by fire when our passenger station burned in 1916." The article did provide some information about the early years of the railroad here.

The Chicago, Rock Island & Gulf was the last major railroad to build into Amarillo, and it was abandoned four decades ago. However, a few signs of the railroad still exist, such as this Rock Island emblem on the Buchannan Street underpass.

In 1903 our line was extended from the western terminus then being near Seventh Street in the old town. Our first passenger station was located on Buchanan Street near the site of our present freight depot. In 1908 a new passenger station was erected on the site of our present station; this building was destroyed by fire on March 23, 1916 and a larger and more commodious building was erected, being completed January 1, 1917, and now contains the offices of division superintendent, trainmaster, chief dispatcher, master mechanic and other operating officials; also the division freight and passenger agent, all of which office are located on the second floor of the building.

Later that year, the Chicago, Rock Island & Pacific put out bids for a new 8-stall roundhouse at Amarillo. The J. E. Nelson Construction Company of Chicago won the contract and had it completed by the end of 1921. The roundhouse had "a mill type of roof with temporary end wall to allow for increasing stalls to 92-foot lengths." The new roundhouse replaced two 70-foot frame engine houses.

By the 1940s, the route west was Subdivision 4 of the Panhandle Division, then the Missouri-Kansas Division. It finished up as Subdivision 36 of the Southern Division. Multiple reorganizations over the years

707

did not greatly impact the operations at Amarillo, but the elimination of passenger trains and the consolidation of freight service reduced the traffic, especially as Southern Pacific routed more and more of its traffic over its own lines to Memphis. Some increases in freight interchange with the Santa Fe did take place at Amarillo, but the traffic never grew to the levels necessary to replace what was lost.

As at many terminals, there were a number of services that had to be performed. In 1929, Amarillo was listed as having a fuel station (40,000-gallon storage capacity), water station, turntable, wye, and a 46-foot track scale with a capacity of 100 tons. Because passenger and freight trains served different locations, train register books were found at those different locations. The 1947 Panhandle Division employee timetable stated that train register books were located at the Amarillo Passenger Station, used by First Class trains, and the Amarillo Yard Office, used by "All except First Class trains." A note was included that there were standard clocks at both locations. There was also an interesting note on the information about the Liberal-Amarillo Line. Although there were no passenger trains listed for the line, it stated that the "siding extending between switch near Buchanan Street and switch west of passenger station" at Amarillo was designated as a siding for first class trains.

In 1979, Amarillo still was listed as having a number of services. For the train crews, this included a standard clock, general order boards and books, a train register station, and a train order station. For the trains, Amarillo was still a fuel and water station. There was a wye that could be used to turn equipment, and a wayside radio. Amarillo was also staffed continuously until the end of operations. All of this was protected by yard limits between Milepost 757 Pole 25 and Milepost 766 Pole 17.

Amarillo was really the west end of the Choctaw Route by the late 1970s. About three million gross tons per year of freight moved to the east of the yard at Amarillo, but less than one million gross tons were moved over the tracks to the west. Amarillo was still a somewhat-friendly interchange point with the Atchison, Topeka & Santa Fe, but the Southern Pacific traffic to and from Tucumcari was steadily declining.

Amarillo Yard was northeast of downtown, located between Ross Mirror Street and Taylor Street, just west of East Tower. The Fort Worth & Denver (BNSF today) yard was immediately to the south. The west end of the yard was at grade with city streets, and some roads were lowered to pass under the tracks (Buchanan Street and Fillmore Street) and others were raised to bridge over the tracks (Pierce Street and Taylor Street). Much of this was done about 1931.

By 1921, the rail routes through Amarillo were pretty well established. The Rock Island had their east-west Choctaw Route, their yard just northeast of downtown, and their Liberal-Amarillo line to the northeast. The Fort Worth & Denver City had their line cutting across the north side of downtown, along with their yard next to the Rock Island yard. The Panhandle & Santa Fe had their mainline come in from the northeast, turn south along the east side of downtown Amarillo, and then head southwest. Another line came in from the north and followed the same route east of downtown.

For the Rock Island, the Chicago, Rock Island & Gulf station was located on the south side of the tracks along N.E. First Street, west of North Taylor. The first floor of the station was brick while the second floor was frame and stucco. The Fort Worth & Denver City tracks were just to the south of the CRI&G station. To the north and across the CRI&G tracks was the poultry facility of Swift & Company, located east of Taylor Street. Also in the area was the Panhandle Mill & Elevator Company, east of Fillmore Street. To the east of this was the CRI&G freight station, located south of N.E. First Street and east of Pierce Street. Across the tracks to the north and east were a number of railroad tool houses. The Rock Island also had a track further north, located just south of N.E. Second Street. This track served the Magnolia Petroleum Company between Johnson and Lincoln streets. For many years, east of Grant Street on the same line was a two-stall roundhouse owned by the CRI&G. None of these buildings remain.

The Farm Security Administration conducted several photo studies of the railroads at Amarillo, but primarily focused on the Atchison, Topeka & Santa Fe Railroad. However, a series of photographs were taken of passengers boarding Rock Island passenger trains in 1942, including this one entitled "Little girl waiting to board the Rock Island Rocket." Vachon, John, photographer. Amarillo, Texas. *Little girl waiting to board the Rock Island Rocket.* Amarillo, Texas, Nov 1942. Photograph. Retrieved from the Library of Congress, https://www.loc.gov/item/2017840316/.

In 1921, the Fort Worth & Denver City had their own passenger station, located on the south side of the mainline at Pierce Street. Today, this station is used as the BNSF north yard office and it is located under the Pierce Street overpass. To the east of the FW&DC station was a building housing a hotel, restaurant, and news stand. To the east of that was the express house building, and then the freight station. Much of the railroad's brick roundhouse still stands south of the FW&DC mainline, just east of East Tower.

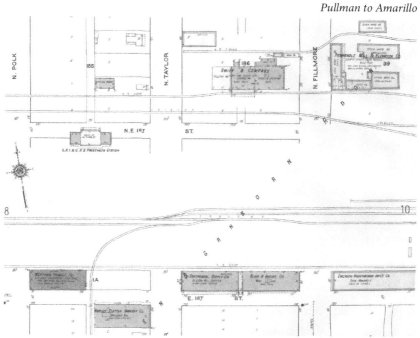

Sanborn Maps – Amarillo CRI&P Depot – 1921. Retrieved from the University of Texas. http://legacy.lib.utexas/maps/sanborn/amarillo_1921_9.jpg

The former AT&SF station and Harvey House still stands in Amarillo, Texas.

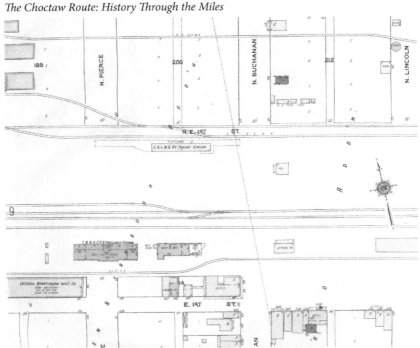

Sanborn Maps – Amarillo CRI&P Freight House Area – 1921. Retrieved from the University of Texas. http://legacy.lib.utexas/maps/sanborn/amarillo_1921_10.jpg

The Santa Fe had the largest collection of railroad buildings in Amarillo in 1921, and many of them still stand. The largest and most recognized is the former Panhandle & Santa Fe station and Harvey House on the west side of the tracks at S.E. 4th Avenue. This large two-story stucco building was built in 1910 and is listed on the National Register of Historic Places. To the south of the station is the former express building, also built with stucco to match the passenger station. Further to the south was once the large ATSF freight house, which started just north of S.E. 5th Avenue and stretched south of S.E. 6th Avenue.

On the southeast corner of Polk Street and 9th Avenue was the general office building of the Panhandle & Santa Fe. This building replaced the earlier general office building that was located on East Second Avenue, east of Johnson Street. The "new" office building is easy to find as it is marked by a large Santa Fe sign on the roof. In 1996, the Texas Historical Commission installed a historical marker with information about the building.

> *Built in 1928-30 at a cost of $1,500,000, this structure was designed by Santa Fe Railroad architect E. A. Harrison. The 14-story building was the tallest in Amarillo until the 1970s, and housed the offices and division headquarters of the Santa Fe Railroad. A significant local example of the skyscraper form ornamented with Gothic Revival style detailing, this edifice is among the few remaining such buildings in the state.*

The former general office building of the Panhandle & Santa Fe remains standing in downtown Amarillo, Texas.

713

During August 1995, Potter County bought the building and restored it over the next four years. Today it houses a number of government offices, including juvenile probation, vehicle registration, and the county tax offices.

Also in Amarillo is ATSF #5000, a 2-10-4 Texas-type steam locomotive built in 1930 by Baldwin Locomotive Works. At the time, few locomotives received a name, but being the first in a new series of locomotives, #5000 was special. The crews that used it soon were calling it Madam Queen after a character on the popular *Amos and Andy* radio show. The steam locomotive was retired in November 1953, and then donated to to the City of Amarillo on April 17, 1957. It is currently located at S.E. 2nd Avenue and Lincoln Street. Several different preservation proposals have been made by both the city and the Amarillo Railroad Museum, which currently maintains the locomotive.

The City of Amarillo

According to the Texas Historical Commission marker, erected in 1973 at the general office building of the Panhandle & Santa Fe, Amarillo was created because of railroads.

> *Construction of a railroad across the Panhandle led to the founding of Amarillo as County Seat of Potter County, Aug. 30, 1887.*
>
> *For the ensuing ten years, Amarillo had a monopoly on trade from the South plains, and was the nation's largest rural cattle shipping point, 1892-97. But in 1898 its trade was threatened and the city's very existence jeopardized when it appeared that the (Santa Fe sponsored) Pecos Valley & North Eastern Railway, to be built to Roswell, N.M. (220 mi. SW), might make junction with the Santa Fe at Washburn (15 mi. SE), cutting off ready access to the South plains.*
>
> *The Santa Fe, however, responded to requests from the citizens to make Amarillo the terminus of the new line. The Santa Fe acquired the Pecos Valley & North Eastern in 1899 and moved headquarters from Panhandle (30 mi. NE) to Amarillo. In 1908 the Santa Fe extended its main line here from Panhandle and built a link from Texico, N.M., to Belen, N.M., making Amarillo a major point on the transcontinental line.*
>
> *These measures, together with construction of branch lines, contributed vitally to making Amarillo the commercial center of the High Plains.*

During the 1880s, the Fort Worth & Denver City Railway was building northwest from Fort Worth and across the Panhandle area. The route crossed a number of cattle trails and trade routes, and several towns were planned along the railroad, many promoted as the soon-to-be capital of the Texas Panhandle. J. I. Berry gambled on a section of land with ample water that was on the route of the FW&DC. A townsite was established during April 1887, briefly using the name Oneida, and then Amarillo. The word Amarillo is Spanish for the color yellow, and different versions state that the city was named for yellow soil along several surrounding bodies of water, or for yellow wild flowers that are common during the spring and summer. Whatever the source, the Amarillo post office opened during August 1887. On August 30, 1887, an election made Amarillo the county seat of Potter County.

A brick courthouse, a hotel, several stores, a saloon and lots of houses were soon built, and a developed courthouse square was created between Fourth and Fifth streets, and Travis and Bowie. This is where the Rock Island tracks now end. However, the construction of the Panhandle & Santa Fe, and the work of Henry B. Sanborn and Joseph F. Glidden, led much of the town to move about a mile to the east to be nearer that railroad, and on higher ground that was less prone to flooding. Because of the move, and the vote in 1893 to officially move the courthouse east, Sanborn is often credited as the "Father of Amarillo."

By 1890, Amarillo had become one of the world's busiest cattle-shipping points, and numerous stockyards and warehouses were erected. Several newspapers were printed starting about this time, but only the *Amarillo News* remains, having started in 1892. An 1893 report on Amarillo stated that the population was "between 500-600 humans and 50,000 head of cattle." On February 18, 1899, the residents of Amarillo voted to incorporate, and the population reached 1442 in the 1900 census. Farming began to take over much of the surrounding acreage, and wheat and other grains began to be shipped through Amarillo. This led to the construction of grain elevators, milling facilities, and food preparation and packaging facilities.

Natural gas was discovered in the area in 1918, leading to several new industries, and then the Gulf Production Company discovered oil on May 2, 1920, on the Burk Burnett 6666 Ranch. The construction of Route 66 through downtown Amarillo led to the construction of the typical service stations, restaurants, hotels and tourist attractions. About the same time, the Federal Bureau of Mines became involved with the area due to helium, a rare material popular at the time for lighter-than-air flying ships.

In 1929, Amarillo became a stop on the nation's first coast-to-coast, scheduled air passenger and mail service. The Great Depression and the Dust Bowl of the late 1920s and 1930s hurt area farming and ranching, and much of the tourism along Route 66 became a migration movement. World War II helped the economy with various government bases and operations, and a nuclear weapons plant opened in 1950.

Today, Amarillo produces about 25% of the country's beef, and almost 90% of that of Texas. A favorite use of the beef is the Big Texan Steak Ranch, "Home of the FREE 72oz steak," a Route 66 attraction since 1960. Amarillo has an estimated population of 200,000, with more than 300,000 in the entire metropolitan area. This makes Amarillo the largest city in the Texas Panhandle, and the 14th-most populous city in Texas.

Home of the Sod Poodles

So, what is a Sod Poodle? In 2019, it became the name of the Amarillo Double-A affiliate of the San Diego Padres baseball team, a member of the Texas League which has a new stadium downtown near the Santa Fe station. However, the name sod poodle dates back to the settlement of the region when the nickname was given to prairie dogs. At the time, prairie dogs covered the area, with one town reportedly covering 25,000 square miles and housing more than 400 million inhabitants. Today, the critters have been pushed back to smaller towns, but some still range up to 1000 acres in size.

The prairie dog towns can be identified by their low mounds, generally cleared of vegetation. A number of these communities can be found along the former Rock Island grade. Normally a few prairie dogs are always on guard, so your presence will be greeted by a few loud barks or chirps. The towns are mostly underground, with rooms used for sleeping, giving birth, food storage, as restrooms, and other uses. According to the Texas Parks & Wildlife, prairie dogs (sod poodles) have one of the most complex underground system of homes and communication methods. This is probably because everything from coyotes to hawks eat them. However, ranchers and farmers also battled the rodent. Ranchers feared them because of their holes, which broke the legs of cattle and horses. Farmers fought them because they often destroyed crops and the fields in which they were planted.

760.7 TAYLOR STREET – The railroad passes under this street. Just to the west was once the Rock Island passenger station, a site that is now a large empty lot.

761.1 FORT WORTH & DENVER CITY RAILWAY BRIDGE – This 81-foot through plate girder span once crossed the Fort Worth & Denver City Railway Company line from Amarillo, Texas, to Trinidad, Colorado, and then on to Denver. Today, the line is the Dalhart Subdivision of BNSF's Colorado Division.

This view of where the Rock Island Railroad once passed over the Fort Worth & Denver City Railway shows the grades and turns involved to make the crossing work.

The Fort Worth & Denver City Railway (FW&DC) was chartered on May 26, 1873, as part of a plan to build a railroad from Colorado to the Gulf of Mexico via Fort Worth. Construction really began when Grenville M. Dodge became involved with the planning. Dodge is considered to be a pioneer of military intelligence, and served as General Ulysses S. Grant's Intelligence Chief in the Western Theater during the Civil War. After the war, he became the chief engineer of Union Pacific and helped direct the construction of the Transcontinental Railroad. After several years, he moved to Texas and then was involved as president or chief engineer of dozens of railroad companies through the rest of the 1800s.

Construction on the FW&DC began on November 27, 1881, and by September 1882, the railroad had completed 110 miles of track to Wichita Falls. There, the railroad built stockyards and helped to end some of the long cattle drives. In 1888, the railroad reached the Texas-New Mexico border, and then built on into New Mexico Territory to meet the Denver, Texas & Fort Worth Railroad, which connected with the Denver & New Orleans Railroad Company at Pueblo, Colorado.

After a reorganization in 1895, Dodge became president of the railroad. He helped to create additional railroads to expand service across Texas that could be fed to the FW&DC. As a part of this, the railroad taught farmers how to work the high and dry land. It also built stockyards and sold land to emigrants. The FW&DC was also responsible for the creation of a number of towns and cities, including Amarillo. As a part of the organization of a number of railroads affiliated with the Burlington System, the Fort Worth & Denver City became the Fort Worth & Denver Railway Company on August 7, 1951. The railroad took over the Texline-Denver line from the Colorado & Southern on December 31, 1981, and then merged into Burlington Northern on December 31, 1982. It then became a part of BNSF when Burlington Northern merged with the Atchison, Topeka & Santa Fe Railway on December 31, 1996. This route is generally used for northbound empty coal trains heading back to the Powder River coal fields in Wyoming, and empty grain trains returning north after unloading at Gulf of Mexico ports.

762.0 END OF TRACK – The rail line is little used west of Amarillo, except for occasional switching and car storage. Bridges are still in place over the Fort Worth & Denver line, the Adams-Hughes Connector, and SW 3rd Avenue. The line is out before the old bridge over SW 6th Avenue.

Starting at the corner of Seventh Avenue and Crockett Street, the next four miles of the railroad grade have been paved and turned into Amarillo's Rock Island Rail Trail. The trail generally follows Plains Boulevard through residential and commercial areas. There are a number of rest stops with benches and picnic tables, but the route could never be called shaded. The west end of the trail is at Coulter Street where the line turns to the west. This area has recently developed and parts of the grade west of Coulter Street are now covered by parking lots, hotels and restaurants.

While the railroad track has been removed just east of the SW 6th Avenue bridge, the railroad bridge carries a fresh coat of paint and Rock Island Lines lettering.

Amarillo (TX) to Tucumcari (NM)
Abandoned

The last 113 miles from Memphis to Tucumcari took seven years to complete, using several different companies and charters. In Texas, it started with the Choctaw, Oklahoma & Texas Railroad Company (CO&T), which was chartered on June 22, 1901, to build the railroad from the Oklahoma State Line west to Amarillo. This charter was amended on November 24, 1902, to build on to the New Mexico State Line. Things became more complicated when the Choctaw, Oklahoma & Texas was sold to the Chicago, Rock Island & Gulf Railway Company (CRI&G) on September 25, 1903, and the CRI&G took full possession of the CO&T on December 1, 1903. The Chicago, Rock Island & Gulf Railway then took charge of the new construction.

Meanwhile, another company, the Chicago, Rock Island & Choctaw Railway (CRI&C), was chartered in New Mexico on January 26, 1903, to build the railroad on to Tucumcari. A contract for the line's construction was issued on March 31, 1903, and grading began. However, all work was stopped on July 16, 1903, and on July 31, 1903, the CRI&C was turned over to the Chicago, Rock Island & El Paso Railway Company (CRI&EP). Despite this change, no work took place again on the Tucumcari to the New Mexico-Texas State Line route until 1909.

The Tucumcari & Memphis Railway Company was incorporated on January 9, 1909, to purchase the Chicago, Rock Island & Choctaw Railway from the Chicago, Rock Island & El Paso Railway. With the purchase, contracts were again issued to start construction of the line, which was completed by May 9, 1910. When completed, the route was conveyed to the Chicago, Rock Island & El Paso Railway Company, which turned the entire route over to the Chicago, Rock Island & Pacific Railway on December 31, 1910.

The tracks between Amarillo and Tucumcari were often included with those of the Golden State Route (Herington, Kansas-Tucumcari, New Mexico). This was because of the Liberal-Amarillo line that essentially made the Amarillo-Tucumcari line an alternative route for the Golden State traffic. For example, in 1925, both were part of the El Paso-Amarillo Division, and the Panhandle Division in 1947.

The track from Amarillo to Tucumcari was closed when the Rock Island shut down in August 1979. The Interstate Commerce Commission did not even assign a carrier to operate the line under the directed service provision as it considered the line to be a secondary branchline. However, the Fort Worth & Denver Railway Company (Burlington Northern – BN) was authorized by the Interstate Commerce Commission to operate the track from "Amarillo to Bushland, Texas, including terminal trackage at Amarillo, and approximately three miles northerly along the old Liberal Line." This last part was the remains of the line from Liberal, Kansas. The 45-mile line from near Amarillo to Stinett, Texas, had been abandoned in 1972.

The line west to Glenrio and on to Tucumcari was officially abandoned in 1982, at about the same time that Burlington Northern bought the CRI&P Amarillo terminal trackage and the line west to Bushland. The line between Amarillo Yard and Bushland was abandoned by 1996 when TrackTech removed it.

762.0 END OF TRACK – The rail line is little used west of Amarillo, except for occasional switching and car storage. Bridges are still in place over the Fort Worth & Denver line, the Adams-Hughes Connector, and SW 3rd Avenue. The line is out before the old bridge over SW 6th Avenue.

Starting at the corner of Seventh Avenue and Crockett Street, the next four miles of the railroad grade have been paved and turned into Amarillo's Rock Island Rail Trail. The trail generally follows Plains Boulevard through residential and commercial areas. There are a number of rest areas with benches and picnic tables, but the route could never be called shaded. The west end of the trail is at Coulter Street where the line turns to the west. This area has recently developed and parts of the grade west of Coulter Street are now covered by parking lots, hotels and restaurants.

764.3 TEAM TRACK – In 1947, a station known as Team Track was located at Avondale Street, shown to have a 10-car capacity. It was gone by the 1970s and is now covered by the Rock Island Rail Trail.

The City of Amarillo Rock Island Rail Trail uses much of the abandoned railroad grade on the west side of town.

766.0 WAREHOUSE SPUR – This track to the north was shown in several documents from the 1970s. It was located just west of Coulter Road. Not far west of here was the end of the Amarillo yard limits, shown as being at Milepost 766 pole 17.

767.1 SONCY – As with many towns along the Rock Island Railroad, the community developed as the railroad was being built. Soncy is one of several stations and towns along the Rock Island that were built on the lands of William Henry Bush. Bush was a businessman involved with barbed wire, hat manufacturing, and ranching. He provided the land for the townsite, and dedicated the town of Soncy on July 6, 1908. As surveyed, the town had five east-west streets, and three north-south streets, and a school was built in 1910. The community never grew much and didn't receive a post office, but it did have an agricultural elevator for many years. It is still an unincorporated community, and is now largely within the city limits of Amarillo, Texas. The area has recently filled with hotels, restaurants, and large business buildings.

Soncy is a Scottish and English term that means lucky, fortunate or thriving. The term may be appropriate for here because William Bush became a millionaire after helium was found on his lands in the area. Soncy Road is still a major thoroughfare in western Amarillo. The Rock Island Railroad depot was once located west of Soncy Road where several hotels now stand. In 1929, Soncy was a flag stop for all passenger trains, and had a 50-car siding, plus a capacity of 15 cars on the other tracks. By the 1970s, there were no tracks at Soncy itself, but there was the warehouse spur to the east and the tracks into a helium plant to the west. The 1979 Rock Island employee timetable stated that these tracks totaled 1897 feet in length.

767.8 GAS SPUR – Just east of Helium Road, the federal government constructed a helium plant during the late 1920s, served by the Rock Island Railroad. With a worldwide shortage of helium, the United States surveyed this area and purchased 50,000 acres for helium extraction. To process the raw gases, an extraction plant was built here on 18½ acres owned by William Henry Bush. Bush was already benefitting from the helium production since much of it was found on his land, so he donated the property needed for the extraction plant in return for a new water well.

Much of the old helium plant west of Amarillo, Texas, still stands. For decades, the plant was a significant customer for the Rock Island Railroad.

The Amarillo Helium Plant was built for the United States Bureau of Mines and the United States Department of War. According to several newspapers of the time, the plant made its first shipment on May 6, 1929. In July of that year, the plant produced 648,850 cubic feet of helium at an average purity of approximately 97 per cent. The plant's history is explained by a historical marker located near the plant.

> *This plant, operated by the United States Bureau of Mines, was the first to produce helium from the extensive helium resources in the Texas Panhandle. From 1929 until 1943, it furnished almost all of the world's supply of helium. Operating around the clock, the plant extracts helium by liquefying the natural gas and separating helium from it at temperatures 300 degrees below zero. The natural reserves in these fields and in extensions into adjacent states contain more than 95 percent of the world's known supply of helium. This is also the site of the world renowned research center which provides fundamental data on the production and uses of helium. Helium is used for a variety of purposes: lighter-than-air craft, low-temperature research, shielded-arc welding; and in national defense, nuclear energy programs and space exploration.*

768.5 WESTERN AMARILLO BOULEVARD BRIDGE – This four-span modern beam bridge was built over Western Amarillo Boulevard, also known as the Amarillo Business Loop of Interstate 40. Heading west, the grade of the Rock Island Railroad is just north of I-40.

To the south and across Interstate 40 is the Cadillac Ranch; ten old Cadillacs half-buried, nose-down, in the middle of a field. It is a popular tourist attraction and easy to find alongside the south I-40 Frontage Road.

While the railroad grade is to the north of Interstate 40, to the south is the Cadillac Ranch.

773.0 FURNICO SPUR – During the 1960s and 1970s, there was a short spur track to the north here. Trains heading west faced a steady grade of 0.6%, and the elevation here was 3800 feet.

774.0 BUSHLAND – "Welcome to Bushland – Home of the Falcons." Bushland is another railroad town that was built on the land of William Henry Bush, and this one was named for him. In 1929, Bushland was a scheduled stop for the *Memphis California* passenger trains (11:43pm westbound, 2:30am eastbound), as well as a water station. At the time, the timetable only showed a 15-car track. By about 1970, there was a short industry siding to the north that measured 1643 feet long in 1979. Today, the Bushland Grain Cooperative elevator remains standing on the north side of the abandoned railroad grade.

This message on the side of a large elevator welcomes you to Bushland, Texas.

The Bushland Grain Co-Op elevator once stood just to
the north of the Rock Island tracks at Bushland, Texas.

A second but smaller Bushland Grain Co-Op elevator stands further to the west, demonstrating the importance of the grain business to the region.

William Henry Bush was born in Martinsburg, New York, in 1849, but moved to Chicago as a businessman. There he got into the hat business, and got to know Joseph F. Glidden, the inventor of modern barbed wire. In 1877, he married Elva Glidden, Joseph Glidden's only daughter. He was soon hired to scout for a ranch where barbed wire would be tested and demonstrated. The result was the Frying Pan Ranch, which included land watered by Tecovas Spring. Managing the ranch and selling barbed wire wasn't enough, as in 1885, he and F. T. Simmons, his brother-in-law, created the Bush, Simmons, and Company, a hat company. Shortly after 1900, Bush founded and served as the president of the Bush Hat Company.

Bush was given the ranch in 1898 by Glidden. At the time, Bush was campaigning for the construction of the Choctaw, Oklahoma & Texas (CO&T), and later for the Chicago, Rock Island & Gulf to acquire the CO&T to do the job. To help with the construction, Bush donated the right-of-way through his ranch, and built several towns around railroad stations. Bush also was a patron of the Art Institute of Chicago, funded the Amarillo Public Library, and helped to establish St. Anthony's Hospital (located in Amarillo and considered to be the first hospital on the High Plains of Texas). William Bush experimented with his ranch, almost single-handedly creating the regional dairy industry when he brought in Guernsey milk cows. He was also heavily responsible for the helium industry, since much of the gas was found on the Frying Pan Ranch. Bush died in Chicago in 1931, and is buried in Graceland Cemetery, the burial place of most of the important people in Chicago's history. In 2001, Graceland Cemetery was placed on the National Register of Historic Places.

The town of Bush was laid out in 1908, with William Bush naming the north-south streets after his friends and relatives. The town was dedicated by Bush on July 3, 1908, and quickly became a rail shipping center for area ranches. A school soon opened, as did a Bushland post office during January 1909. The town was never large, with only about four businesses, a few churches, and 120 residents. A grain elevator was also built for area wheat farmers. Although the town was originally named Bush, it was known as Bush Stop by the railroad. It soon was renamed Bushland, reportedly because William Bush's wife felt that the town was too shabby and small to carry her husband's name. She should see it today, as several new housing subdivisions have been developed here.

Today, Bushland is a growing residential area with its own post office, located at Exit 57 on Interstate 40. Its population was less than 200 from 1965 through 2000, but has grown since. While Bushland itself isn't well-known, the nearby "Cadillac Ranch" is. This "ranch" is located east of town and south of Interstate 40, and is a major tourist attraction that consists of ten Cadillac cars buried nose down in the ground. Bushland is also a stop along Historic U.S. Route 66.

775.0 SOUTHWEST PORTLAND CEMENT – The Rock Island Railroad served a large cement plant north of here, using 13,883 feet of track and a wye at the mainline. This plant was built by Southwestern Portland Cement in 1963 to use local calcium carbonate deposits. Burlington Northern continued to serve this plant until the mid-1990s.

The grade crossing for Cement Road, which closely followed the cement line to the east, still has a crossbuck and part of the bell warning system. It can easily be found by looking for the Cornerstone Ranch sign above Cement Road.

When the railroad was abandoned, everything was taken – rails, ties, signal boxes, and crossing gates. However, the rails and some of the crossing signal parts remain at the Cement Road grade crossing at Milepost 775.0.

Along the north side of Interstate 40, at approximately railroad Milepost 777.5, can be found one of the few signal boxes that was not removed with the abandonment.

729

In a few spots, the carcasses of the old railroad ties can still be found on the former Rock Island Railroad grade. Here, a few lie beside a resting cow at Milepost 779.0.

780.0 COUNTY LINE – The county line between **Potter County**, to the east, and **Oldham County**, to the west, is near the west end of the curve about two miles east of Wildorado. Look for the remains of the five-panel timber pile trestle just north of the freeway, located at an elevation of 3882 feet. Just to the south of Interstate 40 is the large feedlot of Quality Beef Producers.

The remains of a five-panel timber pile trestle remain at Milepost 779.9, just east of the Potter-Oldham county line.

Oldham County was created in 1876 from parts of Bexar County, and it was named for Williamson Simpson Oldham, Sr. Oldham was originally from Tennessee, but moved to Arkansas and served in the Arkansas House of Representatives (1838) and then as a Justice of the Arkansas Supreme Court (1842). After moving to Texas, he represented Texas in the Provisional Congress of the Confederate States (1861-1862), and then was a senator in the Confederate States Congress (1862-1865).

While Oldham County was founded in 1876, it wasn't until 1880 that it was officially organized. At the time, Oldham County had a population of 287, the second most of any Panhandle county, and nearly the entire county was a part of the XIT Ranch. At the time, sixteen other counties were administered by Oldham County officials because of their small populations. The original county seat was Tascosa, but it was moved to Vega after the railroad was built. The county is known for its wheat and livestock production, and in the 2010 census, the county's population was 2052.

XIT Ranch

The XIT Ranch has an interesting beginning. It came about when the Texas legislature paid the Capitol Syndicate of Chicago three million acres of land for building a new State Capitol in 1885. The size of the ranch and the absentee owners led to the ranch being a "stopping place and rendezvous for a large number of bad men and criminals," according to ranch manager A. L. Matlock. This led to the creation of the 23 Rules of XIT Ranch to create a ranch of "sterling honesty and integrity." These rules included prohibitions against carrying arms, alcohol, and gambling.

The original plan of the property owners was to sell the land off for colonization, but to use it for ranching until all of the land was sold. A professional immigration agency was hired in 1890 and wells and dams were built as water sources. However, lower cattle prices and a failure to sell much of the property for farmland led to a financial crisis. Soon, large parts of the property were sold off to other cattlemen, but substantial mineral rights were retained. The operating ranch ended in late 1912, and the last of the XIT cattle were sold on November 1, 1912.

782.0 WILDORADO (WO) – The area around Wildorado was used as part of the Tascosa to Canyon City cattle trail during the 1800s, and was settled in 1900 when a survey for a railroad was made. Eugene Binford and John R. Goodman had already settled in the area and started to create a townsite where the railroad had designated a station location as a shipping point for grain and livestock. While the railroad wasn't immediately built, the town did develop, and a Wildorado post office opened in 1904 with John Goodman as its postmaster.

The name Wildorado came from nearby Wildorado Creek, but the source of the original name is not known. Some speculate that it is a combination of "wild" and "Eldorado" that created a term for a golden place in the wild, possibly a reference to the water along the cattle trail.

The railroad finally arrived in 1908, and the town was laid out and more lots sold. Goodman continued to invest in the town and organized the Wildorado State Bank and built the Wildorado Hotel. In 1909, the *Wildorado Progress* began publishing. A report stated that in 1915, Wildorado featured a grocer, a general store, a lumber company, a blacksmith, a hardware store, a school, two churches, and a telephone system. Over the next several decades, the population grew and then shrank during the Great Depression, but it never exceeded 200 residents. The late 1920s were an especially rough time for the town, as its bank was robbed eight times between 1925 and 1928. The creation of Highway 66 led to stores, hotels and gas stations opening at Wildorado, and the population finally exceeding 200. Today, the town is unincorporated, but still has its post office and the remains of the grain elevator that once operated here.

During the 1920s, the railroad had a 36-car siding at Wildorado, plus other tracks with a capacity of 49 cars. In 1929, the railroad had both an agent and telegrapher here, working the 8:30am-5:30pm shift on weekdays and using the station code "WO". By the 1970s, there were two industry sidings shown as being a total of 3467 feet long. The remains of the old elevator are just west of Main Street. The old station has been moved and now sits on the west side of Main Street about a block north of the old grade.

Heading west, the former Rock Island Railroad grade stays just north of Interstate 40, making it easy to follow using the frontage road.

789.5 EVERETT – Everett is located at Exit 42 on Interstate 40, where Everett Road bridges across the freeway. There is a small feedlot here today, and there was never much more than a small traditional wooden grain elevator. During the early 1900s, there was a 37-car siding to the north. Later, the siding was used for the elevator, measuring 1437 feet long in 1979.

This downtown store tells much of the story of Wildorado; the town is mostly closed.

Parts of several old grain elevators remain at Wildorado, marking the grade of the Chicago, Rock Island & Pacific.

The former CRI&P depot at Wildorado, Texas, has been moved about a block north of the old grade and is used as a house.

Although the exact location isn't identified in this Russell Lee photo from July 1939, it is identified as being a Texas Wheat Pool elevator west of Amarillo. Small elevator complexes like this were located at most stations along the Rock Island in this area, allowing local farmers to deliver their grain for shipment around the world. Russell Lee was an American photographer and photojournalist who worked for the Farm Security Administration (FSA), the Air Transport Command, and the Department of the Interior. In 1965, Lee became the first instructor of photography at the University of Texas. Lee, Russell, photographer. *Line of trucks at wheat elevator in small town west of Amarillo, Texas.* July 1939. Photograph. Retrieved from the Library of Congress, https://www.loc.gov/item/2017783888/.

795.0 VEGA (GA) – Vega was a sizeable station for the Rock Island, with a siding and a small yard, a wye track, and a train order station. In 1929, the railroad had both an agent and telegrapher here (probably the same person), working the weekday 8:30am-5:30pm shift. It was also a water station for the steam locomotives operating over the line. By the 1970s, there was still a 2940-foot siding, plus 2950 feet of other tracks. A wye at the west end of town allowed a spur track to serve several shippers along today's 15th Street. The right-of-way through town can still be easily found, although a few buildings have recently been built on it.

When Oldham County was organized in 1880, Tascosa, located on the Canadian River, was declared to be the county seat. Its location off the Rock Island Railroad led to the county seat being moved to Vega, Texas, in 1915, using the Oldham Hotel until a courthouse was erected. The Vega area was first settled in 1899, ten years after the land was opened for homesteading. On October 17, 1899, N. J. Whitfield purchased land in what was known as Section 90. In 1903, he sold a 100-foot strip of land across his property to the Choctaw, Oklahoma & Texas so a railroad could be built. Even before the railroad was built, Whitfield began selling land. On some of this land, A. M. Miller and Howard Trigg laid out Vega in May 1903, naming the town after the Spanish word for plain or meadow. In 1904, a post office opened using the name, and Miller opened a store. Soon, a saloon and a school that was also used as a Masonic Lodge were built.

Others also helped to develop the Vega area. Swift & Company owned the nearby LS Ranch, and ranchers Patrick and John Landergin bought part of it in 1907. They worked with the Pool Land Company to make more land available to settlers, and then they opened a bank at Vega. The next year, the railroad built through Vega, and was in full operation by 1909. This led to more growth and several new stores, a blacksmith shop, several churches, and the *Vega Sentinel* newspaper.

The 1920s and 1930s saw more improvements. Vega was incorporated in 1927, soon after telephone service and Route 66 arrived. More improvements came about due to a May 3, 1931, fire that took out much of the downtown on the west side of the courthouse square. The north side of the square burned two months later, and Vega established a city water system. At that time, the population was slightly more than 500, and unlike many area communities, it continued to grow.

A combination of tourism, ranching and wheat farming has allowed Vega to continue to be one of the largest towns in the region, and the largest in Oldham County, with a population of about 900. Vega is still the county seat and its post office remains as one of four in the county. It is also the home of a full school system. A tall concrete grain elevator still stands where the railroad once served it, and several hotels and gas station exist to serve the tourists who stop to explore the town. One of

735

the hotels, the Vega Hotel, is listed on the National Register of Historic Places The town's library is located in a building built in 1911 as a silent movie theater. Downtown near the courthouse is a restored Magnolia gasoline station. Vega also holds the title of "The Solar Capital of Texas," due to being the 7th Sunniest Area in the country.

Vega is another Texas town that can be found by its tall, white grain elevator.

796.9 ONTARIO – Ontario was another effort to create a town along the Rock Island Railroad. It was platted in 1908 by T. Carrabine and Company of Kansas. The firm opened a general store, hotel, and built a few houses, and a post office even opened that year. However, it was soon discovered that there was no water at the townsite, and most of the buildings were moved to nearby Vega. The post office closed during May 1912.

In 1929, there was still a 20-car spur track at Ontario, but there were no railroad agents and it was only a flag stop for passing trains. The name Ontario wasn't found in railroad documents much later.

802.7 LANDERGIN – Some sources show that Landergin is a ghost town, located at Exit 28 of Interstate 40. However, the remains of a truck stop and lots of old trailers, plus the remains of the grain elevator, still mark the location.

Landergin, Texas, can be spotted for miles thanks to the tall elevator that still remains alongside the railroad grade.

Landergin, like most of the stations along the Rock Island across this part of Texas and New Mexico, was created as the railroad was built. During the 1840s, the Landergin family migrated from Ireland to Oxford, New York, to avoid the infamous potato famine. In New York, they established a dairy farm. Their sons, Patrick and John, moved to Indian Territory (Oklahoma) during the 1870s, bought longhorn cattle, bred them and began ranching along the Red River. They later ranched in Kansas, buying cattle from further south, fattening them on the Kansas prairie and then selling them in the big cities back east. As the business shrank due to better transportation and the creation of feedlots,

737

the Landergin brothers leased part of the LS Ranch in 1904, and later bought the property.

The land that the Patrick and John Landergin bought happened to be along the planned route of the Choctaw, Oklahoma & Texas. In 1906, the brothers opened a store near their ranch headquarters, and the railroad later built a siding there, starting the town of Landergin. The Landergin brothers also invested in other parts of the region, including the first State Bank in nearby Vega, which they opened in 1909. By the 1930s, Landergin included one store and a grain elevator, and the population peaked at 36 residents. By the 1980s, the town featured a highway exit and a grain elevator, a filling station, a roadside café, and an antique store. Today, they are gone or are simply empty shells.

For the railroad, Landergin was never a major stop, being known as Landergin Spur in the 1929 timetable. At the time, there was simply a seven-car spur track. By the 1970s, there was an 802-foot elevator siding to the south.

808.8 ADRIAN (DR) – Adrian began when surveyors for the Choctaw, Oklahoma & Texas identified the location as a future station and shipping point in 1900. Some of the early settlers were Calvin G. Aten, a former Texas Ranger, and Adrian Cullen, for whom the station was named. In 1909, the railroad built through the area to a point about a mile west of Adrian, and the American-Canadian Land and Townsite Company began to promote the community and the surrounding land. In 1910, the Chicago, Rock Island & Gulf built 22.54 miles of track westward from Adrian all the way to the New Mexico border, connecting with the line to Tucumcari.

Two improvements to Adrian came about due to J. P. Collier, an owner of a number of lots in the town. Collier dug a city water well and installed several water lines to serve a number of homes and businesses. He also started printing the *Adrian Eagle* newspaper. The available water attracted residents and businesses, and by 1910 there was a post office (opened in 1908), general store, bank, lumberyard, blacksmith shop, brick factory, pool hall, school, and two churches. Within a few more years, there was also a drugstore and telephone service.

A grain elevator was built alongside the railroad in 1929, and Adrian became the location of railroad wheat shipments. The construction of Route 66 helped the town to survive, and a few services such as gas stations were built. Adrian was finally incorporated in 1953 with a population of less than 200, making it one of two incorporated communities in Oldham County. The population peaked at 220 in 1990, and was 166 in the 2010 census. The post office still operates, Adrian School is still open, and several cafes and other businesses still serve the community, which proclaims itself to be the "Midpoint of Route 66 between

Chicago and Los Angeles." Look for the painted stripe on the old highway at the west end of town.

A painted stripe on the road and this sign marks what is claimed to be the "Midpoint of Route 66 between Chicago and Los Angeles."

The old Wheat Growers elevator still stands and marks where the railroad used to pass through town. Just west of there, the Midpoint Campground also sits on the old railroad right-of-way. In 1929, the railroad had an agent-telegrapher here (station code "DR"), working the 8:30am-5:30pm shift on weekdays. At the time, there was a 57-car siding and other industry tracks with a 27-car capacity. Adrian was also a designated fuel stop on the railroad in 1929. In 1973, there was still a long siding to the south, with a house track off the siding. There was also a short industry siding to the north of the mainline. The 1979 employee timetable listed only 1442 feet of spur tracks.

Like most Texas towns in the panhandle area, wheat was shipped by rail from Adrian, Texas, using large elevators.

A railroad depot remains in the area, but it can be hard to find. Many years ago, the Panhandle & Santa Fe depot from Umbarger (southwest of Amarillo) was moved to the Ivy Grapevine Ranch and turned into a storage building. The Ivy Grapevine Ranch can be found by heading north from Exit 18 on Interstate 40. Go north about 2½ miles and start looking. Be careful in the area as there are a number of side roads that head out to all of the windmills.

West of Adrian, the railroad begins a three-mile climb of 0.6%, with the grade cresting near Milepost 814 at an elevation of 4186 feet. Heading west from the crest, the line used to then drop at 0.6% for more than five miles to Boise at 3993 feet of elevation.

813.0 GRUHLKEY – This station was shown to be an 18-car spur track in 1929, and was named for Rock Island Roadmaster W. H. "Sorghum Bill" Gruhlkey. According to the January 1951 issue of the *Rock Island Lines News Digest*, Bill Gruhlkey "started to work for the Rock Island as a section laborer at Marseilles, Illinois, in 1885 at the age of 15. At 17, he was a section foreman." Gruhlkey obtained his nickname when he began using sorghum cane to stabilize soft grade in the Boydston area (Milepost 713) that was described as being not even as thick as buttermilk. When the process worked, it was used along the line throughout 1912, fixing spots that were soft due to the heavy snows and rains earlier that year. A unique part of the process was the fermenting smell of the sorghum throughout the hot summer. Gruhlkey retired from the railroad in 1933.

Located at Exit 18 on Interstate 40, Gruhlkey was reportedly built on land owned by "Sorghum Bill" to be a shipping facility for the Carter Stohs Company. It is the halfway point between Tucumcari, New Mexico, and Amarillo, Texas. Heading west, the railroad runs along the edge of the slope, near Piedra Creek, which breaks up the country. This terrain is common north of Interstate 40 and the former Rock Island grade, as streams flow north to the Canadian River.

815.0 CAP ROCK SPUR – Cap Rock was a 15-car siding in 1929. It was located just east of where the railroad once turned south to pass under Interstate 40.

The term cap rock, or caprock, applies to a harder or more erosion-resistant rock layer that is set on top of softer rocks or soil. In this area, cap rock produces buttes or small hills, generally surrounded by dry washes. The railroad runs along this caprock in this area, with high ground to the south, and ground that has been washed away to the north.

Starting about Milepost 814, and heading west to near Milepost 819.5, the railroad drops from an elevation of 4186 feet to 4025 feet. This is the ruling eastbound grade and averages 0.6%.

816.3 INTERSTATE 40 – The railroad grade passes under Interstate 40, sharing the route with Ivy Road at Exit 15. Interstate 40, which stretches from Barstow, California, to Wilmington, North Carolina, is 2560 miles long, making it the third-longest Interstate Highway in the United States. I-40 connects Memphis and Little Rock, crossing east to west across the center of Arkansas, and then on across Oklahoma, the panhandle of Texas, and through New Mexico. Texas has the shortest state segment, while Tennessee has the longest. West of Oklahoma City, I-40 closely follows Historic Highway 66.

The construction of I-40 started in 1957 just as the Rock Island was starting to suffer economic issues. The highway was noted several times as having taken business off of the railroad, leading to less rail service and financial losses.

Heading west, the railroad loops to the south and doesn't return to Interstate 40 until Mile 6 on the highway.

821.5 BOISE – Boise is located south of Interstate 40 at the Bridwell West Ranch exit on Interstate 40. Exit might be an exaggeration, as it is actually a simple intersection involving the ranch road and I-40. Boise is properly described as a ghost town, with only a few stock pens and

741

buildings to mark its location. The location was primarily a shipping point for area ranchers and farmers, and no real town ever existed here.

Boise was located on the open plains at an elevation of 4003 feet. During the early 1900s, there was a 52-car siding to the south of the mainline. There was a water tower here for the trains to use. In 1979, the Rock Island Railroad reported that there was a 2450-foot siding.

In 1929, Boise was an important siding for train operations. At 1:05am, trains No. 111 and No. 112 (*Memphis Californian*) were to meet and pass here. At 12:05pm, freight trains No. 991 and No. 992 were to meet and pass here. Train No. 991 was known as the *California-Oklahoma-Louisiana Gold and Red Ball*, while No. 992 was the *California-Memphis Gold Ball*.

825.4 MUJARES CREEK BRIDGE – This bridge is located well south of Interstate 40, possibly explaining why it still stands over the stream. From east to west, it includes a three-panel open deck pile trestle, two 44-foot deck plate girder spans, and then a two-panel open deck pile trestle.

While there is little access to the Mujares Creek bridge, the remains of several smaller wooden trestles can still be found nearby, located just south of Interstate 40. These remains are of the five-span trestle at Milepost 828.5.

Mujares Creek, also spelled Mojares and Mujeres, flows north into Trujillo Creek, which then flows into the Canadian River. Because of streams like this, Oldham is reported to be the best watered county in the western part of the Texas Panhandle. Mujares Creek is fed by springs, and its water level varies greatly by the amount of recent rainfall. In English, mujares and mujeres means women.

829.8 COUNTY LINE – In this area, the railroad grade is located just south of Interstate 40, and heading railroad-west, it is actually heading to the compass southwest. To the north (railroad-east) is **Oldham County**, while to the south (railroad-west) is **Deaf Smith County**. The county line is clearly marked on I-40.

Like Oldham County, **Deaf Smith County** was created in 1876, but its lack of population kept it from being fully organized for several years, 1890 in this case. La Plata was the original county seat, but it later moved to Hereford, the "Beef Capital of the World." The county has a population of almost 20,000, large for this region of Texas.

The name Deaf Smith honors Erastus "Deaf" Smith. Smith was born in New York, and moved to Port Gibson, Mississippi, with his family in 1798. He moved to Texas for his health, but lost some of his hearing, providing the reason for his nickname, which was pronounced DEEF. He soon developed a reputation in the Texas area, participating in a number of business efforts, including the introduction of muley (polled) cattle from Louisiana to the San Antonio area. During the Texas Revolution, he was a scout and soldier, and is known for being the first member of the Texan forces to reach the Alamo after its fall.

832.2 GLENRIO – Glenrio is a station town that is split between Texas and New Mexico. The location, which is simply a home or two along with a number of abandoned structures, is unincorporated, but has been listed on the National Register of Historic Places since 2007. The community grew thanks to the railroad, and then the construction of Route 66, and has died because of their failure.

The community was founded in 1903 as a planned railroad siding on the Rock Island Railroad, using the name Rock Island. In 1908, the railroad started grading again, with separate railroads handling the track in each direction. According to the December 31, 1910, issue of *The Railway and Engineering Review*, the Chicago, Rock Island & El Paso built the line west from Glenrio to Tucumcari, and the Chicago, Rock Island & Gulf built the line eastward to Adrian, both completed in 1910. As a part of this work, the community was renamed Glenrio by the railroad. The name is an interesting mix of the Scottish "glen" for a narrow valley, and the Spanish "rio" for river.

Before the railroad arrived, the area was opened to farming in 1905. Wheat soon became a popular crop. Ranching was also important, and the railroad quickly built stock pens to handle the livestock off of local ranches. The *Glenrio Tribune* newspaper started publishing in 1910, and a few other businesses also located near the railroad station. In 1915, the Rock Island post office, which opened in 1909, became the Glenrio post office. In 1917, the Ozark Trail was built through Glenrio, adding tourism and highway travel to the businesses in the town. The Ozark

743

Trail was a series of locally maintained roads that ran from St. Louis, Missouri, to Santa Fe, New Mexico. The network of roads was coordinated by the Ozark Trails Association, and this was the major highway in the area until it was replaced by U.S. Highway 66, which used parts of the route starting on November 11, 1926.

Little remains at Glenrio, located on the Texas-New Mexico border, except several abandoned buildings.

Local farms and ranches led to the establishment of several grocery stores, a hardware store, a land office, a hotel, and several cafes and service stations by the 1920s. Travel helped build several additional filling stations, a restaurant, and a motel by the early 1930s. However, where the various businesses were located depended upon the laws in Texas and New Mexico. The State Line Bar and Motel were built in New Mexico, since Deaf Smith County, Texas, was a dry county at the time. The gas stations were in Texas since its fuel taxes were much lower. The railroad station was in Texas, but the mail delivered there had to be hauled to the post office in New Mexico. There was also a welcome station built in Glenrio to handle the traffic on Route 66. The roadway attracted travelers of all kinds, and parts of the movie *Grapes of Wrath* were filmed here.

Despite the tourism and local farms and ranches, the population of Glenrio didn't grow to be more than several dozen residents. The *Glenrio Tribune* stopped publishing in 1934. The end of World War II and improvements in Route 66 helped the community, and the Joseph Brownlee House was moved to Glenrio from Amarillo in 1950. Several other restaurants, service stations and hotels were also built about this time, many using modern art deco or art moderne styles. One of the most noted was the Texas Longhorn Motel, advertised as both the

"First Motel in Texas" and the "Last Motel in Texas." Additionally, the owner, Homer Ehresman, operated the State Line Café and Gas Station.

When the third highway was built – Interstate 40 – it bypassed Glenrio. It also ended the need for many of the area services as travelers could travel farther in less time. This led Ehresman to move his operations to the freeway exit at Endee, New Mexico, while others simply moved north to the nearest exit. Even many of these failed to last, and Glenrio is simply a ghost town with a number of deteriorating building shells, a very wide main street, and a population of five in the 2000 census.

For the Rock Island Railroad, Glenrio was a dividing line for many years. In 1929, it was a scheduled stop for both passenger and freight trains. The railroad had an agent-telegrapher here, working the 8:30am-5:30pm shift on weekdays and using the station code of "GN". There was a 65-car siding, plus other tracks with a capacity of 15 cars. It was also a water stop thanks to a well built by the railroad. This was the last water stop heading west before Tucumcari, so most trains stopped to water. A unique note in the 1929 employee timetable was that the track to the east in Texas was the Chicago, Rock Island & Gulf Railway, while the track to the west was the Chicago, Rock Island & Pacific Railway.

In 1945, the railroad installed a new water tank and windmill in New Mexico, replacing Rock Island Lines deep well No. 2 in Deaf Smith County, Texas. Records show that the Rock Island depot closed in 1955. During the 1960s, there was a siding on the north side of the mainline, and a spur track to the south. As passenger service ended and the number of freight trains dwindled, the siding was removed and only a 771-foot spur track remained by 1979.

832.2 STATE LINE – The former location of the west switch of Glenrio siding is the state line between Deaf Smith County in **Texas** (to the east) and **New Mexico** (to the west). The elevation at the state line is approximately 3850, and the railroad has been climbing and dropping over low ridges throughout this area. The state line between Texas and New Mexico has been a source of conflict since 1859. The line was supposed to be the 103rd Meridian, but the 1859 survey missed the line, and was generally between two and four miles too far west. While New Mexico has made several attempts to regain the hundreds of square miles of territory, it is still officially a part of Texas.

New Mexico became the 47th state on January 6, 1912. Today, it is the fifth-largest and sixth-least densely populated of the states. Its nickname is the Land of Enchantment, and its flag is the distinctive yellow banner with the traditional red sun symbol of the Zia in its center. New Mexico is heavily dependent upon its natural resources, with oil, mining, dryland farming, cattle ranching, and timber being major parts of the economy. Tourism and trade also play a major role. Santa Fe, founded in 1610 as the capital of Nuevo México, is the state capitol, with the largest city being Albuquerque.

Quay County, New Mexico, was created on February 28, 1903, from parts of Guadalupe County. Quay County was named for Pennsylvania senator Matthew Quay. Quay had led the campaign of Benjamin Harrison for president, and Harrison called him a "kingmaker" for his political power. Quay, who died in 1904, had been a major supporter of New Mexico statehood. The county seat is Tucumcari. The county's population has never been large and peaked in the 1910 census at 14,912. As railroads and ranching moved out, the population dropped and then climbed again through the 1940s and 1950s, but has dropped to 9041 in the 2010 census.

Heading southwest from here, the Rock Island and Route 66 were often side-by-side. Today, the grade of the railroad can be seen immediately south of the historic highway, while Interstate 40 curves off to the west. Also curving off to the northwest is the upgraded Route 66 from 1952.

This March 1940 photo by Arthur Rothstein for the Farm Security Administration looks east across the state line at Glenrio. To the south of the highway are the water tanks, well house and tracks of the Rock Island Railroad. Rothstein, Arthur, photographer. *State line. New Mexico – Texas*. United States New Mexico Texas, 1940. Mar. Photograph. Retrieved from the Library of Congress, https://www.loc.gov/item/2017774771/.

834.5 SAND POINT DRAW BRIDGE – The concrete headwalls of this bridge still remain, where once three 45-foot home-built spans crossed this draw. This bridge was built relatively late in the history of the Choctaw Route, with a 1941 date cast into the east and west headwalls.

Sand Point Draw drains the hill to the south and takes any waters north into Martha Creek, also known as Trujillo Creek.

Driving the old Route 66 gravel road west of Glenrio, the concrete headwalls of the old Sand Point Draw bridge can easily be found.

836.9 ENDEE – The remains of Endee can be seen where New Mexico State Highway 93 crosses Route 66 and the grade of the Rock Island. Highway 93 heads north to Interstate 40, where the Russells Truck & Travel Center is located at Exit 369. While there are a few foundations and lots of scrap materials, and even a nearby house or two, Russells is what is left of Endee after it moved to the new Route 66 to the north, and then Interstate 40.

Endee was founded in 1882 as a local trade center, supported by the nearby ND ranch, thus its name. John and George Day organized the ND ranch in the same year and needed a supply and shipping point. Endee was early on a true wild west town with bars, gunfights, and true cowboys. However, it was tame enough to have several stores and a post office, which it obtained in 1886. A favorite claim by many was that "a trench was dug on Saturday to bury the gunfight losers on Sunday."

The population was never large, with 110 in 1946. The Route 66 boom did help as the population was up to 187 in 1950. However, in 1952, an improved Route 66 was built to the north and much of the town began to move. The post office closed in 1955 and little of Endee still remains.

The remains of this house are not far north of the old railroad grade at Endee, New Mexico.

Not long after the railroad was built, the station here used the code of "ND". In 1947, the railroad had a spur track with a capacity of 15 car lengths. It was all gone by the 1960s. Heading west, the railroad starts to climb at about 0.5%, and generally follows San Jon Creek to the station at San Jon.

839.0 MARTHA CREEK BRIDGE – Just west of Quay County Road G, the railroad crosses Martha Creek/Trujillo Creek. The remains of this 26-panel open deck pile trestle can still be seen from adjacent Historic Route 66.

Just to the north, San Jon Creek flows in from the west. While heading west, Route 66 and the railroad grade separate a short distance. The railroad once headed through a large cut while Historic Route 66 runs around and over the ridge.

While the bridge deck is gone from the Martha Creek bridge, most of the pile bents still remain.

840.4 SAN JON CREEK BRIDGE – Like the nearby San Jon station, there is conflict on what the meaning of this stream's name really is. Some sources claim that the name could be a corruption of the Spanish "zan-jon" which means "deep gully," an appropriate name for parts of this stream, which can be big and roaring after a rain.

The remains of this bridge also still can be found. This was a 14-panel open deck pile trestle, and the railroad crossed the stream several more times as the Rock Island used the slope to keep grades at 0.6% or less for westbound trains. At Mileposts 843.3 and 844.3 were more open deck pile trestles over San Jon Creek; they were 12-panel and 15-panel trestles, respectively.

845.3 BARD – Bard is an unincorporated community scattered around Exit 361 of Interstate 40. The town started alongside the railroad grade about 1906. On January 30, 1908, the Bard post office opened, which changed its name to Bard City on October 8, 1909, to avoid conflict with Bard, Texas. The post office went back to Bard on April 23, 1913, and the post office remained open until November 26, 1991.

Early stories about Bard center on the cowboy days and the wildness of the community, but the base of the town was the general store and post office. There is some conflict about where the name Bard came from, with some saying that it came from Bard, Texas. However, the

749

Bar-D Ranch was nearby when Bard was founded, so it was probably the supply center for that ranch.

By the 1940s, Bard was fairly healthy with about 200 residents, being a trading center for local ranchers. Besides a number of scattered houses, there was also a store, gas station, garage and post office. The town originally focused on the railroad, and then moved north to be on Route 66. It then moved further north to be on the new Route 66 and Interstate 40. This explains that scattered community between the Rock Island Railroad grade and Exit 361 on Interstate 40.

In 1947, Bard had a short 6-car house track. The track was gone not long after and Bard was removed from timetables and track charts.

850.3 SAN JON (SJ) – In the 1979 employee timetable, San Jon was the first Rock Island Railroad station in New Mexico. There were 976 feet of spur tracks listed. However, in 1947, the railroad had a 51-car long siding and other tracks with a capacity of 22 cars. There was also a depot with office hours of 8:30am-5:30pm daily except Sunday.

Like many of the towns along the abandoned Chicago, Rock Island & Pacific, little remains of the railroad at San Jon, New Mexico. However, this former railroad sign can still be found in the brush.

Look for the tall community water tower at Exit 356 on Interstate 40. The Village of San Jon was founded in 1902 in advance of the railroad, with the first building erected by Tom Jones. The railroad grade arrived in 1904, and the community became an important ranching and shipping center when the railroad was completed in 1910. The community received its name in October 1906 when the post office opened and W. D. Bennett, the first postmaster, named it. Some sources claim that the name could be a corruption of the Spanish "zanjon" which means "deep gully."

With the arrival of Route 66, San Jon became an important stop with gasoline service stations, restaurants, lodging, and attractions. During this time, San Jon was the largest New Mexico town east of Tucumcari and was the social hub for cowboys from across the region. The population peaked during the 1960 census with 411 residents, and then remained about 300 until 1981, when Interstate 40 was completed through the area. Almost immediately, much of town moved north to the Interstate and the population dropped, with an estimated 200 residents currently. Several gas stations remain at the freeway exit, and there is still a small hotel along Route 66, near the post office which is still open. A few business remain that support area ranching, as well as the San Jon Municipal Schools. The abandoned railroad grade runs along the south edge of today's San Jon community.

Heading west, the railroad crossed some very rough country, requiring high fills, some deep cuts, and tall trestles over several large washes. The grade climbed a bit, then dropped using a set of stair step grades of 0.6% and then level and then 0.6% again. The top of the grade just west of San Jon is at 4035 feet, and it drops down all the way to Barancos Creek at an elevation of 3882 feet.

857.9 BRIDGE – Basically impossible to get to without a long walk, this bridge once featured a 37-panel pile trestle, but little remains today. The bridge crossed a dry wash that could become roaring after a good rain, flowing northward into Barancos Creek just south of Interstate 40. A unique feature is that the stream obviously tried to wash out the railroad numerous times, and the west bank of the gorge is lined with old railroad cars.

859.0 OIL SPUR – A seven-car siding was shown here in 1929. The name of the track probably explains its purpose. During the 1920s, there was a lot of activity in the area exploring for oil.

860.5 BARANCOS CREEK BRIDGE – Barancos is Spanish for gorge, an appropriate name for this stream as it has carved a deep channel in a number of places. Barancos Creek starts on the south side of Mesa Redonda, located south of Tucumcari. The stream flows east and then north to here, and then further north to join Plaza Larga Creek.

The bridge is still standing and is used as part of a private ranch road. From east to west, there is a 50-foot deck plate girder span (DPG), two 75-foot DPGs, a 60-foot DPG, and an 80-foot DPG. All sit on concrete piers, a replacement for the original bridge which was limited to ten miles per hour in 1929.

862.8 PLAZA LARGA CREEK BRIDGE – Plaza Larga is Spanish for long or large town square. It has been reported that the name came about because of the wide flat areas created by the stream. The stream flows northward and merges with Barancos Creek before flowing into Revuelto Creek, also known as Revuelto River.

The railroad bridge still stands. From east to west, the bridge consists of four spans of open deck pile trestle, two 90-foot deck plate girder spans, and four more spans of open deck pile trestle. This is another bridge that was rebuilt due to its ten-mile-per-hour speed limit in 1929.

865.3 LESBIA – Located where the railroad grade now crosses road QR Ag less than one-half mile south of Interstate 40 was the railroad station of Lesbia. In 1947, when Lesbia was a flag stop for the *Memphis California* No. 111/No. 112, the Rock Island had a 51-car siding here. In 1979, there were 1053 feet of spur tracks at Lesbia.

The name of this location changed a number of times. As plans to finish the railroad were being made, a post office opened in 1908 using the name Rudulph, named for Carolina Rudulph, the first postmaster. In 1910, the post office became Castleberry, named for the new postmaster Ritta Castleberry. In 1913, the post office and the community again changed names, this time to Lesbia. The name Lesbia reportedly comes from an Aegean island famed as the home of the Greek poetess Sappho. How the name got here is unknown.

This new name for the post office didn't last long as it closed in 1918. There were greater plans, since in 1915 there was drilling for oil, but the plans did not materialize. However, the railroad kept some tracks at Lesbia to serve area farms and ranches.

868.2 UNDER INTERSTATE 40 – This large concrete tunnel through the I-40 fill is located just west of Exit 339 and the Tucumcari Municipal Airport. In this area, I-40 was built on the grade of U.S. Highway 66.

The railroad underpass just east of Tucumcari is big, and has become the home of a large colony of cliff swallows.

Near here, the former railroad grade is lined with laterals, such as the Simmons Lateral and the Gaudin Lateral. A lateral is an irrigation and drainage ditch. With little rainfall, irrigation is commonly used to grow crops around Tucumcari.

871.7 WYE TO GOLDEN STATE ROUTE – There used to be a switch here that created a wye to the Dalhart-Tucumcari line. To the south is the Tucumcari Wildlife Management Area.

872.5 LAKE JUNCTION – Lake Junction was located at Milepost 636.8 of today's Union Pacific, just north of the U.S. Highway 54 overpass at the northeast end of Tucumcari. In this area today is also Union Pacific Control Point TC637, the east end of the Tucumcari Siding.

In 1947, this was the junction between Subdivision 42 from Dalhart, Texas, and Subdivision 4 from Amarillo, Texas, for trains heading towards Tucumcari. At the time, both were part of the Panhandle Division, Second District. The grade for the Tucumcari leg of the wye can still be found, but the northbound leg's fill has been removed as it once crossed several fields.

874.2 TUCUMCARI (XN) – Even if you have never been to Tucumcari, you have probably seen it referred to in a number of movies, books and songs.

> *"I couldn't help hearing you're going to Tucumcari. I sell goods around here, and I gotta tell you, you're on the wrong train... you see the train doesn't stop at Tucumcari."*

> *"This train'll stop at Tucumcari..."*

> *For a Few Dollars More*

Tucumcari was Milepost 874.2 on the Amarillo line, measured from Memphis, Tennessee. It was also Milepost 638.5 on the Dalhart line, measured from St. Joseph, Missouri. The Dalhart line is still in operation, used by Union Pacific as their Tucumcari Subdivision, which stretches from Dalhart (Milepost 544.0) to Vaughn, New Mexico (Milepost 739.6).

This area has had several names. The first white settlement was founded about 1880 as Liberty, and it was located about three miles to the north alongside Pajarito Creek. About 1901, a railroad construction camp was based here, and the siding used the name Ragtown, and then Six Shooter Siding. When the town was being created, the name Douglas was used briefly before Tucumcari became the name of the post office in 1902.

The Tucumcari name came later for the town, but the name actually predates white settlement by generations. There are at least four legends about the source of the name – one from an early railroader, one from the Jemez Indians, one from the Apache, and one from the Comanche. The railroader version claims that when the first train arrived, a Comanche was impressed with the lantern that a brakeman carried. The story states that the Comanche told the brakeman "tuka? manooril, carry the light!" The Brakeman then responded "'tukama ... carry" which became the town's name.

The Jemez Indian version is credited to historian Herman Moncus. Moncus determined that the Jemez Indians, who lived in the Rio Grande Valley, hunted buffalo and other animals in eastern New Mexico before 1800. Moncus' research found that Tucumcari could mean "a place of the buffalo hunt." However, he also stated that the name may even predate that, and the Jemez Indians probably learned the name from other tribes.

The Apache legend is credited to Geronimo. He reportedly stated that there was an Apache Indian maiden named Kari who had two suitors, Tocom and Tonapon. Her love was Tocom, but Tonapon killed him in a fight over her. Kari then killed Tonapon, and then took her own life. Her father Wautonomah, then in great sadness stabbed himself while crying "Tocom! Kari!" A very similar version of the story states that

Tocom and Tonapon were fighting to replace Chief Wautonomah, and the winner would be chief and earn Kari as their wife.

As stated, some credit the Apache legend to Geronimo. However, some sources credit the tale to others looking for a good story. This list includes a Methodist minister, a group of locals drinking at a bar swapping stories, and even a group of local businesspeople creating stories at the local Elk Drugstore. No matter the source, the story has the romantic angle of Romeo and Juliet. However, this was Comanche territory. The Comanche version of the name comes from linguist Elliott Canonge. He has written that the name is the Comanche term "tukamukaru" which means "to lie in wait for something approaching." The Tucumcari name came from the nearby Tucumcari Mountain, which was often used as a lookout by the Comanche. This version has the support of the 1794 publication of the diary of Pedro Vial, who had traveled through the area during the late 1700s.

Liberty and Fort Bascom

The first settlement in the Quay County area was Tierra Blanca, soon renamed Liberty. The community came into existence as a safe haven for area settlers during the Indian wars around 1864. Liberty was located just north of Pajarito Creek, and benefitted from nearby Fort Bascom, which was established alongside the Canadian River in 1863. Fort Bascom was one of a series of military posts designed to protect the area from Confederate advancements, and later the Comanches and Kiowas, and even Comancheros, who traded stolen goods with local tribes and outlaws. The post also provided troops to patrol the Goodnight-Loving Cattle Trail and the Santa Fe Trail. The post was named for Captain George Nicholas Bascom, who was killed during the Civil War on February 21, 1862, at Fort Craig in the Battle of Val Verde, New Mexico.

The name Liberty came about because the location was used by troops during their off-duty hours (liberty) for drinking and other activities. At the time, alcohol was not allowed within five miles of Fort Bascom, so Liberty had the advantage of being able to do business with the troops. This military business ended in 1870 when the post was abandoned and the land reverted back to John S. Watts, its original owner. There were few uses for the fort as it was poorly constructed and never fully finished. It basically consisted of a sandstone officers' quarters and a few adobe buildings, and nothing remains today.

Despite the loss of the fort, local ranches and farms kept Liberty active. By 1879, Liberty was a regular stage stop for the Overland Stage Company. In 1880, the Liberty post office opened at the E. D. Bullard General Store, which also served as a dry goods store, saloon and stage ticket office. The town never grew much, and with the construction of the railroads and the creation of Tucumcari, many of the leading businessmen moved to the new railroad town. The Liberty post office closed in 1902.

The City of Tucumcari

The junction of several railroads and trails made Tucumcari an important town in northeast New Mexico. Even before the railroads reached the location, the plans of the railroad were known, and a railroad construction camp was created here. Based upon the advantages of being on a railroad, five businessmen from nearby Liberty, located just three miles to the north, filed on land in the area and created the Tucumcari Town Site and Investment Company. These businessmen, M. B. Goldenberg, A. D. Goldenberg, Jacob Wertheim, J. A. Street, and Lee K. Smith, immediately donated 120 acres of land for a new townsite. While several names were used for the townsite, the first official one was Douglas, which had a post office that used that name 1901-1902. However, Tucumcari was soon officially founded on November 22, 1901.

Named for Tucumcari Mountain, located several miles to the south of the new town, Tucumcari became a tent city almost immediately. According to the city's history, J. A. Street was the first person to erect a tent, and thus has the honor of being the first resident. An initial problem was that there were no wells or nearby streams that could be used to provide water for drinking, cooking and bathing. Additionally, while a plat of the town was available, many people just threw up tents or shacks. However, railroad jobs attracted workers, and an organized community soon started to develop. Some of the first businesses recorded include the A. B. Simpson hardware store, the A. A. Blankenship livery barn, the Monarch Saloon, the Barnes & Rankin furniture store, and an unnamed hotel. The Tucumcari post office also opened in 1902.

A report from less than a year later listed the Turner boarding house, the Pioneer Bakery, the Arcade Restaurant, the Waldorf-Astoria Hotel, the Owl Saloon, the Exchange Bank, the Jackson & Foxworth Lumber Company, and Weldon & Young Real Estate and Investments. Quickly more businesses opened and homes were built. By 1910, there were schools, churches, doctors, lawyers, and more than seventy businesses. Tucumcari had also become the county seat of Quay County, New Mexico, and was an important railroad junction.

Starting in the late 1920s, Tucumcari became a popular stop for many traveling the Ozark Trail, and later Route 66. Being the largest city on the highway between Amarillo, Texas, and Albuquerque, New Mexico, Tucumcari soon filled with service stations, restaurants, hotels, and other businesses that catered to travelers. Because of the wide-open country available, many of the scenes in the television show *Rawhide* were shot in the Tucumcari area. Many of these historic businesses, or at least their structures, still exist in Tucumcari today. For decades, the city was famous for its "Tucumcari Tonite" promotions, and Tucumcari also called itself the "Gateway to the West." Travelers on the modern Interstate 40 still see many of the same promotions, and with a population of 5363 in the 2010 census, Tucumcari is still the largest city between Amarillo and Albuquerque. It is also the home of over 50 murals, popular with visitors.

This sign – Home of the Tucumcari Rattlers – can be found on a water tank at Tucumcari, New Mexico.

The Railroads at Tucumcari

At one time, Tucumcari had rail lines heading off in four directions. The original Rock Island Railroad line came in from the northeast, passed through Tucumcari, and headed to the southwest toward El Paso. The line started from the end of track at Liberal, Kansas, and ran through Dalhart, Texas, to here. It then headed to the southwest where it met the El Paso & Northeastern at Santa Rosa, New Mexico. On February 1, 1902, what became the Golden State Route from Chicago to Los Angeles opened. During October 1902, the *Golden State Limited* passenger train started service along the route. This route is now operated by Union Pacific.

To the northwest was the Dawson Railway. The 1901 *Report of the Governor of New Mexico* had an early report about this line. "As soon as the main line of this Rock Island and the El Paso and Northeastern extension is completed, a branch line will be built from Liberty, in San Miguel County, to the Dawson coal fields in eastern Colfax County, a distance of 110 miles. This line is to be pushed ultimately to Trinidad, Colo., thus giving Denver and Colorado points an air line to El Paso and Mexico."

This line, initially owned by the El Paso & Northeastern Railroad (EP&NE), served the large coal mine on the property of J. Barkley Dawson and L. S. Dawson. The mine opened in 1899, and was sold to the Phelps-Dodge Corporation in 1906. The railroad actually started construction at French, New Mexico, on the Santa Fe mainline. The line was first extended northward to the coal mine, and then to Tucumcari to connect with EP&NE, acquired by the El Paso & Southwestern Railway (EP&SW) in July 1905. At first, the Rock Island hauled the connecting freight between Tucumcari and Santa Rosa, but a threat of a new EP&SW line led the Rock Island to lease the Santa Rosa to Tucumcari line on May 1907. This made Tucumcari the primary interchange point between the EP&SW, and later the Southern Pacific when it purchased the company in November 1924. The Dawson Railway, also known as Southern Pacific's Roy Branch, was abandoned from Tucumcari to French in 1954. It was abandoned on to Dawson in 1961, but was rebuilt north of French as the Atchison, Topeka & Santa Fe's York Canyon Line in 1965.

The fourth route was the Choctaw Route, eastward to Memphis, Tennessee. This made Tucumcari an important junction for both passenger and freight trains. Large amounts of coal came off the Dawson Railway, while agricultural and consumer products moved east and west. The Golden State Route provided a Chicago to Los Angeles passenger route, and passengers could transfer from the various trains using the Choctaw Route.

The heralds of Southern Pacific, Union Pacific and Rock Island are painted on a wall near the railroad station at Tucumcari, New Mexico.

Tucumcari was a joint facility, shared by the Rock Island and the Southern Pacific. The costs were split with the Rock Island covering 51% of them. A 1908 Sanborn map showed how the tracks fit into the new town. The original passenger station was located on the south side of the tracks at the north end of 2nd Street, where the newer station now stands. At the west end of the platform was a kitchen and the railroad restaurant. The station was served by a single track, with eight tracks further to the northwest, behind a row of businesses along Railroad Avenue. Sanborn showed that the yard was all CRI&P.

On the north side of the yard about 7th Street were several major shippers, located on a long spur track. From east to west was the electric light plant and the "freight depot" of the Public Service Corporation. To the west was the Tucumcari Wool Sourcing Company, connected to the Public Service building by a long platform. Further west was the Tucumcari Public Service Water Company. On the south side of the yard were a series of grain elevators and farm supply warehouses.

East of the Rock Island yard was where the Dawson Railway headed northwest. Here, the facilities of the El Paso & Southwestern and the Rock Island & El Paso were located. On the east side of a six-track yard was a four-bay engine house. To the west was the railroad's depot. Further west was a machine shop, turntable and a 15-bay roundhouse. Later, a balloon track circled much of this area.

In 1929, Tucumcari was at its peak of activity. The Tucumcari train order station was open 24 hours a day, seven days a week. It was shown to be a fuel and water station, and that there was a turntable and a wye. There was also a 90-car siding listed, as well as a yard with a capacity of 1928 freight cars. To weigh the cars, the railroad had a 46-foot track scale with a capacity of 100 tons.

During this time, the Rock Island was converting steam locomotives from coal to oil. Additionally, the larger locomotives required larger facilities. In 1928, the Chicago, Rock Island & Pacific awarded a contract to the Railroad Water & Coal Handling Company of Chicago to build a new 5000-barrel (210,000 gallons) fuel oil station at Tucumcari, as well as one at Dalhart, Texas, and a 40,000-gallon (950 barrel) facility at Amarillo, Texas.

At the same time, eight Rock Island passenger trains served the Tucumcari station, but almost all of them in the middle of the night. The passenger train activity in 1929 started with the arrival of the westbound *Memphis Californian*, No. 111. It arrived at 2:30am, with the westbound *Golden State Limited* (No. 3) arriving at 2:50am. The next train was No. 11, the *Apache*, which arrived at 3:25am. Twenty minutes later, the eastbound *Golden State Limited* (No. 4) was scheduled to depart at 3:45am. Thus, half of the Rock Island passenger trains that served Tucumcari arrived within about an hour of each other early in the morning. The final morning train was an unnamed No. 2 eastbound passenger train at 9:20am, the only train that regularly served Tucumcari during daylight hours. The first evening train was westbound No. 1, also unnamed, which arrived at 8:10pm. At 11:05pm, the eastbound *Apache* (No. 12) departed town, with the eastbound *Memphis Californian* (No. 112) leaving five minutes later after making connections.

First Division National Railroad Adjustment Board – Volume 107 provided an interesting explanation of some of the operations during 1946 as part of a claims case involving operating changes that impacted hostlers at the Southern Pacific roundhouse. While the report involved Dalhart line trains No. 3 and No. 4, the *Golden State*, and trains No. 39 and No. 40, the *Imperial*, it still shows how the shops at Tucumcari were operated.

> Rock Island road engine crews operate all trains eastward from Tucumcari and Southern Pacific road engine crews operate all trains westward from Tucumcari.
>
> Terminal forces at Tucumcari, including yard service and roundhouse employes, are Southern Pacific employes working under the jurisdiction of the Southern Pacific, who perform the work for both the Rock Island and Southern Pacific at that point; the roundhouse employes include inside hostlers, who are assigned on a continuous shift basis around the clock, starting at 7:00 A.M., 3:00 P.M., and 11:00 P.M. Vacancies on these assignments and extra hostling jobs are filled from the firemen's extra board at Tucumcari.
>
> Prior to May 16, 1946, steam locomotives handled Rock Island passenger trains Nos. 3 and 39 into Tucumcari, and passenger trains Nos. 4 and 40 from Tucumcari. Engine crews arriving Tucumcari on trains Nos. 3 and 39 handled engines on which employed from train to designated roundhouse track, and engine crews departing Tucumcari on trains Nos. 4 and 40 handled engines on which employed from roundhouse to train.
>
> On May 16, 1946, the Rock Island commenced operating diesel electric locomotives on trains Nos. 3 and 4 into and out of Tucumcari. From May 16th, to and including June 30th, 1946, the Rock Island diesel locomotive arriving Tucumcari on train No. 3 was cut out of train at Tucumcari, to return on train No. 4 same day. On July 1, 1946, the Rock Island diesel locomotive was operated on train No. 3 through Tucumcari on a trial run over the Southern Pacific to El Paso, Texas, and returned from El Paso on train No. 4 through Tucumcari on July 2nd. On July 2, 1946, the

Rock Island diesel locomotive was cut out of train No. 3 at Tucumcari and departed therefrom same day on train No. 4. From July 3rd to and including train No. 4, October 6, 1946, the Rock Island diesel locomotive operated on train No. 3 through Tucumcari to El Paso, and returned on train No. 4 through Tucumcari on the following day. Effective October 7, 1946, the Rock Island commenced operating diesel electric locomotives on Trains Nos. 39 and 4 and steam locomotives on trains Nos. 3 and 40 into and out of Tucumcari, the diesel locomotive being cut out of train No 3. at Tucumcari.

By the mid-1950s, the Rock Island was down to only the *Cherokee* on the Choctaw Route. Train No. 111 arrived from Memphis at 7:30pm, while No. 112 headed east at 6:30am. On the Chicago-Los Angeles route, six trains still stopped at Tucumcari. Westbound No. 3, the *Golden State*, arrived at 10:35am, and departed 15 minutes later. Westbound No. 39, *The Imperial*, arrived at 7:55pm, and then departed 25 minutes later. A third westbound train (No. 43) operated from Kansas City to Tucumcari, and arrived at 6:00pm.

On the Dalhart mainline, there were also three eastbound trains. These were No. 4 (*Golden State*) which arrived at 1:40pm and departed six minutes later; No. 40 (*The Imperial*) which arrived at 5:35am and departed forty minutes later; and No. 44 which departed at 6:45am. It should be noted that these times were Central Time. Tucumcari served also as a time change location, with trains to the west using Mountain Time.

By 1979, the Rock Island and Southern Pacific were not in the best of shape. The Golden State route was still the main route and busy, but operations were becoming unreliable due to slow orders and derailments. The line toward Amarillo and on to Memphis was much less busy. Comments from the time state that Tucumcari-Amarillo was "light density at best," while east of Amarillo, there was some significant local business that kept trains running on a regular basis. However, Tucumcari still provided a number of services for the Rock Island. These included general order boards and books, a train register station, a train order station, a standard clock, and a wayside radio. Tucumcari was also listed as being a fuel and water station, and there was still a wye and turntable.

In 1984, the Tucumcari Union Station was still a busy place, handling the crews and train orders for Southern Pacific's Golden State Route.

The Choctaw Route to the east has been abandoned, while the Golden State Route became an important link to Kansas City and Chicago for the Southern Pacific, which proposed buying the line during the late 1970s, even before the failure of the Rock Island Railroad. In 1996, Union Pacific acquired the Southern Pacific, and today, most Union Pacific trains head on through as Tucumcari is no longer a crew change point. However, the yard is used by locals and a maintenance-of-way crew is based here in a small office just west of the former Union Station.

Tucumcari Union Station

The current train station, used for many years as the Tucumcari Railroad Museum at 100 Railroad Avenue, is not the original station at Tucumcari. The current station opened in 1927, and featured passenger services, space for freight and express, and railroad offices for both companies. It was built in the traditional Spanish Mission-style, popular for the era and location. The west end of the station featured a restaurant, operated 24 hours a day by the Van Noy Interstate Company as *The Interstate*. The restaurant later became the Beanery Restaurant, a part of Southern Pacific's restaurant chain.

The Tucumcari Union Station is a large building which also included a restaurant and railroad offices. This view is of the street side of the building.

This is the west end of the Tucumcari Union Station, still displaying its Tucumcari lettering.

In 2002, Union Pacific, which had acquired Southern Pacific on August 11, 1996, donated the station to the City of Tucumcari. The city later worked to restore the station and allowed the Tucumcari Railroad Museum to use the building. On September 22, 2014, the Tucumcari Railroad Museum was incorporated as a 501.c.3 non-profit organization. In 2020, Tucumcari MainStreet, which has offices in the building, was working to take over the museum and to expand it as part of their downtown redevelopment project. Therefore, even though the west end of the Choctaw Route has been gone for forty years, change is still taking place.

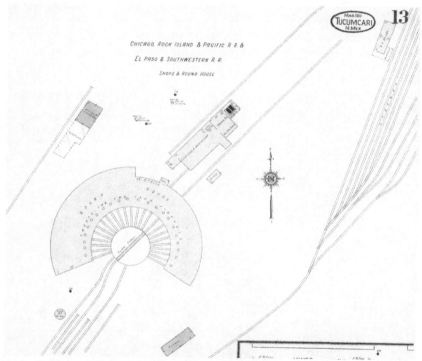

Sanborn Map – CRI&P Shops at Tucumcari – March 1919. *Sanborn Fire Insurance Map from Tucumcari, Quay County, New Mexico.* Sanborn Map Company, Mar, 1919. Map. Retrieved from the Library of Congress, https://www.loc.gov/item/sanborn05717_003/.

Sanborn Map – CRI&P Passenger Station and Railroad Restaurant at Tucumcari – March 1919. *Sanborn Fire Insurance Map from Tucumcari, Quay County, New Mexico.* Sanborn Map Company, Mar, 1919. Map. Retrieved from the Library of Congress, https://www.loc.gov/item/sanborn05717_003/.

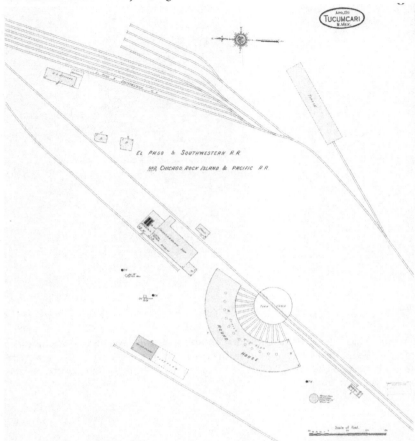

Sanborn Map – CRI&P Shops at Tucumcari – April 1911. *Sanborn Fire Insurance Map from Tucumcari, Quay County, New Mexico.* Sanborn Map Company, Apr, 1911. Map. Retrieved from the Library of Congress, https://www.loc.gov/item/sanborn05717_002/.

About the Author

Barton Jennings grew up in Arkansas, spending years in the Little Rock area exploring the various railroad lines. However, the Chicago, Rock Island & Pacific was always just a few years out of reach, and Bart was only able to experience the last few sad years of the company.

For almost three decades, Barton Jennings has been organizing charter passenger trains and writing the route descriptions, both for planning purposes and for the enjoyment of the passengers. These trips have been in all areas of the United States, often covering operations that haven't seen a passenger train in decades. Some of these trips have been on the routes of the Rock Island Railroad, such as on Farmrail between Clinton and Elk City, Oklahoma, in 2002.

In addition, he has written a number of articles about various railroads for rail hobby magazines. His house has several rooms full of books, timetables and other documents about this and other railroads – important research items from a time long before today's internet. Today, Bart Jennings, after years working in the railroad industry, is a professor emeritus of supply chain management and teaches transportation operations. He also still teaches regulatory issues for the railroad industry, a way to stay in touch with the industry he loves.

The author at Wheatley, Arkansas. Photo by Sarah Jennings.

Printed in Great Britain
by Amazon

18963577R00434